Possible Pasts

Becoming Colonial
in Early America

Edited by

ROBERT BLAIR ST. GEORGE

Cornell University Press / Ithaca and London

First published 2000 by Cornell University Press
First printing, Cornell Paperbacks, 2000

Printed in the United States of America

Library of Congress Cataloging-in-Publication Data
Possible pasts : becoming colonial in early America / edited by Robert Blair St. George.
     p.   cm.
   Includes bibliographical references and index.
   ISBN 0-8014-3344-4 (cloth) — ISBN 0-8014-8392-1 (paper)
     1. America—Colonization—Historiography—Congresses.   2. America—Colonization—Social aspects—Congresses.   3. United States—History—Colonial period, ca. 1600–1775—Congresses.   4. America—History—To 1810—Congresses.   5. Culture diffusion—America—History—Congresses.   6. Culture conflict—America—History—Congresses.   7. Intercultural communication—America—History—Congresses.   8. Acculturation—America—History—Congresses.   I. St. George, Robert Blair.
E101 .P67 2000
973.2—dc21
                                                                                    99-089817

Cornell University Press strives to use environmentally responsible suppliers and materials to the fullest extent possible in the publishing of its books. Such materials include vegetable-based, low-VOC inks and acid-free papers that are recycled, totally chlorine-free, or partly composed of nonwood fibers. Books that bear the logo of the FSC (Forest Stewardship Council) use paper taken from forests that have been inspected and certified as meeting the highest standards for environmental and social responsibility. For further information, visit our website at www.cornellpress.cornell.edu.

Cloth printing   10 9 8 7 6 5 4 3 2 1
Paperback printing   10 9 8 7 6 5 4 3 2 1

Ambiguity . . . is a fundamental attribute of power.

—*Georges Balandier*, Political Anthropology

Contents

Acknowledgments

IT IS a pleasure to thank the many individuals who have helped this collection of essays become a book. It was Richard R. Beeman who first suggested that the McNeil Center for Early American Studies hold a major conference to explore the effects of recent critical theory on the practice of early American historical scholarship and writing. Richard S. Dunn and Ronald Hoffman, as the respective directors of the McNeil Center and the Omohundro Institute of Early American History and Culture, offered unqualified collegiality and the resources necessary for the two institutions to cosponsor an international gathering of scholars at the "Possible Pasts: Critical Encounters in Early America" conference, held in June 1994 at the University of Pennsylvania. This volume is the eventual result of that conference.

Like any intellectual project, this one went through numerous planning stages. Owing in large part to the generosity of the Omohundro Institute and the Colonial Williamsburg Foundation, an initial meeting was held in Williamsburg, Virginia, in 1992. A second meeting was held in the Department of History at the University of Pennsylvania, and a final one at the Maryland Historical Society. As these planning sessions developed, I was helped particularly by the comments of Roger D. Abrahams, James Axtell, Timothy H. Breen, Kathleen M. Brown, Jon Butler, Cary Carson, Richard and Mary Maples Dunn, Arnold Krupat, Michael McGiffert, Jon Sensbach, Carroll Smith-Rosenberg, Darren Staloff, Fredrika Teuta, Lorena Walsh, and Michael Zuckerman. Additional substantive criticism and administrative skill were contributed throughout the process by Sally Mason and Donna Rilling.

At these planning sessions, other individuals were also present—the ones whose commitment to the project went beyond discussion to submit papers for the conference and then for this volume. In large part because of their sustained engagement, the focus of this book moved from a vague interest in various trajectories within cultural studies and poststructural methodologies to its present focus on the negotiative processes of "becoming colonial." I am especially indebted to Carroll

Smith-Rosenberg, whose collegiality and friendship meant so much to me as this work proceeded, to Irene Silverblatt, and to David D. Hall. And it has been a professional delight to work with the other contributors to this book. I learned from each of them, profited from their theoretical expertise and critical acumen, and hope that their essays, as presented here, gain support from one another. Although their contributions are not registered in this volume, the commentators at the conference also brought specific theoretical issues into sharper focus; I am indebted to the thoughtful comments of Rosanne M. Adderly, Jean-Christophe Agnew, Houston Baker, Richard Bauman, Nancy Bentley, Kathleen M. Brown, Peter Burke, Richard L. Bushman, Joyce Chaplin, Eric Cheyfitz, Natalie Z. Davis, Jay Fliegelman, Joseph Koerner, Arnold Krupat, Ann M. Little, Wyatt McGaffey, John Murrin, Barry O'Connell, James Rice, Daniel K. Richter, Jolene Rickard, Ines Salazar, James Scott, Patricia Seed, Jon Sensbach, Ivy Schweitzer, Michel-Rolph Trouillot, Kathryn E. Wilson, and Michael Zuckerman. I am particularly indebted to Timothy H. Breen for offering insightful concluding remarks for the entire conference. Although finally not contributors to this volume, Jane Kamensky, Carol F. Karlsen, and Roberta Pearson presented papers that helped to clarify the critical emphasis of this project.

Finally, I am grateful to the team put together by Cornell University Press to bring this volume to completion, especially Peter Agree. Anne Marie Plane and Matthew Dennis served as critical readers for the press, and their sound judgment and supportive critique have improved the final product. To work with such a group of people is a blessing.

R. B. S.

Possible Pasts

Introduction

ROBERT BLAIR ST. GEORGE

> Colonization: bridgehead in a campaign to civilize bar-
> barism, from which there may emerge at any moment the
> negation of civilization, pure and simple. . . . I am talking
> about societies drained of their essence, cultures trampled
> underfoot, institutions undermined, lands confiscated,
> religions smashed, magnificent artistic creations
> destroyed, extraordinary *possibilities* wiped out.
>
> — AIMÉ CÉSAIRE, *Discourse on Colonialism*

IN 1 6 1 6, the Jesuit priest Father Pierre Biard published his *Relation of New France*. In many respects a careful, proto-ethnographic account of the societies and cultures met by French missionaries as they advanced up the St. Lawrence Valley, Biard's commentary concentrated on native beliefs and social customs that signaled a readiness to heed the Gospels. But at times what the Jesuit father learned was downright surprising, especially in light of assurances Europeans had long held to be true. Take, for example, the role played by early-seventeenth-century concepts of bodily deformity in New World colonial encounters. Taking Christ's perfectly symmetrical, male figure as the template for their own physical and moral regulation, French colonists no doubt expected the Native Americans they met to be physically deformed and thus both morally misshapen and spiritually unregenerate. Yet according to Biard, "you do not encounter a big-bellied, hunchbacked, or deformed person among them: those who are leprous, gouty, affected with gravel, or insane, are unknown to them." What Biard observed was also noted by missionaries and travelers in other colonial situations, and reports by Spanish, German, and English explorers all reveal a single, unifying assumption. While Europeans, with their graceful carriage and ease of discourse, valued hierarchic embodiment as an emblem of political order, the native peoples they conquered bore the signs of political disorder and moral depravity: mutilated physiques, distorted lips, flat noses, short necks, irregular head shapes, or, in the most exaggerated play on a lack of political leadership, complete headlessness.[1]

But what Biard found called European assumptions of natural grace and ease into question. For in Quebec the Natives were perfect and the colonists deformed. "Any of our people who have some defect," he observed, "such as the one-eyed, squint-eyed, and flat-nosed, are immediately noticed by them and greatly derided, especially behind our backs and when they are by themselves." Certainly French colonists, along with their English counterparts farther south, were familiar with such strategies of ridicule; they used the same indices of distortion—especially of the eyes, the nose, or the mouth—to diagnose and deride unfortunate members of their own communities as witches. Perhaps hearing Indians turn the same weapon on them, thus recognizing one strand of similarity amid the tangled lines of intercultural miscommunication, was tough to take; typically, colonists worked hard to find measures of difference, not tissues of connection, between themselves and the "barbarians" whose cultures they fragmented but whose land they desired so as to anchor their own transplanted "civility." Perhaps. But Biard pointed to the final irony of colonial encounters. "You will see these poor barbarians, notwithstanding their great lack of government, power, letters, art and riches," he stated, "yet holding their heads so high that they greatly underrate us, regarding themselves as our superiors."[2]

In this volume I begin by asking what seems like a simple question: What are we to make of Father Biard's assertion? Two short phrases suggest his complicated mixture of motives. When he insisted that "you do not encounter" any physical deformities among native people, he seems to have been idealizing their social order, perhaps in a way similar to the utopian gloss that Roger Williams imposed on the Narragansets in the 1640s. For example, Biard asserted that the Indians were "handsome and well-shaped, just as we would be if we continued in the same condition in

---

1. Father Pierre Biard, *Relation of New France, of Its Lands, Nature of the Country, and of Its Inhabitants* (Lyon, 1616), rpt. in *The Jesuit Relations and Allied Documents: Travels and Explorations of the Jesuit Missionaries in New France, 1610–1791*, ed. Rueben Gold Thwaites, 73 vols. (Cleveland, 1896–1901), 3:75. On bodily deformity as an index of political order and moral improvement, see Robert Blair St. George, *Conversing by Signs: Poetics of Implication in Colonial New England Culture* (Chapel Hill, 1998), pp. 163–73.

2. Biard, *Relation of New France*, 3:75.

which we were at the age of twenty-five." What seems a compliment to their bodily strength, however, instead becomes a sign of stasis, an aging cleric's suggestion that an entire culture remained twenty-five years old forever, an imperial theory of arrested development in which colonized people somehow never attain the wisdom of accumulated experience. Here, Biard's final comment constitutes a warning that seems familiar. "Although you may regard yourselves as our superiors," he seems to be saying, "do not underestimate us."[3]

The symbolic inversion performed by casting colonists as deformed invaders—restless expansionists whose militaristic ethnocentrism prevented them from grasping the symbolic density of the "government, power, letters, art and riches" of the cultures they tore open—provides an opportunity for reimagining colonialism's divergent pasts and presents. As its title suggests, this book makes an assertion. New pasts that reveal the cultural processes of becoming colonial in early America are still possible. In a spirit of methodological experimentation that seeks to hold various trajectories within cultural studies in equipoise with empirical data, the essays in this volume share a consciousness of the possibilities for rewriting existing stories of the past. Perhaps they may provoke contemporary students—whether historians, literary critics, archaeologists, or anthropologists—of cultural contact and intercultural exchange, aesthetics and material culture, slavery, environmental change, religious practice, or textual production to be more reflexive about the ways they perform their own craft. The claim that new pasts of colonialism's cultural contours are still possible suggests those pasts are creatively invented rather than "discovered" in the arid climate of the archive. If, as historian Greg Dening has recently suggested, "history is all the ways we encode the past in symbol form to make a present," the pasts we deem possible are deeply implicated in the ways we respond to the continuing presence of colonialism's long shadow. On one hand, the essays in this book demonstrate the difficult, contradictory cultural positions occupied by colonized people—as objects of imperialism expansion, conquest, confiscation, and colonization and as ambivalent subjects of local rule and resistance strategies—in search of new centers of legitimacy and self-possession. They also attempt, on the other hand, to describe changes wrought in the culture of colonizers through critical encounters with new societies, new environments, new chances for imagining political and social alterity. In different ways this volume explores the "*extraordinary possibilities*" that Aimé Césaire, writing the delicate counterpoint between his native

3. Ibid.; on the utopian strain in Roger Williams, *Key into the Language of America* (London, 1643), see St. George, *Conversing by Signs*, p. 159.

Martinique and the Franco-Algerian conflict in 1955, claimed colonialism had completely "wiped out."[4]

We may begin an exploration of possibility by examining the paired key words in this book's subtitle, "becoming colonial" and "early America." These words are dense with possibility and historiographic challenge for many scholars engaged in critically rethinking colonialism in the Atlantic world. How can we dissect their meanings? As editor, let me chart some of the zones of interdisciplinary contact these terms make visible. "Becoming colonial" suggests an emphasis on the negotiative processes that characterize symbolic exchange in colonial cultures. Adjustments to conflicting value systems, ways of organizing labor, alternative sexualities and gender responsibilities, strategies for family continuity, patterns of normative demographic movement, the shaping of belief systems and religious practice over time, and ways of speaking, reading, and writing did not somehow automatically just "happen." They were protracted processes that, in different ways and with different intensities, affected Europeans, native peoples, and imported slaves in colonial situations. While the experience and governing asymmetry of intercultural contact and exchange varied widely, "Indians," *indios, indigenes, mestizos, Creoles,* and *conquistadores* all inhabited new worlds, middle grounds of which they were all to some degree makers.[5]

"Becoming" colonial actively displaces any lingering structuralist faith in colonies operating as steady-state, closed cultural systems, as "being" in any particular configuration over time. Change was constant. Becoming colonial therefore pushes analysis toward examination of particular projects; historically specific, variable, and open-ended, these initiatives placed individuals and the intertextuality of objects, languages, and actions at the public, observable center of interpretation. By developing detailed and comparative examinations of different colonial projects, the essays in this volume present an opportunity to use history critically to

4. Greg Dening, *The Death of William Gooch: A History's Anthropology* (Honolulu, 1995), p. 14; Aimé Césaire, *Discourse on Colonialism* (1955), trans. John Pinkham (New York, 1972), p. 21; Richard Smith, "Césaire's Balancing Act: Surrealism in Fort-de-France during the War," in *The Literature of Colonialism,* ed. Vanessa Davies and Richard Griffiths (London, 1996), pp. 63–80. See also Nathan Gardels, "Two Concepts of Nationalism: An Interview with Isaiah Berlin," *New York Review of Books,* November 21, 1991, pp. 19–23, esp. p. 19, where Berlin observes that for many cultures nationalism involves "the process of recovering their submerged pasts stifled by imperialism."

5. See James H. Merrell, *The Indians' New World: Catawbas and Their Neighbors from European Contact through the Era of Removal* (Chapel Hill, 1989); Richard White, *The Middle Ground: Indians, Empires, and Republics in the Great Lakes Region, 1650–1815* (New York, 1991); and Daniel H. Usner Jr., *Indians, Settlers, and Slaves in a Frontier Exchange Economy: The Lower Mississippi Valley before 1730* (Chapel Hill, 1992).

subvert the present. As anthropologist Nicholas Thomas has suggested, they implicitly explore how "former colonial discourses and the present might be related."[6]

Becoming "colonial" was an intricate process. It involved both vernacular theories of and lived experience of race and racial mixture, commercial exchange, kinship alliance, aesthetics, creolization, language, civility, savagery, and ambiguity concerning one's social position and personal power. If these and other symbolic practices figured in many colonial projects, how can we articulate our understanding of the range of places, imperial agents, intercultural exchanges, and local compliance and resistance through which we witness the process of becoming colonial? Certainly *colonial* refers to a relationship in which a majority indigenous (or forcibly imported) population is politically dominated by a minority of foreign invaders. *Colonial situation*, its close companion, refers to a "complex of rule, exploitation, and cultural conflict in ethnically heterogeneous political structures that had been created by influence from without."[7] The word "project," however, has a wider array of possible meanings that make it a more useful term for representing the density of experience in contact zones. According to the *OED*, "project" suggests a plan or scheme, a "design or pattern according to which something is made," a "mental conception, idea, or notion." From this meaning flows the concept of a colony as a plan for settlement, a scheme for the extraction of environmental resources or labor; from it too comes the notion of a pattern—for plantation, building construction, religion, law, and government—that would ensure, at least in theory, the predictability and stability of any colony over time. As a verb, "to project" references the enlightened motives with which many monarchs and administrators established colonies and the inversion of their own culture this frequently revealed. One definition meant "to throw or cause to fall (light or shadow) upon a surface or out into space." Another—also a verb, but one borrowed from alchemy—suggests that profitability was a motive; it meant to cast or

6. Nicholas Thomas, *Colonialism's Culture: Anthropology, Travel, and Government* (Princeton, 1994), p. 20. See also Robert F. Berkhofer Jr., *Beyond the Great Story: History as Text and Discourse* (Cambridge, Mass., 1995).

7. Jürgen Osterhammel, *Colonialism: A Theoretical Overview*, trans. Shelley L. Frisch (Kingston, Jamaica, 1997), p. 26. On "colonial situation," see the initial use in Octave Mannoni, *Prospero and Caliban: The Psychology of Colonization* (Paris, 1950; New York, 1956), pp. 9, 10–11. Mannoni's book, written during the Franco-Algerian colonial conflict, introduced a problematic concept of a "dependency complex" on the part of colonized people that has been severely critiqued by, among others, Césaire, *Discourse on Colonialism*, pp. 39–44. Mannoni's term was quickly appropriated and analytically expanded in George Balandier, "La situation coloniale: Approache théorique," *Cahiers Internationaux de Sociologie* 11 (1951): 44–79.

"project" powder into a crucible of molten iron "for the purpose of transmuting it into gold or silver."[8]

The concept of a *colonial project* helps to tie these different essays together. It suggests that concerns of colonial discourse, on one hand, and an interpretive commitment to preserve human agency and subjectivity, on the other, can be brought into sustained and productive contact. When they are, as Nicholas Thomas presciently observes, they establish a useful "analytical tension, a reading that is stretched between regimes of truth and their moments of mediation, reformulation and contestation in practice." "Project" implies a novel theoretical approach, drawing attention "not towards a totality such as a culture, nor to a period that can be defined independently of people's perceptions and strategies." Instead, a colonial project highlights "a socially transformative endeavour that is localized, politicized and partial, yet also engendered by longer historical developments and ways of narrating them." Representational codes are thus a part of the way any project insinuates itself in a landscape; narration articulates the power and authority that colonization demands. And while colonial projects are specific in time, place, and political configuration, they bring into view tactics of imperial domination that have a long evolution in political theory and popular memory. The concept of a colonial project is consistent with the possibility of redressing histories that have been "wiped out." According to Thomas, the term calls attention to the fact that "in colonial circumstances the interest in creating something new, on the part of settlers or a colonized population or both, is widespread; and even if resistance on the part of the colonized seems to entail merely a return to former circumstances . . . the struggle to recreate such conditions nevertheless engenders novel perceptions of identity, action and history; even what appears to be simply reactive or retrogressive thus amounts to a project, to a whole transformative endeavour."[9]

Drawing inspiration in large part from the work of Pierre Bourdieu, Thomas argues that colonial projects highlight the practical expression of

---

8. *The Oxford English Dictionary*, ed. J. A. Simson and E. S. C. Weiner, 20 vols. (Oxford, 2d ed., 1989), 12:597–98, cf."project,""projection." Hereafter *OED*.

9. Thomas, *Colonialism's Culture*, pp. 58, 105–6. Thomas's attention to historical specificity runs productively counter to the globalizing claims of some postcolonial theorists; see also J. Jorge Klor de Alva, "Colonialism and Post-Colonialism as (Latin) American Mirages," *Colonial Latin American Review* 1, nos. 1–2 (1992): 3: "In short, the Americas were neither Asia nor Africa; Mexico is not India, Peru is not Indonesia, and Latinos in the U.S.—although tragically opposed by an exclusionary will—are not Algerians." See also Anne McClintock, "The Angel of Progress: Pitfalls of the Term 'Post-colonialism,' " *Social Text* 10, nos. 2–3 (1992): 87: "But 'post-colonialism' (like postmodernism) is unevenly developed globally. Argentina, formally independent of imperial Spain for over a century and a half, is not 'post-colonial' in the same way as Hong Kong (destined to be independent of Britain only in 1997). Nor is Brazil 'post-colonial' in the same way as Zimbabwe."

discourse, the continual performance and practical mastery of representa-tional codes. The widespread appropriation of Bourdieu's work in con-temporary anthropological writings on colonialism is nothing new to early Americanists. Just two years after *Outline of a Theory of Practice* appeared in English (1977), James Henretta suggested that by refusing to accommodate to prevailing fashions in French structuralism, Bourdieu's concept of *habitus* could help American social historians connect their implicit pragmatism to a body of morally grounded critical theory."Habi-tus," which Bourdieu glosses as "the durably installed generative princi-ple of regulated improvisations," stands at the uncharted intersection of subjectivism and objectivism, the respective realms of rule and structure, and individual will and group response. By combining elements of affect and value with cognitive models of classification, Bourdieu's concept of habitus seems intellectually familiar to American scholars, perhaps for good reason. He had spent time in the 1960s at the Institute for Advanced Studies in Princeton and, at Erving Goffman's invitation, lecturing at the University of Pennsylvania; references in his work to Goffman and Harold Garfinkel, among others, suggest American sources for Bour-dieu's disenchantment with the limiting binarism of structuralist thought and his rejection of any romantic fetishization of individual subjectivity or agency. Historians of the Atlantic world, in particular, may find it espe-cially useful to transplant Bourdieu's concept of habitus to colonial social fields, contact zones where languages meet other languages, where texts can be read from different perspectives for different truths, and where emergent cultural forms articulate the fluidity of social groups as they meet, conflict, borrow from one another, and generate symbolic represen-tations of mixed, hybrid origins.[10]

Indeed, early American historians find in Bourdieu's theory of habitus a way of approaching intersections of individual agency and social fields that embraces their own faith in detailed empirical description. Bour-dieu's attention to the generative and improvisational qualities of habitus

10. Pierre Bourdieu, *Outline of a Theory of Practice*, trans. Richard Nice (New York, 1977), p. 78; James Henretta,"Social History as Lived and Written," *American Historical Review* 84, no. 5 (1979): 1312. The term *colonial practice* was first introduced by Jean-Paul Sartre in his intro-duction to *The Colonizer and the Colonized* (1957), by Albert Memmi, trans. Lawrence Hoey (New York, 1965), p. xxvi: "Colonial practice has engraved the colonialist idea into things themselves; it is the movement of things that designates colonizer and colonized alike." See Sherry B. Ortner, "Theory in Anthropology since the Sixties," in *Culture/Power/History: A Reader in Contemporary Social Theory*, ed. Nicholas B. Dirks, Geoff Eley, and Sherry B. Ortner (Princeton, 1994), p. 392; Bourdieu, *Theory of Practice*, pp. 20, 21, 94, 231; Craig Calhoun, Edward LiPuma, and Moishe Postone, "Introduction: Bourdieu and Social Theory," in *Bour-dieu: Critical Perspectives*, ed. Calhoun, LiPuma, and Postone (Chicago, 1993), p. 2; and Pierre Bourdieu, *Distinction: A Social Critique of the Judgment of Taste* (Cambridge, Mass., 1984), pp. 463–65.

defines it "first in relation to a system of objective potentialities, immediately inscribed in the present, things to do or not to do, to say or not to say, in relation to a *forthcoming* reality which . . . puts itself forward with an urgency and claim to existence excluding all deliberation." Habitus is a lived reality of strategic calculation, a learning curve that balances conservation against change, resources against risk, inaction against interest. As a result, culture itself is reimagined as a repertoire of strategic practices that are carefully deployed through both symbolic and instrumental exchange; habitus is an empirically informed "practical evaluation of the likelihood of the success of a given action in a given situation." Used to conceiving of authority and resistance in terms of strategies, risk, and calculations of interest, early American historians discover here a brand of local theorizing that seems remarkably familiar. At the same time, Bourdieu is careful to note that like culture itself, the shaping through time of habitus is not impervious to interest and calculation:

> One of the fundamental effects of the orchestration of habitus is the production of a commonsense world endowed with the *objectivity* secured by consensus on the meaning (*sens*) of practices and the world, in other words the harmonization of agents' experiences and the continuous reinforcement that each of them receives from the expression, individual or collective (in festivals, for example), improvised or programmed (commonplaces, sayings), of similar or identical experiences. The homogeneity of habitus is what—within the limits of the group of agents possessing the schemes (or production and interpretation) implied in their production—causes practices and works to be immediately intelligible and foreseeable, and hence taken for granted.

Thus while habitus is a organized means of calculating interest and reproducing normative assumptions about everyday life, it does not ensure any equal social distribution of this "generative principal." Habitus is thus a "regulated improvision" for potentials of domination, for the shaping of a commonsense, everyday life—its languages, material artifacts, beliefs, bodily regimes, ritual acts, assumptions about social class, gender, or race—through which politics almost invisibly moves. And Bourdieu's claim that the homogeneity of habitus ineluctably establishes a taken-for-granted reality implies a close connection between strategic practices and cultural hegemony. Yet what makes Bourdieu's concept particularly elastic is the range of overlooked symbolic activities that may play a part in both making and maintaining the dialectic process of "harmonization" between individual experience and social reinforcement: festivals, sayings, commonplace adages—in short, he contends that folklore plays a central part in the articulation of flexible adaptations to hegemonic strategies.[11]

To follow Bourdieu and posit the practical mastery of representational codes in quotidian situations, however, demands some reckoning with colonial discourse. The discourse of power, domination, and rule attempts to limit the languages available for countering imperial force, to curtail the strategies available for local resistance. As Peter Hulme has explained, "Underlying the idea of colonial discourse . . . is the presumption that during the colonial period large parts of the non-European world were produced for Europe through a discourse that imbricated sets of questions and assumptions, methods of procedure and analysis, and kinds of writing and imagery, normally separated out into the discrete areas of military strategy, political order, social reform, imaginative literature, personal memoirs and so on." This approach moves across a range of social activities that have long been used to shape disciplinary interests—military history, politics, social change, literature, and art—to suggest that these fields themselves may be artifacts of the same "methods of procedure and analysis" that colonial regimes used to demarcate, diversify, and screen the unifying logic of imposed rule. Following in part the lead of Edward Said, Hulme emphasizes the role discourse plays in naturalizing hegemonic relations of inequality through tactics of government, discipline, and bodily regulation. Yet neither Said's nor Hulme's work legitimizes an approach to the abstract force of discourse at the cost of attending to individuals as historical "actors" possessed of and conscious of their own agency. Said's *Orientalism* (1978), for example, bears the traced imprints of Michel Foucault and Antonio Gramsci, particularly concerning the political quality of knowledge and its forms of representation and reproduction. Explaining the theoretical basis of his literary approach, however, Said is at pains to distance himself from Foucault's claim that discourse functions at a level that discounts the human agency of any particular text or author, a point typically overlooked by his critics. Instead, the relations between individual intention and the "complex collective formations" that a depersonalized discourse articulates are fully dialectical. And as Hulme's contribution to this volume makes clear, he

---

11. Bourdieu, *Theory of Practice*, pp. 76, 77, 80. Compare Bourdieu's articulation of "habitus" and "commensicality" in this regard with understanding of the latter and "hegemony" in Antonio Gramsci, "Critical Notes on an Attempt at Popular Sociology," in *Selections from the Prison Notebooks*, ed. Quentin Hoare and Geoffrey Nowell Smith (New York, 1987), pp. 419–25; for Gramsci's appreciation of folklore, unfortunately cast in the model of *gesunkeneskulturgut* but still potentially radical, see Gramsci, "Language, Languages, Common Sense" and "Observations on Folklore," both in *An Antonio Gramsci Reader: Selected Writings, 1916–1935*, ed. David Forgacs (New York, 1988), pp. 347–49 and 360–62.

too is careful to construct an approach to colonial discourse that takes the intentions of authors and the mediating work of their texts or documents fully into account. Discourse from this perspective is historically constituted and acquires its normative, governmental force by appearing to have always been a "natural" part of quotidian language. Even for Foucault discourse was double-sided, developing through time and operating, through rupture, against the allegory of historical continuity it helps to manufacture.[12]

Power is creative as well as coercive. Said's *Orientalism*, a work many critics hail as the foundation text of colonial discourse and postcolonial theory, develops the creative tension between abstract discourse, with its critical assumption that the actions of an individual subject or intentions underlying any utterance can be functionally erased, and the myriad, material details of everyday life. If we extend the genesis of studies critical of colonial discourse backward in time from Said's pathbreaking study to include such Caribbean writers as Roberto Fernández Retamar and Aimé Césaire, the Antillean critic Frantz Fanon, or the Mexican historian Edmundo O'Gorman, we discover that the productive analytic tension has a historiography extending back into the early 1930s.[13] As Michael Warner demonstrates in his essay in this volume, this historiography extends back to late-sixteenth-century debates between advocates of British colonization such as Sir Humphrey Gilbert, George Carew, and Thomas Smythe and the "ghost discourse" of critics including Richard Eburne and assorted balladmongers.

Imperial states and authors strategically used the politics and poetics of colonial discourse to produce ways of seeing, talking, writing, painting,

---

12. Peter Hulme, *Colonial Encounters: Europe and the Native Caribbean, 1492–1797* (London, 1986), p. 2; Edward Said, *Orientalism* (New York, 1978), pp. 23–24. See also Said, "Orientalism Reconsidered," in *Europe and Its Others*, proceedings of the Essex Conference on the Sociology of Literature, July 1984, 2 vols. (Colchester, England, 1985), 1:14–27; Said, "Representing the Colonized: Anthropology's Interlocutors," *Critical Inquiry* 15, no. 2 (1989): 205–25; "An Interview with Edward W. Said," *Boundary 2* 20, no. 1 (1993): 1–25; and Said, *Culture and Imperialism* (New York, 1993). On discourse, see Michel Foucault, *The Archaeology of Knowledge*, trans. A. M. Sheridan Smith (New York, 1972), pp. 31–76. On the formative relationship of language, philosophy, and consciousness in political discourse, see J. G. A. Pocock, *Politics, Language, and Time: Essays on Political Thought and History* (New York, 1971), pp. 233–35.

13. Roberto Fernández Retamar, *Caliban and Other Essays*, trans. Edward Baker (Minneapolis, 1989); Césaire, *Discourse on Colonialism*; Frantz Fanon, *Black Skin, White Masks* (1952), trans. Charles Lam Markmann (New York, 1967); Fanon, *Studies in a Dying Colonialism* (1958), trans. Haakon Chevalier (New York, 1965); Edmundo O'Gorman, "Hegel y el moderno Pan-Americano," *Journal of the University of Havana* (January 1937), republished as O'Gorman, "Do the Americas Have a Common Future?" trans. Ángel Flores, *Points of View* 3 (December 1941). This early essay was the seed for Edmundo O'Gorman, *La invención de América: El universalismo de la cultura de occidente* (Mexico City, 1958); see Edwin C. Rozwenc, "Edmundo O'Gorman and the Idea of America," *American Quarterly* 10, no. 2, pt. 1 (1958): 99–115.

and thinking so as to promote acquiescence to political subordination and enforced discipline. There are limits to this discourse. An obvious one is that its perspective is Eurocentric, concerned more with the metropolitan making of power than with its transformation or outright rejection in colonized places by people with their own vision of appropriate social order. Much of colonial discourse was aimed less at the colonized population than at shaping public opinion among the occupying population and at "home" in the imperial state. The literary historian and postcolonial critic Homi K. Bhabha has argued that colonial discourse, while perhaps internally cohesive, is nonetheless partial and open to reworking and dissection. Although he often employs such categorical oppositions as "colonizer" and "colonized," "self" and "other," Bhabha has demonstrated the ways in which subalterns can mimic the performance style and register of their colonial overlords and thereby develop a doubled discourse of their own that both nominally obeys and parodically undercuts the assumed authority of imperial presence. But Nicholas Thomas points to a still more basic and pressing concern. Many scholars uncritically assume that individuals living under the imperial yoke in different locations will somehow be able to make sense of colonial discourse, which is not necessarily the case. As a result, Thomas's abiding faith that "colonialism can only be traced through its plural and particularized expressions" requires at every step that local recognition of discourse in colonial projects is happening. The possibilities for misrepresentation and fragmentary understanding define the project itself. "Colonialism is not a unitary project," he concludes, "but a fractured one, riddled with contradictions and exhausted as much by its own internal debates as by the resistance of the colonized."[14]

These cautions notwithstanding, studies of culture and colonial projects are of late a growth industry, to which this volume adds new voices and critical challenges. Two recent anthologies provide an overview of the range of issues the field now subsumes. The first is modest in scope and thematically focused. In 1992 anthropologist Nicholas B. Dirks edited *Colonialism and Culture*, containing ten essays by anthropologists and historians that previously had been published in the journal *Comparative Studies in Society and History*. The essays range widely in emphasis, from sixteenth-century England to seventeenth-century Tagalog society in the Philippines, to nineteenth-century India, to state violence against the

14. Thomas, *Colonialism's Culture*, pp. x, 51. Homi K. Bhabha, "Of Mimicry and Man: The Ambivalence of Colonial Discourse," in Bhabha, *The Location of Culture* (New York, 1994), pp. 88–91. The liberal construction of "self" vs. "other" opposition is problematic for Bhabha, whose method otherwise owes much to psychoanalytic theory; see Paul Heelas, "Introduction: Indigenous Psychologies," in *Indigenous Psychologies: The Anthropology of the Self*, ed. Paul Heelas and Andrew Lock (New York, 1981), pp. 3–18.

Putumayo people in twentieth-century Colombia. Dirks's introduction to this volume cast light on possible reasons for the surge of recent interest in colonialism (say, since the publication of Said's *Orientalism*). He pointed to the fact that the topic had become somehow "safe" now that "decolonization and the twentieth-century transformations of the world order have rendered colonialism a historical category, linked to the present more by such terms as *neo* and *post* than by any formal continuity." And he rhetorically asked whether by linking colonialism and culture—a connection central to the present volume—we might "ignore the extent to which colonialism has become irrelevant due to transformations in the world economy having to do with the hegemony of superpowers and the internationalized structures of late industrial capitalism."[15]

The call for a critique of colonialism in the modern West has points of origin in the changing international positions and roles of the United States, Great Britain, France, and, increasingly, the states of the former Soviet Union. Under the dispensation of the "New World Order," political power no longer seems the proprietary domain of any single nation; as the Gulf War or the presence of UN forces in Bosnia suggests, single nations now must establish a web of alliances in order to affect political or economic hegemony in the global arena; the older model of a single state exercising unchallenged superiority over others is bankrupt. But for this latter type of domination, the colonial project was the prototype. The critical reassessment by historians and anthropologists begun in *Colonialism and Culture* is thus part of a large-scale reevaluation of forms of colonial domination, crucial in part to guard against their possible return around the globe and in part to provide a way out of a postimperial crisis in ethnographic disciplines concerning the appropriate subjects of study.[16]

15. Nicholas B. Dirks, "Introduction," in *Colonialism and Culture*, ed. Dirks (Ann Arbor, 1992), p. 5; for other early anthologies, see Chris Tiffin, Bill Ashworth, and Helen Griffiths, eds., *The Empire Writes Back: Theory and Practice in Post-Colonial Literatures* (New York, 1989), and Ian Adam and Helen Tiffin, eds., *Past the Last Post: Theorizing Post-Colonialism and Post-Modernism* (Calgary, Canada, 1990). The real distinction between "neo" and older forms of colonialism blurs, however, when one considers the frequent intervention of one state in the affairs of sovereign nations; see McClintock, "Angel of Progress," p. 89: " 'Post-colonial' Latin America has been invaded by the United States over a hundred times this century alone."

16. As early as 1951 Balandier foresaw the pressures that imperial decline would put on anthropology: "The process of decolonization has immediate consequences for the peculiar scientific practice of social anthropology," he argued, especially "on the classical representation of this category of societies." See Balandier, "Situation coloniale," pp. 45–46 (my translation). Over twenty years later, the scale of anthropology's complicity in imperial systems of knowledge production was suggested by Wendy James, "The Anthropologist as Reluctant Imperialist," in *Anthropology and the Colonial Encounter*, ed. Talal Asad (London, 1973), pp. 41–70.

The second anthology suggests how rapidly the field expanded. *Colonial Discourse and Postcolonial Theory*, edited by Patrick Williams and Laura Chrisman, appeared in 1994. It is divided into six major sections and contains thirty-one essays. The sections bear such headings as "Theorizing Colonized Cultures and Anti-Colonial Resistance," "Theorizing the West," "Theorizing Gender," and "Reading from Theory," all of which are explicitly about "theorizing," the implications being that colonial discourse demands a direct engagement with critical theory and that the field was perceived in 1994 as being essentially without theory. The semantic burden to be carried by the term *postcolonial theory* remains unresolved, however. It cannot be defined in such a way as to suggest it merely came "after colonialism." As Peter Hulme makes clear in his contribution to this book, colonialist strategies are not easily displaced either during or after independence movements. They can persist long after so-called national emergence, shaping relations by defining internal colonies within consolidated nation-states. Postcolonial theory adds to our exploration of colonial projects by locating representational strategies at the center of transnational economics and diasporic identity constructions. It attempts to describe the subject matter and circuits of social relations through which discourse works to shape relations of power and knowledge, hegemony and consent, resistance and ritual, and thus makes problematic any ethnocentric assumptions concerning center-periphery models of empire, population movement, and the flow of capital.[17]

Postcolonial theory also prevents us from witlessly assuming that colonial projects are somehow a thing of the past. Why, one might ask, is it useful to restrict this volume to essays that explore the process of becoming colonial in early America, given that later colonial projects across the globe continue to witness similar moments when, as Césaire described, local societies are being systematically "drained of their essence"? The historical investigations gathered in this book effectively tie the past to ongoing colonial practices. These initiatives include not only the expan-

17. Patrick Williams and Laura Chrisman, eds., *Colonial Discourse and Postcolonial Theory: A Reader* (New York, 1994). See also Bill Ashcroft, Gareth Griffiths, and Helen Tiffin, eds., *The Post-Colonial Studies Reader* (New York, 1995); Bart Moore-Gilbert, *Postcolonial Theory: Contexts, Practices, Politics* (London, 1997); and Michael Hechter, *Internal Colonialism: The Celtic Fringe in British Nationalist Development, 1536–1966* (Berkeley, 1975). A recent sign of the institutionalization of postcolonialism is the appearance in 1998 of the journal *Postcolonial Studies*. On the nonlinearity of attitudes in postcolonial history, see Partha Chatterjee, *The Nation and Its Fragments* (Princeton, 1993), p. 6, where he argues that in the realm of the "spirit" of nationalism, national sovereignty may exist before the actual political battle for statehood; the nation can already exist within the colony. Inderpal Grewal and Caren Kaplan, "Introduction: Transnational Feminist Practices and Questions of Postmodernity," in *Scattered Hegemonies: Postmodernist and Transnational Feminist Practices*, ed. Grewal and Kaplan (Minneapolis, 1994), pp. 15–16.

sionist spasms of so-called postimperial states, including England's invasion of the Falkland Islands and continuing French intervention in Indonesia, but also those of former colonial possessions that, as creole elites changed into national leaders, have now become significant colonizing forces in their own right. In former Spanish colonies such as Bolivia, Colombia, and Venezuela, the *independencia* movements of San Martín and Bolívar in the 1820s typically brought nominal relocations of political authority and autonomy, while harsh treatment of Indios, mestizos, and lower-class citizens working in mines, in forests, or on plantations continued unabated; in these places, colonialism survived to inform new nationalist regimes. Or take, for example, the United States of America and the long, tragic history of disease, death, and displacement that both colonial and federal officials have written and then erased—and are still writing and still erasing—across the bodies and landscapes of Native North American peoples. These colonial muscles, remarkably untired, continue to flex: the recent invasions of Grenada and Kuwait; repeated interventions to guarantee democracy in Haiti; the continuing blockade of Cuba long after the cold war has melted into the Caribbean's creole waves; the devastating impact of U.S. economic and environmental policies and the corporate "development" advantages they afford to reduce Brazilian rain forests and villages to ciphers in a global calculation of profit.[18]

An examination of the comparative history of colonial projects in these places makes apparent the contingency of the past and the present, as well as the unsettling duration of plantation schemes for colonial rule with conceptual origins in the sixteenth century. Detailed historical exploration increases sensitivity to variations in colonial administration and in the cultures of domination, dependency, and resistance they help to spawn. And it sheds light on contradictions in contemporary nationalism. There are ethical contradictions between an avowed faith in democratic freedom and the cultivation of a virtuous republican citizenry, on one hand, and the calculations of advantage and interest that support colonial interventions, on the other hand. The conflict in the United States no doubt undergirds a lively tradition of dissent, but also an introspective fascination

---

18. On environmental developments, see the essays collected in Toshie Nishizawa and Juha I. Uitto, eds., *The Fragile Tropics of Latin America: Sustainable Management of Changing Environments* (New York, 1995), esp. Emilio F. Moran, "Rich and Poor Ecosystems of Amazonia: An Approach to Management" (pp. 45–67); Betty J. Meggers, "Archaeological Perspectives on the Potential of Amazonia for Intensive Exploitation" (pp. 68–93); Robert Motta, "A Fragile Capitalism in a Fragile Environment: Entrepreneurs and State Bureaucracies in the Free Zone of Manaus" (pp. 180–200); and Christine Padoch and Wil de Jong, "Subsistence- and Market-Oriented Agroforestry in the Peruvian Amazon" (pp. 226–37).

with national anxiety and the stylistics of political paranoia: apathy, cynicism, disenchantment, disavowal.

What of "early America," the second couplet of the book's subtitle? In common parlance, "early" America means anything from the late sixteenth through the mid–nineteenth century, or roughly from the period of exploration, discovery, or invention of America through the irregular, debated consolidation of nation-states following the wars of independence in both British and Latin America (circa 1825). A strictly chronological approach to the meaning of early America promptly runs into trouble, however, concerning the irregular quantities of available documentary texts representing the positions or identities of indigenous societies under pressure to adapt, however selectively and on their own terms, to the presence of armed and capitalized European colonists. Early English colonial history could thus begin in earnest by about 1620, when sufficient texts generated for and by colonial planters were first penned. But early colonial history for Mohegan or Pequot peoples in Connecticut perhaps did not begin in earnest until after 1750, when the letters of Joseph Johnson and Samson Occum and the writings of William Apess open ambivalent native subject positions to view.[19]

Another difficulty with stabilizing the meaning of "early America" ensues when one realizes that "early" implies something more than mere chronological placement or sequence. It refers also to the ways in which temporal framing may be manipulated to allegorize the undertaking of colonial and early national projects, usually by European creole subjects but occasionally by Native peoples complicit in imperial regimes. Using temporal strategies, Creoles transform the colonial sphere into an imag-

19. On the lack of inclusion of indigenous resistance or agency being ascribed to a lack of suitable sources, see John H. Elliott, "Introduction: Colonial Identity in the Atlantic World," in *Colonial Identities in the Atlantic World, 1500–1800*, ed. Nicholas Canny and Anthony Pagden (Princeton, 1987), pp. 5–8; the exception in this work to the "screening out" of native positionality is Stuart B. Schwartz, "The Formation of a Colonial Identity in Brazil," pp. 15–50. On Joseph Johnson and Sansom Occum, see *To Do Good to My Brethren: The Writings of Joseph Johnson, 1751–1776*, ed. Laura L. Murray (Amherst, 1998); see also Barry O'Connell, *On Our Own Ground: The Complete Writings of William Apess, a Pequot* (Amherst, 1992). The translation of native Massachusett and Natick versions of English legal formulary texts suggests that a Native "colonial" textual tradition might begin in the late seventeenth century; see Ives Goddard and Kathleen Bragdon, eds., *Native Writings in Massachusett*, American Philosophical Society Memoir no. 185 (Philadelphia, 1988). For a contrasting view of native societies in the postcontact period through Native written and pictorial sources, see the exemplary work of James Lockhart, *Nahuas and Spaniards: Postconquest Central Mexican History and Philology* (Stanford, 1991), esp. pp. 2–22, 183–201; Arthur J. O. Anderson, Frances Berdan, and James Lockhart, eds. and trans., *Beyond the Codices: The Nahua View of Colonial Mexico* (Berkeley, 1976); Louise M. Burkhart, *The Slippery Earth: Nahua-Christian Moral Dialogue in Sixteenth-Century Mexico* (Tucson, 1989); and Karen Spalding, *Huarochirí: An Andean Society under Inca and Spanish Rule* (Stanford, 1984).

ined ancient Arcadia; thus positioned as early classical landlords, the America they actually inhabit is separated metaphorically from the timeless zone inhabited by their indigenous workforce and slaves. In this scenario, to claim an "early" temporal location is a strategy to demarcate foundational authority rather than merely label one's location in the sweeping arc of history.[20]

A final difficulty with "early America" is disciplinary. How should the "early" in early America relate to the "early" in early modern Europe? As I have suggested, both fields share an interest in the period from roughly 1500 to about 1800, three centuries in which concepts of selfhood, traditions of spatial representation and illusion, bureaucratic national governments, self-regulating market economies, and the slave trade underwent major transformations in scale and moved toward systematic integration. But as its name implies, "early modern European" culture refers to an overarching period of inchoate modernity; it is marked by a rich overlap and interpenetration of markets, moral reform, and metaphysics. Occasionally early Americanists argue for interpretive continuity between early modern European studies and their own investigations, and given the engagement of the former field with critical theory, such an insistence may help convince skeptical Americanists to overcome their antitheoretical training. Two contributors to this volume make such a claim. Irene Silverblatt, for example, has shown how sixteenth-century Spanish concepts of witchcraft were superimposed on Andean societies in colonial Peru in order to stigmatize indigenous beliefs as immoral and, in particular, to demonize native women. And David D. Hall's study of popular religious belief in colonial New England is strengthened by its ties to early modern Europeanists' approaches to local religion and lay piety.[21]

The lines of continuity in the sixteenth and seventeenth centuries between early modern Europe and early America were not always drawn from the Old World to the New. Specimens of natural history such as animals, plants, and minerals, the material culture and symbolic practices of "exotic" peoples, and occasionally the people themselves could and did move from the colonial margins to metropolitan centers in Spain, Italy,

---

20. Connection of "early" and the temporality of colonial projects is suggested in Homi K. Bhabha, "DissemiNation: Time, Narrative, and the Margins of the Modern World," in *Nation and Narration*, ed. Bhabha (New York, 1990), pp. 298–99, and Johannes Fabian, *Time and the Other: How Anthropology Makes Its Object* (New York, 1983). On temporality and its political uses, see St. George, *Conversing by Signs*, pp. 326–35.

21. Irene Silverblatt, *Moon, Sun, and Witches: Gender Ideologies and Class in Inca and Colonial Peru* (Princeton, 1987), pp. 159–96; David D. Hall, *Worlds of Wonder, Days of Judgment: Popular Religious Belief in Early New England* (New York, 1989), pp. 5–12, 50–52, 71–80, 166–69. See also Kenneth A. Lockridge, *On the Sources of Patriarchal Rage: The Commonplace Books of William Byrd and Thomas Jefferson and the Gendering of Power in the Eighteenth Century* (New York, 1992), p. x.

France, and England. One American Indian, a "Young Man from Virginia," in 1614 roamed with deer and peacocks in the pleasure park of his collector-owner James I. Or consider the Brazilian village erected on the outskirts of Rouen to celebrate Henry II's entry into the town in 1550. According to Margaret M. McGowan, who has studied this entry procession in detail, as the king and his retinue neared the town "they could see a most uncommon scene laid out before them. A meadow (two hundred feet long and thirty-five feet wide), planted with natural and artificial shrubs and trees, provided a home for exotic birds, for monkeys and squirrels, and for fifty Brazilian men and women who has been brought to France in the ships of Rouen merchants." Imported just for the festivities, these Tabagerres and Toupinaboux Indians were augmented by 250 French sailors and merchants who had been to Brazil. Rouen's bourgeoisie had underwritten the building of two complete native villages. McGowan continues:

> At each end of the meadow primitive huts made of solid tree trunks had been erected. For a long time the royal visitors contemplated the activities in which these natives were absorbed: running after monkeys, firing their arrows at birds, lazing in cotton hammocks strung from one tree to another, chopping wood and carrying it to the fort near the river, where French sailors would customarily trade with them. . . . Most alarming was the battle between two tribes—the Tabagerres and the Toupinaboux—which suddenly broke out. They fought furiously with arrows, clubs, and other warlike instruments until the Tabagerres were finally repulsed. The conquerors made good their victory by burning the homes of their opponents to the ground. The show was so arresting that even those who knew the country of Brazil were constrained to comment on its authenticity.[22]

For the monarch, as for the assembled inhabitants of Rouen that had gathered to witness the spectacle, these "collected" Natives and the animals and plants surrounding their villages helped to define the civility of French culture through its symbolic inversion: absence of technological sophistication ("huts made of solid tree trunks"), proximity to nature (people alongside monkeys, birds, squirrels), bellicosity ("warlike instruments," burning homes to the ground), and the penultimate European sign of savagery, nakedness. At the same time, however, a strange famil-

---

22. Margaret M. McGowan, "Forms and Themes in Henry II's Entry into Rouen," *Renaissance Drama* 1 (1968): 218–19. For more on the entry in the context of early modern spectacles, see Stephen Mullany, *The Place of the Stage: License, Play, and Power in Renaissance England* (Chicago, 1988), pp. 65–67. For the 1614 watercolor *The Young Man from Virginia* by Michael van Meer, see Rosemary Weinstein, "Some Menagerie Accounts of James I," *Transactions of the London and Middlesex Archaeological Society* 31 (1980): 134–35, and St. George, *Conversing by Signs*, pp. 162–63, fig. 58.

iarity marked these same indices of otherness; identical qualities might be mapped in the recesses of popular culture that bourgeois reform was then actively trying to suppress. As Peter Mason has argued, in a tradition of poststructural critique that includes Bhabha and Tzvetan Todorov, popular culture had the power to put people in uneasy contact with the "internal other." Ethnographic images of "exotic" or colonized peoples played the "part of a negative self-definition of ego." Out on the margins of empire, Peter Hulme has observed, European "civility" could only "guarantee the stability of its own foundations by denying the substantiality of other worlds and other words."[23]

The new worlds articulated by colonial projects played formative roles in the construction of early modern imperial authority as an exclusive realm of imagined cultural purity and autocratic will; moments of uncanny recognition—involving what Freud termed a "doubling, dividing, and interchanging of the self"—invaded the calm reverie of metropolitan culture, punctuating daily life with both inner instabilities and violent disavowals of uncertainty. Viewing colonial projects from this angle places them in a new zone of possibility; we thus might imagine colonial influence on the practice of "metropolitan projects" in early modern Europe. Yet despite the efforts of scholars such as Hulme, Mason, Todorov, Bhabha, and Stephen Mullany—built in part on the pioneering work of Fredi Chiappelli's *First Images of America: The Impact of the New World on the Old* (1976), and Germán Arciniegas's *America in Europe: A History of the New World in Reverse* (1975)—most early modern Europeanists have been strangely silent on the formative impact of colonial projects on European culture. Even *The New Cultural History*, an influential collection edited by Lynn Hunt, abstains from critical engagement with the topic.[24]

If new worlds had been present as a semiotic force in Europe by the mid–sixteenth century, how should we approach the meaning of early

---

23. Peter Mason, "Classical Ethnography and Its Influence on the European Perception of Peoples of the New World," in *The Classical Tradition and the Americas*, ed. Wolfgang Haase and Meyer Reinhold (Berlin, 1994), pp. 145–46; Peter Hulme, "Polytropic Man: Tropes of Sexuality and Mobility in Early Colonial Discourse," in *Europe and Its Others*, 1:25. See also Mason, *Deconstructing America: Representations of the Other* (New York, 1990), pp. 41–68; Tzvetan Todorov, *The Conquest of the Other*, trans. Richard Howard (New York, 1984); and Bhabha, "DissemiNation," p. 298. For a Native perspective, see Fritz W. Kramer, "The Otherness of the European," *Culture and History* 6 (1989): 107–23.

24. Sigmund Freud, "The Uncanny" (1919), in Freud, *Studies in Parapsychology* (New York, 1963), pp. 19–60. See Fredi Chiappelli, ed., *First Images of America: The Impact of the New World on the Old*, 2 vols. (Berkeley, 1976), esp. Suzanne Boorsch, "America in Festival Presentations," 2:503–15; Stephen J. Greenblatt, "Learning to Curse: Aspects of Linguistic Colonialism in the Sixteenth Century," 2:561–80; and Yakov Malkiel, "Changes in the European Languages under a New Set of Sociolinguistic Concerns," 2:581–94; Germán Arciniegas, *America in Europe: A History of the New World in Reverse*, trans. Gabriela Arciniegas and R. Victoria Arana (New York, 1975); and Lynn Hunt, ed., *The New Cultural History* (Berkeley, 1989).

"America" in this volume? Because the evaluation of colonial projects depends on comparison and because transculturation was a pivotal process for individuals as they moved back and forth across cultural frontiers, "America" in this book includes North America, Latin America, and the Caribbean. Three essays—those by Louise M. Burkhart, Irene Silverblatt, and José Antonio Mazzotti—address projects in Mexico and Latin America, while the contributions of Peter Hulme and Carroll Smith-Rosenberg contain sustained discussion of colonial and early national practices in the Caribbean. While this volume is not intended as an exhaustive survey of different contact zones throughout the Western Hemisphere between the late sixteenth and early nineteenth centuries, these essays raise provocative questions about comparative colonialism. By widening the lens of "early America" to include colonial projects in which British, Spanish, and various Native cultures produced new social syntheses, these essays capture images that raise questions concerning assumptions of comparative method based on cultural convergences and strategies of differentiation.[25]

Convergences suggest useful comparisons. Consider the tactics Native peoples used to strengthen the positions they occupied in nascent colonial economies. In southern New England in the early seventeenth century, the Pequots and Narragansets struggled against each other to establish hegemony over access to English technology and military strength, making scholarly generalizations about the "unified culture" of colonized peoples premature. In late-sixteenth-century Peru, alliances were continually being remade, as Indians in the Huamanga area fought against one another to control access to certain resources and trade with colonial agents. Native merchants sought alliances with Spanish *encomenderos*, or new colonial landholders, in order to expand the Huancavelica mines. According to Steve J. Stern, before the Incas effected their own imperial control over these diverse native groups in 1640, the mines "were a site of impressive native initiative." The Indians, "impelled by the hunt for money and com-

25. For previous attempts at historical comparison, see David G. Sweet and Gary B. Nash, eds., *Struggle and Survival in Colonial America* (Berkeley, 1981), which used specific individuals to explore four kinds of historical struggle—collective struggle, individual defiance, individual accommodation, and competition. See also David B. Quinn, "European Perceptions of American Ecology, 1492–1612"; Anthony Pagden, "Shifting Antinomies: European Representations of the American Indian since Columbus"; Luca Codignola, "The French in Early America: Religion and Reality"; and David Murray, "Through Native Eyes: Indian History/American History," all in *Visions of America since 1492*, ed. Deborah L. Madsen (New York, 1994), pt. 1, pp. 3–22, 23–34, 35–56, and 57–72. For monographic treatments hemispheric in scope and scale, see Max Savelle, *Empires to Nations: Expansion in America, 1713–1824* (Minneapolis, 1974); Lester D. Langley, *The Americas in the Age of Revolution, 1750–1850* (New Haven, 1996); Ronald Syme, *Colonial Elites: Rome, Spain, and the Americas* (London, 1958); and, with a greater emphasis on Latin American economic dependencies, Alan K. Smith, *Creating a World Economy: Merchant Capitalism, Colonialism, and World Trade, 1492–1825* (Boulder, 1991).

mercial profit, joined in the creation of a colonial economy," an economy in which native participants saw advantage in new commercial ventures. Thus while *españoles* and indios had contradictory motives for building a new economy, they created it together. "The Indians embraced the entry of commercial capital on the Andean stage," Stern concludes, and "only later would they discover that the embrace was deadly."[26]

Crowd actions provide a later point of comparison. Eighteenth-century England and Spain witnessed major colonial riots, as each nation attempted to rationalize their imperial administrative practices. In North America, while British support of commercial expansionism and a free market increased, a range of new duties imposed during the 1760s made cider, sugar products, and paper goods increasingly prohibitive in cost. When these burdens fell on shoulders already struggling under the weight of underemployment, something had to give. In such colonial ports as Boston and Newport, mobs took to the streets in August 1765, burning effigies, burying tax bills in mock funerals, and attacking houses. These outbreaks of public violence drew participants from a wide social spectrum, but artisans troubled by inflation, out-migration, and worthless bills of credit played a key role.

That same year, thousands took to the streets of Quito to protest the imposition in March 1764 of a new system for taxing sugar cane production. On May 22 and June 24, 1765, butchers, small farmers, and petty retailers destroyed the customhouse. As the riots broadened through the politically radical lower classes of mestizos and native Indians, their cultural meaning changed. The violence increasingly threatened and alienated españoles (called "peninsulars") and powerful Creoles. In the Túpac Amaru rebellion in Peru in 1780–83, a riot that in different ways culminated two decades of native insurgency, the participants came from different social ranks. According to Lester D. Langley, they supported Amaru's insistence on "total war against Europeans, abolition of slavery, and reconsideration of property laws." Members of the mob, however, had differing agendas for attaining these radical ends, and their fragmentation finally brought the action to an unsuccessful halt, but not without first surprising and frightening creole leaders.[27] On both continents, a tra-

---

26. Steve J. Stern, "The Rise and Fall of Indian-White Alliances: A Regional View," *Hispanic American Historical Review* 61, no. 3 (August 1981): 476–77. On conflicts between northeast Algonquian societies, see Neal Salisbury, *Manitou and Providence: Indians, Europeans, and the Making of New England, 1500–1643* (New York, 1982), pp. 203–35. On native imperial initiatives in Latin America, see Geoffrey W. Conrad and Arthur A. Demarest, *Religion and Empire: The Dynamics of Aztec and Incan Expansionism* (New York, 1984), esp. pp. 152–90 ("Precolombian Imperialism: Theories and Evidence"). This work, along with that of Stern, makes clear that Aztec, Incan, and European imperialisms coexisted.

27. Langley, *Americas in the Age of Revolution*, p. 164; Kenneth J. Andrien, "Economic Crisis, Taxes, and the Quito Insurrection of 1765," *Past and Present* 129 (November 1990): 125–27. For the 1712 riot of the Tzeltal, Tzotzil, and Chol Maya of highland Chiapas, in which insur-

dition of crowd actions dating back a century shaped a common dynamic for political independence during the period 1775–1825. In colonial projects throughout the Western Hemisphere, imperial rule was rejected not by native peoples but by propertied Creoles attempting to balance a rejection of colonial patterns of political and economic hierarchy with a need to guarantee their own use of such preferential patterns after independence had been won. British-American Creoles and their Spanish-American counterparts were equally frustrated by the social and political implications of imperial economic change.[28]

The 1765 riots suggest the rough parallelism of colonial projects in New Spain and British North America. But when they came into direct contact, as when Latin Americans came north to such port cities as Philadelphia, Baltimore, or New York or when Americans went south, cultural difference provided a counterpoint to convergence. In 1784 Francisco de Miranda, an early exponent of a Venezuelan independence movement, visited the new United States. "Good God," he exclaimed. "What a contrast to the Spanish system!" Or in 1807 traveler John Mawe found in Buenos Aires a stratified society of Europeans, Creoles, mestizos, indios, "brown mixtures of Africans and Europeans," and "mulattoes of various degrees." He paused to consider a level and tolerance of miscegenation never seen in either England or the United States. "All these races intermix without restraint . . . so that it is difficult to define the minor gradations, or to assign limits to the ever-multiplying varieties," he commented. "This may be regarded as a momentary evil; but may it not be conducive, in the long run, to the good of society by concentrating the interests of the various classes?"[29] As these voices suggest, however, the differences between colonial projects—and thus their national effects—in Spanish, Portuguese, and British America were striking. Creole families in Venezuela, Colombia, or Mexico were in a more perilous position than those in Virginia, Pennsylvania, or Connecticut because Bourbon imperial policies imposed in 1763 had actively worked to increase taxes while disentailing the estates of older families. Because the economic system they struggled to control bound them at once more tightly to native labor and to a system of taxation in many Spanish colonies, Creoles were more

---

gents gathered and declared "Ya no hay Dios ni Rey" (Now there is neither God nor king!), see Kevin Gosner, *Soldiers of the Virgin: The Moral Economy of a Colonial Maya Rebellion* (Tucson, 1992), pp. 122–59. For an overview, see Leon G. Campbell, "Recent Research on Andean Peasant Revolts, 1750–1820," *Latin American Research Review* 14, no. 1 (1979): 3–50. See also Nancy M. Farriss, *Maya Society under Colonial Rule: The Collective Enterprise of Survival* (Princeton, 1984).

28. Langley, *Americas in the Age of Revolution*, pp. 150–55.

29. Quoted in Peggy K. Liss, *Atlantic Empires: The Network of Trade and Revolution, 1713–1826* (Baltimore, 1983), p. 143; John Mawe, *Travels in the Interior of Brazil* (Philadelphia, 1812), pp. 47–48.

dependent on native peoples and more tightly bound to the Crown than were their northern counterparts.

It is a short step from creole politics to the politics of creolization or to the syncretic fusion of cultures that occurred to some degree in colonial projects based on plantation or settler society. As it suggests intercultural mixing, blending, and cross-fertilization, creolization was directly related to the miscegenation observed by Mawe. But in its precise linguistic meaning, "creolization" refers to the state a contact or "pidgin" language attains when it develops its own grammatical and syntactic rules; a creole language has the structure necessary to produce native speakers and thus to guarantee its reproduction through time. Whether creolization occurs in language, music, body movement and gestural style, or architecture, it demands sustained, intense intercultural exchange. While trade languages and informal ways of bridging worlds occurred in almost all early modern colonial encounters, creolization across different expressive genres resulted with particular frequency from the asymmetries of Caribbean colonial exchange. Scholars and critics including Césaire, Retamar, Fanon, Edward Kamau Brathwaite, and George Lamming, among others, have explored the process by rewriting Shakespeare's *The Tempest*, a canonical yet contested work that casts the interdependency of colonial projects, territorial dispossession, race, and gender in high relief.[30]

However restricted its precise linguistic meaning might be, creolization recalls terms that describe a fusion of diverse forms without reference to temporal duration—*blending, mixing, colliding, blurring, syncretism*, and *compositional heterogeneity*, for instance—but that may occlude forms of individual representation that were emergent, short-lived, and strategically unrelated to the use of pidgins. The word to cover such phenomena

30. On distinctions in language structure, see David DeCamp, "Introduction: The Study of Pidgin and Creole Languages," in *Pidginization and Creolization of Languages*, ed. Dell Hymes (New York, 1971), pp. 15–17. See also Edward Kamau Brathwaite, *The Development of Creole Society in Jamaica, 1770–1820* (New York, 1971), and Brathwaite, *Kumina* (Boston, 1976). For a discussion of the rewriting of *The Tempest* by Césaire and Fanon, see Hulme's paper in this volume, and Brathwaite, "Caliban, Ariel, and Unprospero in the Conflict of Creolization: A Study of the Slave Revolt in Jamaica in 1831–32," in *Comparative Perspectives on Slavery in New World Plantation Societies*, ed. Vera Rubin and Arthur Tuden, Annals of the New York Academy of Sciences, vol. 292 (New York, 1977), pp. 41–62. For recent critical work on *The Tempest* and colonialism, see Charles Frey, "*The Tempest* and the New World," *Shakespeare Quarterly* 30, no. 1 (1979): 29–41; Trevor R. Griffiths, " 'This Island's Mine': Caliban and Colonialism," in *Yearbook of English Studies* 13 (1983): 59–80; Paul Brown, " 'This Thing of Darkness I Acknowledge Mine': *The Tempest* and the Discourse of Colonialism," in *Political Shakespeare: New Essays in Cultural Materialism*, ed. Jonathan Dollimore and Alan Sinfield (Ithaca, 1985), pp. 48–71; John Gillies, "Shakespeare's Virginian Masque," *English Literary History* 53 (1986): 673–707; and Alden T. Vaughan, "Shakespeare's Indian: The Americanization of Caliban," *Shakespeare Quarterly* 39, no. 2 (1988): 137–53. See also Peter Hulme, "The Profit of Language: George Lamming and the Postcolonial Novel," in *Recasting the World: Writing after Colonialism*, ed. Jonathan White (Baltimore, 1993), pp. 120–36.

is *hybridity*. The concept has its earliest roots in nineteenth-century biology and botany but was metaphorically extended to the realm of language by Mikhail Bakhtin. In his essay "Discourse in the Novel" (1934–35), he used the term to describe a "mixing" of linguistic form and the "double-accented, double-styled" qualities of parodic discourse. In two passages he defined it more closely. "What we are calling a hybrid construction," Bakhtin noted,

> is an utterance that belongs, by its grammatical (syntactic) and compositional markers, to a single speaker, but that actually contains mixed within it two utterances, two speech manners, two styles, two "languages," two semantic and axiological belief systems. We repeat, there is no formal— compositional and syntactic—boundary between these utterances, styles, languages, belief systems; the division of voices and languages takes place within the limits of a single syntactic whole, often within the limits of a single sentence. It frequently happens that even one and the same word will belong simultaneously to two languages, two belief systems that intersect in a hybrid construction—and, consequently, the word has two contradictory meanings, two accents.

And, "What is an hybridization? It is a mixture of two social languages within the limits of a single utterance, an encounter, within the arena of an utterance, between two different linguistic consciousnesses, separated from one another by an epoch, by social differentiation or by some other factor." It is crucially important to keep "hybrid expression," in which two or more "languages" inhabit a single utterance as a "syntactic whole," theoretically distinct from its close cousin and frequent cotraveler, "dialogic expression." Unlike hybridity, dialogism depends on maintaining tension between multiple and "formally distinct competing voices." According to Deborah A. Kapchan, it follows that hybridity is perceived at the level of the "primary genre"—within a single utterance, for instance—whereas dialogism works at larger level of intergeneric reference, entailing an interface in a single utterance between, say, a novel and local gossip. "It is clear," she adds, "that hybridization is more than a conversation between genres; hybridization effects semantic ambiguity in the poetic domain."[31]

31. Mikhail Bakhtin, "Discourse in the Novel," in *The Dialogic Imagination: Four Essays*, ed. Michael Holquist, trans. Caryl Emerson and Michael Holquist (Austin, 1981), pp. 304–5, 358; Deborah A. Kapchan, "Hybridity and the Marketplace: Emerging Paradigms in Folkloristics," *Western Folklore* 52, nos. 2–4 (1993): 304–5. On the nineteenth-century origins of hybridity in natural science, see Robert J. C. Young, *Colonial Desire: Hybridity in Theory, Culture, and Race* (New York, 1995), pp. 5–17, 20–22. For an argument that hybridity is a highly individuated, "special case" of syncretism which "can remain an idiosyncratic form of adaptation whose influence may fail to reach across time," see Hamid Naficy, *The Making of Exile Cultures: Iranian Television in Los Angeles* (Minneapolis, 1993), p. 189. See also N. G. Canclini,

Bhabha has at times both effaced the critical distinction between these two strategies and extended their analytic range to colonial projects. Colonial hybridity was a subaltern countermove against the evasion of humanity and moral responsibility present in the discourse of colonizers. "Hybridity is a *problematic* of colonial representation and individuation," he maintains, "that reverses the effects of the colonialist disavowal, so that other 'denied' knowledges enter upon the dominant discourse and estrange the basis of its authority—its rules of recognition." And although his arguments for the utility of the term are specifically intended to describe strategies of representation in colonial India, they have suggestive implications for how emergent forms of vernacular expression may have worked in other colonial places. By focusing less on creolization, with its qualifications of reproducibility through time, and more on hybridity and dialogism—terms that position representation as emergent, individual, internally dense, and potentially evanescent and therefore useful as an art of resistance—we are able to examine diverse colonial projects in early America where such informal moments of creative alterity happened within the ambiguity of power relations.[32]

Hybridity is a useful approach to thinking about the expressive, constituent elements of colonial encounters. But if the process of becoming colonial created new formations, how are we to approach them in methodological terms? As colonial projects accomplished political ends, they often did so through the subtle, indirect route of aesthetics to insist on the naturalization of domination and submission. Thus many of the authors of essays in this volume argue the utility of examining what Mary Louise Pratt has called the "arts of the contact zone": "Autoethnography, transculturation, critique, collaboration, bilingualism, mediation, parody, denunciation, imaginary dialogue, vernacular expression—these are some of the literate arts of the contact zone," writes Pratt. But any articulation of marginality in relation to imperial culture implies risk of "miscomprehension, incomprehension, dead letters, unread masterpieces, absolute heterogeneity of meaning."[33] Contact zone symbolic strategies

---

Hybrid Cultures: Strategies for Entering and Leaving Modernity, trans. Christopher L. Chiappari and Silvia L. Lopez (Minneapolis, 1995), and Nikos Papastergiadis, "Tracing Hybridity in Theory," in *Debating Cultural Hybridity: Multi-Cultural Identities and the Politics of Anti-Racism*, ed. Pnina Werbner and Tariq Modood (London, 1997). For one historical treatment, see William L. Andrews,"The Novelization of Voice in Early African-American Narrative," *PMLA* 105, no. 1 (1990): 23–34.

32. Homi K. Bhabha, "Signs Taken for Wonders: Questions of Ambivalence and Authority under a Tree outside Delhi, May 1817," in Bhabha, *Location of Culture*, p. 114.

33. Mary Louise Pratt, "Arts of the Contact Zone," *Profession* 91 (1991): 37. See also Pratt, *Imperial Eyes: Travel Writing and Transculturation* (New York, 1992), and Rolena Adorno, *Guaman Poma: Writing and Resistance in Colonial Peru* (Austin, 1986). It is important to note that the concept of "contact zone" was itself first theorized by Bakhtin as a means of describing the semiotics of novelization, in which different languages and literary genres come into sus-

examined in this volume include such expressive forms as a Nahua version of a Christian drama (Louise M. Burkhart); witchcraft in Andean society (Irene Silverblatt); Mohegan Joseph Johnson's letters (Laura J. Murray); translation in early Rhode Island (Anne G. Myles); the writing of Inca Garcilaso de la Vega and Guaman Poma (José Antonio Mazzotti); hybrid and monologic speech by lawyers (Robert Blair St. George); women's theatrical performances in Philadelphia, Boston, and New York (Susan Juster, Sandra M. Gustafson); and letter writing, novels, colonial portrait painting, and bodily discipline in Philadelphia (Toby L. Ditz, Carroll Smith-Rosenberg, Margaretta M. Lovell, and Michael Meranze).

Several of these arts are familiar and require little comment: parody, critique, bilingualism, denunciation. Others, including autoethnography, transculturation, and vernacular expression, may be more difficult. An *autoethnographic text* is one in which an author attempts to narrate his or her culture and society in ways that "engage with representations others have made of them." The idea is an inversion of classical ethnography. As Pratt observes, "if ethnographic texts are those in which European metropolitan subjects represent to themselves their others (usually their conquered others), autoethnographic texts are representations that the so-defined others construct *in response to* or in dialogue with those texts. Autoethnographic texts are not, then, what are usually thought of as autochthonous forms of expression or self-representation (as the Andean *quipus* were). Rather they involve a selective collaboration with an appropriation of idioms of the metropolis or the conqueror." These works are often hybridizations, combining disparate elements into emergent forms that articulate the double-voiced problematic of becoming colonial. "These are merged or infiltrated to varying degrees," Pratt continues, "with indigenous idioms to create self-representations intended to intervene in metropolitan modes of understanding. Autoethnographic works are often addressed to both metropolitan audiences and the speaker's own community. Their reception is thus highly indeterminate. Such texts often constitute a marginalized group's point of entry into the dominant circuits of print."[34]

Transculturation is the active process of moving across or through cultural boundaries to affect autoethnographic understandings and hybrid formations. In anthropology the term is frequently used to describe the communicative processes by means of which members of subaltern or marginalized social groups select from the cultural repertoires of dominant groups and invent something new of their own making. Transcul-

---

tained contact and potential dismemberment. See Mikhail Bakhtin, "Epic and Novel: Toward a Methodology for the Study of the Novel," in *Dialogic Imagination*, ed. Holquist, p. 39; see also "Glossary," p. 434.

34. Pratt, "Arts of the Contact Zone," p. 35.

turation is the action whereby a politically dominated culture appropri-
ates some of the symbolic forms of a dominant or imperial culture in
order to articulate its own continuing vision of autonomy; as such, it designates a movement less linear and predictable than either "acculturation" or "adaptation."[35] Cuban sociologist Fernando Ortiz invented the
word in 1940 to describe more precisely the internal logic and expressive
dynamics of cultures living under conquest.

At one level, *vernacular expressions* are those written or performed in the
local or national language. Yet "vernacular" is an adjective that refers to
local epistemologies, working theories of reality, and circuitries of transmission that derive more from collisions of imperial interest and
autoethnographic resistance than from any imposition of "high theory" in
a critical, academic sense. If studies of vernacular architecture or music are
indicative, then the processual realm of vernacular expression does not
reside solely in forms that diffuse from the top of European society downward or outward to the colonial sphere. Nor does it reside solely in strategies of local critique, as demonstrated in art historian Julius Lips's classic
study of modernism's domestication of "primitive" art, *The Savage Hits
Back* (1937). Instead, and in a manner consistent with both autoethnography and transculturation, vernacular expressions move both down from
the top and up from the bottom of colonial society. Shaped by this double
movement, vernacular forms—a people's folklore—are always mixtures;
"to vernacularize," a verb known since the opening years of the nineteenth
century, references uneven and uneasy attempts to create artifacts or texts
that address simultaneous but divergent social realities.[36]

By attending to these and other arts of the contact zone, a final concern
comes into view. If autoethnographic texts can be paintings or maps as
well as novels, or if vernacular expression includes buildings, music,
body movement, and foodways, why should what is typically defined as
"colonial discourse" remain so tightly bound to the spoken and written
word? There is no doubt that most cultural historians find written documents convenient. Words seem reassuringly precise. Words promise an
intentional interlocutor on the other side of time's passage. Words offer an

35. Ibid., pp. 35–36. Along with *counterpoint*, this term was initially coined by Fernando
Ortiz, *Cuban Counterpoint: Tobacco and Sugar* (1940), trans. Harriet de Onís (Durham, N.C.,
1995).

36. Julius Lips, *The Savage Hits Back* (New Haven, 1937); for a more recent meditation on
the same theme, see Marianna Tovgornick, *Gone Primitive: Savage Intellects, Modern Lives*
(Chicago, 1990). On the nature of vernacular buildings, see Eric Mercer, *English Vernacular
Houses* (London, 1975), pp. 1–7, and *OED*, 19:549–50. On the utility of folklore of ethnic conflict among the Maya for exploring their interpretation of colonial rebellions—for the highland Chiapas rebellion (1708–13), the Indian king in Quisteil (1761), and the Indian king in
Totonicapan (1820)—see Victoria Reifler Bricker, *The Indian Christ, the Indian King: The Historical Substrate of Maya Myth and Ritual* (Austin, 1981), pp. 53–83.

opportunity to practice the intellectual athletics of poststructural methodology. Languages may be read "against the grain" or "in reverse," with
attention to metaphor, stylistics, and polysemous, unstable meanings.
Ordinary written documents, from court depositions to diaries, have their
own symbolic forms as written genres and thus cannot be abstracted into
useful quotations without violating the integrity of the intended form.
Written discourse always implies a specific locus of enunciation, or social
and political position, on the part of writer and reader, and the impact of
any written or spoken text can only be assessed in relation to others of its
type; as Umberto Eco has observed, "no text is read independently of the
reader's experience of other texts." But at the same time, the emphasis on
language may prove to be a Eurocentric bias when dealing with contact
situations in which one (or more) culture used images or pictographs
rather than any system of writing. A more inclusive analytic approach
would therefore recognize the limits of discourse and demand embracing
the study of colonial semiosis across different fields of expression; such a
move would entail linking the ethnography of communication, particularly in its emphasis on performance as a frame in which heightened or
stylized expressive registers call attention to the cultural power of what is
being transacted, to the comparative exploration of colonial projects.[37] As

37. Umberto Eco, *The Role of the Reader: Explorations in the Semiotics of Texts* (London, 1981),
p. 21. On poststructuralism and postcolonial discourse, see Patricia Seed, "Review Essay:
Colonial and Postcolonial Discourse," *Latin American Research Review* 26, no. 3 (1991): 182–83,
and Seed, "Poststructuralism in Postcolonial History," *Maryland Historian* 24, no. 1 (1993):
25–26. On narrative fragmentation as a postcolonial strategy, see Gyanendra Pendey, "Voices
from the Edge: The Struggle to Write Subaltern Histories," *Ethnos* 60, nos. 3–4 (1995): 223–42.
On colonial semiosis as an alternative to the limits of discourse, see Walter D. Mignolo,
"Colonial Situations, Geographical Discourses, and Territorial Representations: Toward a
Diatopical Understanding of Colonial Semiosis," and Mignolo, "Afterword: From Colonial
Discourse to Colonial Semiosis," both in *Dispositio* 14, nos. 36–38 (1989): 93–140, 333–38. For
the earlier formation of the ethnography of communication, including how different regis-
ters of speech, material culture, and body movement were envisioned as interrelated, see
Dell Hymes, "Introduction: Toward Ethnographies of Communication," in "The Ethnogra-
phy of Communication," ed. Dell Hymes and John J. Gumperz, special issue of *American
Anthropologist* 66, no. 6, pt. 2 (1964): 1–34; on performance, see Richard Bauman, *Verbal Art as
Performance* (Rowley, Mass., 1977), and Deborah A. Kapchan, "Performance," *Journal of
American Folklore* 108, no. 430 (1995): 479–508. Studies using images and artifacts as an alter-
native to written discourse include Serge Gruzinski, *Painting the Conquest: The Mexican Indian
and the European Renaissance* (Paris, 1992); R. Tom Zuidema, "Guaman Poma and the Art of
Empire: Toward an Iconography of Inca Royal Dress," and Rolena Adorno, "Images of *Indios
Latinos* in Early Colonial Peru," both in *Transatlantic Encounters: Europeans and Andeans in the
Sixteenth Century*, ed. Kenneth J. Andrien and Rolena Adorno (Berkeley, 1991), pp. 151–202,
232–70; John Rowe, "The Chronology of Inca Wooden Cups," in *Essays in Pre-Columbian Art
and Archaeology*, ed. Samuel K. Lothrop et al. (Cambridge, Mass., 1961), pp. 317–41, 473–75,
598–600; John Steckley, "The Warrior and the Lineage: Jesuit Uses of Iroquoian Images to
Communicate Christianity," *Ethnohistory* 39, no. 4 (1992): 478–509; Laurier Turgeon,
"Échange d'objets et conquête de l'autre en Nouvelle-France au XVIe siècle," in *Transferts cul-
turels et métissages Amérique/Europe, XVIe–XXe siècle*, ed. Laurier Turgeon, Denys Delage, and

the essays in this book demonstrate, becoming colonial in early America did not happen strictly at the level of discourse alone. It happened in many places where the realms of discourse and daily practice converged to define regimes of authority and techniques of parodic subversion and resistance.

The structure of this book introduces a way of thinking about becoming colonial in early America that foregrounds neither chronology nor a fragmenting overview of social or institutional development—of family history, religious history, legal history, environmental history, women's history, ethnohistory, political history, economic history, and the like. Rather, this volume encourages the reader to think about how, for Europeans, Natives, mestizos, slaves, Creoles, and mulattoes, living in colonial projects transformed basic cultural assumptions and working concepts: of authentic self and essentialized other; of communication through spoken word, written text, performed drama, images, and material things across different and emerging symbolic systems; of the ways that sustained contact both undermined and attenuated the stable subject positions of both Natives and Creoles in transnational colonial projects and emergent nation states; and of the ways in which these novel subjectivities first emerged, were rehearsed, and were affirmed through public performances. The four sections of this book make this process of intercultural change apparent. In part one, Hulme and Michael Warner argue that "interrogating America" is an essential first step in analysis. What is America? How should we think about America in relation to postcolonial theory or to received truths about what being colonial involved? How should we think about languages, textuality, imagery? Part two attempts to demonstrate, using paired essays, how the linked arts of "translation and transculturation" shaped the interacting cultures of both Europeans and native peoples; "translation" in this instance references both the interpretive revaluation of a spoken or written text into another language and the phenomenon of "heavenly translation," or the revaluation of an individual's soul in resurrection. The process of moving through alternative realities subsumed a variety of linked cultural practices that current work is reassessing: religious dissent and difference (essays by Burkhart and Myles), literature and witchcraft (Silverblatt and Mazzotti), family piety (Hall and Murray), and race (John K. Thornton and Dana D. Nelson). The colonial places these authors explore range from seventeenth-century New England to sixteenth-century Peru, eighteenth-century Africa and America, and post-Revolutionary Philadelphia. Philadelphia serves as the centerpiece of part three, "Shaping Subjectivities." Here, essays by Ditz,

Réal Ouellet (Quebec, 1996), pp. 155–68; and Turgeon, "The Tale of the Kettle: Odyssey of an Intercultural Object," *Ethnohistory* 44, no. 1 (1997): 1–29.

Smith-Rosenberg, Lovell, and Meranze, respectively, examine the ways that experience with inequalities of gender, interracial contact, and the regulation and enforced discipline of the human body (through portraits, in prisons) constructed individual identity and agency in North America's largest urban center. Philadelphia is particularly useful for this focus because it drew people from throughout Britain's northern colonies, from the Caribbean, and from Latin America. It was a city that, despite Quaker antipathies, had a heavy investment in the slave trade and represented independence throughout the Western Hemisphere. The fourth and final part of this book argues that "oral performance and personal power" in early America were closely tied. Performance implied theatricality and the possibility of artifice and misrepresentation. Yet these stagings—of ritual speech and legal theatrics (in the essay by St. George), gendered religion (Juster), and gendered nationalism (Gustafson)—helped to produce the auratic or charismatic effects that in colonial projects frequently proved pivotal in claiming leadership and building the ideology of community on which class relations, labor relations, and the aesthetics of exchange intimately depend.

When Aimé Césaire cautioned in 1955 that colonialism demanded the wiping out of historical possibilities, he had in mind the possibilities that vanished from colonized cultures—to worship as they chose, to manage economies as they chose, to shape the pasts they symbolically used to interpret their present. Colonial projects, however, also constricted the historical possibilities of the cultures in control of imperial expansion. Indeed, what Césaire called the "boomerang effect of colonization" epitomized the process by which Europeans, extolling their own civility while castigating the brutish manners of native peoples, revealed their own inner barbarism. The imperial agent, the planter, the settler, "in order to ease his conscience gets into the habit of seeing the other man as *an animal*, accustoms to treating him like an animal, and tends objectively to transform himself into an animal."[38]

The essays in this volume survey contested terrains on which colonial projects developed and how literature, religious practices, languages, medical and penal theories, and gendered dramatic performances offered social arenas through which Europeans and different Native cultures became colonial in early America. They try to catch the boomerang in midflight, to turn it in the winds of time. Disappeared pasts emerge, slowly, back into the light.

38. Césaire, *Discourse on Colonialism*, p. 20.

part one

Interrogating America

Postcolonial Theory and Early America: An Approach from the Caribbean

PETER HULME

IF THE Caribbean impinges at all on the conventional picture of "early America," then it is through the image of Tituba, the "dark Eve" from Barbados who brought her region's "wild and strange superstitions" to the Puritan innocence of Salem, sparking off the witchcraft hysteria of 1692, one of early America's defining moments, sometimes seen in mythological terms as a "national fall." Tituba's origins have always been mysterious—sometimes Carib Indian, sometimes African—but she has always been a teller of tales and an agent of voodoo, qualities sufficient to ensure her role as "the central, generating figure" in the origins of the witch-hunt.[1] In this essay I take on two challenges suggested by the figure of Tituba. The first is to consider some of the conceptual vocabulary that has recently been brought to the analysis of colonial societies and cultures under the general rubric of "postcoloniality." The second is to look at early America through the lens of the Caribbean—particularly of its native cultures—in a way that may connect to questions of continental range. I will approach both issues by reference to debates within the broad fields of cultural studies and cultural history.

This paper was given as the keynote lecture at the conference on which this volume is based, and retains most of its original shape and language. Warm thanks go to Robert Blair St. George for the invitation to the conference and to Richard S. Dunn—chair of that keynote session—whose landmark work, *Sugar and Slaves*, was in large part responsible for my own initial fascination with the Caribbean.

1. "Dark Eve," "national fall," and "central generating figure" are terms from Bernard Rosenthal, *Salem Story: Reading the Witch Trials of 1692* (New York, 1993), pp. 10–13, on which I draw for this opening section. "Wild and strange superstitions" is a phrase used by Charles W. Upham in his influential *Salem Witchcraft* (1867), quoted by Rosenthal (p. 10).

I.

Questions of terminology warrant attention first, because the process of naming is always one of delimiting a subject for inquiry, and both *early America* and *postcolonial* are far from unproblematic terms. "Early" is one of those words that becomes increasingly puzzling the more you look at it. It might initially appear to make sense only as one part of a completed sequence, as in "early Victorian literature," say, as opposed to "late Victorian literature." To use a temporal marker to describe an incomplete process is almost always a sign of wish fulfillment—"late capitalism," we sometimes say, with its attractive if misleading connotations of "recently deceased." To describe the "early" part of a *nation*'s history as opposed perhaps to its "recent" history seems less problematic, but is a nation being described in "early America"? Presumably not, for the "early" period of U.S. history would run from 1776 to 1877 or 1898, ruling out of bounds many of the papers included in this volume. In the field of literary history, William Spengemann has submitted to withering critique attempts to turn a selection from the literature of British colonial America into "early" U.S. national literature,[2] and I imagine analogous critiques must exist in other disciplines. No doubt too much nit-picking about terminology serves to paralyze thought altogether. In any case, I take the phrase "early America" to be not quite as self-evident as it used to be, and some of the credit for that change should go to the many practitioners in the field who have broadened its range over the last three decades. Richard S. Dunn's pioneering work on the Caribbean was just one example of a willingness to look beyond the bounds of "the future United States" when considering "early America."[3]

At the end of the day, it is enough—or almost enough—to recognize that the existence of a volume of essays such as this one is a sign that the word "America" is regaining, at least within the humanities, its proper continental scope, with the resultant possibilities for the kind of comparative work pursued by the authors of the essays in this collection. So just one further point on America. It should be self-evident—but sometimes seems not to be—that if America is the name for the continent, then the United States of America should be known by its full name or by its initials. In recent years there has been a trend toward two perhaps analogous and defensive moves at the beginning of essays and books. One makes a point of bringing up the question of gendered pronouns only to claim that the male pronoun is unfortunately unavoidable in English to designate the ungendered agent, and the author—always male—then proceeds with

2. See, most recently, William Spengemann, *A New World of Words: Redefining Early American Literature* (New Haven, 1994).
3. Richard S. Dunn, *Sugar and Slaves: The Rise of the Planter Class in the English West Indies, 1624–1713* (Chapel Hill, 1972).

a sigh of relief to use "he" throughout. The other move recognizes the political significance of the rhetoric of "America" and then proceeds to use the terms "America" and the "United States" as synonyms. The real problem here, however, is the adjective. According to some geographers, one of the few points to be made in favor of the North American Free Trade Agreement (NAFTA) is that it applies the "North American" with proper geographic precision, rather than using it as the adjective for the United States. (Spanish at least has *estadounidense* [(citizen) of the United States], though it is a bit of a mouthful.) A recent study dedicated to the myths and stereotypes generated in the United States about Latin America finds no alternative but to use "American" and "Latin American" as the two relevant adjectives for those entities without considering that the usage "American" to refer to the United States deprives the continent of its adjective. By perpetuating the idea of a standard "America" from which everything else is a deviation, this usage further consolidates the stereotypes the book is supposed to be analyzing and contesting.[4]

There are only two controversial parts to the word "postcolonial"—one is "post" and the other is "colonial"—so let me offer a tentative definition as well as a defense of the usefulness of the term. "Postcolonial theory" describes a body of work which attempts to break with the colonialist assumptions that have marked many of the projects of political and cultural criticism launched from Europe and the United States, at the same time as it learns from and frequently refigures those projects in its analyses of the networks of imperial power that continue to control much of the world. The growing popularity of the term *postcolonial* has put questions of colonialism and imperialism onto the agenda of literary and cultural studies, helping implicate "culture" with "imperialism" (to use Edward Said's title) more effectively that many of us had imagined possible.[5] Nonetheless, the relevance of postcolonial theory to America is, to put it mildly, not yet well established.

There are several separate problems here, though they tend to overlap. First is the problem of the time depth of imperialism. In *Culture and Imperialism*, Said recognizes only the age of high imperialism, ignoring the earlier colonial period—what used to be called "the first British Empire"; Said discusses Jane Austen's *Mansfield Park*, published in 1814, as a work from what he calls the "pre-imperialist age."[6] The relationship between

---

4. See Fredrick B. Pike, *The United States and Latin America: Myths and Stereotypes of Civilization and Nature* (Austin, 1992). An admission: I belong to a small but noisy society in England campaigning for the adoption of the adjective "Usean" to apply to the United States.

5. Edward Said, *Culture and Imperialism* (New York, 1993). Contemporary postcolonial theory is usually dated from Said's *Orientalism* (New York, 1978).

6. Said, *Culture and Imperialism*, p. 69. See also my review of *Culture and Imperialism* in "Imperial Counterpoint," *Wasafiri* 18 (1993): 57–61.

"imperialism" and "colonialism" is complicated, but because, generally speaking, "imperialism" is taken as the broader term, Said can—and does—broach the phenomenon of postcolonial theory within a wider discussion of the relationship between "culture" and "imperialism." Fair enough: this is a logical starting point. In practice, however, the field studied in *Culture and Imperialism* is not significantly broader than what was studied in *Orientalism*. The geographic fulcrum of *Culture and Imperialism* is certainly very similar to that of Said's earlier book: the Middle East, with a stretch east to India and west to Algeria. The temporal fulcrum of the book is 1902—the year of Joseph Conrad's *Heart of Darkness*—with about a century on either side given any real weight of analysis. The temporal limitation explains the geography of the book, given the disposition of the British and French empires at the end of the nineteenth century. But the temporal limitation has itself no *obvious* explanation given that these empires both began in the seventeenth century, in America. One consequence of this temporal limitation is that issues of slavery and racism, so inextricably associated with European culture and empire, make only the briefest of appearances in Said's work.

What happens in *Culture and Imperialism*, as it had in *Orientalism*, is that the United States—which Said casually refers to as "America"—appears on the scene to assume the imperial mantle from Britain and France after the Second World War, but without any substantial consideration of the country's own origins as a set of British, Spanish and French colonies; its own imperial beginnings in the Pacific during the mid–nineteenth century; its own history of "internal colonialism"; its own genocidal wars against the indigenous population of North America; or of its own twentieth-century adventurism in Central America and the Caribbean. Said's insistence on placing U.S. foreign policy within a discussion of imperial projects may be entirely salutary, but his analysis of U.S. imperialism lacks the historical and cultural time depth he brings to the European material. Consideration of such time depths would inevitably have brought early America onto his imperial map.

My argument so far might suggest that America's relative absence from the postcolonial debate has been accidental. Said's work is usually seen as inaugurating the discourse, and he focused—for personal as well as cultural reasons—on the Middle East; in addition, postwar struggles against European colonial empires have mostly taken place in Africa and the Indian subcontinent and therefore the most prominent postcolonial theorists have come from those places. Yet there is a contention, articulated, for example, in contributions to a symposium on postcolonial theory in the *Latin American Research Review*, to the effect that the Latin American countries simply do not fit into the postcolonial paradigm at all, indeed that the very notions of colonialism and imperialism came from the *modern* experiences of the non-Hispanic colonial powers and were only subsequently and improperly imposed by historians onto the Spanish American experience.[7] If this argument were correct, then certainly Latin America, and probably the whole of the continent, would fall outside the bounds of this discussion; Said's oversights would turn out to be intuitively correct emphases, and American exceptionalism would be justified with a vengeance.

The argument seems fundamentally flawed, however. Its basis is the point that the wars of independence were not primarily fought by people who were colonized against the people who had colonized them. This point is undoubtedly true, but the real question is, Why take that model of colonizer and colonized as providing the sole definition of colonialism and decide that because America does not fit the model you cannot talk about decolonization, colonial discourse, or postcolonial theory? If distinctions are going to be made—and they should be—then there are plenty of important distinctions that do not simply remove America from the colonial map, as the work of Patricia Seed and others demonstrates.[8] For one thing, the etymology of the word "colony" does not suggest that only *people* are colonized. *Land* is so often the crucial issue. John Locke's *Second Treatise* is a justification of the appropriation of land *from* its original inhabitants; it stands as a classic document of colonial discourse, irrespective of whether the invaders whose actions were justified by the arguments in such documents saw themselves as "colonists" according to narrower definitions of the word.[9] To say, rightly, that the wars of independence were followed by wars of extermination against the indigenous populations of North and South America does not—under this argument—entail calling subsequent discourses justifying such extermination

7. The key articles here are Patricia Seed, "Colonial and Postcolonial Discourse," *Latin American Research Review* 26, no. 3 (1991): 181–200, and Rolena Adorno, "Reconsidering Colonial Discourse for Sixteenth- and Seventeenth-Century Spanish America," *Latin American Research Review* 28, no. 3 (1993): 135–45. Adorno draws on the arguments of J. Jorge Klor de Alva, "Colonialism and Post-Colonialism as (Latin) American Mirages," *Colonial Latin American Review* 1, nos. 1–2 (1992): 3–23. Klor de Alva has expanded these arguments in "The Postcolonization of the (Latin) American Experience: A Reconsideration of 'Colonialism,' 'Postcolonialism,' and 'Mestizaje,' " in *After Colonialism: Imperial Histories and Postcolonial Displacements*, ed. Gyan Prakash (Princeton, 1995), pp. 241–75.

8. See, for example, Seed, *Ceremonies of Possession in Europe's Conquest of the New World, 1492–1640* (Cambridge, 1995).

9. See Hulme, "The Spontaneous Hand of Nature: Savagery, Colonialism, and the Enlightenment," in *The Enlightenment and Its Shadows*, ed. Peter Hulme and Ludmilla Jordanova (London, 1990), pp. 16–34, and James Tully, "Rediscovering America: The *Two Treatises* and Aboriginal Rights," in Tully, *An Approach to Political Philosophy: Locke in Contexts* (Cambridge, 1993), pp. 137–76.

noncolonial but means that from the indigenous perspective colonialism is not over when a particular state becomes "postcolonial" in some formal sense.

II.

Like most scholars who regard their work as offering something different, practitioners of postcolonial theory make explicit claims to read texts with greater attention than they have previously been afforded. The fact that it is called a "theory" and that the notion of "colonial discourse" has been central to its development would seem to place postcolonial theory firmly on *this* side of the so-called discursive or linguistic turn. The U.S. academy has been polarized around this issue in the late twentieth century, as has—to a lesser degree—the academy in Britain, and I hardly suggest that postcolonial theory offers a way forward that will satisfy all parties; it probably would not be worth much if it did satisfy all. But in some important ways, postcolonial theory is very different from other work that has been enabled by that discursive turn, differences I would like to explore.

Postcolonial theory should not, for a start, simply be conflated with postmodernism. Said's work might appear to some people as contradictory in its attempt to combine an investigation of the questions about representation enabled by poststructuralism with an undoubted commitment to the possibility of writing certain kinds of cultural history grounded in material realities, but—following Said's example—postcolonial theory has proved willing to struggle with such apparent contradictions rather than opt to dwell in the intoxicatingly pure but ultimately sterile atmosphere of postmodern epistemological skepticism.

One of the concerns of postcolonial theory has been with identifying the *locatedness* of European theoretical vocabulary as a way of challenging the falsely universal claims of that theory. To *ground* conceptual language is to make it work harder to grasp the world beyond its locality. In part because of its analyses of the locatedness of scholarship, postcolonial theory is always likely to contain arguments to the effect that even the most seemingly "transparent" or "innocent" scholarship is underwritten by a theoretical project. To that extent it is to be placed firmly within the camp of "theory." Yet one of the most interesting aspects of postcolonial theory is that its "theory" often tends to be written, as it were, with a lowercase *t*. Walter Benjamin once wrote that words are sails and that the way they are set turns them into concepts.[10] Postcolonial theory has in that sense

---

10. Benjamin's words are quoted as an epigraph in Paul Gilroy, *The Black Atlantic: Modernity and Double Consciousness* (London, 1993), p. xiii.

often been *vernacular* theory in something like the original sense of that fascinating word, seeking to develop a conceptual vocabulary by setting its vernacular resources. Vernacular theory is not necessarily high theory in the usual First World sense. Rigorous thinking, political consciousness, and cultural acumen are not necessarily dependent on a conceptual vocabulary sedimented from many centuries of metaphysics. Vernacular theory will tend both to grow closer to the ground and to be self-reflexive to the extent that it is studying its own genesis, trying to name the processes that brought it into being—that is, though "local," it is never in any simple sense "pure" or "autochthonous."

In the postcolonial context the arguments for giving due consideration to the local are, first, that the discourses of colonialism have always operated by making the local (colonized) place secondary to the metropolitan center, with local history calibrated according to an external norm; and, second, that the stereotypic simplification of colonial discourse works by a similarly reductive dismissal of "local" distinctions: the theater of colonial discourse is populated by such figures as "the Oriental," "the savage," and "the Indian," figures who have been divorced from particular times and places. Thus postcolonial work is to a degree reconstitutive; to begin to understand local geographies and histories and to allow them to count in a way previously denied are crucial counterhegemonic moves. The notion of the postmodern has tended to homogenize the world, to see the forces of postmodernity extending even into corners of the world seemingly most remote from centers of capitalist development; post*colonial* work has been committed in practice to the elaboration of vernacular distinctions, to the giving of full weight to local developments.

Perhaps the most intriguing of the ways in which postcolonial theory may help break down what have become established academic oppositions lies in its commitment to some of the most entrenched areas of what has often passed for traditional scholarship. "Scholarship" is the key word here. The opponents of Theory (with an uppercase *T*) have usually set themselves up as defenders of Scholarship (with an uppercase *S*). That may always have been a false opposition, but it certainly became more difficult to perpetuate after—to take just the most salient example from early American studies—the publication in 1991 of David Henige's devastating book *In Search of Columbus*, which is a sustained indictment of "traditional" scholarship for its sloppiness and uncritical thinking about the *diario* of Columbus—which after all has so often been called the foundational text of America, however that America has been conceived.[11] Henige's larger point is that scholars in general (and historians in particular) have paid too little attention to matters of text, accepting inaccu-

---

11. David Henige, *In Search of Columbus: The Sources for the First Voyage* (Tucson, 1991).

rate texts as the basis for their analyses and interpretations and not thinking hard enough about the interpretative steps they make while reading.
More interesting for my argument here is that Henige's project clearly
connects—even to the point of joint publication—with that of somebody
such as Margarita Zamora, whose own fine book about Columbus makes
use of theoretical work in pragmatics and linguistics to *read* Columbus's
texts with more attention than they have usually been granted, thereby
both complicating and illuminating the more traditional "historical"
problems of reliability and authenticity.[12] Zamora's notion of the text is
well removed from the narrow framework within which new critical or
deconstructive formalisms have usually worked. Her concern for pragmatics, for example, puts her in the company of such critics as Valentin
Volosinov for whom the "word" is always a social event.[13] She directs our
attention to fundamental but often unasked questions concerning the circumstances under which a text was produced, to whom it was addressed,
what questions it was answering, pushing—as does Henige's complementary work—against the boundary between the disciplines of historical and literary studies. Here, as always, "scholarship" by itself is never
enough.

Let me offer a specific example that relates to the establishment of the
European picture of Native Caribbean cultures at the end of the fifteenth
century, which I take to be the beginning of "early America" as defined in
this volume. One of the perennial subjects of debate about the Native
Caribbean concerns the topic of "cannibalism" and whether some native
inhabitants, in particular those called Caribs, whose supposed name was
taken to describe the practice in the European languages, did eat human
flesh. Whenever this subject is assessed by historians, a key text is always
the letter written by Dr. Alvarez Chanca during Columbus's second voyage to the Caribbean in 1493–94. One of the best recent books about
Columbus has Dr. Chanca reporting "the discovery of human arm and leg
bones in the houses [on Guadeloupe], presumably the remains of a canni-
bal feast," an interpretation the book supports through a sharp contrast
drawn between Columbus's hyperbolic accounts of the wonders of the
Caribbean and what it calls the "firsthand, hardheaded testimony" of
people such as Dr. Chanca and others who sailed with Columbus. These
alternative accounts are offered as valuable correctives to Columbus's
overblown descriptions: "Chanca's matter-of-fact reporting of these horrors leaves little doubt of their authenticity." Case closed. For historians,

---

12. Margarita Zamora, *Reading Columbus* (Berkeley, 1993); David Henige and Margarita
Zamora, "Text, Context, Intertext: Columbus's *diario de a bordo* as Palimpsest," *The Americas*
46 (1989): 17–40. Rosenthal, *Salem Story*, shares this general approach.

13. See Valentin N. Volosinov, *Marxism and the Philosophy of Language*, trans. Ladislaw
Matejka and I. R. Titunik (New York, 1973).

as for public prosecutors, the very best evidence is eyewitness evidence. A footnote divides scholars as it divides witnesses. Historians and social scientists have hard heads and therefore accept the existence of cannibalism in pre-1492 America. Some anthropologists and literary critics, the softheaded, suggest that cannibalism existed only in the minds of Europeans, an attitude said to defy reason, logic, and the available evidence.[14]

This, then, is one of the primal scenes of early America: indigenous savagery observed and reported on by a European eyewitness, with Chanca's status as a medical doctor equipping him with the kind of knowledge and approach that mark him as an appropriate forerunner of the objective historian. On closer inspection the "horrors" that Chanca reported turn out to have been four or five human bones collected—that is to say, stolen— by one of Columbus's officers from a deserted hut on the island, along with some cotton, some food, and two large parrots. "When we saw [the bones]," Chanca actually wrote, "we suspected that the islands were those islands of Caribe, which are inhabited by people who eat human flesh."[15]

Columbus's plan in the fall of 1493 was to take up his exploration of the Caribbean islands almost exactly where he had left off earlier that year, having supposedly heard about the existence of cannibalistic Natives but without actually having encountered any. The working assumption was already that the second expedition had arrived at the islands of the supposed cannibals, an assumption rapidly confirmed by the sight of the human bones. The "reality" or otherwise of Caribbean cannibalism is not at issue here; the point is how carelessly texts tend to be read. To begin with, Chanca was not an eyewitness to cannibalism at all, however that practice might be defined: he is, at best, an eyewitness to the presence of human bones inside a hut, which is not the same thing at all, particularly given Caribbean mortuary practices. In any case, Chanca had not been on the first voyage, so he himself had no expectations, let alone any knowledge. When he writes "We suspected that . . ." he can be referring only to a collective view promoted principally by Columbus himself as source of authority and as main conduit of information and opinion between first voyage and second. Chanca was clearly not writing as an independent and clear-sighted witness; he was promulgating an official position into which he himself had been inducted. The supposed division between Columbus and Chanca falls at the first hurdle for want of a certain care in textual reading, a care that would owe something to a hermeneutics of

14. William D. Phillips and Carla Rahn Phillips, *The Worlds of Christopher Columbus* (Cambridge, 1988), pp. 196–97, 295 n. 21. For a fuller version of this argument, see Peter Hulme, "Making Sense of the Native Caribbean," *New West Indian Guide* 67, nos. 3–4 (1993): 189–220.

15. Diego Alvarez Chanca, "The Report of Dr. Chanca," in *Wild Majesty: Encounters with Caribs from Columbus to the Present Day*, ed. Peter Hulme and Neil L. Whitehead (Oxford, 1992), p. 32.

suspicion and something to a concern for the pragmatics of writing in the fifteenth century. This kind of reading contains reference to the regularities suggested by such a term as *colonial discourse* but can hardly be seen as having been concocted on the wilder shores of postmodern theorization. Without such attention to the textuality of source material, contemporary historiography and anthropology are likely to replicate the self-serving truths of colonial discourse, to the detriment—*como siempre*—of the indigenous population. As Patricia Galloway puts it in her analogous assessment of the de Soto narratives, "With few exceptions these sources portray Indian peoples and their motivations as . . . Europeans' preconceptions demanded that they be; and these verbal images are embedded in a Western European discourse that is still so congenial to our own modes of apprehending reality that we often fail to recognize the problematic aspects of the texts themselves."[16] Postcolonial studies push for that recognition of problematicity against the congeniality of our "common" sense.

III.

In the early years of its development, postcolonial theory tended to leave America off its map, to the detriment both of that theory and of studies of America. Where American postcolonial theory does exist— where, to be more precise, postcolonial theorists are now beginning to recognize or create its precursors, its own retrospectively produced genealogy—that theory often stems from the Caribbean. But in many ways the historiography and anthropology of the Caribbean, at least as they pertain to its indigenous inhabitants, are perhaps the least developed in all the continent. So let me try in this section to explain the seeming disparity, in the hope that it will find some reflections outside the Caribbean.

One of the ironies of Edward Said's lack of attention to America in *Culture and Imperialism* is that the word that does most work for Said in establishing the kinds of connections he wants to make between "culture" and "imperialism" is "counterpoint." "Counterpoint" has a long history within musical terminology, but within postcolonial theory it has a very precise origin in Fernando Ortiz's *Contrapunteo cubano*, published in 1940, which also introduced the term *transculturation* into anthropological and historical discourse.[17] This is an irony rather than an oversight: there is no

16. Patricia Galloway, "The Archaeology of Ethnohistorical Narrative," in *Columbian Consequences*, ed. David Hurst Thomas, vol. 3, *The Spanish Borderlands in Pan-American Perspective* (Washington, D.C., 1991), p. 453.

17. Fernando Ortiz, *Contrapunteo cubano del tabaco y el azúcar* (1940); *Cuban Counterpoint: Tobacco and Sugar*, trans. Harriet de Onís, with a new introduction by Fernando Coronil (Durham, N.C., 1995).

reason why Said's already encyclopedic knowledge and range of references should extend to the Caribbean. But I do want to make a larger
point out of the irony.

In the middle part of the twentieth century much of what we can now
see as Caribbean postcolonial theory and criticism clustered around readings of Shakespeare's *The Tempest*, a play originally written at that crucial
early American juncture just before the first major English settlements on
both mainland and islands. Particularly in Aimé Césaire's powerful
rewriting of the play, the dominant relationship came to be seen as that
between Prospero and Caliban, colonizer and colonized, a model taken
from the Caribbean to Africa in the 1950s and grounded in anticolonial
struggle in the work of Frantz Fanon.[18] In this "Third World" reading the
key words of the play are "This island's mine," Caliban's assertion of his
rights to the land that has been taken from him by Prospero's usurpation.[19] I remain committed to the continuing valence of this model and to
the relevance of Caliban's words. However much we might want to complicate the picture, that claim to land rights is still fundamental to indigenous groups throughout the world, and nowhere more so than on the
American continent.

But the conflict between Prospero and Caliban cannot be definitive of
the colonial situation. Caliban is an overdetermined figure who—like
Tituba—can be read as American or African or both, but his compacted
character obviously cannot suggest the triangular relationship—between
white, red, and black—that defines so many parts of the continent during
the colonial period.[20] In addition, feminist critics have rightly pointed out
that the marginalization of Miranda and Sycorax within the anticolonial
criticism and appropriations of *The Tempest* has tended to deliver an
entirely masculine world of heroic struggle equally inadequate to historical realities and to postcolonial critical ideals.[21]

To my mind the limitation of *The Tempest* for postcolonial work comes
from the very clarity with which it articulates one of the most powerful
fears running through at least English America, here in the interdiction
that Prospero puts on what might have been seen as the "natural" or per-

18. Aimé Césaire, *Une tempête: D'après "La tempête" de Shakespeare. Adaptation pour un théa-
tre nègre* (Paris, 1969); Frantz Fanon, *Black Skin, White Masks*, trans. Charles Lam Markmann
(New York, 1967). See also Rob Nixon, "Caribbean and African Appropriations of *The Tempest*," *Critical Inquiry* 13 (1987): 576–78.

19. William Shakespeare, *The Tempest*, ed. Stephen Orgel (Oxford, 1994), 1.2.331.

20. On the need for that red-black-white triangulation, see David Murray, "Racial Identity
and Self-Invention in North America: The Red and the Black," in *Writing and Race*, ed. Tim
Youngs (London, 1997), pp. 80–101.

21. Abena P. A. Busia, "Silencing Sycorax: On African Colonial Discourse and the
Unvoiced Female," *Cultural Critique* 14 (1989–90): 81–104, and, more generally, the essays in
"The Tempest" and Its Travels, ed. Peter Hulme and William H. Sherman (London, 2000).

haps "inevitable" relationship between Caliban and Miranda on the island. One reading of the play would see Prospero's willingness to lose his beloved Milanese kingdom through Miranda's marriage to the heir of Naples as indicative of the high price he is willing to pay to avoid miscegenation. Ultimately, *The Tempest* turns its back on what at a possibly unconscious level the play is aware will become one of the defining factors of Caribbean and, indeed, American culture: *mestizaje*.

Ortiz's counterpoint between sugar and tobacco, which manages—in ways too complicated to be briefly described—to be a triangular relationship, provides one example of how Caribbean cultural theory has embraced what most European and colonial thought, from Shakespeare onward, has found most dangerous about the Caribbean. Apart from Ortiz, that relatively small geocultural area of the Caribbean has produced postcolonial theorists of the significance of Fanon and Césaire, already mentioned, as well as Edouard Glissant, George Lamming, Roberto Fernández Retamar, and C. L. R. James, to name just a few.[22] One possible reason for the wealth of this kind of writing in the Caribbean is the fact that all theorizing in the Caribbean is articulated across—even if it sometimes ignores—the genocide of the area's native population. *Native* is always a fraught term, certainly so in Algeria and India, which often provide the paradigms for the colonizer / colonized relationship, and equally so in Mexico and Peru. The Caribbean is perhaps exceptional inasmuch as no discourse (with minor and recent exceptions) can claim to embody a genuinely native point of view, in the sense of "indigenous," however much *indigenismo* of various colors can be a political or cultural card to play at certain junctures, as it was in Cuba and the Dominican Republic in the late nineteenth century or as it has been in Puerto Rico in recent years. So what may be the case is that precisely this *lack* of a native positionality has put Caribbean theorists in the forefront of the articulation of a conceptual vocabulary that can make sense of at least certain sorts of cultural developments during and after the colonial period.

The Caribbean has certainly been a fertile ground for the vernacular developments that might be seen as very much in tune with the dominant notes of a more international postcolonial theory. The language of transculturation and counterpoint, of creolization and *métissage*, sits quickly and comfortably alongside the language of hybridity and ambivalence, migration and diaspora. Instead of the "frontier," for so long the defining concept for cultural contact, with its implications of expansion and contraction, a kind of cultural hydraulics, the early Caribbean can now be

22. Edouard Glissant, *Le discours antillais* (Paris, 1981); George Lamming, *The Pleasures of Exile* (London, 1960); Roberto Fernández Retamar, *Calibán: Apuntes sobre la cultura en nuestra América* (Mexico, 1971); and C. L. R. James, *The Black Jacobins: Toussaint L'Ouverture and the San Domingo Revolution*, 2d ed. (New York, 1962).

seen as a "contact zone," a phrase Mary Louise Pratt uses to refer to the *space* of colonial encounters, in which peoples geographically and historically separated come into contact with each other and establish ongoing relations, usually involving conditions of coercion, radical inequality, and intractable conflict. *Contact* is a term that Pratt takes from linguistics, where "contact languages" are improvised forms of communication which develop among speakers of different native languages who need to communicate with one another and which become "creoles" when they have native speakers of their own.[23] As one of the region's leading anthropologists has put it, the Caribbean is "nothing but contact"[24]—and therefore soon, in a cultural sense, nothing but "creole." Whether the Caribbean should in this respect stand as a metonym for America as a whole is a difficult question; some theory undoubtedly travels well, but we do not as yet understand much about the cultural baggage that all terms inevitably carry with them, and the language of creolization, for example, is probably open to quite as reactionary usage as the language of mestizaje has been in Latin America.[25]

IV.

Only very slowly are postcolonial imperatives beginning to alter our picture of the Native Caribbean and of the part that it played in the "contact zone" which is Caribbean history. The still paradigmatic account of the Native Caribbean is characterized by three features: first, initial contact in the Caribbean is between well-defined groups that become smaller or larger during the colonial period—Native Caribbean groups become smaller, African and European groups become larger; second, the indigenous population has certain characteristics which do not change over the period and which were brought from original homelands in the Amazon and Orinoco basins; and third, the indigenous population is marked by a radical dichotomy between two groups, one naturally aggressive, one naturally peaceful, now usually called by the supposedly ethnic names "Carib" and "Taino." This account is based on sixteenth-century Spanish sources and on seventeenth-century French missionary accounts, although it was articulated in its contemporary form in the aftermath of

23. Mary Louise Pratt, *Imperial Eyes: Travel Writing and Transculturation* (New York, 1992), pp. 1–11; see also Pratt, "Transculturation and Autoethnography: Peru 1615 / 1980," in *Colonial Discourse / Postcolonial Theory*, ed. Francis Barker, Peter Hulme, and Margaret Iversen (Manchester, 1994), pp. 24–46.

24. Michel-Rolph Trouillot, "The Caribbean Region: An Open Frontier in Anthropological Theory," *Annual Review of Anthropology* 21 (1992): 22.

25. For the debate around *créolité* in Martinique, see Richard Price and Sally Price, "Shadowboxing in the Mangrove," *Cultural Anthropology* 12, no. 1 (1997): 3–36.

1898; in many ways, it is a U.S. imperial view of the Caribbean, deeply marked by late-nineteenth-century ideas of race and warfare. This is—to borrow a phrase from Nancy Farriss—a labor-saving theory, at least for historians, because the indigenous populations are denied any history at all. They fall from the almost exclusively ceramic heaven of "prehistory" into the hell of modern time in which they supposedly shrink and melt.[26]

A postcolonial ethnohistory is beginning to challenge this picture. The old picture was a snapshot, taken in October 1492, which then gradually faded over the years as the native presence registered there became less easy to discern. The new picture is more like a film; at least it has a narrative and some character development. More recent scholarship, some of it based in the Caribbean itself, is now beginning to study 1492 not as the start of a genocide that the native population suffered passively or as the start of a heroic but doomed defense of native strongholds but rather as the start of a set of original political and cultural *responses* marked by small- and large-scale population movements throughout the islands. There were massive amounts of slave raiding that moved huge contingents of Native Americans from Florida, Central America, Mexico, Colombia, Venezuela, and Brazil, onto the Caribbean islands in the early sixteenth century. New political and military alliances were formed, including a degree of ethnic soldiering. There was adaptation to peasant life under Spanish control, possibly within such forms as the *guajiro* and *jíbaro* traditions of Cuba and Puerto Rico. There was participation in unofficial creole communities on the margins of authorized areas of settlement, sometimes (especially in the eighteenth century) involving guerrilla warfare in conjunction with African Maroons. Finally, there was ethnic reconstruction and identity reformulation. Indeed, the Caribs themselves, one of the staple ingredients of the colonial picture, may have been a *product* of what anthropologists now call the "tribal zone."[27] What is beginning to emerge is a wide-scale Native Caribbean diaspora in the early colonial period. It is always necessary, however, to remember that this is not a glorious story of survival and adaptation but a desperate story of trauma and adaptation in which many hundreds of thousands died.[28]

26. See, most recently, Irving Rouse, *The Tainos: Rise and Decline of the People Who Greeted Columbus* (New Haven, 1992). See also Hulme, *Colonial Encounters: Europe and the Native Caribbean, 1492–1797* (London, 1986), pp. 45–87. On labor-saving theories, see Nancy M. Farriss, "Sacred Power in Colonial Mexico: The Case of Sixteenth-Century Yucatan," in "The Meeting of Two Worlds: Europe and the Americas, 1492–1650," ed. Warwick Bray, special issue of *Proceedings of the British Academy* 81 (1993): 146.

27. R. Brian Ferguson and Neil L. Whitehead, eds., *War in the Tribal Zone: Expanding States and Indigenous Warfare* (Santa Fe, 1992).

28. For examples of this postcolonial ethnography, see the essays in Neil L. Whitehead, ed., *Wolves from the Sea: Readings in the Anthropology of the Caribbean* (Leiden, 1995).

The significance of this emerging paradigm is not easy to gauge. Scholarship is never static; there are always reassessments, new models, as each generation makes its subject anew, finds new materials, invents new methodologies. I am suggesting something more: that deeply embedded colonial assumptions about native passivity, lack of native polities, native military incompetence, allied with the kinds of unreflective reading of texts that I have discussed and compounded by a conflation between archaeological and linguistic and ethnographic evidence, have prevented European and U.S. scholarship from understanding the history of the Native Caribbean, a history that continues to be made, since that native population still survives. It is probably the case that people working with mainland material in the Andes or Mexico or with the history of slavery in the Americas will find this argument familiar, if not already dated. There is, I think, a discernible pattern here. The colonial assumptions with the deepest roots are those with the longest history. Postcolonial theory has a part to play in this continuing reassessment, but not one divorced from the kind of empirical investigations that can take a generalization such as "diaspora," "transculturation," "hybridity," or "creolization" and begin to show how it might function in particular sets of circumstances.

V.

In *Almanac of the Dead*, Leslie Marmon Silko's great American novel of the borderlands, there is a character called Clinton, a black Vietnam War veteran with one foot who is the chief recruiter for the army of the homeless that will welcome and join the great Indian and Latino invasion of the United States through its southern border. Clinton plans to dedicate his first radio broadcast in a reborn United States to children born of escaped African slaves and Carib Indians—the Black Caribs, the one recognizably *new* ethnic group in the Caribbean that the colonial powers could not ignore, although, as would happen with the Miskito and the Seminole, their "Africanness" would be emphasized by colonial authorities over their "Indianness" as a way of downplaying their legal rights to the land they occupied.[29] If postcolonial theory and early American history are to come into the kind of fruitful conjunction I have been advocating here, then the most productive area may well be that covered by the term "transculturation." And no transculturated groups and their cultures have been more ignored in the Caribbean and possibly in other parts of

29. Leslie Marmon Silko, *Almanac of the Dead* (New York, 1992), p. 410. On the Black Caribs, see Nancie L. Gonzalez, *Sojourners of the Caribbean: Ethnogenesis and Ethnohistory of the Garifuna* (Urbana, 1988).

America than those composed of African and Native American mixes—in Jack Forbes's resonant phrase, the "red-black peoples."[30]

Tituba has, over the years, been emblematic of much that has threatened white America. Recent research suggests that she might belong in this red-black grouping.[31] Born in the 1660s somewhere near the mouth of the Orinoco, a member of the group called the Tibetibe by the Spanish, captured by slavers and taken to Barbados where her name is recorded as Tattuba, sold again and taken to New England where she became briefly infamous at Salem, this Amerindian woman, who could well have been part African or part Spanish, can perhaps be allowed to embody the complexity of Caribbean and early American "roots," a word that—at least in English backwaters—is still, appropriately, a homophone of routes.

30. Jack D. Forbes, *Africans and Native Americans: The Language of Race and the Evolution of the Red-Black Peoples*, 2d ed. (Urbana, 1993).

31. Elaine Breslaw, "The Salem Witch from Barbados: In Search of Tituba's Roots," *Essex Institute Historical Collections* 128, no. 4 (1992): 217–38; and Breslaw, *Tituba, Reluctant Witch of Salem: Devilish Indians and Puritan Fantasies* (New York, 1996).

What's Colonial about Colonial America?

MICHAEL WARNER

I F W E were to ask what was colonial about colonial Africa, the answers might be complex: different European powers behaved differently in different colonies, or at different times, and with a different mix of motives. But we would at least know that it meant something to ask the question. We would know that whatever the local variants, they were part of a larger pattern of domination in which the international nation-state system and world capitalism created imbalances of power and wealth that continue to this day, long after the formal arrangements of colonialism ended. We would know that any discussion of the subject would be frivolous if not engaged with the disastrous legacy of colonialism in the historical present. Discussions about colonial Anglo-America seldom have a perceptible relation to that context, despite the importance of the old Imperial school and a revival of transatlantic topics in recent historiography.[1] Among literary critics in particular, very few sentences about colonial America would be significantly altered if the word "colonial"

---

1. For the Imperial school, see especially Charles Andrews, *The Colonial Period of American History*, 4 vols. (New Haven, 1934–38); Andrews, "On the Writing of Colonial History," *William and Mary Quarterly*, 3d ser., 1, no. 1 (1944): 27–48; George Louis Beer, *The Origins of the British Colonial System, 1578–1660* (New York, 1908); Laurence Henry Gipson, *The British Empire before the American Revolution*, 15 vols. (Caldwell, Idaho, 1936–70); Gipson, "The Imperial Approach to Early American History," in *The Reinterpretation of Early American History: Essays in Honor of John Edwin Pomfret*, ed. R. A. Billington (San Marino, Calif., 1966), pp. 185–200; and J. Holland Rose et al., eds., *The Cambridge History of the British Empire*, vol. 1, *The Old Empire, from the Beginnings to 1783* (Cambridge, 1929). For examples of a more recent focus on empire, see Ian K. Steele, *The English Atlantic* (New York, 1986); Stephen Saunders Webb, *The Governors-General: The English Army and the Definition of the Empire, 1659–1681* (Chapel Hill, 1979); David Hackett Fisher, *Albion's Seed: Four British Folkways in America* (New York, 1989); and Bernard Bailyn, ed., *Strangers within the Realm: Cultural Margins of the First British Empire* (Chapel Hill, 1991). D. W. Meinig, *The Shaping of America*, vol. 1, *Atlantic America, 1492–1800* (New Haven, 1986), goes far toward theorizing a transatlantic focus.

were simply replaced by the word "early."[2] At a time when historians have so much to say about the politics, economics, and everyday life of empire, the problem of colonialism in literary culture remains cloaked in banality—at least where American Indian relations are not explicitly thematic.

Historians can rely on the intrinsic interest of any aspect of the past; it is all history. But literary critics must ask questions of value and interest about what we study, not all of which is literature—at least not in the sense that inspires reading. Why, after all, does anyone want to read colonial Anglo-American literature? The standard and usually implicit answer is national. Early modern Atlantic writing is read because it is the cultural heritage of Americans. A nationalist impulse is an almost preinterpretive commitment of the discipline. In the first paragraph of *The Americans* (1958), for example, Daniel Boorstin quotes the famous "city on a hill" passage from John Winthrop's "Modell of Christian Charity." The text is given such prominence because "no one writing after the fact, three hundred years later, could have better expressed the American sense of destiny." This sense of destiny, Boorstin writes, is "the keynote of American history."[3]

Such arguments—and more generally the implicit assumption of national culture—motivate some people to read colonial texts. But not necessarily to read them very well. Boorstin was asking a national question and seeing a nation. In so doing he obscured most of what would now be interesting in Winthrop's text. In the time since Boorstin's book, historians have turned sharply away from the national narrative, having been preoccupied with the localism of early modern colonists, on one hand, and the transatlantic contexts of empire and trade, on the other. They would now be less inclined to let a member of the Massachusetts Congregational elite stand for all the colonies, to forget that some British American colonies remain colonies to this day, or to assume that colonial history had an inner propulsion toward modern nationalism. Given the complex picture of an early modern Atlantic world that historians have developed over the past two or three decades, Winthrop's text might seem to be marked less by the seeds of national destiny than by transitional narratives, a concern for discipline, the consciousness of a nascent imperial culture not fully recognizing itself as such, and a marked silence about those to be dispossessed.

When Winthrop says at the conclusion of his sermon, "Wee shall be as

2. There are, of course, important exceptions, especially Myra Jehlen, "The Papers of Empire," in *The Cambridge History of American Literature*, ed. Sacvan Bercovitch (Cambridge, 1994), pp. 13–168. See also Gauri Viswanathan, "The Naming of Yale College: British Imperialism and American Higher Education," in *Cultures of United States Imperialism*, ed. Amy Kaplan and Donald Pease (Durham, N.C., 1993), pp. 85–108.

3. Daniel Boorstin, *The Americans: The Colonial Experience* (New York, 1958), pp. 3–4.

a Citty upon a Hill," the "we" is neither American nor national. He has been invoking a specific audience in the context of the previous paragraph—namely, church members in the Massachusetts Bay migration. Yet the sense of membership grows broader and more vague in the phrase "our selves and posterity." It grows broader still when Winthrop invokes the world-historical Protestant struggle ("wee shall be made a story and a by-word through the world"), with its fundamentally *transnational* self-understanding, or when he invokes an English national sense of audience through his use of the still novel term "New England." The whole passage is also marked by an uneasy yoking of geographies and temporalities: English traditionalism, the globalizing modernity of Protestant historical narrative, the timeless space of divine judgment, and the migratory spaces of empire and capital. None of this amounts to an "American sense of destiny," particularly as each of the final three paragraphs of the sermon ends rhetorically on a spectacle of failure: "the Lord will surely breake out in wrathe against us"; "we shall shame the faces of many of gods worthy servants, and cause theire prayers to be turned into Cursses upon us"; and "Wee shall surely perishe out of the good Land whither wee passe over this vast sea to possesse it." The nationalist reading papers over not only the implicit aggression of this anathematizing rhetoric but even its explicitly regulative intent. The language suggests not so much shared confidence as a will to authority, power, discipline, and restraint.[4]

These and other features of the text will stand out to any reader interested in colonial American history as a colonial history. But literary critics are only beginning to reimagine the literary history in general as one of a colonial culture. Nationalist criticism has always had a repertoire of themes by means of which colonial writing could be seen as essentially American: the wilderness, natural man, the social covenant, individualism, the rise of democracy and the self-made man, the revolt against Europe and the sublimity of new beginnings. These themes have been worked up with such mythic potency that undergraduates can reliably find them in colonial texts with practically no coaching—especially since the colonial archive has been anthologized to highlight them. There are almost no corresponding themes, in common currency, by which early modern writing might be seen as essentially colonial or Anglo-American. By asking new questions about colonial texts, scholars are currently moving to a new conception of the field—one of colonial literatures of the Atlantic world rather than of a future nation.[5] But when the glorious his-

4. John Winthrop, "A Modell of Christian Charity" (1630), in *The Puritans*, ed. Perry Miller and Thomas H. Johnson, 2 vols. (New York, 1963), 1:197–99. For more on this passage and its subtexts, see Michael Warner, "New English Sodom," *American Literature* 64, no. 1 (March 1992): 19–47.

5. A somewhat similar point is argued by William C. Spengemann in his *A Mirror for Americanists: Reflections on the Idea of American Literature* (Hanover, N.H., 1989) and *A New World*

tory of the nation is set aside, it remains to say what the story of colonial literatures in Anglo-America might be or how to read any given text in its colonial setting—let alone how to read it with pleasure. It is unlikely that any colonial themes will ever have the ego satisfactions of national belonging.

I.

We have only to pose the question seriously to see that the concept of "colonialism" is itself a problem. There have been many colonialisms, and any venture into postcolonial theory should begin with a comparative historical sense of their differences.[6] Historians sometimes distinguish between the "first" British Empire, to which the American colonies belonged, and a second empire that took shape partly in response to American independence. Even within the first empire there was enormous variation in British practice from one colony to another, as well as in the interaction of different peoples. Postcolonial critics often write in the singular of "colonialism," "the colonial condition," "colonial discourse," and "the colonial Other." Yet there are few constants in the history of colonialisms or even of European colonialisms in the early modern period. The northern white settler colonies of America only rarely used a native labor force for the extraction of wealth, and they never saw themselves as administering a native nation, as the British did in India and Africa. Many colonialisms were centrally defined by racism, but not all.[7]

---

of Words: Redefining Early American Literature (New Haven, 1994). Spengemann emphasizes the Britishness of American writing rather than colonial relations. For an example of how the study of colonial literature might include texts from the West Indies, Canada, and London itself, see Myra Jehlen and Michael Warner, eds., The English Literatures of America, 1500–1800 (New York, 1997).

6. Anne McClintock, "The Angel of Progress: Pitfalls of the Term 'Post-Colonialism,' " Social Text 10, nos. 2–3 (1992): 84–98, reprinted in Colonial Discourse and Post-Colonial Theory, ed. Patrick Williams and Laura Chrisman (New York, 1994), pp. 291–304, argues that applying the term postcolonial to the United States not only fails to recognize the variety of colonialisms in modern history but also "actively obscures the continuities and discontinuities of US power around the globe." McClintock sees the United States as a "break-away settler colony," in which colonial control was transferred from the metropolis to the colony but where decolonization did not happen and is not likely to happen (p. 295). See also Vijay Mishra and Bob Hodge, "What is Post(-)colonialism?" in Colonial Discourse, ed. Williams and Chrisman, pp. 276–90.

7. J. G. A. Pocock argues for a history of the British Empire not driven by a unitary conception of empire, in "The Limits and Divisions of British History: In Search of the Unknown Subject," American Historical Review 87, no. 2 (1982): 311–36; see M. I. Finley, "Colonies—an Attempt at a Typology," Transactions of the Royal Historical Society, 5th ser., 26 (1976): 167–88. The Portuguese, for example, involved as they were in the slave trade, showed much more willingness than did other Europeans to use African and Indian languages, to interbreed, and to take on Indians and mixed-race offspring in administrative positions. The English were inconsistent on the degree of difference between themselves and the Irish, the Welsh,

Some colonies involved settlement, others did not. Some colonies were driven by merchant capital, others were not. The English in North America tried settlement before they had more than a vague idea of transatlantic commerce, whereas the French developed a commercial policy that limited settlement.[8] Most of the great colonial powers—the Portuguese, the Dutch, the French, and the English, for example—had contrasting kinds of colonies at the same time, in some cases on opposite sides of the globe. They took slaves to some colonies but not to others. They used native labor in some but not in others. They conquered some at the outset, but others they first traded with as partners for long periods. Some they saw as savage and stateless; others, such as the Moghul Empire, were civilizations more advanced and complex than those of the Europeans, and the future colonizers found themselves dependent on the future colonized for financial and administrative systems.

Nor did Europeans act with one mind in relation to the same colonial venture. The Virginia Company inconsistently treated American Indians as wild savages and as feudal states, as when they sent a robe and crown with which to enthrone Powhatan as an ally, partly in imitation of a similar gesture made by Cortés to the Aztecs. Modern notions of race and nation took shape only gradually in colonial practice; they did not drive colonization consistently. It is not even easy to draw a sharp line between national ventures in colonialism and the practices of national unification that one historian has called "internal colonialism." Within England itself, the draining of the fens under Charles I gave rise to a state program of settlement "plantations" in East Anglia modeled directly on English colonialism in North America and Ireland.[9]

Even in the familiar context of English dispossession of Indians in America, recent scholarship has emphasized how misleading it is to speak of a direct conflict of two cultures. In cultural criticism, such scenes have been singled out for special attention since the Columbus quincentenary, and critics of Anglophone texts have done much to show how the racial and cultural divide organizes colonial writing.[10] But colonial culture is not

---

and the Scots. See J. H. Parry, *The Establishment of the European Hegemony: 1415–1715* (New York, 1966); Parry, *The Age of Reconnaissance: Discovery, Exploration, and Settlement, 1450 to 1650* (Berkeley, 1981); and Bailyn, *Strangers*.

8. On this point see Neal Salisbury, *Manitou and Providence: Indians, Europeans, and the Making of New England, 1500–1643* (New York, 1982), pp. 85–86, and W. L. Morton, *The Kingdom of Canada* (Toronto, 1963). An eloquent version of the contrast runs throughout Francis Parkman, *France and England in North America*, 2 vols. (New York, 1983).

9. See Michael Hechter, *Internal Colonialism: The Celtic Fringe in British National Development, 1536–1966* (Berkeley, 1975), and H. C. Darby, *The Draining of the Fens* (Cambridge, 1956).

10. Notably in Peter Hulme, *Colonial Encounters: Europe and the Native Caribbean, 1492–1797* (New York, 1986), and Anthony Pagden, *European Encounters with the New World* (New Haven, 1993); see also Hulme's essay in this volume. For similar studies of Anglophone writing, see Larzer Ziff, "Conquest and Recovery in Early Writings from America," *American Lit-*

simply racially bipolar. Neal Salisbury, for example, has shown how different tribal factions played out rivalries and conflicts with one another by adopting different relations with rival European groups; in his narrative, the most powerful effects of colonialism come not in a direct relation of force or domination between whites and Indians but in the transformation of Indian groups as they are drawn into an unequal economy. Richard White, tracing similar patterns, has given the name "the middle ground" to all the rites, negotiations, customs, and understandings that emerged neither from European nor from Indian culture but from these local interactions.[11]

In light of such scholarship, it becomes harder to reduce the conflicts of empire to simple scenes of the European and the Indian. And in the variety of colonialism that distinguishes the English mainland colonies—settlement plantation—the relation of settlers and indigenes does not take the visible form of super- and subordinate so much as of center and margin (that is, frontier). That is why Anglo-American settlement does not look like colonialism in the usual sense. Creole culture was able in general to ignore the context of dispossession. Unlike other white settlers in colonies such as Ulster or South Africa, white Americans did not leave in place a native majority to whom their colonial relation would be visibly troubling. Even in colonies with an imported slave population, the white Creoles learned to think of themselves as the locals. They learned to think of the story of their own entrenchment and expansion as the story of a developing local civilization. Indeed, the question of who gets to be local was always the brutally contested question of colonial American history.[12]

It would be helpful in this context to know more about the history of the territorial imagination in Anglo-American culture. In the case of the Span-

---

erature 68, no. 3 (1996): 509–26, and June Namias, *White Captives: Gender and Ethnicity on the American Frontier* (Chapel Hill, 1993).

11. Salisbury, *Manitou and Providence*; Richard White, *The Middle Ground: Indians, Empires, and Republics in the Great Lakes Region, 1650–1815* (New York, 1991).

12. Historians such as Michael Zuckerman and Timothy H. Breen have written eloquently of the "persistent localism" of English settlers, who built in the Caribbean the sharply pitched roofs ready to withstand the snows that never came. In part that localism represents the assertion of Englishness and in some colonies was accompanied by an extremely high rate of back migration in the first generation. But for those who stayed, the story is one of a developing territorial and cultural imagination that localized creole culture—to the disadvantage of both displaced natives and imported Africans. And this is localism in a different sense: not just the carrying over of English habits (which, as Zuckerman notes, was deliberately conservative rather than unreflectively traditional) but also the cultivation of a new version of the local, an imagination of space and identity that was at every moment political and transitive. The point about the roofs is Richard Dunn's, quoted in Michael Zuckerman, "Identity in British America," in *Colonial Identity in the Atlantic World, 1500–1800*, ed. Nicholas Canny and Anthony Pagden (Princeton, 1987), p. 135. See also Timothy H. Breen, *Puritans and Adventurers: Change and Persistence in Early America* (New York, 1980).

ish colonization of Mexico, a brilliant example of such work has been provided by Serge Gruzinski in *La colonisation de l'imaginaire*. Gruzinski
painstakingly shows how Spanish administration, over a period of several generations, eroded and replaced Amerindian pictorial and narrative
practices for representing space and time. Nothing of comparable sophistication has been done for Anglo America, though a similar colonization
of the territorial imaginary was obviously at work at least as early as the
Virginia Company's negotiations with Powhatan.[13] A history of that
process would have to coordinate shifts in the imagination of land tenure,
state administration of land, empiricist geography, and English relations
to both Irish and Indian habits of territorialization. One of the most striking common threads between the Irish and American cases, for example,
is the English insistence that the locals in each instance failed to possess
the land fully. The Irish were "wild" because of the importance of trans-
humance in Irish land use. And the English frequently justified settlement
by claiming that the Indians did not farm and possess the land, even
though the same English circulated Théodor de Bry's engravings of
Indian farming villages and depended on Indian agriculture for their own
survival. In both cases the colonial project was linked to a restructuring of
territorial thought, beginning with the surrender and regrant policy in Ireland in the 1540s and continuing in the long process of colonial charters,
Indian treaties, and experiments in land appropriation.[14]

Cultural historians have a long-standing fondness for themes of wilderness, land, nature, settlement, and civilization in early Anglo-America.
How would these themes be transformed if viewed as part of a complex
but in important ways colonialist process of territorialization? Would it
escape attention, for example, that William Byrd's works are structured
by enterprises of surveying, conducted against a divided but constantly

---

13. On territorial imagination, see Margarita Bowen, *Empiricism and Geographical Thought:
From Francis Bacon to Alexander von Humboldt* (Cambridge, 1981), and Serge Gruzinski, *La
colonisation de l'imaginaire* (Paris, 1988). A useful study in this context is Patricia Seed, *Ceremonies of Possession in Europe's Conquest of the New World* (Cambridge, 1995). See also David
Grayson Allen, "*Vacuum Domicilium*: The Social and Cultural Landscape of Seventeenth-
Century New England," in *New England Begins: The Seventeenth Century*, ed. Jonathan L. Fairbanks and Robert F. Trent, 3 vols. (Boston, 1982), 1:1–10.

14. Nicholas Canny, "The Ideology of English Colonization: From Ireland to America,"
William and Mary Quarterly, 3d ser., 30, no. 4 (1973): 575–98. See also Canny, "The Irish Background to Penn's Experiment," in *The World of William Penn*, ed. Richard S. Dunn and Mary
Maples Dunn (Philadelphia, 1986), pp. 139–56. Howard Mumford Jones shows that perceptions of Natives and landscapes in America were framed by previous accounts of the Irish,
in *O Strange New World* (New York, 1964), pp. 173–75. See also Kenneth R. Andrews et al.,
eds., *The Westward Enterprise: English Activities in Ireland, the Atlantic, and America, 1480–1650*
(Detroit, 1979). David B. Quinn, *The Elizabethans and the Irish* (Ithaca, 1966), pp. 14–15. Canny,
The Elizabethan Conquest of Ireland (New York, 1976).

refreshed sense of metropolitan consciousness?[15] Or that Crèvecoeur's image of the yeoman farmer inescapably refers to the long process of possession, dispossession, the restructuring of land governance, and the struggle to be local? Or that the informational use of travel organizes so many colonial texts, from the early migrant histories to the narratives of Sarah Knight and Alexander Hamilton, captivity narratives, and the soldierly narratives of the imperial wars? Or, less literally, that a cosmopolitan sense of audience can be implicit even in some of the most local and private forms of writing, whenever that writing aspires to the politeness of belles lettres or the urbanity of the modern?

These patterns in the spatial imagination of colonial culture have tended to be ignored or distorted in nationalist criticism, partly because national culture has a different territorial imagination of its own. It demarcates American culture from the magical moment at which white folks begin inhabiting the future United States, which they are said to have "settled." The benign idea of settlement continues to be the main obstacle against recognizing the history of the British American colonies as a story of colonialism rather than of mere colonization. Settling is intransitive, or, if it has an object, the object is merely the land. The narrative of settlement was developed in British colonial theory before any serious colonizing efforts got under way and before North America was its principal site. In the context in which the British first understood themselves as colonial settlers, the natives were very much local, very willing to fight back, and very white. Settlement colonization was a deliberate political strategy for subduing ancient neighbors, the Irish. Not only does the English literature of America begin long before settlement of America; English *settlement* begins before settlement of America. "Settling" North America had not removed the white creoles from English imperial culture; it had made them part of that culture, and they sustained an awareness of the rest of the empire throughout the colonial period. Some of the North American colonies, of course, quickly began thinking of themselves as independent from London, but at their most independent—Massachusetts in the 1640s, for example—they were far from renouncing the English imperial project. They were still in the process of inventing it.

An imperial culture does not even require a political doctrine of empire. As late as 1782 the British House of Commons resolved that "to pursue schemes of conquest and extent of dominion, are measures repugnant to

15. See, for example, Wayne Franklin, *Discoverers, Explorers, Settlers: The Diligent Writers of Early America* (Chicago, 1979). An essential study of Byrd from this point of view is Norman S. Grabo, "Going Steddy: William Byrd's Literary Masquerade," *Yearbook of English Studies* 13 (1983): 84–96; see also the other essays on "colonial and imperial themes" in part 1 of this issue. See Michael Greenberg, "William Byrd II and the World of the Market," *Southern Studies* 16, no. 4 (1977): 429–56.

the wish, the honour, and the policy of this nation."[16] The ease of this disavowal shows how indirect and mediated colonial culture can be. In the
American colonies the settlers often rejected political empire for their own
reasons. But their struggle for autonomy, formerly much celebrated by
nationalist historians, did not imply a rejection of what we might now
call"the colonial project." Resisting political administration by the Crown
and Parliament, they tended to envision an English Atlantic world held
together by means of market, religion, and other cultural mediations—
one that led equally to a future of English dominion. The nature of the
empire was one of the principal subjects of conflict within the empire.

The challenge before us is to render the differences between versions of
colonialism while still asking how the British American colonies were part
of a larger British culture of colonialism and how that larger project
informs creole culture in America despite the differences between American emigrants, creoles, and British colonials elsewhere. Because the objective economic structures and political administrations differ so much
from one colony to another or from one period to another, we should be
particularly attentive to the cultural patterns by which such disparate
ventures were able to elaborate, for all their differences, a European colonial project, distinct from each of its manifestations but necessary to each.

One way to call attention to the colonialist pattern in these mediate
areas of culture is to ascribe to them the integrity of *colonial discourse.*[17] But
colonial discourse has no more unity than colonialism. To speak of it in
the singular hypostatizes a political intention that belongs to no one. It is
indeed sometimes possible to speak of a sharply delineated discourse.
The sixteenth-century English literature of planting, for example, might
be called the oldest branch of American literature in English. It produced
the notion of emigrant settlement colonies oriented to trade, first for Ireland and then for the New World; in doing so it created an entirely different model of colonialism from the Iberian plan of armed conquest and
the extraction of wealth from a native population. The literature of planting has a notable consistency of reference points, assumptions, and formal

16. Quoted in Peter Marshall, "British Expansion in India," in Marshall, *Trade and Conquest:
Studies on the Rise of British Dominance in India* (London, 1993), p. 31.

17. The term has not always been used to imply the integrity of discourse. Indeed, it seems
to have gained its appeal initially from the way it pointed to mediated, or indirectly related,
fields of culture. Edward W. Said, for instance, writes in *Culture and Imperialism* that "there
was a commitment to [colonies] over and above profit, a commitment in constant circulation
which, on the one hand, allowed decent men and women to accept the notion that distant
territories and their native peoples *should* be subjugated, and, on the other, replenished metropolitan energies so that these decent people could think of the *imperium* as a protracted,
almost metaphysical obligation to rule subordinate, inferior, or less advanced peoples" (*Culture and Imperialism* [New York, 1993], p. 10). This sense of imperial culture as metropolitan
consciousness obviously could not be restricted to one discourse among others.

features. It is complex and varied, having to solve scientific problems of geography, new problems of economic theory, and unprecedented issues of national, racial, and Christian identity. It draws on sources in Roman history and Machiavelli, but in England and Scotland its major figures for the first century or so include the Hakluyts, Christopher Carleil, Sir Humphrey Gilbert, Edward Hayes, George Peckham, Sir Walter Ralegh, Thomas Hariot, Francis Bacon, Sir William Alexander, Richard Eburne, Thomas Mun, John White, Josiah Child, and the like.[18] It is a clear example of colonial discourse that is a discourse—an intertextual horizon, a way of talking and writing rather than simply some things said and written.

We can tell that resistance to this literature existed from the beginning because some pro-plantation tracts contain responses to common objections. In addition, some cheap published ballads satirize it.[19] And writers such as Hariot and Captain Smith vividly express their anxiety about the reception of their works in London opinion circles. But the objections to planting mostly remained unpublished. This second, ghost discourse may have had some written expression, now mostly lost, and it almost certainly had a wide, mercantile rather than exactly popular circulation. It partly structures the published literature, as antithesis, but does not occupy the same space. The dialogue between the two is oblique and distorted. Printed speculations about cosmography and colonies give a false appearance of unity to colonial discourse because they have been prefiltered by the ability and need to print. One might want to define colonial discourse as both sides of this asymmetrical dialogue, including the asymmetry as one of its key discursive features. But where does one discourse stop and another begin? Other texts or kinds of language may prove to be ghosts in colonial discourse because they elaborate colonial culture not so much through argument as through narrative or fantasy; for example, literary romances such as Spenser's *Faerie Queene* or Thomas Lodge's *A Margarite from America*.[20] But then the meaning of colonial discourse has no unity *as a discourse*; it is at best a retrospective mapping of sometimes overlapping but sometimes incommensurate contexts.

And because colonial culture is not a framework of shared meaning but multiple contexts of discourse in shifting relations, the indirect mediations of empire sometimes have to be found far from official debate. Laura

18. The literature on planting is summarized in Klaus E. Knorr, *British Colonial Theories, 1570–1850* (London, 1963). On sources, see David Quinn, "Renaissance Influences in English Colonization," in Quinn, *Explorers and Colonies* (London, 1990), pp. 97–118.

19. See, for example, "A West Country Man's Voyage to New England" (ca. 1632), in *English Literatures of America*, ed. Jehlen and Warner, or Richard Eburne, *A Plaine Pathway to Plantation* (London, 1624).

20. This is the subject of a fair amount of more recent scholarship. See, for instance, Jeffrey Knapp, *An Empire Nowhere* (Cambridge, Mass., 1989).

Brown and Felicity Nussbaum, for example, argue that eighteenth-century narratives of women elaborate an imperial culture not only through the obvious exoticization of "native" women but also through the empire's growing concern with reproduction, population, and domestic space.[21] In settler colonies, reproductive sexuality acquires even more importance—and anxiety—than in the imperial home. (The contrast between French and English practice in this regard could not be sharper.) But the colonial context of sexuality has been best studied only in the early period and very seldom with attention to the different role of settlement in different places.[22]

Of all the mediating forms of Anglo-American colonialism, the market culture of the Atlantic may have been more responsible than anything else for the practical sense of belonging to an imperium. When the Scotsman William Robertson wrote his *History of America* (1777), it seemed natural to begin with an overview of "the progress of men, in discovering and peopling the various parts of the earth." Robertson thought that this progress should be credited less to empire than to trade. With the spread of navigation and commerce, he wrote,

> The ambition of conquest, or the necessity of procuring new settlements, were no longer the sole motives of visiting distant lands. The desire of gain became a new incentive to activity, roused adventurers, and sent them forth upon long voyages in search of countries whose products or wants might increase that circulation which nourishes and gives vigour to commerce. Trade proved a great source of discovery; it opened unknown seas, it penetrated into new regions, and contributed more than any other cause to bring men acquainted with the situation, the nature, and commodities of the different parts of the globe.[23]

In a way, Robertson was right. Some contemporary cultural critics have a tendency to speak of empire and capital as being the same. But from a very early point the commercial empire of Europe had exceeded the political empires of the European nations. Spain, which had pioneered the

---

21. Laura Brown, *Ends of Empire: Women and Ideology in Early-Eighteenth-Century Literature* (Ithaca, 1993), and Felicity Nussbaum, *Torrid Zones: Maternity, Sexuality, and Empire in Eighteenth-Century English Narratives* (Baltimore, 1995).

22. For the early period, see Jonathan Goldberg, *Sodometries* (Stanford, 1992), or Richard Trexler, *Sex and Conquest: Gendered Violence, Political Order, and the European Conquest of the Americas* (Ithaca, 1995). See also Mary Beth Norton, *Founding Mothers and Fathers: Gendered Power and the Forming of American Society* (New York, 1996). There are also useful studies from different colonial contexts, such as Anne McClintock, *Imperial Leather* (New York, 1996), or Ann Stoler, "Carnal Knowledge and Imperial Power: Gender, Race, and Morality in Colonial Asia," in *Gender at the Crossroads of Knowledge: Feminist Anthropology in the Postmodern Era*, ed. Micaela di Leonardo (Berkeley, 1991), pp. 51–101.

23. William Robertson, *History of America*, 2 vols. (Dublin, 1777), 1:1, 4.

art of conquering and administering other lands across the ocean, had been surpassed by England, which in the words of Fernand Braudel was "the first territorial state to complete its transformation into a national economy or national market."[24] Merchants—as well as soldiers, settlers, and subjects—made the Atlantic world. The early modern economy had become, for the first time, a global economy. Cultural relations among different parts of the modern world increasingly took place through markets and commerce rather than through the administrators and courts of the state. Empire and commerce linked the world in different, sometimes incompatible ways. Colonists, constantly looking to get around the Navigation Acts, would never have confounded the two.

In 1986, Timothy Breen was still able to propose, as a controverted point, that export markets and luxury imports mattered to eighteenth-century colonists.[25] While it may be true that colonists became more market oriented after 1690, it is hard to believe that they were ever unrelated to transatlantic markets. More specifically, an asymmetrical core / periphery economy was central to English colonialism from the outset.[26] Wallerstein attributes much of the imperial crisis to a creole determination not to have the kind of asymmetrical economy that was already beginning to underdevelop much of the world. The structuring of the transatlantic economy as a colonial economy had deep consequences for almost every aspect of Anglo-American culture, from the routing of cultural and political life through London to the local politics of staple economies. Breen has shown how the structuring of colonial society as an imperial market underlay intercolonial relations and political consciousness. And David Shields has ably demonstrated the preoccupation of American poetry in the early eighteenth century with themes of imperial commerce.[27] The provincial relation to London can be observed in almost any piece of Anglo-American writing and certainly in any colonial newspaper or travel account.

24. Fernand Braudel, *Civilization and Capitalism, Fifteenth–Eighteenth Century*, vol. 3, *The Perspective of the World*, trans. Siân Reynolds (New York, 1984), p. 51.

25. Timothy H. Breen, "An Empire of Goods: The Anglicization of Colonial America, 1690–1776," *Journal of British Studies* 25, no. 4 (1986): 467–99. See also Jean-Christophe Agnew, *Worlds Apart: The Market and the Theater in Anglo-American Thought, 1550–1750* (New York, 1986).

26. As described, for example, in Immanuel Wallerstein, *The Modern World-System: Capitalist Agriculture and the Origins of the European World-Economy in the Sixteenth Century* (New York, 1974); Wallerstein, *The Modern World-System II: Mercantilism and the Consolidation of the European World-Economy, 1600–1750* (New York, 1980); and Wallerstein, *The Modern World-System III: The Second Era of Great Expansion of the Capitalist World-Economy, 1730–1840s* (San Diego, 1989).

27. Wallerstein, *Modern World System*, pp. 335–40; Timothy H. Breen, " 'Baubles of Britain': The American and Consumer Revolutions of the Eighteenth Century," *Past and Present*, no. 119 (1988): 73–104; David S. Shields, *Oracles of Empire* (Chicago, 1990).

It is in this indirect, provincial belonging to the world of the empire that Anglo-American commercial culture had its strongest links to the contrasting form of colonialism on the other side of the English imperial world. England's movement into America was in most ways parallel with its movement into India.[28] The East India Company (EIC), for example, was headed after its chartering in 1600 by Thomas Smythe, who also oversaw the Virginia Company. The first major English emissary to India was Sir Thomas Roe, who had earlier made three voyages for Ralegh to the Caribbean and whose letters to the EIC draw explicit analogies between what Abbé Raynal would later call "the two Indies."[29] For the remainder of the century, American and Indian ventures overlapped, just as they did earlier between America and Ireland. In many cases the investors were the same, as were some of the interlopers. The administrative problems were similar, and international imperial rivalries often made them equivalent—as in the Anglo-Dutch feuds of the 1630s or again in the 1660s, both times played out equally on the Hudson and in South Asia. Clive, before his death in 1774, was slated to quell American unrest following the Boston Tea Party; Cornwallis compensated for the loss of America by consolidating Bengal.

In other ways, of course, America and India are contrasting images of English colonial practice. The contrast was deliberately preserved by the English policy of bureaucratic rotation. (Burke, whose career neatly encapsulates the close relation of Ireland, America, and India, claimed that "the natives scarcely know what it is to see the grey head of an Englishman.")[30] Partly because of the deliberateness of this contrast, it is surprising how invisible India has been in the history of Anglo-American colonialism. Two world-historical ventures into colonialism: begun at the same time, by the same people, with the same infrastructures, elaborating the same world economy, contributing equally the intoxicating staples in the English drug empire (tea, coffee, sugar, tobacco, rum, opium), sources of the same city's metropolitan self-understanding, the same claims of imperial Crown sovereignty in relation to the English nation, linked by the same wars—in all these ways India and America were inescapably tied for merchants, generals, and statesmen. And American consumers were hardly unaware of their involvement in a world colonial system,

28. Synoptic accounts since the Imperial school include Angus Calder, *Revolutionary Empire: The Rise of the English-Speaking Empires from the Fifteenth Century to the 1780s* (New York, 1981); C. E. Carrington, *The British Overseas: Exploits of a Nation of Shopkeepers* (Cambridge, 1968); and, from the English point of view, Linda Colley, *Britons: Forging the Nation, 1707–1837* (New Haven, 1992).

29. Abbé (Guillaume-Thomas) Raynal, *Histoire philosophique et politique des établissemens et du commerce des Européens dan les deux Indes*, 10 vols. (Geneva, 1780).

30. Quoted in Peter Marshall, "The Whites of British India, 1780–1830: A Failed Colonial Society?" in Marshall, *Trade and Conquest*, p. 75.

even though the empire's goods came through London. For all the historical differences between America and India as examples of colonial practice, they were in many ways mutually defined, and Anglo-Americans were certainly part of the English culture of colonialism.

A kind of forgetfulness about this relation settled in during the early national period. The British American mainland colonies were the first to mount a critique of colonial administration and break away from it; yet the United States was also to become the last great colonial and imperial power—which of course it still is. The United States entered colonial relations with the rest of the world only after it became a nation (in 1803 by one reckoning, 1898 by another, but continuing through the present in any case). But how did all other arenas of colonialism manage to remain invisible in the anticolonial political writing of the Revolutionary period—so rich in anticolonial thought that Thomas Paine would become a sacred name throughout Latin America? Americans had been aware of their place in a global English colonial project since before they were Americans. And the transatlantic debates about colonial regulation are full of comparisons between American and other colonies; usually these comparisons were made as arguments against independence. If we think about the so-called founding era as a moment of anticolonial critique, we will have to ask how such an opportunity passed from view, leaving scarcely a trace in the imperial century that followed.

This is not really surprising unless we try to identify the emergence of nationalism as a sharp break with colonial culture. White creoles in British America learned to think of themselves as colonized rather than as colonizers. But they were not colonized subjects in the sense intended by theories of colonial and postcolonial discourse.[31] The shift from British colonies to American nation was a shift mainly for white men: the Revolution is a poor period marker of decolonization. As Wallerstein puts it:

> This [eighteenth-century] "decolonization" of the Americas occurred under the aegis of their European settlers, to the exclusion not only of the Amerindian populations but also of the transplanted Africans, despite the fact that, in many of these newly sovereign states, Amerindians and Blacks

31. Lawrence Buell, "American Literary Emergence as a Postcolonial Phenomenon," *American Literary History* 4, no. 3 (Fall 1992): 411–42, esp. 434, describes American literature as "the first postcolonial literature." He acknowledges that this argument would seem to mystify the imperial direction of American culture and to blur the distinction "between the European settler as colonial and the indigene as colonial" (412). But he chooses to "bracket" such questions, he says, to show, borrowing from Ashis Nandy, how American literature "arose out of 'a culture in which the ruled were constantly tempted to fight their rulers within the psychological limits set by the latter' " (415). I take it that for Buell this condition *defines* the colonial relation. He argues, for example, that "the imperfectness of Cooper's break from Scott might be seen as a mark of the 'colonized mind' " (422). The rise of national culture in America, for Buell, was a process of decolonization. But if Cooper's mimicry of Scott is colonial, then the colonial is hard to distinguish from the merely provincial.

constituted a substantial proportion (even a majority) of the population. . . . In any case, this decolonization differed strikingly from the second great "decolonization" of the modern world-system, that which
occurred in the twentieth century, the difference being precisely in terms
of the populations who would control the resulting sovereign states.[32]

Not only did the Americans fail to develop an anticolonial culture, but
as Peter Marshall notes, Cornwallis's post-Yorktown triumphs in India
were the turning point in British public opinion on empire. After the early
1790s, he writes, "British activities in India were never again, at least
before the twentieth century, to be subjected to prolonged hostile scrutiny
from within the mainstreams of British opinion."[33] If this change in British
opinion seems like a willful deafness to the American critique, as well as
to Burke's great speeches on both American and Indian issues, we should
note that the American anticolonial theorists were just as deaf to anticolonial thought after independence. National culture began with a moment
of sweeping amnesia about colonialism. Americans learned to think of
themselves as living in an immemorial nation, rather than in a colonial
interaction of cultures.[34]

II.

Colonial culture does not imply a unity of shared meaning or a will to
dominate. It is a set of spatial and temporal hierarchies. The imperial culture of English America could therefore be experienced in many indirect
ways—as an orientation to the modern, a spatial imagination, a moral language of civility, even as a prose style. Unequal economies of space and
capital—including a territorial awareness that presupposed dispossess-
sion—were the condition both of colonial consciousness and of literary
circulation. William Robertson's history might serve as an example.
Robertson, though a Scot by birth, writes from the seat of empire. His
prose rings with the confidence that he and his readers are its most
informed and freely inquiring members. Only a commercial civilization
such as the one Robertson describes could result in the erudition and pol-
ish of *History of America*, let alone provide it with a receptive audience. His
is the voice of cosmopolitanism.

A different style is to be found in the journal of Sarah Knight, a Boston
schoolteacher and shopkeeper of the early eighteenth century who had

32. Wallerstein, *Modern World-System III*, p. 193.

33. Peter Marshall, " 'Cornwallis Triumphant': War in India and the British Public in the
Late Eighteenth Century," in Marshall, *Trade and Conquest*, p. 73.

34. For a beautiful illustration of this amnesia, see Alan Taylor's analysis of William
Cooper's *Guide to the Wilderness*, in *William Cooper's Town: Power and Persuasion on the Frontier of the Early American Republic* (New York, 1996), esp. pp. 30–34.

never been to Europe but was no less a subject of the British Empire. As she traveled the countryside she could not help dreaming: "The way being smooth and even, the night warm and serene, and the Tall and thick Trees at a distance, especially when the moon glar'd light through the branches, fill'd my Imagination with the pleasent delusion of a Sumpteous citty, fill'd with famous Buildings and churches, with their spiring steeples, Balconies, Galleries and I know not what: Granduers which I had heard of, and which the stories of foreign countries had given me the Idea of."[35]

Knight here longs for exotic sights and for a better context for her own consciousness. Her journal is filled with anecdotes of the boorish behavior of the colonials around her. Writing is her resource for survival. When the drunken provincials in the room next door will not shut up, she writes satiric verse about them. She does so to remind herself that there is a larger world than the one these locals know. The closest she can come to living there is to fill her journal with wit and poetry, manufacturing an urbane consciousness with the borrowed resources of a style she imported through reading. But she cannot escape the double bind of the colonial: because the style that makes her journal urbane is a borrowed one, it also makes her provincial. The metropolis of her imagination is a jumbled picture, full of indistinct balconies, galleries, "and I know not what."[36]

Twenty-five years before Knight wrote her journal, another Massachusetts Puritan named Mary Rowlandson wrote a famous narrative of her captivity among American Indians. Rowlandson had not returned to England since her infancy. Yet she interrupts her wild tale with a note of familiarity: "I saw a place where English Cattle had been. That was a comfort to me, such as it was. Quickly after that we came to an English path which so took with me that I thought I could have freely laid down and died. That day, a little after noon, we came to Squaukeag where the Indians quickly spread themselves over the deserted English fields, gleaning what they could find."[37]

This, too, is colonial language, and not just because of the value scale— English good, Indian bad. At a time when the English and Indians were at war over the right to the land, Rowlandson defines Englishness through evidence of settlement, glimpsed only in transit as the wild Indians ceaselessly move through unfelled forests. Cattle, path, and fields make Englishness local, even while they struggle to make local places

---

35. "The Journal of Sarah Knight," in *The Puritans*, ed. Miller and Johnson, 2:430.
36. Ibid.
37. Mary Rowlandson, *The Soveraignty and Goodness of God, Together, with the Faithfulness of His Promises Displayed; Being a Narrative of the Captivity and Restauration of Mrs. Mary Rowlandson* (1682), in *Puritans Among the Indians: Accounts of Captivity and Redemption, 1676–1724*, ed. Alden T. Vaughan and Edward W. Clark (Cambridge, Mass., 1981), p. 45.

English. These imprints on the countryside are the markers of Rowlandson's identity, and she unhesitatingly calls them English even though she
had not been within three thousand miles of England in the time of her
memory and would not talk this way about Englishness if she had.[38] Her
captors tease her for the strength of her feeling: "What, will you love English men still?"[39]

Virtually every colonial writer looks both homeward to the seat of
imperial culture and outward to the localities that would remain for them
subordinate. They were also gradually developing their own patterns of
culture. Already in the seventeenth century, English writers made sport
of colonials in different regions. In Ned Ward's satirical sketches of
Jamaica (1698) and New England (1699), in Aphra Behn's play about Virginia (1689), or in Ebenezer Cooke's satirical poem of Maryland (1708),
colonials had come to be recognizable as comic types.[40] By 1705 Robert
Beverley of Virginia could even embrace the stereotype with partial seri-
ousness. "I am an *Indian*," he declared, though it may be doubted whether
he ever meant to cast doubt on his own credentials as an Englishman.[41]
Toward the middle of the eighteenth century, the word "American"
began to appear more frequently in reference to white creole settlers
rather than to Indians. Ironically, just as the English finally emerged the
victors in the long struggle over North America, the sense of colonial
identity had become strong enough to force a crisis in the imperial system.
Colonial culture had begun to produce one of its least anticipated but
most momentous effects: creole nationalism.

For the past two centuries, those colonists who happened to live in the
future United States have been scrutinized for promising germs of Americanness; their provinciality has often been tactfully overlooked. Even
Benjamin Franklin, regarded by many as the original American, spent
twenty years of his life in London and as late as the 1760s fully intended
to live there permanently as a happy Englishman. Portraits of him
throughout most of his life show him in the powdered wig of a London
gentleman. This is not the Franklin of nationalist criticism. But it is the
Franklin who wrote most of the *Autobiography*. Later in life, particularly
on his second trip to France, Franklin changed his image and played the
American, a role he invented for the occasion.[42] It was such a successful
performance that critics cannot always see past it to recover the English

38. On this point see Benedict Anderson, "Exodus," *Critical Inquiry* 20, no. 2 (1994): 314–27.
39. Rowlandson, *Soveraignty and Goodness of God*, p. 36.
40. Ned Ward, *A Trip to Jamaica* (1698); Ward, *A Trip to New England* (1699); Aphra Behn,
The Widow Ranter; or, the History of Bacon in Virginia (1689); and Ebenezer Cooke, *The Sot-Weed
Factor* (1708) can all be found in *English Literatures of America*, ed. Jehlen and Warner.
41. Robert Beverley, *The History and Present State of Virginia, in Four Parts* (1705), ed. Louis
B. Wright (Chapel Hill, 1947), p. 9.
42. Esmond Wright, " 'The Fine and Noble China Vase, the British Empire': Benjamin
Franklin's 'Love-Hate' View of England," *Pennsylvania Magazine of History and Biography* 111,

colonial author whose narrative of a transatlantic mercantile career is addressed to the royal governor of New Jersey.

Olaudah Equiano, by contrast, was dragged toward Englishness: he was taken from Africa to Montserrat and other West Indian islands, and from thence to Georgia, South Carolina, Pennsylvania, Virginia, and finally to London. There, renamed Gustavus Vassa, he began to write English prose. Equiano himself was now not only an author but an English subject, no longer fully African or American. His life history outstripped the labels of identity in a way that paradoxically makes him more typical of his world than those who had a more comfortable home in it. Equiano's long involuntary progress covered the full circuit of the commerce and colonies of the Atlantic rim. He saw and endured the force of its imperial order, perhaps more thoroughly than any other author in the period.

By the same token it would be a stretch to call Samson Occom a Native American. That term was coined much later, a conscious gesture designed to exploit the symbolic resonance of American nationalism. Occom was a Mohegan; in English terms, he was an Indian, an American, a Native. Only in the middle of his life did some Englishmen begin calling themselves American, and toward such disputes among the English as the Revolution he preferred to remain neutral. Toward English culture, however, he was far from neutral. He had made a significant break with most of his fellow Mohegans when he converted to Christianity and an even greater break when he pursued an English education and then traveled to England for two years. When he wrote a sketch of his own life, he began, "I was Born a Heathen and Brought up in Heathenism."[43]

Robertson, Knight, Rowlandson, Franklin, Equiano, and Occom—all occupied different positions in the same imperial culture. They might have had little else in common, but each writes in the language of England's dominion, and each invokes the reference points of empire, of the transatlantic economy, of Christendom, of modern history. In what sense was it the same culture? And was that culture colonial in the same sense in each case? I choose these examples to illustrate the variety of colonial settings. Not everyone in the period was swept up in the unfolding time of world history, like the ever modern Franklin; many lived in local worlds of less moment, relatively indifferent to markets, wars, printing, and other venues of the English Atlantic. No national identity really underlies these authors' writings. Indeed, as soon as we stop looking for

no. 4 (1987): 435–64. See Alfred Owen Aldridge, *Franklin and His French Contemporaries* (New York, 1957).

43. Samson Occom, "A Short Narrative of My Life" (1768), in *The Elders Wrote: An Anthology of Early Prose by North American Indians, 1768–1931*, ed. Bernd Peyer (Berlin, 1982), p. 12.

Americanness, we see that none is aptly described as American. Most have conflicted, transitional identities. But these writers also illustrate some of the most prevalent patterns of early modern Anglo-American colonial writing: a struggle over identity, but also the dialectic of provincialism and cosmopolitanism, the remapping of space, and the experience of life against a background of world-historical time. For all but Rowlandson—and arguably for her as well—literary culture provides an indefinitely urbane sense of audience, a fundamentally extralocal imagination that, for each except Robertson, has to be poised somehow against the very local imagination of territorial possession and the invention of a creole community. This divided spatial attention has a distinctive tension in settlement colonialism, one that informs Anglo-American writing not only in content but in style, voice, intertextual reference, and audience address.

III.

Literary culture has a highly conflicted place in the spatial and temporal hierarchies of colonial culture. Nationalist criticism blurs the issue insofar as it tries to view colonial writers as distinctively American. It sees them as consciously or unconsciously expressive of a larger, proto-national culture. The difference between writers and nonwriters recedes from view. Literary culture is seen as representative rather than distinctive. A denationalized criticism of English Atlantic writing will need to pay special attention to the transatlantic arena of literary culture and the appeal it had for colonists, even when that arena is understood as, say, the community of the saints rather than as the secular audience of the imperial capital. Scholars have long noted the importance of writing in the development of empire, providing an informational and imaginative matrix for worlds that could not be experienced in any other way.[44] But the spatial imagination of the English Atlantic in turn underlies cultures of letters, giving writing an extralocal appeal.

A striking example is this 1619 letter from John Pory, then secretary of the Virginia Company in Jamestown:

> At my first coming hither the solitary uncouthnes of this place, compared with those partes of Christendome or Turky where I had bene; and likewise my being sequestred from all occurrents and passages which are so rife there, did not a little vexe me. And yet in these five moneths of my continuance here, there have come at one time or another eleven saile of

44. Harold Innis, *Empire and Communication* (Oxford, 1950); J. Parker, *Books to Build an Empire: A Bibliographic History of English Overseas Interests to 1620* (Amsterdam, 1965); and Jehlen, "Papers of Empire."

ships into this river; but fraighted more with ignorance, then with any other marchandize. At length being hardned to this custome of abstinence from curiosity, I am resolved wholly to minde my busines here, and nexte after my penne, to have some good book alwayes in store, being in solitude the best and choicest company. Besides among these Christall rivers, and oderiferous woods I doe escape muche expense, envye, contempte, vanity, and vexation of minde. Yet good my lorde, have a little compassion upon me, and be pleased to sende mee what pampletts and relations of the Interim since I was with you, as your lordship shall thinke good, directing the same (if you please) in a boxe to Mr. Ralfe Yeardley, Apothecary (brother to Sir George Yeardley our governour), dwelling at the signe of the Hartychoke in great Woodstreet, to be sente to me by the first, together with his brothers thinges.[45]

Pory finds himself depending on London for material written goods; he also expresses a heightened self-consciousness about a broader cultural dependence. Like Sarah Knight, he looks to letters for a consciousness broader than his locale. Jamestown, he takes pains to say, is not completely savage: "Nowe that your lordship may knowe, that we are not the veriest beggers in the worlde, our cowekeeper here of James citty on Sundays goes accowtered all in freshe flaming silke; and a wife of one that in England had professed the black arte, not of a scholler, but of a collier of Croydon, weares her rough bever hatt with a faire perle hatband, and a silken suite thereto correspondent."[46] The urbane style of this sentence helps to place Pory in a map of the Jamestown streets through which this cowekeeper and this collier's wife parade, while equally placing him in relation to London and the Levant. Like the finery of his fellow colonists, Pory's style and humor invite us to see a progress in civilization. And this same geography of culture that makes Jamestown civilized, English, makes it provincial.

In his classic study *Savagism and Civilization*, Roy Harvey Pearce argued that the mixed uses of "civilization" in the colonial period gave way, shortly after the Revolution, to a racialized narrative legitimating dispossession.[47] "Civilization" came to be understood not as something that might exist in different versions but as Christianity, the wearing of clothing, table manners, or other positive contents of Englishness. Its implication of progress took on invidious implications for those whom it classed as "savage." Often it was used as synonymous with Christianity even by missionaries whose practice—aiming at conversion but not at literacy or

45. Lyon G. Tyler, ed., *Narratives of Early Virginia* (New York, 1907; rpt., New York, 1952), p. 286.

46. Ibid., p. 285.

47. Roy Harvey Pearce, *Savagism and Civilization: A Study of the Indian and the American Mind* (Baltimore, 1953; rpt., Berkeley, 1988).

refinement—implied a sharp distinction. And like so many normative concepts, it required a continual labor of ejecting from oneself all that is wild or savage—a labor that for the civilized person can produce what John Barrell calls "the psychopathology of empire." For these reasons, the narrative of civilization has often been seen as a prime example of colonialist thought.[48]

Yet in 1619, Pory does not see civilization as the defining identity of white Europeans (though this meaning is no doubt also available, on reserve). Writing makes him civilized. It also separates him from his fellow colonists. He has a clerk's sense of class. The civilization he craves is opposed not to savagism but to uncouthness. He sees it as remaining foreign to the settlers, at least compared with "those partes of Christendome or turky where I had bene." Civilization, for him, is neither national nor racial. It is a marker of social identity shared with Turks, exactly because literary practice is said to supersede merely local forms of sociability; he seeks "best and choicest company" with "some good book." Books are resources that would allow a progress in self-culture. The "curiosity" that Pory values may be a defining ideal for the moral consciousness of an explorer and colonist; yet its promise of indefinite self-fashioning points elsewhere. For Pory it pointed to London, and he did not stay long in the Chesapeake.

The aspiration to civilization has contradictory meanings, each equally visible in Pory's letter and heightened by his dependence on his patron for print. Colonial writers are always inventing the meaning of civilization in this way. Even when the idea of civilization begins to afford the colonizer's sense of calling and destiny, it also separates the writer from the "solitary uncouthness" of his or her place. Its narrative assumption—human beings move from savagism to civility—leads, not inexorably, to the ideological perception of Indian cultures as inferior because primitive. But the same narrative orientation implies another possibility, powerfully expressed in Pory's letter, to which no modern reader of colonial texts can be altogether indifferent: a possibility of cumulative self-cultivation through the historical resources of arts and letters. Civilization at its most ideological is *also* a horizon of worldliness, a faraway port from which supplies can be recruited for a struggle against the "abstinence from curiosity" that is everyday local culture. Literate culture, in short, helped to define more than one cognitive geography. And because the stakes in the narrative of civilization were so high, the colonial writer could find him- or herself confronted with sweeping questions of value. Reflecting on the colonial project three years before Pory's letter, for example, John

48. John Barrell, *The Infection of Thomas DeQuincey* (New Haven, 1991); Stanley Diamond, *In Search of the Primitive: A Critique of Civilization* (New York, 1974).

Smith was led to an extended meditation on what makes living interesting: "Then, who would live at home idly (or thinke in himselfe any worth to live) only to eate, drink, and sleepe, and so die?"[49] The writers of early modern Anglo-America had to map and narrate themselves in ways that could be more or less contradictory but were never without tensions.

Need it be added that this dialectic between colonial geographies and the critical inquiry of literate culture is also the context in which Anglo-American texts might now be reread?

49. *A Description of New England*, in *The Complete Works of Captain John Smith (1580–1631)*, ed. Philip L. Barbour, 3 vols. (Chapel Hill, 1986), 1:344.

part two

Translation and Transculturation

The Native Translator as Critic: A Nahua Playwright's Interpretive Practice

LOUISE M. BURKHART

IN 1536, a hundred years before the founding of Harvard College, Franciscan friars in Mexico established the first European-style institution of higher learning in the Americas. Although Harvard College was intended in part as a school for Native Americans and its Indian College did graduate some Natick students in the 1660s, its primary clients were the sons of British colonists. In contrast, the College of the Holy Cross in Santiago Tlatelolco, the northern sector of Mexico City, was open only to indigenous boys. Here sons of the native nobility, as well as an occasional exceptionally talented boy of commoner status, received an education in the traditional liberal arts curriculum, plus some training in theology and medicine.

Among the graduates were a cohort of scholars and teachers who worked with the Franciscans on the production of Christian literature in Nahuatl, the principal native language of central Mexico. Some of these same Nahua men, like many of the other graduates, also held prestigious offices in the colonial governments of the native communities. Several assisted with ethnographic investigations of native culture. A privileged elite acting as interpreters between cultures, the Nahua scholars were also an affront to Spanish colonists, whose sense of cultural superiority was threatened by native men who knew Latin and who prayed in church several times a day. In this essay I examine the translation of a Spanish religious drama into Nahuatl by one (or possibly more) of these native schol-

My work on the Nahuatl drama was supported by a grant from the Translations Program of the National Endowment for the Humanities. I thank Robert Blair St. George and the anonymous reviewers for their comments and suggestions on this paper.

ars.[1] The Nahuatl text dates to approximately 1590, or about seventy years after the Spanish invasion, and was intended for performance on Wednesday of Holy Week. This text is the oldest extant dramatic script in a Native American language. A handful of other Nahuatl dramas that may be of sixteenth-century origin survive, but only in much later copies or versions.

The first theatrical performances of Christian narratives in native languages, with native actors, were produced under Franciscan auspices in the 1530s, a practice later adopted by other religious orders. Subject matter ranged from the Fall of Adam and Eve to the Last Judgment, with stories from the lives of Christ and the saints accounting for the bulk of the scripts. This early missionary theater has been the subject of various studies, hampered not only by the paucity of available texts but often also by a "spiritual conquest" perspective: the friars are invested with agency and authority, while the indigenous people are treated as obedient performers and passive spectators, so impressed by the spectacles that they willingly accept Christianity.[2]

The Nahuatl play, written in a native scribal hand, lies at the end of a 220-leaf manuscript compiled by an anonymous Franciscan friar, containing notes for sermons, short theological commentaries, and other materials. It bears the heading *miercoles santo*, "Holy Wednesday," but no information on authorship, source, or actual performances (fig. 3.1). The drama was first recognized in 1986, by David Szewczyk of the Philadelphia Rare Books and Manuscripts Company, when the manuscript—taken from Mexico after the fall of Maximilian and sold in London in 1869—went on the market from a private collection. The Princeton University Library purchased the manuscript, specifically because of the play it contains.[3]

Because it was adapted from a specific, known Spanish source, this script provides insight not only into the nature of early Nahua-Christian drama but also into the practice of translation by native interpreters. Friars who gave their trusted assistants Christian texts to translate into

1. This play is the subject of my book *Holy Wednesday: A Nahua Drama from Early Colonial Mexico* (Philadelphia, 1996), which contains complete translations of the Spanish and Nahuatl plays; background information on Spain and Mexico; discussions of the Nahuatl play's social, textual, and performance contexts and possible authorship; parallel text materials; and a fuller treatment of the points presented here. The Spanish and Nahuatl texts are published on a disk, also available from the University of Pennsylvania Press.

2. On Mexican missionary theater, see especially Fernando Horcasitas, *El teatro náhuatl: Épocas novohispana y moderna* (Mexico City, 1974); Marilyn Ekdahl Ravicz, *Early Colonial Religious Drama in Mexico: From Tzompantli to Golgotha* (Washington, D.C., 1970); Othón Arróniz, *Teatro de evangelización en Nueva España* (Mexico City, 1979); Robert Ricard, *The Spiritual Conquest of Mexico*, trans. Lesley Byrd Simpson (Berkeley, 1966); and Richard C. Trexler, *Church and Community, 1200–1600: Studies in the History of Florence and New Spain* (Rome, 1987).

3. The manuscript is now in the Princeton Collections of Western Americana, Visual Materials Division, Department of Rare Books and Special Collections, Princeton University Library.

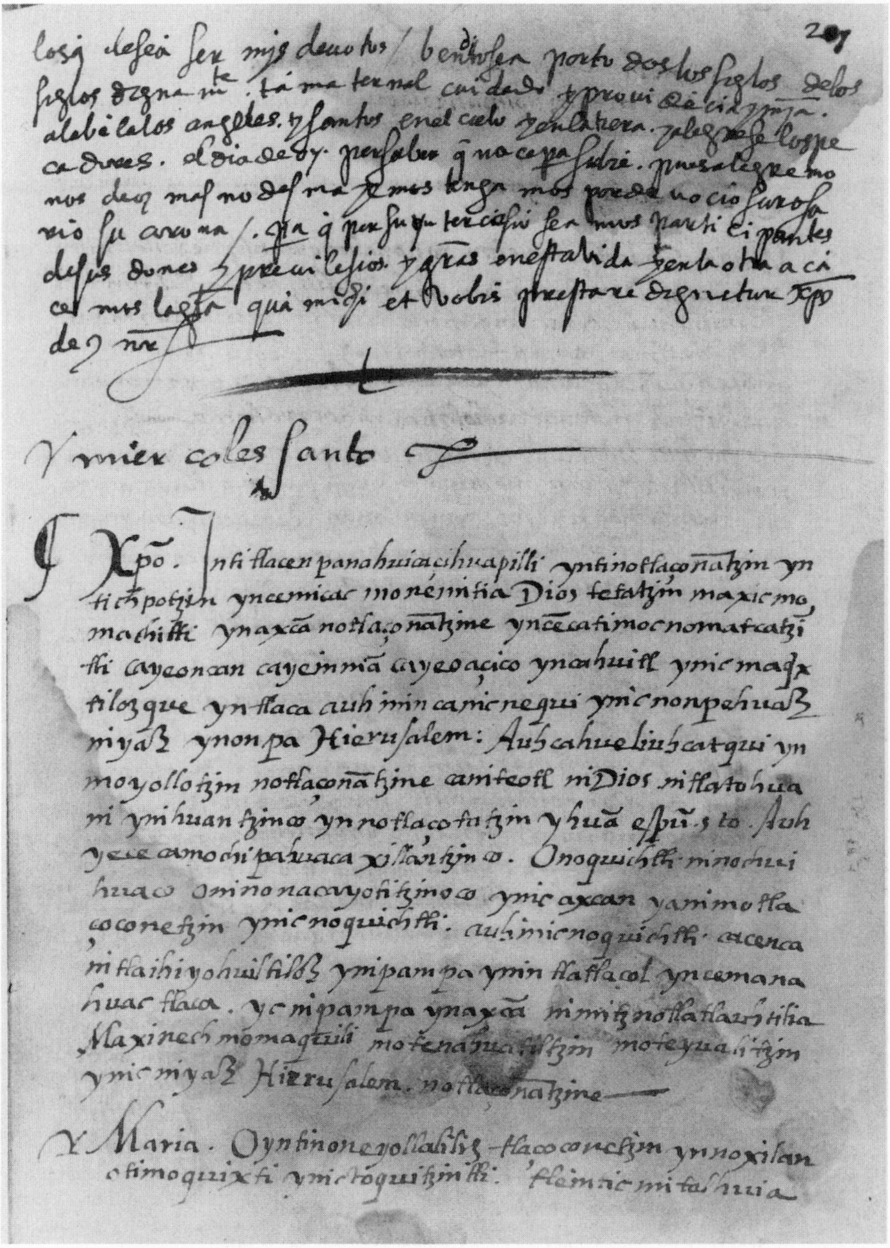

Fig. 3.1. The first page of the "Holy Wednesday" drama. (Photo: Princeton University Libraries.)

Nahuatl assumed that the resulting translations adequately conveyed the immutable truths of the Christian faith. Statements such as "I dictated . . . the songs; the Latinists wrote them" and "by his hand has been written and passed all that I have published" assert the friars' control over the texts.[4] This was a necessary fiction, given that the friars' authority as men of God and masters of the native languages enabled them to gain permission to publish books in these languages. Native voices thus are masked behind those of the friars. But by directly comparing a native translator's work with its source, one can reconstruct something of the translation process and view it as a highly creative rather than a mechanical act.

Studies of colonial discourse often focus on the hegemonic formulations and justifications of the European colonial powers and their inscription into the early accounts of indigenous peoples and their cultures. Anticolonial discourse by indigenous peoples is much more difficult to recover, and not just because the writing of history was concentrated in European hands. It is also a question of what we are prepared to recognize as anticolonial discourse. John and Jean Comaroff stress that native expressions of resistance are often formulated outside of the register of verbal debate. Furthermore, they state, "when the colonized respond in the genre of rational debate—at least as defined in European terms—the hegemony of the colonizing culture may be well on its way to instilling itself in its new subjects." Indeed, some of the most articulate Native American critics of European domination write in the conqueror's own language and exploit contradictions within the dominant culture's own discourses: the Pequot preacher William Apess uses Christian ethics to expose Anglo-American racism; the Andean chronicler Felipe Guaman Poma de Ayala uses the Spanish legal concept of the "just war" to challenge the legitimacy of the conquest of Peru.[5]

But we need not locate anticolonial manifestos or overt resistance movements in order to find counterhegemonic intent in native discourse and

---

4. The first statement is from fray Bernardino de Sahagún on the composition of the *Psalmodia christiana*, a book of Nahua-Christian chants; the original wording is "dicte la postilla, y los cantares: escrjujeronlos, los latinos" (Bernardino de Sahagín, *Florentine Codex: General History of the Things of New Spain*, trans. Arthur J. O. Anderson and Charles E. Dibble, 12 vols. [Santa Fe, 1950–82], introductory volume, p. 54). The second is fray Juan Bautista, in the prologue to his *Sermonario en lengua mexicana* (Mexico City, 1606). Referring to the Nahua scholar Agustín de la Fuente, Bautista states, "Por su mano ha scripto, y passado todo quanto he impresso" (unpaginated). Unless otherwise noted, all translations are by the author.

5. John Comaroff and Jean Comaroff, *Ethnography and the Historical Imagination* (Boulder, 1992), p. 257; William Apess, *On Our Own Ground: The Complete Writings of William Apess, a Pequot*, ed. Barry O'Connell (Amherst, 1992); Rolena Adorno, *Guaman Poma: Writing and Resistance in Colonial Peru* (Austin, 1986); Felipe Guaman Poma de Ayala, *El primer nueva corónica y buen gobierno*, ed. John V. Murra and Rolena Adorno, trans. Jorge L. Urioste, 3 vols. (Mexico, 1980).

practice. There are many strategies by which the dominated may actively negotiate their relationship to the colonizing culture: James Clifford suggests "appropriation, compromise, subversion, masking, invention, and revival." We must also be aware that resistance may speak in muted tones. The colonial record consists largely of what James Scott calls "public transcripts," within which protest may be masked in various manners; "hidden transcripts," the private discourses and actions in which resistance is expressed more openly, only rarely find their way into the historical record.[6]

As the adoption of Christian religion by native peoples has come to be seen less as a "spiritual conquest" and more as a strategy for collective survival, scholars, including myself, have emphasized the gaps between native and European Christianity and the continuities between preconquest and colonial religious belief and practice.[7] Pre-Columbian traditions are seen to exert a constraining and directing force on how native people understood Christianity and adapted its creeds and customs to their own use. This approach is superior to those that treat Christianity as a thin veneer loosely glued on a reified and essentialized native culture. Yet it too has essentializing, deterministic tendencies: certain preexisting cultural traits appear to act in the manner of an unseen hand, leading the colonized people to interpret Christianity in a particular fashion.

Without denying that pre-Columbian cultural expressions, as well as colonial realities, affected native practices of Christianity, I would like to suggest another way of looking at the situation, one that grants more agency to the native actors. In developing their versions of Christianity, Natives employed their own symbolic repertoires to construct informed critiques of European culture. A native version of Christianity is not simply what the people were capable of understanding, given their linguistic and conceptual categories, or what they found useful and meaningful as they coped with their colonized status. Counterposed to the religious practice of their conquerors, it stands as a commentary on it. For all native practice, in a colonial context, participates in the ongoing negotiation of power relations.

Europeans can claim, as they often did in colonial Mexico, that the Natives got it wrong. But the native version persists—often with considerable tenacity on the part of its practitioners—as a muted challenge to European cultural hegemony. A refusal to practice Christianity in the

6. James Clifford, *The Predicament of Culture: Twentieth-Century Ethnography, Literature, and Art* (Cambridge, 1988), p. 338; James Scott, *Domination and the Arts of Resistance: Hidden Transcripts* (New Haven, 1990).

7. The classic work in the "spiritual conquest" mode is Ricard, *Spiritual Conquest of Mexico*. Examples of work emphasizing collective survival are James Axtell, "Some Thoughts on the Ethnohistory of Missions," *Ethnohistory* 29, no. 1 (1982): 35–41, and Nancy M. Farriss, *Maya Society under Colonial Rule: The Collective Enterprise of Survival* (Princeton, 1984). On my own work, see especially Burkhart, *The Slippery Earth: Nahua-Christian Moral Dialogue in Sixteenth-Century Mexico* (Tucson, 1989).

European mode implies that there is something unsatisfactory, even inferior, about the European version. And given that European Christianity was represented to native people as the eternal and immutable Word of God and as the legitimating purpose for colonial domination, native mutations thereof amount to a destabilizing critique of one of colonialism's dominant discourses.

I will use the case of the Nahuatl play to illustrate these general points. Entrusted with the translation of a Spanish religious text into Nahuatl— overtly an act intended to further Spanish cultural hegemony—the native translator created a very different text. In doing so, he acted not only as translator but also as critic, evaluating the adequacy of the Spanish source and correcting its perceived defects by making his own changes, additions, and omissions. Thus, the Nahuatl version can be read as both an adaptation and a critique of its source.

The corrected, translated text, intended for performance by Nahua actors, was directed toward a public domain of native religious practice, characterized by elaborate processions and dramas, through which native people represented themselves to one another and to non-Natives as pious Christians.[8] Because many priests and some other non-Natives could understand Nahuatl and because written scripts were subject to priestly review, the texts for these dramatic performances may be considered part of the "public transcript" of colonial religious life.

The Spanish source for the Nahuatl play is an *auto* (one-act religious drama) entitled *Lucero de nuestra salvación* (Beacon of our salvation). Composed by a Valencian bookseller named Ausías Izquierdo Zebrero, it was first published probably in 1582.[9] It is written in five-line stanzas of rhymed verse. Set at the home of Mary Magdalene and her sister, Martha, in Bethany, near Jerusalem, the drama enacts a farewell scene between Jesus Christ and the Virgin Mary. Christ asks his mother's leave to depart for Jerusalem, where he knows he will be arrested and executed. In the presence of Mary Magdalene, Mary begs her son not to leave her; he protests that he must carry out his father's will. An angel then arrives bearing letters to Mary from five Old Testament personages who, imprisoned in the Limbo of the Holy Fathers, wait anxiously for Christ to come

8. See Louise M. Burkhart, "Pious Performances: Christian Pageantry and Native Identity in Early Colonial Mexico," in *Native Traditions in the Postconquest World*, ed. Elizabeth H. Boone and Tom Cummins (Washington, D.C., 1998).

9. The earliest extant edition I could locate, which I have used for this analysis, is a circa 1590 but undated imprint now in the Houghton Library at Harvard University. The full title of this imprint is *Auto llamado Luzero de nuestra Saluacion, que trata el despedimiento que hizo nuestro Señor Iesu Christo de su bendita madre estando en Bethania, para yr a Hierusalen, en que se contienen passos muy deuotos, y razonamientos contemplatiuos de la passion de Christo, y de su bendita madre.*

and liberate them. This refers to the Christian tradition of the harrowing of hell, the belief that on Holy Saturday, while his body lay in the sepulchre, Christ descended to hell and brought forth the souls of all who had been faithful to the true God, from Adam and Eve down to Saints Joseph and John the Baptist.

The authors of the five letters are Adam, David, Moses, Abraham, and Jeremiah. Each one encloses with his letter one of the implements that will be used in the Passion of Christ: the cross, the crown of thorns, the three nails, the column, and the lance. After reading the letters, Mary no longer attempts to detain Christ but quibbles with him over smaller matters, such as whether she may accompany him and where in Jerusalem she will be able to find him. Finally they bless one another, and as Christ prepares to leave, Mary collapses into Mary Magdalene's arms.

The most immediately striking difference between the Spanish play and its Nahuatl adaptation is the latter's length, which is much more than double that of its source. Even so, the Nahua playwright followed the organization of the Spanish play in regard to the characters' turns at speech. There are only two discrepancies between the plays in this respect, one of which may be due to scribal error in the extant copy of the Nahuatl play. Oral-poetic analysis of the Nahuatl indicates that the Nahua interpreter also tended to respect the stanza structure of the Spanish: stanza boundaries in the Spanish are frequently echoed by discursive breaks in the Nahuatl. The fact that the Nahua playwright was paying such close attention to his source makes it clear that his alterations were quite deliberate.

The Nahua playwright supplements the cast with six small boys costumed as angels, one to read the letters aloud to Mary—thus sustaining dialogue, where the Spanish play presents a lengthy monologue—and five to carry onstage the five implements of the Passion. This influx of angels may be linked to native representations of the sacred as a garden paradise filled with birds and flowers; some Nahua-Christian texts equate angels with brightly feathered tropical birds. Children were also dressed as angels for masses and processions.[10] Depictions of angels carrying the Passion implements were common in contemporary Indo-Christian art (fig. 3.2). Native artists developed a distinctive style of mural painting and

---

10. Louise M. Burkhart, "Flowery Heaven: The Aesthetic of Paradise in Nahuatl Devotional Literature," *Res: Anthropology and Aesthetics* 21 (Spring 1992): 89–109. Diego Valadés, *Retórica cristiana*, ed. Esteban J. Palomera, trans. Tarsicio Herrera Zapién et al. (Mexico City, 1989), pp. 423–33; Andrés Pérez de Ribas, *Historia de los trivmphos de nvestra santa fee entre gentes las mas barbaras, y fieras del nuevo orbe: Conseguidos por los soldados de la milicia de la Compañia de Iesvs en las missiones de la provincia de Nueva España* (Madrid, 1645), p. 737.

Fig. 3.2. An angel with the crown of thorns. Relief sculpture, Huexotzingo, Puebla, Mexico. (Photo: Louise M. Burkhart.)

relief sculpture, modeled after European woodcuts, with which they ornamented churches, chapels, and friaries built in the colony. Mary, Mary Magdalene, and the crucified Christ, as well as Saint John, appear in a mural in Tepeapulco (fig. 3.3); such images provided models for the play's props and costumes.

One particularly substantive change concerns the respective authors' treatment of dramatic action. The Spanish play, though it hardly constitutes a masterpiece of suspense, does follow the classical Western model for drama: it centers around a conflict that is resolved into winners and losers. The angel arrives at the height of the dispute between mother and son, acting as mediator and initiating the process by which Mary gives up and Christ prevails.

This basic plot structure is disrupted in the Nahuatl version. The Nahua playwright downplays the disagreement between Christ and Mary. The Nahuatl Christ treats his mother with notably more deference; the Nahuatl Mary is less argumentative and is invested with more knowledge and authority than her Spanish counterpart. The second stanza of Christ's opening speech shows this contrast, as well as illustrating how the Nahua playwright fleshed out the terse Spanish verse into more elaborate oratory:

Fig. 3.3. The Crucifixion. Mural painting, Tepeapulco, Hidalgo, Mexico. (Photo: Louise M. Burkhart.)

Spanish: And although I am the sovereign God
            I come to you obediently,
            as son in a human sense,
            I ask that you give me permission,
            and your hand, sacred Virgin.[11]   (1r)

Nahuatl: And well do you understand,
            oh my precious mother,
            that I am a divinity, I am God, I am sovereign,
            along with my precious father and the Holy Spirit.
            However, it was in your pure womb
            that I came to become a man, I came to assume flesh.
            Hence, now I am your precious child,
            in the sense that I am a man.
            And in the sense that I am a man,
            I will be made to suffer great fatigue,
            because of the misdeeds of the people of the world.
            Thus, because of them I now beseech you:
            may you give me your command, your send-off,
            so that I may go to Jerusalem,
            oh my precious mother.   (207r)

The Nahuatl Christ does not seek his mother's permission, "although" he is God and, therefore, does not really need to do so. Rather, he acknowledges her understanding of his situation and seeks her compassion for the people of the world.

Just before the angel arrives, the Spanish Mary does nothing but complain of her own imminent suffering:

> Oh sad, afflicted Mother,
> with maddening and strong pain,
> as there is a definitive sentence
> that you must suffer death
> how might I continue living?
> Oh my broken heart
> Oh my anguished soul,
> Oh my much beloved son

11. The translation of the Spanish auto is from the circa 1590 Houghton Library imprint and was done with the collaboration of Dr. Maurice Westmoreland, Department of Languages, Literatures, and Cultures, University at Albany, State University of New York. The translation from the Nahuatl is my own, from the manuscript at Princeton. Page numbers from the original manuscripts are given in the text. The complete texts in English are published in my book *Holy Wednesday*.

> do not die an ignominious death,
> this alone I ask you.   (2v)

The parallel text in the Nahuatl is as follows:

> My precious child,
> how very piercing, how profound is the affliction
> that will befall you!
> Nothing whatsoever matches it, is equal to it,
> the aching, the hurting
> that your heart will know.
> How very strong is the sovereign command that was set down,
> the sentence of divinity!
> How will I be even a little bit happy?
> For I will see you then,
> when they tie you to the stone column by your hands.
> Not just four hundred times will they flog you.
> Oh, my heart,
> it is as if it is about to issue forth,
> it is so distressed, I am suffering so much,
> with sadness, with aching.
> My precious child,
> may you not become very short of breath,
> as you are made to suffer fatigue,
> but truly with all your heart, according to your wishes,
> in this way the torments will befall you.   (211r)

The Nahuatl Mary first expresses solidarity with her son by describing his suffering as well as her own. She repeats, nearly word for word, part of his immediately preceding speech to her, where he said, "Oh my precious mother, oh, how very piercing, how profound is the affliction that will befall me in that time, at that moment! Nothing is equal to it." Nowhere else in either version does one character repeat another's words so closely. Mary then predicts the flogging that her son will undergo and utters an optative statement, which may likewise be considered to have prophetic force, asking that his torments proceed as he wishes and not prove more than he can endure. Coming after this empathetic and prophetic statement, the angel's letters lose their mediating function. The conflict between mother and son seems already to be resolved.

At the end of the Spanish play, Mary attempts to throw herself into Christ's arms. He rejects her, stating, "Do not throw yourself into my arms / Hold onto her, Magdalene" (4v). On that abrupt note, Izquierdo closes his play. In the Nahuatl play, Christ tells Magdalene to hold onto Mary, lest she fall, but does not himself reject her embrace:

> May it not be that you will fall,
> oh my mother!
> Oh Magdalene,
> take hold of her, embrace her!
> May it not be that she will fall!   (215r)

The Nahua playwright then appends to the end of his text four speeches that are not in the Spanish source but in which Mary and Christ make further declarations of mutual love and support. These include one of Mary's longest speeches—and arguably her most eloquent—in the entire Nahuatl play. She asks to die with her son, even though he earlier explained to her that she must remain alive. Christ gives his mother a long blessing full of praises, even though he already blessed her in the text that parallels the Spanish. In terms of the resolution of the plot, these final speeches are unnecessary and redundant. At the very end, the playwright inserted these stage directions: "And they encouraged each other, then they took leave of each other, they said goodbye to each other, they embraced each other" (215v). The drama thus ends with a show of mutual affection.

Why this de-emphasis on conflict in favor of mother-son solidarity? The change can be interpreted in several ways. For one thing, the Nahua playwright has cast the text in the discourse genre of Nahuatl oratory. This speaking style emphasized the exchange of polite and deferential speeches organized nonlinearly as what its practitioners described as "a scattering of jades," or a sequence of independent, artistically executed utterances. One argued by employing more persuasive rhetoric than one's interlocutors, not by overtly contradicting them. The characters in the Spanish play evidently seemed rude, argumentative, and unschooled in proper social intercourse—as, no doubt, did many Spanish colonists. By carefully reforming his characters' speech according to Nahua conventions, the playwright offers a critique of Spanish-style social interaction.

By investing Mary with more authority and representing Christ as more obedient, the playwright also comments on intergender and intergenerational relations. The gender complementarity that characterized native society and its deities was under siege as colonial authorities sought to impose more patriarchal forms of family organization and as women were barred from most public and official roles. Priests preached against the evil idolatries of the elders, and colonial administrative policies emphasized the conjugal pair and the nuclear family over the extended family and the lineage; both practices undermined the authority of parents over their children. But here we have a Nahuatl Christ who is able to respect and obey his human mother as well as his divine father.

Family harmony may be considered a positive value under Spanish-Christian ethics as well, but moral responsibility is a higher one. In addition to downplaying the mother-son conflict, the Nahua playwright repeatedly places more emphasis on the role of prophecy than does the Spanish text. Christ must go through with his plans because everything has been laid out in the ancient prophecies. For example, where the Spanish Christ says, "Truly it seems to me / that that which is prophesied / cannot fail to come to pass" (2v), the Nahuatl playwright composed this more emphatic evocation of the power of the prophecies:

> It is true that I will cause to come true
> that which the prophets left foretold.
> Regarding me they left it said
> that I would rescue people here on earth.
> It will certainly come true,
> that I will endure everything
> that they left declared, which lies written in the sacred book.
> Nothing whatsoever will be lost,
> even if it is a little spatter of ink.
> It will all come true.   (210r)

Combined with his filial obedience, this deference to the prophecies leaves Christ acting with virtually no will of his own. Whereas the Spanish Christ contradicts and corrects his mother and admits that he could choose to redeem humanity without undergoing death, the Nahuatl Christ gives no indication that he has free will, that he could go against the desires of his father and the prophets, that in complying with his prophesied death he is making a moral choice. In so humbly submitting to the pattern laid out by his elders, Christ is following behavioral norms represented in the Nahuatl moral exhortations recorded in the sixteenth century, which emphasize filial obedience and the transmission of ancestral wisdom. These teachings directly contradict the friars' emphasis on individual moral responsibility, on the contest between good and evil carried out, like a classical dramatic conflict, within the individual soul.

The emphasis on past prophecies and intergenerational continuity is also evident in the Nahua playwright's treatment of the Old Testament figures. Having lost their function as mediators in the Christ-Mary dispute, they appear as ancestral figures with foreknowledge of the upcoming events. The Nahua playwright adds references to their kinship ties to Mary and to people in general; they are her fathers, they are people's first fathers. They describe their situation as one of suffering and torment, to a greater extent than their counterparts in the Spanish text and in terms that echo the descriptions of Christ's own upcoming ordeal—itself given added emphasis in the Nahuatl text. According to Church doctrine, the Holy Fathers in Limbo did not suffer any pain or torment. The Nahuatl text treats them as if they were actually in a deeper level of hell where sinners are punished. They speak in penitent tones of their own misdeeds, as Nahuas were encouraged to do in the rite of confession.

Two specific passages are especially noteworthy. David's letter states that, after Christ fulfills his destiny, "our riches, our prosperity, will return" (212v). This wealth-and-riches couplet was used in Nahuatl oratory as a metaphor for happiness and prosperity in a general sense. The corresponding line in the Spanish refers to Christ's founding of a new law—that is, to replace the law of Moses. Thus, where the Spanish text suggests the replacement of a past order with a new one, the Nahuatl refers to a return to an earlier state.

The second passage occurs in Christ's first speech after the reading of the letters. The Spanish Christ tells his mother:

> Allow me now to rescue
> these my beloved children.
> Consider how lost they are.
> And in the spilling of my blood
> they will be redeemed.   (4r)

The Nahuatl text follows the Spanish in having Christ continue to importune his mother, even though this is redundant given her previous acceptance of his fate. But he plans to rescue a more broadly defined group of souls than does his Spanish counterpart:

> May this be all that you say,
> may you yield to me,
> may it be that I go!
> It is for this reason:
> my precious ones and a great many others
> who were confounded, were confused by error,
> I will rescue with my precious blood.   (214r)

Not just his "precious ones"—that is, the Holy Fathers—are to benefit, but also an undefined group of "others" who had fallen into moral error.

By representing the Limbo correspondents as ancestral figures and as penitent sinners, suffering in the underworld, who will be rescued along with a "great many others" and have restored to them their former prosperity, the Nahua playwright very subtly suggests that the fate assigned to the colonial Nahuas' own non-Christian ancestors might be revised. The friars taught that all the ancestors were imprisoned in hell and were suffering eternal torment for their idolatries and other misdeeds. Yet the story of the harrowing of hell provided a narrative model of escape from the underworld. If Christ was willing to rescue the non-Christian prophets, patriarchs, and kings of the Old Testament, then why should that favor not be extended to "a great many others"? Instead of abandoning the past in favor of a wholly new Christian order, as the friars demanded, why should Christianizing Nahuas not incorporate it into the new order and maintain continuity with it?

Simply by being translated into Nahuatl and performed by Nahua actors, a Spanish text becomes culturally ambivalent. It is first displaced from its original performance context in Spain to enter the multivocal and contested realm of social relations in the Mexican colonial context. It is then removed from the immediate control of the missionary friars to enter a Nahua universe of discourse and practice. Here, Nahua performers can manipulate its meanings, subverting the unidirectional transfer of European culture by intruding their own interpretive stance, even if only on a metalinguistic level.

But when native interpreters approach the practice of translation—or what Nahuas called *tlahtolli icuepca*, or "the turning around of words"—in the manner of this particular playwright (and other Nahua scholars), we see the extent to which translation can accommodate an assertion of native ideas and values. These enter the translated text not simply as a by-product of the passage between languages and cultures but also because the translator has deliberately inscribed them there in accordance with definite ideas about what native Christian discourses should be. This presumes a critical evaluation of the original text, decisions regarding how best to adjust it to the interpreter's ends, and strategies for implementing those changes in the process of producing the translation.

The translator must also understand and work within the limits imposed by priestly censorship and the public performance context. A text that digressed too blatantly from its model might not be accepted for public performance; the written text itself could be subject to confiscation. Much had to be said through double meanings, ambiguity, and other subtle reworkings of the original texts. Yet at least some of these translators found it possible to construct meaningful cultural critiques under the guise of translating Old World Christian texts. In this case, a Christian religious drama intended for performance during Holy Week—the high point of the Catholic ritual cycle—was made to encode validations of native cultural practices and subversive reworkings of Christian teachings.

Dissent and the Frontier
of Translation:
Roger Williams's *A Key into the*
Language of America

ANNE G. MYLES

TO BE a religious dissenter in an orthodox society is to reside at
the margin of cultural experience, to be at once a member of that society
and to stand over the line—over the line of acceptable speech or behavior
and sometimes, through banishment or other forms of forced marginalization, over the line geographically as well. To occupy such a position
can provide dissenters with a unique vantage point on the ragged edges
of a society's institutions, settlements, and discourses. Often, dissent
brings with it a firsthand encounter with the connections between language and power, as difference leads to polemical battles and the compelling sentences uttered by institutions of law. Having passed through
such an encounter, dissenters gain both a sophisticated ability and deep
commitment to unraveling the construction of orthodox authority, exposing both its rhetorical origins and its very real effects.

In colonial New England, society's margin was literally and symbolically the frontier between "civilization" and "wilderness." It was the border where European and native cultures met and where, in turn, European culture was in the process of defining itself through and against this
contact, counting on its own power to represent verbally—and in so doing
to assimilate and possess—the New World. Ironically, this critical border
was also the place to which those who rendered themselves intolerable by
their dissent were banished, befitting the view that they were themselves
wild and barbaric. What orthodoxy could not have predicted was the pos-

sibility that dissenters might appropriate their uniquely decentered position and cast it back on their accusers in transgressive refigurations of American symbolic and moral space.[1]

Roger Williams stands as the most important representative of these dimensions of early American dissent. The most educated and articulate opponent of New England's religious and political orthodoxies, he was also the closest to orthodoxy theologically, rendering him the most comprehensible—and hence the most dangerous—to those he criticized. He was also among the individuals in seventeenth-century New England most actively engaged with the indigenous realities of American existence. Banished from Massachusetts in 1635 for a complex of positions springing from his insistence on absolute separation between church and state, Williams was exceptionally aware of the way Puritan orthodoxy both grounded itself in and expressed itself as discourse. In his view, the unchristian language of historical typology led inexorably to the "bloody" rhetoric of his chief disputant John Cotton and others in support of civil punishment of religious nonconformity.[2] Returning to England for the purpose of securing a charter for his settlement of Providence Plantations, Williams published several writings, among them the most unusual work of his career, *A Key into the Language of America* (1643). The first extended translation of Native American language to come from New England, a detailed anthropology of Narraganset Indian society, and a vigorous interrogation of the meaning of Christianity and humanity in a colonial context, after long neglect *A Key* has recently drawn increasing attention for its complex cross-cultural articulations.[3] But it has not yet been fully situated in relation to Williams's own dissenting insistence on establish-

---

1. See John Canup, *Out of the Wilderness: The Emergence of an American Identity in Colonial New England* (Middletown, Conn., 1990), pp. 105–48. Canup offers detailed readings of Thomas Morton and Roger Williams as figures whose "threat to the Puritan order carried a suggestion of wilderness contamination and accommodation with Indian savagery" and who in turn "retaliated with . . . an ironic inversion of Puritan rhetoric" (p. 125).

2. On the logic of Williams's opposition to orthodox language, see Anne G. Myles, "Arguments in Milk, Arguments in Blood: Roger Williams, Persecution, and the Discourse of the Witness," *Modern Philology* 91, no. 2 (1993): 133–60.

3. The first major step toward a reevaluation of *A Key into the Language of America* was the publication of a critical edition with an extensive introduction by John J. Teunissen and Evelyn J. Hinz (Detroit, 1974), from which my textual citations in this essay are drawn (references are given parenthetically in the text). Additional analyses of the text include Canup, *Out of the Wilderness*, pp. 137–48; Christopher D. Felker, "Roger Williams's Uses of Legal Discourse: Testing Authority in Early New England," *New England Quarterly* 63, no. 4 (1990): 624–48; Ivy Schweitzer, *The Work of Self-Representation: Lyric Poetry in Colonial New England* (Chapel Hill, 1991), chap. 5; and Eric Wertheimer, " 'To Spell Out Each Other': Roger Williams, Perry Miller, and the Indian," *Arizona Quarterly* 50, no. 2 (1994): 1–17. For several recent discussions of *A Key*, see Anne Keary, "Retelling the History of the Settlement of Providence: Speech, Writing, and Cultural Interaction on Narragansett Bay," *New England Quarterly* 69, no. 2 (1996): 250–86; Larzer Ziff, "Conquest and Recovery in Early Writings from

ing the limits of true Christian expression or within the context of the Renaissance ideas about language and colonization that would have loomed large for contemporary readers.

Although in an age of multiculturalism Williams's *A Key into the Language of America* stands as a central colonial text, it remains a frustrating one. While it comes as close as any seventeenth-century Anglo-American work to a sympathetic representation of Native American culture and at moments seems almost to give that culture a chance to speak for itself, it always remains firmly anchored in a Eurocentric perspective. In the words of one recent commentator, "Ultimately, it is still the Anglo-Puritan poet who . . . arrogates the language of the other in the service of a conversion culture bent on political and religious hegemony."[4] If we read it looking for traces of authentic indigenous presence or compare it to texts authored by Native Americans themselves, *A Key* falls painfully short. But to produce such a work was never Williams's intention. My approach here will focus on the lasting strength of *A Key*, which is the way, within a set of practical, instrumental goals, it demonstrates the resources that dissent liberates within a culture for self-critique. Engaging in the work of literal linguistic translation while challenging the dominant application of translation as a trope, *A Key into the Language of America* articulates a separatist vision of Christian communication in America that offers a profound challenge to the ideological norms of the colonial mind.

I.

Roger Williams began to study the language of the Narraganset Indians soon after his arrival in New England in 1632, with the original aim of participating in the work of Indian conversion. By the winter of 1635–36, when he fled the jurisdiction of the Massachusetts Bay Colony by heading out to unsettled lands near the Narragansett Bay, his knowledge became essential. In his account of the deed to lands he purchased from the sachems Miantonomi and Canonicus, Williams asserted that "by God's merciful assistance, I was the procurer of the purchase, not by moneys nor payment, the natives being so shy and jealous that moneys could not do it; but by that language, acquaintance, and favor with the natives, and other advantages, which it pleased God to give me." Though framed in terms of thankfulness for God's special providence to his persecuted wit-

America," *American Literature* 68, no. 3 (1996); 509–25; and David Murray, "Using Roger Williams' Key into America," *Symbiosis* 1, no. 2 (1997): 237–53.

4. Wertheimer, " 'To Spell Out Each Other,' " p. 13. For a critical reevaluation of Williams's complicity with the colonizing project, see Keary, "Retelling the History of the Settlement of Providence."

ness, Williams's testimony still suggests that God helps those who know the language.[5] Language and favor, both gained by Williams's ongoing willingness to immerse himself in Narraganset society, influenced much of his subsequent life in New England. His linguistic skills served to advantage not only in his relations with the Narragansets, among whom he made his living as a trader, but also with the Massachusetts authorities, both prior to and following his exile. Massachusetts found that Williams's theological irregularity could be overlooked when it came to his services as a mediator in English-Indian relations. He served as an interpreter for the Narraganset sachems and their allies in a number of treaties and trans-actions with the Massachusetts government in the critical years around the Pequot War, and for decades he advised the colony on the courses it should pursue.

According to his own account in the preface to *A Key into the Language of America*, he drew together the text's materials "in a rude lumpe at Sea" during his voyage to England (p. 83). He states his hope that, if English-men learn to converse with the Indians, "it may please the *Father* of *Mercies* to spread *civilitie* (and in his owne most holy season) *Christianitie*; for *one Candle* will light *ten thousand*" (p. 84). Indian mission was, of course, one of the rationales for the settlement of New England. The royal patent for the Massachusetts Bay Colony announced that "the principall Ende of this Plantacion" was "to wynn and incite the Natives of [the] Country, to the Knowledg and Obedience of the onlie true God and Savior of Mankinde, and the Christian Fayth." But by 1643 the colony still could not

---

5. "Confirmatory Deed of Roger Williams and his wife, of lands transferred by him to his associates in the year 1638," *Records of the Colony of Rhode Island*, 10 vols. (Providence, 1856–65), 1:23. If the syntax of this passage leaves ambiguous whether Williams attributes his "language, acquaintance, and favor" to God, Williams would later stress the laborious nature of normal language acquisition, asserting that one could learn an Indian language only by "constant use or a Miracle." He writes, "[Experience] testifie[s] how hard it is for any man to attaine a little proprietie in common things (so as to escape Derision amongst them) in many years, without abundance of conversing with them, in Eating, travelling, and lodging with them, &c., which none of [New England's] Ministers . . . ever could doe" (*The Complete Writings of Roger Williams*, 1st ser., 6 vols. [Providence, 1866], 4:372–73). The means by which Williams chose to study—living and interacting with the Indians over an extended period of time—are themselves revealing. Since the days of discovery, the more customary practice was for Europeans to kidnap Natives, who would be expected to learn the relevant European language and then teach their own language to their captors. According to Francis Jennings, the missionary John Eliot was taught by an Indian captured during the Pequot War. See Jennings, "Goals and Functions of Puritan Missions to the Indians," *Ethnohistory* 18, no. 3 (1971): 197–212. As Stephen J. Greenblatt insightfully remarks, "To learn a language may be a step toward mastery, but to study a language [particularly when done not by kidnapping but by linguistic and cultural immersion] is to place oneself in a situation of dependency, to submit" (*Marvelous Possessions: The Wonder of the New World* [Chicago, 1991], p. 104). For a more recent discussion of the complexities of linguistic conquest, see Ziff, "Conquest and Recovery."

point to any serious missionary efforts, although funds had been sent for this purpose since the 1630s and pressure was mounting.[6]

Despite his wish to see his Narraganset acquaintances saved, by the 1640s Williams explicitly refused to take this work upon himself, expressing grave doubts about the validity of any large-scale conversion attempts. First, there was the problem of mastering the language adequately. Committed to precise expression and more aware than most of his contemporaries about the difficulty of speaking across the barrier of language and culture, he argued that he himself needed more practice before he would "be able in propriety of speech to open matters of salvation" to the Indians: "In matter of Earth men will help to spell out each other, but in matters of Heaven (to which the soule is naturally so averse) how far are the Eares of man hedged up from listening to all improper language?"[7] Second, if, as he believed, there could be no pure, visible church in the present age, gathering Indians into worshiping congregations would serve little purpose. Only full individual contrition and conversion, the same demanded of any English Puritan, were worth anything at all. Williams pointedly refused to venture whether this kind of conversion had taken place in America, citing evidence of "no small preparation" in the Indians' hearts, but concluding cautiously, "I know not with how little Knowledge and Grace of Christ, the Lord may save, and therefore neither will despaire, nor report much" (p. 87). Ultimately, he was uncertain whether universal conversion was even an appropriate goal before the Second Coming, questioning where in the present the power might lie to spiritually authorize such a mission. From the outset, then, informed readers would have confronted the unsettlingly resistant status of *A Key into the Language of America* as an aid toward the project of Indian conversion, written by someone who endorsed the hope but refused to support the effort.[8]

But the goal of Indian conversion did not stand as an end in itself for the seventeenth-century settlers of the New World. It also existed as part

6. Nathaniel B. Shurtleff, ed., *Records of the Governor and Company of Massachusetts Bay in New England,* 5 vols. (Boston, 1853–56), 1:17. Roy Harvey Pearce offers a good introduction to the history of missionary efforts in New England in *Savagism and Civilization: A Study of the Indian and the American Mind* (Berkeley, 1988), chap. 1. See also Alden T. Vaughan, *New England Frontier: Puritans and Indians, 1620–1675* (Boston, 1965), pp. 235–59. Francis Jennings criticizes inaccuracies and biases in Vaughan as he discusses the political considerations underlying the initiation of active conversion efforts in the 1640s; see "Goals and Functions of Puritan Missions," p. 199.

7. Roger Williams, *Christenings Make Not Christians, or A Brief Discourse concerning that name Heathen, commonly given to the Indians,* in *The Complete Writings of Roger Williams,* ed. Perry Miller, 7 vols. (New York, 1963), 7:40.

8. For an excellent discussion of Williams's views on Indian mission in the context of his views on the millennium, see W. Clark Gilpin, *The Millenarian Piety of Roger Williams* (Chicago, 1979), pp. 116–34.

of a larger religio-historical vision, the *translatio imperii et studii*. The concept of the translatio, which dated from the Middle Ages, was based in the idea that, in the words of Ernst Robert Curtius, "the renewal of the Empire by Charlemagne could be regarded as a transferal of the Roman *imperium* to another people. This is implied in the formula 'translatio imperii' with which the 'translatio studii' (transferal of learning from Athens to Rome or Paris) was later coordinated."[9] For Protestants, while the idea of the Roman imperium no longer applied directly, the vision persisted in the idea of the shifting dynamic center of the Christian world. From an English Puritan perspective, this center had moved to England's churches; if civilization could be brought to America, this locus would be extended or even—the most thrilling possibility for New Englanders—relocated altogether. The millennial hope of New England Puritanism was that America had become the special site where the first fulfillment of God's promises would occur. As Sacvan Bercovitch and other scholars have established, this belief came to wind itself inextricably with the exceptionalist rhetoric that was to be a central force in shaping American identity from the seventeenth century to the present.[10]

Language and rhetoric play a central role in the ideology of the "translatio imperii et studii." Although in its origins it was an entirely European concept, by the age of discovery the translatio had become, as Eric Cheyfitz explains, "inseparably connected with a 'civilizing' mission, the bearing of Christianity and Western letters to the barbarians, [who are] literally . . . those who do not speak the language of the empire."[11] Within this ideology, to civilize and Christianize are seen as inextricable features of a single project, and both dimensions posit an essential link between civilization and language. This link springs from and inscribes a radical binarism at the center of the colonial endeavor; if bringing civilization means bringing language, then language and civilization must be taken as essentially absent in "uncivilized" societies. And indeed, as Stephen Greenblatt has demonstrated, the dominant Renaissance European view of native societies was that they were lacking in recognizably human language. What Greenblatt calls "linguistic colonialism" was not incidental arrogance but rather a cornerstone of the foundations of empire.[12] Within this

9. Ernst Robert Curtius, *European Literature and the Latin Middle Ages* (Princeton, 1983), p. 29, as quoted in Eric Cheyfitz, *The Poetics of Imperialism: Translation and Colonization from "The Tempest" to "Tarzan"* (New York, 1991), pp. 111–12.

10. This argument was defined most influentially in Sacvan Bercovitch, *The Puritan Origins of the American Self* (New Haven, 1975). See also Cheyfitz, *Poetics of Imperialism*, pp. 111, 122–23.

11. Cheyfitz, *Poetics of Imperialism*, p. 112.

12. Stephen J. Greenblatt, "Learning to Curse: Aspects of Linguistic Colonialism in the Sixteenth Century," in *First Images of America: The Impact of the New World upon the Old*, ed. Fredi Chiappelli, 2 vols. (Berkeley, 1976), 2:562.

schema, eloquence—the knowledge of and ability to use the principles of rhetoric, which in Renaissance terms signifies more generally the ability to speak properly, accurately, and persuasively—becomes both a mark of civilization and a technology of domination. The connection between eloquence and European prerogative was further underlined by powerful metaphoric resonances; since classical times the principles of rhetoric had been figured as "clothing"—the "dress" of rhetoric. It was an easy step to see the world as divided into the dual categories of clothed Europeans and naked barbarians, whose relative physical bareness stood as a natural sign of their spiritual, cultural, and linguistic lack.[13]

Despite Williams's specific reservations about conversion, the feasibility of Indian mission as such was not a focal point in his quarrel with New England. More urgent to him was the broader problem of the blurring of nation and church, of civilization and Christianity, implicit in the totalized cultural-religious-linguistic transferal implied by the translatio. His resistance to this conflation is reflected in the subtle but critical distinction he expresses when he hopes that God will spread civility "and in his owne most holy season" Christianity to the Narragansets: the two are separate elements, temporally disjunct, and the first does not automatically produce the second. In the important companion text to *A Key*, the pamphlet *Christenings Make Not Christians* (1645), Williams furiously assaults the pernicious confusion he saw encoded in the conventional European concept of the "Christian world": "Yea if the Lord Jesus himselfe were heare . . . what would he say to a CHRISTIAN WORLD? To CHRISTENDOME? And otherwise then what He would speak . . . must no man speak that names himselfe a Christian."[14] Exploding the oxymoron, Williams attacks the underlying premise and, through it, the legitimacy of English participation in the translatio, arguing that precisely because the idea of a "Christian world" derives from the model of the Roman Empire and was carried over into current usage via Catholicism, it is not a legitimate Protestant view. From this point, he goes on to one of his central arguments in the piece, that England's Protestant "heathen" must complete their own conversion from the idolatrous remnants in their worldview before they have any business trying to convert Indians "from *Antichristian Idols*" to true faith.[15]

13. On eloquence as a technology of imperial domination, see Cheyfitz, *Poetics of Imperialism*, chaps. 2 and 6, esp. p. 120, and Greenblatt, "Learning to Curse," p. 562. To an English reader, the Narragansets themselves would have seemed to endorse this distinction; in *A Key into the Language of America*, Williams notes that they called all Europeans *Wautaconâuog*, or "Coatmen," derived from "*Waûtacone*, one that weares clothes" (p. 133).

14. Williams, *Christenings Make Not Christians*, 7:32.

15. Ibid., 7:31–33, 37. For further discussion of the argument in *Christenings*, see Gilpin, *Millenarian Piety*, pp. 125–28. Williams never mentions the "translatio imperii et studii" by name, but his attack on the idea of a Christian imperium embodied in the term "Christendom" and

This abstract, stringently separatist argument is animated by Williams's recognition of how it manifests itself in real and consequential speech. Williams opens the pamphlet with the dramatically expressed insight that a dualistic world in which "men stand upon their tearmes of *high opposition*" between Christian and heathen does not encourage the work of conversion at all but instead promotes a very different agenda. "How often have I heard both the English and Dutch . . . say," he stated, that "these *Heathen* Dogges, better kill a thousand of them then that we *Christians* should be indangered or troubled with them; Better they all were cut off, & then we shall be no more troubled with them: They have spilt our *Christian* bloud, the best way to make riddance of them, cut them all off, and so make way for Christians."[16] We hear in this language the grim, repetitive automatism of imperial violence, a violence predicated on and subtly authorized by the polarization that Williams insists is an act of false naming. It is a discourse of power, one that uses the category of Christian (but really national and racial) identity to legitimize obliteration of the threatening and inconvenient Other. As Williams describes this speech, it sounds little different from what in other writings of the period he calls "the language of the Dragon," the discourse of orthodoxy claiming its right to persecute dissent.[17]

The argument that runs throughout *A Key into the Language of America* is essentially the same as that of *Christenings Make Not Christians*. While the Narragansets certainly stand in need of conversion, the English do too; while they may be civilized in the secular sense (the extent to which they *were* in fact civilized in the true sense of the word Williams would debate), as a group they, like the Indians, are no more than natural men and can claim no divine prerogative. At the level of language, *A Key* summons the trope of translation as translatio, of colonial speech as civilizing imperial eloquence, to effect a radical turn. Countering the standard representation of the New World Other as lacking the eloquence that European / Christian civilization only can bring, in dialogue-like vocabulary sections and interwoven comments on culture and linguistic usage Williams records the presence of a complex, competent, and morally dis-

---

the idea that this could be extended to America makes his familiarity with the concept quite evident.

16. Williams, *Christenings Make Not Christians*, 7:31–32.

17. In ibid., Williams explains that the original meaning of "heathen" is simply "nation" or "gentiles" and insists that "although men have used to apply this word Heathen to the Indians that go naked . . . yet this word Heathen is most improperly[,] sinfully, and unchristianly used in this sence" (7:31). In *A Key into the Language of America*, Williams pointedly contrasts the names the English give the Indians ("wild-men," "barbarians," "heathens," and the like) with the ways they name themselves, as "People" and as distinct tribes (pp. 84–85). For one prominent use of "heathen," see Williams, *Mr. Cotton's Letter Examined and Answered*, in *Complete Writings*, ed. Miller, 1:326.

cerning Narraganset speech and society. In the general observations and short didactic poems that conclude each chapter, Williams then shifts the gaze to explore the instruction to be gained by English readers from the phenomena he records and to offer *them* an education in the properties of Christian eloquence in the New World.

Although Williams's poems have been rightly identified as the "site[s] of the most disturbance and the most revelation" in *A Key*, it is important to consider how the text handles its central task of translating and teaching the Narraganset language.[18] In his opening "Directions for the use of the Language," Williams explains the rationale for the most obvious of his practices, the dialogic form in which he presents his material: "1. A Dictionary *or* Grammer way *I had consideration of, but purposely avoided, as not so accomodate to the Benefit of all, as I hope this Forme is.* 2. *A* Dialogue *also I had thoughts of, but avoided for brevities sake, and yet (with no small paines) I have so framed every Chapter and the matter of it, as I may call it an Implicite Dialogue*" (p. 90). Williams's pedagogical thinking here suggests acquaintance with the most progressive contemporary ideas about the teaching of foreign languages, such as that promoted by Jan Comenius in his *Janua Linguarum* (1631). Comenius offered a new approach to learning Latin, which became vastly popular, based on repeated readings of a text that discourses in simple terms on the names of things. Comenius's text covered encyclopedically the natural, social, intellectual, and spiritual realms in a manner of which Williams's *Key* is distinctly reminiscent. A dialogic approach to language instruction also seems to have had political resonance for Williams. In a 1654 letter to John Winthrop Jr., he comments on his experiences as a language learner and teacher: "[Mr. Milton] for my Dutch I read him read me many more languages. Grammar rules begin to be esteemed a Tyrannie. I taught 2 Young Gentlemen[,] a Parliam[en]t mans Sons (as we teach our children English) by words, phrazes, and constant talke etc."[19]

Williams's sense that grammar abstracted from speech is "a tyranny" resonates in suggestive ways with the other forms of tyranny he opposes, such as orthodoxy imposing a single "rule" of acceptable belief with no regard to the human costs of compulsion; fittingly, his own arguments for toleration in *The Bloudy Tenent of Persecution* and other polemical writings

---

18. Schweitzer, *Work of Self-Representation*, p. 207.

19. Glenn W. LaFantasie, ed., *The Correspondence of Roger Williams*, 2 vols. (Providence, 1988), 2:393. Williams became friends with Milton during his second trip to England in 1652–53. On Williams's debt to Comenius, see Will S. Monroe, *Comenius and the Beginnings of Educational Reform* (New York, 1971). Interestingly, Comenius had a long-standing interest in the question of Indian education, beginning no later than 1641–42, when he spent time in England and was apparently invited by John Winthrop Jr. to visit New England; see Robert Fitzgibbon Young, *Comenius in England* (New York, 1971).

were also presented in various dialogic forms.[20] But this passage also reminds us that dialogue is prototypically a child's way of learning language. In the pains he takes over the pedagogy that will render his text most *"pleasant* and *profitable* for *All"* (p. 83), Williams puts his readers in the position of elementary learners rather than accomplished speakers, a relationship to language that must have felt regressive and unfamiliar to anyone conceiving of their position within the logic of colonialism. It is, however, a positioning that establishes a potential for openness and teachability that would provide an essential basis for the more demanding instruction of the text's observations and poetry.

Williams's handling of the "implicit dialogue" form is striking and suggestive. To take one example from the first chapter:

Túnna Cowâum, Tuckôteshana?	*Whence come you?*
Yò nowaûm.	*I came that way.*
Náwwatuck nóteshem.	*I came from farre.*
Mattaâsu nóteshem.	*I came from hard by.*
. . . .	. . . .
Acâwmuck nóteshem.	*I came over the water.*
Otàn.	*A Towne.*
Otânick notéshem.	*I came from the Towne.* (P. 94)

Perspectives on the rhetorical implications of such exchanges have varied, although modern readers share the desire to find in these passages some analogy to the text's overall perspective on cross-cultural exchange. John Canup argues that the distance between the columns signifies the incompatibility of Narraganset and English expression and the impossibility of genuine communication between them, although he observes that "the counterbalancing effect of the English translation also suggests that the ground between is potentially a place of meeting, a linguistic neutral zone in which meanings can converge and blend." Ivy Schweitzer sees the use of the dialogue form in largely positive terms, as "a powerful metaphor for the entire text as a dialogue between two cultures and two different cultural constructions of subjectivity."[21]

How might the text's linguistic placements register in the particular

20. Discussing these issues, Schweitzer, *Work of Self-Representation,* p. 199, contends that "Williams's use of dialogue [is] characteristic of his notion of fallen epistemology: until further divine revelation, truth is merely provisional, in this world engaged in a continuous dialogue with peace. Thus, the principle of dialogue can be seen as a structural effect of Williams's belief in the freedom of conscience, a freedom he extended to his Narragansett hosts."

21. Canup, *Out of the Wilderness,* p. 143; Schweitzer, *Work of Self-Representation,* p. 194.

context of the translatio and linguistic colonialism? Initially striking is that the Narragansets are, to a nearly unprecedented degree, unsilenced here, as equal room is made for their unfamiliar speech in the domain of "Western letters." Still, the two columns may not be quite so equivalent as they first appear. Placing the Narraganset words consistently on the left and the English ones on the right may be convention or a mapping of the West-East positions of America and England, but it is a convention that enforces the sense of translating *from* Narraganset *to* English as a final destination. This effect is consolidated by the fact that the English words are printed in italics; in a seventeenth-century text this practice signifies emphasis and importance rather than foreignness. Still, while these considerations affect the status accorded the two languages, there is no suggestion that the goal is to have English erase the Narraganset language; they appear above all as *two* potentially coexistent sites—and mediums—for partaking of God's blessings.

With the partial exception of a catechistic exchange buried in the chapter on religion, what is presented in *A Key* is not official language but practical and secular speech, that which is spoken by individuals. Perhaps most striking in these vocabulary passages is that it is frequently impossible to assign stable positions for Narragansets or Englishmen. (In the passage above, for example, one might at first assume that the phrase "I came from the Towne" would logically be spoken by an Englishman, but the assumption is immediately challenged by the observation that follows, which explains that "in the Narigánset Countrey . . . a man shall come to many Townes" [p. 95]). In a sense, the very fragmentation of the dialogue forces the reader to recognize the universality of the role of speaking subject. The brevity of the exchanges paradoxically works to cultural advantage, limiting the chance that the English translation will fall into the typical trap of obscuring what Indian speakers really said or intended. All we are given is the elements of speech and the capacity to uncover the hidden syntax of the speaking "I" that would remain otherwise inaudible in the "barbarisms" of a non-Indo-European language.[22]

The text's vocabulary / dialogue sections are accompanied by interwoven observations on various elements of Narraganset society, including, significantly, the powers and flaws of Indian speech. There is no question

22. Williams's representation of Narraganset speech stands in an interesting and problematic relation to his occasional recording of the Narragansets' broken English. For example, he relates that "[his] old friend Wequash" confessed on his deathbed *"Me much pray to Jesus Christ. . . . Me so big naughty Heart, me heart all one stone!"* (p. 88). Although Williams validates the content of this utterance without regard to its linguistic errors—he observes that these are *"Savory expressions* using to breath *from compunct and broken Hearts"*—the Narragansets' English still puts them in danger of derision from readers for whom speaking English properly and speaking at all are not readily separable.

but that Williams's voice, his subjectivity, is ultimately the superior one that organizes, interprets, and judges Indian speech and culture. Yet the text would indicate that this interpretive dominance is legitimized not by race, colonial relations, or even Christian profession but solely by the need for all human beings to transfer judgments to the higher personhood of Christ. Only those who can integrate within themselves this translation of perspective, Williams insists, can claim the authority to speak from a position above the Narragansets' status as natural men. In the "General Observation[s]" and above all in the poems that conclude each chapter of *A Key*, Williams pulls together the "facts" and themes established in his linguistic and cultural treatment of each topic and translates them into Protestantism's universal dialectic of nature and grace. Through this process, the automatic projection of the *translatio* is preempted by a project of reflective English self-examination, in which readers are forced to scrutinize the truth of their own lives and naming and determine whether they themselves stand with God or, like those they seek to convert, are still caught in the wilderness of the world.

II.

Poetry serves in several ways as a technology in Williams's project of reverse conversion. To write competent verse is a clear indicator of rhetorical and cultural mastery. Williams the banished dissenter here steps forth from the wilderness in the full dress of verse to insist most forcefully on the need to rewrite colonial meaning. Further, poetry bears a profound relationship to the imperial vision, considered by at least some in the Renaissance as the most ancient form of civilizing eloquence.[23] Yet the audience here is clearly English: suddenly we have not a nation of orators but one, who labors to purify the dialect of his own tribe. Last and probably most important, the verbally precise nature of lyric poetry itself—especially as practiced in Williams's compressed, analytic, at times almost Dickinsonian lyrics—compels readers into unusually close attention to the act of naming and the syntax of relationship.

Virtually all poems in *A Key* repay close examination, but I focus here on two that I believe offer Williams's most explicit attack on the discursive domination of the *translatio* and his attempt to establish an alternative form of Christian eloquence. Thematically similar, both poems deploy colonialism's crucial organizing metaphors of clothing and nakedness. Working at this fundamental ideological juncture, Williams repeatedly reminds his readers how complex and reflexively challeng-

23. See Greenblatt, "Learning to Curse," p. 565.

ing these metaphors can be once stripped of projected assumptions of European superiority.[24] The first poem comes at the end of chapter 20, "On [The Indians'] Nakedness and Clothing," in which Williams reviews clothing-related terms and comments on both the Indians' custom of sometimes choosing to go naked and their "freedom from any wantonesse" (p. 185). The chapter concludes with a "Generall Observation" that, typical of the volume, enacts a translation from culture to spirit; here, the movement is made through a metaphoric extension of the category of clothing, as Williams wonders at the fact that the "Sonnes of men" in *Europe, Asia,* and *Africa* . . . should have such plenteous clothing for Body, for Soule!" whereas those in America "neither have nor desire clothing for their naked Soules, or Bodies."[25] Immediately following, the poem reads:

> [1.] O what a Tyrant's custom long,
> How doe men make a tush,
> At what's in use, though ne're so fowle:
> Without once shame or blush?

> [2.] Many thousand proper Men and Women
> I have seen met in one place:
> Almost all naked, yet not one,
> Thought want of clothes disgrace.

24. Williams was not the only writer to take up the trope of nakedness and clothing in countering the traditional European view of the Indian. Much of Williams's challenging juxtaposition of native and European cultures echoes Montaigne's essay "Of the Caniballes," which Williams must have known. After a substantial representation of his subjects' good sense and proper expression, Montaigne concludes ironically: "All that is not verie ill; but what of that? They weare no kinde of breeches nor hosen" (*The Essayes of Montaigne* [1603], trans. John Florio [New York, 1933], p. 229). The strategies of the Montaigne essay are discussed at length in Cheyfitz, *Poetics of Imperialism,* chap. 5.

25. At a literal level the observation is somewhat perplexing; in this chapter Williams has established that the Narragansets *do* have different kinds of clothing, even if it is mostly "beasts skin" that they often choose not to wear. In *Christenings Make Not Christians,* Williams used clothing as a metaphor of merely external conversion: "It is not a suite of crimson Satten will make a dead man live, take off and change his crimson into white he is dead still, off with that, and shift him into cloth of gold, and from that to cloth of diamonds, he is but a dead man still" (7:37). Outward clothing was, in fact, a matter of considerable importance to Williams. As a trader, he expressed his view that letting the Narragansets wear the wrong kind of European clothes could have a negative influence on them: "I have long had Scruples of selling the Natives [aught] but what may bring or tend to Civilizing. I therefore neither brought nor shall sell them Loose Coats nor Breeches" (Williams to John Winthrop Jr., July 1654, in *Correspondence of Roger Williams,* ed. LaFantasie, 2:392–93). Williams's scruples suggest a connection in his mind between loose clothes and loose principles; writing in 1676, he noted that "it is commonly known that as [the Indians'] garments hang loose around their Bodyes, so hangs their Religion around their Souls" (in *Complete Writings,* ed. Miller, 5:258).

[3.] Israell was naked, wearing cloathes!
The best clad English-man,
Not cloth'd with Christ, more naked is:
Then naked Indian.   (Pp. 187–88)[26]

> Exod.
> 32.

Structurally similar to the majority of poems in *A Key*, this one reflects the text's characteristically complex movement between natural observation, cultural comparison, and spiritual allegory. Most immediately, the poem rebukes the skirt-tucking distaste with which Europeans tend to encounter the foreign spectacle of naked Indians: odd as it is to *us* that they do not have clothes, the poem points out humanistically, it is no [dis]grace in their eyes; all people see through the tyrannical blinders of their own customs. In the final stanza, the poem picks up on the "Observation"'s shift from literal to spiritual clothing to remind readers of what as Christians they should believe—that being "cloth'd with Christ" is the only kind of dress that really matters.

But, like many poems in *A Key*, this one is more complex than initially appears. The first stanza appears to mean that custom obscures from people something "in use" *among themselves* that is "fowle," about which they are insufficiently ashamed. What are those who "make a tush" failing to blush at? What form of custom tyrannizes them? The clue comes in the reference to Exodus 32, placed prominently next to the third stanza. This scripture bears no direct relationship to matters of nakedness or clothing; rather, it deals with Aaron's creation of the golden calf, the primordial instance of idolatry. The custom the poem is concerned with, that leaves people naked while wearing clothes, is the habit of idolatry. Europeans decry Indian customs without blushing at the much greater foulness of their own false worship.

Williams here cites custom as a "tyrant," a word that suggests problems of domination. The main form of tyranny for Williams was the persecuting theocracy of Massachusetts and the language through which it authorized itself, in which he saw the idolatrous remnants of Catholicism and the Roman Empire; this is the "custom" in which Englishmen are clothed and about which they "make a tush." By contrast, the "proper" physical nakedness of the Americans suggests that there is a concomitant natural propriety to their expression. They may worship idols, but they know no better; naked of pretense, they have, indeed, no cause to feel disgraced. Without putting it in so many words, Williams is announcing that, for all their aggressive cultural and rhetorical assertion, the translators of empire have no clothes.

Interestingly, the poem also alters one of the founding images in the

---

26. The poems in *A Key into the Language of America* are printed predominantly in italics in the original text, which I have removed for ease of reading.

tradition of imperial eloquence. Scholars have identified as a central locus of linguistic colonialism the "scene of primal colonization" in Cicero's *De Oratore*, in which an orator gathers an assemblage of "wild savages" in a field and civilizes them by instructing them "with reason and eloquence" in the meaning of social order.[27] The scene Williams portrays in the second stanza of the poem, a gathering of thousands of naked yet proper Indians, at once recalls and subverts this precedent. In *A Key*, we repeatedly encounter Williams's persona as a solitary, often needy wanderer, encountering a complex and well-established Narraganset world; here, we must presume that the Indians are "met in one place" to conduct in discourse the affairs of their own society. There is no sense that they are gathered to listen to Williams's persona orate; he casts himself syntactically in the passive position of the observer, who, "hav[ing] seen," directs his instruction and civilizing eloquence entirely toward his compatriots.

Another poem in *A Key*, however, offers an even more explicit and eloquent refutation of false figuration. It comes in the brief chapter 30, "Of their paintings." One of only three poems in the book written in a pentameter line, its fuller sound reflects the larger scope of its content. Williams explains in the immediately preceding observation: "It hath been the foolish Custome of all barbarous Nations to paint and figure their Faces and Bodies (as it hath been to our shame and griefe, wee may remember it of some of our Fore-Fathers in this Nation[).] How much then are we bound to our most holy Maker for so much civility and Piety? And how should we also long and endeavour that *America* may partake of our mercy[?]" (p. 241). This is a challenging passage, for here Williams sounds close to an orthodox position, juxtaposing civility and piety and using the word "barbarous" in a way that does not register his skeptical analysis elsewhere of such imperialist terminology. At the same time, he invokes the memory of a barbaric early England, emptying out pride in national origins in favor of gratitude to God. In the poem itself, the terms used to describe the dangers of "paint[ing] and figur[ing]" are mingled to the point where Indian and English practices can no longer be readily distinguished:

> [1.] Truth is a Native, naked Beauty; but
> Lying Inventions are but Indian Paints,
> Dissembling hearts their Beautie's but a Lye.
> Truth is the proper Beauty of God's Saints.

27. See Cheyfitz, *Poetics of Imperialism*, chap. 6, esp. pp. 113–17; Greenblatt, "Learning to Curse," p. 565.

2. Fowle are the Indians Haire and painted Faces,
   More foule such Haire, such Face in Israel.
   England so calls her selfe, yet there's
   Absoloms foule Haire and Face of Jesabell.

[3.] Paints will not bide Christs washing Flames of fire,
   Fained Inventions will not bide such stormes:
   O that we may prevent him, that betimes,
   Repentance Teares may wash of all such Formes.   (P. 241)

In contrast to the previous poem, what covers nakedness here is not clothing but paint. This change shifts the metaphorical valence and the initial appearance of Indian custom: nakedness no longer represents shameful bareness but rather beauty. Although it declares nothing unorthodox, the first line of the poem at least momentarily implies a stunning reversal of the imperial schema. Most directly, the truth of the gospel is "naked" in the sense of being simple and unadorned and "native" in the sense of being intrinsic and familiar to its possessors, and of course, to a believer it is beautiful. Christian truth is, the fourth line dually suggests, the basis of the saints' spiritual propriety, and it is a beauty that is their proper possession. But in the American context, it is impossible not to hear in the phrase "a Native, naked Beauty" an association between truth and the Natives themselves. I do not know whether it was Williams's intention, but the line also evokes the image of a beautiful Indian woman, standing as an emblem of the proper, chaste nakedness of Truth. Such an image would fit with Williams's choice to present the arguments of *The Bloudy Tenent* through the voice of the personified sisters Truth and Peace.[28]

Any Indian / Truth analogy, however, is immediately undercut beginning with the disjunctive "but" at the end of the first line, as the false beauty of "Lying Inventions" is immediately compared to "Indian Paints," a practice labeled outright as "foul." But once again, attentive readers are compelled to ask, exactly what "lying inventions" is Williams concerned with? The fact that this is a chapter on painting establishes a critical context. Following "Wussuckhòsu / *A painted Coat*," Williams comments, "Of this and *Wússuckwheke*, (the English Letters, which comes neerest to their

28. America was also frequently emblematized in the form of a naked Indian woman, a tradition of which Williams would surely have been aware. This further supports the idea that for Williams it is not just individuals but also the colonial enterprise itself that is being sullied with "paints." The best-known version of this visual motif, showing Vespucci awakening a sleeping America, comes from Johanes Stradanus, *Nova Repertus* (Antwerp, 1600). It appears, among other places, in Jack N. Greene, *The Intellectual Construction of America: Exceptionalism and Identity from 1492 to 1800* (Chapel Hill, 1993), p. 9.

painting) I spake before in the Chapter of their Clothing" (p. 240).[29] In context, then, this chapter on painting is also a chapter about the nearest thing to writing that can be expressed in the "language of America." Painting is also a traditional analogy for the "colors" of rhetoric, an analogy further elicited by the echo of the rhetorical term "invention"—the systematic finding of persuasive arguments, also known as "discovery." As "Indian paints," then, "lying inventions" are lying language, corrupt "figures" and falsely formed arguments. Hence, I would suggest, the poem is about the dangers of all forms of spiritual "dissembling" and especially the falsity within English verbal representation.[30]

This critique of English customs and English rhetoric becomes more pointed in the second stanza. Falsity and decadence are illustrated through biblical references to Absolom and Jezebel. As earlier scholars have noted, these references would suggest to a Puritan strong parallels with the son and wife of Charles I and the corrupt English court.[31] Yet the reference to Jezebel is also clearly linked to New England's suppression of dissent: a worshiper of the idol Baal and wife of the corrupted King Ahab, Jezebel "cut off the prophets of the Lord" and threatened Elijah—the prophetic figure with whom Williams repeatedly identifies in A Key—with a similar fate (1 Kings 18–19).[32] For Williams, these errors are tangled up with a more fundamental lie. England (by extension, New England) "calls herself" Israel. But Williams held rigorously to the belief that since the coming of Christ the only true Israel was the pure church, criticizing throughout his writing the pernicious effects of ever locating God's Israel in a nation. Thus the particular "invention" being attacked, I would argue, is the typological and imperialist discourse that permits such flattering conflations of the spiritual and secular. It is this that is a "paint" on the naked truth of the gospel. For Williams, this language is what always lies,

29. Williams is in error here; his previous reference comes in chap. 8, "Of *Discourse* and *New[e]s*": "Wussuckwhèke, Wussúckwhonck. / A *letter* which they so call from Wussuckwhómmin, *to paint*, for, having no letters, their painting comes the neerest" (*Key*, p. 138). The Bible, he notes elsewhere, is "Manittóo wússuckwheke / *Gods Booke* or *Writing*" (p. 198).

30. Wertheimer, " 'To Spell Out Each Other,' " also discusses this poem in the context of issues of linguistic representation, seeing it as exploring a conflict between "imaginative poetic language and the imaginative symbol-making of the Indian" in the generalized context of Puritan opposition to the language of the imagination (p. 10). Wertheimer rightly observes that allegiance to metaphor was an integral feature of Williams's dissent (p. 5). But throughout his writing Williams is always engaged in a highly particularized struggle against the figurative discourse of orthodox historical typology and never appears to be engaged in questions about metaphoric language in and of itself.

31. The specifics and overriding theme of moral decadence in these stories would, as Teunissen and Hinz point out, make the "parallels to the son and wife of Charles I . . . only too obvious to the good Puritan." See their introduction to *A Key into the Language of America*, p. 66.

32. All biblical quotations are from the King James Version.

in a practice of spiritual naming that reality cannot substantiate; moreover, it is a naming that—analogously, perhaps, to the Indian custom of painting "in Warre" (p. 240)—inevitably declares itself in blood.

In the third stanza of the poem, the ideas in motion are reprised and resolved in a cry of separatist piety. Neither native custom, national identity, nor typological discourse can stand before "Christ's washing Flames." Williams propounds his view that a saving grace can be found only in repentance, marked in its sincerity by tears. As accounts of his conflict with New England orthodoxy make clear, Williams understood repentance not just as sorrow for present sins but as active repudiation of the institutions of the past.[33]

But this is not quite all. The poem's most stinging attack on orthodox signification is veiled in its biblical reference to the "face of Jezebel." Jezebel's notoriously painted face and her final downfall are described in 2 Kings 9:30–37. In this passage, which Williams would certainly have expected his readers to know, the word of the Lord comes through Elijah that Jezebel will be eaten by dogs. Elijah prophesies that "the carcase of Jezebel shall be as dung upon the face of the field in the portion of Jesreel: so that they shall not say, This is Jezebel." Jezebel's terrible punishment for attempting to silence God's truth combines what we might call "effacement" and "erasure." Her painted face and her body are obliterated, and her name becomes impossible to speak; in multiple physical and linguistic senses, her figure becomes indistinguishable from the ground. This rhetoric of violence against figures, it has been argued, was systematically deployed by orthodoxy against the persons of both Indians and dissenters in New England.[34] Williams's poem shows that dissent enacts

33. This was one of the bases of Williams's earliest contention with New England. John Winthrop records Williams's refusal to join the congregation at Boston after his arrival in 1631, "because they would not make a public declaration of their repentance for having communion with the [nonseparated] churches of England, while they lived there" (Winthrop, *History of New England*, ed. James Kendall Hosmer, 2 vols. [New York, 1908], 1:62).

34. Appropriately, Eric Wertheimer, " 'To Spell Out Each Other,' " p. 11, points out that in the seventeenth century the word "foul" had the meaning of "ignominious" or "unnameable." This kind of figural iconoclasm is the subject of Ann Kibbey's *The Interpretation of Material Shapes in Puritanism* (New York, 1986). Drawing especially on the writings of John Cotton, Kibbey argues that the destruction of verbal figures is deeply implicated in Puritan violence against the "figurative" otherness of both Indians and women. Williams's practice seems to subvert this norm by altering the object of destruction. The figure of Jezebel is a key point of contact, for the most immediate association for a New Englander would be Anne Hutchinson, whom John Winthrop called an "American Jesabel" (Winthrop, "A Short Story of the Rise, reign, and ruine of the Antinomians, Familists, and Libertines," in *The Antinomian Controversy, 1636–38: A Documentary History*, ed. David D. Hall [Durham, 1990], p. 310). Kibbey focuses on Hutchinson, along with the Pequot Indians, as prime objects of Puritan rhetorical violence (on this association and the use of 2 Kings 9 authorization for the extermination of dissenters, see *Interpretation of Material Shapes*, pp. 107–8). Could Williams also be alluding to Hutchinson in his Jezebel reference? I see no basis for such a reading in either

its own rhetorical violence, yet the animus here is directed pointedly against an ideological system. In this poem and in the larger context of *A Key*, Jezebel's death stands as an allegory for God's destruction of the idolatrous symbolism that assigned spiritual meaning to nations and licensed them a priori to extend themselves over the non-Christian world.

III.

A Key into the Language of America is a complex text, working on many other levels than the comparatively subtle one I have been discussing here. Williams refuses to be pinned down to a single location among the multiple sites he can occupy as humanistic New World observer, sincere Protestant Englishman, disaffected cultural critic, and impassioned separatist Elijah. Likewise, it is difficult to reach a single, stable conclusion about what he achieved in this work. *A Key* had a significant impact on Williams's life and the history of New England, but its measurable effect was directly political rather than persuasive. When Williams returned to New England in 1644, he carried with him a letter from Parliament to the Government of Massachusetts, granting him "a free and absolute Charter of civil government" for Providence Plantations. One factor that Parliament cited in its decision to grant the charter was Williams's "great industry and travail in his printed Indian labours . . . the like whereof we have not seen extant from any part of America."[35] Whether intended or not, the comment was a slap in the face to the orthodox, who would not come through with any visible efforts in the direction of Indian missions for several more years. More important, the charter led the way for the rocky but ultimately successful establishment of principles of toleration and civil government on the resolutely desacralized ground of Rhode Island— a space where, in the words of one scholar, the inhabitants had a chance to design an alternative American reality, "experiment[ing] with new political and social forms that befitted the harsh realities of their lives on the frontier."[36]

We have no evidence whether *A Key* ever seriously convinced anyone to reconsider the relationship between nationality, Christianity, and European presence in the New World. If it failed to do so, perhaps this might

---

the poem or in Williams's writing generally; Hutchinson, like Williams, was a dissenting victim of the Puritan state and had little to do with what he saw as the real ills of society. One of the poem's tactics may well be a contentious redirection of the figure of Jezebel. On the Hutchinson-Jezebel connection, see also Amy Schrager Lang, *Prophetic Woman: Anne Hutchinson and the Problem of Dissent in the Literature of New England* (Berkeley, 1987).

35. Reproduced in Winthrop, *History of New England*, 2:198.

36. LaFantasie, "Introduction," in *Correspondence of Roger Williams*, ed. LaFantasie, 1:xxxix.

have dismayed Williams less than we would think. In *The Simple Cobler of Aggawam* (1647), the orthodox satirist Nathaniel Ward would complain that religious "opinionists" such as Williams "desire[d] not satisfaction, but satisdiction, whereof themselves must be judges."[37] Though his intent is scornful, Ward's neologism—"satisdiction," a sufficiency of *saying*—captures something of the verbal drive and grounding of dissent, its drive to construct a subjectively viable counterreality in words and texts. For himself and for careful readers of his text, Williams used all the linguistic resources at his disposal to formulate an alternative cultural poetics of colonial settlement and Christian eloquence.

Finally, it is significant that Williams engages with this task not only as a dissenter but also as an artist.[38] Whether or not he was conscious that he was exploring aesthetic questions, the first stanza of "Truth is a Native, naked Beauty" echoes the opening of one of the greatest poems about Protestant poetics "Jordan (I)" by Williams's contemporary and fellow Cambridge scholar George Herbert:

> Who says that fictions only and false hair
> Become a verse? Is there in truth no beauty?
> Is all good structure in a winding stair?
> May no lines pass, except they do their duty
> Not to a true but painted chair?[39]

Herbert's allusions to the false fronts of hair and painted inventions and the way he links truth and beauty suggest a Protestant sensibility remarkably close to Williams's own.[40] Yet throughout the poems of *A Key*, Williams does something that Herbert does not do by relocating this search for truly beautiful "forms" from the comparatively safe aesthetic realm to the conflicted and consequential site of colonial struggle. This is in its small way a significant act. If colonialism and the linguistic and physical violence that accompanies it perpetuate themselves through a cultural poetics of eloquence, then dissent cannot stop at demystifying a culture's ideological "inventions" but must further attempt an alternative *poesis*—an imaginative remaking, if you will—of rhetorical

---

37. Nathaniel Ward, *The Simple Cobler of Aggawam in America*, ed. P. M. Zall (Lincoln, 1969), p. 17.

38. For an extended discussion of Williams's attitude toward art, see Keith W. F. Stavely, "Roger Williams: Bible Politics and Bible Art," *Prose Studies* 14, no. 3 (1990): 76–91.

39. George Herbert, "Jordan (I)," in *The Works of George Herbert*, ed. F. E. Hutchinson (Oxford, 1967), p. 56.

40. On general issues in Protestant poetics, see Barbara K. Lewalski, *Protestant Poetics and the Seventeenth-Century Religious Lyric* (Princeton, 1979). On George Herbert as a poet of Puritan sensibility, see Richard Strier, *Love Known: Theology and Experience in George Herbert's Poetry* (Chicago, 1983).

authority. In *A Key into the Language of America*, Williams struggles to go beyond the disgust and outrage at English behavior that is a dominant note in his prose and to counter a nascent exceptionalism with the disarming representation of holy beauty as well as holy truth. He reminds his Protestant readers that their own professed allegiance is not to metaphors of imperialism but to God, whom he figures as the ultimate Poet, the one who "gives [the] Stars their Names" and who, finally, is himself inexpressible (p. 156). If anywhere, he here gives voice to the different register of eloquence that lies in what he describes elsewhere as "the Simplicitie, the plainnes[s], the Meekenes[s], and true Humilitie of the Learning of the Son of God."[41] Whether in prose or poetry, Williams called for a world in which readers would remember that *this* was the transformative learning that had to be translated both among themselves and to America.

41. *Correspondence of Roger Williams*, ed. LaFantasie, 1:375.

The Inca's Witches: Gender and the Cultural Work of Colonization in Seventeenth-Century Peru

IRENE SILVERBLATT

Coca k'intucha, hoja redonda, coca k'intucha, hoja
redonda, ¿por que delito padesco tanto?
(O my dear perfect *coca*, round leaf, perfect *coca*, round
leaf, for what sin am I suffering so?)

—*Peruvian folk song*

WRITING IN 1625 and 1626 to the Supreme Council in
Madrid, Juan de Mañozca, one of the priests in charge of the Spanish
Inquisition's Lima office, bemoaned the colony's abysmal lack of faith. He
blamed Peru's degradation on two things: witchcraft and the penchant of
criollos (men and women of Spanish descent, born in the colonies) to take
on the customs, even the dress, of the colony's uncivilized Natives.[1]

Three years later, Mañozca's concerns were reinforced by a novel edict
of faith. Following tradition, this edict, or statement of the heresies and
immoral habits that Catholics were obliged to report to the Holy Office of
the Inquisition, was read in Peru's churches and publicly displayed on

I thank the John Simon Guggenheim Foundation for support of the research and writing
of this essay, the McNeil Center for Early American Studies and the Omohundro Institute of
Early American History and Culture for their invitation to participate in the "Possible Pasts"
conference, and Robert Blair St. George for his work in organizing the conference and as an
editor. Unless otherwise noted, all translations in this essay are my own.

1. José Toribio Medina, *Historia del Tribunal de la Inquisición de Lima* (1877), 2 vols. (Santiago, 1956), 2:18.

church doors. Like others, it contained the standard warnings about hidden Jews, Muslims, Protestants, and followers of heretical sects as well as about bigamists, fornicators, priest solicitors, and practitioners of other sex-related transgressions. The Peruvian version, however, diverged from others read throughout the Spanish empire as it went on to list the particular problem of women

> given to superstitions . . . who with grave offence to God . . . [and] who do not doubt . . . their adoration of the devil, they invoke and adore him . . . and wait for images . . . of what they want [to know] for which the aforesaid women . . . go to the countryside and . . . drink certain potions of herbs and roots, called *achuma* and *chamiço*, and *coca* with which they deceive and stupefy the senses and the illusions and fantastic representations that they have, they judge and proclaim afterwards as revelations or as a certain sign of what will happen in the future.

The Peruvian case is striking because of the importance given to witchcraft at a time when the Spanish Inquisition, at least in peninsular judgments, tended to minimize its dangers. Equally remarkable is the attraction attributed to native customs and fashions, said to seduce Peru's non-Indian populations, and to native herbs and lore, claimed to be prized by non-Indian women for use in sorcery and witchcraft.[2]

In this essay I argue that one way to make sense of the bewitchment of Indian customs, along with the inquisitor's deep chagrin, requires placing both in the broader swirl of Spain's imperial project. The economic and political transformations that marked colonialism's legacy were inseparable from its profound cultural charge: the task of refashioning the humanity of women and men in consort with the processes of colonial state making. Philip Corrigan and Derek Sayer envisioned the making of

2. Ibid., 2:37; Gustav Henningsen, *The Witches' Advocate: Basque Witchcraft and the Spanish Inquisition, 1609–1614* (Reno, 1980); Brian Levack, *The Witch-Hunt in Early Modern Europe* (New York, 1987), pp. 201–6. Studies of colonial women accused of practicing witchcraft in the New World constitute a relatively small but growing field. For an important first examination of women tried for witchcraft in colonial Peru, see María Emma Mannarelli, "Inquisición y mujeres: Las hechiceras en el Perú durante el siglo XVII," *Revista Andina* 3, no. 1 (1985): 141–56. See also the pioneering analysis of the gendered aspects of New England witch-hunts of women of European descent in Carol F. Karlsen, *The Devil in the Shape of a Woman: Witchcraft in Colonial New England* (New York, 1987). For important feminist analyses of witchcraft practices among *españoles* and mestizos in eighteenth-century Mexico, see Ruth Bejar, "Sex and Sin, Witchcraft and the Devil in Late-Colonial Mexico," *American Ethnologist* 14, no. 1 (1987): 35–55, and Behar, "Sexual Witchcraft, Colonialism, and Women's Powers: Views from the Mexican Inquisition," in *Sexuality and Marriage in Colonial Latin America*, ed. Asunción Lavrín (Lincoln, Nebr., 1991), pp. 178–206. For an analysis of indigenous women accused of practicing witchcraft in colonial Peru, see Irene Silverblatt, *Moon, Sun, and Witches: Gender Ideologies and Class in Inca and Colonial Peru* (Princeton, 1987). The Inquisition's jurisdiction did not extend to the colony's native populations; see Medina, *Historia del Tribunal*, 2:27–28.

the nation-state as a kind of prolonged cultural revolution.[3] Following their lead, I conceptualize the emerging social selves, relations, and classes of humanness in seventeenth-century Peru as party to a colonial cultural revolution—a protracted process of building Spanish hegemony in which broad contests over cultural boundaries, social identities, and social relations bore the colors of political dominion and legitimacy (fig. 5.1).

Spanish policies supported a variety of political, economic, and religious institutions to facilitate the colonial enterprise. At their core lay the insinuation of new social relations and human categories (such as *español, indio,* and *negro*) essential to the forging of colonial beings. Outside the interactions required for the successful running of the colonial enterprise, Spanish policies envisioned the colonial order as a triad of racial cultures, separated by strong social boundaries.[4] The realities of colonialism's social and political dynamics, however, could not be thus contained; hybrid racial classes (such as *mestizo, mulato, sambo* [a person of a mixture of African and Indian ancestries]) entered the Spanish political ken. So did colonial subjects who did not fit the moral imperatives of their "race," such as (uncivilized) Spanish vagabonds, rebellious Indians, and non-Indian, coca-chewing, Inca-worshiping "witches." The protracted skirmishes between inquisitors and witches in seventeenth-century Peru were part of colonialism's enduring—and always incomplete—cultural mission.

The Peruvian Inquisition, perhaps the colony's premier institution of many involved in moral regulation, was responsible for the rawest displays of cultural force. In its great theater of power, the *auto-de-fé,* and in smaller, daily theaters of reputation and fear, the Inquisition clarified cultural blame, arguing who among the colony's human beings held beliefs or engaged in life practices that threatened the colony's moral and civic order. The testimonies of its accused witches, however, provide a window on the subtler domains of the colony's cultural arguments as well as on their unintended consequences. In other words, they reveal much about the vagaries, the seesawing, of hegemony building. For even as some witches exposed the limitations of imperial teachings, even as they suggested ways the cultural order of colonial hegemony could be turned against colonial rule, they laid bare the tenacious hold that colonial categories of humanness exerted on Spain's Peruvian subjects. Colonial

3. Philip Corrigan and Derek Sayer, *The Great Arch* (Oxford, 1985).

4. Building on the experiences of a developing absolutist state, Spanish colonial statecraft imposed broad, universal classifications on their subjects; all natives of the "New World" were Indian subjects of Spain, whereas descendants of Iberia, regardless of social distinctions, were privileged Spanish colonists. Economic pressures spurred the creation of a third cultural category of colonial order—that is, *negro*—which was applied to all Africans and their descendants brought to Peru as slaves. See Juan de Solórzano Pereira, *Política Indiana* (1647), Biblioteca de Autores Españoles, vols. 252–56 (Madrid, 1972).

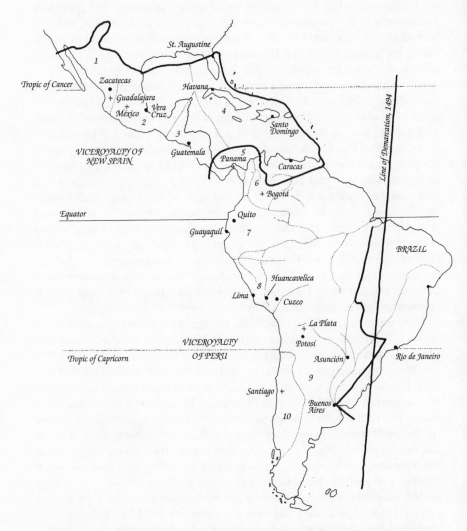

Fig. 5.1. Principal territorial divisions and towns, ca. 1650. Key to *audiencia* districts:
1. Guadalajara; 2. México; 3. Guatemala; 4. Santo Domingo; 5. Panama; 6. Bogotá; 7. Quito;
8. Lima; 9. Charcas; 10. Chile. After Mark A. Burkholder and Lyman L. Johnson, *Colonial Latin America* (New York, 1994), p. 73. (Map: Robert Blair St. George.)

witches who saw power in indio herbs, indio mountains, and even, as we shall see, the vanquished Inca were arguing about (among other things) the illegitimacy of Spanish rule, its limits, and its impossibilities. Nevertheless, they were using the categories of colonial rule to order their skirmishes; colonial ideology scaffolded political critique. Witches' illegal, if rich, montage of cultural productions were part of an appraisal that was forceful—and inspired fears—precisely because of the contradictions of colonialism as well as the pervasiveness of its cultural designs.[5]

I.

First, a brief chronology of Peruvian witchcraft is needed. When Spanish inquisitors came to Peru in the last twenty years of the sixteenth century, they brought a range of heresies punishable by their offices. These included activities associated with superstition, the "mixing" of sacred and profane activities, and implicit or explicit pacts with the devil known as witchcraft. Early cases of witchcraft prosecuted by Peru's inquisitors corroborate some of these patterns. Like their peninsular cohorts, witches chanted spells and prayers, threw beans and read their hidden meanings, and mixed potions of herbs and powders primarily for ends of love.

Many of the accused were of Spanish descent and born either on the peninsula or in the growing South American cities of Lima or Potosí; although some were mestizas with Indian mothers, as were Francisca Espinosa, Francisca Gómez, or Doña María de Aguilar, others, such as Ana Pérez, had mothers of African descent. A few were married, but most

5. This dynamic underpinned the building of a colonial hegemony. During the last twenty years students of the processes of nation-state building have been exploring the dynamics of class relations, state formation, and cultural practices. Although these students have explored, for the most part, the roads to nation-state building and capitalist development, I believe Gramscian insights are germane to the early colonial state. The literature on these processes has grown enormously, and I will cite here those works that most influenced my work. Along with Corrigan and Sayer, *The Great Arch*, see E. P. Thompson, "Eighteenth-Century English Society: Class Structure without Class?" *Social History* 3, no. 1 (1978): 133–65; Raymond Williams, *Marxism and Literature* (Oxford, 1978), pp. 75–144; Eugene D. Genovese, *Roll Jordan Roll: The World the Slaves Made* (New York, 1974); and T. J. Jackson Lears, "The Concept of Cultural Hegemony: Problems and Possibilities," *American Historical Review* 90, no. 3 (1985): 567–93. Jean and John Comaroff have used Gramsci's insights in their discussions of the English colonial state in South Africa; see their *Ethnography and the Historical Imagination* (Boulder, 1992) and *Of Revelation and Revolution*, 2 vols. (Chicago, 1991 and 1997). Gramsci inspired my exploration of the crises of social classifications in colonial Peru; see Silverblatt, "Becoming Indian in the Central Andes of Seventeenth-Century Peru," in *After Colonialism: Imperial Histories and Postcolonial Displacements*, ed. Gyan Prakesh (Princeton, 1995), pp. 279–98. Michael T. Taussig's astute *Shamanism, Colonialism, and the Wild Man: A Study in Terror and Healing* (Chicago, 1987) stimulated the analysis of colonial *indio* witchcraft and the genesis of its power.

were single, widowed, or had husbands only on paper and were involved in unconventional (but not uncommon) arrangements with lovers, or *galanes*. While early records may indicate "race," ancestry, and marital standing, they do not always show whether or how women supported themselves; later cases, however, suggest that many worked as seamstresses, laundresses, or street vendors. And, in accord with church expectations, they all worked witchcraft in covens.

Like their peninsular contemporaries, a principle source of transgression lay in mixing the sacred with the profane by conjuring with the Lord's Prayer, the Ave Maria, or the Credo or by making special appeals to Saint Martha, the Holy Trinity, or "Saint Erasmus."[6] Like others accused of witchcraft in the century to follow, these women set special store in items from the repertoire of Catholic ritual, such as *ara*, or scrapings of a church altar made into powders, mixed with beverages, and given to fickle men to make their hearts true. Similarly, women bribed *chrism* from clerics, using it to seek similar ends.

Some of the accused flirted with more dangerous sources of power, the knowledges and icons of Iberia's enemies within. Isabél de Espinosa, who left Seville to escape her husband, learned how to tell the future from *moriscas*, or women of Moorish descent. Another Sevillana transplanted to Potosí, the widow Doña Francisca Maldonado, admitted to knowing Spanish conjures that called up the priesthood as well as the Tablets of Moses. One of her coconspirators, the mestiza Francisca Despinosa, also admitted to calling up the Tablets of Moses and Israel. An accomplice had warned her, however, about the added dangers of Judaizing heresies: "calling on items associated with Jews," she cautioned, "might not be a very good thing."[7]

Living in the colonies opened up a Pandora's box of knowledge—herbal cures, divining tricks, and potions for love and power—that began to complement European wisdom. The same women who were accused of conjuring the Laws of Moses and the Tribes of Israel were also experimenting with indigenous lore. Whether migrants from Spain or born in the colony, they actively sought out the knowledge of Indian women, especially regarding questions of herbal healing and *hechizos*, or bewitchments. Francisca Gómez, married to an español and the daughter of an immigrant man and an india, turned herself in after two Cusqueñans strenuously denounced her for running off to join native pilgrimages in order to learn "Indian witchcraft." Doña María de Aguilar, a mestiza from Cochabamba, married to a solicitor and accused of participating in the so-

6. For the period 1592–98, see "Inquisición," lib. 1028, ff. 233v–34, 234v–35, 262–64v, 282v, 319v–21, 330v–31, 515–16, 517–19, 522–23v, Archivo Histórico de la Nación (hereafter AHN), Madrid, Spain.

7. Lib. 1028, ff. 233–34, 502–6v, 521v, AHN.

called conspiracy of *hechizeras*, or "sorceresses," from Potosí, was condemned for speaking "Indian" with her cohorts and for trying to find
Indian hechizeras to assist in their "sorcery" sessions.[8] Again, testimony
against Doña María stressed the "Indianness" of her lore. Inquisitors and
their objects were increasingly drawn to Indian magic's apparent allures
and dangers. The years before 1600 would find this magic playing a growing but not yet ubiquitous role.

Although men were infrequently charged with witchcraft (they tended
to be accused of blasphemy or of speaking heretical propositions), by 1622
two had been condemned for using sorcery to uncover another magical
attraction of Indian life: *guacas*, the native burials rumored to conceal vast
quantities of treasure. Both men enjoyed substantial reputations as clair-
voyants who could find lost property—from pilfered silver trays and
stolen merchandise to escaped slaves and the colony's "lost" property of
underground Indian riches.[9]

Ana de Castañeda, one of the more notorious Lima witches of the second decade of the seventeenth century, wore her religious commitments
in the form of a San Franciscan habit and lived them through marriage to
a Dominican friar. With a long history of dealings with the Inquisition—
she had been tried and punished twenty years before in Cartagena—Castañeda had moved to Lima where again she ran afoul of inquisitional
authorities. She was brought before the court for casting spells—invoking
demonios, saints, and God and using powders of consecrated altars to see
into the future. But her special skills were in the arena of love, and in her
love cures she made use of an indigenous seed called *palla palla*. *Palla*, also
the Quechua term for "noblewoman," had singular abilities to calm angry
husbands and stop them from fighting with their wives. Inquisitors also
noted that Ana de Castañeda claimed a following from among women "of
all social conditions and ranks."[10]

Who were these women, seeking out Ana de Castañeda, from backgrounds that cut across colonial Peru's social and cultural hierarchies? And
how could they have so freely consulted someone under suspicion? Testimony identified them as *atapadas* or *tapadas*, "the covered ones," these
women who would shamelessly walk the streets of Lima, go to its public

8. Ibid., ff. 505v, 326, 512, 514; see also ff. 507–11.

9. Ibid., lib. 1030, ff. 225–25v. *Guaca* means "shrine," "place of worship," or "adored deity"
in Quechua. Colonials, more concerned with the metal adornments than with their holiness,
equated guacas with burials. In today's Peru a *guaquero* is someone who illegally hunts for
pre-Columbian burial sites in search of treasure. The fame of Señor Navarrete, one of Peru's
male witches, extended to Lima's indio artisans. Navarrete was actually brought in front of
the Inquisition because a native tailor charged him with taking a silver picture frame in payment for services (to find who had stolen bolts of cloth from his shop) that were never
rendered.

10. Lib. 1029, ff. 500v, 501, 504, 504v, 502v, AHN.

Fig. 5.2. Figure of tapada, Trujillo, Peru, eighteenth century. From Baltasar Jaime
Martínez de Compañon, *Trujillo del Perú a fines del siglo XVIII: Dibujos y acuarelas que mandó
hacer el Obisbo D. Baltasar Jaime Martínez de Compañon*, ed. Jesús Dominguez Bordona, 5
vols. (Madrid, 1936), vol. 2, plate E5.

plazas, or flirt from balconies masked by very carefully and seductively draped veils (fig. 5.2). Lima's tapadas were notorious, serenaded in poetry and censured by the Third Lima Council. The council was concerned that tapadas, able to traverse the city incognito, were enjoying improper liberty and promoting public scandal and disgrace.[11] Issued at the end of the sixteenth century, council decrees prohibiting women from wearing veils during public festivals seemed to have had little impact on colonial fashion. Peru's viceroys entered the moral fray. In 1624 the Marquez Guadalcázar published an edict, "the Decree of the Tapadas," in an attempt to bring some propriety to Limeñan customs. The decree "prohibited women regardless of status, quality, or rank from wearing veils in the streets, or Lima's public promenades . . . either when on foot or in carriages." And "they should all reveal their faces so that they can be seen and recognized and esteemed and held for who they are." Punishments, which varied according to the standing of the offender, were steep but impossible to enforce. Viceroys continued their charge against the immorality—the potential for social disorder—that tapadas seemed to encourage, and in 1634 they even had civic authorities place some women under arrest. Three years later another ban on veils was proclaimed, suggesting, once more, the hollowness of royal edicts.[12]

Ana de Castañeda's accomplices appear repeatedly in colonial witchcraft trials throughout the century. Although tapadas found themselves the object of decrees in Madrid as well as in Lima, they were perceived to be most dangerous in the colonial capital. As scramblers of social hierarchy, tapadas were everywhere a potential threat to public order; however, colonial soil magnified the dangers they posed. Built on gendered and increasingly racialized economic and political hierarchies, the colonial enterprise was particularly vulnerable to the mockery of women who would not recognize their place. It should not be surprising, then, that hechizos involving tapadas and love magic could be blamed for inciting political havoc. At the time when the mining center of Potosí was jolted by riots between Spanish nationals, it was said that Ana de Castañeda had turned "the whole city upside down . . . with her sorcery, tricks, and lies, and that even the convents of friars and nuns were not safe."[13]

11. In his 1602 epic poem La Argentina (Buenos Aires, 1912), Martín del Barco Centenera wrote of the untoward accessibility of the tapadas and of the attempts of the Third Lima Council to censure them (pp. 192–92v); see Concilios Limenses, ed. Rubén Vargas Ugarte, 3 vols. (Lima, 1952), 1:273–74.

12. Juan Antonio Suardo, Diario de Lima de Juan Antonio Suardo (1629–1639) (Lima, 1936), pp. 10, 46, 158. Sermons preached by Joseph Aguilar at the turn of the century again singled out tapadas for their veiled threat to moral and civic order in Lima; for the sermons, see Rubén Vargas Ugarte, La eloquencia sagrada en el Perú en los siglos XVII y XVIII (Lima, 1942), p. 48.

13. Lib. 102, f. 503v, AHN; see Antonio León Pinelo, Velos antiguos i modernos en los rostros de las mugeres sus con veniencias, i daños (Madrid, 1641).

At the end of the decade, after edicts were posted on church doors warning all Peru of the danger of witchcraft, the number of "witches" who either turned themselves in to the Inquisition or were denounced by others (often clients) grew. Most of those tried for witchcraft were either Spanish or mulatas, and their concerns, abilities, and clientele mirrored those of the mid-1620s. Witches' special skills addressed the daily stuff of life, love and justice. They could foretell if much-missed husbands would arrive with the next fleet and if they would have married another. They claimed to be able to ensure that lovers would remain passionate, that men would treat their kinswomen well, that royal officers would be impeded from carrying out a sentence, or even that the Inquisition's proceedings would stop.[14]

Catalina de Baena was one of eleven women chastised during the period from 1627 to 1631 for a variety of witchcraft offenses. Born in Jérez de la Frontera, Spain, and living in Potosí, hers was a hybrid lore, drawing on Christian prayers, special masses, native herbs, and indigenous frotations. In addition, Catalina searched in Indian burial sites for a most powerful conjuring ingredient—the bones of *gentiles*, or native peoples who had never been baptized or touched by the Christian world in any way.[15]

It was a mulata, known only by the name Francisca, who taught Catalina de Baena lessons in the powers of bones from such ancient Indian sites. Catalina admitted that "in the company of an Indian man and woman [she] had gone to some guacas . . . and brought back a sack full . . . and left them in the home of a negra, Isabel . . . who then told the mulata Francisca, who was supposed to prepare them, as she had promised." Like all others accused of witchcraft, de Baena denied ever having made a pact with the devil; indeed, "this thing about pacts seemed like latin to her." She would never, she insisted, use Indian bones for malefic ends; they were for good fortune. And de Baena, who believed in both the magic of Indian bones and the knowledge of a mulata hechicera, appealed to the court for leniency, on traditional racial and gender grounds. She, after all, "was well born of honorable (Spanish and old Christian) parents, who had done this out of necessity and simpleness."[16] Catalina de Baena ran foul of inquisitional authorities once more: while imprisoned, she was accused of allowing one of her slaves to give some writing material to another inmate. De Baena argued that she did this under duress, cowed by María Martínez, a renowned witch with whom de Baena had a history of conjuring.

María Martínez, born in Portugal and daughter of the priest of her vil-

---

14. See, for example, lib. 1029, ff. 500v, 501, and lib. 1030, ff. 194v, 201v, AHN.
15. Ibid., lib. 1030, f. 360.
16. Ibid., ff. 360v, 361, 361v.

lage and Andresa Martínez from Guinea, had a fierce reputation for straightening out questions of love and justice. She was *zahori*, "could see right into peoples' insides," and because of her gifts she was sought after by españoles, *doñas*, free blacks, and slaves alike. One witness saw many women "with cloaked faces" visiting her at night "to do witchcraft business." Even under guard in the Inquisition's secret cells, Martínez caused a great stir. According to Pedro Bermúdez, on one night over fourteen women tried to seek her out, causing such an outcry that even the prisoners began to shout in protest.[17]

Speaking in her own defense, María Martínez claimed to be a baptized Christian. Like all the women interrogated by inquisitional courts, she was very much a participant in orthodox Catholicism. She went to confession, regularly took communion, and, having been confirmed, was conversant in the basics of the Catholic faith. Perhaps she was too well versed; she would speak the words of Holy Communion, *corpus meum*, in conjures of love. Martínez worked with españoles and with indios. In fact, her zahori skills were not sufficient (either in her view or by the reigning discourse pairing witchcraft abilities and "race") to effect the darkest of hechizos. Indian lore was dangerous, and she admitted to having tried, through a native intermediary, to track down an indio *hechicero* who she believed would be able to kill a man who had raised terrible testimony against her.[18] In the end, Martínez decided not to pursue the vendetta. But the courts dealt with her harshly, having her paraded through the streets, whipped two hundred times, and then exiled from Peru for ten years. In contrast, the court treated Catalina de Baena with greater leniency. Attentive to de Baena's racial arguments (she was, after all, a "Spanish" woman) and receptive to her claims that Martínez exercised power over her, Inquisition judges did not make her suffer corporal punishment or the humiliation of public penance. Catalina de Baena was, however, exiled for four years.

The arrest and punishment of these colonials—after witchcraft edicts directing attention to women and their use of Indian hechizos were first posted on Peru's church doors—was an attempt to stop the "plague of women" that seemed so threatening to colonial order. Such indio herbs as coca and palla, Indian "bones" and "gentile" burials, even Indian "witches" (and some zahori) continued to mark colonial witchcraft in the years to follow.[19] So too did the contradictory tangle of colonial relation-

17. Ibid., ff. 380v–82. At this period, as slave labor was becoming increasingly important to the Peruvian workforce, so were the divining gifts of women and those of some men, forcibly taken to Peru from Africa.

18. Lib. 1031, ff. 381, 380v, 382v, AHN.

19. Medina, *Historia del Tribunal*, 2:35. These records have given us few examples of men accused of witchcraft, but many examples exist of men who availed themselves of witchcraft magic. These cases also show the gendered basis for making charges. Women who consulted

ships which, on the one hand, brought together women from a variety of ranks and ethnic groups for collective healing / divining and which, on the other, marked breaches between them grounded in the official and magical practices of "race."

By 1645 and through the century's close, trials against non-Indians accused of witchcraft—whether Spanish, mulata, or mestiza, free or slave—show a remarkable turn in "Indianness." Coca was becoming the centerpiece of collective conjuring rites, paired with a new group of personages in the colonial hechizo repertoire. Now, joining saints and credos, we find the Inca and sometimes the coya, or Inca queen. Often, they appear in tandem with a set of special *diablos*, "devils" representing colonial "offices" or "professions." Cuzco royalty first appeared in the trial of Ana María de Contreras, penanced by the Inquisition in the *Gran Auto* of 1639 and charged again, seven years later, with diabolic conjuring. This mulata slave explained that the many women who sought her out, lavishing money and food, pushed her return to old "deceits and tricks." Contreras's trickery included "having worshiped the mountain peaks and rocks in memory and signification of the Inca and his wife."[20] Mountain peaks and rocks were the soul of the native sacred landscape and the scourge of priests sent to extirpate Indian idolatries. They rarely, however, embodied the Inca or his wife; Contreras was voicing an emerging colonial contribution to the meaning of mountains.

Doña María de Córdoba's coca readings—always conducted with several friends, *maestras* (teacher / mentors), and relatives of the person to be healed—were built around deciphering images made from wads of coca leaf. Although she denied ever praying to the devil or even seeing his figure in her porcelain bowl, de Córdoba did sing to the colonial diablos. Like the Inca she conjured with them, this cohort of devils cut rather "stately" figures. The devils, however, were tied to colonial trade, colonial markets, and to colonial bureaucracies: "the devil of the fish market, the devil of shopkeepers, the devil of the notary publics, and with those who trick the lawyers." While the devils were tied to colonial institutions, the Inca was king of the indios, wearing "an Indian costume, with a star in his forehead." To conjure these figures with coca leaf, songs were chanted: "Coca, my mother, please do this, what I ask you to do, for the faith I have in you, for the one who sows your seed, for the one who cultivates you, for all who worship you, for the Inca, for the Colla [queen], for the sun and the moon that illuminated you in the earth where you were sown."[21]

---

witches were often accused as coconspirators or accomplices, whereas men were not (see, for example, lib. 1030, ff. 354–59, and lib. 1031, ff. 1–147v, AHN).

20. Lib. 1031, f. 332v, AHN. No trial records for accused witches during this time period exist in the record group I worked with. Although witches were penanced, their beliefs cannot be determined until trial records appear again in 1646.

21. Ibid., ff. 374–75v, 376, 446v; see also lib. 1032, ff. 417–18, 458–64.

Like Doña María de Córdoba, her occasional accomplice, Doña Luísa de Vargas—alias Doña Luísa *Quarterona* (the quarteroon, in 1648), alias Luísa Blanca (Luísa White, in 1656)—had an extensive history in front of the Inquisition's tribunal. In early testimony she revealed how she first learned about certain herbs and ointments for love magic from a negra, about other plants from indios, and about "coca and the drink Indians call *chicha*" from a negra. Doña Luísa, who boasted a clientele as diverse as her teachers, was a specialist in "domesticating" (*amansar*) men (and occasionally women, as in hechizos performed for a colonial magistrate). Chants joining coca and the Inca stressed his royalty and sovereignty: "O my coca, I conjure you with the Inca, with all his vassals and court."[22]

The Inca, as king of the "Indian gentiles," had never been baptized. And clerics, writing at the time when the Incas were being condemned by royal authorities for their tyrannical practices, had them fated for an eternity in hell. Doña Luísa's prayers, however, invoked these "gentile," pre-Christian, kingly powers even as she brought the Inca into her known, civilized world through baptism: "O my Inca, o my father, I baptize you with this wine, in exchange for the chrism and the water that you never had . . . I drink to you and I call for your help and I call for your vassals help . . . and I ask for you, don Mélchor." *Coca* took on powers in these women's hands that it did not have in indigenous ones. One incantation to the Inca adored him along with a powerful, bewitching coca: "I conjure you with the *palla* [noblewoman] and with your ancestors, with the idols whom you believed in, my father, I drink to you with this wine, [and] with this coca that you used in your sorcery."[23] As king of Indians—"gen-

22. Ibid., lib. 1031, ff. 349v–50, 383. Other accused witches with similar stories of meeting in groups, praying to the Inca, and using coca, included Antonia Abraca (a free mulata), ibid., ff. 378–91; Doña Anna Balleja, ibid., ff. 388v–91; and Antonia de Urbina, ibid., f. 392. Another set of witches processed by the Inquisition between 1660 and 1667 included Doña Petronilla de Guebara, ibid., f. 498; Doña Ana de Sarate, ibid., ff. 497–97v; Doña Josepha de Lievana, ibid., f. 498v; Doña Magdalena Camacha, ibid., ff. 499v–501; and Doña Cataline Pizarro, ibid., f. 501.

23. Ibid., ff. 383, 399v. Don Mélchor Carlos Inca, the last direct descendant in the male line from the Inca kings, was the grandson of Paullu Thupa Inca, who was son of Huayna Capac. Paullu allied with the Spanish, and Don Mélchor spent part of his life at the Spanish court trying to claim what he considered to be due recompense from the Crown for his royal blood and for his ancestor's assistance in "pacifying" the Andes. See El Inca Garcilaso de la Vega, *Royal Commentaries of the Incas and General History of Peru* (1609, 1616–17), trans. Harold V. Livermore (Austin, 1987), pp. 620, 625, and José Antonio Mazzotti's essay in this volume. Don Mélchor traveled to the Spanish court in 1602 to start the claims proceedings. The incantations of some non-Indian "witches," along with those of native Calchaquis, make clear the potency of his memory. Doña Luísa was a woman of great strength. One witness overheard her telling a *comadre* that the Inquisitors were going to have her tortured, and Doña Luísa counseled that "she should have womanly valor" (*valor de muger*). "Trying to hearten her comadre, she taught her a special charm against Inquisitors to give her strength to face the judges when called in front of the tribunal." See lib. 1031, ff. 385v–86, AHN.

tiles" and idol worshipers—the Inca had accrued powers of witchcraft, effected through the most "Indian" of plants, coca.

Coca was (and is) used for divining and curing in the indigenous Andes, but not in ways described here. Drawing on European witchcraft beliefs, these women with Inca guidance had transformed coca into an instrument of sorcery; drawing on European auguring beliefs, they also transformed coca into an image capable of revelation. Inquisitional authorities, however, converted coca chewing (with no known addictive properties) into a "vice" or kind of depravity: "Women who chew coca, do not pray, do not commend themselves to god, do not say 'good day' to one another . . . they do not cook, or clean , and sell everything they have in order to buy coca."[24] For non-Indian colonials, coca was the key to a merging Indian / Inca domain, and they infused it with powers grounded in the "magic" their colonizing world had foisted on native experience. And as an instrument of sorcery, prophecy, and vice, coca chewing—thus bathed in an Indian aura—fanned women's perceived abilities to threaten and disrupt public order.

II.

Coca conjuring increasingly tied "Indianness" to the figure of the Inca monarch. This ideological union echoed broader strains shaping the Andean cultural milieu, in which the Inca, acquiring an "absolutist" taint, began to typify the keystone of colonial cultural fiction: the Peruvian "Indian." The Inca inspired ambivalent and contradictory feelings among Peru's non-indio populations, and debates raged throughout the colonial period about the nature of the empire and its political legitimacy. These debates tended to cast the Incas as either utopian exemplars or tyrannical despots, yet both postures shrouded the monarch in a mystique of unlimited authority. Contemporary analysis, critical of "big men" theories and sensitive to the social matrix of Inca government, has suggested that much of the Incas' reported absolute power actually rested in the local Andean "ethnic" polity, or *ayllu*.[25]

24. Lib. lo32, f. 534, AHN. Common medicinal claims for coca were that it was a good dentifrice and helped stomach disorders (see ibid., lib. 1031, f. 460). Some women who claimed to have developed an addiction, such as Doña María de Córdoba, said they began chewing for health reasons. Francisca de Bustos, tried in 1669, claimed that when she was very ill some Indian women, *curanderas*, helped her by having her chew coca. Once she saw how much it did help her, she continued, until she chewed it *"por vicio"* (because it was a terrible habit) (ibid., lib. 1032, f. 114–14v). Coca (as opposed to cocaine) is not considered to be physiologically addictive; see Catherine J. Allen, *The Hold Life Has: Coca and Cultural Identity in an Andean Community* (Washington, D.C., 1988), pp. 221–23.

25. See Pedro Sarmiento de Gamboa, *Historia general llamadaíndica* (1572), Biblioteca de Autores Españoles, vol. 135 (Madrid, 1960), pp. 189–279, and Diego de Córdoba y Salinas,

In the colonial world, Inca charisma also drew on the mystery of the unbaptized and perhaps the powers of hellishness. By reigning church calculations of the seventeenth century, all unbaptized Andeans were destined for hell. Religious authorities, echoing secular findings, declared the Inca, his family, and ancestry to be partners in the devil's kingdom. One of the century's renowned missionaries and "extirpators of idolatry," Hernando de Avendaño, made clear in his sermons that devilry and Inca political spuriousness were closely entwined. "Tell me children [*hijos*]," he asked, "how many Inca kings have gone to hell?—Everyone[.] How many ccoyas?—All of them. Why? . . . [B]ecause they worshiped the devil in guacas."[26]

But if seventeenth-century colonial authorities believed Inca rule opened doors for the devil, they also were increasingly understanding this rule as a wonder of absolute authority. "Indians worked harder under the Incas than they do now under the Spanish," preached Avendaño, providing a lesson in supposed European benevolence touched with a hint of wishful thinking. Avendaño, who used the Incas as hell-bent examples of idolatry's errors, also presented them as powerful rulers capable of inspiring the love, fear, and respect that were supposed to model sentiments toward the spiritual realm. Similarly, the homilies of Francisco de Ávila, whose evangelizing activities in Huarochirí spurred further missionary campaigns, suggest that Inca activities on earth would inspire deference in Indian subordinates to contemporary Spanish kings and to the universal Christian God. Colonials marveled at Inca dominion and at their creations; an account written by a Portuguese crypto-Jew states that the Incas "were the most feared and respected and well served by their vassals of any we know about in the world. . . . That's why they constructed works that seem *impossible* to mankind."[27] Looking with amazement on Inca ruins, they imagined the kind of unconditional control over human beings that could have produced wonders beyond human (that is, Spanish) prospects.

Inca mystique prompted some colonials—with rights over Indian labor or holding administrative positions that touched on Indian life—to fashion themselves Inca rulers. Felipe Guaman Poma de Ayala, the native

---

Crónica franciscana de las provincias del perú (1651; Washington, D.C., 1957). See John V. Murra, *La organización económica del estado Inca* (Mexico City, 1978).

26. Hernando de Avendaño, *Sermones de los misterios de nuestra santa fé católica, en lengua castellana y la general del inca* (Lima, 1648), pp. 114–15. Note that the double *cc* here represents the aspirated *c* in native pronunciation.

27. *Ibid.*, pp. 24v, 33v–34; Francisco de Ávila, *Tratado de los evangelios, que nuestra madre la iglesia* (Lima, 1648), pp. 43, 63, 126; Anónimo, *Descripción del virreinato del Perú* (1610), ed. Boleslao Lewin (Rosario, Argentina, 1958), p. 91 (emphasis added). See also Bernabé Cobo, *History of the Inca Empire* (Austin, 1983), p. 239.

chronicler and critic of the colonial regime, tells of *encomenderos* (holders of labor grants) who made themselves into Incas, insisting even on being carried around in Inca-style litters: "The aforesaid encomenderos and their wives have themselves transported in litters, as if they were saints in procession. They are received [and feted] with dances . . . and songs. Better said, they order themselves carried about like the Inca." Guaman Poma continued his critique of the seemingly limitless abilities of such other colonial officials as priests, *corregidores* (magistrates), and lawyers to impose their will on Indian populations without check or constraint. "They have all become 'Incas,' " he decried in irony.[28]

The colonial allure of Inca authority, with its promises of power over "Indians," prompted one Andalusian gentleman to become an Inca, of sorts. Don Pedro Bohorquez claimed that the Calchaquí, thorns in the side of the colonial frontier, believed him to be the last Inca king, Don Mélchor Inca, and, as a result, their sovereign. Under his jurisdiction, they were now willing to abandon their rebelliousness, join the Catholic fold, and embrace the authority of the Spanish Crown. The Crown was willing to accept this unusual turn of events as a short-term modus vivendi. But the entente collapsed when Bohorquez, taking on the accoutrements of an Inca king and in the name of his Indian kingdom, began to challenge Spanish sovereignty.[29] The Calchaquí were sometime allies of the Inca but never completely colonized by them; Bohorquez was immersed in the colonial Inca's ideological force, as well as in the universalist concept of Indian, to which it was bound.

The ideological union of "Indianness" and Incas, of native powers and an Indian king, had a growing appeal to non-Indians living in Spain's Inca colony. The fantastic power over human beings and fortune that a colonial Inca seemed to promise sparked colonial imaginations. While encomenderos carried on Inca-style litters were legitimate bearers of a colonial Inca custom and the "Inca andaluz" was accepted by colonial officials until he promoted sedition, colonial women, who sang to the Inca and sought out Indian herbs, were branded as witches and decried as public menaces. They all, nevertheless, drew on a shared source of Inca allure and the mystique of Inca power. During the middle decades of the seventeenth century and the years to follow—when the strength of Span-

28. Felipe Guaman Poma de Ayala, *El primer nueva corónica y buen gobierno* (1615), critical ed., ed. John V. Murra and Rolena Adorno, trans. Jorge L. Urioste, 3 vols. (Mexico City, 1980), 2:524, 525, 558, 857 (the quotations are on pp. 524 and 525).

29. "Historia peregrina de un inga andaluz" (1658), ed. Constantino Bayle, in *Razón y Fé*, ed. Bayle (Madrid, 1927). For Calchaquí-Spanish conflict, see *Colección de las memorias*, ed. Altolaguirre, p. 111, and Suardo, *Diario de Lima*, pp. 231, 289. The Andalusian Inca was captured and executed by royal authority in 1667. Bohorquez's treason must have added fuel to colonial fears, coming as it did on the heels of an aborted uprising by Indians from the empire's civilized center.

ish imperial dominion was battered by internal dissension, economic downturns, and foreign challenges—the Inca's powers in love, luck, and even government began to grow. Ana María de Ulloa prayed to fix the outcome of a civic trial, "O my coca, o my princess, o my Inca, since for you nothing was impossible."[30]

III.

For the non-indio world, the Inca's (and Indianness's) seeming omnipotence was a seesaw jockeying with the Crown's and the church's (perceived) weaknesses. The vaunted political "stability" of the seventeenth century (the mature colonial state) stretched over gnawing contradictions. Bankruptcies and fiscal crises periodically shook seventeenth-century economies, particularly at midcentury. The precipitous and continued decline in Peru's native population, whose labor in mines was crucial for state revenue, posed additional threats. And while colonial churchmen and authorities railed against the abuses suffered by Natives or the blatant inequities and skewed morality of fellow clergy, local officials, and colonial entrepreneurs, they seemed incapable of implementing meaningful reforms.[31]

The Spanish enterprise had its enemies, threatening to sabotage the endeavor from without and within. Foreign policies and wars had colonial consequences; royal officials were confronted with the impossible task of policing the South American coastline, ever subject to British and Dutch raids. Moreover, they viewed with great apprehension one clear advantage that colonial conditions put in the lap of foreign rivals: the ability to form allegiances with either native peoples still to be "pacified" (to use the Spanish term) or with "Indian" subjects, disgruntled with colonial rule. Royal energy was spent fighting constant frontier wars as well as curtailing the occasional seditious activities of Indians, who, by seventeenth-century Spanish estimates, should have been loyal subjects. Foreign policies enhanced the cachet of the native "enemies within." And it

30. Lib. 1031, f. 529v, AHN.
31. Peru's seventeenth century has often been called a century of political stability. But it took decades for the Crown to assert its dominion, challenged as much by an Inca resistance as by colonists who refused to submit to royal sovereignty. Colonial efforts to consolidate Spain's institutional presence, inspired by the successes and failures of Spanish state making in the Iberian peninsula, ushered in what many historians have called the "mature" colonial state. The measure of "maturity" of the Peruvian colony lay in the relative political calm marking the following century and a half of Spanish hegemony (Karen Spalding, *Huarochirí: An Andean Society under Inca and Spanish Rule* [Stanford, 1984], pp. 168–238). See Kenneth J. Andrien, *Crisis and Decline: The Viceroyalty of Peru in the Seventeenth Century* (Albuquerque, 1985). See also Diego de León Pinelo, *Mando que se imprimiesse . . . cerca de la enseñanza y buen tratamiento de los indios* (Lima, 1661).

is in this regard that public debates over the existence of idolatries and the subversive qualities attached to native religion take on relevance, including for colonial witches who had turned to Indian heresies.

Native practices were not subject to the Inquisition's scrutiny, although many Natives were well aware of its presence and some awed by its reputed powers. Indigenous peoples found their ethics and beliefs subject to probing by *doctrineros* (clergy sent to proselytize in native settlements) and "idolatry" inspectors, who, under diocesan jurisdiction, were sent out to "visit" Indian communities. The most famous (or infamous) attempts to root out native idolatries and heretical customs were sponsored by the Lima archdiocese. Coming in waves throughout the seventeenth century, these campaigns, whose procedure and practices took the Inquisition as a model, were marked by an intent and fervor that would have matched any inquisitorial efforts.[32]

To get the ecclesiastical and state support needed to mount campaigns equal to the task, colonial missionaries first had to convince potential sponsors that idolatries existed. Peru harbored a long tradition of naysayers, and Jesuit missionaries, supported by regulars such as Francisco de Ávila, lobbied hard to convince secular and religious authorities of the pervasiveness of idolatry and the twinned heresy of native witchcraft. They argued that idolatrous practices, a kind of devilry, constituted a danger to the realm and thus it would behoove royal government to support the missionary activities necessary to "extirpate . . . discover and remedy so hidden an evil." And more provoking, their discoveries suggested that if idolatries were rampant in Lima, the capital of the colonial world, the civilizing presence would be even more imperiled in the colony's vast hinterlands.[33]

Both in clerical tracts and in the ecclesiastical trials in which native heretics were judged, idolatrous behavior was often paired with political dissension, even revolt. It was the idolatrous who tended to leave their state-mandated *reducciones*, or "settlements," to be closer to their gods; it was the idolatrous who would promote disrespect toward local officials; it was indios abused and angered by colonial practices who would leave the company of Christians to join the infidels' ranks; and it was the infi-

---

32. Guaman Poma, *El primer nueva corónica*, 2:276–79. These inspections varied in their intensity, scope, and frequency; we know that idolatry inspections existed in Cuzco, for example, but their legacy is unclear. See *Cuzco 1689. Documentos. Informes de los párrocos al obispo Mollinedo*, ed. and transcribed by Horacio Villanueva (Cuzco, 1982). For a comprehensive study of the extirpation of idolatry campaigns, see Pierre Duviols, *La destrucción de las religiones andinas* (Mexico City, 1977), p. 213. Pablo José de Arriaga, *The Extirpation of Idolatry in Peru* (1621), trans. L. Clark Keating (Lexington, 1968).

33. See *Colección de las Memorias*, ed. Altolaguirre, pp. 26–27, 229–30; José de Acosta, "Escritos Menores" (ca. 1571–78), in *Obras*, Biblioteca de Autores Españoles, vol. 73 (Madrid, 1954), pp. 249–386. Arriaga, *Extirpation of Idolatry*, pp. 96 (quotation), 145, 152.

dels who were fighting the wars of the frontier and exacting such a high price for Spain's colonial venture.[34] Idolatry breathed sedition.

Idolatry was also twinned with witchcraft, and extirpators, finding witchcraft in native religious practices, were quick to find native women doing the devil's work. Juan Pérez Bocanegra's telling conflation of gender stereotypes with European and native religious practice pointed to one of the devil's guises. Pérez called the women who presided over indigenous (and sacrosanct) confessional rites *"alumbradas aturdidas"*; in inquisitional records, on the other hand, the alumbradas aturdidas were subversive, morally perturbed, and heretical illuminists. Imbued with grace, they could hear God's word without ecclesiastical mediation and would preach his will, prophesy the future, and, of course, confess without priestly benefit. Alumbradas enjoyed significant followings among Peru's populace, even its nuns and clergy. Decried by Inquisitors during the seventeen century's third decade, they were classed with witches as the premier subverters of moral and civic order.[35] Native and nonnative heretical disorders, particularly when they involved women, were seen as cut from the same cloth.

Women were often perceived to do the devil's worst work in the realms of love and politics. Martín de Murúa, a notorious *doctrinero*, along with Father Acosta, who penned much of the Third Lima Council, understood native women to be the most likely to use the black arts to cause death, and extirpators uncovered plots that linked female sorcery to the death of officials and landowners.[36] Heresies of indigenous women—including outright mockery—with specialties in magic that could both transform domestic life and take revenge on the powerful, were in some church eyes beginning to cross cultural boundaries. All the more reason to see non-india women, turning to Indian habits, as growing threats to the colonial enterprise.

Colonial cultural politics, honed by the ethics and zeal of Spain's Counter-Reformation, were as preoccupied with sexual matters as with religious heresies. This thrust reflected the Counter-Reformation's focus on domestic life as an arena in which it hoped to assert its authority and dominance. Clerics, perturbed by the love magic practiced by native and

34. Arriaga, *Extirpation of Idolatry*, p. 63; Rodrigo Hernández Príncipe, "Mitología andina" (1621), in *Inca* 1 (1923): 24–68; Leg. 4, exp. 14, Archivo Arzobispal de Lima (hereafter AAL), Lima, Peru; *Colección de las Memorias*, ed. Altolaguirre, pp. 71–72, 194, 297, 298.

35. See Juan Pérez Bocanegra, *Ritual formulario e institución de curas para administrar a los naturales* (Lima, 1631), p. 112; Silverblatt, *Moon, Sun, and Witches*, pp. 159–96; Rubén Vargas Ugarte, *La eloquencia sagrada en el perú en los siglos XVII y XVIII* (Lima, 1942), p. 7; Medina, *Historia del Tribunal*, 2:28–35.

36. Silverblatt, *Moon, Sun, and Witches*, pp. 169–81; Martín de Murúa, *Historia del origen y geneología real de los Incas* (1590), ed. Constantino Bayle (Madrid, 1946), p. 301; José de Acosta, *Historia natural y moral de las indias* (1590), in *Obras*, p. 172. Leg.1, exp. 12, AAL.

nonnative witches, preached the importance of chastity and the sacredness of the marriage sacrament to their colonial parishioners, of whatever origin.[37] Colonial witches, whose herbs and ointments were frequently tied to heretical love practices laced with indio magic, rivaled church sovereignty in domestic affairs and, no doubt, played on colonial fears of native subversion, gender subordination, and cultural disorder.

The colony was seen to be threatened by another set of internal enemies whose history was explicitly linked to that of indio evangelization. Peru's missionaries saw their efforts in light of Spain's tumultuous religious past, understanding early church strategies to convert pagans and especially later attempts to convert Moors and Jews as rehearsals for ventures in the Americas. Evangelists, such as Arriaga, were sobered by the herculean task of rooting out the hidden evil of Judaism in a country as pious as Spain: "For it has scarcely been possible to extirpate so evil a seed even in so clean a land, where the Gospel has been so continuously ... and thoroughly preached and where the Most Righteous Tribunal of the Holy Office has been so diligently and solicitously watchful."[38] Christian vigilants found heresy to be as strong among the Moors and their descendants, expelled from Spain just a little more than a decade before the publication of Arriaga's treatise on the extirpation of idolatry. Continuing in his comparative vein, Arriaga wrote, "The problem of setting aright and causing to be forgotten errors of belief learned at a mother's breast and inherited from father to son can readily be seen in the recent example we have had ... in the expulsion of Moors from Spain." With no spiritual remedy possible "it became necessary," he explained, "to avoid the temporal damage that was feared and to expel them from the country."[39] Moors, who like Jews could remain in the peninsula only on the condition of baptism, rebelled against the Crown when inquisitorial officials insisted that their customs (of dress, eating, and the like) were as heretical as their beliefs.

Nevertheless, the "disease of the Indians" was not "so deeply rooted a cancer" as that of Moors and Jews, Arriaga assured his readers. Yet the indio disease magnified concurrent anxieties over Peru's New Christians as it did over Peru's Old Christians turned Native.[40] The revived aware-

37. See Anne J. Cruz and Mary Elizabeth Perry, eds., *Culture and Control in Counter-Reformation Spain* (Minneapolis, 1992); Mary Elizabeth Perry, *Gender and Disorder in Early Modern Seville* (Princeton, 1990); Silverblatt, *Moon, Sun, and Witches*, pp. 159–80; and Ana Sánchez, *Amancebados, hechiceros, y rebeldes: Chancay, siglo XVII* (Cuzco, 1991), pp. viii–xi; *Doctrina christiana y catechismo para instrucción de indios* (1584, 1585), ed. Luciano Perena (Madrid, 1985), pp. 126–32, 143–44, 198; Pérez Bocanegra, *Ritual formulario*, pp. 211–50.

38. Arriaga, *Extirpation of Idolatry*, p. 9; Duviols, *La Destrucción de las Religiones Andinas*.

39. Arriaga, *Extirpation of Idolatry*, p. 9; see also Henry Kamen, *Inquisition and Society in Spain in the Sixteenth and Seventeenth Centuries* (Bloomington, 1985).

40. Arriaga, *Extirpation of Idolatry*, p. 6. Lib. 1030, f. 426, AHN; Medina, *Historia del tribunal*, 2:145–46.

ness of the hidden threats of Old and New World heresies, with their potential temporal damage, and the novel combinations of cultural ties made possible by conditions of colonial existence, played into anxieties over Spain's hold on the viceroyalty. But they also pointed to other tensions within colonial cultural politics: between "heresies" and legitimate cultural difference; between beliefs and the practices of daily living; between religious orthodoxy and ancestry; and between official policies that bounded "culture" in racialized boxes and the whirlwinds of colonial experience that belied them.

IV.

Inquisitor Mañozca's anxieties over witchcraft and "Indianness" were concerns regarding the cultural work of Spanish hegemony. On one hand, colonial rule, inscribed in cultural terms and through cultural hierarchies, was threatened by witchcraft ideologies that reached into the political and cultural arenas of empire building. The imagined threat of colonial witchcraft swelled as it absorbed fears surrounding idolatries, New Christians, women's disorderliness, native subversions, and allegiances of slaves, foreign enemies, and Indian malcontents. Colonial witches, on the other hand, conjured hechizos that firmly placed them in the colonial world of seventeenth-century Peru. With remarkable gifts of cultural improvisation, they addressed the disappointments, failures, and hopes—in love and justice—of their contrary colonial circumstances. Not Indians by any official calculus, they were drawn to "heresies" of Incas and native lore.

Yet, in spite of (or along with) heresies that crossed boundaries of "race" and social standing, these women engaged the categories of colonial rule. Colonial witches, coupling Inca and coca with "Indian," were forging a stereotype of Peruvian "Indianness" (and an ideology of *indigenismo*) that is with us to this day. Moreover, their perception of the social universe was parsed by the cultural divisions of the colonial state. As Doña Ana Ballejo would pray: "To the three souls of calvary, one of a negro, the other of an indio, the other of an español. I conjure you with the lord father, the lord son, the lord holy ghost."[41] The colonial universe was conceptualized as a triumvirate of cultures.

Colonial witches might have been skeptical of the kind of authority over domestic life that the church was attempting to establish. Yet even while dubious about aspects of orthodoxy, women, in their prayers and conjures, never doubted the efficacy of saints, of Catholic symbols, or of certain features of state power. It was the diablo of colonial tradesmen, merchants, notaries, and bureaucrats who had the power to fix fortunes of love and luck or to intervene when colonial institutions of government

41. Lib. 1031, f. 389v, AHN.

touched their lives. So did the Inca, increasingly described in a regal, absolutist form. But while monarchy ruled, even in heresies, Inca monarchs pointed to the limits of colonial authority and to the illusions of colonial rule. Harboring Inca dreams and praying to indio ancestors, colonial witches at least glimpsed the fiction of cultural boundaries as they reconfigured the possibilities of their pasts.

Mestizo Dreams: Transculturation and Heterogeneity in Inca Garcilaso de la Vega

JOSÉ ANTONIO MAZZOTTI

> Verdad es que tocan [los escriptores Eſpañoles] muchas cosas de las muy grandes que aquella republica [de los Incas] tuuo, pero escriuen las tan cortamente, q̃ las muy notorias para mi (*de la manera que las dizen*) las entiendo mal.
>
> —INCA GARCILASO DE LA VEGA, *Commentarios Reales [Royal Commentaries]* (emphasis added)

> It is true that these [Spanish writers] have dealt with many of the very remarkable achievements of that empire [of the Incas], but they have set them down so briefly that, *owing to the manner in which they are told*, I am scarcely able to understand even such matters as are well known to me.]
>
> —INCA GARCILASO DE LA VEGA, *Royal Commentaries*

AMONG THE many approaches to Latin American cultural and discursive phenomena in recent decades, two have been especially useful. The first is the theory of transculturation derived from the works of Cuban anthropologist Fernando Ortiz. In his 1940 response to the concept of acculturation proposed by Robert Redfield and other North Americans to describe processes of "cultural contact," Ortiz argued that such a concept describes processes of assimilation only within a dominated culture but fails to encompass fully the transformations that occur when two cultures come into contact. While Ortiz recognizes that his use of "acculturation" somewhat narrows Redfield's use of the term, he nonetheless finds in the neologism "transculturation" a better tool for describing not the substitution of one (dominated) culture by another (dominant) one but an ideally syncretic and harmonious transformation of the two cultures into a third entity. Many years later, Ángel Rama, one of Latin America's leading literary critics, would develop this same concept to describe what he called "narratives of transculturation" in such writers as José María Arguedas, João Guimaraes Rosa, Juan Rulfo, and Augusto Roa Bastos. In Arguedas's novels, for example, Rama encountered a manifestation of an "authentic national culture."[1]

The second approach to Latin American literature which has proven very useful in recent decades derives from theories of cultural and discursive heterogeneity that refer to a preexisting condition on which any process of transculturation takes place. As initially formulated by Antonio Cornejo Polar, this approach posits that many discursive systems can coexist independently; their coexistence need not suggest a harmonious synthesis. In the case of *indigenista* novels, for example, the internal contradictions of some Latin American societies become transcribed within the heterogeneous character of the narratives, which purport to present an external portrait of the indigenous world within the parameters of a Western literary genre.[2] What these novels ultimately achieve, then, is not

1. For an early definition of "acculturation," see Robert Redfield, Ralph Linton, and Melville J. Herskovits, "Memorandum for the Study of Acculturation," *American Anthropologist* 38, no. 1 (1936): 149–52. For the first formulation of "transculturation," see Fernando Ortiz, *Contrapunteo cubano del tabaco y el azúcar* (Havana, 1940). The first English translation, by Harriet de Onís, is *Cuban Counterpoint: Tobacco and Sugar* (New York, 1947). Mariano Picón Salaz, in *De la conquista a la Independencia* (Mexico City, 1944), chap. 4, incorporates the use of "transculturation" as conceptual tool to explain early cases of cultural contact in the New World. A detailed summary of the concept of transculturation can be found in Sylvia Spitta, *Between Two Waters: Narratives of Transculturation in Latin America* (Houston, 1996), chap. 1. See Ángel Rama, *Transculturación narrativa en América Latina* (Mexico, 1982), esp. chaps. 3–4.

2. See, for example, Antonio Cornejo Polar, "El indigenismo y las literaturas heterogéneas: Su doble estatuto sociocultural," *Revista de Crítica Literaria Latinoamericana* (hereafter *RCLL*) 7–8 (1978): 7–21; Cornejo Polar, "La literatura peruana: Totalidad contradictoria," *RCLL* 19 (1983): 37–50; and Cornejo Polar, "Los sistemas literarios como categorías históricas: Elementos para una discusión latinoamericana," *RCLL* 29 (1989): 7–23. Two lucid comparisons of theories of transculturation and of cultural heterogeneity can be found in Raúl Bueno, "Sobre la heterogeneidad literaria y cultural de América Latina," and Friedhelm Schmidt, "¿Literaturas heterogéneas o literatura de la transculturación?" both in *Asedios a la heterogeneidad cultural: Libro de homenaje a Antonio Cornejo Polar*, ed. José Antonio Mazzotti and U. Juan Zevallos-Aguilar (Philadelphia, 1996), pp. 16–32, 33–40.

always a dialectic fusion of different cultural elements but rather a Westernized presentation of the Indian world.

In this paper I explore one of the first Latin American mestizo writers, a historian who has traditionally been considered a typical representative of the assimilation process of mestizo and criollo elites. But I argue that in the *Royal Commentaries of the Incas*, Inca Garcilaso de la Vega wields a canonical historiographic discourse in such a way as to express a new perspective on the indigenous past and the colonial future, thus creating the bases for a discursive heterogeneity in later Latin American literature.[3] By focusing on particular aspects of Garcilaso's discourse, I will underscore some elements of the style or *manera* he uses to achieve an authoritative voice—not only before a European public but also before his Andean relatives and acquaintances. Beyond simply rephrasing his defense of Inca organization and desire for mestizo privilege that are so recurrent and obvious in the *Royal Commentaries*, from his discursive strategies I will derive the image of a colonial subjectivity that challenges the most traditional interpretations of Garcilaso's style and perspective as totally Europeanized or "acculturated."[4]

I.

A few pieces of information about the world of this member of the first mestizo generation in Peru may be useful. Inca Garcilaso de la Vega was born in 1539, six years after the occupation of Cuzco by Spanish troops. He was the offspring of the concubinage of a Spanish noble captain and an Incan princess and was raised in his mother's family and taught the

3. Garcilaso de la Vega, *Primera Parte de los Commentarios Reales, que tratan del origen de los Incas, Reyes que fueron del Peru, de su idolatria, leyes y gobierno en paz y en guerra: De sus vidas y conquistas, y todo lo que fue aquel Imperio y su Republica, antes que los Españoles passaran a el* (Lisbon, 1609); the second part was published as Garcilaso, *Historia General del Peru: Segunda Parte de los Commentarios Reales* (Córdoba, 1617). In this essay, most citations are from Garcilaso, *Royal Commentaries of the Incas and General History of Peru, Part One*, trans. Harold V. Livermore (Austin, 1966), with the corresponding part, book, and chapter in the Spanish volume also provided.

4. Since the beginning of this century, it has become commonplace to read Garcilaso's work in opposition to those of more apparently "authentic" indigenous authors, such as Felipe Guaman Poma de Ayala and Joan de Santacruz Pachacuti. For examples of this opposition persisting in the works of contemporary historians, see Nathan Wachtel, "Pensamiento salvaje y aculturación: El espacio y el tiempo en Felipe Guamán Poma de Ayala y el Inca Garcilaso de la Vega," in Wachtel, *Sociedad e ideología: Ensayos de historia y antropología andinas* (Lima, 1973); Patricia Seed, "Failing to Marvel: Atahualpa's Encounter with the Letter," *Latin American Research Review* 26, no. 1 (1991): 1–24; and Jacques Lafaye, "¿Existen 'letras coloniales'?" in *Conquista y Contraconquista: La escritura del Nuevo Mundo. Actas del Congreso Internacional del Instituto Iberoamericano en Providence, Rhode Island, 1990*, ed. Julio Ortega and José Amor (Mexico City, 1994), pp. 641–50.

Inca language of Quechua during his first years. During the later years of his youth, he was educated in his father's culture and learned the Spanish language. Although bilingual in Spanish and Quechua, all his later works were written in Spanish more than twenty years after he left Peru in 1560 to live with his father's family in Spain.

Most studies of Garcilaso's oeuvre emphasize the gap between his so-called late-Renaissance style and his defense of Inca administration and its non-Western traditions of expression. He has even been accused by several historians of romanticizing and manipulating the European utopian tradition in order to present the image of an ideal government that was lost with the Spanish invasion.[5] Most of these readings contextualize Garcilaso's works—especially the *Royal Commentaries*—within a European canonical tradition. A principal shortcoming of such interpretations is that they pay no attention to the subtleties of the first edition of the work. The most important editions produced during this century— those of Ángel Rosenblat in 1943–44, Carmelo Sáenz de Santa María in 1960, and Carlos Araníbar in 1991—have served as the exclusive source for many contemporary studies of the *Royal Commentaries*. Yet without exception these editions severely modify Garcilaso's original punctuation, assuming the potential receptor of the text to be a learned, Westernized reader. As a result, Garcilaso's prose becomes transformed into a clear example of how well a mestizo subject of the Spanish king was able to master the Castilian written language.

To present Garcilaso as a heterogeneous writing subject, I must explain some of the features of the *princeps*, or first, editions of the two-part *Royal Commentaries* and how they enable us to encounter a problematic mestizo subjectivity and its expression through a polyphonic discourse. Despite the apparent mistakes and misprints of the first editions, I argue that the rhetorical mechanisms embedded in the *Royal Commentaries* achieve a high degree of authority by evoking not only some of the most prestigious European literary and religious *topoi* but also some important symbols of Incan imagery and resonances with an Incan mode of narration. With this understanding of history as a double-voiced discourse, we can deduce the conformation of a writing subject who is dealing with a European audience and censorship but who, at the same time, is transforming original Andean themes and styles to accommodate them within a projective future.

One important factor to note with respect to this double-voiced discourse is that an aural reception of the work was considered as a possi-

5. See, for example, Marcelino Menéndez y Pelayo, *Historia de la poesía hispanoamericana* (Madrid, 1913), and, more recently, Juan Durán Luzio, "Sobre Tomás Moro en el Inca Garcilaso," *Revista Iberoamericana* 96–97 (1976): 349–61.

bility during its production process. This is verifiable especially in those chapters of the text which narrate Incan territorial expansions and which presumably were written and added after the initial conception of the work. José Durand establishes that the diachronic narration of the war campaigns and the deeds of the Incas was written after the synchronic description of their rituals and customs. Thus, the narrative voice of the text simulates some features of an ancient tradition of narration, one that Jan Vansina has termed the *historical poems*. This form of "epic" and historical reciting of the past was an institutionalized and formal practice among the Incas, one controlled by the state to strengthen the power of the sovereign. The *khipukamayuq*, or professional accountants and historians in charge of the composition of the poems, were supported by the royal families as a specialized staff that contributed to the glorification of the royal ancestors.[6]

It is now possible to know with a fair degree of certainty some characteristics of this celebratory genre. Following studies by Mario Florián and Jean-Phillipe Husson, we have learned that, like most Native American poetry, Quechua poetry was organized through semantic and syntactic couplets. These couplets have also been examined by Dennis Tedlock and Dell Hymes in the poetry of some North American native cultures, and by Ángel María Garibay and Miguel León-Portilla in the Nahuatl and Maya cases.[7] The complementary character of these pairs of verses is achieved

6. José Durand, "Garcilaso y su formación literaria e histórica," in Centro de Altos Estudios Militares, *Nuevos estudios sobre el Inca Garcilaso de la Vega* (Lima, 1955), pp. 76–77; Jan Vansina, *Oral Tradition: A Study in Historical Methodology*, trans. H. M. Wright (Chicago, 1965), p. 155. There are many testimonies from early and late chroniclers regarding the existence of this indigenous "genre." Juan Díez de Betanzos, *Suma y narración de los incas* (1548–56), ed. María del Carmen Martín Rubio (Madrid, 1987), p. 86, is very explicit about the origin of these poems, attributing them to the initiative of Inca Pachakutiq, the great reformer of the Inca state. Possibly because of the formalized structure of the poems, Betanzos compares them with the Spanish "romance" poetic form and calls them *cantares*. For recent approaches to Betanzos's text and its relationship to an oral indigenous "epic" source, see Martin Lienhard, *La voz y su huella* (Havana, 1989), chap. 6, and Mazzotti, "Betanzos: De la 'épica' incaica a la escritura coral: Aportes para una tipología del sujeto colonial en la historiografía andina," *RCLL* 40 (1994): 239–58. References to these poems are also detailed in Pedro de Cieza de León, *El Señorío de los Incas* (ca. 1552; Madrid, 1985), chaps. 11–12, and appear in Bartolomé de las Casas, *Apologética historia sumaria* (1552), Biblioteca de Autores Españoles, vol. 2 (Madrid, 1958), pp. 391, 422; Antonio de la Calancha, *Chronica Moralizada del Orden de San Agustín en el Perú con sucesos exemplares vistos en esta Monarchia* (Barcelona, 1638), pp. 90–92, and, among others, Garcilaso himself in *Royal Commentaries*, pt. 1, bk. 6, chap. 5.

7. See Mario Florián, *Panorama de la poesía quechua incaica* (Lima, 1990); Jean-Phillipe Husson, *La poésie quechua dans la chronique de Felipe Guamán Poma*, Serie Ethnolinguistique Amerindiene (Paris, 1985); and Jean-Phillipe Husson, "La poesía quechua prehispánica: Sus reglas, sus categorías, sus temas a través de los poemas transcritos por Waman Puma de Ayala," *RCLL* 37 (1993): 63–86. See Dennis Tedlock, *The Spoken Word and the Work of Interpretation* (Philadelphia, 1983); Dell Hymes, "Discovering Oral Performance and Measured Verse

by forms of syntactic parallelism and by the intersection of semantic fields that create the impression of a dual conception of time and space. For example, two verses in a poem collected by the Yaru Willka chronicler Guaman Poma de Ayala are as follows: "Like a reflection of water, you are an illusion / Like a reflection of lymph, you are an appearance." The verses refer to the same entity, a "you" that is divided in two different images which refer to similar and complementary spaces.[8]

It would be interesting to develop a more detailed description of the mechanisms of pre-Hispanic Quechua poetry and the different lyric genres that survived as discursive practices after the arrival of the Europeans. The semantic and rhythmic complexity of such poetry was directly linked to ritual contexts, and its full understanding would imply constant references to the political and cultural circumstances from which they derived and in which they functioned. Unfortunately, however, very few lines have survived from the specific genre of "historical poems." Only Cieza transcribes in Spanish prose a short fragment of one of these texts. It is possible to deduce their political intention and direction, however, if we accept texts by Betanzos and Titu Cusi as having such an oral "hipotexte." On one hand, Betanzos devotes the first part of his history of the Incas to glorify the deeds of Pachakutiq Inka, while Titu Cusi does so by tributing homage to his father, Mankhu Inka. Yet both are hardly "translations" of an original "epic" genre. According to what Betanzos himself declares, these "poems" were also sung and represented in ritual festivities. On the other hand, there are non-Incan versions (such as those gathered in *The Huarochirí Manuscript*) about the Andean past and the *cuzqueño* government. But we cannot afford to describe here their peripheral vision of the Cuzco regime.[9]

in American Indian Narrative," in Hymes, *"In vain I tried to tell you": Essays in Native American ethnopoetics* (Philadelphia, 1981), pp. 309–41; and these works by Ángel María Garibay: *Llave del náhuatl* (Mexico City, 1940); *Épica náhuatl* (Mexico City, 1945); *La literatura de los aztecas* (Mexico City, 1970); and *La poesía lírica azteca: Esbozo de síntesis crítica* (Mexico City, 1937). Miguel León-Portilla has written on this topic in *La filosofía náhuatl estudiada en sus fuentes* (Mexico City, 1956); *Literatura del México antiguo: Los textos en lengua náhuatl* (Caracas, 1978); *Tiempo y realidad en el pensamiento maya* (Mexico City, 1968); and *Literatura maya*, comp. Mercedes de la Garza, chronology by Miguel León-Portilla (Caracas, 1980).

8. Felipe Guaman Poma de Ayala, *El primer nueva coronica y buen gobierno*, ed. Rolena Adorno and John V. Murra, trans. Jorge L. Urioste, 2 vols. (Mexico City, 1980), 1:290. Translations of several Quechua couplets into Spanish can be found in Husson, "La poesía quechua prehispánica," pp. 65–66. These couplets are taken from the numerous poems Guaman Poma transcribed throughout his long chronicle.

9. Cieza de León, *El Señorío de los Incas*, p. 57. I derive the concept of "hipotexte" from Gérard Genette's *Palimpsestes: La littérature au second degré* (Paris, 1982), p. 39. Díez de Betanzos, *Suma y narración de los incas*, ed. Martín Rubio, p. 86. *The Huarochirí Manuscript* is a compilation of myths and legends from the late sixteenth century in the central Andean region of Yauyos, made by the mestizo friar Francisco de Ávila during his campaigns for the "extirpation of idolatries." A summary of its discursive particularities can be found in the recent

It is useful to review the specific origins of Garcilaso's Incan oral sources during his life in Cuzco before 1560. He claims in his work that the main narrator of the foundation of Cuzco and the conquests by the Incas was a great-uncle of his, the prince Kusi Wallpa, son of Garcilaso's great-grandfather, Tupaq Inka Yupanqi, the eleventh monarch of the empire (*Commentarios Reales*, pt. 1, bk. 4, chap. 16). In the chapters of the work devoted to the foundation of Cuzco (pt. 1, bk. 1, chaps. 15–17), interruptions in the text caused by abundant punctuation make its visual reading a very uncomfortable activity. This is why most modern editions of the *Royal Commentaries* have simplified the prose, making the text much more readable in terms of long phrases and fluidity.

In this first edition of 1609, the pace of the narration resembles a system of recitation that can easily be compared with what we know about the historical poems of the Inca court. The semantic couplets can be localized only by paying attention to the pauses and silences that are explicitly marked in the narration through comas, colons, and semicolons. In that period, many of the punctuation marks derived from copiers and typesetters during the process of the transcription of a text from its original form to the page proofs. But even if we accept that Inca Garcilaso did not read and correct the galleys of his book, it is still very telling that many other contemporary texts with similarly chaotic punctuation do not present pairs of couplets with the same frequency and in "foundational" or war passages. Some of the histories consulted by Garcilaso (such as those by José de Acosta or Francisco López de Gómara) are good examples. It is possible, of course, to find poets of the so-called Spanish literary Golden Age using similar forms of parallelism. But the frequency of dual structures in Garcilaso's prose coincides not only with the abundant use of this accepted rhetorical device but also with a simulated form of "recitation," which evokes an oral indigenous source; Garcilaso's old great-uncle Kusi Wallpa refers to his own narrative form as a *recitado* (pt. 1, bk. 1, chap. 16).[10]

Thus the localization of semantic couplets is almost impossible to accomplish in modern editions of the *Royal Commentaries*, which tend to privilege the longer cadences and visual scansion of an assumed Westernized reader. But the use of formulas as variations of a "mental template," as Michael N. Nagler defines them, also remains visible in the narration of the Incan conquests throughout the work. In this sense, the

---

English edition by Frank Salomon and Jorge Urioste (Austin, 1991), esp. the introduction by Salomon.

10. For a more detailed explanation of this argument, see Mazzotti, "En Virtud de la Materia: Nuevas consideraciones sobre el subtexto andino de los *Comentarios Reales*," *Revista Iberoamericana* 61, nos. 172–73 (1995): 388–99; see also Mazzotti, *Coros mestizos del Inca Garcilaso: Resonancias andinas* (Lima, 1996), pp. 133–67.

resonance of a Quechua orality gives the text, in its original form, the authority to establish its arguments about the Incas and its premodern proposal of *nación*, *patria*, and social organization as one of a legitimate and familiar nature before an Andean public. Traditionally, the "oral" quotations in Garcilaso have been heard as "echoes of Thucydides" and re-creations of classic historians. This is an undeniable point; however, my reading of the princeps editions suggests a different kind of eloquence, especially given that Garcilaso dictated the *Royal Commentaries* to his son, Diego de Vargas; Durand argues the same point for at least the second part of the *Royal Commentaries*. And in the last years of his life, Garcilaso was not able to write because of his "shaky" hands.[11]

This authority, achieved through the imitation of a specific type of orality, is consistent with the semantic aspects of certain images used in the work to describe the Andean spiritual ages. These images have generally been identified only with prestigious literary and rhetorical topoi such as the *præparatio evangelica* and the Augustinian scheme of the human ascension to the City of God. The metaphors used in the work to talk about Andean spiritual history also reveal a syncretic but contradictory conformation of Incan and European images. Garcilaso used the allegory of the climatic and temporal phenomena of obscure darkness, the morning star, and the sun of justice to refer to the ages of barbarism, the Incas, and the Christian faith (pt. 1, bk. 1, chap. 15). In his own words:

Viuiendo, o muriendo aquellas gentes de la manera que hemos viſto, permitio Dios nueſtro Señor, que dellos miſmos ſalieſſe vn luzero del alua, que en aquellas eſcuríſsimas tinieblas les dieſſe alguna notícia de la ley natural, y de la vrbanidad y reſpetos, que los hombres deuian tenerſe vnos a otros, y que los deſcendientes de aquel, procediendo de bien en mejor, cultiuaſſen aquellas fieras, y las conuirtieſſen en hombres, haziendoles capaces de razon, y de qualquiera buena dotrína: para quando eſſe miſmo Dios, Sol de juSticia tuuieſſe por bien de enuiar la luz de sus divinos rayos a aquellos idolatras, los hallaſſe no tan ſaluajes, ſino mas dociles para recebir la fe Catholica, y la enſeñança, y doctrina de nueſtra ſancta madre Ygleſia Romana.[12]

11. For the concept of "mental template," see Michael N. Nagler, "Towards a Generative View of the Oral Formula," *Transactions and Proceedings of the American Philological Association* 98 (1967): 269–311, esp. 297. For an explanation of orality in Garcilaso based on Western sources, see, for example, María Antonia Garcés, "Lecciones del Nuevo Mundo: La estética de la palabra en el Inca Garcilaso de la Vega," *Texto y Contexto* 17 (1991): 125–51, esp. 135–38, and Margarita Zamora, *Language, Authority, and Indigenous History in the Royal Commentaries of the Incas* (Cambridge, 1988), p. 45. For an argument about Garcilaso's dictation of his work, see José Durand, "Respuesta," *Nueva Revista de Filología Hispánica* 3 (1948): 168, and José de la Torre y Cerro, *El Inca Garcilaso de la Vega: Nueva documentación* (Madrid, 1935), doc. 94.

12. Garcilaso, *Commentarios reales*, pt. 1, bk. 1, chap. 15, f. 13v.

[While these peoples were living or dying in the manner we have seen, it pleased our Lord God that from their midst there should appear a morning star to give them in the dense darkness in which they dwelt some glimmerings of natural law, or civilization, and of the respect men owe to one another. The descendants of this leader should thus tame those savages and convert them into men, made capable of reason and of receiving good doctrine, so that when God, who is the sun of justice, saw fit to send forth the light of His divine rays upon those idolaters, it might find them not longer in their first savagery, but rendered more docile to receive the Catholic faith and the teaching and doctrine of our Holy Mother the Roman Church.][13]

The succession of the amount of light, presented here as a progression in terms of spiritual advancement, is a commonplace within the framework of Renaissance culture. The same metaphor was widely used elsewhere, from the Apocalypse to Albrecht Dürer's engraving of Sol Justitiae to Jesuit Pedro de Rivadeneira's late-sixteenth-century Spanish political treatise *The Christian Prince*, which Garcilaso mentions in other passages of the *Royal Commentaries*.[14]

But if we compare the images of Garcilaso's allegory with the Inca pantheon as described by Cristóbal de Molina, Blas Valera, Bernabé Cobo, and other chroniclers who wrote about Inca religion, we find that Garcilaso's images were not at all unknown for the surviving Inca aristocracy of the early seventeenth century. The morning star, or Venus, was generally characterized as a servant of the moon; it presided over the dawn and the spring as a symbol of fertility. The sun represented a dual entity, divided according to the solstices of summer and winter. In the case of the summer, *Apu Inti*, "major sun," was the symbol of the power of the higher celestial god Wiraqucha. It announced the climax of the rain and harvest times during the months of December to May. The other sun, *P'unchaw*, represented the weak sun of winter, when the celestial body lies at its furthest distance from Cuzco, the point of observation in the southern hemisphere. It represented a time of preparation and renovation of the cosmic cycle and was worshiped during the Inti Raymi celebration of June (figs. 6.1, 6.2).[15]

13. Garcilaso, *Royal Commentaries*, p. 40.

14. For the Dürer painting, see Erwin Panofsky, *Albrecht Dürer*, 2 vols. (Princeton, 1943), 1:78, and vol. 2, plate no. 101; see also Pedro de Rivadeneira, *El Príncipe Christiano* (1595), in *Obras Escogidas*, Biblioteca de Autores Españoles, vol. 60 (Madrid, 1868), p. 256. For other reminiscences of the morning star from the Apocalypse, see William D. Ilgen, "La configuración mítica de la historia en los *Comentarios reales* del Inca Garcilaso de la Vega," in *Estudios de literatura hispanoamericana en honor a José J. Arrom*, ed. A. Debicki and E. Pupo-Walker (Chapel Hill, 1974), pp. 37–46, esp. pp. 41–42. For references to the "sun of justice" within Christian tradition, see also Ernst Kantorowicz, *The King's Two Bodies: A Study in Mediaeval Political Theology* (Princeton, 1959), p. 101.

15. See Cristóbal de Molina ("El Cuzqueño"), *Ritos y fábulas de los incas* (ca. 1573; Buenos Aires, 1959); Blas Valera ("el Jesuita Anónimo"), *Relación de las costumbres antiguas de los naturales del Pirú* (ca. 1595), in *Tres relaciones de antigüedades peruanas*, ed. Marco Jiménez de la Espada (Madrid, 1888; rpt., Asunción, 1950), pp. 133–203; and Bernabé Cobo, *Historia del*

258

DEZIEMBRE
CAPAC·INTI·RAIMI

lagran pascua
solene del sol

capac

Fig. 6.1. Celebration of the major "Feast of the Sun" or summer solstice (Capac Inti Raimi) in the month of December. From Felipe Guaman Poma de Ayala, *El primer nueva corónica y buen gobierno* (Paris, 1936).

Fig. 6.2. Celebration of "Feast of the Sun" or winter solstice (Inti Raimi) in the month of June. From Felipe Guaman Poma de Ayala, *El primer nueva corónica y buen gobierno* (Paris, 1936).

The two Inca suns suggest a complexity that any linear reading of the Christian "sun of justice" does not show. For which is the sun implied in the text if we consider Incan references to the major sun of December or the weak sun of June? If we follow a narrative succession based on the temporality of the day, the arrival of the españoles would represent the sun immediately following the dawn and thus could be compared to a sun that has not yet arrived at its potential maturity and power. In this sense, the text would be implying a "fourth age" surpassing the colonial order, a projective era represented by a major sun not present within the threefold description of the Andean spiritual ages. The example of the metaphoric suns illustrates the possibility of a subtextual reading of Garcilaso's work that decenters and even contradicts a purely Europeanized reading of the text. By attending to the Andean resonances of style and semantic fields within the work, we can begin to discern some of the features of a writing subject who is much more complex than the traditionally accepted commonplace of the "acculturated" and "harmonious" mestizo.

II.

It is possible to notice the existence of a polyphony that is not only successive but also simultaneous—that is, the subject represented in the work includes his own "other" speaking under the same formulas and style that are apparently univocal. A similar argument has been made by Rolena Adorno in one of her most recent works on Guaman Poma, in which she posits the overlapping of different positions of the colonial subject who must negotiate with Spanish censorship.[16] The concept of polyphony is appropriate for the analysis of a "plurality of independent and unmerged voices and consciousness [in which the heroes] are not only objects of the authorial discourse but also subjects of their own directly signifying discourse." In the case of Garcilaso's work, we must remember that we are dealing with a profoundly elitist and Cuzcocentric version of the Andean past and the colonial present. The concept of polyphony, then, becomes insufficient because the Andean subtext and the Spanish superficial or explicit text overlap and imply a simultaneous intercultural discourse.[17]

Nuevo Mundo (1653), ed. Marco Jiménez de la Espada, 4 vols. (Sevilla, 1890–93). See also R. Tom Zuidema, "La imagen del sol y la *huaca* de Susurpuquio en el sistema astronómico de los incas en el Cuzco," *Journal de la Societé des Americanistes* 63 (1976): 199–230, and Arthur Demarest, *Viracocha: The Nature and Antiquity of the Andean High God* (Cambridge, Mass., 1981), pp. 13–15.

16. See Rolena Adorno, "Textos imborrables: Posiciones simultáneas y sucesivas del sujeto colonial," *RCLL* 41 (1995): 33–49.

17. Mikhail M. Bakhtin, *Problems of Dostoevsky's Poetics*, trans. Caryl Emerson (Minneapolis, 1984), pp. 6–7. Bakhtin, "Discourse Typology in Prose," in *Readings in Russian Poetics: Formalist and Structuralist Views*, ed. Ladislav Matejka and Krystyna Pomorska (Ann Arbor,

At the same time, because the writing subject becomes decentered, it cannot be completely considered within the framework of a transcultural national subject, as Ángel Rama has stated for such representative twentieth-century Latin American novelists as José María Arguedas and Juan Rulfo. The mestizo described by Rama is a culturally unified being, an affirmative and *atomic* mestizo, in the etymological sense of the word "atomic," meaning nondivisible. On the contrary, our mestizo colonial subject is highly divisible and therefore lives in a constant and chameleonic oscillation between worlds and cosmological visions.[18]

To explain why the oscillatory position of the writing subject acquires such an original status in Garcilaso's work, it is helpful to refer to the political direction of the text. According to David A. Brading, the proposal of a "Holy Incan Empire" underlies the entire conception of the *Royal Commentaries*.[19] This is especially visible in the second part of the work, which presents a clear exaltation of the principal Spanish conquerors and even a political program of the 1540s conceived by Carvajal, one of the lieutenants of Gonzalo Pizarro (*Commentarios Reales*, pt. 2, bk. 4, chap. 40). The latter was a younger brother of Francisco Pizarro and led a major rebellion in Peru against the Spanish Crown between 1544 and 1548. He and mostly all of the *encomenderos*, or new Spanish landowners, opposed the New Laws decreed by the Crown. The New Laws, inspired by Bartolomé de las Casas, were intended to protect the Indians by limiting the privileges and possession of land by the conquerors.

In the program that Carvajal proposes to the rebel, he argues that Gonzalo Pizarro should proclaim himself king of Peru in alliance with the Inca nobility hidden in the mountains of Vilcabamba. Such a declaration would immediately presuppose the articulation of the mestizo group as the legitimate inheritor according to this political program. Yet we cannot be certain of the origins of this text, which Garcilaso puts in Carvajal's mouth. The sources quoted by Garcilaso are insufficient for establishing the veracity of the text. Nonetheless, Emilio Choy argues that the interest in the "progressive force" of the conquest (conceived as of the emergent

1978), pp. 176–96, refers to the related concept of "convergent discourses." It is still important to point out, however, that in the case of Garcilaso the multipositionality of the subject includes a highly problematic convergence of positions, some of them repressed by the official rhetoric and values of the period; see also Paul Smith, *Discerning the Subject* (Minneapolis, 1988), p. xxxv.

18. For transcultural modern authors, see Rama, *Transculturación narrativa en América Latina*, chaps. 3–4. Approaches to Garcilaso's cultural oscillations and incomplete harmony can be found in Nicolás Wey-Gomez, "¿Dónde está Garcilaso? Las oscilaciones del sujeto colonial en la formación de un discurso transcultural," *RCLL* 34 (1991): 7–32, and Cornejo Polar, "El discurso de la armonía imposible (El Inca Garcilaso de la Vega: Discurso y recepción social)," *RCLL* 38 (1993): 73–80.

19. David A. Brading, "The Incas and the Renaissance: The *Royal Commentaries* of Inca Garcilaso de la Vega," *Journal of Latin American Studies* 18, no. 1 (1986): 1–23, esp. 22.

proto-bourgeoisie of the encomenderos) was an option considered by Garcilaso as a desirable factor in his reconstruction of Andean history.[20] Brading and Choy concur on the general sense of the *Royal Commentaries* as a political text, and not only as a historical account of the facts of the conquest and the Incan past. Indeed, one of the ultimate aims of the work is to defend requests for some privileges and tributary exemptions that the Inca descendants in Cuzco made to the Spanish Crown.[21] But it is also important to keep in mind the general problem of the social conditions of the mestizo group during the first decades of the Spanish conquest. As was obvious then, the mestizos seemed different from both the white conquerors and the vanquished Indians, and surviving testimonies bear witness to the scorn mestizos suffered from both European and Indian groups. Most of Garcilaso's generation were born from Spanish fathers and Indian mothers, through relationships of rape, concubinage, or, very rarely, Christian marriage. Thus the social status of the mestizos was generally described as "marginal." They were not allowed to carry guns, possess land, or have Indians for their own servants. In general, they were reduced to practicing minor jobs as shoemakers, blacksmiths, or horse keepers; if lucky they might eventually serve the Spanish Crown as translators, owing to their knowledge of the indigenous languages. Only in very exceptional cases could mestizos inherit lands and properties from their Spanish "fathers"—when an Indian mother was a very important princess, for example, or when a father belonged to the peninsular aristocracy.[22]

20. A letter from Carvajal to Gonzalo Pizarro is quoted in a passage from one of Garcilaso's sources, El Palentino's *Historia del Perú*, in *Crónicas del Perú*, ed. Juan Pérez de Tudela Bueso, Biblioteca de Autores Españoles, vol. 164 (Madrid, 1963), pp. xx, xlix. However, Carvajal does not refer there to an alliance with the Incan aristocracy or to the succession by a mestizo nobility. See also Juan Pérez de Tudela Bueso, "Observaciones generales sobre las guerras civiles del Perú: Los cronistas Diego Fernández, Pedro Gutiérrez de Santa Clara y Juan Cristóbal Calvete de Estrella," in *Crónicas del Perú*, ed. Pérez de Tudela Bueso, p. xlviii. Emilio Choy, "Quiénes y por qué están contra Garcilaso," in Choy, *Antropología e historia*, 2 vols. (Lima, 1985), 2:20–21.

21. See Manuel Burga, "El Inca Garcilaso de la Vega: Exilio interior, ambigüedad y segunda utopía," in Burga, *Nacimiento de una utopía: Muerte y resurrección de los incas* (Lima, 1988), p. 282, and John H. Rowe, "Probanza de los Incas nietos de conquistadores," *Histórica* 9, no. 2 (1985): 193–245.

22. On the legal status of mestizos, see Ángel Rosenblat, *La población indígena y el mestizaje en América*, 2 vols. (Buenos Aires, 1954), 2:151–55; and Richard Konetzke, "El mestizaje y su importancia en el desarrollo de la población hispanoamericana durante laépoca colonial," *Revista de Indias* 7, no. 23 (1946): 7–44, and Konetzke, "El mestizaje y su importancia en el desarrollo de la población hispanoamericana durante la época colonial (Conclusión)," *Revista de Indias* 7, no. 24 (1946): 215–37. For the case of Doña Francisca Pizarro, a mestiza who was the oldest daughter of Francisco Pizarro and an Incan princess, see María Rostworowski de Diez Canseco, *Doña Francisca Pizarro, una ilustre mestiza* (Lima, 1989); Doña Francisca was recognized as "legitimate" by the Crown even though her parents were not married.

As a privileged mestizo, Garcilaso was not exactly a bastard, as were most of his generation. He was recognized as a "natural son" by his father, even after the Spanish captain married a very young Spanish woman when Garcilaso was ten years old. In this sense, his case was unusual compared with the normal conditions of mestizos. Even Indians referred to mestizos as *sacha runa* (*Commentarios Reales*, pt. 1, bk. 9, chap. 31), or "false men," men from the jungle not conceivable in terms of civilization and culture. The signification of the name "sacha runa" is enormous given that this minority of "monstrous" mestizos during the first decades of the invasion was going to become the great majority during the Republican era.

The *Royal Commentaries* appears, then, not only as a product of the process of colonization but also as an alternative view to that process and an articulation of a foundational perspective against the colonial, bureaucratic, and Crown-directed system. But it does not give initial impressions about the Inca culture such as those found in works by Cieza de León or Betanzos, who wrote in the early 1550s. Rather, it includes a general transformation of Incan knowledge as an important component of its reconstruction of the past. There is clearly an interest in underlining a harmonious but frustrated past in the general proposal of a Holy Incan Empire, conceived in terms of a strategic alliance between Spanish and Incan aristocracies. Although this political program is not explicitly supported by the writing subject, it becomes clear through the analysis of the subtext and the mythical exaltation of the rebel figures of Carvajal and Gonzalo Pizarro, during the narration of their military campaigns (*Commentarios Reales*, pt. 2, bks. 4 and 5). These figures no doubt occupy a pivotal role in the imagination of what could have happened in the mid–sixteenth century as an aftermath of the encomendero rebellion. But at the same time they represent a lost possibility, a separation of subject from object, which could explain the contemporary status of a marginal mestizo historian within the Spanish world. Nevertheless, as Max Pensky argues, this separation "subtly presupposes that [the union of the subject with object] is, however feebly and unsatisfactorily, accessible through memory, through intentional or unintentional discoveries of correspondences or traces, through the repetitive allegorization of the objects of experience. Memory and forgetting settle as constituent, mournful properties of the realm of objects of intuition and knowledge."[23] The "allegorization of the objects of experience" to which Pensky alludes may, in the case of Garcilaso, be understood as the expression of an imaginary point in the past that projects itself into the future only through overcoming the meaninglessness

23. Max Pensky, *Melancholy Dialectics: Walter Benjamin and the Play of Mourning* (Amherst, Mass., 1993), p. 27.

of life.[24] This melancholic subject, contrary to the many melancholic subjects of the late Renaissance, finds signification in the chaotic signs of the present through the practice of a specific "manera" or style of writing that represents a new voice and a new perspective: stylistically polyvocal, ideologically contradictory, and culturally mestizo in the diverse and complex sense already described.

The marginal subject expressed in Garcilaso's works, as José Rabasa states, challenges the canonical tradition of the wise and European authorized historian by means of an insistence on his Indian origins; this subject thus achieves a high degree of authority before his potential Andean readers.[25] But as we well know, the interpretations of his work have had diverse political and social consequences. One was the Great Rebellion of Tupaq Amaru the Second in 1780, which sought to reestablish an Incan aristocracy; another was the criollo war for independence, during which José de San Martín wanted to publish the *Royal Commentaries* for its understanding and dignifying view of the Andean past. Both political leaders recognized Garcilaso's work as a provocative base for a new independent state but no doubt took from the work very different projects and perspectives for the future of the nation. Indeed, the concept of nation has very specific racial and cultural meanings in the *Royal Commentaries*. For Garcilaso, nación is merely an ethnic group and still far from our modern concept of nation state as a fusion of different groups into one single, imagined cultural identity. For Garcilaso, there is a nation of *cuzqueño mestizos*, a nation of mulattos, a nation of criollos, and many non-Incan Indian nations. Garcilaso's text presupposes an implicit hierarchy in which the cuzqueño mestizo group, to which Garcilaso belonged, would be recognized as a ruling cast at the top of the social pyramid.[26]

24. Julia Kristeva describes the state of "asymbolia" as typical of melancholic subjectivities in contemporary literature; see her *Black Sun: Depression and Melancholia* (New York, 1989), p. 9.

25. José Rabasa, "On Writing Back: Alternative Historiography in *La Florida del Inca*," in *Latin American Identity and Constructions of Difference*, ed. Amaryll Chanady (Minneapolis, 1994), pp. 130–48.

26. We are, of course, not dealing here with an enlightened "imagined community." Although Benedict Anderson, *Imagined Communities: Reflections on the Origin and Spread of Nationalism* (London, 1983), chap. 4, alludes to the formation of modern nation-states in Latin America, he discusses principally the role of newspaper printing and Westernized criollo elites at the end of the eighteenth century. Garcilaso's premodern conception of a Peruvian community may be more related to the "ethnic origins of [a] nation," which the *curacas* (indigenous local chiefs) could also embrace as their own; see Anthony Smith, *The Ethnic Origins of Nations* (New York, 1986), chap. 1. Within Garcilaso's "ethnic nation" the racial and cultural groups (including the dominant criollos) became subordinated to a mestizo aristocracy. In the case of Garcilaso's text, the renewable function of signs in written language allows for different readings, depending on the social and cultural subject who consumes it; see Homi K. Bhabha, "Introduction: Narrating the Nation," in *Nation and Narration*, ed. Bhabha (New York, 1990), pp. 1–7. An initial approach to Garcilaso's reception by both criollo and mestizo readers during the seventeenth and eighteenth centuries can be found in

After having explored several elements of Garcilaso's work, one thing seems clear: the mestizo subject is neither only the Europeanized aristocrat that patronizes the Indian population nor only the representation of an Incan cosmic force that organizes reality according to a mythic conception of time and space. His discourse involves both elements and at the same time something else—the enigmatic manifestation of a dream—a dream that is, like any dream, the allegorization of a repressed desire marked by a diversity of voices and semantic fields readable in different ways. Despite the political programs that the official criollo cultures of the Andean countries have constructed over the fictional model of the harmonious and "acculturated" mestizo, the specificity of Garcilaso's subjectivity remains an open question. This brief journey, through an avenue of interdisciplinary analysis, has hopefully offered a tool for understanding one of the most interesting cases of historical possibility that existed during Latin America's early colonial period. This analysis has also hopefully underscored the need both to reformulate the concept of transculturation for early modern colonial discursive expressions and to explore the notion of discursive heterogeneity for texts such as the *Royal Commentaries*, born along the border of contradictory cultures, subjectivities, and political interests.

Pedro Guíbovich, "Lectura y difusión de la obra del Inca Garcilaso en el virreinato peruano (siglos XVII–XVIII): El caso de los *Comentarios reales,*" *Revista Histórica* 37 (1991): 103–20, and in Mazzotti, "Garcilaso y los orígenes del garcilasismo: Notas sobre el papel de los *Comentarios reales* en la formación de un imaginario nacional peruano," *Fronteras: Revista del Centro de Investigaciones de Historia Colonial* 3 (1998): 13–25.

From "Religion and Society" to Practices: The New Religious History

DAVID D. HALL

IN THIS essay I describe and reflect on the rhythms of affiliation and participation in the congregational, gathered churches of early New England, my particular concern being participation in the sacrament of infant baptism. Before turning to the task of description, however, I want to locate myself in several contexts. First and foremost is the field of Puritan studies. What I borrow from this field is the concept of a religious or theological tradition that stretches, essentially unbroken, from sixteenth-century Protestant reformers to certain Protestants in Elizabethan and Stuart England, and from these Protestants—or Puritans as we usually term them—to the English who transplanted this tradition to New England in the mid–seventeenth century. In taking over and reaffirming this concept, I do not endorse its homogenizing tendencies—that is, its representation of Puritan theology as coherently systematic and, more generally, of Puritanism as a nearly perfect fusion of ideas and practice. Historians of doctrine have dismantled the first of these representations, and social historians have angrily dismissed the second. Let me affirm, therefore, that the tradition was hybrid and multivocal and that Puritanism as culture or tradition varied according to the local setting, the social field, in which it played itself out.[1]

A second context in which I situate myself is the field of popular reli-

---

1. See, in general, E. Brooks Holifield, *The Covenant Sealed: The Development of Puritan Sacramental Theology in Old and New England, 1570–1720* (New Haven, 1974); Charles Lloyd Cohen, *God's Caress: The Psychology of Puritan Religious Experience* (New York, 1986). Perry Miller's study *The New England Mind* (Cambridge, Mass., 1939; rpt., Cambridge, Mass., 1954) can be reclaimed in support of this statement. Mary Beth Norton demonstrates the importance of local custom over against normative, theological ideas for the practice of marriage among the colonists; Norton, *Founding Mothers and Fathers: Gendered Power and the Forming of American Society* (New York, 1996), chap. 1.

gion. What I take from this field is the proposition that in certain specific historical situations—and I have argued elsewhere that seventeenth-century New England represents such a situation—the relationship between high and low, the learned and the unlearned, the elite and "the people," was characterized by negotiation or give-and-take rather than by extremes of "domination" and "resistance." To explore the workings of popular religion is also to assume that ordinary people—or, in churches, the laity—were actors in their own right.[2] A third context is the social history of small-scale communities, the "new social history" that emerged with such force in early American history at the beginning of the 1970s. From this literature I take two interrelated premises: that the essential social unit was the family, and that families in these early modern rural communities were centrally concerned with self-preservation over time.[3] Thus I arrive at certain framing words or categories: tradition, ambivalence, negotiation, family strategy. Moreover, I am especially interested in the role of wives and mothers within the structure of the family. In this essay, therefore, I will examine certain cultural practices—joining the church, renewing covenant, participating in the sacraments of baptism and the Lord's Supper—and, via these practices, reconceive the relation between religion and society.

Now to the task of description. On a March day in 1705 the towns people of Taunton, Massachusetts, gathered in their meetinghouse for a ceremony of covenant renewal. "We gave Liberty to all Men and Women kind, from sixteen years old and upwards to act with us," the minister of the town reported, "and had three hundred Names given in to list under Christ." Remarkable for its size, encompassing nearly all the town's adults, the ceremony also stirred up emotions of unusual intensity among a particular group; in the words of the same narrator, the scene included "Parents weeping for Joy, seeing their Children give their names to Christ."[4] Some twenty-five years later, Jane Turell, a married woman and a church member living on the outskirts of Boston, gave birth to her second child (the first had been stillborn), whom she took almost immediately to the meetinghouse to be baptized. The infant lived but eleven days. From Jane Turell's father came the following report of his daughter's response to this sad event: "All the family remember the many tears of Joy and thankfulness she shed at the presentation of this child to God in holy

---

2. David D. Hall, *Worlds of Wonder, Days of Judgment: Popular Religious Belief in Early New England* (New York, 1989).

3. Here I have in mind the community studies that employed historical demography and in particular Philip J. Greven, *Four Generations: Population, Land, and Family in Colonial Andover, Massachusetts* (Ithaca, 1970).

4. *Christian History for 1743* (Boston, 1744), pp. 110–11.

Baptism, and her more than common composure of mind and quietness at its death and funeral."[5]

"Tears of joy": in each of these narratives parents rejoice as their children are incorporated into the (symbolic) body of Christ, the social body of the congregation, and the intergenerational body of the family. The high emotion of these parents presumes the possibility of great danger, that the children of the next generation will be lost—lost to Christ, the community, and the family that brought them into being. The narrative of covenant renewal in Taunton in 1705 implies the very real likelihood that the ordinary, ongoing mechanisms of family incorporation or preservation across generations have not been working well, for it has taken this extraordinary ceremony to reunite the youth of the town with their parents. The story of Jane Turell is certainly about loss but also about gain, for the act of incorporating her infant son into the body of Christ had for her the significance of ensuring that she would "meet [him] at the right hand of Christ another day."[6]

In these same years infant baptism was much on the mind of the Reverend William Williams of Hatfield, Massachusetts. In the 1720s the religious uniformity of the Connecticut River Valley was disturbed by the emergence of a handful of persons who questioned the legitimacy of infant baptism. Taking up the challenge of responding to these Baptists, Williams and his neighboring colleagues turned to the many passages in the Old Testament, the most important of them Genesis 17:7, in which one or another of the prophets described the covenant between God and his people, a covenant that these ministers represented as continuing, unbroken, from Abraham to the dispensation of the New Testament and the visible church of their own day. As in the case of old Israel, so in the new this covenant encompassed not only parents but their "seed," or children: "God is unchangeably the same, keeping covenant and mercy with his people and their seed even to a thousand generations." And although in some sense faith was a condition of entering into this covenant, Williams assured his readers and listeners that the mere being in covenant through their parents made it likely that children would be saved. The "promise" of the gospel, the promise of redeeming grace, unfolded intergenerationally: "The *Children* of visibly penitent Believers, *are by the rich Grace of God comprehended in the same covenant with their parents.*"[7]

---

5. Benjamin Colman, *Reliquiae Turellaie, et Lachrymae Paternae. Two Sermons Preach'd at Medford . . . The Lord's Day After the funeral of his beloved daughter Mrs. Jane Turell* (Boston, 1735), p. 101.

6. Ibid., p. 103. The reference in the text is to "them," meaning her firstborn and the third of her children.

7. William Williams, *An Essay to Prove the Interest of the Children of Believers in the Covenant* (Boston, 1727), p. 4.

A parent himself, Williams underscored the significance of this message for the parents in his audience. To forgo infant baptism was, he argued, "uncomfortable" to parents because it deprived them of the expectation that "God will take . . . care of" and provide "Covenant-Mercy to their seed." To Williams this expectation was "an inestimable blessing." Shifting to the rhetoric of inheritance, he invoked the experience of others in reporting that "some [parents] *when dying* have express'd more comfort in this, than *all else* they could leave with [their children] in the world."[8] Another minister writing about baptism in these years made the same point: "Inasmuch as Christ blessed such infants, and said, of such is the Kingdome of God; I think it gives great ground to believe and hope, that if such die while infants (and so not having rejected the covenant) their souls would go to the Kingdom of God in Heaven."[9]

William Williams was speaking to a local situation; it was the behavior of persons in his and neighboring congregations and towns that most directly concerned him. But in justifying infant baptism he drew on a long-standing theological tradition and its hermeneutics of the Bible. Starting in the 1720s, we may follow that tradition back through time to the origins of Puritanism in Elizabethan England, pausing on the way to acknowledge the famous debates at the turn of the century between the Mathers and Solomon Stoddard, the deliberations of the Cambridge Synod of 1662, and the treatise on baptism that Thomas Shepard wrote in the 1640s. Throughout this century and a half, certain arguments became standard. I have already indicated one of these, that the covenant between God and his people included children even though they could not consciously or voluntarily enter into it. The ministers differentiated between two forms of covenant: the "federal," which children entered through the sacrament of baptism and adults did also, provided they were of a "godly conversation," and the covenant of grace, which in terms of church membership was limited to persons willing and able to describe the "work of grace." Notwithstanding this distinction, which rested on the underlying difference between the reprobate and the elect, the ministers insisted that the external covenant functioned as a means of grace: far better that infants and adults come within this covenant and receive its benefits than stay outside and increase the risk of remaining unredeemed. It was in keeping with this theme that Thomas Shepard II likened the visible church, with its external covenant, to a garden where Christ nurtured tender plants, and that Richard Mather took up the theme of inheritance, specifying what it was "that Parents should lay up for their Children, and

8. Ibid., pp. 15, 33, 22, 9, and preface.
9. Benjamin Wadsworth, *Some Considerations About Baptism, Manag'd By Way Of Dialogue Between A Minister And His Neighbor* (Boston, 1719), p. 54.

leave such an estate behind them, that their posterity after them may comfortably bee provided for."[10]

Every household in Mather's Dorchester congregation was actively pursuing such a strategy—a strategy based on acquiring enough land to pass on sufficient economic resources to each child. Mather acknowledged the material dimensions of inheritance only by way of transition to his particular theme: agreeing it was "requisite for the outward subsistence of Children in temporal regards" for parents to strategize about inheritance, he insisted that it was even more important that they plan and prepare for the "spiritual" inheritance of the next generation. That task was peculiarly the responsibility of mothers:

> Mothers, you are more with your children whilest they are little ones, then their Fathers are, therefore be still teaching them as soon as ever they are capable of learning. You are at much paines with the bodyes of your children, and suffer not a little while you bear them in your wombs & when you bring them into the world, and will you not be at some paines for the saving of their soules? You are naturally of tender and dear affection for your children, and God mistakes it not that it be so; but will you shew no affection to them in respect of their soules, which is the principal matter[?] [W]ill it not move you to think that the children of your own bowells should everlastingly perish, and be in inconceivable misery world without end? I beseech you have pitty upon them, and do your best to teach them, and pray for them, weep for them ... who knowes but the prayers and teares of a faithfull Mother may be the salvation of the childs soule?[11]

If mothers wept in expressing their concern for the safety of their children, fathers, though more self-composed, felt a similar responsibility. Richard Mather invoked that responsibility in designating himself as a "Spiritual Father" burdened with the obligation of preventing the apostasy of the next generation. Would the children of Dorchester claim the inheritance that was theirs as children of the covenant, or like erring generations in old Israel, would they forfeit their privileged status and expose themselves to doom and destruction?

As we listen to Richard Mather speak about mothers, fathers, and children, we hear intrude some of the classic themes of "practical divinity"— that judgment awaits every one of us in our hour of death and that its outcome will be disastrous unless we as sinners repent, accept Christ, and

10. Thomas Shepard, *The Church-Membership of Children, and Their Right to Baptism* (Cambridge, 1663), p. 14; Richard Mather, *A Fare-wel Exhortation to the church and people of Dorchester in New-England. But Not unusefull to any others, that shall heedfully Read and Improve the same, As Containing Christian and Serious Incitements, and perswasions to the Study and Practice of Seven principal Dutyes* (Cambridge, 1657), p. 10.

11. Mather, *Fare-wel Exhortation*, p. 13.

strenuously pursue the moral life as obligated by the covenant. We hear him reiterate the premise that salvation depends on divine grace. And he also describes certain steps that we can take, for God works through "means," including our own agency.

Mather and his fellow clergy applied this several-sided message of benefits, obligations, and danger to baptism and the Lord's Supper. Wherein lay the danger of participating in the sacrament of baptism, either as parents or as children? It lay in the possibility that, as children grew up and became adults, they would not fulfill the obligations of the covenant. The Boston minister Samuel Willard spoke at great length about this danger in a sermon series based on the parable of the fig tree that bears no fruit. Were children of the covenant to do likewise, were they to break the conditions of the covenant, God would cast them off. Should this happen, the blame would fall first on parents for failing properly to rear their children and, second, on these children turned adults— or "youth," for Willard seemed most concerned about persons in this intermediate stage of life. Willard was sharply monitory of parents for their "great neglect . . . of doing their Duty to their Children, in order to their being fruitful. They love to have Church priviledges for their Children; they cannot bear that they should not be acknowledged Christians, and not have the badge of Christs Covenant upon them; but alas! this is all they mind; how wo[e]ful neglects of Duty are there in such Parents?[12] Turning to "young persons," he admonished them for preferring "evil practices" and ignoring the pursuit of godliness. In so doing, they jeopardized their future state before God, even though they were church members. To parents and children alike, he offered this chilling moral:

> Learn hence, that visible-Church Membership give to no man security of his Salvation. It is therefore a vain thing for any man to boast of, or put their confidence in it: and yet alas! how many are there who so do? . . . If this be a truth, that there may be barren fig-trees in Gods vineyard; it then necessarily follows, that men may belong to the number of God's visible church, and enjoy all the outward advantages of it, and yet after all that, fall short of eternal life.[13]

Yet the covenant also provided benefits. And Willard lingered on these, using, yet again, the theme of inheritance and evoking the emotions of parents concerned with family preservation:

> They leave the *entail* of these blessings to their posterity. God is wont to receive parents with their children into his Covenant, and the promise

12. Samuel Willard, *The Barren Fig Trees Doom* (Boston, 1691), p. 82.
13. Ibid., pp. 87–88.

runs down to *generations*: and where God hath given saving grace to parents, they count it an high favour of God to them, that if their children die
in infancy, they have the covenant to comfort themselves in concerning
them; if they outlive them, though the times are evil and threatning, yet
they shall leave them plants in the Vineyard, under the covenant protection of God, and the visible Heirs of all the means of Salvation.[14]

Safety was thus intermingled with danger. In these sermons, as in
countless others preached in the same decades, ministers proclaimed that
persons brought within the covenant via infant baptism faced higher
expectations and consequently ran a greater risk of displeasing God than
did those on the outside.

A similar doubleness surrounded the sacrament of the Lord's Supper.
Here the two-sided message of safety and danger was exaggerated by the
premise, fundamental to evangelical Calvinism, that a radical difference
existed between true or sincere faith and hypocrisy and that persons who
came to the Lord's Table should have some expectation of being sincerely
within the covenant of grace. To come otherwise, to come "unworthily,"
was to expose yourself to the terrifying message of 1 Corinthians 11:28–29,
a message insistently reiterated by the clergy: "Wherefore whosoever
shall eat this bread, and drink this cup of the Lord, unworthily, shall be
guilty of the body and blood of the Lord. . . . For he that eateth and drinketh unworthily, eateth and drinketh damnation to himself."[15]

These sketches of sacramental theology help make a point which
should be obvious and which has become central to Puritan studies: the
theology of the clergy in regard to baptism, the Lord's Supper, and the
process of redemption involved a mixture of motifs. The historian Brooks
Holifield has aptly characterized the sacramental theology of the Puritans
as "ambidextrous": the sacraments *were* efficacious, yet the sacraments
were *not* efficacious. The implications of this point are large, as I hope to
suggest in what follows.[16]

To return to the laity, we can ask the simple question, to be answered
on the basis of the serial (quantitative) data in church records: how did
they behave with respect to the two sacraments? The local variations of
practice (and principle) were innumerable. But the evidence in the case of
the Lord's Supper is fairly consistent from one town or parish to the next:
most adults who were members of the church by virtue of baptism
refrained from participating in the other sacrament. At the turn of the century Solomon Stoddard estimated that the ratio of baptized adults to

14. Ibid., p. 32.
15. King James Version. The uses of this text are described in Hall, *Worlds of Wonder*,
chap. 3.
16. Holifield, *Covenant Sealed*, pp. 45–48, chaps. 4–5.

those coming to the Lord's Table was four to one. In a good many places the ratio was more extreme. In searching personal records to determine reasons for this difference, we encounter, consistently, a deep sense of uncertainty about assurance of salvation that translated into a reluctance to participate. Hearkening to the horrific language of 1 Corinthians 11:28–29, laypeople reasoned that they were safer abstaining from the sacrament even though their ministers urged them in the strongest terms to come to Communion.[17]

Church records suggest a different attitude about baptism. More often than not, families where one parent was in covenant brought all their children to this sacrament. Two other aspects of this practice are remarkable. One is that a majority of parents brought newborn children to the church within two weeks of birth.[18] The other is that the practice of renewal of covenant, when adults again pledged to walk in holiness and thereby reaffirmed their eligibility—and the eligibility of their children—for the covenant, coincided with the events of marriage or pregnancy. As a minister alert to these practices noted, it was "visibly a prevailing custom" for persons to renew the covenant when "they come to be married, and then to do it for their credit's sake, and that their children may be baptized." The first of these facts underscores the sense of risk that parents lived with, as well as their expectation that baptism *somehow* benefited newborn children. The second fact highlights the close relationship between family formation, family extension (via childbirth), and the sacrament of baptism.[19]

A third body of data is relevant. Throughout the seventeenth century, when townspeople founded a church, men were the initial members. But within a period as brief as a few years, women preponderated, by a ratio of three to two or greater. The really interesting data concern who joined when and in what sequence. In families where the husband and wife each became members, it is strongly the case that the wife joined first and the husband followed after an interval of years. In households where but one adult (or parent) was a member, wives outnumber men by a significant factor. When we look for explanations of these patterns, the pertinent data

---

17. Solomon Stoddard, *The Inexcusablenes of Neglecting the Worship of God* (Boston, 1708), p. 21. Other evidence may be found in David D. Hall, "Introduction," in *The Works of Jonathan Edwards*, by Edwards, vol. 12, *Ecclesiastical Writings*, ed. Hall (New Haven, 1994), pp. 1–90. On abstinence, for example, see Colman, *Reliquiae Turellaie*, pp. 110–15; Hall, *Worlds of Wonder*, p. 161.

18. I base this statement on my own intermittent research and on the systematic study of Essex County, Massachusetts, church records by Anne S. Brown in "Bound Up in a Bundle of Life: The Social Meaning of Religious Practice in Northeastern Massachusetts, 1700–1765" (Ph.D. diss., Boston University, 1995).

19. Edwards, *Ecclesiastical Writings*, p. 257.

may be, once again, the conjunction of church membership with marriage and, for women, with the risks of pregnancy and childbirth.[20]

From this data, as well as from the public and private statements of ministers and laypeople,[21] emerges my principal argument: that the rhythms of affiliation and participation in the congregational churches of early New England were closely tied to strategies of family formation and family preservation. To phrase this differently, the "work" that church membership and the sacrament of baptism performed in the religious culture of early New England was to secure for families something they badly wanted: that their children and their children's children live in safety and health after them. As we know from the social and family historians, these families also wanted their children to live in prosperity. Thus it happened that families passed on two kinds of goods: the symbolic goods of membership within the covenant, a goods that fell especially within the purview of mothers, and the "real" goods of land, cattle, houses, and movable property.

Social historians have suggested that the second of these systems of inheritance came under strain in some communities in the closing decades of the seventeenth century. Strain also appears in the other system—evident in the sharp debate, encompassing both laity and clergy, that arose around the decision of the Synod of 1662 to allow the privilege of baptism to descend within families, then in the propagandizing of the 1670s, initially clergy-led, for the ceremony of renewal of covenant[22]; in the uneasiness about "youth" that appears in many places from the 1650s onward; in the "tears of joy" that parents shed in Taunton; and especially

20. Mary McManus Ramsbottom, "Religious Society and the Family in Charlestown, Massachusetts, 1630–1740" (Ph.D. diss., Yale University, 1987).

21. Statements by laypeople that place family preservation in the context of religious duties, including church membership, may be found in several of the "relations" in George Selement and Bruce C. Woolley, eds., *Thomas Shepard's Confessions*, Publications of the Colonial Society of Massachusetts, vol. 58 (Boston, 1981); in Sarah Goodhue, "Valedictory and Monitory Writing," in Thomas F. Waters, *Ipswich in the Massachusetts-Bay Colony*, 2 vols. (Ipswich, 1905), 1:519–24; in Samuel Sewall, *Diary of Samuel Sewall*, ed. M. Halsey Thomas, 2 vols. (New York, 1973); and in Mary Rowlandson, *The Sovereignty and Goodness of God, Together with the Faithfulness of His Promises Displayed; Being a Narration of the Captivity and Restoration of Mrs. Mary Rowlandson* (Cambridge, Mass., 1682), in *Puritans among the Indians: Accounts of Captivity and Redemption*, ed. Alden Vaughan and Edward W. Clark (Cambridge, Mass., 1981). Some of these references are brought together in Hall, *Worlds of Wonder*, chap. 3.

22. Inheritance practices are addressed, for example, in Paul Boyer and Stephen Nissenbaum, *Salem Possessed: The Social Origins of Witchcraft* (Cambridge, Mass., 1974). The corrections to this argument are many; see in particular John J. McCusker and Russell R. Menard, *The Economy of British America, 1607–1789* (Chapel Hill, 1985), chap. 5. On propagandizing, see especially the statement issued by the "reforming" synod of 1679, in Williston Walker, *The Creeds and Platforms of Congregationalism* (New York, 1893), pp. 435–36.

in the many reports dating from the Great Awakening of the surprise and pleasure older people felt at the high participation of youth in the revivals.[23] Keeping in mind the anxieties expressed by parents during these decades, we must take a fully historical approach to the nexus of family preservation and religious practices, recognizing that during the century from 1640 to 1740 families and churches tried out several different strategies of incorporation and discovered, as they did so, that each strategy was variously effective or ineffective. What worked in one town or parish did not always work as well in another; what succeeded for a while could gradually lose its effectiveness.

The expectations behind these strategies, together with the inevitable unevenness or unpredictability of any practice, are the realities that lie behind the talk of *declension*. Students of American Puritanism have wrestled mightily with this word, the current trend being for revisionists to deny that declension occurred—to deny, in other words, that Puritanism weakened over time.[24] In the context of this essay I want to propose another interpretation: when ordinary people use that term, we may understand them as saying, "Our family strategy isn't working quite as we had hoped"; when clergy use that term, they have their own worries about incorporation or preservation in mind. These worries, these signs of strain, do not signify that Puritanism was becoming ineffective; rather, they illustrate the truism that no culture, no family, exerts thoroughgoing or complete control over the succeeding generation.

What are the "possible pasts" on which this essay impinges? There is the past of mainstream Puritan studies, a past I have anchored in a description of the complex theologizing of the clergy about grace and how it was experienced, transmitted, and made evident in the visible church. There is the past of Congregational church history, the classic story of gathered congregations wrestling with the question of how to incorporate the children and grandchildren of the first-generation members and deciding, most of them, to accept a family descent–based system of infant baptism as their means of doing so. There is the past that foregrounds popular religion, or the actions and attitudes of the laity, wherein we see lay men and women carefully differentiating between the two sacraments of baptism and the Lord's Supper and preferring to participate in one far

---

23. See, for example, the many reports of local revivals in various years of *Christian History* (1743–45).

24. See especially Stephen Foster, *The Long Argument: English Puritanism and the Shaping of New England Culture, 1570–1700* (Chapel Hill, 1991), and for another critique, Harry S. Stout and Catherine A. Breckus, "Declension, Gender, and the 'New Religious History,'" in *Belief and Behavior: Essays in the New Religious History*, ed. Philip R. VanderMere and Robert P. Swierenga (New Brunswick, 1991), pp. 15–36.

more than in the other. And there is the past of the new social history, in which families strategized about modes of inheritance, both spiritual and material.

Collectively and in their interrelationships, these several pasts teach us a good deal about the workings of the religious in early New England and, I would argue, about the workings of the religious more generally. As steps toward a larger framework of interpretation, let me conclude with four propositions.

1. The official religious system—what we conventionally refer to as Puritanism with a capital *P*—offered a good deal of resources to ordinary people. In particular, it provided the image and idea of an intergenerational covenant richly beneficial to each succeeding stage of the family. Amanda Porterfield has suggested that Puritanism may have been especially appealing to wives and mothers because it made available, via the model of maternal piety and devotion within the context of the family, a "means of attaining status and exercising influence" in an otherwise patriarchal culture. These assumptions seem warranted not only by the manifest behavior of lay men and women and the evidence we have of their mentality but also by the contents of the ministers' sermons and treatises and *their* expectations as parents and family members.[25]

2. Benefiting from the official system, these laypeople nonetheless marked out a middle space for themselves, one in which they could operate selectively and, as they wished, moderate the more rigorous demands of that system. We have seen them distancing themselves from the tensions that surrounded the Lord's Supper and, in contrast, eagerly participating in other rituals addressed to family preservation. This analysis can be extended beyond church history to incorporate Richard Godbeer's account of eclectic modes of healing (or what he terms the intermingling of "magic" and "religion"), Carla Pestana's description of the de facto toleration of Baptists in local communities, and my own of the reading public, the marketplace of print, and the lore of wonders.[26] This body of work

25. Amanda Porterfield, *Female Piety in Puritan New England: The Emergence of Religious Humanism* (New York, 1992), p. 86. It was always possible for certain persons (whether clergy or laypeople) to repudiate the nexus between family culture and religion. First-generation Quakers, expecting the imminent triumph of Christ, willingly left their families to become witnesses to the Truth. Baptists also modified that nexus, and in 1749 Jonathan Edwards attacked it in calling for a restoration of "sincere" profession as the sole basis for admission to the sacraments. But the Quakers soon moved to birthright membership, thereby restoring the nexus, Edwards was dismissed by his congregation, and New Light congregations also began to compromise. For this last point, see Susan Juster, *Disorderly Women: Sexual Politics and Evangelicalism in Revolutionary New England* (Ithaca, 1994).

26. Richard Godbeer, *The Devil's Dominion: Magic and Religion in Early New England* (New York, 1992); Carla G. Pestana, *Quakers and Baptists in Colonial Massachusetts* (New York, 1991); Hall, *Worlds of Wonder*, chap. 2.

reveals that laypeople moved selectively through many layers of meaning, abetted in doing so by the very multiplicity of possibilities that persisted within even the most orthodox version of Puritanism.

3. Where this middle space or process of appropriation became concrete was in the family. As Mary Ramsbottom has aptly observed, with reference to the remarkable evidence she amassed concerning gender and family structure in relation to church membership, "In the orchestration of church rituals, we see families making their own religious identities."[27] Historians may hold different views on the internal structure of these families. My own interpretation is one that foregrounds the initiating roles of wives and mothers, most of whom were literate, and the evident restlessness of "youth." When we move out beyond the family to consider the political workings of the church, town, and colony, the evidence points to a dispersion and decentralization of authority as manifested, for example, in the congregational structure of the church. In this instance, dispersion served to limit the authority of each parish minister. Forms of hierarchy persisted, but so did a capacity within families, kinship networks, and small-scale communities to enact their own version of official policies.[28]

4. My final point brings us back to religion. That very word is problematic; as it is now truistic to observe, no one has or believes a "religion." Instead, the religious lies in what we do—in practices and in the meanings that energize such practices. In a preliminary way I have sketched how we could recast the history of Puritanism as a history of practices and meanings, my object lesson being the practices of affiliation and participation in the gathered church and its sacraments. To move in this direction is also to overcome the classic (and paralyzing) duality of "religion" and "society"; in the stream of everyday experience, in the unfolding of local or popular culture, that duality gives way to the fusion of the religious and the social in the rhythms of affiliation and participation. The task ahead is to extend this perspective to other practices, to other local cultures. In doing so we will fashion a better understanding of society, religion, and authority.

27. "Households, I believe, were not only the key units of New England society in the seventeenth century but also the main constituents of ecclesiastical institutions. . . . When the household is used as a primary category of analysis, church membership becomes an even more revealing example of religious behavior. . . . In the orchestration of church rituals, we see families making their own religious identities. In Charlestown, the laity participated in the ongoing definition of public religious institutions" (Ramsbottom, "Religious Society," p. 10).

28. One example among many: when the Springfield, Massachusetts, church invited Robert Breck to become its minister, the church got its way despite the strenuous opposition of the majority of clergy, along with their allies among the magistrates, in Hampshire County; the local church took advantage of differences of opinion among the Massachusetts clergy as a whole.

What Did Christianity Do for Joseph Johnson? A Mohegan Preacher and His Community

LAURA J. MURRAY

I desire the continuance of your prayers dayly that God would make and keep me humble minded and willing to Submit to his will and pleasure & to dispose of me as Seems good to him and most for his own Glory.

—JOSEPH JOHNSON *to Eleazar Wheelock,*
December 29, 1767

This morning Exceeding Pleasant. After I had read some of the holy Scriptures, I thought Proper to wash my Cloaths. Accordingly I have spent the day in washing my Shirts, and Stockings.

This Evening had a Meeting here. Several young People assembled, and Samuel Ashpo Prayed and Spoke, and after the meeting broke up John Nanepome and Robert Ashpo came in. We went to Sleep very late.

—JOSEPH JOHNSON, diary, *November 22, 1771*

FOR TODAY'S secular student of Native American culture and history, the writing of Joseph Johnson, an eighteenth-century Christian Mohegan from Connecticut, may not initially be satisfying or compelling. His letters, diaries, and sermons rarely offer direct critiques of

colonial actions and institutions, and hardly ever does he foreground cultural practices or spiritual beliefs particular or traditional to his people.
Rather, Johnson's writing is marked by fervent Christian self-abasement
and a firm desire to conform to English modes of behavior and social
organization. Johnson's humility with respect to both heavenly and
earthly superiors is so insistent that the first question that arose for me
as I tried to respond to his writing was not my title question but, What
did Christianity do *to* Joseph Johnson? How did it set the terms for him
to describe himself as a "good for nothing Black Indian"?[1] How did
rhetorics of racism and religion interact and intensify each other in his
writing?

The answers at first seemed all too clear: this was a case of religion as
colonialist ideology. Jorge Noriega has written that "Indian students tar-
geted for training in the early stages of U.S. colonialist education were
used essentially as a virus, a medium through which to hurry along a calculated process of sociocultural decay 'from within' "; Johnson, this interpretive framework would suggest, betrayed his people to his teacher
Eleazar Wheelock and his Savior, Jesus Christ. Yet despite its power—and
even despite Johnson's remarks about the ignorance of his pagan ancestors—this kind of interpretation quickly proves too blunt an instrument.
For Joseph Johnson was one of a group in his community whose reasons
for participating in Christian worship may or may not have accorded with
those of the local white clergy. Noriega's virus metaphor does not
acknowledge that a wide range of meanings can be attached to a common
practice by different individuals or communities. In this essay, I emphasize Christianity's materiality as part of Johnson's lived experience, rather
than its falsity as ideology. To do so is not to deny the close ideological
and practical ties between Christian missions and colonialism but to recognize the inhibiting *and* enabling power of belief on its own terms, as
well as the ways disempowered individuals, as members of communities,
acted—within, despite, and sometimes because of ideological and material
constraints.[2]

---

1. Joseph Johnson to Eleazar Wheelock, April 20, 1768, Wheelock Papers, Dartmouth
College.

2. Jorge Noriega, "American Indian Education in the United States: Indoctrination for Subordination to Colonialism," in *The State of Native America*, ed. Annette Jaimes (Boston, 1992),
p. 379. Joseph Johnson clearly does present a contrast to such Native spokespeople as Red
Jacket, who stood up for the well-being of his people by arguing against Christian missionaries; see Peter Nabokov, ed., *Native American Testimony: A Chronicle of Indian-White Relations
from Prophecy to the Present, 1492–1992* (New York, 1991), p. 57. For discussions of more
empowering relations of aboriginal people to Christianity, see James Treat, ed., *Native and
Christian? Native Voices on Religious Identity in the United States and Canada* (New York, 1996),
and Barry O'Connell, ed., *On Our Own Ground: The Complete Writings of William Apess, a
Pequot* (Amherst, 1992). Terry Eagleton has observed that "in order to be truly effective, ide-

Johnson's early letters, from one of which is taken my first epigraph, are in many regards set pieces written as exercises for his teacher and thus dramatize his subordination to Eleazar Wheelock's will and discourse. But his later letters and diaries show a greater range of tone, substance, and occasion. The second epigraph, an entry from Johnson's diary, matter-of-factly places his solitary and communal Christian devotions in sequence with other activities of a day's work. As I have become more familiar with the texture of Johnson's writing and the outlines of his life, my emphasis has shifted to the question, What did Christianity do *for* Joseph Johnson? Why and how did he believe in it? If it made him suffer, how did his faith also help him in spiritual or material ways?

In addressing these questions, I explore one Native person's Christian belief and the power it produced and resisted. I begin with biography, considering various dimensions of prevailing doctrine as Johnson understood them, as well as the particular goals and audiences of Johnson's writing. But the Christian practice of Johnson's community, as documented in his diaries, is also key. Johnson's religious identity can be understood only in the context of the Native American Christian communities of New England in which he came to Christ and of which he became a passionate, though youthful, leader. Comparison with later Mohegan Christians may also offer insight into Johnson's circumstances and discourses; thus I close with a discussion of the early-twentieth-century diaries of Fidelia Fielding, which manifest a different but equally intimate relationship between Mohegan identity and Christian belief.

I.

Joseph Johnson was born to Joseph and Betty (Garrett) Johnson, both Mohegans, at Mohegan, Connecticut, in 1751. The family had a history of leadership in that community and beyond: Augh Quant Johnson, probably Joseph Johnson's grandfather, had gone to England in 1736 to further Mohegan land claims; an uncle was a vocal counselor to the sachem; and Johnson's father was a leader of scouts in the French and Indian War. Joseph Johnson Sr. died in that war, whereupon Betty Johnson sent her seven-year-old son Joseph to Eleazar Wheelock's Indian Charity School at nearby Lebanon. She may have done so partly out of financial distress, which is well documented among Mohegan war widows of this period.

ologies must make at least some minimal sense of people's experience, must conform to some degree with what they know of social reality from their practical interaction with it" (*Ideology: An Introduction* [London: Verso, 1991], p. 14). There is, then, always an element of "sense" in people's acceptance of ideology; this element may be minuscule or large, depending on the degree of coercion and control, but it merits consideration either way.

However, Betty Johnson was a church member and was perhaps disposed to give her son a Christian education in any case.[3] The fact that Joseph Johnson was not a first-generation Christian is important to note.

At the Charity School Wheelock trained both Indian and white boys for missionary work among the Six Nations; he also schooled Indian girls to be good Christian wives to the Indian boys.[4] In lieu of a history of Wheelock's involvement in missionary work and Indian education, an excerpt from one of Wheelock's letters may stand as sufficient introduction to his pedagogical philosophy and attitudes toward students. Writing to evangelist George Whitefield, Wheelock complained with gusto:

> None know, nor can any, with out Experience, Well conceive of, the difficulty of Educating an Indian. They would soon kill themselves with Eating and Sloth, if constant care was not exercised for them at least the first year.—They are used to set upon the Ground, and it is as natural to them as a seat to our Children—they are not wont to have any Cloaths but what they wear, nor will they without much Pains be bro't to take Care of any— They are used to a Sordid Manner of dress, and love it as well as our Children to be clean. They are not used to any regular Government, the sad consequences of which you may a little guess at—they are used to live from Hand to Mouth (as we Speak) and have no care for Futurity—they have never been used to the Furniture of an English House, and dont know but that a wineglass is as strong as an HandLoom. Our Language when they Seem to have got it is not their Mother Tongue and they cannot receive nor communicate in that as in their own. It is a long time before they will learn the proper Place, & use of the Particles, A, an, the & c. and they are as unpolished & uncultivated within as without. However experi-

3. Thomas Coram to "Augh Quant Johnson Otherwise Cato," September 21, 1738, William Samuel Johnson Papers, Connecticut Historical Society, Hartford. For evidence of the active role of Johnson's Uncle Zachary from the late 1730s to the 1770s, see "Indian Papers," ser. 1, vol. 1, pp. 247–50; ser. 1, vol. 2, pp. 35, 94, 99, 291, 293, 310, 326; ser. 2, vol. 1, p. 36, Connecticut State Library, Hartford. For Joseph Johnson Senior's commission, instructions, and letter to Betty Johnson, see William Allen, "Memoir of Joseph Johnson," Wheelock Papers. On the financial distress of war widows, see Zachary Johnson petition, 1755, "Indian Papers," ser. 1, vol. 2, p. 94. The 1774 census listed 142 Indian men and 244 Indian women in New London County; the large discrepancy between the numbers for men and women is at least partly the result of war casualties (*Collections of the Massachusetts Historical Society* 10 [1809]: 117). Record of the 1743 baptism of Johnson's mother can be found in Records of the New London Church, vol. 1, p. 34, Connecticut State Library, Hartford.

4. Johnson uses the terms *English* and *white*, *Native* and *Indian*, to describe the people he encounters; I also use a combination of terms, aware that each has its inadequacies or particular slant. The basic published sources for Wheelock's school and Johnson's education and life are William DeLoss Love, *Samson Occom and the Christian Indians of New England* (Chicago, 1899), and James Dow McCallum, ed., *The Letters of Eleazar Wheelock's Indians* (Hanover, N.H., 1932). For more recent accounts of Wheelock's school, see James Axtell, "Dr. Wheelock's Little Red School," in *The European and the Indian: Essays in the Ethnohistory of Colonial North America* (New York, 1981), pp. 87–109, and Margaret Connell Szasz, *Indian Education in the American Colonies, 1607–1783* (Albuquerque, 1988), chaps. 8, 9, 10.

ence has taught us that it may be done, And they be as open to conviction of the Truth of their State, when proper Matter of Conviction is communicated to them as any.[5]

This letter vividly displays the poverty of Wheelock's cross-cultural imagination and suggests the material poverty of indigenous people in New England, but it also reveals a high degree of cultural survival in New England Native communities at this time, communities that because of missionary presence, integration into colonial economies, and military alliances have often been assumed to be highly assimilated to all European ways. Despite itself, the letter contains positive evidence of the persistence of Native languages, as well as Native child-rearing, house-furnishing, and eating practices. It is hardly surprising, then, that Wheelock had a difficult time in his efforts to "purge all the Indian" out of his students.[6] Furthermore, the school's proximity to Mohegan permitted Mohegan students' families to visit the school, and several sets of siblings came to the school together. At least one of Joseph Johnson's sisters attended the school. So although Johnson left Mohegan at a tender age, he was by no means cut off from his home.

In 1767, at the age of sixteen, Joseph Johnson was sent to teach among the Oneidas. He worked in upstate New York for two winters, despite the recalcitrance of his Oneida students and the vigorous demands of his supervisor, Samuel Kirkland, but then quit amid charges of drunkenness and misbehavior. For the next two years, Johnson taught and traveled well away from Wheelock's watchful eye:

Afterwards I left the School intirely Rev[d] Eleazer Wheelock D.D. intirely, and from that time, I been wandering up, and down, in this Delusive World. Some of my time, I Spent at Providence Town, keeping a School. Some of my time, I have Spent upon the Ocean wide. I have been down Eastward, as far as to the Western Islands twice. Curvo, & Florus, I have Seen, and to the South ward I have been as far, to the West Indies. Seen also the Islands between Antigua and Granades, and again from Antigua I have Sailed down leward Sailed by the Virgin Islands, also by Sandy

---

5. Wheelock to Whitefield, July 4, 1761, Wheelock Papers. Wheelock later took in Iroquois students, but at this time his students were all Mohegans, Montauks, and Delawares, and thus these observations do apply to New England Indians specifically (McCallum, *Letters*, app. A).

6. Wheelock to Mr. Pemberton, October 10, 1764, Wheelock Papers. On cultural survival, see also Ezra Stiles's 1761 sketches of wigwams at Niantic in *Extracts from the Itineraries and Other Miscellanies of Ezra Stiles, D.D., LL.D., 1755–1794*, ed. Franklin Bowditch Dexter (New Haven, 1916), p. 131; and a 1773 reference to Mohegan women making "yoke hegg," a traditional form of parched corn, to feed a delegation on their way to Oneida, in Farmington Indians to "All Our Indian Brethren," October 13, 1773, Wheelock Papers.

Cruize, Portireco, down as far as to Mona. And after So long time Even in my 21st year I Safely arrived to my Native place. Their I Spent one year in working upon my farm.[7]

Johnson represents his return to Mohegan as the resolution of a heroic journey, and in the diary Johnson kept that year he noted every week, sometimes in the margin as well as in the main text, the anniversary of this return. The diary details his daily labors, medical treatments, conversion to Christ, an amorous adventure, and in general the social texture of the Christian community at Mohegan and its relations with neighboring native Christian groups. Johnson continued his diary during the year he taught among Native people at Farmington, near Hartford; several of his sermons from that year also survive. Thereafter the surviving documents of Johnson's life are letters he wrote to governors and other benefactors, to the Oneidas, and to other New England Indians, letters he composed to forward the project of moving a group of Christian New England Indians to the Oneida country.[8]

In retrospect this emigration has been called "the Brotherton movement," after the town that was eventually founded in upstate New York, the main credit for which is usually given to Samson Occom—Wheelock's most famous student, Johnson's father-in-law, and an important leader among the New England Indians in this period. Occom was indeed involved and did move a group of people there after the revolution. It was Johnson, however, who made the initial arrangements, including obtaining a deed of land from the Oneidas. Johnson's letters about these affairs are numerous; suffice it to say that whether his audience was Oneida or English, he was extremely good at tailoring his pleas to its expectations and customary rhetoric. In the Revolutionary years, for example, the loyalty to God shown in his earlier letters to ministers is replaced by loyalty to liberty, even though other evidence shows Johnson's commitment to that cause was lukewarm at best.[9] But because he needed freedom of

---

7. Johnson to Wheelock, August 30, 1773, Wheelock Papers.

8. The published source for all Johnson's writing so far located is Laura J. Murray, *To Do Good to My Indian Brethren: The Writings of Joseph Johnson* (Amherst, 1998); in the essay I cite manuscript sources.

9. For Johnson's efforts, see "To the Indians Concerning Oneida Lands," December 24, 1773, Wheelock Papers; record of a meeting, *Papers of Sir William Johnson*, ed. Sullivan et al., 12:1060; Johnson to Oneidas, January 20, 1774, Wheelock Papers; deed in Love, *Samson Occom*, pp. 222–23. In the summer of 1774 Johnson implored Sir William Johnson to intervene and convince the New England Indians not to fight for the Americans (Joseph Johnson to Sir William Johnson, July 8, 1774, Wheelock Papers); in 1775 he was criticized for visiting Guy Johnson (*Minutes of the Albany Committee of Correspondence*, 1:182–83); and in 1776 he named his second son William—that is, William Johnson—a common enough name but, under the

movement, Johnson carried messages back and forth between Revolutionary leaders and the Oneidas; when questioned, he protested that he would be willing to lay down his life for American liberty. Perhaps he did: Johnson died at the age of twenty-five sometime in 1776 or 1777, in unknown circumstances.[10]

II.

Most studies of connections between colonialism and Christianity focus on the dramatic collision of contrasting worldviews and on early converts or the conversion of leaders.[11] But it is crucial to understand that at the time of Joseph Johnson's birth, Christianity was already a part of the fabric of his Mohegan community. His mother was a Christian, and she had her son baptized as an infant. Many neighbors were Christians. The sachem, Ben Uncas, was a Christian. Many Mohegans no doubt continued to hold more traditional beliefs (either in opposition to or alongside Christian beliefs), and others perhaps participated only intermittently in the

circumstances, likely not a coincidence. The fullest source on Occom to date is Love, *Samson Occom;* a full history of Brotherton has not been written.

10. Johnson made the claim of loyalty on July 22, 1775 (*Minutes of the Albany Committee of Correspondence*, 1:164). The only known record of Johnson's death is a postscript to a letter from David McClure: "The Churches this way who had a taste of Mr. Johnson's ministerial Gifts feel for the public in the loss of that zealous, pious and very promising Indian Preacher" (McClure to Wheelock, May 8, 1777, Wheelock Papers). For a larger picture of the effects of the Revolution on Native peoples, see Colin Calloway, *The American Revolution in Indian Country: Crisis and Diversity in Native American Communities* (New York, 1995).

11. See, for example, Homi Bhabha, "Signs Taken for Wonders: Questions of Ambivalence and Authority under a Tree outside Delhi, May 1817," in *"Race," Writing, and Difference*, ed. Henry Louis Gates Jr. (Chicago, 1985), pp. 163–84, and Tzvetan Todorov, *The Conquest of America*, trans. Richard Howard (New York, 1984). In the New England context specifically, examples of studies of collision and conversion include William S. Simmons, "The Great Awakening and Indian Conversion in Southern New England," in *Papers of the Tenth Algonquian Conference*, ed. William Cowan (Ottawa, 1979); Elise M. Brenner, "To Pray or to Be Prey, That Is the Question: Strategies for Cultural Autonomy of Massachusetts Praying Town Indians," *Ethnohistory* 27, no. 2 (1980): 135–52; and Harold W. Van Lonkhuyzen, "A Reappraisal of the Praying Indians: Acculturation, Conversion, and Identity at Natick, Massachusetts, 1646–1730," *New England Quarterly* 63, no. 3 (1990): 396–427. For treatments of colonialism and Christianity more concerned with ongoing process, see (in various contexts) Jean Comaroff and John Comaroff, *Of Revelation and Revolution: Christianity, Colonialism, and Consciousness in South Africa* (Chicago, 1991); James Axtell, *The Invasion Within: The Contest of Cultures in Colonial North America* (New York, 1985); Ake Hultkrantz, *Belief and Worship in Native North America* (Syracuse, 1981); William K. Powers, "When Black Elk Speaks, Everybody Listens," in *Religion in Native North America*, ed. Christopher Vecsey (Moscow, Idaho, 1990), pp. 136–51. As more historians research eighteenth- and nineteenth-century Native American history, models of the relationship between change and continuity will necessarily become more important than "first-encounter" models; see, for example, Daniel Mandell, " 'To Live More Like My Christian English Neighbors': Natick Indians in the Eighteenth Century," *William and Mary Quarterly*, 3d ser., 46, no. 4 (1991): 332–79.

church (like most of their white neighbors), but conflicts at Mohegan were often played out between Christians. The Mohegan leaders of opposite camps in the ongoing land dispute known as the "Mason case" were Ben Uncas and Samson Occom. Occom, a Christian "separate" preacher, was calling for the return of lands lost to the Mohegans, whereas the sachem Ben Uncas, a member of the Montville Congregational Church, sided with the government of Connecticut. The political disputes overlapped with the intra-Christian ones. In 1765 Uncas charged Occom with plotting a bloody rebellion should the Mason case fail, complaining that Occom "incourage[d] exorting . . . after his sermon" in a Mohegan home and drew Mohegans away from the sermons of Reverend David Jewett.[12]

Johnson's diary from 1771 and 1772 contains little evidence of overtly political activity, but it does confirm that a group of Mohegan Christians were worshiping in Mohegan homes as diligently as they did at church. For example, Johnson reports that they "met again at one Sarah Wayoiges at the Desire of her Daughter Sarah, who lie at the Poin of Death, and had a very agreable meting." The diary also shows prayer meetings as an occasion for socializing between local native Christians (Mohegan, Tunxis, Pequot, Montauk, Narraganset, Niantic)—ties that were the foundation for the intertribal Brotherton alliance Johnson soon worked to foster. "We spent the Evening in Singing," Johnson wrote on November 14, 1771, during a visit from some Montauk and Pequot friends; "David Fowler of Long Island was the Chief, and Some of the young women belonging to Stonington also." Sometimes the Mohegans did the traveling: "This morning I went over to meeting at Groton," he notes on November 24, "with my Uncle, aunt, Imanuel, Hannah, Olive, and an Old woman. We catchd a Rabbit, after we had Crossed the River." At the home prayer meetings, authority was not vested in one individual but

12. According to David Conroy, "In 'Times' Turned 'Upside Down': Race and Gender Relations in Mohegan, 1760–1860," paper presented at Sturbridge Village, Massachusetts, Spring 1995, pp. 8–9, Mohegans who farmed, worshiped at the church, and had some degree of literacy are better documented than those who moved from place to place and never attended church or school. I do not mean to underestimate the number of Mohegans who refused involvement in the church, but I do wish to make clear that the conflicts at Mohegan were not simply or primarily "traditional vs. Christian" conflicts as might be assumed. As opposites, both terms are far too simple to describe the Mohegan situation. For a full discussion of the various non-Mohegan interests involved in Mohegan land controversies, see Conroy, "The Defense of Indian Land Rights: William Bollan and the Mohegan Case in 1743," *Proceedings of the American Antiquarian Society* 103, pt. 2 (1994): 395–424. On the Jewett / Ben Uncas / Occom dispute, see Sarah Mohomett deposition, March 8, 1765, and Ben Uncas to General Court of Connecticut, May 18, 1765, William Samuel Johnson Papers; Wheelock to David Jewett, January 29, 1765, Wheelock Papers; Robert Clelland to Thomas Fitch, December 24, 1764, in "The Fitch Papers: Correspondence and Documents during Thomas Fitch's Governorship of the Colony of Connecticut, 1754–1766, Vol. II, January 1759–May 1766," *Collections of the Connecticut Historical Society* 18 (1920): 313–15.

shared; thus on one occasion "Mr. Occom preach't, Sampson Pray'd, John Exhorted, and Sinners heard." Occasionally Johnson mentions the presence of white people, but usually the worshipers were Native people. The meetings may have even been held in the Mohegan-Pequot language. "This Evening had a meeting here," he writes on November 13, 1771. "Henry Spoke first concerning the goodness of God in Sending his son in to the world for us Sinners, more Especially Gods goodness in makeing himself known to us poor Indians, that now we may hear of Jesus Christ in our own Language, and therefore there can be no Excuse for those that Remain Impenitent."[13]

I noted earlier the dramatic importance Johnson gave in his autobiographical sketch to his return to Mohegan. In contrast to his emphasis on this homecoming and also to the thickness of his diary descriptions of prayers and religious meetings, Johnson's depiction in the diary of his conversion to Christ, about a month after he returned to Mohegan, is decidedly unresounding; he notes almost in passing that after a day alone boiling pumpkin for the fatting hogs, "This night I began to call upon the Name of the Lord." We know from his other writing that this conversion was extremely important to Johnson, and certainly other diary entries elaborate his religious struggle, but I take his underplayed initial statement as evidence that Johnson thought of his conversion more as the consequence than the culmination of his return to Mohegan. Conversion was, however momentous, a secondary event. After all those years of catechism at Wheelock's school, Johnson could not be born again until he was home again. His personal faith was a part of a collective faith, and it was supported and recognized on December 2 when, as he reported, "This Evening was desired to pray by my Uncle, and I took it as a great favour."[14]

How do we reconcile the diary's representation of religion as intensely social with the common claim that the evangelical Christianity of the Great Awakening depended on "the notion of the solitary believer standing naked before an all-powerful, all-knowing God" and insisted that "family and community meant little because the sovereign God tried and tested each sinner"?[15] Indeed, Johnson emphasizes solitary striving in the many diary entries in which he faces the depravity and darkness of his soul. But even there we find hints of community resonance. The building and falling cadences of his series of questions and pleadings to his soul are the cadences of spoken prayer, of "groanings that Can not be let-

13. The undated citations are from Johnson diary, Dartmouth College, November 17, 1771, and January 19, 1772. This diary begins in October 1771 and ends in March 1772.

14. Johnson diary, November 13, 1771, and December 2, 1771.

15. James P. Ronda, "Reverend Samuel Kirkland and the Oneida Indians," in *The Oneida Indian Experience*, ed. Jack Campisi and Laurence M. Hauptman (Syracuse, 1988), p. 25.

tered." When Johnson admonishes his soul—"Hast thou chose the Pleasures of Time, and Sence, Before the Glories of another world? Examine
yourself of these Matters and know thou the State of your Condition"—
he is practicing for a more public exhortation. One passage in the second
diary ends with Johnson's signature, as if he were writing a letter: "I am
as Ussual, the Mohegan Indian, now keeping a School among the Indians
at farmington. in good health. & Endeavouring to use it for the good of
my fellow Indians, &c. &c. &c."[16] On another occasion, Johnson addresses
an outside reader directly as he describes a dream:

> What think you, who ever, here after may peruse these Lines—I am Joseph
> Johnson who do you think was the Subject of my Meditation—or the
> Object on whom my Soul Delighted—or what impression think you, was
> left upon my heart? I felt love glow in an ardent manner in my heart. To
> whome do you think? Methinks one might guise I awoke in some Uncom-
> mon Surprize. So I did—no sonner [sic] I awoke but got directly up—and
> Dressed me and followed the Blessed Lamb out, and there I worshiped
> him. It was Jesus Christ, who was the subject of My first Meditation, and
> the only Object of my Love, & in whom my Soul truly Delighted.

This direct address ("What think you, who ever, here after may peruse
these Lines") is rather startling. Excerpts of Johnson's first diary (in addition to the entire first diary) found among Eleazar Wheelock's papers suggest that Johnson may have shared his daily records with his mentor; perhaps, then, he anticipates here a very particular audience. But whichever
audience was expected—a stranger, a colleague, a future congregation, or
a future self—Johnson's private writing always had some kind of public
manifestation, imagined or applied.[17]

A few months after filling the first diary notebook, Johnson left Mohegan for Farmington, as "a child in the knowledge of Jesus my Lord, and a
babe in Understanding," being "but one year, and three months old properly." "My friend," he wrote in a sort of public declaration, "you Cant

16. Johnson diary, December 1, 1771, November 19, 1771, December 3, 1772, and December 28, 1772. The second diary, November 1772 to February 1773, is at the New York Public
Library.

17. The diary excerpt in the Wheelock Papers is dated January 2, 1772. Diaries in the eighteenth century were generally not considered private, and missionaries were often required
to keep them to document their work. Samuel Kirkland, a white student of Wheelock's with
whom Johnson spent two years teaching at Oneida, recalled in his later years that "review-
ing, correcting, and transcribing these documents [his diary] . . . is certainly an irksome &
disagreeable task. . . . Yet I am conscious it is a part of my *duty*" (*The Journals of Samuel Kirkland*, ed. Walter Pilkington [Clinton, New York, 1980], p. 43). The style and content of Johnson's diaries (for example, his account of a romance in Newport) suggest they served purposes other than duty, but certainly one cannot assume he did not expect others to read
them.

expect that in such a short time, I have arrived to manhood. No. . . . Neither do I Speak, when I have a Call, with a vain Conceit of being Endowed with a Superiour Understanding in any thing. No. Neither have I any worldy gain in view. No. But I am labouring for a Crown of Righteousness, which was laid up for Saint Paul."[18] Johnson was apparently bound for upstate New York, where he had worked as a teacher a few years earlier. But as he records in his diary, Providence intervened on the road just past Hartford in the form of three men, reminiscent of a parable or *Pilgrim's Progress*, offering him a chance to take a leadership role among the Native people at Farmington:

> I went 3 Miles. There I was much at a stand whether to call at Farmington or no, as my design was to go to the Mohawk Country. There I Stood at a Stand some time. At last . . . Came 3 men. I enquired of them, whether it was much out of the way, to go by Farmington, to go at Canaan, through Norfolk. They told me, that now it was the nighest way I could go from here. So I concluded to go by Farmington, the more because I was desired by the Revd Samson Occom. . . . This Evening Several Indians assembled themselves together at the house of Thomas Occurrum. I read the Sermon, which Mr Occom Preacht, at the Execution of Moses Paul; they heard with much Solmnity, after that we Sang, after that I spoke little of the goodness of God to all his Creatures, to us in a Perticular manner. Than I Acquainted them of a Proposal, which Mr Occom proposed Concerning my keeping a School amongst them if the School was void of a Teacher. They all rejoiced, to think of the Proposal. They Continued asking me if I could Content myself with them, so after we had Prayed; we Concluded the ensueing Day to go [to] their overseer, to get his Approbation and to Confirm all.[19]

All of a sudden, Johnson has become not a mere apprentice but also a schoolteacher, preacher, and prayer leader in his own right. His appointment was initiated by Occom, a Native preacher, and the Farmington Indian Christians themselves; when Johnson was put through his paces by Timothy Pitkin the following day, "some of the headmen of the Indian tribe was present"—to oversee the overseer, as it were.[20]

At Farmington, the private prayers Johnson had recorded in his diary at Mohegan expanded into public sermons; the diary ceases to be concerned primarily with inward turmoil, as Johnson, at the tender age of twenty-one, stands as a man of some "Considerable Influence in this Place":

18. Johnson to All Enquiring Friends, 1772 or 1773, Wheelock Papers.
19. Johnson diary, November 18, 1772.
20. Ibid., November 19, 1772. The "Farmington Indians," as they were called by this time, included people of Tunxis, Quinnipiac, and Mattabeeset or Wangunck descent (Murray, *To Do Good to My Indian Brethren*, pp. 32–33).

About dusk one of the chiefs of this town, and one of the young men, brought a Stragling man to me, and desired me to Examine him. I thought myself not Capable, not knowing the Customs of People Enough. . . . But I did my uttermost Endeavour that he should not be abused, as it seemed to me that all there design, was to make a sport of him. But I remembered Joseph & his brethren, how Joseph Said, for I fear God, do this. And I remembered Our Saviour, when he was brought before Pilate, he answered not a word. My heart was arous'd with Compassion towards the Pitifull Object, and as I had Considerable Influence in this Place I endeavour'd to use it, for his safety. And after we had Examined him, at the school house, alone, he was led to another place, whire another of the chiefs dwelt. There I Spoke boldly, on his behalf, and desired them to require no further Inteligence from him, and use him as becoming rational Creatures or Christians. For my part I must be gone, So[?] I went out, & they Said they would not abuse him, and would harken to all my advice, & words.[21]

Here Johnson is learning to speak "boldly" on public matters, emulating the mercy of his Old Testament namesake, and reminding himself of the silence of Jesus before Pilate. In his diary he tells the story of the "stragling man" as a parable, and his own dramatic exit—"For my part I must be gone"—is reminiscent of Jesus going out to pray at Gethsemane. Like Jesus, Johnson tests his followers' faith by leaving them to make their own decision. The story is a multivalent allegory: both Johnson and the stranger represent Jesus under judgment, and Johnson plays the multiple roles of Old Testament Joseph, Jesus, and Pilate.

It is in the context of this kind of incident in the diaries that I interpret Johnson's letters to white political and church officials as "speaking boldly" on behalf of his people, even as they are thick with humility or contempt. In his letters, Johnson's attitude to his non-Christian ancestors or fellow Native people is often condescending or disrespectful. Yet this contempt is elaborately rhetorical and may not represent his own feelings so much as those expected of him. For as a Christian Johnson was expected to be humble before God, and as a laborer in God's vineyard he was expected to be humble toward his church superiors, but as an *Indian* Johnson was expected to be humble before white people. He delivers meticulously on all counts; most of his letters had particular ends in view, usually pecuniary, and their humility is highly ritualized. For example, he begins a letter to Governor Trumbull of Connecticut with a lengthy diatribe against sinning Indians:

I confess, that but little respect belongs to an Indian. I am an Indian. I am of a Nation little respected in these days, and for good reason. My forefa-

21. Ibid., December 2, 1772.

thers, the Natives of this land, brought this disrespect upon themselves & theirs. When your forefathers intreated them as brothers, and recieved [sic] them into their friendship, and in a brotherly manner declared unto them the mind and will of God, they paid no regard to your Worthy Ancestors, nor to their words, but walked, every one according to the Imagination of their own wicked & unchristianized hearts; and lived in Intemperance, Excess, rioting, and other desolate Practices.

The passage continues in this vein. By the end of the letter, however, Johnson is agitating for higher wages, having observed that white teachers are being paid much more than is he. He returns to the earlier theme, but now only to qualify and undermine it:

I did Acknowledge, & do Acknowledge again, that a very little respects belongs to an Indian. But must men [have?] so much respect of Persons, in so small trifles, may not every one that tryeth to do good, and be serviceable to his fellow Creatures, be Suitably Encouraged whether English, or Indian? Suffer me to ask your Honour, in a humble Manner, a Question more. If an Indian is Capable, is faithfull, & is Serviceable as and English man in the bussiness, and answers the End as well? Why [is it not] reasonable that an Indian Should meet with the same Encouragement? And be made Equal Shearer of the bounty with the English man. Since they are both labouring in one Noble Cause, and Since it was given freely for the good, of the poor Indian Natives in Perticular.[22]

It is clear from this letter that self-abasement was one of Johnson's most important *skills*, a skill of subterfuge that looks like subservience but acts like its opposite. When Johnson abruptly interrupts these questions to plead that Trumbull "forgive my boldness, & familiarity, I *desire* to keep in Remembrance that I am an Indian, & I *desire* to be Submissive before your Honour" (emphasis added), his frustration is evident even as he apologizes. Johnson implicitly equates remembering that he is an Indian with being submissive, but the "&" between the phrases also leaves potential for an opposite interpretation; it was legitimately difficult for Johnson to be humble and an Indian at the same time, when he saw the unfairness being dealt him because of his race. In another double-voiced example of the rhetoric of humility, he begins a letter to Wheelock by insisting that he is "very thankfull in very deed" and promising that "a law of Gratitude is wrote as it were upon the table of my Once Savage heart"; he then refers to this section of the letter as "this my Indian introduction"—a prefabricated unit to be inserted as needed.[23]

22. Johnson to Trumbull, draft, early summer 1773, Occom Papers, Connecticut Historical Society, Hartford. I have not located a recipient's copy of this letter.

23. Johnson to Wheelock, August 30, 1773, Wheelock Papers. Melissa Fawcett, Tribal Historian of the Mohegans and a central participant in their recent successful bid for federal recognition, was amused at the similarity between the tone of Johnson's letter to Trumbull

The intensity of Johnson's Christian rhetoric of self-abasement and earthly misery also becomes less striking and disturbing in the context of religious doctrine of the time. The Puritan-derived Protestant theology of eighteenth-century New England required *all* Christians to be humble before God. Many religious diaries of white Puritan and Great Awakening preachers demonstrate an intense form of self-disgust. An exaggerated but widely published and admired case of self-loathing was that of David Brainerd (1718–47). Brainerd dwelt daily on his "great vileness" and "unspeakable unworthiness"; on the occasion of his examination for the post of missionary to the Indians, he recorded that "I thought myself the worst wretch that ever lived: it hurt me, and pained my very heart, that anybody should show me any respect." Compared with the tortured Brainerd, Johnson appears relatively calm and confident. Furthermore, although Johnson wrestled with his conscience at length, we never hear from him protests such as Brainerd's: "Of late, I have thought much of having the kingdom of Christ advanced in the world; but now I saw I had enough to do within myself." Johnson seems never to have had time for such concentrated introspection: he followed the "separate" practice of preaching as soon as he received the call. As an Indian, he was under constant pressure from various groups of Indian Christians to preach and instruct; he became involved in the Brotherton project early in his short life as a preacher; and his poverty prevented him from ever retreating to studious piety.[24]

In examining Johnson's exertions on behalf of the Mohegans and other New England Indians, we need not conclude he operated against the terms of his Christianity.[25] As he did when defending the "Stragling man"

and the strategy of her own correspondence with the Connecticut governor of her own day (Fawcett to the author, April 1994). For a more elaborate analysis of the rhetorical strategies of a Montauk student of Wheelock's, whose humility is also ritualized, see Murray, " 'Pray Sir, Consider a Little': Rituals of Subordination and Strategies of Resistance in the Letters of Hezekiah Calvin and David Fowler to Eleazar Wheelock, 1764–1768," *Studies in American Indian Literature* 4, nos. 2–3 (1992): 48–74.

24. Jonathan Edwards, *The Life of David Brainerd*, ed. Norman Pettit (New Haven, 1985), pp. 189, 188, 203. Johnson once asked Wheelock to assist him in private study: "In order that I might be rendered more usefull to the world it is necessary, that I should employ the ensuing winter to the Steady Study of divine Truth," he wrote, "and in order for me to devote myself to a steady Study, it is very necessary that I should have help from some quarter" (Johnson to Wheelock, October 17, 1774, Wheelock Papers). But even this attempt—which met with no success—seems to be as concerned with effects on others as it is with personal salvation.

25. No doubt some Native people harnessed Christian rhetoric selectively for purely pragmatic reasons. Van Lonkhuyzen argues, for example, that John Eliot's first convert, Waban, was motivated largely by a desire to learn various English craft skills and to enhance his personal power ("Reappraisal of the Praying Indians," pp. 399, 402). This may have been the case; however, Van Lonkhuyzen has a difficult time accounting for the conversion of the rest of the tribe, which suggests, I think, a common academic discomfort with nonsuperficial, socially reinforced spiritual belief.

in Farmington, Johnson's letters often invoked the Bible to give weight to his own actions. The middle section of the letter to Governor Trumbull already discussed is a particularly potent example:

> Most Noble Governor, when I was admited into thy Presence, and stood before thee my Mind turned upon Nehemiah of old, who once was the kings Cup-bearer, and I considered of the time when he took up the wine, and gave it unto the king, being Sad; and I reflected upon these words of king Artaxerxes unto him, for what dost thou make request? & I remembered that Nehemiah the Son of Hachaliah, made an Ejaculatory Prayer to the great god of heaven & Earth, and found favour both from the King of Heaven, and of Artaxerxes the king. And thus O Governor was my Soul Exercised, before I sat out from home, and while I was by the way, before I arrived to the Place of your Residence, also while I stood before thee. And I humbly hope that I, the Indians, and the children which the Lord hath given them, shall likewise find favour in his gracious sight, and in the Eyes & hearts, of his Servants to whom we made our wants known in our Petition.[26]

In the Old Testament, Johnson finds a model to add dignity to his begging for money, which he needed to support his travels in setting up and peopling the new settlement of Christian Indians in New York. Although Johnson does not spell out the parallel, both he and Trumbull would have been familiar with Nehemiah, who as a servant far away from his native Jerusalem was shattered to be told by his brethren that "the remnant that are left of the captivity there in the province are in great affliction and reproach: the wall of Jerusalem also is broken down, and the gates thereof are burned with fire." In his prayers, Nehemiah acknowledges to God that "we have dealt very corruptly against thee, and have not kept the commandments, nor the statues, nor the judgments," but he asks for forgiveness nonetheless.[27] The implied comparison of Mohegan or Brotherton and Jerusalem is quite bold, as is the implied degree of assistance Johnson is asking from the governor; King Artaxerxes was extremely generous with Nehemiah, giving him letters of credit to many merchants for materials with which to rebuild the city and sending captains of the army to protect him. In most of his letters petitioning for financial assistance, including this one, Johnson asks for amounts of a few pounds. The biblical

26. Johnson to Trumbull, early summer 1773, Occom Papers.

27. Neh. 1:3, 7 (King James Version). When the King asked Nehemiah why he was sad, he was "sore afraid" and replied, "Let the king live for ever: why should not my countenance be sad, when the city, the place of my father's sepulchres, lieth waste, and the gates thereof are consumed with fire?" Like Nehemiah, Johnson prefaces his lament with praises to God and governor.

parallel, however, makes it clear to us—as it no doubt did to Trumbull—that Johnson saw his project in grand terms. His people may indeed be only a "remnant," he implicitly concedes, but they are also a "nation" like the children of Israel.

The Bible was not Johnson's only source of Christian models for action. For along with the messages about the unimportance of earthly things, tolerance of human suffering, and quiescence and passivity, the New England church supported another strain of thought. In his diary, Johnson makes frequent mention of Richard Baxter's *The Saints' Everlasting Rest*, a Puritan guide to personal salvation republished in abridged form many times through the eighteenth century. Baxter insists that entry into heaven requires continual self-examination, prayer, imagination, and learning, and his metaphor for such processes is "motion." Although this motion, as Baxter explains, is to be entirely inward, it is described in the language of physical exertion and thus can offer a call to address earthly as well as heavenly goals: "Up, and be doing; run and strive and fight and hold on, for thou hast a certain, glorious prize before thee. God will not mock thee: do not mock thyself, nor betray thy soul, by delay or dallying, and all is thine own." "I know it must be God that must change men's hearts," Baxter acknowledges, "but I know also that God worketh by means, and when he meaneth to prevail with men, he usually fitteth the means accordingly, and stirreth up men to plead with them in a prevailing way." It was perhaps on Baxter's model that Johnson set himself the task of pleading "in a prevailing way" for the spiritual and material betterment of the Native people of New England. Indeed, he almost quotes Baxter directly when he writes to Governor Trumbull that "tho I say I trust kind Providence, yet I think it my duty, not to stand Still, but to be up and be doing, and be using all Proper Means for my own good and the good of others."[28]

To be sure, some of Johnson's communications with Native audiences seem to preach quiescence. When Johnson chose Colossians 3:2 ("Set your affection on things above, not on things on the earth") as his text for a sermon in Farmington, we might reasonably assume him to be preaching complacency and acceptance of poverty. Indeed, this is the burden of his argument. But a remark at the beginning of the sermon suggests another universe of meaning. Johnson prefaces his exegesis with the promise that he has not come "to Seek your Lands, Cattle, or what ever you Call yours"; the promise implies a critique of other ministers who have used this message to steal from the Indian people or to rationalize prior theft.

---

28. Richard Baxter, *The Saints' Everlasting Rest* (1650; rpt. of Benjamin Fawcett's abridged 1758 ed., Westwood, N.J., 1962), pp. 83, 98; Johnson to Jonathan Trumbull, spring 1773, Occom Papers.

Johnson, a Native minister, may have occupied the only position from which the Tunxis people could find any meaning in the message of denying earthly gain. He was one of them, an Indian explaining the value of their suffering, not a white man trying to quiet them. Furthermore, this congregation would have known full well that Johnson himself *was* devoting immense energies to "things on the earth"—that is, to obtaining new land for the Brotherton settlement. The message of acceptance and the practice of action were for Johnson deeply interdependent rather than contradictory. It was unlikely that Native people would graciously accept the miserable conditions under which they lived, as Christians asked them to do, so he needed to change those conditions to help them become accepting Christians. Johnson's own sense of humility was in turn helpful in effecting those changes, because it gave him patience—he *expected* to be "despised, yea hated, & looked upon as an Enimy"—and because it was what white political and religious leaders wanted to hear.[29]

I have not intended in this discussion to pretend that Joseph Johnson was not constrained by his Christian beliefs or that they did not sometimes limit his goals and methods for improving his own life or the lives of his people. What I have been eager to show, rather, is that Christianity was, for Johnson and for his "brethren," a way of being Mohegan, or being Indian—whatever its burdens or benefits. It is telling in this regard that Johnson uses the word "brethren," from the lexicon of evangelical Christianity, to mean "Christian Indians" or even simply "Indians" (as in "my Brethren, the poor Natives of New England" or "I maintain a good Character both among the English and also, among my brethren"),[30] and never to mean Christians in general. Johnson's brethren were apparently all Native people: "his relations," as Native people today would say, or "his brothers," in the terminology the Oneidas taught Johnson as they offered land and friendship. Missionaries tended to assume that Indians were reprobates and outsiders until they had proved themselves ten times over, but the word "brethren" as used by Johnson carries a contrary assumption of inclusion on the grounds of race. Of course Johnson hoped that all Indians would become Christians, but he considered them his brethren in a racial sense even before they became brethren in a religious one.

---

29. Johnson sermon, August 14, 1773, Occom Papers; Johnson, Dedication to Christ, May 24, 1772, Wheelock Papers.

30. Johnson to the Citizens of New Haven, February 21, 1774, Occom Papers; Johnson to All Enquiring Friends, 1772 or 1773, Wheelock Papers. Johnson's most common use of "brethren" is in conjunction with the adjective "Indian"; while this usage might suggest that "brethren" on its own means simply "Christians" to Johnson, he never uses it alone in that sense.

III.

The bulk of my research on Joseph Johnson was undertaken during the spring of 1994, when, after years of Mohegan lobbying and gathering of documents, the continuing existence of Mohegans was officially recognized by the United States government. Christianity, community, and politics have evidently continued to interconnect at Mohegan. For example, Mohegan council meetings throughout the years of struggle for federal recognition were held in the hall of the Mohegan church. Some historians would no doubt find these latter-day events irrelevant or even dangerous to my study of an eighteenth-century Mohegan, but with caution I admit their influence and would like to present a couple of earlier-twentieth-century intersections of Christian and Mohegan identity, to add resonance to my reading of Joseph Johnson.

In the context of subsequent Mohegan history, it becomes clear that Johnson's combination of Mohegan and Christian identities did not represent a transitional phase toward total assimilation. Indeed, since 1831, when it was built under the sponsorship of a group of white and Mohegan women, the Mohegan church has been a major community focus and force for Mohegan cultural survival. In the late nineteenth century, the Mohegan Ladies' Sewing Society began to meet regularly at the church, like their ladylike white counterparts in Norwich. In 1917 the Sewing Society participated in the dedication of the "Mohegan Trail"—the newly named highway from Webster, Massachusetts, to New London, Connecticut. When the white businessmen of various Chambers of Commerce drove into Mohegan wearing "Indian" headdresses and waving brightly colored toy tomahawks, the Mohegan women served them *yokhegg*, a traditional Mohegan food. I would read the incident, even though it was undoubtedly orchestrated by non-Mohegans, against itself, as a mark of a Mohegan cultural survival in the spirit of parody, community, and continuity. Like Joseph Johnson in the pulpit, perhaps, these women of the Sewing Society made for themselves something which looked to white observers like imitation or agreement but which reserved room for "insider" meaning. The Mohegan women's self-understanding as they participated in this odd event (or their conversation as they cleaned up afterward) is amusing to contemplate.[31]

31. The dedication ceremonies are recounted in Arthur L. Peale, *Memorials and Pilgrimages in the Mohegan Country* (Norwich, Conn., 1930), pp. 27–28. See also James W. Fitch, "The Mohegan Church: A Historical Address, Delivered at the Seventy-Fifth Anniversary of the Building of the Chapel at Mohegan, Conn., November 23, 1906" (pamphlet, n.d.), Connecticut State Library, Hartford; Russell Handsman, "Resisting Those Who Would Civilize: Gender Ideologies and the Women of Mohegan Hill," paper presented at the Ninety-First Annual Meeting of the American Anthropological Association, San Francisco, 1992. The dif-

The diaries of Fidelia Fielding, sober and concerned with spirituality, speak more directly to issues that arise in Joseph Johnson's writing. Born in 1827, Fielding was the granddaughter of Martha Uncas, who, a generation younger than Johnson, nonetheless remembered childhood encounters with shamans and spirits and evidently taught her granddaughter to value Mohegan knowledge and culture. Fielding in turn passed on Mohegan beliefs, legends, and medical practices to the next generation. She grew up speaking Mohegan and kept a diary in the Mohegan language as late as 1903; the diary was translated by the white anthropologist Frank Speck, to whom she had taught the language, in the 1920s.[32]

Speck considered Fielding's mind "erratic," "superstitious," and "self-centered." The diary, however, eludes such judgments, being more measured than erratic, more prayerful than superstitious, and no more self-centered than any diary is by definition. Its first entry kaleidoscopes each moment in an unfolding December day: "This early morning the sun I can see. Nearly noon, the sun is hot. The sun is warm, nearly night, already it is night, the sun is gone." The diary is centrally a document of Fielding's relation to the natural world; in it she records the daily cycle of sunrise and sunset, within which she fishes, finds and kills "spirit" snakes, burns over her field, listens to the birds, and watches the rain. It displays various non-Christian beliefs; for example, Fielding claims that a large rock in the area was stolen by witches—Speck, in a footnote, claims it was blasted away. The explanations may concur more than Speck understands, because Fielding's witches are evidently *white*, taking advantage of the "Poor Indian" who "has not money, he has not anything because he can not steal [or] lie!"[33] Fielding's story does provide an explanation of contemporary reality. Interestingly—and perhaps like Joseph Johnson's concern about the meaning of a black spot on his aunt's hand—the witch story itself may represent a hybrid of European and indigenous folk traditions. Mohegan oral tradition was resilient, as it was passed on from generation to generation in the Mohegan language, but its resilience was partly an effect of its flexibility.[34]

ference in the gender profile of the church in the two periods deserves to be researched further.

32. Accounts of Martha Uncas's experiences with a *moigu* (shaman) and the *makiawisag* (little people) can be found in Frank G. Speck, "Notes on the Mohegan and Niantic Indians," *Anthropological Papers of the American Museum of Natural History* 3 (1909): 197, 201. Fielding's diary was published as "Native Tribes and Dialects of Connecticut: A Mohegan-Pequot Diary," ed. Speck, *Annual Report of the Bureau of American Ethnology* 43 (1925–26): 199–287. Joseph Bruchac's poetic adaptation of Fielding's diary and Speck's commentary dramatizes the vast chasm of understanding between Fielding and her white student; see Bruchac, "Mu'ndu Wi'Go: Mohegan Poems," *Blue Cloud Quarterly* 24, no. 3 (1978).

33. Speck, "Native Tribes and Dialects," pp. 224 (Speck's comments), 229, 233–47.

34. Johnson's worry is in his diary, December 22, 1771. See William S. Simmons, *Spirit of the New England Tribes: Indian History and Folklore, 1620–1984* (Hanover, 1986), and Gladys

It should not be surprising, then, that despite Fielding's strong identification as Mohegan and her use of the Mohegan language, she was also a Seventh Day Adventist and a member of the Methodist Mohegan Church.[35] As the months pass Fielding's diary shows an increasing concern with her intimate relationship with *mundu*. Speck hesitated at this Mohegan word for God in an unusual gesture of interpretive humility, deciding not to translate it, "being unable to define her concept of the deity."[36] What *mundu* meant to Fielding is also beyond my presumption to know, but I would suggest, as I did in reading Joseph Johnson's writing, that the meaning(s) may not lie so much in any one anthropological definition as in the diary's structure and in Fielding's lived days. While the longest single passage in Fielding's diary concerns God, the devil, and Jesus, many months pass before the next entry, a Mohegan rendering of the Lord's Prayer. Many months pass again before one more cluster of entries, and the diary ends as it begins, with observations about the land: "January 7.—Saturday. Rain last night. Snow half gone, can see the ground again." *Mundu* is one part of this *grounded* cycle of elements and seasons, as an earlier entry confirms: "The sun is good, rising clear. I can not find anything. Already noon, I must eat my dinner. I must say 'Thank you' [for] my food because *Mundu* gives me all things [I] have here on earth. I must be strong. I went to meeting to-day at Mohegan."[37] Fielding's *mundu* no doubt converges in many ways with the God of non-Mohegan Seventh Day Adventists or Methodists. But as in Johnson's Mohegan diary, there is a profound sense of *place* in all Fielding's writing. Given the struggles over Mohegan land tenure that began before Johnson was born and ended after Fielding died (or have perhaps not ended), we can safely assume that place for these writers was differently inflected than it would have been for their non-Native Connecticut neighbors.[38]

In reading both Fielding and Johnson, it is difficult to pin down spe-

Tantaquidgeon, "Mohegan Medicinal Practices, Weather-Lore, and Superstition," in "Native Tribes and Dialects," ed. Speck, pp. 264–75.

35. Fielding identified as Mohegan against both Pequot and white alternatives: "I am from Mohegan! I am not Pequot!" she writes. "White men think [they] know all things. Half [the things they are] saying not are so. Poor white men. Many want all this earth" ("Native Tribes and Dialects," ed. Speck, p. 247).

36. Ibid. Speck's complete sentence is admittedly less than humble in tone: "Being unable to define her concept of the deity, as if she could even do it herself, I adhere to the original name in the English translation, preferring to permit the reader to reach his own conclusion as to the content of her mind" (p. 247).

37. Ibid., pp. 237, 251. "I can not find anything" probably refers to gathering food, an activity described throughout the diary.

38. See Constance A. Crosby, "From Myth to History, or Why King Philip's Ghost Walks Abroad," in *The Recovery of Meaning: Historical Archaeology in the Eastern United States*, ed. Mark Leone and Parker Potter (Washington, D.C., 1988), esp. p. 199; Crosby claims that place became an important focus of spiritual as well as practical power as pressures from non-Native people and cultures increased.

cifically Mohegan ideas or beliefs. Johnson does not ever seem to have written in the Mohegan language, and he may have had little sense of a specifically Mohegan spiritual power; the particular version of Christianity he practiced was inflexible and intolerant of syncretism.[39] But then again this very intolerance would have required Johnson to withhold any more Mohegan thoughts from his writing. That Fielding, writing as an old woman one hundred and thirty years later, was immersed in non-Christian beliefs and the Mohegan language, draws us beyond textual analysis to wonder about the kinds of things Johnson either rejected, did not know, or did not see fit to write about. Perhaps these silences are related to gender, age, or family as much as to religion. While there is more to be learned concerning these and related issues, even the cleverest detective work is unlikely to light on a "true Mohegan tradition" lying unnoticed between the lines. I do not refer here to the problems of limited or biased documentation, problems though they remain. Rather, Fielding's diary confirms an idea I have tried to demonstrate in reading Johnson's writing: that Mohegan tradition often lies, unrecognized, before our eyes, in routine accounts of routine practices, and even in letters written according to the specifications of non-Mohegans. Like their "brethren" before and after them—in all the complexity that term implies—Joseph Johnson and Fidelia Fielding defined themselves as Mohegans partly through norms of behavior imported from Euro-American culture. Along with family ties and old stories, this daily improvisation has long been a central part of Mohegan tradition.

39. For references to non-Christian beliefs, see Johnson to Wheelock, May 2, 1768, Wheelock Papers, and Johnson diary, December 22, 1771.

War, the State, and Religious Norms in "Coromantee" Thought: The Ideology of an African American Nation

JOHN K. THORNTON

HISTORIANS OF Afro-America have often tried to link the African background of American slaves to their American behaviors. Most often this has taken the form of discussion of "African survivals" in material culture; rarely has it sought to understand the African contribution in political thought and in ideology outside of a fairly narrowly defined set of religious norms, often themselves seen as "survivals." In large measure the focus on survivals has been created by a relative ignorance on the part of Americanists about seventeenth- and eighteenth-century Africa, as well as the inability of many Africanists to provide this information. The tendency has been, for many years, to look at modern cultures in both regions through an anthropological telescope rather than a historical one.

This problem is heightened when one examines the question of political ideology, which is often colored by the issue of the role of slavery to such an extent that all other ideology is placed aside—that is, African Americans are seen as having as their sole ideology a struggle against slavery as a legal institution. It might be useful, however, to see African political ideology as having a positive rather than a negative outlook; Africans and African Americans had worldviews that included political ideals about the right and just ordering of society. The issue of slavery was only one of several matters touched on by the worldview, and perhaps was not even the most important one. Instead, Africans focused on what they thought an ideal state might be as much as what was wrong about their present state.

The issue of the ideal state, which I have examined elsewhere with regard to the Haitian Revolution, often came up in revolts or in plots, where people actually began acting on their ideas about what a good or at least a better society might be.[1] It also happens that revolts and plots are well documented, and African Americans often speak more clearly and frequently in their own voices in these events than elsewhere. While focusing on revolts and plots, however, we should imagine that the ideologies which underlie these dramatic moments were probably also present in more passive forms at all times among Africans living in the Americas. In Haiti, I examined the role of the ideology of Kongolese in making the revolution; here I will focus on another nation at a slightly different time, the Akan or "Coromantee" nation.

During the seventeenth and eighteenth centuries, the Coromantee nation obtained a fearsome reputation among the slaveholders of the Americas. Coromantees, the New World, English national name for the Akan of modern Ghana, although often stereotyped as hard and loyal workers among English-speaking slaveholders, were implicated in dozens of slave rebellions and plots. Edward Long, the Jamaican planter who published an extensive treatise on life in the West Indies in 1774, was particularly disdainful of the Coromantees, whom he suspected of being behind most mischief in his country. His anti-Coromantee feelings were heightened by his demonstration that they played the role of leaders in the 1760 slave rebellion, and he was anxious that the colony import no more Gold Coast slaves.[2]

In America, the Coromantee nation (or "country," as it was often called) was defined as people who shared a common language, today known as Twi or Akan, and this language formed the basis for membership in a loosely structured organization of conationals who socialized with and aided one another.[3] As Long and other colonists noted, the national organization also played an important role in organizing plots and rebellions, because geographic dispersion across different plantations and possession of a common language made organization on a large scale possible. Thus, the nation made an important part of the social identity of African-born slaves and sometimes even of their American-born descendants, at least in the first generation. It was one of the most important social institutions, for the process of enslavement had broken the family or larger kinship organizations as a social institution, and gender imbalances would inhibit their rapid reemergence for many slaves. As a means of

1. John Thornton, " 'I Am the Subject of the King of Congo': African Political Ideology and the Haitian Revolution," *Journal of World History* 4, no. 12 (1993): 181–214.

2. Edward Long, *The History of Jamaica*, 3 vols. (London, 1774; rpt., London, 1970), bk. 3, chap. 3, pp. 470–75. A description of his proposed bill is found on pp. 470–71.

3. For additional background, see John Thornton, "The Coromantees: An African Nation in the Americas," *Journal of Caribbean History* (forthcoming).

social organization, it allowed Africans to remain a part of a larger community that was neither restricted to a single estate nor under the control of the masters. It was at the same time a religious organization, where principles brought from Africa could inform life and worship as much as the local environment would allow.

Its dual role as social glue and religious institution made the national organization an ideal place for plotting and staging revolts, and for Coromantees, it clearly did perform that function from time to time. But it also provided a more mundane and day-to-day set of rules and activities that were always present, even if the revolts highlighted them for a few moments. Mutual aid society, burial group, and place to enjoy social entertainment: these were also functions performed by the nation in America and by the Coromantees in particular.[4]

As important as the national organization was in the Americas, however, there was no exact equivalent in Africa. The Akan-speaking people, whose society is well described in a series of seventeenth- and eighteenth-century accounts, clearly did not organize themselves by linguistically defined "tribes" or nations; indeed, they did not even have a common name for the language in Africa. The terms "Akan" and "Twi," the most common modern names for the language, are creations of the mid– to late nineteenth century. Instead, Akan speakers were found in dozens of independent states, which effectively cut the linguistic community into many pieces.[5]

But while the nation as an American institution did not have a direct African model, the ideology and organizational ideals of Coromantee nations did draw on Akan political ideology and even fairly specific modes of organization drawn from the immediate past of Akan slaves in the New World. In exploring these ideological models, we will uncover both the dynamic of political organization on the eighteenth century Gold Coast and the way in which the ideological struggles over these forms in Africa carried over into the Americas.

4. The daily functioning of the nation is revealed particularly in the inquest into the Antigua plot of 1736–37 found in Public Record Office (London; hereafter PRO), Colonial Office (hereafter CO) 9 / 10, and analyzed in Thornton, "Coromantees."

5. On modern names, see Thornton, "Coromantees." I have favored the use of Akan rather than Twi in this work because Akan is less specific to a particular dialect, whereas Twi refers primarily to the eastern dialects of this language. The best evidence for language and language nomenclature in the eighteenth century comes from travelers' accounts and a series of linguistic studies created by native speakers Jacobus Capetein and Christian Protten in the mid–eighteenth century; see Jacobus Elisa Joannes Capetein, *Vertaaling van het Onze Vader, de Twaalf Gefloofs-Artykelen, en det Tien Gebonden des Herren* (Leiden, 1744), and Christian Protten, *En nyttig Grammaticalsk Indledelse til Tvende hindintil gandske unbekiendte Sporg, Fanteisk og Acraisk* (Copenhagen, 1764). Both these catechisms are reproduced in the original languages, along with some translation and commentary, in H. M. J. Trutenau, *Christian Protten's 1764 Introduction to the Fante and Accra (Gã) Languages*, 2d ed. (London, 1971).

I.

In Africa, Akan political organization was dominated by the state. Akan states, however, were not all precisely the same, not surprising given that more than forty such political units existed in the mid–seventeenth century along the Gold Coast. Although each state differed, they did possess a sort of common political language and, more important, a common set of political disputes and problems. In particular, there was a long-lasting conflict within Akan states over the issue of the constitution: should the state be autocratic or more decentralized, should office be hereditary or achieved, and how should decisions be made?

Willem Bosman, a Dutch factor with long experience on the Gold Coast, wrote in 1704 of Gold Coast governments as being a mixture of "Republican" and "Monarchial" forms. Generally this mixture reflected the various constitutional places of the hereditary elite and those nobles who had achieved status through their merit and wealth. In describing the government of Axim, on the western end of the coast, he noted two bodies, the "Caboceros," corresponding to the hereditary elite, and the "Manceroes," or the wealthy new nobles. Axim contrasted with other states where the government was more despotic.[6]

The relations between the two bodies were often turbulent; indeed, Bosman believed that most wars were caused by this governmental impasse. Each of these social groups, in turn, possessed their own ideas of what the proper ordering of government ought to be, which gave ideological weight to their material struggle. The problems of contrasting ideological and social principles predated the slave trade and may have lain at the root of the wars that would eventually come to fuel the slave trade. That they were in some ways anterior to the slave trade both temporally and philosophically may explain how they could be transported to America and become building blocks for a Coromantee society.

Every society likely has two sets of contrasting and often contradictory norms: those which maintain stability (conservative or reactionary ones) and those which emphasize change (liberal or radical ones). In stable, peaceful societies, conservative norms tend to prevail, whereas in disturbed or changing societies, the norms of change prevail. In addition, social groups with contrasting stakes in the status quo are likely to gravitate toward norms that maintain or enhance their position.

Conservative norms came from the Akan elite. Theirs was a class of hereditary nobles that ruled most towns and states. They believed in birth-given rights and duties, forming a group known in Akan as *ohenes*. They idealized a time of stability when everyone knew their place and

---

6. William Bosman, *A New and Accurate Description of the Coast of Guinea* (London, 1705; orig. Dutch, 1704; facsimile, London, 1967), pp. 164–65.

order prevailed. In referring to the area around Accra, for example, Ludevig Rømer, a factor of the Danish West India Company who resided on the Gold Coast in the mid–eighteenth century, noted that they looked back to a Golden Age, when the Kingdom of Benin ruled the area, order and discipline prevailed, and population was exceedingly dense. There was ample food, no one needed to steal as food was provided, and there were no jewels and expensive clothes, except those provided by the emperor.[7]

Rømer's informant on these matters, an elderly nobleman named Noyte, blamed the end of this state of affairs partly on the withdrawal of Benin and partly on droughts sent as divine punishment by God.[8] What elderly nobles, whose wealth and position were guaranteed by heredity, did not emphasize was that such a Golden Age would also have been socially stable and kept most people in subordinate positions, and to that end there was a clash between an ethic of social mobility and one of stability.

While conservative norms emphasized hereditary wealth and power, change-oriented norms emphasized that a person could acquire title through the possession of wealth; wealth, in turn, was the product of hard work and especially carefully managed commerce, not simply inherited or given by the state. The ethic of social mobility was in some ways represented by the many stories of "Nannj" or Anansi, the trickster spider.[9] Other informants told Rømer of the antics of this spider, beloved today in

7. In using Akan, I pluralize according to English usage—that is, by adding s to the singular. Akan pluralizes sometimes through changing the prefix, thus the plural of *ohene* is properly *ahene*, and other times through addition of -*num* as a suffix, which would complicate exposition in this presentation. For eighteenth-century rules, see Protten, *Grammaticalsk Indledelse*, pp. 38, 40. There is some evidence that Benin rule did indeed extend into the Accra area, probably in the mid–sixteenth century, although Rømer's informants are dealing more with a mythical Golden Age than historical facts; see Robin Law, "Trade and Politics behind the Slave Coast: The Lagoon Traffic and the Rise of Lagos, 1500–1800," *Journal of African History* 24, no. 3 (1983): 320–26. Note that the language of Accra and surrounding areas was not Akan but Gã, a related but to Akan speakers unintelligible language. In the New World, however, the Gã speakers, most of whom were able to speak Akan as a second language in the eighteenth-century Gold Coast, were a part of the Coromantee nation; an Antiguan slave named Court, whose "coronation" is highlighted below, took the throne name Tackey, a Gã name, as did the leader of the 1760 Jamaica revolt. Ludevig Ferdinand Rømer, *Le Golfe de Guinée, 1700–1759: Récit de L. F. Rømer*, ed. and trans. Mette Dige-Hess (Paris, 1989), pp. 90–93.

8. Rømer, *Golfe de Guinée*, p. 93.

9. On the wealth ethic in Akan society, exemplified by the proverbs "sika sene, biribi nsen bio" (wealth surpasses everything) and "sika ne ohene" (wealth is king), see T. C. McCaskie, "Accumulation, Wealth, and Belief in Asante History: I. To the Nineteenth Century," *Africa* 53 (1983): 23–43; see also Ivor Wilks, "The Golden Stool and the Elephant Tail: An Essay on Wealth in Asante," *Research in Economic Anthropology* 2, no. 1 (1979): 1–36. Rømer gives the spider's name in its Gã form (for both forms, see Protten, *Grammaticalsk Indledelse*, p. 63 [extra sheets found attached to back of copy at National Library of Copenhagen]) as "Naninga" and its Twi form as "Annansae"; see also Trutenau, *Protten's 1764 Introduction*, p. 72 n. 3. Bosman,

Ghana, the West Indies, and South Carolina, whose primary joy was the upsetting of established rules and order. In Rømer's version of the stories, which he summarizes at some length, God had ordered Anansi to create people, whom he had spun out from his web material until he had used it almost all up. But when the people he had created failed to show gratitude, he took the rest of the material and created a little man to whom he gave his name and who served as a trickster, living "without working in the world by fooling the others."[10]

The junction of the conservative and the change-oriented conceptions of society took place in the creation of nobles, in which someone with personal wealth could acquire a title of nobility. One of the earliest descriptions of Gold Coast society, published by the traveler Pieter de Marees in 1602, described this ceremony. In a legal system in which land could not be owned to let out to tenants for profits and in which taxation was the crucial form of land revenue, ownership of slaves was a critical means of converting liquid assets into reproducing wealth. The title of nobility gave a newly wealthy person access to power and decision making, as well as legal advantages in acquiring more wealth, especially the right to buy and own slaves.[11]

Willem Bosman's eighteenth-century description of a later and more complicated set of ennobling ceremonies reveals the contrast between the norms that underlie this form of nobility and the older, hereditary norms. After detailing the ceremony, Bosman goes on to note "that in reality they are not so [noble] is plain, because no Person can Enoble himself, but must be so by Birth, or by the creation of another: In both which they are deficient; for by Birth they are only Slaves, and consequently widely distant from Nobles."[12]

Although these two contrasting routes of wealth and power, with their corresponding norms, coexisted on the Gold Coast, conditions in the late seventeenth century caused the more open, change-oriented norms to be

Description, p. 146, notes in passing that some people believed men were created by "Anansie, that is, a great Spider" but gave no further details.

10. Lawrence Levine, *Black Culture and Black Consciousness: Afro-American Folk Thought from Slavery to Freedom* (New York, 1977), p. 103. Rømer, *Golfe de Guinée*, pp. 57–58; other stories continue to p. 60.

11. Pieter de Marees, *Beschryvinge ende historische verhael vat Gout Koninckrijck van Guinea* (Amsterdam, 1602), translated by Albert van Dantzig and Adam Jones under the title *Description and Historical Account of the Gold Kingdom of Guinea* (London, 1987), pp. 85b–87a. For a more lengthy discussion of the legal structure of Africa with regard to slavery, see John Thornton, *Africa and Africans in the Making of the Atlantic World, 1400–1680* (New York, 2d ed., 1998), pp. 72–97; for more details specifically on the Gold Coast, see Ray A. Kea, *Settlements, Trade, and Politics in the Seventeenth-Century Gold Coast* (Baltimore, 1982), pp. 104–10. This social structure is described, based on careful study of many sources, in Kea, *Settlements*, pp. 101–4.

12. Bosman, *Description*, pp. 135–36, 137.

reflected in politics. Not only were those people who came to America drawn from the most disturbed and changing elements of Akan society, but the very circumstances of their enslavement and transportation also reinforced the tendency toward change-ordered norms. It was this package of norms that characterized Coromantee society and made it different from their Old World Akan society.

Commerce and war were the two elements that had the most to do with change in Akan society. Commerce, especially the Atlantic commerce, was a route that made it possible for commoners to acquire wealth and for lesser nobles to become greater ones. As a gold-producing region, the Akan world produced its share of suddenly wealthy gold strikers, and these people, in turn, hoped to turn their good fortune into reproducing wealth through the acquisition of slaves, titles, and a share in the government. The ennobling ceremonies described by Bosman provided the vehicle whereby these things could be done. At the same time, the insecurity of commercial wealth and the imperfect fit between wealth and power made for some wild social mobility (upward and downward) and a turbulent history that resulted in both the use and purchase of slaves and the export of slaves.[13]

Warfare was another feature of the period, even in the seventeenth century, before the region became a major exporter of slaves. Many wars were commercially motivated and had been from the time before the slave trade. Portuguese records from the sixteenth century onward reveal the role the Portuguese played in attempting to mediate disputes, for war interfered with the gold trade, and it was in Portugal's interest to prevent them. And when the Dutch took over Portuguese positions in the Gold Coast early in the seventeenth century, they also inherited a policy of attempting to allay frequent warfare in order to open trade routes.[14] Other

13. Kwame Daaku, *Trade and Politics on the Gold Coast, 1600–1720* (Oxford, 1972), is a classic study of the role of commerce in creating turmoil in the region.

14. There has not been a systematic study of the wars that are revealed in the fragmentary records of the Portuguese factor at Mina. See Arquivo Nacional de Torre do Tombo, Lisbon (hereafter ANTT), "Cartas Missivas," maço 2, documento 180 (2/180), 1502, and "Corpo Chronológico" (CC), parte I, maço 9, documento 60 (I/9/60), Factor and Officials of Mina to King, September 2, 1510; CC II/85/9; and Order of Fernão Correia to Factor, September 26, 1519, in *Monumenta Missionaria Africana*, ed. António Brásio, 1st ser., 15 vols. (Lisbon, 1952–88), 1:427; Gonçalo Francisco de Almeida to King, April 14, 1548, and Afonso Gonçalves Botafogo to Queen, April 18, 1557, both in *East of Mina: Afro-European Relations on the Gold Coast in the 1550s and 1560s*, ed. and trans. Avelino Teixeira da Mota and P. E. H. Hair (Madison, Wisc., 1988), pp. 64, 101 (I/101/25). This list should not be taken as exhaustive, given the very fragmentary nature of the evidence. With the archives of the first West India Company having largely been lost, there are few records for this early period of Dutch occupation, just as the Portuguese documentary record is virtually nonexistent after ca. 1540. A useful summary of wars from 1618 to 1631 can be found in the entries of the monthly news summary published in Amsterdam by Nicholas van Wassenaer, *Historisch verhael aller*

wars derived from the struggles within Akan states over power and wealth, such as the war between Okay, the ruler of Accra, and his cousin and other noblemen between 1622 and 1627, which also involved the Akan-speaking states of Sabou and Fante. Naturally, others still resulted from the political and diplomatic aims of states seeking to expand and enlarge themselves or to defend themselves against the inroads of others.[15]

The wars of the period of export slave trade do not seem much different from this cycle of wars known from the 1620s, except that many more slaves were sold to European buyers by the victors. One such war that matched the coastal state of Fetu against its interior neighbor Abrem was reported by several travelers in the 1660s. For four years, 1662–66, the war was a standoff, but at the end the Fetu army won a battle, which resulted in many prisoners, "all of whom are slaves," according to the French traveler Nicholas Villault.[16] Villault's opinion was seconded by Johann Wilhelm Müller, a German Lutheran minister who served the Danish Company in the 1660s and who also witnessed the war and contended that the sale of prisoners was responsible for the growing slave trade of the region. Only a few years later Fetu was involved in another war, which involved a complex alliance of Fetu and Wassaw against the "Accanys" (Akan) in the interior. This war had just ended when the *James*, a Royal Africa Company ship, arrived at Coromantee in 1675 and the captain learned that Fetu and Wassaw, the victors, would soon provide ample slaves, which the *James* subsequently carried to Barbados.[17]

The slaves captured in these wars might well be cycled back into the slave-consuming Akan society—war and trade had grown, and the possibilities for the newly wealthy to use slaves was increasing. At the same time, the commercial possibilities resulting from an increased demand for slaves for shipment overseas also created Akan society's wealth and con-

---

gedenckwaerdiger geschiedenissen die in Europa (Amsterdam, 1621–31), 22 Deelen (parts) foliated separately, bound in 8 vols.; see pt. 4, fols. 87–87v (December 1622); pt. 6, fols. 67–68v (December 1623); pt. 9, fols. 59–59v (May 1625); pt. 10, fols. 36v–37 (April 1626), and fols. 49v–50 (May 1626); pt. 13, fol. 24 (May 1627, retrospective back to 1622); pt. 14, fol. 53v (December 1627); and pt. 17, fols. 60–61 (June 1629).

15. Wassenaer, *Historisch verhael*, pt. 4, fol. 87–87v (December 1622); pt. 6, fol. 68 (December 1623); pt. 11, fol. 49v–50 (May 1626); pt. 13, fol. 24 (May 1627); pt. 17, fol. 61 (June 1629).

16. Nicholas Villault, *Relation des costes d'Afrique appelées Guinée* (Paris, 1669), pp. 359–61; an English translation of this source was published in London in 1670.

17. Wilhelm Müller, *Die Afrikansche auf der Guineischen Gold Cust gelegene Landschafft Fetu* (Hamburg, 1668; rpt., Graz, 1968), pp. 138, 142–43. A fully annotated translation of this work, with the original pages marked, appears in *German Sources for West African History, 1599–1669*, ed. and trans. Adam Jones (Wiesbaden, 1983), pp. 134–259."Voyage of the *James*" (ship's book), 1675–76, in *Documents Illustrative of the History of the Slave Trade*, ed. Elizabeth Donnan, 4 vols. (Washington, D.C., 1935; rpt., New York, 1965), 1:200–201.

tributed to war. As the society heated up, so did the social struggle among the free.

Bosman, describing war as he saw it at the end of the seventeenth century, noted that the division of Akan societies into the hereditary nobles with their conservative views and the more change-oriented mercantile elite was itself the cause of wars. Both groups had different views about the role of war and peace, and both were also anxious about trade and trade disputes. Consequently, the two bodies of the "republican" institutions in Gold Coast society often disagreed about when and how to go to war, sometimes even fighting among themselves.

There were multiple possibilities for disgruntled members of either body to raise mercenary forces or to arm their slaves and use them against the state; alternatively, sometimes participants would actually hire whole states to engage in the war on their side, making gold payments for the soldiers. These complications led to long and often very complex wars of which the Komenda War of the 1690s served Bosman as an excellent example. These wars involved not only various African states and mercenary groups but also European factors, who had raised their own armies to protect the gold awaiting shipment and were often hired as mercenaries, a practice dating back to the early seventeenth century at least. Different European nations frequently served on opposite sides in the conflicts, while hired African states did the same, sometimes switching their alliances, as occurred several times in the Komenda War. A similar war involving private merchants with armed slaves, participants from various states, and the hiring of allies took place on the other end of the Gold Coast in 1711–12.[18]

This pattern of wars and their connections to commercial wealth suggests that change-oriented norms were becoming more common on the Gold Coast. That these wars often pitted relatively small states against each other was complicated by the fact that these small states were sometimes unable to maintain public order such that banditry became quite

18. This practice also predated the development of the export slave trade; for example, in 1614, Dutch soldiers helped the king of Accra against his enemy the king of Atty. See Samuel Brun, *Schiffarten* (Basel, 1624; modern ed., Amsterdam, 1913), English translation in *German Sources*, ed. Jones, pp. 46–96 (with original 1624 pagination marked), esp. p. 36; Wassenaer, *Historisch verhael*, pt. 4, fol. 87 (December 1623), where the Dutch sent soldiers to help Coromantijn, Achera, and Commendo against "the Moorish kings who lay inland." Bosman, *Description*, pp. 164–80, and his account to the West India Company, Elmina Council minutes, March 10, 1700, in *The Dutch and the Guinea Coast, 1674–1742: Selected Documents from the General State Archives in the Hague*, ed. and trans. Albert van Dantzig (Accra, Ghana, 1978), pp. 60–61; the testimony of Roharts, at the same time, reveals the practice of hiring states to fight, which led to frictions over payments, pp. 61–62. Minutes of Elmina Council Meeting, February 15, 1712, in *Dutch and the Guinea Coast*, ed. and trans. Dantzig, p. 164.

widespread. Jan Kango, for example, a lesser *caboceer* (noble) of the state of Adom undertook a long career of banditry in the early eighteenth century, soon growing so powerful that he threatened neighboring states, and had to be brought to heel by a powerful army.[19] Sometimes even powerful states, such as Asante, could not fully control their armies, for in 1715 groups of deserters from that army and other soldiers from Wassa, a nearby state, were encamped in the small district of Ouwien, plundering it and passersby. They were led by Asante generals, but without the consent of the ruler of Asante. Bandits, professional soldiers, and mercenaries could, by service and acquisition of wealth, gradually acquire title and security or even found their own states, especially in the lands east of Accra, between the Gold and Slave Coasts.[20]

Because each state was small, internal order was difficult to maintain and, given the few soldiers in their professional armies, many rulers hired mercenaries to fight these wars. Rebels and rivals, lacking access to the professional armies, also threw their lot in with bandits and mercenaries. Mercenaries, in turn, fueled and were drawn from a floating band of soldiers and highway robbers who contributed to a certain level of lawlessness. One Dutch report noted that one war of about 1708 might be the end of the state of robbery and plundering that existed in the area behind the coast, but only if Asante won the war and established order. War and disorder posed problems that predated the late-seventeenth-century export of slaves; a Dutch report of 1627 notes the activities of Corakijn, "between Acanien [the nucleus of the future state of Asante] and the sea as an Alarbo or robber."[21] Collectively, however, these provided routes to social mobility, while resulting in an increasing confusion between the commercial and military routes to success.

The imperial states, such as Asante, that emerged in the late seventeenth century were able to impose their authority by mobilizing larger and more loyal military forces, which in turn made a new impact on the general population, especially those now vulnerable to enslavement and export. Being somewhat larger, the inland states drew on their general population rather than on professional soldiers to create their armies.

19. For an important study of banditry, see Ray A. Kea, " 'I Am Here to Plunder on the Great Road': Bandits and Banditry in the Pre-Nineteenth-Century Gold Coast," in *Banditry, Rebellion, and Social Protest in Africa*, ed. Donald Crummey (London, 1986), pp. 109–32. Protest by Cuep and Schoonwitz on behalf of General Hendrik Lamey from Prussia, Minutes of Council, Elmina, September 16, 1707, in *Dutch and the Guinea Coast*, ed. Dantzig, p. 132.

20. Elmina Journal, October 25, 1715, in *Dutch and the Guinea Coast*, ed. Dantzig, p. 186; Kea, *Settlements*, pp. 130–33, 134–37; and Robin Law, *The Slave Coast of West Africa, 1550–1750: The Impact of the Atlantic Slave Trade on an African Society* (New York, 1991), pp. 225–59.

21. Wassenaer, *Historisch verhael*, pt. 14, fol. 53v (December 1627). See also Kea, *Settlements*, pp. 134–35; Letters and Papers from the Gold Coast, Englegraff Robberts to X, August 15, 1712, in *Dutch and the Guinea Coast*, ed. Dantzig, p. 168.

They changed tactics to allow large groups of soldiers with relatively few military skills in hand-to-hand fighting to take on the smaller professional armies of the area whose hallmark had been virtuosity in close fighting with swords and lances. At the same time, they drew large numbers of people into military service through mass levies, in this way revolutionizing warfare. They also gave new opportunities for the most able of the fighters to achieve new status, which in turn promoted a change-oriented set of norms in the armies.[22]

The confusion of status caused by mass mobilization, mercantile wealth, and military advancement contributed to the prevalence of change-oriented norms and had important religious implications as well as social and political ones. Akan religion, like its politics, possessed both change-oriented and conservative norms. Conservative ethical principles were embodied in the regional shrines and the *obosom* (spirit of a god or ancestor) who was incorporated in them, of which Rømer provided a detailed description as they existed in the 1740s.[23] These deities guarded lasting principles, promoted communal solidarity, and frowned on ambition and disruption.

By contrast, change-oriented principles were found in the personal *sumang*. These were lesser spirits who were able to work on behalf of an individual or a small group. Some were inherited from a family and looked over its interests; others could actually be purchased in the marketplace and would serve whoever paid the price. Obtaining powerful sumang was roughly the equivalent in the religious sphere as acquiring a title in the political sphere. Thus, competitors often waged supernatural war with each other, each using their own personal charms or hereditary sumang; should these prove too weak, they might also purchase sumang from a priest, who could capture the power of various spirits in charms.[24]

In the change-oriented environment of the late seventeenth and eigh-

---

22. Kea, *Settlements*, pp. 154–68. For biographies of socially mobile generals in Asante, see Ivor Wilks, "What Manner of Persons Were These? Generals of the Konti of Kumase," in Wilks, *Forests of Gold: Essays on the Akan and the Kingdom of Asante* (Athens, Ohio, 1993), pp. 241–58.

23. There have been many recent studies of Akan religion from a variety of perspectives. A more recent attempt to define it historically is found in T. C. McCaskie, *State and Society in Pre-Colonial Asante* (Cambridge, 1995), pp. 102–44. McCaskie has built his interpretation from his own fieldwork and careful reading of the original interviews and papers of R. S. Rattray (from the 1920s) and M. Fortes (from the 1940s), as well as research in older, mostly nineteenth-century, accounts by travelers and missionaries. McCaskie sees the Asante state, especially in the nineteenth century, as playing an important role in determining religious norms, but this was less likely to be true in the earlier periods and in areas outside of or on the periphery of Asante; Rømer, *Golfe de Guinée*, pp. 61–65. See also Müller, *Afrikansche auf der Guineischen Gold Cust*, pp. 47–48.

24. Müller, *Afrikansche auf der Guineischen Gold Cust*, pp. 55–56.

teenth centuries, there was a tendency to focus on personal sources of religious authority, and this emphasis on the personal led to a religious background that favored personal Other Worldly beings. Within the concept of change-ordered religion, however, some ethical principles still transcended either the type of spiritual force that one could employ or the purposes to which it was put. However different these two spiritual forces were, neither one was considered primarily good or primarily evil. The best linguists of the eighteenth century, Jacob Capetein and Christian Protten, chose both terms to translate the "spirit" of the Holy Spirit in their Christian catechisms: Capetein used a form of "sumang," while Protten chose a form of "obosum." This suggests that the distinction between good spirits and evil spirits was lacking. Indeed, this was more or less explicitly stated by the Danish factor Johannes Rask, resident on the Gold Coast from 1709 to 1713, who noted that the local people did not distinguish between a good and an evil god.[25]

Whether this use of Other Worldly, change-oriented beings was ethical or evil (a form of witchcraft) depended on the motivations of the person making use of the being. If, on the one hand, the motive was ethical, protecting a family and forwarding its business, it was legitimate. But when, on the other, spiritual forces were invoked to harm enemies, gain revenge, or win profits at others' expense, they would be considered as witchcraft.[26]

In the generally disturbed and confused conditions on the Gold Coast of the late seventeenth and eighteenth centuries, one would expect witchcraft to be rampant and an atmosphere of distrust to prevail. Part of this insecurity was reflected in the prevalence of oaths in Akan society, much as feudal Europe made elaborate and religiously sanctioned oaths to seek some security in the confused interpersonal relationships of that period.

25. Capetein, *Vertaaling van het Onze Vader*, pp. 8 (Akan) / 9 (Dutch), in the Apostle's Creed, "Die van den goeden Geest ontfangen" (who was made [man] by the Holy [literally good] Spirit) is "Endï Sanmanp, om, onisén," and pp. 13 (Akan) / 14 (Dutch), "Ik geloove in den goeden Geest" (I believe in the Holy Spirit) is "Mivìa Sanmanp," hence employing "sumang" (that is, "good sumang," but note that the Dutch is literally "good spirit") are used. Protten, *Grammaticalsk Indledelse*, p. 28, gives "ofri ninzen vo Abossum kroakroa Panninino nhu na akkatamaziaba Maria" for "through the power of the Holy Spirit was incarnate from the Virgin Mary" (no Danish translation given) and "Mi dang Avvsum kroa kroa paninino" for "I believe in the Holy Spirit," with "obosum" as the form, here literally "Obosum in the form of a great or elder soul." Johannes Rask, *En kort og sandferdig Rejse-Beskrivelse til og fra Guinea* (Tronheim, 1754); the modern edition and Norwegian translation is by Jotein Ovrelid, *Ferd til og fra Guinea, 1708–1713* (Oslo, 1969), p. 59.

26. Müller, *Afrikansche auf der Guineischen Gold Cust*, pp. 50–52, 54, 55–56. Like many priests, Müller equated virtually all forms of African religiosity with witchcraft, arguing that the revelations of African Other Worldly beings were actually manifestations of the Devil and hence a form of witchcraft. For discussion of nineteenth- and twentieth-century concepts of witchcraft in the Akan world, especially its political dimensions, see McCaskie, *State and Society*, pp. 133–35, and T. C. McCaskie, "Anti-Witchcraft Cults in Asante: An Essay in the Social History of an African People," *History in Africa* 8 (1981): 125–54.

Eating fetish and *drinking fetish,* the terms widely used for taking an oath and reasonably accurate translations of *Didi Summän* (*didi sumang*) or *anum summän* (*nom sumang*) were so prominent that European treaties usually included this sort of oath in their promulgation. A typical form was to call on the Other Worldly being in whose name the oath was taken to kill the person taking the oath if he violated it. "When they drink the *Oath-Draught*," wrote Bosman of oathing in his day, " 'tis usually accompanied with an Imprecation, *that the Fetiche* may kill them if they do not perform the Contents of their Obligation." Bosman also noted, however, that such oaths were frequently broken despite their religious sanction.[27]

Warfare and banditry, mercantile wealth, and service in the larger imperial armies were the outcome of conflicting interests and norms, creating situations in which change-oriented norms would prevail in Gold Coast society. They also provided the basis for the slave trade and, in a very real way, contributed to the immediate background of the history of the peopling of the Americas.

II.

The Coromantee nation in the Americas was created out of this social and religious background. Coming as they did mostly from commoner backgrounds, the slaves' ethical and political concepts tended to be change-oriented, even if they had not become slaves and been exported. The conditions of slavery surely helped to reinforce the idea of a change-oriented society.

The religion of the New World Coromantees focused on the norms of flexibility and change. From at least the late seventeenth century, this religion was called *obeah*.[28] more recent scholars have derived this term from the Akan word for witchcraft, *obayi*, which was not attested before the nineteenth century but was likely to have been in use earlier.[29] The priests in the New World were thus obeah men, just as priests in the Old World were either obosom men (*obossum-fu*, according to Müller, meant *obossum* man) or sumang men (*summan-fu*).[30]

27. Bosman, *Description*, p. 149. Müller, *Afrikansche auf der Guineischen Gold Cust*, vocabulary, pp. 83–89, esp. p. 88; see also many archival examples of oaths in Jones, *German Sources*, pp. 176 n. 154, 273. On the history of the concept of fetishism in Africa, see William Pietz, "The Problem of the Fetish, I," *Res* 9 (Spring 1985): 5–17.

28. Its earliest attestation is in PRO, CO 9/10, fol. 89, as "obi," in "Quarcoo, an old Obi man and Physitien." The witness noted he was "afraid of this Obey man, he is a bloody fellow."

29. It can be found in Johann Gottlieb Christaller, *Dictionary of the Asante and Fante Language called Tschi* (Basel, 1881; rev. ed., 1933), making an attestation in the early 1870s.

30. Müller, *Afrikansche auf der Guineischen Gold Cust*, pp. 74–75.

Although Christian commentators in the New World emphasized their evil practices, the priests were perhaps known by Coromantees as witches because they focused more on personal and change-oriented norms than on conservative and regionally oriented norms. In fact, in more recent Akan thought, it is possible to distinguish between good and bad witchcraft, using motives and intentions as well as causing injury as a guide.[31] Such an emphasis would be natural in a new environment, where the obosoms who were territorially based, ancient, and conservative had been left in Africa, and time would have to wait for the discovery of new obosoms in America, if they existed at all.

This would naturally put more prevalence on sumang as a usable spiritual force, and sumang, given its personal emphasis, would be the most susceptible to misuse as witchcraft, especially if it involved, as it often did, poisoning and the settling of personal scores. But at the same time, the obeah man performed roles that would surely be considered ethical, and therefore the use of the term *obeah* in America must have shifted to include public roles and ethical private practice as well as witchcraft. Quarcoo, an obeah man of Antigua, explained the ennobling ceremony to a Coromantee named Court in 1736 when Court was elected as head of the Coromantee nation, and Quarcoo also administered an oath to other Coromantees who colonial officials charged were plotting a rebellion. All this suggests a general adherence to the public and general deities which must have performed roles similar to those of the obosoms but which were now conceived as sumangs.[32] Quarcoo was probably a *sumangfo* in Africa, because one of the witnesses who testified against him said that he knew the old man "in Coromantee country."[33] But many other obeah men also engaged in the more private functions accorded in Africa to the sumangfo, or priest of sumang. Coromantee plotters in a revolt in 1712 in New York had their oath administered to them by a "free Negro who pretended sorcery," possibly a Coromantee himself, perhaps even a Creole who had nevertheless mastered the art of contact with the otherworld and was accepted as such by the Coromantees.[34]

This commitment to a more flexible form of status and change-oriented norms may also explain why Coromantees, even though they came from societies where many people were slaves, might not regard the status of slave as permanent or binding. This is clearly seen in the political philosophy of Coromantees, who like members of other nations in the New

31. McCaskie, *State and Society*, p. 274.
32. PRO, CO 9/10, fol. 89.
33. Ibid.
34. Sharpe to Society for the Propagation of the Gospel, June 23, 1712, in Chaplain Roswell Randall Hoes, "The Negro Plot of 1712," *New York Genealogical and Biographical Record* 21 (1890): 163.

World chose kings for themselves when they could. Yet the iconography of their coronations came not so much for the conservative ceremonies of the ohenes, which would seem appropriate for a "king," but the change-oriented ideology of the commoner ennobling process, in which any worthy person was transformed into a noble and granted political rights.[35]

Many Coromantee "coronations" (as they were often called in the New World) were part of, or at least confused with, slave conspiracies, and therefore it is difficult to determine if these kings were like those chosen in various American societies where there was no conspiracy. Thus, for example, the coronation of a Coromantee king in Barbados in 1675, which included the carving of an elaborate throne, was taken by English colonists to be part of a conspiracy.[36] But Court's coronation in Antigua, the best-documented Coromantee coronation, generally meets our expectations of an ennobling ceremony on the Gold Coast, now masking as a royal coronation.[37]

Court's ceremony was called an *ikem*, or "shield ceremony," by informants of the inquest, which corresponds almost exactly to one of the two (shield and horn) commoner ennobling ceremonies used in the Gold Coast in Bosman's time (1688–1702).[38] The symbolism of the shield ceremony was military in nature, but it was not specifically a military event and was acquired by merchants rather than by soldiers, although the distinction between the two tended to blur in the conscription-oriented societies of the Gold Coast into which Court was born. Court was reputed to be the richest slave in Antigua, wealth that he had acquired in service to his master and in commercial activity over a long period of time, much as one might have expected of Gold Coast merchants.

The judges of Antigua who decided that Court's ceremony was military in nature and produced a potentially real king to take over the island for the slaves were thus surely mistaken. Court was in fact taking a title of

35. On the concept of transformation, though primarily for kingly office, in Akan society, see Michelle Gilbert, "The Person of the King: Ritual and Person in a Ghanian State," in *Rituals of Royalty*, ed. D. Cannadine and S. Price (Cambridge, 1987), pp. 298–330.

36. *Great Newes from Barbados, or a True and Faithful Account of the Grand Conspiracy of the Negroes* (London, 1676), p. 9, quoted in Michael Craton, *Testing the Chains: Resistance to Slavery in the British West Indies* (Ithaca, 1982), p. 109.

37. The case against Court was circumstantial; most of the alleged plotting was the product of rumor and insinuation or jailhouse confessions taken, no doubt, under torture. Court, his close associates, and even his master denied any plot, and it is not unreasonable to suppose that there was none. Modern historiography has tended, however, to accept the reality of the plot; see Craton, *Testing the Chains*, pp. 120–24; D. Barry Gaspar, *Bondmen and Rebels: A Study of Master-Slave Relations in Antigua, with Implications for Colonial British America* (Baltimore, 1985), pp. 215–54.

38. Bosman, *Description*, p. 136. Bosman does not give the name of the ceremony in Twi, but Müller, *Afrikansche auf der Guineischen Gold Cust*, vocabulary, gives "ockym" as the equivalent of "ein Schild" (a shield).

nobility created for mercantile wealth that would not have threatened the political order in his homeland and probably was not intended to threaten that in Antigua. But at the same time, other Coromantees in the Caribbean were undertaking much more dangerous forms of social reorganization in their nations. True rebellions, with radical change of the existing affairs as a goal, surely did take place, drawing on Akan norms as well. It was toward the banditry and military traditions, for example, that the leaders of the various Coromantee Maroon communities looked.

Many of the thousands of Akan-Coromantee slaves were made prisoners of war and subsequently enslaved as a result of military operations. For those slaves who could not acquire much in the way of mercantile wealth and lived in a society that denied them real opportunities for this, the use of their military skills to acquire wealth and power presented a second option. As late-seventeenth-century changes in military recruitment brought larger armies into existence, they also brought citizen soldiers into the slave trade. Not only did Coromantees in America have the model of the mercenary-bandit or citizen-soldier from Africa, but many also had concrete military experience and training behind them. This may account for their fairly remarkable abilities in the field during the full-scale revolts that were led by Coromantees.

The presence of this military tradition and training in the Americas is shown in the rash of Coromantee revolts that wracked Jamaica in the period after 1673. In these revolts, Coromantee military behavior suggested roots in the weapons and tactics of the evolving military culture of the Gold Coast. The rebels knew how to use firearms and displayed the sort of tactics that were characteristic of Gold Coast armies. Thus, in this early 1673 revolt, the two hundred Coromantee rebels took the opportunity to seize guns before fleeing to the mountains;[39] in 1678 guns were again taken. The rebels of 1678 did not only run away but also fought a pitched battle with British colonial forces.[40] In 1685–86 rebels took twenty-five "good guns" and captured more weapons as the revolt spread,[41] while in 1690 they took small cannon as well as muskets, which they could have used if they had served in Gold Coast armies.[42] In the ensuing

39. Craton, *Testing the Chains*, pp. 75–76, citing numerous unpublished documents.

40. Documentation cited in Richard S. Dunn, *Sugar and Slaves: The Rise of the Planter Class in the English West Indies, 1624–1713* (Chapel Hill, 1972), p. 260, and Craton, *Testing the Chains*, p. 76.

41. Lt. Gov. Molesworth to Blathwaite, August 29, 1685, in *Calendar of State Papers, Colonial Series: America and West Indies*, ed. J. W. Fortesque (London, 1899; rpt., Vaduz, 1964), p. 82, no. 339. Fuller documentation, including a lengthy account from John Taylor, "Multum in Parvo" (1688), manuscript in the Institute of Jamaica, is given in Dunn, *Sugar and Slaves*, pp. 260–61.

42. Cannon were often used in Gold Coast wars in the late seventeenth century, though they lost popularity later; see Kea, *Settlements*, p. 159.

fight, the Coromantee rebels, using their muskets and artillery to good effect, were able to repel a first attack of colonial troops, yielding only to a second assault by superior forces before retreating to the mountains.[43]

Considering that Jamaica, unlike some other colonies in the New World, provided no military training for slaves, it is likely that these rebels acquired their skill with gunpowder weapons in Africa.[44] Slaves had to make special forays to acquire guns, yet their own equipment and agricultural tools might have provided weapons (for hand-to-hand combat, however, rather than missile combat, as guns did). Guns require at least familiarity to use, and substantial training to use well (as contemporary accounts maintain they did), yet there was no opportunity for slaves to acquire the requisite training in Jamaica. Furthermore African military training might well have provided them their background in the use of both the weapon and appropriate tactics.

Their tactics also resembled those of the newly emerging military patterns of the Gold Coast; in 1685 (the best-described revolt from a military perspective) the rebels employed a dispersed order of attack, withdrew quickly after the first attacks, but reformed later.[45] They might not have been equally able to stop the determined advance of the colonial troops as they did in 1685 and 1690 (when they also used artillery) without at least some tactical training and the will to stand and fight which comes from experience. The fact that they did not use drills appropriate to European soldiers suggests that it was the Gold Coast experience, rather than anything they might have learned in the colony, which guided their tactics. The Coromantee rebels who fled to the mountains soon built their own estates as Maroons, drawing heavily on the Gold Coast background of military ennoblement. While some Coromantee slaves such as Court managed to acquire wealth and won the support of their fellows to be elected "king" in an American version of the ennobling ceremony, others played to the military tradition of success and ennoblement. Ray A. Kea, studying the slave revolt of 1733 in the Danish West Indies, has argued that there was a direct connection between leaders of the Akan state of Akwamu, captured in war between 1730 and 1732, and their leadership of the revolt.[46]

43. See Craton, *Testing the Chains*, p. 76.

44. On the whole, the English shrank from the prospect of arming their slaves. A brief attempt to set up a slave militia in Barbados in 1673 was quickly abandoned; see Dunn, *Sugar and Slaves*, p. 262. As shown by Gary A. Puckrein, *Little England: Plantation Society and Anglo-Barbadian Politics, 1627–1700* (New York, 1984), pp. 178–79, the problem of defending colonies with militia of European origin only created immense political difficulties for all the English colonies.

45. Molesworth to Blathwaite; documentation cited in Dunn, *Sugar and Slaves*, pp. 261–62.

46. Ray A. Kea, " 'When I die, I shall return to my own land': An 'Anima' Slave Rebellion in the Danish West Indies, 1733–34," in *The Cloth of Many Colored Silks: Papers on History and*

Coromantee Maroons joined existing runaway communities or formed new ones of their own. These towns resembled the new settlements created by bandits, outcast nobles, and wealthy men in the Gold Coast who could not satisfy their political ambitions within the confines of a state. Just as the late-seventeenth-century Gold Coast had a number of these new towns—*crooms* (*krouws*) named after their founders[47]—so the towns of the Jamaican Maroons typically bore the name of their founder—Cudjoe's Town, Nanny's Town, Diana's Town, Molly's Town, Accompong's Town, or Guy's Town.[48] Just as the European sources that describe the Gold Coast often called these nobles "captains," so too did the colonial records of Jamaica.

The Maroon communities were militarily defiant and, like the bandit settlements of the Gold Coast, sometimes lived on plunder, the stealing of slaves, and attracting other people's slaves away to be clients.[49] They were also prepared to submit to authority if it would recognize their right to rule. This point is well illustrated by the surrender of the substantial group of towns founded or led by Cudjoe, who signed a treaty with Britain in 1739.

The treaty and its surrounding ceremonies drew from Akan, European, and local sources, but it performed the same functions as the ennobling process of the Gold Coast.[50] Like nobles on the Gold Coast, Cudjoe was granted freedom from enslavement (as were his subjects), trade concessions, and more or less absolute jurisdiction over his new estate, tempered by the rights of his overlord. The treaty also imposed military obligations but fixed succession in the community.[51] A similar treaty signed with Quao was a bit more restrictive but also provided for local control and succession as well as military duties.[52] In Cudjoe's case, the ending of the treaty was sealed by an act of submission that resembled similar acts of ennobling in the Gold Coast, except that Britain became the overlord rather than an Akan ohene or his representative.

Society Ghanaian and Islamic in Honor of Ivor Wilks, ed. John Hunwick and Nancy Lawler (Evanston, 1996), pp. 159–93.

47. Kea, *Settlements*, p. 106.

48. Mavis Campbell, *The Maroons of Jamaica, 1655–1796: A History of Resistance, Collaboration, and Betrayal* (Trenton, 1990), pp. 48–49, 164–65.

49. Ibid.; Barbara Glamon Kopytoff, "The Maroons of Jamaica: An Ethnohistorical Study of Incomplete Polities" (Ph.D. diss., University of Pennsylvania, 1973). For specifics on this period, see especially Kopytoff, "The Early Political Development of Jamaican Maroon Societies," *William and Mary Quarterly*, 3d ser., 35, no. 2 (April 1978): 287–307.

50. The best description is in Marees, *Beschryvinge ende historische verhael;* see also *Description and Historical Account of the Gold Kingdom of Guinea* (1602), trans. Dantzig and Jones, pp. 85b–87a. See, however, Bosman, *Description*, pp. 135–36.

51. The treaty is printed in full in Campbell, *Maroons of Jamaica*, pp. 126–28.

52. The treaty is printed in ibid., pp. 135–37.

On the Gold Coast, the towns and new settlements founded by rebels or rich men were often eventually incorporated or reincorporated into an existing polity through formal ceremonies.[53] In addition to the shield (*ikyem*) ceremony such as Court had performed, Quao's ceremony may have been inspired in part by the horn Gold Coast ennobling ceremony. According to Bosman, when a person became rich, they made all sorts of horns, which they taught their family to blow. They then showed them publicly and presented a public ceremony for all and sundry. At the end of this they own a title of nobility, and "they are free to blow their horns at plesure, which none are permitted who have not thus aggrandized themselves."[54]

As the diary of the English expedition that made a treaty with Cudjoe indicates, horns played a major role in the celebration, which included sacrifices of animals, a military dance performed by the new noble, and a symbolic submission to the new authority. The English force that went to make the treaty with Quao were led to him by a "hornsman" sent as an ambassador, just as a new noble on the Gold Coast sent horn players out to invite others to his celebration.[55]

III.

Thus, even though slavery imposed stringent conditions on the Coromantee nation, its members continued to seek the kind of social mobility possible in Africa by whatever means were available in America, both peacefully through acquiring wealth or forcefully by breaking free. At the same time, they sought to consolidate these positions with reference to their own emerging cultural symbols rooted in American reality and the Akan past. This Akan past was, as befitted their status both in Africa and in America, interpreted in terms of change-oriented social norms. Ironically, the American vision was more open to achievement and democratic, for a simple noble in the Gold Coast might be a king in America, whereas the community granted this title in America, hopefully (and generally too optimistically) to be accepted by the higher authorities of the British colonial state, as in the African one, but not necessarily dependent on this acceptance. What Court and Cudjoe obtained from their "subjects"

53. Kea, *Settlements*, pp. 114, 126–29.
54. Bosman, *Description*, pp. 135–36.
55. The best description of Cudjoe's celebrated act of submission is found in a letter by a witness printed in 1798 in the *Jamaica Journal and Royal Gazette*, quoted in Michael Mullin, *Africa in America: Slave Acculturation and Resistance in the American South and the British Caribbean, 1736–1831* (Urbana, Ill., 1992), pp. 50–51. For a detailed discussion of the historiography of this act, which is often couched in psychological terms, see Campbell, *Maroons of Jamaica*, pp. 113–17.

was derived entirely from the more radical of the ideas within African society, while being subject to a far more demanding ultimate authority.

Historians have often viewed independent action of African Americans as resistance, arguing that the conditions of slavery were sufficiently odious and constricting that any act of independence constituted "resistance." Certainly it is the right word to use when violent escape and the development of independent communities is the goal, even more so when it is achieved. But, as the Coromantee case shows us, the idea of resistance is also limiting in itself. Coromantees, like all people, had ideas of justice and right that transcended the immediate conditions of the Americas, and they strove for those both in Africa and in America. The degree that the societies from which they came and those to which they were taken accepted those ideals determined how much their achievement required violence or was met with repression. Resistance was an element of the equation but not necessarily the reactive activity frequently implied in the term.

Instead, for Coromantees, exercising their political ideas was a creative activity. When Cudjoe led rebels, he had no doubt that the only way the creative process could be finalized was through violent resistance, but when Court held his coronation on an afternoon in front of thousands of multiracial spectators, he hoped that the same creative ideal could be realized within colonial society.

Consolidating National Masculinity: Scientific Discourse and Race in the Post-Revolutionary United States

DANA D. NELSON

> It has often given me pleasure to observe, that Independent America was not composed of detached and distant territories, but that one connected, fertile, wide-spreading country was the portion of our western sons of liberty. . . . [I]t appears as if it was the design of Providence, that an inheritance so proper and convenient for a band of brethren, united to each other by the strongest ties, should never be split into a number of unsocial, jealous and alien sovereignties.
>
> —PUBLIUS (JOHN JAY), *"Paper no. 2"*

IF COLONIALISM was accompanied by what Robert Miles calls a "civilization project," a process "initiated by a class, or a fraction of a class" that aims "to establish and to legitimate a social hierarchy," the post-Revolutionary United States depended on a cognate symbolic strategy, an "independence project" that sought to establish and to legitimate

I offer warm thanks to many helpful readers: my writing group at Louisiana State University—Rick Moreland, Reggie Young, and especially Elsie Michie—as well as Walt Herbert and Jerold M. Martin. I appreciate the comments of my two anonymous readers at Cornell University Press, and I particularly thank Robert Blair St. George for his insight and wit, his patience and intellectual support. This essay helped me to think about issues that are developed more fully in the first chapter of my book *National Manhood: Capitalist Citizenship and the Imagined Fraternity of White Men* (Durham, N.C., 1998).

a political order.[1] Following Miles, we can usefully conceptualize "independence" as an identity ideal for the civic subject as well as for the corporate body of "nation" (the people)—with a binary structure separating Self (the independent) from its opposite (the dependent). Scientific discourse played a crucial role in U.S. identity formation roughly contemporaneous to the scientific consolidation of "race"; it offered intellectual strategies notably amenable to the psychosocial worries attendant to the enactment of that independence project.

In particular, the Aristotelian paradigm, with its scientific logic of identity and exclusion, perfectly suited the anxious project of civic territorialization. The precise calculations, expansive boundaries, and sensation of mastery provided in the Newtonian universe and Baconian nature similarly provided a positional authority for "independence." Indeed, Gayle Ormiston and Raphael Sassower read the Declaration of Independence as an exemplary text of the scientific enlightenment. They observe that "as is the case with many seventeenth-century narratives—... the texts of Bacon, Hobbes, and Galileo are examples—nature is a book, a text to be deciphered and comprehended. Not only does the text legitimate the laws it claims are 'natural,' it legitimates the 'truths' it cites as 'self-evident,' " The Declaration's scientific objectivism is refined by discourses of math and geometry in Publius's arguments for the Constitution and in that document itself. Publius makes frequent appeals to ever more objective scientific rationality, as in Federalist Paper no. 38, where Alexander Hamilton urges readers to consider the "science of morals and politics" with the same dispassion that allows men to accept geometrical theorems such as "the INFINITE DIVISIBILITY of matter"—a principle the Constitution literally applies in its three-fifths designation of enslaved humans.[2]

Enlightenment scientific discourse facilitated the constitution of a reassuringly bounded yet symbolically expansive white manhood that underlay the consolidation of nation. Although, as Michael Goldfield notes, the Continental Congress rejected South Carolina's attempt to place the adjective "white" in the Constitution, that adjective would come to define the very status of citizenship within a year. When a bill was submitted to

1. Robert Miles, *Racism after "Race Relations"* (New York, 1993), pp. 88–89, 90. See also Homi K. Bhabha, *The Location of Culture* (New York, 1994), p. 2, commenting on the correlation between "cultural difference" and models of "civility": "For at the same time as the question of cultural difference emerged in the colonial text, discourses of civility were defining the doubling moment of the emergence of Western modernity. Thus the political and theoretical genealogy of modernity lies not only in the origins of the *idea* of civility, but in this history of the colonial moment."

2. Gayle L. Ormiston and Raphael Sassower, *Narrative Experiments: The Discursive Authority of Science and Technology* (Minneapolis, 1989), p. 56; Publius (Alexander Hamilton), "Paper no. 31," in *The Federalist Papers by Alexander Hamilton, James Madison, and John Jay,* ed. Garry Wills (New York, 1982), p. 148.

Congress stipulating that naturalization would be restricted to "free white persons," there were no recorded arguments over racial restrictions. Rather, in the two-day debate the wording was refined such that the free white person was pronominally gendered a "he."[3] In the 1990s historians have begun analyzing how the abstracted category of "white manhood" could take hold and become a lived, common reality that superseded the locality, class, and ethnicity of identity in the early nation. Rather than treating "race" as a corollary to culture—as ethnicity—they analyze race and, more specifically, whiteness as a structure or system of privilege and identity, of discrimination and exclusion. It was in the name of precisely such a systematization that enlightenment science stepped forward for the project of racial categorization, a project that would quickly shift from a horizontal ordering of "difference" to a vertical one that soon culminated in such influential initiatives as Samuel G. Morton's racial craniology. That hierarchizing systematization was echoed in and complemented by a national organization of race and gender, in the constitution, in law.

In this essay I trace thematically the emergence of an experimental reorganization, extension, and national incorporation of white masculinity that would identify itself in terms of "individualism" during the early national period. Whiteness—formerly associated primarily with British aristocratic elites—was increasingly extended, actually democratized, to define civic identity in the early national period. This ideological extension functioned in part to manage the divisive effects of interclass and interregional rivalry that characterized this period, which James Roger Sharp has summarized as "a hothouse atmosphere of passion, suspicion and fear."[4] One index to that developing consolidation of white masculine identity becomes manifest in the projection of cultural fears about dependence and rivalry onto groups of people who were excluded from this newly active category. Anxieties about social and political disintegration were increasingly linked to women, racial others, and national "foreigners." Sentiment (one of the philosophical grounds of appeal for the nation's Declaration of Independence) was dissociated from masculinity,

3. Michael Goldfield, "The Color of Politics in the United States: White Supremacy as the Main Explanation for the Peculiarities of American Politics from Colonial Times to the Present," in *The Bounds of Race: Perspectives on Hegemony and Resistance*, ed. Dominick LaCapra (Ithaca, 1991), p. 119. This law remained on the books, surviving an attempt to strike it during Reconstruction, until the McCarran Act of 1952, operating after slavery to exclude Asian immigration; see Benjamin B. Ringer and Elinor R. Lawless, *Race-Ethnicity and Society* (New York, 1989), p. 110.

4. James Roger Sharp, *American Politics in the Early Republic: The New Nation in Crisis* (New Haven, 1993), p. 1. For a brilliant reading of the cultural (and capitalist) articulation of corporate individualism, see Christopher Newfield, *The Emerson Effect: Individualism and Submission in America* (Chicago, 1996).

identified as a source of political "infection," and increasingly projected onto women. European immigrants were increasingly regarded with suspicion as likely sources of contamination to "democratic" spirit, a suspicion that was formalized in the Alien and Sedition Acts. And strikingly, "race" as a category came during this period to be systematically and *negatively* articulated as foreign "otherness," in terms of bodily disease and political exteriority. From these observations, we can begin to assess how the national masculinity of the early national period, buttressed by appeal to scientific authority, established symbolic boundaries on two fronts, defining civic identity—national masculinity—against both femininity and racial otherness.

I offer a reading of Thomas Jefferson's *Notes on the State of Virginia* and Benjamin Rush's essay "Observations . . . [on] Negro Leprosy," focusing specifically on how scientific discourse offered helpful equipment to U.S. identity formation coextensive with its articulation of the concept of "race."[5] For the sake of interdisciplinary communication, I want to be clear at the outset about my aims for this essay. I examine two works by two prominent American politicians and writers for the ways in which they highlight an emerging cultural logic, a logic that, arguably, has been sustained in the United States until today. I am not trying to assess or quantify either Jefferson's or Rush's individual investment in racism; identifying an individual as "racist" is one of the least interesting and least useful things to do in working toward an understanding of how racism works as a structure or a system. Because I am interested in racism as a social structure, my analytic focus on how racism works is not concerned as much to identify moments where it emerges as hatred of or disgust (or romantic admiration, for that matter) for Native and African Americans either individually or generally. Through a thematic reading of two texts that treat race, I will instead foreground the plastic, even contradictory mobility of racial discourse in constructing and negotiating whiteness, as well as the ways in which anxieties generated by the categorical imperatives *of* whiteness were being routed, through the language of science, into worries about female sexuality. I do not suggest that this analysis stands for a complete picture of Jefferson or Rush or of post-Revolutionary U.S. culture. Rather, I isolate and foreground a common

5. Feminist historians of science such as Evelyn Fox-Keller have convincingly demonstrated that Enlightenment scientific paradigms were underwritten by an active misogyny; others, like Londa Schiebinger, have pointed out that Enlightenment science aggressively contributed to the masculinization of both science and power. See, for instance, Evelyn Fox-Keller, *Reflections on Gender and Science* (New Haven, 1985), and Fox-Keller, *Secrets of Life, Secrets of Death: Essays on Language, Gender, and Science* (New York, 1992); and Londa Schiebinger, *Nature's Body: Gender and the Making of Modern Science* (Boston, 1993). For the question of science and race, see also Sandra Harding, *The "Racial" Economy of Science: Toward a Democratic Future* (Bloomington, 1993).

theme, a strong logic in articulations of national and "white male" identities, highlighting key features of their often converging constructions for more extended consideration.

However different their political positions and scientific interests, both Jefferson and Rush contributed to the consolidation of national masculinity through the production of the racial Other. They produced what historian David Theo Goldberg has termed a gendered *social knowledge* and established "a library or archive of information, a set of guiding ideas and principles about Otherness." They tabulated physiological and moral characteristics in the production of racial taxonomy as an epistemological exercise of power / identity. Yet both betrayed an anxiety over the stability of their racial logic and projected that concern onto the bodies of women. Such moments emphasize their participation in a national project, that of installing "race" into the same paradigm of oppositional and absolute hierarchized difference that gender had come to occupy during the eighteenth century.[6] Their fears were manifested in uneasy speculations. Jefferson and Rush insisted that the "best" white women are absolutely distinct from white men—one of their gauges for civility and civilization being absolute gender binarity. Yet they considered those same women liable to a symbolic and an actual deterioration into barbarous strangeness, which reveals them to be, in Felicity Nussbaum's striking phrase, "joined by the genitals" to other races and other species.[7]

I.

Thomas Jefferson has long been at the center of discussions of slavery and racial attitudes in the early United States. In an article on what Edmund Morgan enduringly phrased "the American paradox," Alexander O. Boulton observes that Jefferson's *Notes on the State of Virginia* "to a large degree, was an explication of the Declaration of Independence; it grounded, as he thought, some of the grand philosophical principles of the Declaration in the empirical proofs of science."[8] If science—"an investigation of Natural Laws"—would lead Jefferson to his assertion in 1776 that "all men are created equal," it would be the apparatus of science to which he would turn to stabilize his claims for the distinctiveness of a white civic body politic in the United States.

6. David Theo Goldberg, *Racist Culture: Philosophy and the Politics of Meaning* (Cambridge, Mass., 1993), p. 150. See Schiebinger, *Nature's Body*, and Thomas Lacqueur, *Making Sex: Body and Gender from the Greeks to Freud* (Cambridge, Mass., 1990).

7. Felicity A. Nussbaum, " 'Savage' Mothers: Narratives of Maternity in the Mid–Eighteenth Century," *Cultural Critique* 20 (Winter 1991–92): 129.

8. Alexander O. Boulton, "The American Paradox: Jeffersonian Equality and Racial Science," *American Quarterly* 47, no. 3 (September 1995): 472.

The passage on "laws" in Jefferson's *Notes on the State of Virginia* offers an intellectually and affectively tortured argument for the physical and cultural traits that separate white from black. He begins by asserting absolute and visible difference via a catalogue in which even the pluses he accords to "blackness" turn into minuses. "Whites" are more beautiful and symmetrical, "blacks" are less; "we" have more color, "they" are monotonously monochrome; we have more emotion, they have less; whites have flowing hair and more of it; blacks feel less pain. Blacks secrete more from their skin, but it gives them a less agreeable smell and makes them less tolerant of cold. Blacks have as much bravery, but only because they have less forethought. Blacks court more ardently, but only because they are less tender, and so on.[9] In this racial calculus, Jefferson employs his beloved mathematics as a technique of disembodiment, in the service of splitting social bodies by anatomizing physical bodies. The body is removed from its localized physicality and placed in categorical spaces produced by philosophical abstraction *and* notably suited to population planning.[10]

Yet Jefferson's confidence wanes by the end of this section; he concedes "great diffidence" in offering *any* judgments about ascertaining racial difference through observation. "How much more" difficult it is to observe difference, Jefferson admitted, "then where it is a faculty, not a substance, we are examining; where it eludes the research of all the senses; where the conditions of its existence are various and variously combined; where the effects of those which are present or absent bid defiance to calculation." He concludes that "to our reproach it must be said that though for a century and a half we have had under our eyes the races of black and of red men, they have never yet been viewed by us as subjects of natural history." Jefferson's response to this failure is to appeal for further—and connotatively violent—scientific observation, "where the subject may be submitted to the Anatomical knife, to Optical glasses, to analysis by fire, or by solvents" (p. 143). Here we can see the usefulness of "science" to the psychosocial construction of "race." It provides authority to categorize, restrain, and govern human reality based on abstractions of bodily particularity, and it offers a progressivist hope that today's failure may be overcome in the future, where the future is to be realized, as T. Walter Herbert observes, in "the use of force by white males upon dark bodies."[11]

---

9. Thomas Jefferson, *Notes on the State of Virginia*, ed. William Peden (New York, 1954), pp. 138–39; subsequent page references will be given parenthetically.

10. Denise Albanese has more generally outlined the implications of this scientific strategy in "The Absent Body in Galileo," paper presented at the Modern Language Association conference, Toronto, December 28–31, 1993. See also Albanese, *New Science, New World* (Durham, N.C., 1996).

11. T. Walter Herbert, letter to author, May 25, 1994.

Jefferson's discussion of "blacks" in query 14, with its obsessive concern to locate and delineate bodily difference, elucidates structurally a process of splitting and excorporation. Here he seeks to enable a legal construction of a *white* body clearly separated from the black body, simultaneously striving to construct the scientific individual / observer as distinctively separate from the subject of scientific scrutiny. But splitting and excorporation strategies are psychologically corollary to desires about engulfment and *in*corporation, and the latter paradigm is more useful to understanding Jefferson's treatment of "Indians"—a treatment that, however different from his handling of "blacks," works in parallel ways to consolidate *whiteness*. In the query on "productions," Jefferson calculates the conditional racial *equivalency* of Native Americans. "Were we equal in barbarism," he concludes, "our females would be equal drudges. The man with them is less strong than with us, but their woman stronger than ours; and both for the same obvious reason; because our man and their woman is habituated to labour, and formed by it. . . . They raise fewer children than we do. The causes of this are to be found, not in a difference of nature, but of circumstance" (p. 60). The paradigm of scientific debate epitomized in Jefferson's argument with George-Louis Leclerc Buffon in *Notes on the State of Virginia* has perhaps disenabled us from considering how this passage poses a scientific argument on behalf of American (masculine) identity not simply to legitimate its stability and progression for France and other "world" powers without, but also to justify its imaginative expansion in the form of territorial aggression within. In this case, equivalency functions to project racial *incorporation* and annexation, gesturing toward a construction of an assimilative and expansive "white" body. They are like—or could be like—us; we belong anywhere they are. Arguably, then, Jefferson's discussion of Native Americans in "Productions" has in pragmatic terms as much to do with producing geopolitical identity (confirmation seemingly offered in Jefferson's subsequent and aggressive involvement with westward expansion) as with defending intellectual legitimacy.

These two aims (incorporation and refutation) are mutually confirmative in the exercise of defensive grandiosity that Jefferson calls a "proud theory": American genius. Frank Shuffelton contends that in the section "Productions," Jefferson's "desire to refute Buffon's theory of New World degeneracy leads him to emphasize cultural production, a category in which he can include Logan as well as Franklin and David Rittenhouse."[12]

12. Frank Shuffelton, "Thomas Jefferson: Race, Culture, and the Failure of Anthropological Method," in *A Mixed Race: Ethnicity in Early America*, ed. Shuffelton (New York, 1993), pp. 272–73. In his chapter on "Productions," Jefferson offers the reported rhetorical eloquence of the Mingo chief Logan to refute Buffon's assertion that all humans in the New World were degenerating because of the more primitive environment. Arguing that by factoring in the

It is important to recognize, however, that that Jefferson finally does not lump Logan *together* with Washington, Franklin, and Rittenhouse; rather his treatment of Native Americans is separated from his concluding remarks on the transplanted "white race" by a scientific or anthropologized assertion that he does "not mean to deny, that there are varieties in the race of man"—a pointed qualification of his earlier calculus of equality (pp. 62–63, 64–65). By asserting this hierarchicalized anthropology between Indian "productions" and "white" ones, Jefferson signals his actual regard of Native Americans as a resource for U.S. identity. Thus it seems less coincidental that this discussion appears not in the query on "Aborigines" but on "productions." Despite the objective posture of science, we can see that Jefferson's argument about "Indians" does not function simply as a dispassionate response to Marbois's "cultural questionnaire," or even as a defensive one. Rather, it is a more complex and aggressive argument, one guided by territorializing ambitions.[13]

In the passages on "productions" and "laws," the calculation of difference evokes doubt about the stability of racial definition. Each instance takes up "blackness" in the specific context of sexual reproduction. In "Laws," Jefferson makes an (almost obligatory, for this period) observation concerning "the preference of the oran-ootan for the black women over those of his own species" (p. 138); as many commentators have argued, Jefferson's language here suggests fears about both miscegenation and racial recrimination for the actualized desires of white men for female slaves. In "Productions," he adds to his "catalogue of our indigenous animals . . . a short account of an anomaly of nature, taking place sometimes in the race of negroes brought from Africa." In this section he describes four albino "blacks" he has seen personally and three more of which he has heard reliable accounts. Speculating that albinism is perhaps caused "by a disease in the skin, or in its colouring matter," he concludes that "it seems more incident to the female than male sex" (pp. 70–71).

Jefferson explicitly characterizes variability in skin color as a "disease" projectively disassociated from both masculinity and whiteness. It might seem that a man as preoccupied with quantification and calculation as

---

differences of circumstance, "we shall probably find that they are formed in mind as well as in body, on the same module with the 'Homo Sapiens Europaeus,' " Jefferson backs his argument with a transcript of the speech; see *Notes on the State of Virginia*, pp. 62–63.

13. Jefferson's text participates in a genre that would culminate shortly in such guides as Julian R. Jackson's *On Military Geography: Its Nature, Object, and Importance* (London, 1850) and, in particular, Jackson, *What to Observe; or, The Traveller's Remembrancer* (London, 1841), which advises travelers on how to collect cultural, geographic, and physical information useful to empire building and defense. We have only to consider here how, in answer to the previous query on "rivers," Jefferson is careful to point out the amenability of each he describes to gunboat navigation, a reading that directs us to see how the catalogue of "warriors" in the section on "Aborigines" serves similar interests.

Jefferson would not consider a sample of seven statistically valid. Yet even setting that quibble aside, we must carefully examine the symbolic and pedagogical intersections of "woman" with "race" in these passages on albinism and orangutans.[14] Regardless of Jefferson's explicit intentions, the suggestion of female culpability for racial instability in this passage links it to what was by then an established eighteenth-century tradition of casting misogynistic anxieties about the reproductive powers of women in scientific discourse. Scientist-philosophers such as Nicolas Malebranche, in *De la recherche de la vérité* (Paris, 1712)—a study that went through five more editions between 1721 and 1772—argued that it was the mother alone who was to be held responsible for imposing, in utero, "pathological or teratological horrors" on the developing fetus.[15] More precisely, female emotional vulnerability—*her* penetrable and unstable psyche—were the direct cause of infant marking. Her secret passions literalized themselves on the skin of the offspring; as Barbara Stafford summarizes, "Like a blank sheet of paper, the skin became marbled by pathos, mottled by an alien pattern of interiority."[16] Jefferson's categorization here corresponds to the more apparently optimistic diagnosis that Benjamin Rush would make in 1797: black skin was itself the manifestation of leprosy.

II.

In "On Slave Keeping" (1773), Rush staked a position on Africans quite different from the one Jefferson would take in *Notes on the State of Virginia.* In his essay Rush refutes extensively the very positions his Virginia counterpart would shortly take on African character, sensibility, and "beauty" while fully anticipating the moral energy of Jefferson's thoughts on "manners." Both men were, of course, slave owners, so we would not want to

14. After I first presented this work at the "Possible Pasts" conference, Eva Cherniavsky's fascinating and suggestive book *That Pale Mother Rising: Sentimental Discourses and the Imitation of Motherhood in Nineteenth-Century America* (Bloomington, 1995) was published. Cherniavsky also reads Jefferson's observations on black women albinos—and in terms very similar to my interpretation here—though her interest is less in scientific discourse and national masculinity than in the (national) production of the sentimental (white) mother. For example, she notes that "these women make their appearance in the *Notes* as mute figures, a designated 'anomaly of nature,' wedged in between an entry on native birds and remarks on the importation of the honey bee. They are as such less the agents of resistance than an emblem of Jefferson's disease. But despite their status in the *Notes* as silenced and objectified figures, I would argue that they display an irreducible material remainder of the rationalized black body" (p. 17).

15. See Barbara Marie Stafford, *Body Criticism: Imagining the Unseen in Enlightenment Art and Medicine* (Cambridge, Mass., 1991), p. 313.

16. Ibid.

overestimate the immediate relevance of differences in rhetorical positions on blackness. Yet it would seem initially that Rush is even less invested in what we now identify as "racism" than was Jefferson. Certainly Rush's arguments about "negro leprosy," based in his observation of Henry Moss and careful study, demonstrate his willingness to see the possibility of likeness where Jefferson saw only irremediable difference, whatever its causes. Precisely because of their political and intellectual differences, then, I want to draw attention to significant correlations in each man's scientific contributions to the "race" archive.

For Jefferson, disease apparently functions to destabilize difference, manifesting itself in "cadaverous" whiteness as the corruption of "natural" blackness (*Notes*, p. 70). For Rush it would seem that difference itself is the disease. He characterizes the putative "blackness" of African skin as "morbid" and the physiology as "short, ugly and ill proportioned," problems remedied only by salubrious Nature effecting a recuperation of "healthy" or "natural" whiteness *and* the attempts of a combined "science and humanity" to follow nature's lead in discovering an "artificial" method for "dislodg[ing] the color in negroes."[17] Rush envisions his search for a medical cure as a corrective to the tyranny of "whites" both ignorant and learned, the former supposing that "blackness" is the "mark" of "divine judgment," the latter arguing that it is correlative to the ability of blacks to work in "hot and unwholesome climates" (p. 297).

Beneath Rush's optimism, however, lurks fear of psychosocial dissolution and collapse. As Sander Gilman has incisively argued, the figure of disease itself functions as a category of difference and as such works to "determine the construction of the idea of the patient in a direct and powerful manner, drawing the boundaries between the 'healthy' observer, physician or layperson, and the 'patient.' The construction of the image of the patient is thus always a playing out of this desire for a demarcation between ourselves and the chaos represented in culture by disease."[18]

That science now does not characterize "black" skin as a disease makes my point all the more emphatically. No matter how optimistic, humane, and incorporative Rush might seem, we must consider how, in figuring "blackness" as a disease that is potentially curable, he participates in the deployment of "race" as a white strategy for managing social anxieties about instability, chaos, and fragmentation. If, as Gilman argues, disease is a projective figure for personal disintegration, by ascribing it to black

17. Benjamin Rush, "Observations Intended to Favour a Supposition that the Black Color (as it is called) of the Negroes is Derived from Leprosy," *Transactions of the American Philosophical Society* 4 (1799): 291–92, 295; subsequent page references will be noted parenthetically.

18. Sander L. Gilman, *Disease and Representation: Images of Illness from Madness to AIDS* (Ithaca, 1988), p. 4.

skin Rush engages the black Other as a receptacle for social instability in the early republic and, conversely, makes whiteness available as a recuperative and transclass social order.

Linking "race" to an apparatus for social order and civic reproduction in Rush's thinking does not seem to be unwarranted. In "On Slave Keeping" (1773), Rush raises a similar set of concerns, figured somewhat differently. In taking up the question of apparent biblical sanction for slavery, Rush observes that

> we are told the Jews kept the heathens in perpetual bondage. The design of providence in permitting this evil, was probably to prevent the Jews from marrying among strangers, to which their intercourse with them upon any other footing than that of slaves, would naturally have inclined them. Had this taken place—their Natural Religion would have been corrupted—they would have contracted all their vices, and the intention of providence in keeping them a distinct people, in order to accomplish the promise made to Abraham, that "in his Seed all the Nations of the earth should be blessed," would have been defeated; so that the descent of the Messiah from Abraham, could not have been traced, and the divine commission of the Son of God, would have wanted one of its most powerful arguments to support it.[19]

Here Rush supports the *logic*, if not the practice, of slavery, in the name of social stability and patriarchal order. Notably, he characterizes exogamous relations in terms of infection: "they would have contracted all their vices." And he evokes a most similar argument in his embedded caveat about Negro "leprosy." "The facts and principles which have been delivered," Rush maintains, "should teach white people the necessity of keeping up that prejudice against such connections with them [that is, Negroes], as would tend to infect posterity with any portion of the disorder" ("Observations Intended to Favour a Supposition," p. 295). Rush in effect appeals for a medico-racial quarantine, placing him far closer in conclusion on the topic to Jefferson than their political differences superficially indicate.

Strikingly, Rush locates his anxieties about infected populations and racial "disease" in precisely the same way as Jefferson. Rush hauls in the obligatory orangutan as he quotes Hawkins's observations about African albinos: "The difference of color cannot arise from the intercourse of whites and blacks, for the whites are very rarely among them, and the result of this union is well known to be the yellow color, or mulatto. Many of the natives assert that they are produced by women being debauched

19. Benjamin Rush, "On Slave Keeping" (1773), in *Selected Writings of Benjamin Rush*, ed. Dagobert D. Runes (New York, 1947), p. 8.

in the woods by the large baboons, or ourang-outangs. . . . No satisfactory discovery has been made to account for such singular, but not unfrequent phaenomena in the species" (p. 291). And just before his warning about maintaining the purity of the white population, Rush presents two anecdotes that underscore how women, via sexual contamination, become culpable for racial impurity. "A white woman in North Carolina not only acquired a dark color," he stated, "but several of the features of a negro, by marrying and living with a black husband. A similar instance of a change in the color and features of a woman in Buck's county in Pennsylvania has been observed and from a similar cause. In both these cases, the women bore children by their black husbands" (p. 294). Anxieties about disease are simultaneously projected onto two screens: sexually active females and blacks. Rush assigns responsibility for anxieties about loss of control in the social body of the early republic to the two groups against which civic identity, along with its corresponding entitlements, is increasingly consolidating itself.

Let me return to Gilman's arguments about the cultural work of "disease." In an extended passage that suggestively links the notion of racial "contamination"—evoked by both Jefferson and Rush—to more general issues that surround the cultural project of independence, Gilman explains:

> The basic structure is the reactivation of the fantasy of psychological wholeness that existed in all of us before we distanced ourselves from our first caregiver. It is this fantasy of wholeness which lies at the root of all the bipolar images of difference (health vs. disease; good vs. bad; white vs. black). . . . Our internalized sense of difference is a product of that primal moment in everyone's experience when we first became aware that we were different—different from the caregiver, unable to control our world. We need to project the fantasized source of our anxiety about our original loss of control. . . . This sense of difference is triggered by any deep-seated sense of ontological insecurity. . . . This moment of insecurity reproduces the repressed anxiety of that primal moment.[20]

What literary historian Jay Fliegelman describes as the post-Revolutionary sealing of identity thereby manages national concerns through the defensive privatization of ideals not only of family but also of race.[21] Inasmuch as infection, figured in terms of and *as* "blackness," was sealed out, "whiteness" was affectively sealed *in* the ideal national family, an enclo-

20. Gilman, *Disease and Representation*, p. 5.
21. Jay Fliegelman, *Prodigals and Pilgrims: The American Revolution against Patriarchal Authority, 1750–1800* (New York, 1982), chap. 8 and passim, as well as his discussion of Washington, p. 198, esp. comments on "The Sealing of the Garden."

sure that functioned to consolidate civic masculinity as it countered anxieties about the expansive, potentially disintegrative effects of democracy. And whiteness served nation and citizen in aggressive as well as in defensive capacities. As Collette Guillaumin's analysis of racist ideology suggests, the nonspecificity of whiteness is both what made it work as a cross-class abstraction and what also provided the crucial locus of what she describes as "occluded subjectivity," an authoritative standpoint from which "there is no sense of belonging to a specific group, so the group itself always remains outside the frame of reference, is never referred to as a group."[22] Whiteness as a symbolic guarantee to civic manhood thus assumed a negative definition that offered the control of Other bodies at the same time it required control of white women's bodies to certify their "virtue," typically in the form of reproductive "purity." The cultural dissociation of sentiment from notions of fraternity, the concomitant association of sentiment with penetrable womanly nature during the early national period; the intense turning of white, middle-class women's culture toward first Republican motherhood and then more generally domesticity; the racial calculus of the Constitution; the quarantine logic of the Alien and Sedition Acts; and the increasing reliance on racial demarcation among the working classes[23]—these serve as general examples that support analyzing intersecting ideals of nation, whiteness, and masculinity in the early United States from a more carefully descriptive vantage. Whiteness offered a useful strategy for imagining an independent, fraternally driven identity—a national masculinity.[24] Simultaneously, however, and with corollary ramifications, the negotiation of new models of class and regional masculinities under the umbrella of national belonging bestowed affective and pedagogical functions onto categories of whitened femininity and darkened otherness in the new republic.

22. Collette Guillaumin, *Racism, Sexism, Power, and Ideology* (New York, 1995), p. 50.

23. On sentiment and fraternity, see Fliegelman, *Prodigals and Pilgrims*, pp. 230–35. The post-Revolutionary "whitening" of the working classes is helpfully analyzed in David Roediger, *The Wages of Whiteness: Race and the Making of the American Working Class* (London, 1991); Noel Ignatiev, *How the Irish Became White* (New York, 1995); and Eric Lott, *Love and Theft: Blackface Minstrelsy and the American Working Class* (New York, 1993).

24. T. Walter Herbert phrased the point I am making here in this way: "The interpretive strategies derived from an awareness of cultural factors in neurosis—and in what passes for normality—recognize that processes of repression and projection are organized differently in different cultural eras and sites, and reveal themselves in local particularities. Reading social circumstance as text is not a matter of seeking some universal psychic grammar, but of grasping the interplay of social discourses within it" (Herbert, "Aesthetic Force and Political Complicity: The Example of Hawthorne," paper presented at Modern Language Association conference, Toronto, December 28–31, 1993, p. 13). I am indebted to T. Walter Herbert for sharing a copy of his paper with me.

III.

The scientific discourse that made itself available and amenable to the purposes of identifying and consolidating bodily knowledge of whiteness in Jefferson and Rush's age (for instance, the "objective" stance of the scientist that provides a paradigmatically occluded subjectivity)[25] has tooled the racism inherited by our age. We can see the descendants of Rush's and Jefferson's strategies working today in proposals for gated communities, which so clearly evoke and draw on the logic of the racial quarantine; in demographical calculations that offer warnings about which racial group will gain majority status by what year; in our national obsession with the mythologized benefits and (re)productivity of black "welfare queens": in "bell curve" calculations of "racial intelligence" which offer themselves for policy purposes; or in new, differential calculations of drug-possession sentencing which have resulted in a precipitous rise in male Native American, African American, and Latino inmate populations. We see them too in the media's handling of the Los Angeles riots, in which national attention was focused not toward African Americans' furious sense that the nation's justice served only white America but toward African Americans' and Korean Americans' cultural antagonisms, misunderstandings, and prejudices—a strategy we might call *racist* calculus. And we encounter them in the news coverage of the Oklahoma City bombing, where media and national authorities leaped to speculate that this heinous act of violence committed against the "nation's heartland" was the work of foreign terrorists, only to shift gears quickly, adopting the imagery of another "bodily" alien, *cancer*, when we learned the act was perpetrated by at least two white men who are U.S. citizens. The national- and self-purifying functions of these thematic and rhetorical strategies uncannily echo Jefferson's racial calculus and Rush's quarantine logic.

In similar fashion, within academia it seems worth considering how disciplinary boundaries, strategies, and habits also contribute to a culture of racist disavowal. For instance, with regard to my subject here—racial constructions in the early nation—scholars frequently reference the general prevalence of racism or even its grounding in "human nature" to avoid thinking in specific ways about the involvement of the nation's founding figures in institutionalizing racism. Glancingly acknowledging the racism they have "in common" with their age, we turn instead to focus on those places where they "transcended" it. I suggest that by studying

25. For a provocative analysis of scientific objectivity, see Zuleyma Tang Halpin, "Scientific Objectivity and the Concept of 'The Other,'" *Women's Studies International Forum* 12, no. 3 (1989): 285–94.

closely only that part of their legacy which we find ethically admirable by contemporary standards, we tacitly embrace their involvement in racial consolidation. We project away from them—and thereby our nation and ourselves—an implication in and responsibility for ongoing racist structures.

part three

Shaping Subjectivities

Secret Selves, Credible Personas: The Problematics of Trust and Public Display in the Writing of Eighteenth-Century Philadelphia Merchants

TOBY L. DITZ

THE SCHEMING merchant was a stock figure in the early modern world, sometimes anathematized specifically in the image of the Quaker or Jewish merchant. Assuming that Philadelphia's eighteenth-century merchants actually read or at least riffled through the pages of the sometimes ornately bound volumes that they displayed on the shelves of their townhouse libraries, they may well have come across the following passage from Giovanni Paolo Marana's *Letters Writ by a Turkish Spy*, first published in 1684 but remaining in print and popular on both sides of the Atlantic throughout the eighteenth century:

> As to these modern Seducers [Quaker merchants] . . . they [aim] to heap up Riches in Obscurity. . . . They are generally . . . observ'd to be very punctual in their Dealings, Men of few Words in a Bargain, modest and compos'd in their Deportment. . . . In a word, they are singularly Industrious, sparing no Labour or Pains to increase their Wealth; and so subtle and inventive, that they would, if possible, extract Gold out of Ashes. I know none that excel them in these Characters but the *Jews* and the *Banians*: The former being the craftiest of all Men, and the last so superlatively cunning that they will over-reach the Devil.[1]

---

1. Giovanni Paolo Marana, *The Eight Volumes of Letters Writ by a Turkish Spy*, 9th ed. (London, 1730), 6:17. Frederick Tolles, who also cites this passage, calls the *Turkish Spy* unaccountably popular and finds that at least four prominent Quaker merchants stocked their libraries with Marana's multivolume work; see Tolles, *Meeting House and Counting House: The Quaker Merchants of Colonial Philadelphia, 1682–1763* (New York, 1948), pp. 47, 159–60, 195–96. A full set was also among the Library Company's first acquisitions; Edwin Wolf, "The First Books and Printed Catalogues of the Library Company of Philadelphia," *Pennsylvania Magazine of History and Biography* 78, no. 1 (1954): 67–68.

I wish to call attention particularly to Marana's association of the merchant's seductive guile with hidden motives and actions. In Marana's text, the Quaker merchant ingenuously poses, but only poses, as a sincere man. The conventional signs of sincerity—a "modest and compos'd" exterior, sparing speech, industry, and punctuality—are no longer reliable indications of a virtuous character but veils that hide sincerity's opposite number: a "subtle and inventive" nature. Marana's particular terms of abuse, such as "Seducers," "craftiest," and "cunning," signal that merchants who mysteriously "heap up Riches" are quintessentially theatrical villains. They are clever impersonators capable of misrepresenting their true identities: one thing in public, another when operating in "obscurity." Indeed, by the passage's end, mercantile duplicity becomes virtually demonic. Mercantile cunning, when coupled with overtones of racial exoticism as figured in the Jewish and Indian ("Banian") traders, is "superlatively" great and sufficiently powerful to produce results akin to alchemy's magical transmutations.[2]

Marana's vitriol is symptomatic. His is an extreme version of a broader cultural castigation of the deceiver, who, when figured as a wily merchant, signaled to early modern writers and readers the dangers of commerce: its potentially corrupting effects on character and its disruption, via the disturbing power of money to beget money, of conventional criteria for judging social rank. The passage is also instructive because, in a curious way, the merchants' own view of their market milieu and of their fellow merchants recapitulated Marana's. In the voluminous correspondence that connected Philadelphia's overseas wholesale traders with their partners, suppliers, and buyers in Europe and throughout the British Atlantic,[3] the difficulty of discriminating between true sincerity and its ersatz facsimile is a persistent, often shrilly sounded motif. Like Marana,

2. On the preoccupation with dissimulation, see Katharine Eisaman Maus, "Proof and Consequences: Inwardness and Its Exposure in the English Renaissance," *Representations* 34 (Spring 1991): esp. 35–38. Note that the merchant has met his match in the reader. Like many other early forms of fiction, the *Turkish Spy* purports to be a collection of found letters, in this case those of a "Turkish spy" who is able to observe the morays and foibles of Europeans while remaining unobserved himself. Such fictions, like the immensely popular editions of letters by famous persons, position the reader as a privileged beholder, capable of penetrating the secret or private musings and conduct of others. On this point see Jean-Christophe Agnew, *Worlds Apart: The Market and the Theater in Anglo-American Thought, 1550–1750* (New York, 1986), p. 80, and Patricia Meyer Spacks, *Gossip* (New York, 1985), pp. 65–91.

3. I focus primarily on Philadelphia's largest wholesale merchants, men who were traders on a more or less full-time basis in Caribbean and overseas markets and who had sufficient wealth to appear among the richest 15 percent of all wholesalers active in the last half of the eighteenth century. By the criteria of wealth, kinship affiliations, and political connections, they were, for the most part, also members of Philadelphia's elite. See Thomas M. Doerflinger, *A Vigorous Spirit of Enterprise: Merchants and Economic Development in Revolutionary Philadelphia* (Chapel Hill, 1986), pp. 20–22, 25–26, 31–32.

merchants were apt to write as if they were bedeviled by insinuating deceivers and to emphasize that business success depended on penetrating the masks that hid the true intentions of others.

The widespread preoccupation with dissimulation or false appearances was one of a cluster of concerns underscored by the idiom of theatricality and its model of the divided self. As others have observed, theatricality was itself a response to anxieties about identity and reputation generated by commerce in an imperial age. But it was a response that codified rather than allayed those anxieties. The theatrical idiom's hallmark was a distinction between inner being and an outer, performative self that was said to enact or represent the life of the interior. Despite variations introduced by the idiom's association with a wide range of discourses bearing on practical virtue and personal comportment, most writers using it recommended the assiduous cultivation of a shielding outer persona as the solution to a felt sense of vulnerability. Yet by emphasizing deliberate self-fashioning and the difficulties of properly aligning inner selves and outer characters, this solution exacerbated fears not only about the misrepresentations of others but also about inadvertent self-exposure and the integrity of identity in a world conceived as populated by indifferent observers or spectators.[4]

Certain features of provincial merchants' economic and cultural milieu heightened the salience of theatricality and its problematics. Provincial merchants worked under conditions of unusual risk and uncertainty. They were, after all, in the midst of creating markets at the fringes of an expanding empire, and they did so without the support of a well-developed economic infrastructure. The unpredictability of markets and the lack of institutional guarantees meant that the intensive cultivation of personal ties and patronage connections to obtain credit and to carry out services at a distance was an absolute requirement of doing business. In

4. Agnew, *Worlds Apart*, pp. 9–12; Jean-Christophe Agnew, "Banking on Language: The Currency of Alexander Bryan Johnson," in *The Culture of the Market: Historical Essays*, ed. Thomas L. Haskell and Richard F. Teichgraeber III (Cambridge, 1996), pp. 231–58. David Marshall, *The Figure of Theater: Shaftesbury, Defoe, Adam Smith, and George Eliot* (New York, 1986), pp. 4–6. For a fuller summary and citations to the literature on theatricality, see Toby L. Ditz, "Shipwrecked; or, Masculinity Imperiled: Mercantile Representations of Failure and the Gendered Self in Eighteenth-Century Philadelphia," *Journal of American History* 81, no. 3 (1994): 54–55. On the formation of provincial identity, see T. H. Breen and Timothy Hall, "Structuring Provincial Imagination: The Rhetoric and Experience of Social Change in Eighteenth-Century New England," *American Historical Review* 103, no. 5 (1998): 1411–14, and the essays gathered in Ronald Hoffman, Mechal Sobel, and Fredrika J. Teute, eds., *Through a Glass Darkly: Reflections on Personal Identity in Early America* (Chapel Hill, 1997). On elite culture and its performative aspects, see Richard Bushman, *The Refinement of America: Persons, Houses, Cities* (New York, 1993); David S. Shields, *Civil Tongues and Polite Letters in British America* (Chapel Hill, 1997); and Jay Fliegelman, *Declaring Independence: Jefferson, Natural Language, and the Culture of Performance* (Stanford, 1993).

these circumstances, the need to find trustworthy associates was always pressing; misjudgments could spell financial disaster.[5] At the same time, establishing and maintaining one's own reputation for competence and honesty was equally essential. But these very conditions—the competitive yet still personalized nature of market transactions and their coupling with the scramble for patronage and connection—encouraged the theatrical imagination's fractured understandings of the self and its posture of suspicion. Once adopted, the merchants' use of the theatrical idiom virtually guaranteed that they would articulate this context as the felt experience of peril and vulnerable identity.

I.

My concern is with one particular permutation of the theatrical view of self and its relations with others: a tension between candor and what amounted to a counterethic of secrecy as standards for good character and conduct and for good writing itself. Given what I have called the posture of suspicion associated with theatricality, relationships based on trust often turned on the keeping of secrets. Merchants preoccupied with the dangers of self-revelation in a hostile world treated the sharing and guarding of secrets as a signifier of friendship and alliance. With a trusted friend one could afford to be unreserved and candid and to expect candor in return. Simultaneously, trust involved the sharing of secrets or truths safely revealed only to a handful. The symbiotic relation between candor and secrecy was, in turn, closely linked to an ongoing conceptual and figurative sorting of identity and social relations into domains of public and private experience; to demarcations between friends and strangers, home and world, inner character and worldly comportment; and to anxieties about the cultivation of public personas.

I turn first to the paramount ethic of candor. Given the cultural impor-

5. See especially Doerflinger, *Vigorous Spirit of Enterprise*, pp. 115, 133–43; Harry D. Berg, "The Organization of Business in Colonial Philadelphia," *Pennsylvania History* 10, no. 3 (1983): 157–77; Ditz, "Shipwrecked," pp. 55–58; Marc Egnal, "The Changing Structure of Philadelphia's Trade with the British West Indies, 1750–1775," *Pennsylvania Magazine of History and Biography* 99, no. 2 (1975): 156–79; David Hancock, *Citizens of the World: London Merchants and the Integration of the British Atlantic Community, 1735–1785* (Cambridge, 1995); John J. McCusker and Russell R. Menard, *The Economy of British America, 1607–1789* (Chapel Hill, 1985), esp. pp. 78–88, 189–200, 277–90, 334–41; Gary B. Nash, *The Urban Crucible: Social Change, Political Consciousness, and the Origins of the American Revolution* (Cambridge, Mass., 1979), pp. 72–74, 100–106, 119–23, 127–28, 161–67, 178–80, 235–39, 243–48, 256–60, 265–71; and Tolles, *Meeting House and Counting House*, pp. 88–89, 92–93, 99, 120–22. On the importance of personal connections for a slightly later period, see Naomi R. Lamoreaux, *Insider Lending: Banks, Personal Connections, and Economic Development in Industrial New England* (Cambridge, 1996).

tance of pietistic theology and moral codes in the colonies, most merchants, like other provincials, invoked the model of the divided self only to advocate plain style or sincerity, the perfect concordance of inner being and its outer representation or expression. The rhetoric of candor, sometimes formulaic and sometimes deployed with considerable creativity, came into play with respect to almost every dimension of business conduct as merchants negotiated with one another over pragmatic concerns. When performing services for one another, merchants understood their relations to involve a particular duty to adhere to the virtues of "fidelity" and "honest[y]," the qualities that made a man "fit to be trusted." In this they gave occupationally specific shape to the more widespread ethic of candor.[6]

But the premium on candor perhaps comes into sharpest relief when applied to mercantile writing itself. As the history of bookkeeping in the Weberian mode has made famously clear, occupationally specific imperatives about writing, especially as reinforced by general ethical and religious precepts, had an intimate bearing on mercantile subjectivity. The good merchant operated under a double injunction to keep meticulous records of his business activities and to be willing to exhibit them at a moment's notice to suppliers, buyers, and partners. As a secularized version of spiritual stocktaking and preparedness, this injunction carried a powerful ethical force; sloppy books indicated a level of moral laxness or slovenliness, as well as technical incompetence, while hesitations about their display hinted at fraudulent concealment. The imperative to keep impeccable books was all the more insistent in the case of the factor or commission merchant who bought and sold goods on behalf of others and, therefore, was under a special obligation to give timely "advice" to his principals or employers. Thus, John Mair, who wrote a best-selling manual on bookkeeping, dubbed the commercial agent "Peter Pen," as if to emphasize that his business was as much to write as it was to buy and

6. An early letter-writing manual contains a model letter from one merchant to another recommending a third man in the following terms: "I recommend to you the Person, on whose Fidelity you may firmly rely, as one that is both Just and Honest ... my Experience of his Conduct in many weighty Affairs, makes me confident in his Integrity and Ability, A Man both fit to be trusted and capable of serving so worthy a Person" (Thomas Goodman, *The Experienc'd Secretary or Citizen and Countryman's Companion* [London, 1699], p. 10). On trust, see also John Hill, *The Young Secretary's Guide; or, A Speedy Help to Learning*, 8th ed. (London, 1697), pp. 73, 86. On the eighteenth-century publication history of these two very influential manuals and their imitators, see Katherine Gee Hornbeak, "The Complete Letter-Writer in English, 1568–1800," *Smith College Studies in Modern Languages* 15 (October 1933–January 1934): 77, 84–86, 91–93, 95–99. For early merchants' letters invoking trust ideals, see William Shippen to John Askew, October 30, 1727, Philadelphia, Powel Papers, Historical Society of Pennsylvania, Philadelphia; John Reynell to Michael Atkins, October 1737, Reynell Letterbook, as cited in Berg, "Organization of Business," p. 165.

sell goods, and to underscore the relentless double-checking or self-audit-
ing necessary to produce accurate books.[7]

Even the fundamental accounting requirement that the inevitable error
be corrected with interpolations and strike lines rather than erasures to
avoid the appearance of fraud was indicative of the critical importance of
candor in writing. Nonlinear disruptions to the text—which included not
only interpolations but also marginal notations, almost identical consecu-
tive entries (in which the second entry corrected the first), and so forth—
called the auditing reader's attention to errors, allowing the reader to
visualize the whole chain of recording acts. Thus, the texture of the well-
written text is complex, but it is all surface, displaying both final result
and error-prone process as simultaneously present and undisguised.[8] In
short, the good merchant was ready at all times both to compute and to
show the books that contained the numerical narrative of his life as a
trader.

The importance of bookkeeping and the display of books as a mark of
mercantile competence and morality thus shaded into a more general
exhortation to live life as if it were an open book. Those exhortations often
mobilized distinctions between home and world only to advocate their
abolition. For example, bankruptcy statutes, pamphlet literature, and
mercantile letters alike used the imagery of the home when attempting to
pinpoint the elusive distinction between unfortunate debtors temporarily
unable to meet their obligations and "knavish" bankrupts.[9] William Blackstone's gloss on the recently reformed law of English bankruptcy is representative. He lists eleven deeds tending to indicate that a failing merchant was dishonest; among them were leaving "his own house with
intent to secrete himself" and "keep[ing] in his house privately." Once

7. John Mair, *Book-keeping Moderniz'd, or Merchant-Accounts by Double Entry, according to the Italian Form* (6th ed., Edinburgh, 1793; rpt., New York, 1978), pp. 43, 66–67. Mair's handbook went through over twenty eighteenth-century editions. On its use in the provinces, see McCusker and Menard, *Economy of British America,* and M. F. Bywater and B. S. Yamey, *Historic Accounting Literature: A Companion Guide* (London, 1982), pp. 164–67. On writing and personal identity, see Toby L. Ditz, "Formative Ventures: Eighteenth-Century Commercial Letters and the Articulation of Experience," in *Epistolary Selves: Letters and Letter-Writers, 1600–1948,* ed. Rebecca Earle (London, 1999), pp. 59–78; Margaret Hunt, *The Middling Sort: Commerce, Gender, and the Family in England, 1680–1780* (Berkeley, 1996), pp. 58–62, 172–85; and Donna Merwick, "The Suicide of a Notary: Language, Personal Identity, and Conquest in Colonial New York," in *Through a Glass Darkly,* ed. Hoffman, Sobel, and Teute, pp. 122–53.

8. Mair, *Book-keeping Moderniz'd,* pp. 63–67. On transparency, fraudulent concealment, and writing, see Sandra Sherman, "Credit, Simulation, and the Ideology of Contract in the Early Eighteenth Century," *Eighteenth-Century Life,* n.s., 19, no. 3 (1995): 89, 93.

9. Here, as in other cases, lay and professional discourse and political and mercantile polemics were mutually influential, articulated in overlapping genres and intersecting forums; see Julian Hoppit, *Risk and Failure in English Business, 1700–1800* (Cambridge, England, 1987), esp. pp. 18–28.

accused of bad faith, virtually any behavior could be construed as symptomatic of a devious secretiveness; the dishonest debtor could neither stay nor go. What united these and the other enumerated acts was an intent to "evade" one's creditors and, in particular, "to avoid being seen or spoken to" by them. The fraud refused transparency in favor of private defiance, secrecy, and withdrawal into, what Marana would have called, "obscurity." Blackstone's widely shared association of mercantile immorality with concealment and secrecy helped to define by negation the conduct of the honest debtor. The impecunious merchant who wished to maintain his credibility and avoid further escalation of conflict had to be willing literally to be at home and to open his doors when his creditors knocked. It is, then, no accident that in eighteenth-century Philadelphia and elsewhere, the arbitration proceedings that brought together a failing merchant and his creditors usually took place at the debtor's house, where the conclave of creditors examined the distressed merchant's account books, papers, and correspondence.[10]

Merchants engaged in less formal disputes with one another also associated honesty in bookkeeping with the imagery of thresholds easily crossed. When, for example, John Reynell and Jane Farson, the widow of Reynell's former business correspondent, quarreled over money that she claimed he owed her, both parties stressed mutual visitation and inspection of the merchant's records. Reynell writes to Farson that he had already credited her account with the sums owed as "appears Clearly by my Books," and he upbraids her for not coming to his "Store" to examine his books as he had requested the last time she was in "Town" (Farson lived in Wilmington). Farson did make one trip to Philadelphia to "visit his house" and assumed some of the blame for what turned out to be a protracted dispute on the grounds that she had not visited soon enough. To be "clear of hard thoughts" and "prejudice," she offered to make yet another trip to Philadelphia. The visits did not resolve the dispute. Farson argued that "even the best and most honest" books may be "mistaken," and she offered ancillary documents and letters in support of her position, copies of which she had hand-delivered to Reynell's doorstep. She and Reynell also subsequently disagreed about what they had said when she was "at [his] house." But the visits served a more intangible purpose. Judging from her offer of a repeat visit to dispel "hard thoughts," Farson apparently viewed Reynell's willingness to open his house and books for

10. William Blackstone, *Commentaries on the Laws of England: A Facsimile of the First Edition of 1765–1769*, vol. 2, *Of the Rights of Things* (1766), intro. A. W. Brian Simpson (Chicago, 1979), pp. 477–79. See also Doerflinger, *Vigorous Spirit of Enterprise*, pp. 142–46; Hoppit, *Risk and Failure*, pp. 18–28; and Bruce Mann, *Neighbors and Strangers: Law and Community in Early Connecticut* (Chapel Hill, 1987), pp. 101–7, 128–32.

inspection as a token of his honesty.[11] Although she persisted in calling Reynell mistaken, she never accused him outright of deception.

In this light, the merchant's house (or "store") was a special arena for dispute resolution, one designed to contain conflicts that could then remain private affairs among friends. But as the very persistence of contention and Farson's continued expression of lingering doubt indicate, the merchant's house was sometimes a site for the ongoing vocalization and elaboration of suspicion. As Reynell hints at the height of their bickering when he writes, "If thou thinks I am so bad a Man as to assert things that are not true, its time for thee to have done with me," the meetings at a merchant's house could operate as a relay, a preparation for the moment when his books and conduct would be subject to the scrutiny and judgment of a wider public as the dispute spilled out into open court or circulated in the newspapers that gave notice to the merchant's potential creditors.[12]

Even as merchants articulated an unconditional ethic of candor in their daily dealings, merchant friendships highlighted the capacity to keep secrets. As one might expect, partners routinely circulated among themselves information that they regarded as confidential. Thus, in 1762 Richard Hill warned his brother and partner in Philadelphia, Henry Hill, that his two-page hypothetical "calculation" demonstrating the greater profitability of shipping wines on commission rather than on twelve months' credit, "should not been seen by any body but yourself," as if the relative merits of each practice were not widely discussed in mercantile circles as they hobnobbed at coffeehouses and on the wharves. Years later, Henry Hill would complain to his London partner that a mark of his declining status as an aging senior member of what had proved to be a long-lived firm now recruiting second-generation kinsmen was that the other partners no longer sent him the "Detailed information" suited to his "rank."[13]

Merchants who regularly did business with one another, like partners, underscored their solidarity by creating shared secrets. Thus, in the 1740s a New Jersey wheat supplier pleads with Philadelphia merchant Samuel Powell to keep a buyer's complaint about the quality of a recent shipment "Secret for reasons easily understood," justifying his request partly on the grounds that he and Powell have been longtime correspondents. Or,

11. John Reynell to Jane Farson, May 5, 1775, and July 10, 1776, Philadelphia, Reynell Letterbook, and Farson to Reynell, May 14, 1775, October 1, 1775, April 6, 1776, and May 11, 1777, Wilmington, Coates-Reynell Collection, Historical Society of Pennsylvania.

12. Reynell to Farson, July 10, 1776, Philadelphia, Coates-Reynell Collection.

13. Richard Hill to Henry Hill, January 18, 1762, Madeira, and Henry Hill to Thomas Lamar, October 24, 1788, Philadelphia, Sarah A. G. Smith Family Papers, 1732–1826, Historical Society of Pennsylvania.

again, late in the century Samuel Southern wrote to Samuel Coates, a
Philadelphia wholesaler, that "it will not be communicated to any of your
Friends which will do you any dammage" that Coates had shipped more
than Southern had ordered.[14] In these cases, the keeping of secrets had
practical import for the merchant's reputation for business competence.
But as the example of the hypothetical calculation indicates, the practical
consequences attendant on preserving or failing to preserve secrets were
sometimes of less moment than the organization of social relations
around them.[15] And even when the practical consequences were great, the
sharing of secrets simultaneously marked off a zone of privileged friendship putatively insulated from competition. By the same token, merchants
represented relations outside this zone not only as competitive but also as
tinged with malice.

The association of market competitiveness with potentially humiliating
public exposure comes through clearly in a letter from Robert Bisset, who
was a senior partner in a firm specializing in Madeira wines. He writes to
his London partner and brother-in-law in March 1789, when the firm was
operating at a loss. In an attempt to salvage their deteriorating position,
Bisset tried to convince his partner to accept a new way of handling the
capital he had invested in the firm. Bisset claimed that he would be
driven to distraction should their credit fail and portrayed the consequences of allowing the news of the firm's precarious financial condition
to circulate beyond the confines of the partnership itself as a scene of mor-
tifying defeat. "We shall," he writes, "become the scoff of our Neighbors
who would triumph should they . . . know our present situation." He then
urges the utmost secrecy, while using the strong image of scourged earth
to indicate what will happen should his partner, Lamar, fail to act decisively and discreetly. "My communications," Bisset revealed, "have hith-
erto arisen from my own ideas not chusing to consult with any person on
so delicate a point least the nakedness of the land should be discovered."[16]

The imagery of public exposure and shaming at the hands of hostile

14. Andrew Reed to Samuel Powell Jr., March 17, 1745, Trenton, Powel Papers; Samuel
Southern to Coates and Reynell, December 6, 1783, Newburyport, Coates-Reynell Collection.
Goodman's letter-writing manual contains a paradigmatic example of the constitution of
trust relations around secrecy. The entry begins, "In a confident reliance on your Fidelity, I
am imboldened . . . to communicate weighty Secrets to you. . . . As for the Secrets I formerly
communicated to you, by your faithfully laying them up in the Repository of your Breast . . .
they have in all things . . . succeeded" (Goodman, *Experienc'd Secretary*, p. 38). See also John
Hill, *Young Secretary's Guide*, p. 86.

15. See Stephanie Jed, *Chaste Thinking: The Rape of Lucretia and the Birth of Humanism*
(Bloomington, Ind., 1989), p. 82.

16. Robert Bisset to Thomas Lamar, March 2, 1789, London, Smith Family Papers. For more
on Bisset and scenarios of exposure and shaming generally, see Ditz, "Shipwrecked," pp.
66–69, 72–73.

and judgmental "neighbors" is suggestive. It links the mercantile view of commercial relations, including their all-important networks of credit, with what Jay Fliegelman has called the "culture of performance" and its problematics.[17] More generally, the merchants' articulation of the problem of trust and secrecy, with its vocabulary of friends and enemies and of triumph and humiliation also embeds competition not so much in the logic of *im*personal market dynamics but in a language of honorable service associated with the ties of instrumental friendship and connection that still structured eighteenth-century commerce.

A view of trust centering on secrets, then, contained its own contradictions. As Stephanie Jed has pointed out in her brilliant analysis of Florentine mercantile culture, it generated a preoccupation with the possibility that secrets would be penetrated or violated, and it conjured up an explicit or implied image of those fair-weather "friends" and "neighbors" who might do one "dammage." Similarly, it entailed, as its underside, the problem of treachery by those privy to inside knowledge. This view articulated the insecurities and competitiveness of market life in such a way as to increase rather than dispel distrust and suspicion.[18]

Moreover, the posture of suspicion turned the guarded man into his own nemesis in the end. Construing others as opaque, the merchant defined himself as needing to reveal the secrets of others, to penetrate their dissembling veil of secrecy. The following advice from the successful, if somewhat irascible, merchant John Reynell to Elias Bland, who was just finishing his apprenticeship in 1743, is illustrative. "In doing business be a little on the Reserve," Reynell cautioned, "and Observe well the Person thou has to do with . . . and don't let it be known, who thou dost Business for, or what Sorts of Goods thou Ships off. Some will want to know both, perhaps with a Design to Circumvent thee." He continues: "Endeavour to know what Prices other People give for Goods, but Say nothing of what thou gives thy self, . . . its very Probable some will tell thee, they give more for a thing than they did, on Purpose to make thee buy dear, in Order to do thee an Injury." Frederick Tolles, the historian of Philadelphia's Quaker merchants, cites this letter to confirm the Quakers' reputation for "taciturn" silence, which he attributes primarily to their religiously based premium on plain style. He also notes that (as in Marana's text) the Quakers' reputation for truth telling transmuted easily, via the image of their disciplined silence, into its opposite, a reputation for cun-

17. Fliegelman, *Declaring Independence*. See also Bushman, *Refinement of America*. For the colonial concept of neighborliness, see Mann, *Neighbors and Strangers*, pp. 162–69; Mary Beth Norton, *Founding Mothers and Fathers: Gendered Power and the Forming of American Society* (New York, 1996), pp. 241–44.

18. Jed, *Chaste Thinking*, p. 85. See also Agnew, *Worlds Apart*, pp. 79–87, 96–100.

ning, for "slyness." We might add to Tolles's gloss that Reynell's advice is
a good example of the theatrical imagination at work in the arena of business operations. His world was filled with those who lied or deceived others with a "Design" to gain advantage or profit (again, thought of as
"injury"). The antidote was not only silence but also a vigilant and penetrating gaze of one's own. Such a view underscored the theatrical stance
by implying that every trader's persona was composed of an artful second
nature that masked a carefully guarded self.[19]

Such a model of the self, however well adapted to the problematics of
display and reputation building in commercial port cities, produced a further contradiction. As the foregoing passages suggest, it deeply complicated the ethic of candor by implying, without fully acknowledging, that
straightforward transparency was undesirable and perhaps impossible.
For a final illustration, I turn not to a practicing merchant but to Samuel
Richardson, one of England's foremost advocates of sincerity and plain
style. In the following passage, he anticipates Robert Bisset's preoccupation with secrecy and scoffing "neighbors" in the vilification he heaps on
apprentices to traders who would gossip about their masters. Richardson's jeremiad is perhaps a classic statement of worries over betrayal and
exposure and one in considerable tension with his usual insistence on
candor.

> The Man is not living who is without Faults; and if a Master has ever so
> many, and those ever so gross, it is not a Servant's Duty to expose them, or
> him; but, on the contrary, a kind of Treachery and baseness of Disposition
> for a Person to be guilty of, who is taken into a Family in so intimate a
> Relation, as that of an Apprentice, so that he must needs know the Secrets
> of it. The Names and Crimes of the *Spy-Fault*, the *Back-biter*, the *Detractor*,
> the *Ingrateful*, the *Betrayer of Secrets*, become his.—Besides, of what Avail
> can such Back-biting and Detraction be? If the Master even be an *ill Man*,
> and what is said of him *true*, that Servant is *worse* who exposes him . . . so
> that a Man is *degraded* and made the Subject of *Ridicule* and *Scoff*, not only
> of his *insolent Servants*, but perhaps of his *unfriendly Neighbors*.[20]

19. Reynell to Elias Bland, June 22, 1743, Reynell Letterbook, as cited in Tolles, *Meeting
House and Counting House*, p. 60. For others advocating a protective silence, see Robert Lamar
Bisset to Henry Hill, December 25, 1785, Madeira, Smith Family Papers; Edward Shippen to
Jasper Yeats, July 16 1783, [Lancaster], Edward Shippen Letterbook, Burd-Shippen-Hubley
Family Papers, Historical Society of Pennsylvania. For the history of debates about the rela-
tive merits of silence and polished speech as strategies for dealing with a world of dissem-
blers, see Agnew, *Worlds Apart*, pp. 80–81.

20. Samuel Richardson, *The Apprentice's Vade Mecum; or, Young Man's Pocket-Companion*,
Augustan Reprint Society Publication no. 169–70 (London, 1734; rpt., Los Angeles, 1975), pp.
45–46. See also Richardson, *Familiar Letters on Important Occasions*, ed. J. Isaacs (London, 1741;
rpt., London, 1928), p. 47.

Although Richardson does not ask the servant to lie, he is suggesting that he collude in the concealment of his master's flaws—even vices—and in the maintenance of his untarnished public persona. In his theatrical preoccupation with the master's potential abasement before unsympathetic observers ("unfriendly Neighbors"), Richardson in this passage takes for granted what he elsewhere condemns: a split between the inner and outer persona.[21] Similarly, he unsuccessfully tries to avoid the implication that the faithful servant must exercise a certain guile in serving his master's interests. One also notes the vehemence, typical of the theatrical imagination, with which the risk of exposure (a word Richardson uses twice) is stated. When an "intimate" brings a man's vulnerable inner life into public view, the man becomes "subject" to "ridicule" and scorn; he is "degraded" before his "neighbors," put through an undeserved collective ritual of mortification. No wonder the gossiping intimate is viewed not merely as indiscreet but as a treacherous spy too, for by circulating "secrets" he has committed an act that derogates not his own rank but the public standing of his master.

Finally, like the provincial traders and others to whom Richardson explicitly directs his advice, his own association of trust with secrecy is closely related to distinctions between private and public domains. Richardson, who elsewhere lists taverns, theaters, and the streets as places to be approached with caution or avoided altogether by the industrious apprentice, is particularly distressed that a member of a master's "family" should, through idle talk, circulate household secrets. In this way the endorsement of a shielding secrecy could produce the separation between home and world that the ethic of candor deemed illegitimate; it constituted the household as private space, precisely as a home, by defining it as a place where the secrets of one's blemished self might be at once safely revealed to intimates but hidden from the view of "unfriendly neighbors" beyond the door. Of course, as Richardson's vehemence suggests and as the potent figure of the treacherous servant reminds us, the private places that sheltered unadorned selves were never completely secure. When the theatrical imagination created the border between the public world of potentially jeering neighbors and the private realm of relations founded on faithful service, it simultaneously stirred up apprehensions of its transgression.[22]

21. For a characteristic plea for candor yoked to the ideal of transparency, see Richardson, *Apprentice's Vade Mecum*, p. 37.

22. A charming early-eighteenth-century instance occurs when Isaac Norris writes to his London correspondent and friend John Askew, noting that if he could ask Askew "without seeing it wrote," he "would wisper to send . . . some Shuttle Cocks of the best make" "to Exercise [his] Children in the hall in Cold Weather." Aware that many of his Quaker neighbors would regard the possession of such items as a violation of plain style, Norris trusts

The obsession with privileged information had a further consequence for merchants' writing specifically: even as they equated fraud with the illegitimate concealment of "goods, Books and Cash Notes," merchants could associate their own writing with a needed, protective secrecy.[23] This was certainly true of letters. Eighteenth-century correspondents could not assume that letters would be read only by the addressee; some subgenres were private communications for the delectation of an audience of one, but others were virtuoso displays of writing prowess intended for display or had the qualities of a circulating newsletter. Thus it was not unusual for a merchant's letters, conveying as they did news of markets and imperial affairs, to appear pinned up on coffeehouse bulletin boards or excerpted verbatim in newspapers. In this era, then, one was well advised to signal expressly one's desire for confidentiality, a process that reinforced an association between secrecy and the letter. Accordingly, merchants replicated the advice of letter-writing manuals that routinely devoted several pages to the proper method for applying seals and to introductions for trusted colleagues who hand-delivered letters to distant recipients.[24] More generally, it followed almost by definition that when merchants

Askew to behave as if his letter did not exist, to treat the letter as if it were only an evanescent whisper. Trust also permits a vivid (and, in this case, exculpatory) written scene of domestic life. Isaac Norris to John Askew, March 2, 1716/1717, Philadelphia, as cited in Tolles, *Meeting House and Counting House*, p. 137. For similar complications, see Daniel Defoe, *The Complete English Tradesman* (1726; Gloucester, England, 1987), pp. 162–67.

23. For accusations of fraud and quarrels about profit and loss centering on the illicit concealment of papers, see John Reynell to Daniel Flexney, September 30, 1736, Philadelphia, Reynell Letterbook, Coates-Reynell Collection. (Reynell complains that an indebted merchant and one of his many creditors together committed "a Piece of very great Fraud" on the remaining creditors, when the creditor "Got into his custody all [the] goods, Books and Cash Notes" of his debtor friend.) See also Robert Bisset to Henry Hill, May 15, 1786, Madeira, Smith Family Papers.

24. Censorship of mail and a murkiness in the legal distinction between personal letters and those belonging to the chartered entity for which a merchant worked (for example, the East India Company) could also be issues. Richard D. Brown, *Knowledge Is Power: The Diffusion of Information in Early America, 1700–1865* (New York, 1989); Earle, *Epistolary Selves*; Hornbeak, "Complete Letter-Writer"; Spacks, *Gossip*, pp. 65–91; Keith Stewart, "Towards Defining an Aesthetic for the Familiar Letter in Eighteenth-Century England," *Prose Studies* 5, no. 2 (1982): 179–92. On Philadelphia, see Jay Fliegelman, *Prodigals and Pilgrims: The American Revolution against Patriarchal Authority, 1750–1800* (New York, 1982), pp. 37–69, 83, 89; Tolles, *Meeting House and Counting House*, pp. 161–204. Some advice manuals went so far as to recommend—albeit with tongue half in cheek—secret codes and invisible ink. William Mather, in a section of his *Young Man's Companion*, which went through twenty-four editions by 1775, suggested, for example, that his readers "write [their] Mind[s]" with milk or "Gall Water," while interleaving "that which" they "would have Secret" with innocuous prose written in "common Ink." Thus, his secret letter has an effect precisely the converse of the nubby surface of the account book that displays all: a seemingly straightforward surface of "common Ink" is actually a veneer designed to guard the invisible secrets of the interior life (William Mather, *The Young Man's Companion* [13th ed., London, 1727; rpt., New York, 1939], pp. 14–15). On trusted emissaries, see Hill, *Young Secretary's Guide*, p. 86.

exchanged confidences, the letters and documents recording them were themselves regarded, in effect, as secret papers.

Indeed, merchants sometimes conceived their letters and books in spatial terms, handling their writings as items to be deposited in guarded or hidden places known only to a trusted few. Their treatment of their writing as secret texts to be kept under lock and key contributed to the conceptualization of the household as a private place. Thomas Lawrence's instructions to his sister, Catherine, who is also his sole legatee by his last will and testament (the siblings have outlived both their father and eldest brother), provide an example. In this case, as in others, secret writing is also closely linked to family fate and fortunes. On the eve of a voyage to Providence as a supercargo in 1761, Lawrence writes that he wishes to inform his sister that he has left a "Receipt for £200 Currency which you'll find in a Small Book, lying in my Desk, the Key of which is in a Small trunk left with Mr. Goodwin, where you'll allso find papers of Consiquence Relating to my father, & Brother, which Beg you'll give Mssrs. Crugers the perusal of."[25] In short, he has constructed something of a treasure hunt in which each person holds only one of many clues as to the whereabouts of the secret book (or papers) and its contents. Only the potential nearness of death has led him to give the entire map to his most trusted intimate, his sister. At the same time as the letter reveals the whereabouts of papers, the letter traces a social network of trusted colleagues organized around his dead father's and brother's legacy of paper. Thus the elaborate precautions taken bore not only on the documents' practical importance but also testified to the larger symbolic resonance of secret writing as a way of associating trusted friends with private places (desks, studies, and libraries).

The dominant ideal of candor, structured as it was by the idiom of theatricality, was, therefore, not without its ambiguities. Merchants, like others who advocated sincerity, condemned disjunctures between inner lives and outer character as signs of knavish duplicity. But in their anxiety to protect themselves from the scoffers who would take advantage of their "faults," their writing could hardly avoid reproducing the distance between interior lives and public reputations, domestic scenes and public stages that they otherwise denounced as immoral. A counterethic of secrecy served to distinguish trusted intimates from others, but in such a way as to deem fragile the protection that such a distinction offered. The realm of intimacy, sometimes signified by images of the home, was porous and—as the word "secrecy" suggests—not fully freed from the taint of illicit camouflage.

---

25. Thomas Lawrence to Catherine Lawrence, May 19, 1761, and June 23, 1762, New York, Powel Papers; Jed, *Chaste Thinking*, p. 83.

II.

The emphasis so far has been on mercantile narratives of practical business matters, an emphasis that highlights cultural and social dynamics internal to the mercantile community. Yet merchants were members of a broader provincial elite, thus their public personas were subject not simply to the scrutiny of their class peers but also to the critical evaluation of the artisans, servants, and laborers with whom they interacted. Because men and women of different classes and political persuasions rubbed shoulders with one another on the wharves, at marketplaces, and in taverns, mercantile codes of secrecy and candor had a political, cross-class dimension. This was especially true in the late colonial era, when Philadelphia's public culture was becoming both more broadly inclusive, yet more contested. In particular, the use of secrecy to conceptualize and demarcate zones of intimacy and trust from arenas associated with the hazards of competition, manipulative self-display, and the risk of self-exposure played a direct role in debates about political loyalty and political representation during the Revolutionary era. To illustrate this use of secrecy, I focus on the case of the East India Company tea commissioners.[26]

We may start by recollecting that on both sides of the Atlantic, the republican opposition's critique of monarchy associated secrecy and guile with absolutist pretensions and the corrupt politics of court patronage, while aligning legitimate political representation with "publicity" and "transparency." But, as Dena Goodman has pointed out in her revisionist assessment of Habermasian public sphere analysis, historians should repudiate, for analytic purposes, any such easy associations between republicanism and publicity, on the one hand, and absolutism and secrecy, on the other. Rather, the tension between publicity and secrecy played itself out precisely within the social networks and forms of associational life that Habermas and others identify most closely with an emerging public sphere, in those formally nongovernmental networks and "institutions of sociability" that were of major consequence for both commercial life and oppositional politics in eighteenth-century port cities: taverns and coffeehouses, improvement societies and men's clubs, and such media of communication as newspapers.[27]

---

26. See Timothy H. Breen, "Narrative of Commercial Life: Consumption, Ideology, and Community on the Eve of the American Revolution," *William and Mary Quarterly*, 3d. ser., 50, no. 3 (1993): 491–94; J. E. Crowley, *This Sheba, Self: The Conceptualization of Economic Life in Eighteenth-Century America* (Baltimore, 1974), pp. 142–57; Doerflinger, *Vigorous Spirit of Enterprise*, pp. 167–68, 179, 189–90; and Nash, *Urban Crucible*, pp. 242–46.

27. Dena Goodman, "Public Sphere and Private Life: Toward a Synthesis of Current Historiographical Approaches to the Old Regime," *History and Theory* 31, no. 1 (1992): 4, 6–7, 9, 11–13, 17; see also Peter Thompson, *Rum, Punch, and Revolution: Taverngoing and Public Life in*

These were the same sites that merchants (and others) viewed in highly theatrical terms as requiring the cultivation of guarded public personas and as fraught with the potential for damaging self-exposure. This was the field of social relations unconsecrated by trust or, better, the field within which the necessary distinctions between trusted allies and others were constantly produced. To put this another way, the tension between publicity and secrecy criss-crossed the realms of society and polity, which were in any case interlocking, precisely because the rhetoric of secrecy both marked off absolutist pretensions from legitimate state politics and generated representations of social experience outside the state that tentatively identified intimate domains putatively exempt from the tense logic of social relations lived in "public."

Turning now to the tea commissioners and the political uptake of the merchants' representations of private and public experience, I single out one episode concerning the partners Henry Drinker and Abel James, who ran one of Philadelphia's largest and longest-lived colonial mercantile concerns, and some of their close associates. In the spring and summer of 1773, the assiduous cultivation of their connections in New York and London produced a large payoff for Drinker and James; they became, along with five other prominent Philadelphia merchants, agents for the East India Company, whose ailing financial condition was about to be remedied by Parliament's new Tea Act. Their first practical duty would be to receive and sell an anticipated shipment of tea—the only item still subject to a duty under the terms of the Townshend Acts. Because the merchants now acted on behalf of a semipublic corporation in the midst of the imperial crisis, their views of their duties as commercial agents became a major political issue.

Drinker and James, along with their fellow commissioners in Philadelphia and New York, initially viewed their commissions as prize plums well worth the months of trouble it took to get, conceptualizing their

---

Eighteenth-Century Philadelphia (Philadelphia, 1999), pp. 17–20, 111–19, 159–81, 203–4. On the emergence of a public in late-colonial port cities, see Brown, *Knowledge Is Power*; Breen, " 'Baubles of Britain: The American and Consumer Revolutions of the Eighteenth Century," *Past and Present*, no. 119 (1988): 73–104; Breen and Hall, "Provincial Imagination," pp. 1434–38; Shields, *Civil Tongues and Polite Letters*, pp. xiv–xvii, 315–17; David Waldstreicher, *In the Midst of Perpetual Fetes: The Making of American Nationalism, 1776–1820* (Chapel Hill, 1997); and Michael Warner, *The Letters of the Republic: Publication and the Public Sphere in Eighteenth-Century America* (Cambridge, Mass., 1990), pp. 17–18. On the public sphere generally, see Jürgen Habermas, "The Public Sphere: An Encyclopedia Article," *New German Critique* 1, no. 3 (1974): 49–55; Craig Calhoun, ed., *Habermas and the Public Sphere* (Cambridge, Mass., 1992); Joan Landes, *Women and the Public Sphere in the Age of the French Revolution* (Ithaca, 1988); and Daniel Gordon, David A. Bell, and Sara Maza, "Forum: The Public Sphere in the Eighteenth Century," *French Historical Studies* 17, no. 4 (1992): 882–950.

"trust" in such a way as to meld conventional commercial canons of accountability and fidelity with more general notions of ethical responsibility before men and God. Indeed, as "Men of Integrity who had to answer for their conduct at a future day,"[28] the atmosphere of escalating rumor and mounting opposition to the imminent shipment at first inspired the commissioners to visions of manly firmness on behalf of strategies attempting to reconcile the company's interests with the provincials' hostility to the Parliamentary duty. Thus, Benjamin Booth, a fellow commissioner in New York and a longtime business partner of Drinker and James, writes, "As Agents to the Company, we mean to be very firm to the trust reposed in us, that we will neither be awed by the number of our opponents nor terrified by their threats, fully convinced that they act upon interested motives."[29] In Booth's view, then, although the motives of the radicals were selfish and partial, those of the commissioners were not. As agents who represented the interests of others when carrying out the "trust reposed" in them, the commissioners transcended self-interest. Their service conferred a legitimacy that the opposition could not claim.

The image of steadfast bravery in the face of numerous and threatening opponents may also have been a fortifying tonic for writer and recipient alike, as radical strategy coalesced around forcing all tea-bearing ships headed for any provincial port to return without unloading. Booth would write two weeks later that the "drooping spirits" of his colleagues "too often want a Cordial."[30] As well they might; at least two New York agents would soon be burned in effigy, a fate Booth narrowly escaped.

As the commission merchants, subject to constant pressure from militant American provincials, attempted to preserve their jobs, their reputations, and, even, their necks, they also began to squabble among themselves. They viewed their time of troubles not only as a drama of exposure at the hands of the radicals but also in terms of rifts created among the commissioners by illicit secrecy and the failure of candor. Such acrimony, with its dark undertow of mutual suspicion, was partly responsible for the piecemeal and somewhat desultory response of Philadelphia's moderates and conservatives to unfolding events. In Philadelphia, if not in all places, it contributed to the failure of elites to reassert control over the resistance on behalf of strategies less threatening to the architecture of commercial empire than those which ultimately prevailed, and even to

28. [Henry Drinker on behalf of] James and Drinker to Booth and Pigou, October 29, 1773, Philadelphia, James and Drinker Papers, Historical Society of Pennsylvania.

29. Benjamin Booth to James and Drinker, October 4, 1773, and October 18, 1773, New York, James and Drinker Papers.

30. Booth to James and Drinker, October 18, 1773.

their larger failure to maintain dominance over municipal and provincial government.[31]

Radicals, of course, had a view of the responsibilities of the commissioners different from that of the India Company agents themselves. Moreover, they were willing to mobilize artisans, tradesmen, and laborers on behalf of militant resistance tactics and a more democratic, less deferential vision of politics. Thus "the inhabitants of Philadelphia" who attended a general open-air meeting on October 16, 1773, condemned the Parliamentary duty on the anticipated shipment of tea in a series of resolutions. As is well known, they used the language of radical republicanism to damn the duty as taxation without "consent" and thus as an arbitrary seizure of property in violation of the "inherent Right of Freemen." It was, further, part of a "ministerial plan" that had a "Direct tendency" to introduce "arbitrary Government" by "render[ing] Assemblies useless." It followed that "Every freeman in America" had a duty to show "virtuous & steady opposition" to such a plan and that anyone who participated in "unloading, receiving or vending the Teas . . . is an Enemy to his country." To do otherwise was selfishly to pursue the lure of profits at the expense of the public good.[32]

Although the assembled inhabitants ratified the resolutions by acclamation at the open-air meeting—What could be more public?—the leaders who organized the meeting and drafted the declaration as a means of pressuring moderates and conservatives did much of their planning at Bradford's Old London Coffeehouse and the City Tavern, places favored by elites and especially by merchants. Much political organizing—official and extraofficial—went on in the small back or upstairs rooms provided by many of Philadelphia's taverns. These semiprivate enclaves within the more or less public setting of the tavern were congenial places for gentlemen leaders who preferred a style of politics that resembled regulated conversation among friends. In this respect, the political styles of moderate and radical leaders were not so very different. But this mode of organizing also contributed to mutual recriminations, to accusations of secretive scheming and lack of candor.[33]

The resolutions did not say—but within the framework of republican rhetoric might well have—that the tea commissioners were prime exam-

31. Doerflinger calls the merchants "reluctant revolutionaries" (*Vigorous Spirit of Enterprise*, pp. 167–68, 180–87); see also Nash, *Urban Crucible*, pp. 240–46.

32. "Resolutions of a Meeting of a Great Number of Inhabitants of Philadelphia," October 16, 1773, Enclosure (copy), James and Drinker to Booth and Pigou, October 29, 1773, Philadelphia, James and Drinker Papers. On populist radicals and merchants, see Crowley, *This Sheba, Self*, pp. 142–46.

33. The clientele of taverns tended to split more clearly along political and class lines as the Revolution unfolded; see Thompson, *Rum, Punch, and Revolution*, pp. 145–81. On political styles, see Waldstreicher, *Perpetual Fetes*.

ples of placemen who had been robbed of virtue by the corrupting seductions of patronage, a major weapon in the furtherance of the "ministerial plan." A position which from one vantage point had seemed a just reward for a patronage game well played and in which one could exercise the manly firmness inherent in faithful service was now symptomatic of political parasitism, a literally treacherous failure or alienation of political will. Borrowing from religious antecedents, especially from Quaker practices of friendly conversation and admonishment and, more proximately, from the merchants' own habits of mutual visitation, the eighth and final resolution authorized a delegation of eight leading Anglican and Quaker merchants to "wait on" the "gentlemen" rumored to have been appointed as agents and to ask them to resign their commission.[34]

In the following passages, Henry Drinker recounts the immediate aftermath of this round of visits for the benefit of Benjamin Booth and his new partner, James Pigou (who had been, incidentally, the London "connection" primarily responsible for obtaining the company commissions for Drinker and James). After the committee questioned James and Drinker, it returned to its usual meeting place at the coffeehouse and reported the results aloud to those assembled. According to Drinker, "After reading what related to Thos & Isaac Wharton a hand Clap ensued and upon reading their report of our Answer—a Hiss was heard from Diverse within the House—We [Drinker and his partner, Abel James] have not been able to collect the Answer deliver'd by Thos and Isaac Wharton, they assure us it was the same in substance with ours, but if that was the Case, the Committee must have acted an invidious part."[35] Drinker then notes that the commissioners had met together in advance of the delegation's expected visits to fashion a unified response and wonders whether the other commissioners really had adhered to their private agreement. (The commissioners had apparently agreed to stipulate that the parliamentary duty was a violation of fundamental right but to argue that resignation was premature because they had not yet received formal instructions from the East India Company and, therefore, could not be sure that they would be asked to do anything incompatible with virtue.)[36]

Drinker continues, writing that if the others "did depart from" this

34. On Quaker visitation, censure, and discipline, see Barry Levy, *Quakers and the American Family: British Settlement in the Delaware Valley* (New York, 1988), pp. 57–61, 70–82, 96–100, 129–31, and Jean Soderland, *Quakers and Slavery: A Divided Spirit* (Princeton, 1985), pp. 30–31, 189–93.

35. [Drinker on behalf of] James and Drinker to Booth and Pigou, October 19, 1773, Philadelphia, James and Drinker Papers. See also Committee Report, October 23, 1773, as Enclosure (copy), James and Drinker to Booth and Pigou, October 29, 1773, Philadelphia, James and Drinker Papers.

36. [Drinker on behalf of] James and Drinker to Booth and Pigou, November 20, 1773, Philadelphia, James and Drinker Papers.

agreement, "we can't help it, but as honest Men, who were to account at a future day . . . we could not think ourselves justified in going further in our reply to the Committee. Thus you see we are in the way of trouble, no doubt but that class of Men among us called the Sons of Liberty, will treat us as very bad Men, for Acting a Part which we conceive becomes every good and honest man circumstanced as we are."[37] The theatricality of this narrative is stark. The letter creates a scene, a drama of betrayal and exposure to which the literally absent writer and reader are now spectators. The effect is to heighten a sense of immediacy; the "hisses" and "hand-claps" become very nearly audible registers of the judgment of those assembled. On another level, when Drinker once again declares that he and his partner are "honest Men" who will be held "to account at a future day," though the sentiments are conventional, his emphasis is on the requirement to convey that candor effectively to the hissing and clapping audience. Though Drinker's evaluation of the commissioners' position differed from that of the Sons of Liberty, he too saw himself as "Acting a Part," or assuming or putting on the moral attitude appropriate for those "circumstanced" in a position of trust. This is not to say that when Drinker invoked the canon of faithful service to fortify himself against the vilification he expected to receive that he viewed himself as self-serving (however we or the Sons of Liberty might see it). But he is concerned with the social or public dimension of his virtuous character and with his failed ability to maintain a credible public persona or reputation for candor.[38]

Moreover, when Drinker suggested that the committee must have distorted the answer of the other commissioners or, worse, that the other commissioners "departed" from their prior agreement, he introduced motifs of misrepresentation, secrecy, and betrayal that repeatedly recurred in the ensuing weeks. Drinker continued to suspect Wharton of duplicity, simultaneously suggesting that the committee deliberately fomented a "division among the commissioners" by keeping the exact wording of Wharton's answer a "profound secret from the Public." Here the commissioners' answers become illicitly concealed or secret writing, like a ledger or other record which ought to be a candid account of one's doings but which is stolen and hidden by the very judges assigned to examine it. Against this backdrop of deceitful practice and possible betrayal, James and Drinker continued to avow their adherence to the ideal of candor.[39]

37. [Drinker on behalf of] James and Drinker to Booth and Pigou, October 19, 1773.

38. One also notes that when Drinker provides for his friends a textual version of his public persona and the processes of collective evaluation to which it is subject, his transposition of the culture of performance into writing has the effect of positioning his readers as (hopefully) more sympathetic observers than the coffeehouse audience.

39. [Drinker on behalf of] James and Drinker to Booth and Pigou, October 29, 1773, Philadelphia, James and Drinker Papers. For example, see "Second Answer," signed October

Meanwhile, as Drinker and his fellow commissioners considered several strategies for getting the tea landed safely (some of them quite stunningly far-fetched in their misapprehension of the depth of resistance), they treated other words and writings as closely guarded communications, as they had long done with more conventional business information. For example, in a letter to Drinker and James, Booth detailed a strategy of calling the opposition's bluff by suggesting that the commissioners publicly offer to resign their commissions if all other traders were willing to sign a "solemn" agreement not to receive or sell tea smuggled in from other colonies. Arguing that not ten in one hundred retailers would sign, he assumed that such a tactic would rout the opposition. Naturally, Booth asked that his proposal be kept confidential; the success of his maneuver hinged on acting a public part at variance with private intention.[40] In this way, even as they insisted on publicity and proclaimed their own adherence to the ideal of candor, the commissioners made distinctions between private and public conversation and texts, clothing their efforts to shape the company's definition and rhetorical presentation of its interest to accommodate the mood of the public in the protective garb of secrecy.

Thomas Wharton, the fellow commissioner whom Drinker and James suspected of betrayal, provides a version of the same events that is a curious mirror image of Drinker's. Having consolidated his public position by resigning his commission soon after the visit from the committee, Wharton accused Drinker and James of "ambiguous words" and insisted that they had not "acted a candid part either to the public or to their fellow agents." Like Drinker, who wished he could lay his hands on Wharton's "answer," Wharton also sought out the written documentation that would confirm his suspicions of double-dealing. Thus, when Drinker and James did resign their commissions in early December after the committee found it necessary to visit them a second time, Wharton obtained copies of Drinker and James's second reply, the committee's report, and Drinker and James's resignation, all of which were public documents that circulated widely. But, as if still unsure that all this documentation had adequately demonstrated or exposed his fellow merchant's inexplicit and deceptive conduct, Wharton then asked his brother to get copies of what James and Drinker had written to the company's directors.[41]

Although one might take Wharton's attack on Drinker and James to mean that he supported the views of the "patriots" while his colleagues vacillated, such was not the case. Wharton, like the other agents, had once

22, 1773, Enclosure (copy), James and Drinker to Booth and Pigou, October 29, 1773, Philadelphia.

40. Booth to James and Drinker, October 18, 1773.

41. Thomas Wharton to Samuel Wharton, November 30, 1773, and January 1, 1774, in "Selections from the Letter-Books of Thomas Wharton, of Philadelphia, 1773–1783," *Pennsylvania Magazine of History and Biography* 33, no. 3 (1909): 319, 324.

endorsed the strategy of getting the East India Company itself to pay the duty, along with other moderate schemes designed to land the tea safely. Although Wharton abandoned such schemes because they proved unacceptable to the radical opposition, he claimed in January that he had never budged from the principles underlying them, writing complacently to his brother in London that he himself "never could see the justice of refusing the tea to be landed, but have in all companies and on every occasion spoke my sentiments, that every Englishman has a right to import his property agreeable to law into America ... but its to little purpose to oppose the voice of the multitude."[42] Wharton must have done a masterful job of "coasting" the truth, if he had managed to phrase such sentiments so that they were acceptable to the delegation and the coffeehouse public in mid-October. Yet by now claiming consistency ("in all companies and on every occasion") in his advocacy of conservative and unpopular "sentiments," Wharton avoided the accusation of hypocrisy. Declaring continued fealty to the company's interests, he even assumed that he and several others would be reappointed as tea commissioners in the event that the hated duty was rescinded.[43] Business as usual.

Wharton's retrospective self-representation as a consistent speaker who simply bowed before the weight of public opinion was duplicated by Drinker and James, who, when they finally resigned in December, insisted that they had "steadily and publicly avowed" that the tea "ought to be received and stored" while further attempts were made to get the duties rescinded. They also stressed, however, that they had never "meant to do Any thing that should be disagreeable to their fellow Citizens" and that they now saw that the "General sense" and "Opinion of the people" was that the "tea should not land."[44]

Notice that the merchants' acknowledgment that they ultimately acquiesced to views that were not their own—to views they had repeatedly insisted they did not share—is an afterthought ("its to little purpose to oppose ... the multitude," figuratively shrugs Wharton), an addendum to the overtly more important matter of establishing consistency. What should we make of this rather pro forma acknowledgment? Having initially staked their reputations on faithful service to the company—having cast themselves as David to the public's Goliath—one might imagine that

---

42. Thomas Wharton to Samuel Wharton, January 2, 1774, Philadelphia, in ibid., p. 323.

43. It is in this light that one can read Wharton's stunningly smug statement to his friend Thomas Walpole that "if anything could stimulate me to resign in the early manner I did it was, a belief, that after I had done my duty to my country, I could with more certainty serve the Honorable the East India Company." Wharton to Thomas Walpole, December 24, 1773, Philadelphia, in ibid., pp. 321–22.

44. "Second Answer," October 22, 1773, and "Resignation," December 2, 1773, James and Drinker Papers.

the commissioners would have difficulty escaping a sense of humiliated defeat or craven capitulation before a superior force. But this is not their tone. The merchants implicitly conceded, instead, that the situation demanded the impossible: service to two masters with intractably opposed views. They made a choice and granted superior authority to "the opinion of the people." At the same time, they transferred their (theatrical) notions of trust and service to the new authors of their actions: "their fellow citizens." Although their own views differed from those of their new principals, they could cast their resignations not as capitulation but in the light of their duty to adhere to their new master's public will ("general sense"). It is a remarkable moment. Just here an occupationally specific ethical and psychological vocabulary has aligned with the terminology of Revolutionary era political debate sufficiently well to help to produce new understandings of citizenship.

From this angle, the merchants and their interlocutors were tentatively constituting, despite their continued avowals of candor and their effort to uncover secret inconsistencies, a private zone of "sentiments" and views that were simply irrelevant to the ongoing public drama of trust. What the committee wanted from those it exposed to its scrutinizing gaze and what it got, at least temporarily, was not a convincing portrait of fully candid or transparent men but men who promised, as a matter of duty, to conform their "conduct"—their public personas—to the people's will. The tea commissioners and their like-minded friends were themselves marginalized politically at least temporarily, but not without making their particular contribution to the ongoing revision of concepts of political representation and to the reconfiguration of distinctions between private loyalties and public allegiances.

III.

As men of the market immersed in the social logic of connection and influence, as men who made their living in part by writing, Philadelphia's eighteenth-century merchants were in important respects late heirs of the Renaissance problematics of self-fashioning and theatricality. But they inflected these problematics with an accent peculiar to the cultural and economic milieu of British colonial port cities. In the maelstrom of the Revolution, the merchants' occupationally specific variant of the theatrical idiom and its model of the divided self entered directly into the domain of politically relevant speech and action. In alliance and conflict with others, merchants articulated new variations on the vexed relation between public and private communication and between public and private selves, variations that became available for transposition into the liberal discourses of state and society and of sincerity and domesticity which would become such marked features of the political and cultural land-scape after the Revolution.

In this rearticulation of a rich discursive heritage, we can detect one moment in the historical emergence of what we are wont to call the mod-ern personality: the modern subject's sense of itself as possessing interior, psychological depth. But make no mistake. The representations of self that circulated in the Revolutionary era did not much resemble those we conventionally associate with the ideology of "bourgeois" or "possessive" individualism, an ideology that, according to the now classic literature on commerce and culture, posits as its subject a firmly bounded, autonomous, individual. Rather, the representations bequeathed to the nineteenth century were of a self understood as complex but elusive and precariously integrated. It was, moreover, deeply intertwined with social imperatives: a socially conditioned self. It follows that the nineteenth-century fixation on social masking, "confidence men and painted women," and self-making was not, as some have suggested, a sudden development coinciding with the birth of the new nation.[45] It was instead the result of a complex legacy accumulating from a much longer cultural experience of commerce in an age of empire: the latest permutation in modernity's "discovery" of the psychological subject.

45. Karen Haltunnen, *Confidence Men and Painted Women: A Study of Middle-Class Culture in America, 1830–1870* (New Haven, 1982); Steven Watts, "Masks, Morals, and the Market: American Literature and Early Capitalist Culture, 1790–1820," *Journal of the Early American Republic* 6 (Summer 1986): 127–49; and Larzer Ziff, *Writing the New Nation: Prose, Print, and Politics in the Early United States* (New Haven, 1991).

Black Gothic:
The Shadowy Origins of the
American Bourgeoisie

CARROLL SMITH-ROSENBERG

SOCIAL HISTORIANS traditionally associate the emergence of a Euro-American middle class with the mid–nineteenth century and the beginnings of the industrial revolution.[1] As a cultural historian, I

Scholarship, as my friend Peter Stallybrass argues, is never an isolated effort. The generous support I received from many scholars has made this essay possible, and I am deeply grateful to all of them. My greatest debt is to Philip Lapsansky, Chief of Reference, The Library Company of Philadelphia, for discovering and identifying Leonora Sansay's *Zelica* and for the generosity with which he shares his scholarly expertise about Philadelphia, early American history, and the construction of race in the United States. I also thank Nina Auerbach, Mary Frances Berry, Phyllis Rackin, and Robert Blair St. George of the University of Pennsylvania; Emory Elliott and Sterling Stuckey of the University of California, Riverside; Toby Ditz of Johns Hopkins University; and Viola Sachs of the University of Paris. My special gratitude goes, as always, to Alvia G. Golden for her inspiring fusion of constructive criticism and loving support.

1. See Stuart M. Blumin, *The Emergence of the Middle Class: Social Experience in the American City, 1760–1900* (Cambridge, England, 1989), esp. chap. 1. Social and economic historians have traditionally rooted class identity in socioeconomic experiences. While I think of class as tied to material practices, I also see it as discursively constituted, as a cultural experience, as creative mimicry. As Gareth Stedman Jones argues, class is a "contested point between many competing, overlapping or simply differing forms of discourse" (*Languages of Class: Studies in English Working Class History, 1832–1982* (Cambridge, England, 1983), esp. the introduction. For a treatment of class in a preindustrial American setting, see Gary B. Nash, *Urban Crucible: The Northern Seaports and the Origins of the American Revolution* (Cambridge, Mass., 1979), pp. viii–xiii. For a more traditional association of middle-class formation with the 1830s and 1840s, see Stuart M. Blumin, "The Hypothesis of Middle-Class Formation in Nineteenth-Century America: A Critique and Some Proposals," *American Historical Review* 90, no. 2 (1985): 299–338, and Herbert G. Gutman, *Work, Culture, and Society in Industrializing America: Essays in American Working-Class and Social History* (New York, 1976). For scholars who place middle-class identity formation earlier, see Anthony F. C. Wallace, *Rockdale: The Growth of an American Village in the Early Industrial Revolution* (New York, 1978); Billy G. Smith, *The 'Lower Sort': Philadelphia's Laboring People, 1750–1800* (Ithaca, 1990); and John K. Alexander, "Poverty, Fear, and Continuity: An Analysis of the Poor in Late Eighteenth-Cen-

disagree. A Euro-American middle-class culture and identity developed a half century earlier, the products not of industrial but of commercial and fiscal capitalism. The nascent American middle class was a commercial class, its prosperity and prospects dependent on international trade and the spread of the market economy into farming communities. By the 1780s and 1790s, a bourgeoisie of merchants, shopkeepers, and artisans turned manufacturers, aided and abetted by a supporting cast of lawyers, doctors, publishers, and coffeehouse and tavern renters, emerged in cities and towns along the Atlantic seaboard, engaged actively in producing and reproducing a new commercial economy and new middle-class identities.[2]

Exciting and expansive, the new commercial economy was, at the same time, ambitious, competitive, and unstable. With a weak fiscal infrastructure and perennially undercapitalized, it was repeatedly convulsed by booms and busts, made worse by wild fiscal and land speculation. "Gambling was in the blood of these men," the economic historian Thomas Doerflinger tells us. "When luck ran against them, they were tempted to play double-or-nothing in order to mend their fortunes with a single spectacular deal. . . . Mired in financial difficulties, they concocted grandiose projects in order to stay afloat, and when their calculations proved mistaken, they drowned."[3] Filled with risk, the world of commerce, the cultural historian Toby L. Ditz observes, was also a world of deceit and self-conscious theatricality. Needing one another for information about distant markets or to plan joint ventures, men of commerce knew that, in their cutthroat world, trust was an oxymoron. To mask weakness, outface rumor-driven doubts, and appear what they were not, they learned to play an extensive repertoire of often contradictory characters.[4]

Divergent and conflicting discourses further destabilized their culture, rendering middle-class subjectivity ever more contested, its representations ever more suspect. On one hand, commercial republican discourses praised the new middle-class subject as a forceful man of industry, inde-

---

tury Philadelphia," in *The Peoples of Philadelphia: A History of Ethnic Groups and Lower-Class Life, 1790–1940*, ed. Allen F. Davis and Mark H. Haller (Philadelphia, 1973).

2. See, in particular, Thomas M. Doerflinger, *A Vigorous Spirit of Enterprise: Merchants and Economic Development in Revolutionary Philadelphia* (Chapel Hill, 1986); Paul G. Faler, *Mechanics and Manufacturers in the Early Industrial Revolution: Lynn, Massachusetts, 1780–1860* (Albany, 1981); Charles S. Olton, *Artisans for Independence: Philadelphia Mechanics and the American Revolution* (Syracuse, 1975); and Steven C. Bullock, "The Revolutionary Transformation of American Freemasonry, 1752–1792," *William and Mary Quarterly*, 3d ser., 47, no. 3 (1990): 347–69.

3. Doerflinger, *Vigorous Spirit of Enterprise*, p. 162.

4. See Toby L. Ditz, "Shipwrecked; or, Masculinity Imperiled: Mercantile Representations of Failure and the Gendered Self in Eighteenth-Century Philadelphia," *Journal of American History* 81, no. 3 (1994): 51–80. See also Ditz's essay in this volume.

pendence, talent, and self-control. Classical republican rhetoric, on the other hand, denounced him as an effeminate figure trapped in a theatrical world of representation, appearance, and dependency.[5] Of course, he was both. A man of contradictions, ambivalently gendered, he appeared as unstable and fractured as the economy in which he functioned.[6]

Two questions preoccupied the male world of commerce. Could the eighteenth-century man of commerce ever know the man behind the mask of self-representation, trust appearances, discern who was hardworking and honest and who was fraudulent and conniving? Could he ever know himself? Struggling with such discursive instabilities and economic uncertainties, the new bourgeois press constituted two figures whose otherness was designed to bestow the appearance of coherence on the new middle-class man of commerce and industry. One was the genteel white woman, the other, the enslaved African American laborer. Not surprisingly, however, distinctions between the new, white male, middle-class subject and his negative others proved slippery. As I hope to show in this essay, the white, middle-class man of commerce and his varied others fused on the pages of the new urban press, perhaps even in his fantasies and imagination, refusing him a coherent, unified, middle-class identity.

The middle-class woman's relation to her own class was convoluted and self-contradictory. In many ways, the middle-class woman produced the new middle class. Her desires in the form of domestic consumption drove much of America's import trade and enriched America's great merchants, small shopkeepers, industrious artisans, and printers as the trade in novels, literary magazines, and devotional literature proliferated. Enriching the men of her class, she also embodied their status through her

5. A survey of the historiography of American republican discourses reads like the who's who of great American historians—or of great historical contestations. See, for example, J. G. A. Pocock, *The Machiavellian Moment: Florentine Political Thought and the Atlantic Republican Tradition* (Princeton, 1975); Bernard Bailyn, *The Ideological Origins of the American Revolution* (Cambridge, Mass., 1967); Gordon S. Wood, *The Creation of the American Republic, 1776–1787* (Chapel Hill, 1969); Joyce Oldham Appleby, *Economic Thought and Ideology in Seventeenth-Century England* (Princeton, 1984), and Appleby, "Republicanism in Old and New Contexts," *William and Mary Quarterly*, 3d ser., 43, no. 1 (1986): 20–34; Istvan Hont and Michael Ignatieff, eds., *Wealth and Virtue: The Shaping of Political Economy in the Scottish Enlightenment* (Cambridge, England, 1983); and Michael P. Zuckert, *Natural Rights and the New Republicanism* (Princeton, 1994). For important review essays, see Isaac Kramnick, "Republican Revisionism Revisited," *American Historical Review* 87, no. 3 (1982): 629–64; Kramnick, " 'The Great National Discussion': The Discourse of Politics in 1787," *William and Mary Quarterly*, 3d ser., 45, no. 1 (1988): 3–31; and Linda Kerber, "The Republican Ideology of the Revolutionary Generation," *American Quarterly* 37, no. 3 (1985): 474–95.

6. Ditz, "Shipwrecked," and Carroll Smith-Rosenberg, "Dis-Covering the Subject of the 'Great Constitutional Discussion,' 1786–1789," *Journal of American History* 79, no. 4 (1992): 841–73.

elegant clothing, bearing, and speech, as well as her familiarity with things cultural.[7] Yet just as the middle-class woman's desires and display of self produced her class, so they were perceived as threatening her class's survival—or they at least served to express the fears of merchants, shopkeepers, and master craftsmen in an uncertain, indeed revolutionary, economy. Hundreds of essays warned husbands of the dangers that their wife's social ambitions and material desires posed to their hopes for personal fiscal security.[8]

Virtue further complicated the middle-class woman's relation to her class. Lacking economic independence, the married middle-class woman could never aspire to civic virtue as constituted within eighteenth-century republican discourses. At the same time, bourgeois men used bourgeois women's sexual virtue to constitute their class's ultimate symbol of respectability.[9] Having required the bourgeois woman to be both elegant and nonproductive, how could the bourgeois man ever trust her virtue or rest securely in the symbols of his class? In her turn, how did bourgeois women read these representations of themselves as other?

Simultaneously sign and scapegoat, representations of middle-class women were too deeply implicated in the ideological inconsistencies of their class to do other than reinforce the middle-class man's sense of instability. When actual bourgeois women, increasingly literate and leisured, responded to male representations, inscribing alternative visions of themselves—and men—such instability only multiplied. Seeking to reinforce their own uncertain sense of self, white middle-class spokes*men* turned to a second negative other: enslaved African American laborers. What contrast could be more stark than that of free and unfree labor; the one a willing worker, driven by ambition, the other, a will-less drudge, driven by others; the one talented, the other, unskilled, uneducated? The enslaved African American laborer emerges from this comparison unfree, unwilling, unskilled, uneducated, an un-being—the northern free producer's antithesis, his defining negative other.

Nothing about the Euro-American middle class's construction of self, however, proved that simple. By the late eighteenth century, British attacks on the slave trade had begun to embellish long-standing Quaker

7. Smith-Rosenberg, "Dis-Covering the Subject," pp. 857–61.

8. See, for example, "Consequences of Extravagance," *American Museum* 1 (June 1787): 549–52.

9. The middle class's representation of the middle-class woman as sexually pure makes this picture even more complex, for as the nonproductive consumer of luxuries, the middle-class woman's claim to virtue was suspect at best. See Carroll Smith-Rosenberg, "Domesticating Virtue," in *Literature and the Body: Essays on Populations and Persons*, ed. Elaine Scarry (Baltimore, 1988), pp. 160–84. For the germinal essay on the ways gender complicates the meaning of "virtue," see Ruth Bloch, "The Gendered Meanings of Virtue in Revolutionary America," *Signs* 13, no. 1 (1987): 34–58.

reservations about slavery. Enlightenment insistence that all men are cre-ated equal, revolutionary rhetoric rallying America's Sons of Liberty to resist British efforts to "enslave" them, further complicated the discursive picture[10]—as did the northern urban press's cultural war against the Vir-ginia junto's political and intellectual domination of the new nation. The "true American," the new bourgeois press insisted time and again, was not the southern slaveholder but the northern free producer; he was not Thomas Jefferson but Benjamin Franklin.[11]

As part of their campaign, northern urban editors repeatedly repre-sented the slave south in exotic terms. The planter appears a sybaritic and lethargic, effete and unproductive aristocrat who lives in luxury as others slave for him. "The poor Negro slaves alone work hard," essay after essay argued. Virtually everything produced in the South is produced by slaves. "It is astonishing and unaccountable . . . what an amazing degree of fatigue these poor . . . wretches undergo."[12] In these ways the northern urbane press used the productive black to prove southern whites degen-erate and unproductive. It used the enslaved black to prove them inhu-man and brutish as well, representing southern slaveholders as mutilat-ing slaves who acted only in manly freedom-loving self-defense. Invoking language only recently directed toward British invaders, the pages of the northern press condemned slaveholders and white overseers, alike, as "unfeeling sons of barbarity."[13]

10. Matthew Carey, a leading Republican and editor and publisher of the new nation's most prestigious political magazine, *The American Museum*, printed a number of essays ques-tioning the morality of enslaving Africans. For two examples, see "Address to the Heart, on the Subject of American Slavery," *American Museum* 1 (June 1787): 541–45, esp. 541; and Humanus, "On Slavery," *American Museum* 1 (May 1787): 471. For examples of the northern press's discussion of what I have denominated "political slavery," see three other essays Carey published: Harrington, "Address to the Freemen of America," *American Museum* 1 (January 1787): 4, 91–95; "Thoughts on the Present Situation of Public Affairs," *American Museum* 1 (March 1787): 306–10; and Black Beard, "Ludicrous Plan for the Benefit of R***I****," *American Museum* 2 (August 1787): 171–72, esp. 171.

11. For an essay praising Benjamin Franklin as the "true American," see Noah Webster, "Anecdotal Notices of Dr. Franklin," *American Magazine* 1 (October 1788): 810–11. Carey's *American Museum* published dozens of Franklin's essays in the months leading up to ratifi-cation of the Constitution. A sense of northern frustrations is gained by remembering that four of the first five American presidents were Virginians. See also Michael Warner, *Letters of the Republic: Publication and the Public Sphere in Eighteenth-Century America* (Cambridge, Mass., 1990), esp. chap. 3 ("Franklin: The Representational Politics of the Man of Letters").

12. "Miscellanies. Manner of Living of the Different Ranks of Inhabitants of Virginia. Hard-ships of Negro Slaves. Traits of their Character. Their Passion for Music and Dancing," *American Museum* 1 (March 1787): 245–48 (the quotation is on p. 246).

13. Note the negative play on Sons of Liberty, which the author of "Manner of Living" seeks to show slaveholders were not. For other criticisms of slavery, see "The State of Slav-ery in Virginia and other parts of the Continent, from the Marquis de Chastellux's Travels in America," *Columbian Magazine* 1 (June 1787): 479–80; "Summary View of the Slave Trade," in *Supplement to the First Volume of "Columbian Magazine"* (Philadelphia, 1787), pp. 870–72; "The

A dangerous slippage accompanied the northern press's deployment of African American slaves to constitute southern whites' other to their northern white middle-class readers. A number of essays appearing in Philadelphia magazines, for example, threatened to establish too close a bond between the northern white middle-class reader's self-image as freedom loving and productive and the northern press's representation of the enslaved African American as equally productive and freedom loving. To extricate themselves from so dangerously eroding the racial differences most northerners deeply believed in, northern editors began to emphasize African Americans' distinctive racial characteristics. African women, northern bourgeois readers were told, indulged in repulsive sexual acts, even "mating" with orangutans. They were an inferior species.[14] Still the original slippage (grounded on a shared productivity) haunted northern rhetoric, rendering enslaved African Americans as contradictory and destabilizing an other as the white middle-class woman.

To explore more fully the contradictions embedded in the construction of a Euro-American, middle-class identity in the opening decades of the new nation, I will examine two novels produced by the new middle class: Charles Brockden Brown's paradigmatic novel *Arthur Mervyn; or Memoirs of the Year 1793*, published in two parts (the first in 1799, the second in 1800), and Leonara Sansay's *Zelica*, published in 1820 but based on an earlier semifictional work by Sansay, her *Secret History; or, The Horrors of St. Domingo, in a Series of Letters Written By A Lady at Cape Francois to Colonel Burr, late Vice-President of the United States*, published in 1808.[15]

Slave: Inscribed to James Oglethorpe, esquire, by Theophilus Rowe," *Columbian Magazine* 1 (February 1787): 293–94; and E. H. Smith, *A Discourse, Delivered April 11, 1798, at the Request of and Before the new-york society for promoting the manumission of slaves, and protecting such of them as have been or may be liberated* (New York, 1798).

14. "Observations on the Gradation in the Scale of Being between human and Brute Creation. Including some curious Particulars respecting Negroes. (From a late History of Jamaica)," *Columbian Magazine* 2 (January 1788): 14–22, esp. 14; A Friend to the Fair Sex, "Marriage Ceremonies of different Countries Compared," *Columbian Magazine* 2 (1787): 491–97, esp. 493.

15. Charles Brockden Brown, *Arthur Mervyn, or Memoirs of the Year 1793. First and Second Parts*, Bicentennial ed., 2 vols. (Kent, Ohio, 1980); Leonara Sansay, *Zelica, The Creole; a Novel, by an American. In Three Volumes* (London, 1820); and Sansay, *Secret History; or, the horrors of st. domingo, in A Series of Letters, written by a Lady at Cape Francois to Colonel Burr, late Vice-President of the United States, Principally during the Command of General Rochambeau* (Philadelphia, 1808). All citations are given parenthetically in the text and are from these editions. For a detailed history and analysis of *Zelica*, see Philip Lapsansky, "Afro-Americana: Rediscovering Leonora Sansay," *Annual Report of the Library Company of Philadelphia for the Year 1992* (Philadelphia, 1993), pp. 29–46. I have argued elsewhere that the novel is a particularly useful genre for historians in search of the play of ideological contradiction and rhetorical confusion. The diversity of characters and the novel's reliance on conflict and change for the development of plot and character encourage both the overt and covert expression of ambiguities and contradictions. Its evocative nature intensifies its ability to enact discursive inconsistencies and social conflict. While the prescriptive genres of a culture—sermons, advice books, political magazines—seek to repress ambiguity, the novel

I.

One of Brown's most contradictory works, *Arthur Mervyn* offers a bitter, somber critique of late-eighteenth-century commercial and fiscal capitalism. At the same time, it works to constitute its title character—and through their identification with him, its readers—as subject to and of that capitalist culture. A resistant member of an established Philadelphia mercantile family, Brown graphically portrayed the corruption he saw lying at the heart of Philadelphia's commercial and financial world. Fraud and deceit characterize every commercial venture that the novel portrays; insecurity haunts its counting houses and parlors. In the darkness of night, merchants plot to defraud one another; counterfeit bills of exchange are presented as real—or is it that real ones are represented as counterfeit? Heiresses are seduced and abandoned, fortunes stolen, murders committed, and bodies buried. Self-interest, not the general good, reigns supreme. Hedonistic delight in opulent display drives all before it. How, the book asks, can one detect reality beneath the layered masks of masterful representation? How can one develop a sense of self in a world so filled with deception and secrecy? The answer, Brown's novel suggests, lies in a complex fusion and confusion of race and gender. What type of middle-class subject emerges on pages so haunted by duplicity, so shrouded in darkness? To begin to answer that question, I will focus my analysis on the development of the youthful Arthur Mervyn, the text's central protagonist.

In volume 1 of Brown's novel, Arthur Mervyn, long considered by literary critics an archetypal American Adam, twice studies his reflection in a mirror. The first time occurs toward the novel's beginning, just after Arthur, a barefoot farm boy, is hired as an amanuensis by the merchant manqué and arch trickster Thomas Welbeck, taken into Welbeck's mansion, and dressed in the latest European fashions. Gazing at his transformed self, the poor farm boy muses:

> Appearances are wonderfully influenced by dress. Check shirt, buttoned at the neck, an awkward fustian coat, check trowsers, and bare feet were now supplanted by linen and muslin, nankeen coat, striped with green, a white silk waistcoat, elegantly needle-wrought, casimer pantaloons, stock-

---

plays on dangerous desires. Ultimately affirming the permissible, it makes its readers familiar with the forbidden and the transgressive. I am especially concerned with the complex ways the new bourgeois print culture generally and fiction in particular constituted the normative middle-class subject as white and male. I therefore focus on the white male reader, although we know from Cathy Davidson and other feminist literary historians that middle-class women were avaricious consumers as well as producers of the urban print culture. In the last section of this essay I explore the bourgeois author as a white woman and her representations of both race and gender; see Cathy N. Davidson, *Revolution and the Word: The Rise of the Novel in America* (New York, 1986).

ings of variegated silk, and shoes that in their softness, pliancy, and polished surface vied with satin. I could scarcely forbear looking back to see
whether the image in the glass, so well proportioned, so gallant, and so
graceful, did not belong to another. . . . Twenty minutes ago . . . I was traversing that path a barefoot beggar; now I am thus. . . . Some magic that
disdains the cumbrousness of nature's progress, has wrought this change.
I was roused from these doubts by a summons to breakfast, obsequiously
delivered by a black servant. (1:51)

The second mirror scene occurs many chapters later when a more experienced Arthur Mervyn, representing himself as an exemplar of disinter-
ested benevolence, returns to a Philadelphia ravaged by yellow fever. His
return is motivated solely by altruism, Mervyn tells his mentor, Dr.
Stevens, and his readers; he comes to nurse a young clerk he fears is
stricken by fever.[16] Moving through dark houses that reek of pestilence,
Arthur discovers the hideous remains of a yellow fever victim lying near
a chest broken open and ransacked. At that moment a sudden movement
in a mirror catches his eye. Lurking behind his own white figure, he
glimpses a horrible black form.

One eye, a scar upon his cheek, a tawny skin, a form grotesquely misproportioned, brawny as Hercules and habited in livery, composed, as it
were, the parts of one view. *To perceive, to fear, and to confront this apparition
were blended into one sentiment.* I turned towards him with the swiftness of
lightening, but my speed was useless to my safety. A blow upon my temple was succeeded by an utter oblivion of thought and feeling. (1:147;
emphasis added)

I propose seeing these mirror scenes as fictive pier glasses in which not
only Arthur but also Philadelphia's new urban male readers, generally,
could see themselves transformed as middle-class men of fashion and

16. Yellow fever frequently swept the eastern seaboard in the eighteenth and early nineteenth centuries, brought by ships trading either with the mainland south or the Caribbean.
The late summer and fall of 1793 saw Philadelphia's worst yellow fever epidemic, one pre-
cipitated by the outbreak of the fever in Haiti and the flight of white refugees from the beginning of a black revolution on that island. Roughly 15 percent of Philadelphia's forty-five
thousand inhabitants died from yellow fever between mid-August and the beginning of
November. As the epidemic gathered force, another twenty thousand fled the city, including
most members of the U.S. Congress and of Washington's administration, Pennsylvania state
legislators, and most of the city government. Anarchy reigned for some weeks until a vol-
untary group of merchants and doctors reestablished some degree of medical, social, and
political order. For details, see J. H. Powell, *Bring Out Your Dead: The Great Plague of Yellow
Fever in Philadelphia in 1793* (Philadelphia, 1993), and Martin Pernick, "Politics, Parties, and
Pestilence: Epidemic Yellow Fever in Philadelphia and the Rise of the First Party System,"
William and Mary Quarterly, 3d ser., 29, no. 3 (1972): 559–86.

respectability.[17] Certainly they evoke the Lacanian trope of the mirror as a key moment in the emergence of the individual as subject to language and ideology, a time when the infant, until then experiencing himself only as a series of disconnected body parts, looks into a mirror and first perceives himself as a unified figure.[18]

The initial mirror scene invites the new urban reader first to participate vicariously with Arthur in his meticulously detailed dressing and then to gaze, as he gazes, self-absorbed, in the mirror. Some years earlier in America's economic development, the same reader might have seen himself as a fragmented part of an embryonic middle-class body (a leather-aproned artisan, an awkward farmer newly come to the city, a petty tradesman, a provincial merchant). Now, subject to and constituted by the new urban print culture, he could see himself re-formed in Arthur's trans-formation to a well-proportioned, gallant, and graceful middle-class gen-tleman.[19] Abetting this reformation process is a desire for the luxurious goods in which Arthur Mervyn is garbed, the importation and marketing of which goods played a critical part in Philadelphia's expanding market economy.[20]

Recasting this Lacanian scene in Althusserian terms, let me suggest that through such scenes, the city's popular print culture constituted its new readers as middle-class subjects, instructing them in correct manners, dress, virtues, and desires, setting them off and complementing them by the introduction of the shadowy figure of the obsequious black servant announcing breakfast.[21] White waistcoat, black servant—here, indeed, we see a scene resplendent with a self-congratulatory sense of "tranquillity"

17. As I have noted, I focus primarily on the construction of a male bourgeois subject. The novel does offer numerous representations of genteel women's fashion, which presumably would have interested both women and men readers. Shortly after the first mirror scene, for example, the novel presents a vivid representation of the dress of an elegant urban lady, in the person of Welbeck's mistress, Clemenza Lodi. It also has Mervyn describe the appoint-ments of Welbeck's house in elaborate detail: crystal decanters, Turkish carpets, velvet draperies, mahogany tables, and so forth, all quite enough to whet the imagination and desires of male and female middle-class readers. Yet only the most elite of Philadelphia's bourgeoisie could have afforded the clothing and appointments that Brown describes. These descriptions were teases, invitations to a fantasy world that Brown's readers knew they could never enter; see Doerflinger, *Vigorous Spirit of Enterprise*, esp. chap. 1.

18. See Jacques Lacan, *The Four Fundamental Concepts of Psychoanalysis*, trans. Alan Sheri-dan, ed. Jacques-Alain Miller (New York, 1981). "He" is the correct pronoun to use in sum-marizing Lacan's argument because Lacan's theories deny subjectivity to women.

19. For a sophisticated description of America's late-eighteenth-century print culture, see Warner, *Letters of the Republic*. See also Doerflinger, *Vigorous Spirit of Enterprise*.

20. See Doerflinger, *Vigorous Spirit of Enterprise*.

21. I am influenced by Louis Althusser's concept of "interpellation," his theory that "all ideology has the function (which defines it) of 'constituting' concrete individuals as sub-jects." See Althusser, "Ideology and Ideological State Apparatuses," in his *Essays on Ideology* (New York, 1976), p. 45.

and social order.[22] When the white man is in his waistcoat, "all's right with the world."[23]

What a contrast the second mirror scene presents! Desire is replaced by danger; a young man's pleasurable fantasies, by fears of pestilence and death; the morning sun, by darkness and night. The novel's invocation of the "malignant pestilence" of yellow fever, its representation of a grotesque corpse and a merchant's chest ransacked, suggests that commerce brings not only linen and muslin to America's political and economic capital but also disease and danger, corruption and death.

Strikingly different though they seem, these twinned mirror scenes, read together, reaffirm the new urban reader as a genteel, white middle-class subject. They counterpoise the classic male body of European philosophical thought and the grotesque body of the servant or peasant classes.[24] The classic body, alluringly represented by the young Arthur, is free and independent, self-possessed, a unified, coherent whole, harmoniously proportioned, graceful, white as marble, the forehead, a very "temple" to reason and romantic rhetoric. The servant or peasant body, as caught in the mirror, is by contrast "grotesquely misproportioned," its face deformed. Far from appearing a well-proportioned and coherent whole, it is "composed" of "parts." The servile status of this grotesque and dangerous figure is signed by his livery, which in eighteenth-century Europe identifies a servant but in eighteenth-century urban America most commonly suggests a slave, a suggestion his "tawny" color reaffirms. Contrasting the white gallant to servile blacks, virtue to violence, benevolence to thievery, tranquillity to disease, social order to disorder, these two scenes work in tandem to confirm the new white middle-class subject as the virtuous new "American" and the black man as his grotesque and dangerous other.

In her critical book *Playing in the Dark*, Toni Morrison argues that "the literature of the United States has taken as its concern the architecture of

---

22. "Tranquillity" is the word Mervyn uses when thinking back to his feelings on that day. His memory is ironic, for he quickly loses the sense of tranquillity that Welbeck's wealthy lifestyle first inspired in him. One cannot help but note here that, as Arthur himself tells us, appearances render a man a composite of his clothes, a rendering the rest of the novel will problematize but, in the end, with Arthur's marriage to a rich and urbane widow, reaffirm.

23. Before consideration of these mirror scenes, a brief caveat is in order. In late-eighteenth-century America only the richest urban houses contained large mirrors or looking glasses. For Arthur Mervyn to gaze at himself in a mirror meant that in entering Welbeck's mansion, he had entered the self-referential, magical, looking-glass world of bourgeois identity formation, a world in which reality and representation, endlessly refracting, seemed indistinguishable.

24. M. M. Bakhtin, *Rabelais and His World*, trans. Hélène Iswolsky (Cambridge, Mass., 1968). See also Peter Stallybrass and Allon White, *The Politics and Poetics of Transgression* (Ithaca, 1986), esp. the introduction and chap. 1.

a *new white man.* . . . The process of organizing American coherence through a distancing Africanism became the operative mode of a new cultural hegemony." She continues:

> Africanism [by which Morrison means white figurations of African Americans and of blackness] has become both a way of talking about and a way of policing matters of class, formations and exercises of power . . . meditations on ethics and accountability. Through the simple expedient of demonizing and reifying the range of color on a palette, American Africanism makes it possible to say and not say, to inscribe and erase, to escape and engage, to act out and act on, to historicize and render timeless. It provides a way of contemplating chaos and civilization, desire and fear, and a mechanism for testing the problems and blessings of freedom.[25]

Read in this way, Brown's inscription of the tawny and grotesque apparition in livery provided eighteenth-century Philadelphians with "a way of talking about and a way of policing matters of class . . . power . . . ethics and accountability," a way to "inscribe and erase" the dark underbelly of the city's commercial and agricultural economy. Philadelphia's prosperity, while intimately tied to British and European markets and increasingly benefiting from trade expansion into southern Europe and the Mediterranean, continued in the 1780s and 1790s to rest squarely on its West Indian trade. The city's provision merchants gathered the produce of Pennsylvania's farms and forests, shipped it on Philadelphia-made ships to the West Indies, and brought back sugar and rum for quick profits plus badly needed specie and often questionable bills of exchange.[26] Philadelphia's urbane merchants and bankers, her sturdy Quaker and German farmers, and her industrious artisan-manufacturers all served and benefited from one of the world's richest slave economies.

Philadelphia's eighteenth-century print culture constituted Benjamin Franklin, artisan turned statesman, as the new white American. It valorized free trade and free labor. Still, dark, servile figures shadowed its urban white American, colored its efforts to distance him from connections to and crimes against enslaved African Americans. In this, Philadelphia's eighteenth-century urban print culture is hardly unique. As Morrison reminds us, the "fabrication of an Africanist persona [by white America] is . . . an extraordinary meditation on the [white] self . . . an astonishing revelation of [white] longing, of terror, of perplexity, of

---

25. Toni Morrison, *Playing in the Dark: Whiteness and the Literary Imagination* (Cambridge, Mass., 1992), pp. 14, 7–8.

26. Doerflinger, *Vigorous Spirit of Enterprise*, pp. 100–108. See also Marc Egnal, "The Changing Structure of Philadelphia's Trade with the British West Indies, 1750–1775," *Pennsylvania Magazine of History and Biography* 99, no. 2 (1975): 156–79.

shame, of magnanimity." "It requires," Morrison concludes, "hard work *not* to see this."[27]

Let us spend a few minutes working hard to see the role black figures and figurations of blackness played in making the new white middle-class American man a contradictory and inherently unstable subject, first in the two mirror scenes and then more generally in Brown's complex novel. At first glance, these two scenes constitute an idealized middle-class subject, invoking obsequious and dependent, grotesque and dangerous blacks to reaffirm his coherence—as well as the coherence of a social order based on a racist hierarchy. In the first scene we see Arthur Mervyn, as the elegant young man of fashion, summoned to breakfast by a black servant, the juxtaposition of white master and black servant inscribing a racially based social order of tranquillity and peace. In the second, the selfless and brave white Arthur is struck down by the murderous black ruffian, now the symbol of social order endangered and in disarray.

If we reexamine these mirror scenes, however, we begin to find that race works to erase as well as to inscribe social order, that black figures fuse with and thus fracture the hegemonically constructed white subject. The black servant in the first scene suggests closure. He is not, however, the principal negative other against which the newly urbane Arthur takes form. Rather, "new Arthur's" true negative other is the "old Arthur," the impoverished and naïve farm boy. Far from embodying a noble agrarian ideal, as farm boy Arthur is a barefoot beggar, a dirty, hungry, and penniless son of a Jukes-like rural family. His positioning in the first mirror scene closely parallels the positioning of the tawny servant / slave in the second mirror scene. The one is "awkward," the other "misproportioned." Both are poor; both are unskilled. Both are dependent, Arthur on his master Thomas Welbeck's benevolence, and the servant / slave, in his turn, on *his* master's wealth. Nor do the parallels end there. Both Arthur and the black figure, by stealth and by night, take what does not belong to them. Just as Arthur discovers to the reader the tawny servant / slave ransacking the contents of his master's chest, so does he confess that he also entered a deserted home at night (Welbeck's), taking a fortune in bank notes.[28]

As we glance from one scene to the other, the figures of the poor white farm boy and the liveried servant / slave become twin pawns in a discursive dialectic that establishes the white middle-class subject as the virtuous, true "American." Their interchangeability has significant class

27. Morrison, *Playing in the Dark*, p. 17.

28. Both houses in question are rented by transients, underscoring the instability of Philadelphia's commercial community—and not only during yellow fever summers; see Doerflinger, *Vigorous Spirit of Enterprise*, esp. chap. 1.

implications. Re-fusing their racial distinctiveness, it threatens to color all those dispossessed or marginal to Philadelphia's emerging capitalist economy. Is this the real threat the grotesque tawny monster poses to Arthur and rural Euro-Americans generally (a threat Arthur references with the phrase, "To perceive, to fear . . . this apparition were . . . one sentiment")—that the new commercial and fiscal capitalist economy will make economically displaced rural whites and blacks interchangeable as urbane, middle-class Americans' feared and detested negative others? Read in its entirety, the novel poses that danger, for it positions the rural poor as grotesque, representing them as "clowns," "simpletons," and "rustics," in contrast to the urbane middle class (1:19, 51, 86, 134). Even hardworking farming families are represented as living in "wood hovels," which contrast sadly with the "loftiness" of urban mansions (1:47). Arthur's own rural family consists of an increasingly confused and alcoholic father who dies in debtor's prison, a stepmother turned prostitute, and siblings who are sickly and die young. Only in the city, Mervyn insists repeatedly, can a man strengthen his mind and enlarge his knowledge (1:296).

Yet the novel also represents urban laborers as unthinking and inhuman wretches, socially useful only when subject to discipline and control. Those hired during the yellow fever epidemic to care for the sick "neglect their duty and consume the cordials which are provided for the patients, in debauchery and riot." They were "bloated with malignity and drunkenness." They were "depraved" (1:172–74). Yet, Arthur Mervyn tells his readers, "the cause of it was obvious. The wretches whom money could purchase were, of course, licentious and unprincipled. Superintended and controlled, they might be useful instruments; but that superintendence could not be bought" (1:176). The message is clear. Wage laborers and the working classes, unsupervised, would descend into anarchy and depravity. Supervised by the middle-class man of virtue, they could be made orderly, productive members of society. The urban wage laborer is thus positioned as defenders of slavery positioned the enslaved African American laborer—that is, as undisciplined, licentious, unprincipled, in need of control and superintendence.

The two mirror scenes undermine racial distinctions and social order in even more threatening ways. Carefully examined, the graceful Arthur Mervyn, newly employed as a gentleman's amanuensis, appears to be as dependent as the "other" tawny servant / slave: both wear their master's clothing; they eat their masters' food; they live as dependents within their masters' house; they are at their masters' beck and call. Indeed, only a few pages after Arthur gazes so admiringly at himself, he agrees to submit to Welbeck's request that he tell no man about his past life but rather assume the persona Welbeck creates for him—just as enslaved African Americans assumed the names, personas, and pasts constituted for them by white slaveholders.

If we extend our vision but slightly beyond the frame of Brown's novel, we will see an even more telling parallel between Arthur and Philadelphia's African Americans. *Arthur Mervyn* is in many ways a novel about appearances and representations. Its convoluted plot revolves around the question, Can we believe Arthur's self-representations as virtuous and benevolent?[29] Appearances are against Arthur. At the height of the yellow fever epidemic, the still impoverished Arthur, hearing that Philadelphians are abandoning their homes, flies to town in secret, telling not a soul of his intent. He claims to seek out and succor a youth he does not know. Once there, he wanders through empty houses and attempts to carry off chests. He claims altruism alone drives him, that he risks his life to nurse the sick (Wallace), rescue orphans left by the epidemic (Eliza Hadwick), and deter those who robbed and defrauded the innocent (Welbeck). In return for all his good services, Arthur continues, he took in recompense only what was offered as reward for the return of stolen money. A host of angry voices, however, accuse Arthur of laziness, wantonness, fraud, deception, and robbery.

A bitter conflict divided Philadelphians during the yellow fever epidemic. A number of prominent white citizens charged Philadelphia's African American community with profiteering from the epidemic, charging exorbitant rates to nurse the poor and then neglecting them, robbing the dead, and vandalizing white homes. Their chief representative, Republican politician and publisher Matthew Carey, published the allegations in his widely read *Short Account of the Malignant Fever*. Asserting that he had "aimed at telling plain truths in plain language . . . had taken every precaution to arrive at the truth," and that "most of the facts mentioned have fallen under my own observation," Carey reported that "vile . . . blacks . . . extorted two, three, four, and even five dollars a night for attendance [on the sick as nurses], which would have been well paid by a single dollar. Some of them were even detected in plundering the houses of the sick." Stating at another point in his *Short Account* that

29. *Arthur Mervyn* has, not surprisingly, attracted an extensive body of critical literature focusing on just this point. See, for example, Patrick Brancaccio, "Studied Ambiguities: *Arthur Mervyn* and the Problem of the Unreliable Narrator," *American Literature* 42, no. 1 (1970): 18–27; William Hedges, "Charles Brockden Brown and the Culture of Contradictions," *Early American Literature* 9, no. 2 (1974): 107–42; Emory Elliott, "Narrative Unity and Moral Resolution in *Arthur Mervyn*," in *Critical Essays on Charles Brockden Brown*, ed. Bernard Rosenthal (Boston, 1981). Michael Warner, *Letters of the Republic*, chap. 6, offers a particularly suggestive interpretation of Arthur Mervyn as a classical republican hero. I find Warner's interpretation eloquent, but he effaces racial issues and simplifies Mervyn's complex and ambivalent relation to capitalism.

"many men of affluent fortunes . . . have been abandoned to the care of a negro . . . no money could procure proper attendance," Carey equated black nursing with no attendance at all.[30]

African American leaders Richard Allen and Absalom Jones angrily denounced the charges, pointing out that Carey had fled the city as soon as yellow fever had broken out and, consequently, contrary to his assertion, had observed very little directly. They, on the other hand, had never left the city but rather had worked closely with Dr. Benjamin Rush in his efforts to combat the epidemic. It was under Rush's direction that they had organized African Americans' nursing efforts. Philadelphia's blacks, they asserted, guided by benevolent selflessness, had risked their lives to nurse the sick, care for abandoned orphans, and detect those who robbed and defrauded innocents. Many refused all compensation for their services. Others took only what they were offered.[31]

Arthur Mervyn, asserting his innocence in the face of charges of exploitation and robbery, is positioned precisely as Philadelphia's African Americans were in the city's larger debate about how to perceive virtue and evaluate truth—and precisely as the second mirror scene positions the servant / slave. Like Mervyn, the African American community was accused of laziness, wantonness, deception, and robbery. Thus both within and without the novel, telling parallels exist between white Americans and black Americans.

These parallels exist not only when whites are poor and marginal but even when they are critical players in the emergence of a Euro-American middle class. More telling yet, in terms of destabilizing the white Philadelphian as the true American, Philadelphia's own mercantile elites played a role in this erasure of racial distinctions. Arthur's master, the elegant "nabob" Thomas Welbeck, is in fact not the master of his own fortune. Quite the contrary, the fashionable attire and lifestyle that proclaim Welbeck's upper-middle-class status are secured with money stolen from a man who died of yellow fever. The genteel Welbeck and the tawny servant / slave are thus joined in a brotherhood of thieves who have robbed the fever dead. Indeed, Welbeck's great wealth, which impresses not only the innocent Arthur but Philadelphia's entire commercial community, was, like so many Philadelphia fortunes, originally made in the sugar / slave economy of the West Indies. Quite literally, it was blood money pro-

---

30. Matthew Carey, *A Short account of the Malignant Fever, Lately Prevalent in Philadelphia: with a Statement of the Proceedings that took place on the subject in different parts of the United States*, 2d ed. (Philadelphia, 1793), pp. vii, 31, 76–77.

31. A[bsalom] J[ones] and R[ichard] A[llen], *A Narrative of the Proceedings of the Black People, During the Late Awful Calamity in Philadelphia in the year 1793: And a REFUTATION of some CENSURES Thrown upon them in some late Publications* (Philadelphia, 1794). For a discussion of this controversy, see Powell, *Bring Out Your Dead*, pp. 95–101.

duced by the sale of West Indian slaves, one of whom rose up and killed the man who sold him. The fortune produced by this sale of men stolen from Africa is then stolen by another white man, this time by Thomas Welbeck. It is this stolen blood money, raised by the sale of human lives, that so impresses Philadelphia's commercial community and secures Welbeck's entrée to it and a life of fashionable respectability. The poetic irony is that the world of Philadelphia commerce, fashion, and respectability is financed in large part by the provision trade to the slave economies of the West Indies. Where, the novel repeatedly asks, does thievery (illicit commerce) end and commerce (legal thievery?) begin? What self-image does the novel encourage its aspiring Euro-American, middle-class readers to internalize and enact?

By shifting our gaze from Mervyn to Welbeck, we have turned from our initial examination of middle-class subjectivity to explore the novel's deep-seated fears about the dangers commercial and fiscal capitalism pose to civic virtue, and the ways in which the novel invokes the yellow fever epidemic to symbolize those dangers. In the novel's shifts and turns, blackness shadows the way. In a novel in which not one of the many commercial or fiscal transactions represented is honest or productive, virtually all occur in the dark of night. It is then that merchants plot to defraud one another, seduce innocent women, rob and murder. And it is at night that virtually every one of the novel's numerous defrauding merchants is cut down painfully by yellow fever—in one case, carried screaming to the pest house and, in another, nailed alive in his coffin.

Yellow fever literally signaled Philadelphia's commercial ties to the slave economies of the West Indies. Coloring our understanding of the nature of America's commercial economy, yellow fever constitutes an apt symbol for the ways in which the moral blackness of slavery seeped into the whiteness of Euro-America and of middle-class commercial Euro-Americans. Fortunes secured from the sale of slaves encourage deceit and debauchery in one mercantile family, arrogance and cruelty in another. For, after all, what does yellow fever do to white men's bodies? It turns their skin yellow or coffee colored. It fills them with black bile, which the victims compulsively try to rid themselves of, cannot, and die. Read with eyes informed by Morrison's essays, it would seem that yellow fever provided Brown with "a way of contemplating chaos and civilization" and of problematizing, at the very moment he appeared to consolidate, the coherence and the virtue of the white American subject.

If *Arthur Mervyn* undercuts the apparently clear distinctions between free and slave labor, unveiling the servile and base components of middle-class subjectivity, it renders distinctions between the white man of commerce and the genteel white woman equally uncertain. Ostensibly, the novel establishes the genteel woman as sentimental, innocent, benevolent, and submissive to the guidance of fathers and lovers. She has one secret weakness, however: her vulnerability to the seductions of deceitful men. Multiple seductions attest to this—the various seductions of Clemenza Lodi, merchant Watson's sister, and that of Arthur's own sister. But having constituted Arthur Mervyn as the ideal middle-class subject, the American Adam as Every Capitalist, the novel proceeds to represent Mervyn as equally sentimental, innocent, benevolent, and vulnerable to the seductions of deceitful men. In fact, the novel underscores specific parallels between Mervyn and Clemenza Lodi. Welbeck finds both penniless. He offers each a home, fine clothing, and a genteel appearance, but at the price of their promise to tell no person of their real pasts. Is not Mervyn as much a victim of Welbeck's seductions as Clemenza herself, the defrauded daughter of the man killed in Haiti by the slave he tried to sell?

Mervyn repeatedly represents himself in stereotypically feminine terms. His most enjoyable times, he tells us, are spent in domestic conversation with groups of women, in which he is the only man. Concerning one such experience, Mervyn reported to Dr. Stevens (a barely disguised representation of Benjamin Rush, a physician known for his writings on women) in strikingly erotic phrases: "This intercourse was strangely fascinating. My heart was buoyed up by a kind of intoxication. I now found myself exalted to my genial element, and began to taste the delights of existence.... The time flew swiftly away, and a fortnight passed almost before I was aware that a day had gone by" (2:173). On another occasion he tells Dr. Stevens: "My mind is enervated and feeble, like my body. I cannot look upon the sufferings of those I love without exquisite pain. I cannot steel my heart by the force of reason." And on another occasion he continues, "I enjoy fond appellations, tones of mildness, solicitous attendance." "I am, in that respect," he concludes, "a mere woman" (2:17, 127, 180).

In contrast, the novel's critically important women are represented as decisive and forceful, economically self-reliant, and ambitious for knowledge and worldly experience. Eliza Hadwick, Mervyn's first romantic interest, turns on Mervyn when he patronizes her and treats her as his intellectual and social inferior because she is a woman. Angrily, Hadwick demands, "Have I not the same claims to be wise, and active and courageous as you?" (2:80). Equally significant, the text leads the reader to side with Hadwick.

The most powerful, autonomous, and sophisticated character in *Arthur Mervyn* is not one of the cast of ambitious and deceitful merchants but a woman. Literary critics represent Ascha Fielding as the Oedipal mother, "Mama" to the desiring and youthful Mervyn. As a result, they downplay her phallic, "masculine" characteristics. Fielding, the novel tells us, is "rich," "the absolute mistress of her fortune . . . [with none] to controul her in the use of it" (2:268). Possessed of great capital resources, she is socially autonomous, unencumbered by children, worldly, highly educated, and conversant with European politics. She is so much the master of her own estate that early in their relationship Mervyn pleads with her to employ him as her philanthropic factor or agent—a plea she rejects. An independent woman, Fielding informs Mervyn, she can manage her philanthropic endeavors on her own. She is bold, unconventional, and intrigued by risk. She is, in short, manly. In embracing Fielding, then, Mervyn assumes the role not only of adoring son but of dependent and clinging ingenue.

Subverting distinctions between women and men, Ascha Fielding subverts as well distinctions between black and white. *Arthur Mervyn* envelops Fielding with the mysteries of the Orient. When we first see her, she is "arrayed with voluptuous negligence," reclining at her ease in a seraglio on the outskirts of Philadelphia (2:102). We know nothing of her origins. Indeed, on first meeting her, Mervyn cries out, "Who, where, what are you? . . . Tell me, I beseech you!" (2:105). We soon learn that Ascha Fielding is that archetypal liminal figure who spans East and West, black and white, outsider and insider. She is a Jew. Her father, born in Portugal, moved to London, where he became a wealthy and well-respected merchant. Her Semitic nature, however, makes her an outsider, indeed grotesque. "She is a foreigner," that archetypal spokesman for middle-class respectability Dr. Stevens tells Mervyn, "unsightly as a *night-hag*, tawny as a Moor, the eye of a gipsy, low in stature . . . less luxuriance than a charred log" (2:432). In eighteenth-century imagery, this language represents her as unmistakably black—and desired by Mervyn!

Arthur Mervyn is a relentlessly destabilizing text. Repeatedly interweaving the proto-American capitalist with his black other, it ends with him in *her* intimate embrace. Ascha Fielding's embodied fusion of the white middle-class man's two defining others (women / blacks) requires us to recognize not only the white middle-class man's dependence on them both to define and to stabilize his own subjectivity but also their mutual interdependence. Only by tracing their complex triangularity will we begin to understand the ways power is produced, reproduced, and deployed in America's bourgeois world.

II.

Arthur Mervyn explores the commercial and fiscal revolutions; Leonora Sansay's *Zelica* makes political revolution and the struggle for freedom its framing motif. On her pages brave soldiers struggle to throw off the tyrannical yoke of European imperialism; wives urge husbands, "Let your cry be ever, Liberty or death!" (p. 206). Despite such rhetorical evocations of the American Revolution, however, the United States plays but a shadowy role in this novel. It is Haiti's struggle for freedom, justice, and self-determination that rivets the reader's attention—Haiti's struggle and Haiti's failure. By the novel's end, savage black tyranny casts its dark shadow over the island. Inhuman cruelty makes its streets run red with blood. Its white protagonists have either fled or lie dead and dismembered.

Does Sansay's *Zelica* unambivalently reinscribe the Euro-American racism that *Arthur Mervyn* appears at moments to destabilize, if not overtly question? That is not an easy question to answer, for *Zelica* aggressively decenters race and gender far more than even *Arthur Mervyn*. It represents black Haitians as both valiant freedom fighters and bestial animals bent on the rape of white women. It represents Haiti's white creole elite as both sadistic sybarites savagely exploiting enslaved Africans and pathetic victims of black savagery. French soldiers appear as enlightened advocates of equality and as lascivious colonizers oppressing Creoles and blacks alike. Confusions multiply as *Zelica* represents slavery as inhumane; black self-governance as a chimera; marriage as women's greatest source of happiness; and husbands as unfaithful, indifferent, or sadistic. On its pages women assume male roles, and men loll in voluptuous ease. Whites exceed the savage acts of "savage" blacks: a French general burns black rebels at the stake; a creole wife beheads her husband's slave mistress, cooks the severed head, and then serves it to her husband for dinner. *Zelica* systematically complicates what racism would make simple, decenters subjectivities, and distorts the political picture. How can we weave our way through this novel?

Certainly *Zelica* begins on an unexpected note. Praising black Haitians as valiant freedom fighters, it condemns whites in Haiti as "tyrants [who] abuse . . . their power . . . oppressing the slaves that toiled to supply their extravagant enjoyments." The French are imperialists bent on the exploitation of Haiti's riches and of its women. The island's creole elite are voluptuaries who "live for pleasure only,—pleasures that succeed each other, like waves of the summer sea. As one object loses its power to charm, a new object, as sweet and as shining replaces it" (p. 57). Creole women "combine in their persons all the charms [of the] seraglio" (p. 56).

In stark contrast, black Haitians emerge as classic republican heroes, Spartan in their asceticism, Roman in their bravery and love of freedom. They "had emancipated themselves and broke by their own efforts the fetters of bondage, daring to oppose their undisciplined courage to the bravery of well-appointed troops . . . warriors who had arrested the flight of the Austrian Eagle—subdued the descendants of the Caesars" (p. 4). Initially, at least, the blacks of Haiti appear as new Caesars, earning that title with their bravery and skill at arms. "Having enjoyed the blessings of liberty," we are told, "they had sworn never again to submit to the yoke they had thrown off." Proudly they scorn French efforts to buy their submission. "The people of colour," General Christophe proclaims, will "never submit to the dominion of the Europeans, whilst a single arm retained power to resist it . . . the war between them would be one of extermination, and if the troops from Europe were destined to gain the ascendancy in the island, their empire should be held over mountains of ashes moistened with blood" (p. 4). Overtly and by inference, the opening scenes of *Zelica* appear to associate the Haitian and American revolutions—but they do not. Although the novel begins by praising the martial valor and republican virtue of Haiti's black soldiers, it then undercuts that image almost immediately by presenting a far more powerful counterimage, that of suffering white creole "ladies" inhumanely driven from their homes by these same victorious black soldiers. Smoke from their burning homes rises in the background. In the foreground the "ladies," dressed in white, struggle up a steep hill, prodded on their way by black revolutionaries wielding bayonets:

> Some bearing their children in their arms—some supporting the feeble steps of aged relatives, their feet . . . torn to pieces . . . their steps marked with blood. Creatures who had been nursed in the softest folds of luxury . . . now exposed without shelter . . . suffered excruciating torture; but their physical pains were forgotten in the more exquisite anguish of their moral torments. Every heart was torn with anxiety for some object of its dearest affection; trembled for a father, a brother, a husband, or a son, from whom they had been severed. (Pp. 16–17)

With the entrance of the creole "ladies," the text shifts radically. Dropping its critiques of European imperialism and the excesses of West Indian slavery, *Zelica* becomes a romance that transforms the heroic black republicans into ravening animals threatening white women. General Christophe, first presented to us as a model of Spartan severity and courage, becomes a potential rapist lusting after a creole woman, "the fairest of the race that he had devoted to destruction, and whilst his imagination rioted among heaps of slain, it pointed as the reward of his toils to some distant tranquil bower . . . where . . . he should devote his life to . . . the object of his idolatry" (pp. 22, 25).

Christophe's second in command, a fictional character named General Glaude, is his symbolic double. Like Christophe, Glaude is initially presented heroically as one who "had been among the first to hail the dawn of freedom." But, also like Christophe, he dares to love a white woman, for which arrogance the novel turns him into a savage before our eyes. We are shown him gazing at Clara "with the admiration of a savage for its idol. . . . He burned with the fury of a tiger panting for his prey." He dreams of rape, his brute power overwhelming Clara's resistance. Clara's response is predictable (parallel to that of nineteenth-century readers?). While she had initially lavished praise on Glaude's military prowess and love for liberty, when she discovers that he loves and desires her she is "overpowered by the chill of terror.... To consider herself as the object of an unhallowed passion—to be loved by a half-civilized negro... was appalling.... she shuddered at his name" (p. 148). Never again does Clara speak Glaude's name.

It is not only "fierce chieftains" that the text transfigures as "ruthless barbarians," "half-civilized" "monsters," "beasts of prey," "tigers raging for blood," or "licentious" but also Haitians in general. Haitian soldiers are presented dancing and singing like animals or "slaves" to savage superstition. Though the novel ends with the Haitian soldiers triumphant and their enemies routed, never again does it extend sympathy to those who fight for their freedom and their honor. Rather, it represents black Haitians as obsessed by their lust for white women, who nobly resist the blacks' "unholy feelings" with their last breath. The women's deaths are often cruel, at times sadistic. (Interestingly, the novel presents us with only two black Haitian women—one, an ancient witchlike character, terrifying and intensely loyal to her white owners; the other, erotically represented as a sable Venus [p. 84].) Our last vision of Cape François is of a city again in flames, its streets littered with the dismembered bodies of innocent white women and children.

How can we explain this radical reversal? If the novel's object is simply to condemn the Haitian Revolution as a world turned horribly upside down or to hold it up as a dreadful contrast to the reason and moderation of a glorious Euro-American revolution, why does it begin by so lavishly praising the black Haitians as freedom-loving republicans? Why does it so positively link the two revolutions? Answers to these questions lie in the novel's fusion of political and sexual revolution and in its representations of the two central female protagonists, Clara and Zelica.

Clara St. Louis came from New York to marry one of Haiti's wealthiest white creole commercial leaders. Her apartment recalls the magnificent rooms that Arthur Mervyn found so impressive when he first arrived in Philadelphia. Like Thomas Welbeck's rooms, Clara's rooms "were filled with all that taste and splendour could devise," with mirrors so "superb" that "wherever she cast her eyes, her own beautiful image was reflected" (p. 141). (Do Clara's mirrors reflect a coherent white bourgeois subject, or in their multiplicity do they fragment that subject? Can the white creole subject ever be coherent?)[32] Clara's marriage to a leading Haitian creole

32. In my reading of Charles Brockden Brown's novel of Euro-American / American Indian relations, I suggest that he posits the Euro-American as a white, postcolonial Creole who is always an innately divided and multiple identity, split by race, by his ambivalent rela-

merchant could be read as symbolizing the ties that bound New York's commercial community to a country that, according to the novel, "offered ... commercial resources so immense that all those who conducted business, with however small a capital, soon attained ease" (p. 140). (Is it ironic that Haiti's slave economy appears to represent the realization of "The American Dream"?)

Clara, however, represents more than mercantile America. She stands more overtly for America's commitment to republican principles. Clara longs to return to her own country, "where personal liberty is sacred, and all the rights of man respected" (p. 31). She repeatedly praises the American Revolution and chides the French on the sad comparison of their revolution and military heroes with her revolution and the great George Washington (p. 152). Can we read Glaude's desire for Clara, therefore, as representing not simply uncontrolled black lust for a beautiful white woman but also, more rationally, the black Haitian republic's desire for commercial and political ties to the United States? The white U.S. political leaders and men of commerce had desired to consummate these ties with Haiti's white creole elite (represented by Clara's creole husband), but not with its new black leaders. The text certainly supports such an interpretation, as it tells us explicitly that Glaude values Clara not only for her sexual charms but also for the political and economic ties to the United States that he hopes an alliance with her would procure. Clara's death at the novel's end may thus suggest that the blackness of Haiti's revolution overshadowed both the liberal republic promise of rational self-government—a self-government mainland white American men had achieved, at least for themselves—and the commercial capitalist promise of a union between the two American republics which would bring whites in both countries prosperity and progress. Consider the telling irony of Clara's death: she is unintentionally pierced by a sword wielded by Zelica's white father, whose idealistic but misguided support for Haiti's black leaders, the novel argues, made the revolution's accompanying carnage and destruction possible. Thus Clara's death could be read as marking the death of U.S. commercial connections with black-dominated Haiti.

Zelica, the woman idolized by General Christophe and the novel's title character, is an even more complex figure. Although Zelica appears as fair as the morning sun, she is a "quadroon." Her mother was her father's slave, "but one degree removed from black." Early in her life, Zelica's father had sent Zelica to France to distance her from maternal influences. When Zelica returns to Haiti, she confesses, she finds herself repulsed by the very sight of blacks. "Though their advocate, I am not their admirer,"

---

tion to Europe and America. See Carroll Smith-Rosenberg, "Subject Female: Engendering an American Identity," *American Literary History* 5, no. 3 (1993): 481–511.

she tells a French soldier. "Whilst I think that they have an indisputable right to the freedom that they are struggling to obtain, I feel an involuntary sensation of horror at the sight of a black and never behold one without shuddering" (pp. 138–39).

Zelica's father, de la Riviere, is a white creole radical who embraces the Haitian Revolution and General Christophe in particular. As Zelica tells Clara in one of their intimate conversations, her father "idealizes Christophe . . . talks with enthusiasm of his unspoiled energy, the ardour of his untaught feelings, and the native grandeur of his soul" (pp. 204–5). De la Riviere reaffirms his support of the revolution both by bequeathing his estate to Christophe and by offering Christophe his own daughter in marriage, a marriage Zelica refuses in horror. Pronouncing death preferable to marrying a black man, Zelica proclaims the absurdity of the radical political espousal of racial mixture and denounces her father's patriarchal acts as political tyranny. De la Riviere's relation to Christophe offers another key to reading the novel's complexities. Aiding and abetting the black revolution, de la Riviera plays a critical role in the transfer of the right to govern Haiti from the educated, enlightened creole elite, which he represents, to Christophe's black military. Handing political governance to Christophe, de la Riviera seeks to seal the transfer by handing over his daughter as well.[33]

The feminist political theorist Carol Pateman argues that the social contract, the bedrock of the liberal political state, presumes a sexual contract that confirms women's political inferiority and consequently their exclusion.[34] Thus Zelica's marriage contract with Christophe not only marks the transfer of political power from white to black men but reaffirms women's social, sexual, and political subordination within liberal republics, be they black or white, and the refusal of republican men to reexamine their continued exercise of patriarchal power over women. This, at least, appears to be Sansay's intention, for she represents Zelica's refusal of marriage as a refusal not only of a black lover but specifically of her father's assertion of patriarchal power. Echoing contemporary French feminists' attacks on the misogyny of their own revolution, Zelica angrily denounces her father's "despotic . . . disposition of my hand," pointing out that her father, an "enthusiast for liberty . . . leaves his daughter no choice but the most abhorrent slavery . . . and death" (pp. 201–2).[35] Boldly refusing the sexual contract, Zelica refuses the sexual polarities it affirms. Her

---

33. On the exchange of women to effect political mobility and changing power relations, see Gayle Rubin, "The Traffic in Women: Notes on the 'Political Economy' of Sex," in *Toward an Anthropology of Women*, ed. Rayna R. Reiter (New York, 1975), pp. 157–210.

34. Carole Pateman, *Sexual Contract* (Stanford, 1988).

35. See Genevieve Fraisse, *Reason's Muse: Sexual Difference and the Birth of Democracy*, trans. Jane Marie Todd (Chicago, 1994), esp. chap. 1.

father, she tells Clara, thinks her "all soft, all submissive" (the way the sexual contract constitutes women). But she is not. Rather, she has inherited her father's "own energy." Like him, she affirms, "I will sacrifice my life to save my feelings from violation." Zelica thus proclaims her right to self-determination (pp. 204–5).

This passage recalls the feminist theorist Gayatri Chakravorty Spivak's contention that white women, to assert their right to a liberal humanist subjectivity, joined white men in endorsing racism and imperialism.[36] Sansay wrote too close to her own country's struggle for national liberation to endorse the right of France to control Haiti. As a Euro-American, however, she could easily embrace racism as a way to underscore the legitimacy of Zelica's determination to refuse her father's patriarchal right to transfer his control of her body to the man of *his* choice. Sansay's novel represents that attempt in political terms. "The enthusiast for liberty" is revealed as "despotic" in relation to women. Can we read this as Sansay's protest against women's exclusion from the social contract not only in Haiti but in the United States and France as well?

If so, then why did Sansay make Zelica a "quadroon"? Would not Zelica's enforced marriage to Christophe be even more shocking were Zelica, like Clara, "purely" white? Reading Zelica against the novel's depiction of Clara's America may offer a final clue to the book's many riddles. Recall that Clara sees America as a country "where personal liberty is sacred, and all the rights of man respected." This representation of America obscures the denial of suffrage not only to white women but also, even more ironically, to the large body of enslaved African Americans resident in the United States whose personal as well as political liberty is not sacred and whose economic and sexual rights are not respected. Enslaved blacks are as effaced from this representation of America as Zelica's black blood is by her fair skin. And as enslaved African Americans inspired hatred, fear, and revulsion among Euro-Americans, so Zelica, as already noted, reports hating the very sight of blacks in Haiti. This second analogy, however, causes us to pause. It positions Zelica in relation to blacks as Euro-Americans are positioned. Yet Zelica, as a "quadroon," is not a Euro-American. Might she not stand, then, not for Euro-American women but, even more importantly, for America itself? Does Zelica, fusing black and white and refusing to admit that fusion, embody America in its racial and ideological complexity?

If Zelica refuses to recognize her own blackness, Justine Senat, the ultimate sybaritic Creole, refuses to acknowledge Zelica's whiteness. Delighted over de la Riviere's insistence that Zelica marry Christophe,

36. Gayatri Chakravorty Spivak, "Three Women's Texts and a Critique of Imperialism," *Critical Inquiry* 12, no. 3 (1985): 243–61.

Madame Senat predicts "the enchantress will only return to her native colour, which all the water of the ocean would not wash out of her veins" (p. 139). But Madame Senat is wrong. At the novel's end, seeking to escape the embrace of Christophe, Zelica leaps into the ocean, from which she is rescued by her French white republican lover, who carries her, as his "white" bride, to America and freedom. There, together, the brave white soldier as virtuous republican and the brave quadroon as white "lady" will quite literally embody future Americans.

Simultaneously inscribing and refusing racial polarities, *Zelica* similarly inscribes and refuses gendered polarities. There is only one truly powerful and masterful character in the novel: Zelica. Men, whether French, black, or creole, time and again prove irrational, ineffectual, self-indulgent, ill informed, or impotent—in short, anything but heroic republicans. It is Zelica who assumes the role of the empowered man. It is she who understands and effectively controls the movements of black and white armies and who is able to thwart the plans of French generals and black chiefs. And all to one end: to protect Clara, the woman she has sworn to keep safe from every danger. It is men who endanger Clara and men whom Zelica succeeds in thwarting until the novel's very end, when, as already seen, Zelica's own father tragically stabs Clara to death. Indeed, *Zelica* constructs a fascinating variation on the classic Oedipal plot. Here two women love each other. It is the father of one, the same father who attempts to force his daughter to marry a man the father loves and admires, who ends by killing the other woman and dying himself.

Powerful, protective, and erotic, Zelica plays the male role far more convincingly than do any of the novel's male characters. Certainly, too, Zelica and Clara's love story is the central one of the novel. On first meeting, they turn from all others to wander romantically together through "a wilderness of flowers" (p. 93). Repeatedly each presses the other to her bosom, throws herself into the other's arms. As the text reports, "There was a sympathy of thought and feeling between these two lovely females that united their souls. This sympathy did not require the slow movement of time to call it forth; a look discovered, a glance imparted it" (p. 93). Calling her "my dearest Clara," Zelica pours forth her love. "My sweet, my best loved friend," she tells her, "you . . . above all creatures, I love and honour" (pp. 172–73). For her part, Clara admits "her joy increased at the idea of owing her safety to Zelica. She pressed her face into her bosom" (p. 238). Later Clara declares, "If you [Zelica], had been my constant companion you would have saved me from many errors." Here we find the erotic epicenter of the novel, for compared with each other, these women's male lovers fade into insignificance. Zelica's French lover is a dark figure in a night sea, while Clara's husband is unfaithful, self-indulgent, effeminate, and foolish.

III.

On one level, two texts could not be more dissimilar than Brown's *Arthur Mervyn* and Sansay's *Zelica*. One is canonical, the other forgotten. One addresses the problems faced by a commercial and political capitol poised on the threshold of modernity. The other depicts the nostalgia besetting a stifling colonial town whose elegance is past and whose future will be violent. Read interactively, however, one sees that both novels explore the critical issues besetting the new American nation and its newly bourgeois citizens.[37]

First, they pose questions of *creolité*. Both Philadelphia's Euro-Americans and Haiti's white planters had to carve out identities that would distinguish them from their former colonizers, the English and French (whom they represented alternatively as tyrannical and oppressive or worldly and sophisticated), and the persons of color with whom they shared their brave new world. Second, both novels explore the dependence of the commercial economy of the United States on the slave economies of the Caribbean and American mainland. Most pointedly, they question if a freedom-loving bourgeoisie could ever expiate its guilt for profiting from such trade or, indeed, how real its profit actually was. In answer to that question, both novels insist that the intermixture of slave and liberal republican, black and white, will always bring disease, decay, and death. Clara's life in Haiti as much as her violent death there make this point. The slave labor system corrupted white Haitians as much as it exploited black Haitians. It made white Haitians as savage as the "savages" they exploited, as incapable of civic virtue, reasoned moderation, and intelligent labor as the slaves who rose up against them. Furthermore, by invoking Clara's death and the murder of countless white creole women and children by "black brutes," *Zelica* suggests that the intermingling of black and white would always lead to violence. Similarly, in *Arthur Mervyn* the blood money extracted from the sale of human lives brings only moral degeneration, destruction, and death to all who seek to benefit from it (the Lodi family, Thomas Welbeck) and to those who sought to defraud the defrauding Welbeck. And what could be more chilling than Brown's description of the desolation and horror of the yellow fever that Philadelphia ships trading with the beleaguered Haiti brought home with them to Philadelphia?

At the same time, both novels constitute powerful heroines who boldly fuse black and white, male and female. Each novel's strongest character refuses racist and sexist categories. Ascha Fielding and Zelica are fearless, resourceful, rational, intelligent, educated, and at home in Europe's most

---

37. Note that Sansay's representation of Haiti as sybaritic parallels the northern press's representation of the slaveholding south as such.

sophisticated circles. They represent the best of virtuous republican and bourgeois culture. Yet both are described as black, as alien others to white Protestant "Americans." And both refuse normative bourgeois definitions of white womanhood—Ascha Fielding by her wealth and independence, and Zelica by refusing her father's command to marry the man of *his* desires. White and black, female and male, polyglot, multiple, and conflicted in their identities though they are, they hold the promise of a prosperous and virtuous future in their soft arms.

But they do so only by flying from the dilemmas that the fusion of free trade and slave labor produced for bourgeois white Americans. To preserve her freedom and virtue, Zelica leaps blindly into Haiti's incarnadine sea. Ascha Fielding and Arthur Mervyn also turn their backs on Philadelphia's commercial world, though in a far more genteel manner. But flight, no matter how genteel its form, refuses closure. Certainly their flight refuses resolution to the principal problems facing bourgeois and republican America. The print culture of late-eighteenth- and early-nineteenth-century America apparently could offer no clearer a resolution to the moral dilemmas that the fusion of slave labor and free trade, of black and white, or of male and female presented to the new American bourgeoisie than that press could posit a coherent, unified white American subject.

Bodies of Illusion:
Portraits, People, and the
Construction of Memory

MARGARETTA M. LOVELL

IN THIS essay I look closely at makers commenting on the act
of making (in this case, making portraits) to gain insight into aspects of
eighteenth-century American culture both too basic and too important to
occasion direct comment. In its focus on certain fundamental aspects of a
culture that is close enough to our own in time, geography, and continuity
to need active defamiliarization, my inquiry revolves around a series of
linked, deliberately basic, questions. What is the meaning and impact of
"likeness" and illusion when the object is commissioned and the subject is
a human face and form? What can elaborated self-portraiture tell us about
portraiture as a social practice? What does art have to do with patriarchy?
What, beyond the Veblenian obvious, is the relation between portraiture
and wealth? How is a portrait, once commissioned, executed, paid for,
and hung, understood to act on its human context?

As it addresses these and other questions, this essay moves outside the
realm of creation and reception to consideration of the artwork as a social
participant. It attempts to interrogate a handful of works to inquire into
the ways in which portraits can be read as situating, for their immediate
audience(s), the face and form of individuals in time and space and in history; it attends to the body as the site of identity, physical presence, and
memory. My focus is on the painting of portraits as a cultural practice and
the process by which a person (a body, a physiognomy, and perhaps a

I thank the Henry E. Huntington Library and Art Gallery in San Marino, California, for providing me the opportunity and resources to complete this study, and the McNeil Center for
Early American Studies at the University of Pennsylvania and the Omohundro Institute of Early
American History and Culture for the occasion to begin it. I am grateful to Shelley Bennett, Patricia Hills, Joseph Koener, and Dell Upton for their useful comments on earlier drafts of this essay,
to Jay D. McEvoy Jr. for a facilitation grant, and to Elizabeth Leary for her research assistance.

soul) becomes an object: an object beyond decay, change, death; an object of instruction, affection, continuity, pleasure, duty, perhaps deception; an object in which that-which-has-been can be present with that-which-is. The project is to begin to explore how portraits of and by eighteenth-century Americans operated in the culture that produced them and how they both commented on and helped to formulate that culture. This inquiry looks at self-portraiture as a special kind of play and self-commentary on the creation of illusion, and it sees that commentary positioning portraiture as a constructive fiction with serious social ends.

In 1806 Benjamin West (1738–1820) painted a double portrait that includes the image of his wife, Elizabeth Shewell West (1741–1814), and of himself, the two heads inflected—as is so often the case in portraiture—toward one another (fig. 13.1).[1] She looks out at the viewer, while the keen-eyed West, looking neither at her nor at us, rivets his gaze to the left. The work was painted in England where this pair of Philadelphians made their home. Successor to Sir Joshua Reynolds as the president of the Royal Academy, West was a major player in the British art establishment. But he was also a primary figure in the development of American art during the late colonial and early national period.

In his London studio (pictured—or imagined—in a painting known as *The American School* executed in 1765 by Matthew Pratt, Elizabeth's cousin) West—the standing figure with palette in hand—hospitably taught, advised, and, on occasion, employed three generations of aspiring American artists, including Gilbert Stuart, Charles Willson Peale, John Trumbull, John Singleton Copley, Henry Benbridge, and the artists assembled here (fig. 13.2). They constituted a community of painters, a conscious subculture if not, in fact, a school. These are the artists—Benjamin West and those in his circle in the late 1760s and 1770s—that will be the focus of my discussion here.

That *The American School* is about painting, especially portraiture, is a fairly straightforward reading, and one I will return to shortly. But let us first consider the West double portrait known by the title *Self-Portrait*.[2]

---

1. This painting, signed "B. West 1806," was given by the artist to his friend Robert Fulton (artist, cyclorama entrepreneur, and inventor of the steamboat and the submarine), who brought it to the United States in that year. Two years later it was listed among the works hanging in the newly established Pennsylvania Academy in Philadelphia. The location of the "original" portrait of Elizabeth Shewell West, if one in fact existed independent of its inclusion within the 1806 *Self-Portrait*, is unknown (see Helmut von Erffa and Alan Staley, *The Paintings of Benjamin West* [New Haven, 1986], pp. 453–56). For Robert Fulton as a collector (as well as producer) of art, see Carrie Rebora, "Robert Fulton's Art Collection," *American Art Journal* 22, no. 3 (1990): 40–63.

2. *Self-Portrait* is the title under which the painting is published in von Erffa and Staley, *Paintings of Benjamin West*, no. 530, and in Susan Danly, *Facing the Past: Nineteenth-Century Portraits from the Collection of the Pennsylvania Academy of the Fine Arts* (Philadelphia, 1992), p.

This title immediately raises questions. First there is the artist's oblique gaze. Ordinarily, the mirror-generated aspect of a self-portrait gives us direct and unequivocal eye contact with the artist; in this case he looks intently but decisively past us, excluding us from his act of self-observation. But that is not the only problem. The absence of any reference to the second figure, West's wife, in the title seems awry until we focus on the fact that in this work she is less a "she" than an "it." She is a two-dimensional portrait within West's simulated three-dimensional studio space. The image is a self-portrait because *he* is understood to be a sentient being, whereas "she" is understood to be an object, referential but a mere simulacrum. Within the fiction of the painting the "real" Elizabeth, her body and her being, is outside the frame, offstage to our left; we catch the trace of her location, her inferred situated self, in West's scrutinizing stare.

West's project here is notable. A search for a theory of painting among the texts left us by eighteenth-century American artists yields a thin harvest: a few letters from John Singleton Copley, some remarks by Gilbert Stuart.[3] But while eighteenth-century prescriptive remarks on painting, even descriptive remarks by Americans, are rare, in such images as this we see both practice and comment on practice.

In this work West has positioned himself rather curiously, almost humbly, as a painter of domestic portraits.[4] The hierarchy of genres situated portraiture—as an aesthetic project based on the reportage of visual facts—well below history and religious painting, genres understood to be based in the realms of ideas and civic ideology, and genres which West vigorously and successfully pursued. The difference, as Reynolds in his *Discourses* clarified and codified for eighteenth-century British practitioners and patrons, was not just between the factual recording of real countenances and bodies in portraiture and the imaginative re-creation of tribal tales in history painting but between the lesser world of private life and the nobler social cement of public virtue and corporate ideology.

40; in 1808 it was listed in an inventory of West's works published by the English journal *La Belle Assemblée or Bell's Court and Fashionable Magazine addressed particularly to the Ladies* as "Mr. West painting the portrait of Mrs. West, in one picture, half figures, large as life; in ditto [the Academy at Philadelphia]" (John Dillenberger, *Benjamin West: The Context of His Life's Work with Particular Attention to Paintings with Religious Subject Matter* [San Antonio, 1977], pp. 129, 187). For an account of West's self-portraits as a group, see Ann C. Van Devanter, "Benjamin West and His Self-Portraits," *Antiques* 103, no. 4 (1973): 764–71.

3. John W. McCoubrey, *American Art, 1700–1960: Sources and Documents* (Englewood Cliffs, N.J., 1965), pp. 5–25, 35–43.

4. More appropriate to understanding West's position and his reputation is the portrait of him by Sir Thomas Lawrence that situates him in the robes of the president of the Royal Academy as a lecturer and as a history painter (1810, Yale Center for British Art, New Haven, Conn.).

Fig. 13.1. Benjamin West (1738–1820), *Self-Portrait*, 1806. Oil on canvas; H. 36 1/8″ (91.8 cm), W. 28 1/8″ (71.4 cm). (Photo: Courtesy of the Pennsylvania Academy of the Fine Arts, Philadelphia, Gift of Mr. and Mrs. Henry R. Hallowell.)

Fig. 13.2. Matthew Pratt (1734–1805), *The American School*, 1765. Oil on canvas; H. 36″ (91.4 cm), W. 50 1/4″ (127.6 cm). (Photo: The Metropolitan Museum of Art, Gift of Samuel P. Avery, 1897.)

Moreover, the visual pun in which West is indulging here—his play with spatial ambiguity between two and three dimensions, between object and person—rests on the kind of baroque joke Reynolds had explicitly disdained.[5] But West flies in the teeth of stricture, hierarchy, and precedent to construct a certain kind of double reading in this painting. Clearly, Mrs. West is painted with the same vibrancy, at the same scale as her husband, and she challenges us with her direct gaze; our subjectivity is acknowledged and constructed in hers. West is intent on her seeming "thereness." In this work we sense in the aging, distinguished, and urbane

5. Reynolds, in "Discourse III," insists that deception is not the "business of art" because "it is not the eye, it is the mind, which the painter of genius desires to address." In "Discourse XIII" he states, "Painting is not only not to be considered as an imitation, operating by deception, but . . . it is and ought to be, in many points of view, and strictly speaking, no imitation at all of external nature" (Sir Joshua Reynolds, *Discourses on Art*, ed. Robert R. Wark [San Marino, Calif., 1959, based on the 1797 edition], pp. 50, 232).

veteran at the pinnacle of his profession a residue of the exuberant, playful wonder that we hear best in the account of his backwoods, visually
innocent contemporary Chester Harding:

> I fell in with a portrait-painter . . . one of the primitive sort . . . and was
> enamored at once. I got him to paint me and my wife, and thought the pic-
> tures perfection. . . . I took the pictures home, and pondered on them, and
> wondered how it was possible for a man to produce such wonders of art.
> At length my admiration began to yield to an ambition to do the same
> thing. I thought of it by day, and dreamed of it by night, until I was stimu-
> lated to make an attempt at painting myself. I got a board; and, with such
> colors as I had for use in my trade [he was a sign painter], I began a por-
> trait of my wife. I made a thing that looked like her. The moment I saw the
> likeness, I became frantic with delight: it was like the discovery of a new
> sense; I could think of nothing else. From that time, sign-painting became
> odious, and was much neglected.[6]

Harding, who eventually became a polished and celebrated academic
portraitist, had reached manhood without learning to read, without ever
witnessing a dramatic performance, and without seeing a painting. Harding's comment on his awakening to visual power and West's insistence on
visual wit point to a firm substructure in American eighteenth- and early-
nineteenth-century art, to its practitioners' understanding of the raw
power of illusion to draw the viewer into a state of delight and suspended
disbelief. The successful portrait vividly, almost magically, summons the
subject before the viewer's eyes.

The artist's wizardry is not the only active agent in the achievement of
likeness. As the philosopher and historian David Hume put it in 1739,
"Resemblance depends on the [viewer's] memory by which we raise up
the images of past perceptions. . . . Memory not only discovers the identity but also contributes to its production."[7] The viewer's memory, of
course, is not just of the individual face captured but also of the web of
social relations in which they (the human original of the image and the
viewer of the image) are mutual actors.

West's double portrait, in its differential inclusion of Elizabeth as
painted object and the artist as "real," prefigures that moment when he
(and we) will look at the painting within the painting and know her to be
chronologically, as well as situationally, offstage, dead—a remembered

6. Chester Harding, *My Egotistigraphy* (1866), excerpted in *Twelve Works of Naive Genius*, ed.
Walter Teller (New York, 1972), p. 92.

7. David Hume, "Of Personal Identity," in *A Treatise of Human Nature* (1739), ed. L. A.
Selby-Bigge, 3 books in 1 (Oxford, 1978), 1:260–61. Hume is here arguing against the intuitive
notion of the self and against the concept of a fixed identity.

rather than an apprehended face and being. In this sense West's project points to a reality behind all portraiture: insofar as it images likeness and particularity, it exposes the unrecoverability of the depicted moment and the soon-to-be inanimate character of the likeness's original. As such pointed prints as *Life and Death Contrasted, or An Essay on Woman* make clear, the particularity of physiognomy, costume, and gesture recorded in the portrait are inevitably subsumed into the generic and timeless condition of death (fig. 13.3).

But if West's image gestures forward in the direction of a memento mori—toward the inevitable personal end of the individual subject(s) pictured—it also references backward toward the mythic origins of painting. As recorded by Pliny and as re-imaged by West in an etching of 1791, the "first" artist turns away from the original and toward the subject's shadowed image, which she circumscribes and renders permanent on a wall (fig. 13.4).[8] This turning away from the subject (in West's print) and from the object (in West's painting) mimics the artist's necessary actions in capturing the likeness on which the project of portraiture as a social practice depends. The face and the imaged face are never really interchangeable (as Oscar Wilde would have it in *Dorian Gray*), because the "original" is subject to time, but West proposes in his double portrait that they might be.

West's unusual visual pun in the *Self-Portrait* of 1806, his situating of his art-making capacity in the same universe as Harding's vernacular "likeness"-making "delight," has its counterpart in the work of a few other American painters within the orbit of West's studio at this period. West's younger contemporary and one of his many protégés, Charles Willson Peale (1741–1827), painted a portrait a decade earlier of two of his sons, known as *The Staircase Group* (fig. 13.5). Two life-sized figures, one equipped with the accoutrements of painting (palette, bouquet of brushes, and mahlstick) turn to face the viewer. In a move improbable if not impossible in contemporary European practice, Peale installed the work in his gallery not in a picture frame but within a doorframe, constructing a wooden step below the image. We are told that no less a personage than George Washington, "as he passed it, bowed politely to the painted figures, which he afterwards acknowledged he thought were living persons," and the work was accounted a success.[9] That it was necessarily Washing-

8. For a recent discussion of the role of the myth of the origins of painting and drawing in the eighteenth century, see Ann Bermingham, "The Origin of Painting and the Ends of Art: Wright of Derby's *Corinthian Maid*," in *Painting and the Politics of Culture: New Essays on British Art*, ed. John Barrell (Oxford, 1992), pp. 135–66.

9. Rembrandt Peale, "Reminiscences: The Person and Mien of Washington," *Crayon* 3 (April 1856): 100. For a discussion of Peale's veristic "plain" style, see Brandon Brame Fortune, "Charles Willson Peale's Portrait Gallery: Persuasion and the Plain Style," *Word and Image* 6, no. 4 (1990): 308–24.

Fig. 13.3. Life and Death Contrasted, or An Essay on Woman, ca. 1760. Engraving, printed for Bowles & Carver, London; H. 9 1/2″ (24.1 cm), W. 12 3/4″ (32.4 cm). (Photo: Courtesy of the Newberry Library.)

Fig. 13.4. Benjamin West, designer, *The Origin of Painting* (trade card etched by Francesco Bartolozzi for Thomas Sandby Jr.), 1791. Etching; at platemark H. 9 1/2" (24.1 cm), W. 6 1/2" (16.5 cm). (Photo: The Huntington Library, Art Collections, and Botanical Gardens.)

ton, a living legend of integrity and wisdom, who was fooled by the deception is instrumental in the tale and in the culture's acknowledgment of the power of art to defy empirical experience. Art appears to have the capacity to remove its subjects from the laws by which we read visual data. In Peale's mind it was the artist's métier and his goal to do so: "If a painter . . . paints a portrait in such perfection as to produce a perfect illusion of sight, in such perfection that the spectator believes the real person is there, that

Fig. 13.5. Charles Willson Peale (1741–1827), *The Staircase Group*, 1795. Oil on canvas; H. 89″ (226.1 cm), W. 39 1/2″ (100.3 cm). (Photo: Philadelphia Museum of Art, The George W. Elkins Collection.)

happy painter will deserve to be caressed by the greatest of mortal beings."[10] We could interpret this "staircase" project, its intellectual framing, and its reception as evidence of a kind of hopeless provincial naïveté. Indeed Reynolds had explicitly attributed the erroneous understanding of art as "imitation, operating by deception," to men in "a gross state of nature," such as "people taken from the banks of the Ohio."[11]

On the other hand, Peale's artwork-as-successful-deception might equally be seen as a kind of Duane Hanson move, a calling to consciousness of both the artist's wondrous artistry and the audience's pleasure in recognizing a world congruent with but governed differently from that which we know through our senses. For *The Staircase Group* has both an instantaneous comment to make about deception and a permanent existence as a marker of a certain epistemological stance at a certain moment. The painting, in other words, is not "reflecting" any prior event or social reality but rather commenting on, even actively shaping, habits of mind and ways of knowing through artfully constructed fictions that simulate, with uncanny accuracy, the "real."

Peale's own direct comment on the making of portraits—"the pinning of heads to canvas," as one contemporary vividly put it—is a self-portrait in which an oval image of his wife, Rachel, and the figure of his daughter Angelica flank his own somber visage (fig. 13.6).[12] He holds a palette and cluster of brushes in his left hand while his right hand, holding a single brush, pauses between the flat surface of the palette and the flat surface of the pictured canvas. Again, in scale, coloration, treatment, and direct gaze, the face of Rachel appears to challenge its status as fiction, as flattened, inanimate object in a world of rounded, animate forms. Angelica, with an upraised finger drawing the viewer's attention to her presence and her face, appears to reach behind her father's form (attesting to the three-dimensional character of the world these two occupy) to touch the top of his poised brush, as though she would supplant him as the active agent in the creative process.[13] Or does she? One might equally read that

10. Charles Willson Peale, "Autobiography," typescript, p. 338, American Philosophical Society, Philadelphia, Pa., as cited in *Three Centuries of America Art* (Philadelphia, 1976), p. 167.

11. Reynolds, "Discourse XIII," pp. 232–33.

12. Gilbert Stuart, cited in Jules D. Prown, *American Painting: From Its Beginnings to the Armory Show* (New York, n.d.), p. 47.

13. Models for Peale in this hand-play include William Hogarth's *David Garrick with His Wife*, 1757, Collection of HRM The Queen, Windsor Castle. Angelica Kauffmann Peale (b. 1775) was indeed taught by her father how to paint but discontinued painting after her marriage; see Charles C. Sellers, *Portraits and Miniatures by Charles Willson Peale* (Philadelphia, 1952), p. 159, and Wilbur Harvey Hunter, *The Peale Family and Peale's Baltimore Museum, 1814–1830* (Baltimore, 1965), n.p. For a discussion proposing that Angelica represents divine inspiration, see David Steinberg, "Charles Willson Peale: The Portraitist as Divine," in *New*

Fig. 13.6. Charles Willson Peale, *Self-Portrait with Angelica and Portrait of Rachel*, ca. 1782–85 or 1788–90. Oil on canvas; H. 36" (91.4 cm), W. 27 1/16" (68.7 cm). (Photo: The Museum of Fine Arts, Houston; The Bayou Bend Collection, Gift of Miss Ima Hogg.)

third hand as Rachel's, a fixed, flat picture of a hand (her right hand, reaching across her body to intercept the brush) as incapable of action as her head is incapable of will. This ambiguity, reinforced by the contrast between Peale's gravity and the impishness of his daughter, draws attention to the possibility of substitution and usurpation, as well as to the facts of artistic agency, simulation, and distinctions that do not point to difference (for, in fact, *all* the hands are painted).

Thus far I have addressed Anglo-American portraiture at the end of the eighteenth century and the early years of the nineteenth as visual experience, as pleasurable deception, a status de-emphasized in English art theory but deliberately underlined in this set of "theory" paintings by Americans. Peale's *Self-Portrait with Rachel and Angelica Peale*, however, complicates matters; it also comments on portraiture as social experience, as a family matter. The work incorporates a second visual pun that goes as directly as the device of the canvas-within-the-canvas to the problematic heart of portraiture: Peale situates himself as the active agent between a pair of similar female faces underlining the two ways Rachel's visage can be reproduced—artistically and biologically. The replication of Rachel's features in the living lineaments of Angelica's face guarantees the mother a kind of earthly permanence different from but operatively similar to the artist's finished canvas; both promise that an echo of her presence will outlive her body. Portraiture, then, Peale suggests, is simultaneously about likeness, magical artistic prowess, and family relations.

Likeness was the most straightforward project of portraiture and the first basis on which it was judged by contemporaries.[14] It is the empirical foundation that doomed the genre to lower status in the art hierarchy but it is also the key to its value as mnemonic. Investing the likeness with intellectual and social meaning, then, with qualities beyond the merely observable, potentially can elevate the status of the portraiture project and create meaning beyond the delight of identity. The use of the portrait subject's face, body, deportment, expression, and accoutrements as an index

---

Perspectives on Charles Willson Peale, ed. Lillian B. Miller and David C. Ward (Pittsburgh, 1991), pp. 131–43. The ambiguity concerning the dating of the work revolves around the age of Angelica—either she is aged seven to ten years in 1782–85 (and this seems most reasonable to me as her size, hairstyle, and manner all seem clearly marked as juvenile), or thirteen to fifteen years in 1788–90. In 1782 Rachel was thirty-eight years old; she died in 1790 when Angelica turned fifteen.

14. For an instance of a contemporary discussion of likeness, see Stephen E. Patrick, " 'I have at Length Determined to Have my Picture Taken': An Eighteenth-Century Young Man's Thoughts about His Portrait by Henry Benbridge," *American Art Journal* 22, no. 4 (1990): 68–81.

15. The mystique of the genius portrait painter who could read souls found contemporary expression and popularization in the writings of Johann Caspar Lavater, in which he discussed "the talent of discovering the interior of Man by his exterior—of perceiving by certain

of mind, character, achievements, and experience thus follows naturally.[15] But Peale's painting suggests that likeness aside, even more important than investing the sitter with "character" (always problematic with female sitters in any case) was situating the sitter within a social identity coded for class, gender, and situation within the family.[16]

These two works—Peale's and West's elaborated self-portraits—are unusual paintings. By and large, when paintings occur within paintings in this period, their artifice and their role as images, as shorthand versions of larger realities and relationships, is unambiguous, as in *Mrs. Thomas Lea* by Gilbert Stuart (1755–1828), perhaps the best-known of the American portraitists tutored and encouraged by Benjamin West (fig. 13.7). Mrs. Lea wears a miniature painting (these were usually executed in watercolor on ivory) as a broach. In its scale, its summary treatment of features, and its location decisively within the sitter's accoutrements, it differs from the paintings within paintings we have been looking at. The comment it makes on the role of painting is straightforward—the miniature oval of a boy performs the function of mnemonic for Mrs. Lea in the same fashion that her full-scale image on the wall in her home points its viewers to her face, her form, her role, and her position within a family web.

It is no accident that Stuart's miniature portrait, the image of Peale with his wife, and the West painting with his wife all position women and children as the objects of art, as images rather than beings. More rarely we find images of men within paintings, as in the portrait of Archbishop Robert Drummond included within Benjamin West's portrait of the churchman's two sons and daughter-in-law (fig. 13.8). The elder Drummond, one of West's most important patrons, died the year this

natural signs what does not immediately strike the senses" (Lavater, *Essays on Physiognomy Designed to Promote the Knowledge and the Love of Mankind* [1781], 3 vols. [London, 1810], 1:20). The question remains whether the outward signs of inward state are natural or cultural and how the reading of these signs is acquired. As George Berkeley, *An Essay toward a New Theory of Vision* (1709), in *The Works of George Berkeley Bishop of Cloyne*, ed. A. A. Luce and T. E. Jessup, 9 vols. (London, 1948), 1:195, put it, "Without experience we should no more have taken blushing for a sign of shame than of gladness." For a discussion of the origins and political and ideological uses of veristic (male) portraiture, see Sheldon Nodelman, "How to Read a Roman Portrait," *Art in America* 63, no. 1 (January–February 1995): 26–33.

16. As William Hogarth put it, nature has "afforded us so many lines and shapes to indicate the deficiencies and blemishes of the mind, whilst there are none at all that point out the perfections of it beyond the appearance of common sense and placidity." And the solution of the ancients—to indicate the gods' Olympian sagacity by "giv[ing] them features of beauty"—is, in his view, unsatisfactory (William Hogarth, *The Analysis of Beauty* [London, 1753], pp. 141, 142, as quoted in Richard Wendorf, *The Elements of Life: Biography and Portrait-Painting in Stuart and Georgian England* [Oxford, 1990], pp. 175–76). Richard Brilliant aptly maintains that, of the constituent ingredients of personal identity (appearance, name, social function, and consciousness), only the first is directly picturable; see Brilliant, *Portraiture* (Cambridge, 1991), p. 9.

Fig. 13.7. Gilbert Stuart (1755–1828), *Mrs. Thomas Lea*, ca. 1798. Oil on canvas; H. 74″ (188.0 cm), W. 29″ (73.7 cm). (Photo: Corcoran Gallery of Art, Anonymous gift.)

group was painted and may have been too ill to sit, but the expedient of including his visage as a framed canvas creates an unsettling and aesthetically unsatisfactory solution.[17] This, after all, is the family patriarch,

17. The internal portrait of Archbishop Robert Drummond (d. December 1776) which West reproduces here was executed by Sir Joshua Reynolds and is now in the St. Louis Art Museum. As the West *Drummond Family* was painted in 1776, the year West succeeded Reynolds in the presidency of the Royal Academy, this portrait may obliquely comment on professional as well as family succession.

and his reduction to inert object displaces him in scale and presence to a kind of cypher, which brings us to the gender and power relations within the family that lie at the core of portrait practice in the eighteenth century.

Let us return for a moment to Pratt's *American School* and to the question of links between visual proprieties, family order, and the function of the portrait as social participant (see fig. 13.2). As mentioned above, this ambitious work is by Matthew Pratt, seen in profile at the easel, and its subject is his wife's kinsman, Benjamin West (in the hat) mentoring a young artist on the left. This painting, more straightforwardly than any others considered here, is a "theory" painting. Susan Rather sees it as Pratt's account (derived from Continental theorists) of the appropriate education of the artist, the auspicious leadership role projected for American painters in Dean George Berkeley's account of the westward migration of culture (published a decade earlier), and Pratt's

Fig. 13.8. Benjamin West, *Three Members of the Drummond Family*, 1775. Oil on canvas, H. 60" (152.4 cm), W. 72" (182.9 cm). (Photo: The Minneapolis Institute of Arts.)

own potential role as coequal with Benjamin West in that happy development.[18]

The work was exhibited in London with its current title, *The American School*, in 1766, and it clearly proposes for Pratt a role larger than that of the one-notable-work artist he became. On the right we note Pratt's profile figure silhouetted against an almost blank canvas on which we find his signature. On his palette, colors are arranged, with recent vigorous activity suggested in the blue and green pigments. These are the colors found in the costumes of the more distant pupils (suggesting Pratt's authorship of the whole canvas), as well as those found in the conventional drapery swag bracketing the upper corner of the studio canvas against which his head stands out or, read another way, onto which his head is laminated.

Ultraviolet photography of the work suggests that the outlines of a figure were painted on that now vacant canvas, lines that their author apparently intended to be legible but that have subsequently faded to invisibility to the naked eye (fig. 13.9).[19] Rather interprets this partial outline (in light of the absence of a female sitter in the room) as the figure of an imaginative Muse, suggesting that the newly begun project—and the practice of art in general among these artists—was history painting.

Given the disposition of this fugitive figure and the convention for portraits—not history paintings or allegorical works—to be set off with drapery swags, however, it is more reasonable to read these traces of white zinc pigment as the initial steps in making not an allegorical work but a portrait, one similar in scale and pose to that of Mrs. Robert Shewell Jr. (fig. 13.10). This work and its pair, *Robert Shewell*, have been attributed to Henry Benbridge, another artist in West's orbit at this time (and another cousin of Mrs. West), but they may have been painted by the author of *The American School*, Matthew Pratt (fig. 13.11).[20] Mrs. Shewell was Pratt's cousin and the sister of Elizabeth Shewell West; in this linkage between family and patronage we see a pattern typical of eighteenth-century artistic and commercial life. In the spandrels of her roundel portrait, white and red paint outlines on a buff ground reveal initial steps similar to those recorded in *The American School*. That there is no female sitter present in Pratt's group of busy artists can be explained by the painter's work on the

18. Susan Rather, "A Painter's Progress: Mathew Pratt and *The American School*," *Metropolitan Museum Journal* 28 (1993): 169–83.

19. See also Trudy E. Bell, "Technology: Ultraviolet Detection," *Connoisseur* 210, no. 843 (1982): 140–41.

20. Questions concerning the authorship of this pair of portraits and the identity of the sitters are addressed in the curatorial file, Fine Arts Museums of San Francisco. One notes here that, as in the case of work on Peale's self-portrait with Rachel and Angelica, the impetus in recent scholarship has been to upgrade these portrait projects into the more "elevated" realm of history painting.

Fig. 13.9. Matthew Pratt, detail of *The American School*, 1765, showing right side of painting under ultraviolet light. (Photo: The Metropolitan Museum of Art, Gift of Samuel P. Avery, 1897.)

drapery rather than on the sitter (the sitter's presence was not required during the painting of accoutrements) and the general focus in the project on stages of instruction and development in the life of the artist.

What I am proposing is that *The American School* may well prescribe and endorse the traditional stages in art education from drawn copies after

Fig. 13.10. Henry Benbridge (1743–1812), attributed, *Sarah Boyer Shewell (Mrs. Robert Shewell, Junior)*, ca. 1775. Oil on canvas; diameter 25 7/8" (65.7 cm). (Photo: Fine Arts Museums of San Francisco, Gift of Mr. and Mrs. John D. Rockefeller 3rd.)

plaster casts to painted figures after life, but the end product is the *portrait*, complete with such visual clichés as the drapery swag. With the notable exception of John Singleton Copley, who volubly chafed (at least in his correspondence with those who devalued portraiture) at the social and aesthetic role of the portraitist, the artists that West befriended and advised, including Pratt, Benbridge, Stuart, and Peale, went on, apparently happily, to careers as portraitists.[21] They were familiar with the hierarchy of genres and its bias against portraiture; indeed they must have watched West formulate, design, and execute his complex history paint-

21. McCoubrey, *American Art*, pp. 17–18. By the early nineteenth century it was a standard trope of English artists to decry the bread-and-butter portraiture business. See Desmond

Fig. 13.11. Henry Benbridge, attributed, *Robert Shewell, Junior,* ca. 1775. Oil on canvas; diameter 25 7/8" (65.7 cm). (Photo: Fine Arts Museums of San Francisco, Gift of Mr. and Mrs. John D. Rockefeller 3rd.)

ings. One recalled "a gallery filled with sketches and designs for large [history] paintings—the spacious room through which I passed to the more retired atelier—the works of his pencil surrounding me at every side—his own figure seated at his esel [*sic*], and the beautiful composition at which he was employed."[22] Yet they became portraitists. It has been presumed that their "settling" on portraiture represents a lack of ambition or talent, a surrender to expediency or to their patrons' unworthy taste.

Shawe-Taylor, "This Mill-Horse Business," in *The Georgians: Eighteenth-Century Portraiture and Society* (London, 1990), pp. 7–20.

22. William Dunlap, *A History of the Rise and Progress of the Arts of Design in the United States,* 3 vols. (New York, 1834; rpt., New York, 1969), 1:67. Concerning Peale's experience in West's

But perhaps they understood portraiture and its uses, indeed its necessity, differently from how we understand it. Perhaps, in a sense, they saw it as so common, so embedded in social structures of individual, class, and family identity, that it had no need for the elaboration of theory constructed around the more obviously political and ideological project of history painting.

The fact that Pratt's *American School* was exhibited shortly after its completion—as were West's *Self-Portrait* with Elizabeth and Peale's *Staircase Group*—suggests that these paintings, despite their familial subject, were to a degree public statements and therefore potentially about the art of painting and the meaning of painted portraits.[23] Most obviously, exhibited portraits were statements about the artists' technical skills and availability for portrait commissions. Each of these three works is signed, indicating not that the artists took particular pride in claiming the work but perhaps that each artist wished to communicate his identity directly to potential patrons who would note this information in the relative novelty and anonymity of the public exhibition hall.[24] As one contemporary put it, "These [exhibitions] are all for honour—there is no prophet [*sic*] arising from it. It only tends to Create a name that may hereafter produce business."[25] These three name-creating, business-enhancing works also have in common one additional characteristic—they were not commissioned and therefore they could accrue monetary value to the artists only as billboards, as mechanisms to expand patronage. But they were also actors in the theater of social values, and it is in this realm that I wish to place them,

London studio, see Jules D. Prown, "Charles Willson Peale in London," in *New Perspectives on Charles Willson Peale*, ed. Miller and Ward, pp. 29–50. For a discussion of the theory and patronage of these two genres in eighteenth-century Britain, see Louise Lippincott, "Expanding on Portraiture: The Market, the Public, and the Hierarchy of Genres in Eighteenth-Century Britain," in *The Consumption of Culture, 1600–1800: Image, Object, Text*, ed. John Brewer and Ann Bermingham (London, 1995), pp. 75–88.

23. Benjamin West, *Self-Portrait*, 1806, exhibited 1807, Pennsylvania Academy of the Fine Arts; Matthew Pratt, *The American School*, 1765, exhibited 1766, Society of Artists of Great Britain; Charles Willson Peale, *Staircase Group*, 1795, exhibited 1795, the Columbianum or American Academy of the Fine Arts.

24. Pratt signed only this, a for-exhibition painting; on signatures, see Margaretta M. Lovell, " 'Such Furniture as Will Be Most Profitable': The Business of Cabinetmaking in Eighteenth-Century Newport," *Winterthur Portfolio* 26, no. 1 (1991): 44–48. Portrait prints that were unblushingly commercial ventures utilizing public figures were invariably signed and (as the likeness was almost certainly unknown to the purchaser) labeled.

25. Robert Fulton to Mary Smith, January 20, 1792, Semple Collection, Historical Society of Western Pennsylvania, Pittsburgh, as cited in Rebora, "Robert Fulton's Art Collection," p. 41; see also Matthew Pratt, "Autobiographical Notes," in William Sawitzky, *Matthew Pratt* (New York, 1942), p. 22. In London, as Marcia Pointon has put it, "the successful portrait painter . . . employed the Royal Academy as his chief publicity agent" (*Hanging the Head: Portraiture and Social Formation in Eighteenth-Century England* [New Haven, 1993], p. 41).

Fig. 13.12. Charles Willson Peale, *The Peale Family Group*, 1773 (with changes 1808). Oil on canvas; H. 56 1/2" (143.5 cm), W. 89 1/2" (227.3 cm). (Photo: Collection of the New-York Historical Society.)

as documents about the meaning of painted faces and painted bodies. That portrait painting was, to a degree, about conjuring, is clear; it provided an aura-bearing object that hovered on the threshold between personhood and objecthood. But to what end? I propose that the portrait primarily marked and negotiated critical relations within communities.

A fourth painting that seems intended at least in part as an essay on the art and practice of painting, especially portrait painting, is Charles Willson Peale's monumental *The Peale Family Group* of circa 1770–73 (it is over seven feet long), perhaps the most elaborate painted text of this kind (fig. 13.12). It was executed a few years after Peale's return to the colonies from West's London studio and includes the artist's brothers (St. George and James), his wife (Rachel), sister (Elizabeth), mother, and two of his children seated at a table. Peale himself, his sister Margaret Jane, and the family nurse (Peggy Durgan) stand.[26] Most obviously, "family" for Peale and his contemporaries signaled a more heterogeneous group of individuals than it usually does today; not only the nuclear group of parents and their

26. Charles C. Sellers, *Charles Willson Peale* (New York, 1969), pp. 80, 104, 122; Sellers, *Portraits and Miniatures*, pp. 157. It was apparently executed in 1773 (some evidence suggests as early as 1770) and exhibited in his painting gallery. He returned to the canvas in 1808–9, and

children but also grandparents, adult siblings, and even servants were incorporated easily within this elastic concept. Less obvious but equally familiar to Peale and foreign to us is the codified hierarchical order of family governance that clarified the relation of each of these individuals as subordinate to, deferential to, and legally dependant on a single, male head of household who was responsible for the well-being of the whole.[27] And beyond the expanded cohabiting family unit, ties of kinship—as seen in the integration of Elizabeth West's family within her husband's student and client groups—bound even larger kin networks into communities of mutual support and collective interest.

Peale's *Family Group* gathers a circle of figures before the gaze of the onlooker, whose implied presence closes the ring. It also depicts a number of artworks. An oil painting in a gilt frame is suggested in the upper right, where we also find three sculptural busts Peale modeled in England: Benjamin West, Peale himself (it is reported that he used this bust as a model in the difficult task of painting his obliquely foreshortened self-portrait here), and an important British patron.[28] Behind the painted figure of Peale, a stretched canvas on an easel bears the outlines of an allegorical work in progress, and two chalk drawings—one of foliage partially rolled in Margaret Jane's hand and one of figures on which St. George labors—complete the assemblage of media and genres, unless we also include the ephemeral artwork of the carved eponymic fruit peel in the foreground. The identification of family with art, especially its production (at least three members of the household are identified here as art makers), is reiterative and central to our reading of the image.

At the center of the canvas and at the core of the family group is Rachel, who calmly anchors the composition and returns the viewer's gaze. In their role as mothers, women in this period were pictorially privileged; while the organization of the painting around Rachel's serene countenance may be an indication of Peale's personal regard, it is also characteristic of its era.[29] Similarly, Peale's seeming reticence about his own presence (his body blocked by other figures, his face obscured by shadow) is also common in this period, while subtle markers of his patriarchal status that would have been quickly legible to his contemporaries—his hand on

---

alterations at this time include painting out a verbal legend, work on the background and on his self-portrait, and the addition of the dog and the palette with brushes.

27. Carole Shammas, "Anglo-American Government in Comparative Perspective," *William and Mary Quarterly*, 3d ser., 52, no. 1 (January 1995): 128–29, 132–34; Shammas suggests that patriarchal power did not wane or falter in the United States as a result of the Revolution.

28. Edward P. Richardson, Brooke Hindle, and Lillian B. Miller, *Charles Willson Peale and His World* (New York, 1982), p. 28.

29. See Margaretta M. Lovell, "Reading Portraits: Social Images and Self-Images in Eighteenth-Century American Family Portraits," *Winterthur Portfolio* 22, no. 4 (1987): 46–71.

Rachel's shoulder, the gold frogging and buttons on his jacket—do much to reconstitute his true status in this circle. From three vantage points— the bust on the mantelpiece, the palette-wielding instructor on the left, and the unseen recorder of the scene returning Rachel's gaze—Peale and his proxies observe, surround, and control the tableau of extended family.

The Peale Family Group is a tight, well-ordered, symmetrical universe orbiting around Rachel; five figures on her right are balanced by five figures (if we count the dog, Argus) on her left. The table and her shoulders are aligned with the picture plane. There are eight adults in the family group and eight mature fruits before her. The exact center of the canvas and the painting's vanishing point coincide in the patch of skin revealed at Rachel's throat. The metaphors here for harmony, linkage, and congruency—and their cognates, stability, order, and permanence—resonate and reverberate. And yet there are also notes of disorder, contingency, and temporality: St. George's red erasure cloth and the fruit knife, tipping precariously over the table's edge, the peach pit and its peel evidencing if not a death certainly the disappearance of a player. These metaphors and countermetaphors signal the world as this culture strove to construct itself—ordered, stable, hierarchical, symmetrical—but they also acknowledge the world as its denizens knew it to be—liable to accident, temporality, and decay.

The Peale Family Group, then, was neither constructed to be nor understood to be the record of a single event, a "real" day or site, but rather the record of that world as art can make it, a diagram of how it ought to be and, at halcyon moments, might seem to be. Most "real" are the family members—they are described volumetrically and in color. The artworks, for all their proliferation, are monochromatic, linear, "unreal" by comparison. They belong, Peale suggests, to the realm of abstraction, in a realm beside and linked to but not to be mistaken for life. Of the three artworks in process here—the landscape, the portrait, and the allegory—only two need concern us.

The first is St. George's drawing of his mother and her grandchild, an exercise and lesson in portraiture reaching across and out of the canvas. (In Charles's portrait the child gives us eye contact; in St. George's, Mother Peale does so.) The second is a group of drapery-clad, "classical" women who have been identified as the Three Graces and whose figures with linked arms and hands provide a model for the Peale family's affectionate touching. Goddesses personifying charm, grace, and beauty (physical, intellectual, artistic, and moral), these celebrants were also associated with favor and gratitude for favor, and as such, in this context, they evoke reciprocity and mutual obligation as well as benefit. When Peale returned to this canvas in 1808, his alterations included the elimination of the words "Concordia Animae" (harmony of the soul) originally painted across the Three Graces, "the design being sufficient," as he put it, "to tell the subject." That is, he felt, the relation between the abstract allegory and the concrete cluster of Peales was sufficiently clear without this verbal legend.[30]

This work has been interpreted as a record of Charles Willson Peale's personality and unfailing good-fellowship.[31] I would suggest instead that it is not so much recording a personal bonhomie as reiterating a familiar cultural message, one ensconced in law and normative social relations as well as architecture and painting: the well-ordered hierarchical family unit, bound by ties and recognized structures of mutual obligation and duty as much as affection, was the primary unit and the mirror of the well-ordered, peaceful, prosperous state. Order, not personality, created harmony, and the project of painting in the eighteenth century was not to record things as they are but to "teach us," as John Barrell puts it, "a way of *conceiving* of our relations to other people."[32] Peale's project was not to show methods of art instruction, to disclose his frustrated longings to paint allegories, or to record an especially warm moment in his family's history but to engage in memory construction, to imagine and project a more generalized prescriptive code of behavior, using his kin as exemplars.

The widely read eighteenth-century British theorist Jonathan Richardson remarked that a portrait "may be instrumental to maintain and sometime augment Friendship, and Paternal, Filial, and Conjugal Love, and Duty."[33] This instrumental social role of the mute canvas served to remind the viewer and reiterate for his or her benefit not just bonds of affection and details of physiognomy but the more critical bonds of family duty.

30. Sellers, *Portraits and Miniatures*, p. 157. Charles Willson Peale intended the canvas to be "emblematical of family concord"; see Charles C. Sellers, *Charles Willson Peale: Early Life* (Philadelphia, 1947), p. 116. Not surprisingly, Peale's concept of nature also evidenced this enthusiasm for linkage, order, and harmony: species were linked by "the same chain . . . manifesting the most perfect *order* in the works of a great *Creator*—who's [*sic*] ways are wisdom, her paths are peace, harmony and Love"; animals similarly provided "models of friendship, constancy, parental care, and every other social virtue" (quoted in Richardson, Hindle, and Miller, *Charles Willson Peale and His World*, p. 196). While mythological figures are relatively rare in American art of this period, Henry Benbridge's tableau of *The Three Graces* survives from the West circle (Winterthur Museum).

31. Wayne Craven, *Colonial American Portraiture: The Economic, Religious, Social, Cultural, Philosophical, Scientific, and Aesthetic Foundations* (New York, 1986), p. 386; for another perspective on Peale's familial personality, see Phoebe Lloyd, "Philadelphia Story," *Art in America* 76 (November 1988): 154–203.

32. John Barrell, "Sir Joshua Reynolds and the Political Theory of Painting," *Oxford Art Journal* 9, no. 2 (1986): 38, and Barrell, *The Political Theory of Painting from Reynolds to Hazlitt: The Body of the Public* (New Haven, 1986). See also Dell Upton, *Holy Things and Profane: Anglican Parish Churches in Colonial Virginia* (New York, 1986), pp. 199–232.

33. Jonathan Richardson, *An Essay on the Theory of Painting* (London, 1725; rpt., Menston, England, 1971), p. 13.

Mutual obligation, then, and the codified harmony it constructed at the bedrock of social order, is at the heart of the portraiture project.

Portraits were, in the eighteenth century, family matters. Often commissioned in pairs, in which husband and wife complement or mirror each other in pose, scale, and format, they were frequently commissioned at the time of and to mark transitions in status, especially the birth of an heir, the attainment of majority, or, most often, marriage. Death, on the other hand, was marked among families of substance not by a rectangular canvas commissioned to hang within the orthogonal envelope of the family's daily experience but by a lozenge-shaped canvas hatchment posed outside, above the front door (fig. 13.13). Dramatically askew to the architectural order of the structure's spatial volumes and forms, these very different products of the same colonial painters' efforts summarized in two dimensions, in the abstract language of heraldry, the concrete daily-enacted familial relations that had been terminated by death. No further marriages, achievements, or progeny could alter the human (and hence economic) relations so diagrammed. Hatchments (a corruption of

Fig. 13.13. Christian Remick (1726–after 1783), detail of *A Perspective View of Part of the [Boston] Commons,* 1768. Watercolor; H. 19 1/2" (49.5 cm). W. 28 1/2" (72.4 cm). (Photo: Courtesy of the Concord Museum, Concord, Mass.) The painting is dedicated to John Hancock, whose house, seen here, bears a hatchment over the front door.

"achievements") expressed, in armorial code, the key aspects of the deceased person's lineage, honors, and relations to closest family—whether spinster or bachelor, wife, husband, second wife, and so on—and in doing so clarified not only the familial state of the deceased but also the resulting status of survivors. In a society in which rights and expectations were based on familial state as well as age, gender, and wealth, such clarification before the community was not superfluous display, and such clarification within the community and economy of the family unit was equally important. It is apparent that while the issue of lineage was frequently (but not always) moot in America, the issues of inheritance, familial state, power, and honor were not and therefore this English tradition survived the Atlantic crossing.[34] Although they performed different functions, portraits and hatchments were related forms; the former was a private, simulated likeness of life, whereas the latter gave, in two-dimensional public code, personal and familial résumés in death. In those canvases marking shifted relations among the living, paired, balanced, and reciprocally inflected images of husband and wife predominate. Characteristic is the pair consisting of the portrait of Benjamin West's sister-in-law considered earlier and that of her husband, Robert Shewell, painted by either Benbridge or Pratt (figs. 13.10 and 13.11).

Today the practice of portraiture is often associated with the basest aspects of human nature—vanity, pride, an appetite for self-aggrandizement, narcissism, and attempts to claim undue status; the purported vices differ for males and females, but the specter of overweening self-love is constant. Little evidence argues that this is how painted portraits were understood in the eighteenth century. Others have proposed that eighteenth-century portraiture was about self-fashioning among competitive elites, specifically older, established merchant elites locating ways to evade the challenges of their nouveaux riches rivals. David Solkin, for instance, speaking about English (male) portraiture, sees the portrait project as primarily about style, the battlefield on which class emulation, the retreat of the elite, and visual quotation duke it out for political and social capital.[35] While I would agree that eighteenth-century Anglo-American portraits were centrally about money, I do not see them, at least among

34. Julian Franklyn, *Shield and Crest: An Account of the Art and Science of Heraldry* (London, 1960), pp. 294–98; C. W. Scott-Giles, *Boutell's Heraldry* (London, 1958), pp. 146–49; Jonathan L. Fairbanks, "Portrait Painting in Seventeenth-Century Boston: Its History, Methods, and Materials," in *New England Begins: The Seventeenth Century,* ed. Jonathan L. Fairbanks and Robert F. Trent, 3 vols. (Boston, 1982), 3:413; and Abbott Lowell Cummings, "Decorative Painting in Early New England," in *American Painting to 1776: A Reappraisal,* ed. Ian M. G. Quimby (Charlottesville, 1971), pp. 91–101.

35. David H. Solkin, "Great Pictures or Great Men? Reynolds, Male Portraiture, and the Power of Art," *Oxford Art Journal* 9, no. 2 (1986): 42–49; see also Timothy H. Breen, "The

Americans, as fundamentally structuring competitive relationships among anxious patriarchs.

Only people with discretionary money bought portraits in the colonial and early national period. But portraits were a curious sort of purchase, one that resulted in a temporary congruence between an owner and his property. And, unlike other items of expense and display such as clothing or silver teaware which retained commodity value after purchase, portraits cost substantial amounts but had no residual market value.[36] The burgeoning market for portraits during this period reflects the straightforward fact that more people had wealth, by which I mean inheritable substance beyond that required to sustain a household. But the relation between portraits and money is not a simple matter of the rich finding yet another commodity to buy. Consider, for instance, Copley's monumental *Pepperrell Family* and West's *Arthur Middleton Family*. These are canvases on which more than money was expended and in which more than competitive bravura was invested (figs. 13.14 and 13.15). Both mark, more than any other quality, the hoped-for eventual transition of substance to an heir pictured at the dead center of both the images and the families.

As important to the portrait project as wealth was the genetic path along which it moved. The key anxiety was not which elite had the most cash or which power structures were in the ascendancy. The anxiety at the base of the patriarchal system among the wealthy was that its weakest link coincided with its greatest benefit. Around the sexual behavior of women the culture erected complex legal, ideological, and aesthetic codes, dictating and confirming through her person the orderly transfer of wealth and power to rightful heirs.[37] Patriarchal authority expressed in legal codes, in social behavior, in architecture, and in the arrangement and form of furnishings was also encoded in portraits, where it assisted in the clarification and essentialization of potentially ambiguous, potentially contested relations that if disordered might lead to chaos, animosity, discontinuity, and aggression—those qualities so rigorously edited out of and controlled by these paintings. With exaggeration but precision, essayist William Hazlitt critiqued the intentions of these portrait patrons:

Meaning of 'Likeness': American Portrait Painting in an Eighteenth-Century Consumer Society," *Word and Image* 6, no. 4 (1990): 325–50.

36. As an index of their lack of residual value for the artist, note such poignant evidence as the inventory of Sir Joshua Reynolds's closet, "where there were a great number of portraits which had been rejected and were left upon his hands," cited in Pointon, *Hanging the Head*, p. 50 n. 123.

37. For an insightful discussion of portraiture and legitimacy, of "family pieces" and generational continuity, see ibid., pp. 61, 158–75; for a discussion concerning the tangential subject of naming in relation to progeny-substitutes in the eighteenth century, see the provocative essay by Gauri Viswanathan, "The Naming of Yale College: British Imperialism and American Higher Education," in *Cultures of United States Imperialism*, ed. Amy Kaplan and Donald E. Pease (Durham, N.C., 1993), pp. 85–108.

Fig. 13.14. John Singleton Copley (1738–1815), *Sir William Pepperrell and His Family*, 1778. Oil on canvas; H. 90" (228.6 cm), W. 108" (274.3). (Photo: North Carolina Museum of Art, Raleigh, Purchased with funds from the State of North Carolina.)

"They wish to be represented as complete abstractions of persons and property."[38] The double helix of persons and property, twining with prescribed harmony, is mapped in fixed form on these portraits. Small countermetaphors of disruption and contingency are permitted in these canvases alluding to the accidents of nature, but the realm of ordered human relations which these images labor to maintain is seamless. The first job of the portrait was to depict a unique, almost magical likeness so as to bring

38. William Hazlitt, *The Complete Works of William Hazlitt*, ed. P. P. Howe, 32 vols. (London, 1933), 18:108–9, as cited in Nadia Tscherny, "Likeness in Early Romantic Portraiture," *Art Journal* 96 (Fall 1987): 193–99; see also Margaretta M. Lovell, "Painters and Their Customers: Aspects of Art and Money in Eighteenth-Century America," in *Of Consuming Interest: The Style of Life in the Eighteenth Century*, ed. Ron Hoffman and Cary Carson (Charlottesville, 1994), pp. 284–306.

the sitter into the presence of the viewer. The second task was to situate the individual within recognizable, easily legible and replicable codes of dress, address, and social order.

The commissioning and hanging of these works in the domestic setting resulted in a situation in which the patron owned his own replica, anticipating that it would in time be owned, along with the substance it "represented," by his true (biological) replicas, his descendants. While the future was unpredictable to a degree, if family members dutifully maintained the order prescribed by and encoded in these works, the correct, harmonious outcome would, as much as possible, be ensured.

The primary audience for eighteenth- and early-nineteenth-century portraits was not ourselves, unknown strangers wandering in museums hundreds of years after the fact. Nor was it the patrons' neighbors. The primary audience was the domestic circle of the participants themselves, those familiar with the players, their likenesses, their foibles, their inevitably changing, aging selves, and the architectural markers (symmetry, hierarchy, and harmonious variation) that reiterated the portraits'

Fig. 13.15. Benjamin West, *Arthur Middleton, His Wife Mary (née Izard), and Their Son Henry,* 1770–71. Oil on canvas; H. 44 3/4" (113.7 cm), W. 66" (167.6 cm). (Photo: Dr. Henry Middleton Drinker; portrait on display at the Middleton Place National Historic Landmark, Charleston, S.C.)

design. The paintings remained present as mute, changeless witnesses and reminders not of a specific moment in a family's history—indeed, the Pepperrell family pictured here had already lost to death the mother who forms its columnar core when this portrait group celebrating the arrival of the heir was painted—but of a proposed way of being, a way of understanding themselves as a family bound by invisible lines of mutual obligation if not by more affectionate ties. These paintings represent a manufactured memory but not a falsified record.

In American hands, perhaps because the practice of painting in the colonies was so singularly a matter of painting heads and families, the lower genre of portraiture began to invade the higher calling of history painting. In British theory and practice, these were exclusionary practices; the first set out private individual instances and familial relations, while the second told tales critical to public memory. But beginning in the 1760s, West, Copley, and that pupil of both, John Trumbull, all injected portraits into history painting and succeeded by this innovation in catching the attention, and sometimes the acclaim, of those more firmly schooled in genre distinctions.[39] Why they made this move rather than reiterate the protocols of those presumed to be more knowing is unknown, but it is reasonable to believe that they did so as a result of early schooling in that strong tradition of capturing faces—to the exclusion of all other genres—that flourished in the colonies.

Despite their subsequent training in Italy and London, these Americans retained an enthusiasm for the authenticity of a particular, recognizable face, for the pleasure of the artist's wondrous capacity to double that which was unique, to freeze the clock for distinct individuals destined to change and die. In these eccentric self-portraits we can glimpse this group

39. While the portrait-based history paintings of Copley, West, and Trumbull are easily recognized, vernacular versions are less well known. Notable in this context is an account of an effort by Matthew Pratt in this line recorded by his son: "I think about 1785 the Fine arts, were very poorly encouraged in Philad[elphi]a and during which time, my Father, having little to do in that Line, was prevailed upon, by a number of his particular friends, to paint some signs, and he consented thereto. The first which he painted, was a very large one called 'The representation of the Constitution of 1788,' which contained excellent portraits of the Gentlemen, composing that convention. And which was hung up, at the South west corner of Chestnut & Fourth Sts where the Philadelphia Bank, was afterwards erected. Which attracted very great attention. Persons pointing out particular likenesses, such, as Washington, and others. At the bottom of which, the following lines were written by my Father. 'Those 38 great men have signed a powerful Deed / That better times to us, should very soon succeed,' " as quoted in Sawitzky, *Matthew Pratt*, p. 23. The subgenre of public portraits of worthies intended for specific sites of display to encourage emulation and regard—which I do not discuss here—grew considerably in importance on both sides of the Atlantic at this time. The project in this case, of course, was to familiarize, heroicize, and individualize notables who were personal strangers to their audience; see Pointon, *Hanging the Head*, pp. 52–104.

of artists theorizing their face-painting practice, consciously playing with and commenting on their extraordinary toolbox of illusion and visual deceit. In such paintings as West's *Self-Portrait* (with Elizabeth) and Peale's with his daughter (and Rachel) or with his assembled family, the artist wonders out loud, as it were, at what he can do. He not only casts himself as the recorder of specific truths, the ingenious creator of recognizable images that will outlive death, but even positions himself as Pygmalion, infusing his creation with life and endowing the beloved artwork with existence. These works also suggest a kind of self-consciousness, visual wit, and irony that seems very comfortable with our postmodern habits of mind. And the commissioned portraits in which they exercised these skills of duplicating the immediacy of present persons are still, in a sense, convincing. Indeed, one of the key problems in approaching eighteenth- and early-nineteenth-century painting today is that we resist making it strange, distant, the borrowed property of a culture other than our own.

In portraits by the extraordinary group of Americans who passed influential years in Benjamin West's studio, we see faces, poses, and gestures—in short, persons—who appear to be immediately accessible and straightforward. We are taken in by their apparently frank gazes, by the artists' seeming fidelity to visual facts, by our own presumption of cultural continuity. But the portrait project is as Chester Harding suggested, a kind of wondrous deception. Portraiture deals in visual facts, but to its own ends; it is a kind of truth-telling, but one that moves by indirection in its honesty. The truth it tells is a certain set of prescribed cultural truths to which we might not otherwise have access, as well as a localized physiognomic truth. Its business is, these images tell us, to displace the aura of individual beings onto an inert object with an eye to the construction of the immediate future's long-term memory. In this group of eccentric self-portraits we glimpse the awareness among these artists of their power to raise the dead, fool the living, and describe a truth that is simultaneously recognizable and invented.

A Criminal Is Being Beaten:
The Politics of Punishment and
the History of the Body

MICHAEL MERANZE

> The ego is first and foremost a bodily ego; it is not merely
> a surface entity, but is itself the projection of a surface.
>
> —SIGMUND FREUD, *The Ego and the Id*

ON THE morning of June 27, 1833, Mathias Maccumsey, an inmate at the Eastern State Penitentiary in Philadelphia, met his fate. Samuel Wood, the penitentiary's warden, ordered that Maccumsey have the "iron gag" placed on him.[1] The gag, an "iron instrument resembling the stiff bit of a blind bridle, having an iron palet in the centre, about an inch square, and chains at each end to pass round the neck and fasten behind," was in this instance "placed in the prisoners mouth, the iron palet over his tongue, the bit forced in as far as possible, the chains brought round the jaws to the back of the neck; the end of one chain was passed through the ring in the end of the other chain to 'the fourth link,' and fastened with a lock." Maccumsey's "hands were then forced into

Portions of this essay have appeared in Michael Meranze, *Laboratories of Virtue: Punishment, Revolution, and Authority in Philadelphia, 1760–1835* (Chapel Hill, 1996). An earlier version was presented to the Research Seminar of the Department of History at the University of California, San Diego. I thank Nancy Bentley, Michael A. Bernstein, Helen E. Deutsch, Steven Hahn, Rachel N. Klein, Stephanie McCurry, Robert Blair St. George, Kathryn Wilson, and the readers for Cornell University Press for their comments.

1. See "Warden's Daily Journal," June 27, 1833, and June 28, 1833, Eastern State Penitentiary, Record Group 15, Pennsylvania Museum and Historical Commission, Harrisburg.

THE IRON GAG.

Fig. 14.1. The Iron Gag. From Thomas B. McElwee, *A Concise History of the Eastern State Penitentiary* (Philadelphia, 1835), facing p. 17. (Photo: The Library Company of Philadelphia.)

leather gloves in which were iron staples and crossed behind his back; leather straps were passed through the staples, and from thence round the chains of the gag between the neck and the chains; the straps were drawn tight, the hands forced up towards the head" (fig. 14.1).[2] This was not the first time that Maccumsey had been subject to the gag. But this time it proved fatal. Shortly after it had been secured, he suffered seizures and collapsed. All efforts to revive him proved futile, and within the hour he was dead.[3] The prison physician, Franklin Bache, reported that Maccum-

2. Thomas B. McElwee, *A Concise History of the Eastern State Penitentiary. Together with A Detailed Statement Of The Proceedings Of The Committee, Appointed By The Legislature, December 6th, 1834. For The Purpose Of Examining Into The Economy And Management Of That Institution* (Philadelphia, 1835), pt. 1, p. 18.

3. For information on the incident, see "Warden's Daily Journal," June 27, 1833; testimony of Silas Steel, Leonard Phleger, William Griffith, and Charles S. Coxe, in McElwee, *Concise History of the Eastern State Penitentiary*, pt. 1, pp. 158–59, 149–50, 177–78, and 186–87, respectively.

sey had died of apoplexy.[4] At the time of his death, Maccumsey was forty-four years old and serving the second year of a twelve-year sentence for murder.[5]

Maccumsey was neither the first nor the last individual to die in the Eastern State Penitentiary. But his death poses, in particularly stark form, the contradictions of enlightened penal reform.[6] The modern system of penal incarceration emerged over and against older forms of corporal and capital sanctions—especially the pillory, the rope, and the whip, "those cruel and vindictive penalties which are in use in the European countries," as Roberts Vaux put it.[7] The opening of the Eastern State Penitentiary in 1829 culminated fifty years of penal experimentation (fig. 14.2). The new penitentiary, its proponents insisted, would replace cruelty with compassion, suffering with solitary reflection, and render ferocity unnecessary. The architectural imposition of solitary confinement would enable authority to remake character and modify the spirit (fig. 14.3).

This new carceral system, as Michel Foucault demonstrated in his still unparalleled *Discipline and Punish*, produced a "real, non-corporal" soul. This soul, Foucault insisted, was not "an illusion, or an ideological effect. On the contrary, it exists, it has a reality, it is produced permanently around, on, within the body by the functioning of a power that is exercised on those punished." In Foucault's telling, the "soul" became the hinge on which the modern penal system turned. The modern penal soul, Foucault wrote, "unlike the soul represented by Christian theology, is not born in sin and subject to punishment, but is born rather out of methods of punishment, supervision, and constraint." The entry of the soul enabled punishment to do more than punish bodies. No longer aimed at the degradation of the body, penitentiary punishments would lift up the inmates' souls, preparing them for their return to society remade. The penitentiary would spiritualize punishment.[8]

4. *Fifth Annual Report of the Inspectors of the Eastern Penitentiary of Pennsylvania, Accompanied with the Table of Prisoners in the Western Penitentiary, Read in Senate February 12, 1834* (Harrisburg, 1834), p. 9.

5. Information on Maccumsey's biography and sentencing is drawn from the *Fourth Annual Report of the Inspectors of the Eastern State Penitentiary* (Philadelphia, 1833), p. 17.

6. For discussions of penal reform in the early national United States, see David J. Rothman, *The Discovery of the Asylum: Social Order and Disorder in the New Republic* (Boston, 1971); Thomas L. Dumm, *Democracy and Punishment: Disciplinary Origins of the United States* (Madison, Wisc., 1987); Louis P. Masur, *Rites of Execution: Capital Punishment and the Transformation of American Culture, 1776–1865* (New York, 1989); Adam J. Hirsch, *The Rise of the Penitentiary: Prisons and Punishment in Early America* (New Haven, 1992); and Michael Meranze, *Laboratories of Virtue: Punishment, Revolution, and Authority in Philadelphia, 1760–1835* (Chapel Hill, 1996).

7. Vaux quoted in [George Washington Smith], *Description of the Eastern Penitentiary of Pennsylvania* (Philadelphia, 1829), p. 7.

8. Michel Foucault, *Discipline and Punish: The Birth of the Prison*, trans. Alan Sheridan (New York, 1977), p. 29.

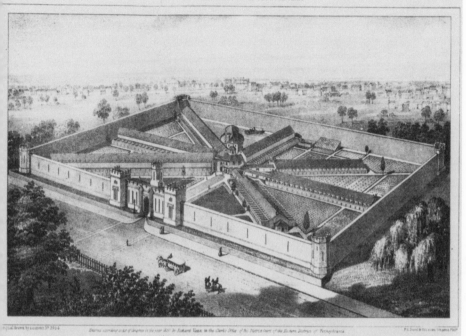

THE STATE PENITENTIARY,
FOR THE EASTERN DISTRICT OF PENNSYLVANIA

Fig. 14.2. The State Penitentiary, for the Eastern District of Pennsylvania (the "Cherry Hill State Prison"). Drawing by convict no. 2954, printed by P. S. Duval, 1855; H. 6 1/2" (16.5 cm), W. 10: (25.4 cm). (Photo: The Library Company of Philadelphia.)

Yet less than five years after the penitentiary opened, Maccumsey died at the hands of prison officials, and his death revealed a penal world of violence. The gag was only the most extreme measure that prison officials imposed on noisy or refractory inmates. Punishments in the penitentiary ranged from depriving inmates of their time in exercise yards to increasingly severe reductions of food, confinement in a "dark cell" or dungeon, and restraint in a straitjacket or the gag.[9] Each penalty aimed to accomplish what solitude could not: to compel prisoners to submit without question to the regulations of the institution. If the Eastern State Penitentiary had

9. McElwee, *Concise History of the Eastern State Penitentiary*, pt. 1, pp. 16–18.

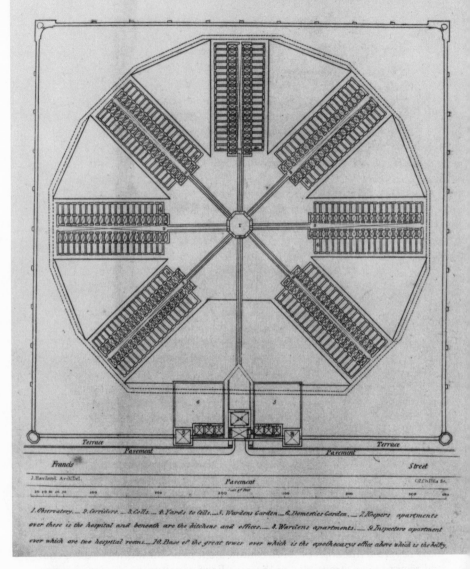

Fig. 14.3. *Plan of the Eastern Penitentiary*. Engraving, ca. 1830, after original drawing by John Haviland; H. 8 1/16" (20.5 cm), W. 5 1/8" (13.1 cm). From George W. Smith, *A View and Description of the Eastern Penitentiary of Pennsylvania* (Philadelphia: C. G. Childs, 1830). (Photo: The Library Company of Philadelphia.)

been designed to make corporal and capital punishments superfluous, physical violence had reemerged at the heart of its disciplinary practices.[10]

Why was this so? How did Pennsylvania legislators, prison officials, and penal reformers deploy physical sanctions against the bodies of prisoners and maintain their belief that punishment had been spiritualized? The answer, I contend, is that the elaboration and intensification of penitential restraint took place in a world dominated by slavery and monarchy. Proponents of penitential punishments were preoccupied with the scaffold and whipping post because each condensed the social characteristics of monarchy's excess and slavery's debasement. The hanged and whipped body, or so the proponents of penitential punishments argued, marked a society as inhumane; the insensibility of the beaten convict signified the lack of sensibility of the social form itself. "Humanity" and "sensibility," those two key words of late-eighteenth- and early-nineteenth-century reform, demanded an end to the use of the rope and the lash.[11]

The scaffold and the whipping post helped delegitimate monarchy and slavery. And the imaginative fusion of these punishments with these social forms meant that as rope and whip were cast aside other forms of punishment—forms that were corporal in a different way—could emerge and avoid the charge of cruelty. If whipping and hanging signified brutality, the defenders and organizers of the Eastern State Penitentiary believed, then other forms of corporal discipline were not necessarily violent or barbaric.

I.

Several different concerns intersected in the shift from public punishment to solitary penitence. Most important, in the late eighteenth century at least, was anxiety about the nature of public communication and personal virtue. Late-eighteenth-century critics condemned public punishments for their uncontrollable and contradictory meanings and argued that public penalties disseminated violence and criminality throughout society. Pointing to the frequent cases of crimes committed at the foot of the scaffold, the *Pennsylvania Evening Herald* insisted that "the place of execution in London . . . is perhaps a scene of as much villainy, picking

10. In fact, Maccumsey himself had been subject to physical violence—a beating—at the hands of Wood on a previous occasion. On this, see testimony of William Griffith in ibid., p. 177.

11. The movement to eliminate whipping within the penal system was only one moment of a wider campaign to abolish corporal punishments in the northern United States during the antebellum period. For an analysis of this larger context, see Myra C. Glenn, *Campaigns against Corporal Punishment: Prisoners, Sailors, Women, and Children in Antebellum America* (Albany, N.Y., 1984). For an analysis of the importance of "sensibility" to bourgeois Anglo-American culture and society, see G. J. Barker-Benfield, *The Culture of Sensibility: Sex and Society in Eighteenth-Century Britain* (Chicago, 1993).

pockets, etc. as the city affords."[12] Indeed, "A Citizen of the World" argued, London's capital punishments effectively brought authority itself into disrepute, allowing a reversal in which the condemned were transformed into heroes.[13] Public punishments addressed to the body and designed to resuture the community and teach submission to the law did neither.

These concerns were real enough. The years of the American Revolution made manifest the instabilities of public punishments. Crowds resisting imperial authority drew on the repertoire of public punishments as they carted, tarred and feathered, and hanged in effigy supporters of British policy. In contrast, say, to the thespians at the Boston Tea Party, Philadelphia's lower sorts—not its upper-class resistance leaders—organized these crowds.[14] But the divisiveness of public punishments was not limited to popular appropriation of the ritualized forms of legal penalties. Pennsylvania executed more people during the Revolutionary era than at any other time in its history. Some of these executions merely indicated a general disruption of authority accompanying the struggle for independence. But many were clearly connected to political conflicts. And whereas a rough consensus on the defense of property and persons surrounded the more conventional exercise of public punishments, this consensus did not extend to executions for political purposes.[15]

Pennsylvanians, then, did not have to look far afield to demonstrate the contradictory quality of public, corporal, and capital penalties. Yet that is just what they did. Throughout the 1780s and 1790s, Pennsylvania's penal reformers engaged in an ongoing ideological labor to undermine these punishments by casting them as foreign, monarchical practices.[16] The les-

12. *Pennsylvania Evening Herald*, July 16, 1785, n.p. Unless otherwise noted, all the newspapers cited in this essay were published in Philadelphia.

13. "The populace depart, either applauding the criminal's hardness, or as they term it, his spirit, in dying 'like a cock'—or else condemning his weakness—'He died like a d—d chicken hearted dog.' " See "A Citizen of the World," *Pennsylvania Mercury*, November 27, 1788, n.p.

14. For example, see the tarring and feathering reported in John Hughes to Customs Commissioners, October 13, 1769, in "Custom House Papers," vol. 10 (May 1769–November 1770), Historical Society of Pennsylvania, Philadelphia. On this issue more generally, see Steven Rosswurm, *Arms, Country, and Class: The Philadelphia Militia and the "Lower Sort" during the American Revolution* (New Brunswick, N.J., 1987), pp. 32–34, 46–48.

15. This lack of consensus can be seen, for example, in the controversy and agitation surrounding the executions of Quakers Abraham Carlisle and John Roberts in 1778. See Samuel Hazard et al., eds., *Pennsylvania Archives* (Harrisburg, 1874–1935), 1st. ser., 7:21–58, Harrisburg, Pa.; Masur, *Rites of Execution*, pp. 75–76.

16. The *Pennsylvania Evening Herald*, for instance, insisted that "in some countries the legislators, like Draco of old, seem to make a sport of human life, and declare it forfeit on the most trivial occasions" (April 30, 1785, n.p.). William Bradford Jr. argued that capital punishments were a violation of Pennsylvania's spirit, their presence a result of their imposition by a rapacious British Crown; see William Bradford Jr., *An Enquiry How Far The Punishment of Death Is Necessary In Pennsylvania. With Notes and Illustrations, To Which Is Added, an Account*

son was clear: the new republican order should eliminate these ritualized and violent seizures of the body. After all, as an "Essay on Capital Punishment" noted, those countries "most remarkable for severe punishments" were not those "distinguished by a regard to their laws."[17]

Yet this effort to condemn and distance spectacular penal embodiment was not the entire story. Throughout the 1780s (and beyond) these condemnations of the rituals of corporal and capital sanctions coexisted in the public papers with descriptions of these horrific punishments. These were, in the late eighteenth century at least, descriptions not of public penalties in Philadelphia but of these punishments elsewhere. It was almost as if, while condemning bodily sanctions as foreign monarchical remnants, Philadelphians could not take their eyes off of them. Somehow these rituals, when mediated through print, could be turned to the advantage of humanity. In the public view but extruded from the public presence, the punishments would serve to mark the difference between Pennsylvania and, for example, England, and to maintain the pleasure produced by that difference.[18]

The dynamic of this satisfied distance can be seen most clearly in Benjamin Rush. A consistent and principled opponent of all forms of capital punishment, Rush also offered the most complex critique of public punishments articulated in late-eighteenth-century Philadelphia.[19] Rush argued that public punishments inevitably degraded those subject to them, replaced respect for the law with admiration or sympathy for the condemned, and inured the crowd to the evils of criminality and violence while violating both reason and Revelation. But Rush's critique of public penalties—his efforts to tie them to older forms of ignorance and policy— opened up a space for new forms of bodily sanction and for the relish of

---

of the Goal and Penitentiary House of Philadelphia, and of the Interior Management Thereof by Caleb Lownes, of Philadelphia (Philadelphia, 1793).

17. "Essay on Capital Punishment," *Freeman's Journal*, September 7, 1785, n.p.; see also *Pennsylvania Evening Herald*, April 30, 1785, n.p.

18. This tendency contained the additional disavowal of the fact that in England as well, the 1780s marked a crucial turning point in the history of public punishments. Most noticeable in this regard was the ending of the procession to Tyburn and the removal of the scaffold to Newgate Prison in 1783. On the punitive crisis of the 1780s and its implications, see John Beattie, *Crime and the Courts in England, 1660–1800* (Princeton, N.J., 1986), pp. 629–32; Peter Linebaugh, *The London Hanged: Crime and Civil Society in the Eighteenth Century* (New York, 1992), pp. 333–70; and Douglas Hay, "The Laws of God and the Laws of Man: Lord George Gordon and the Death Penalty," in *Protest and Survival: Essays for E. P. Thompson*, ed. John Rule and Robert Malcomson (New York, 1993), pp. 60–111.

19. See Benjamin Rush, "An Enquiry into the Effects of Public Punishments Upon Criminals, and Upon Society, Read in the Society for Promoting Political Enquiries, Convened at the House of Benjamin Franklin, Esq. in Philadelphia, March 9th, 1787," and "An Enquiry Into the Consistency of Murder by Death, with Reason and Revelation," both in Benjamin Rush, *Essays: Literary, Moral, and Philosophical*, ed. Michael Meranze (Schenectady, N.Y., 1988), pp. 79–105.

imagined punishments. In his proposed "house of repentance," Rush suggested a gradation of punishments consisting of "bodily pain, labour, watchfulness, solitude, and silence."[20] Rather than the ferocious and vicious pain of the public punishment, pain that led to misplaced sympathy on the part of the crowd, now pain rooted in knowledge would work in the service of reformation.

The knowledge of pain would operate for reformation on two levels. If subjection to pain could help lead to repentance, then knowledge of that subjection could spare people the necessity of repentance in the first place. "Children," Rush insisted, "will press upon the evening fire in listening to the tales that will be spread from this abode of misery. Superstition will add to its horrors: and romance will find in it ample materials for fiction, which cannot fail of encreasing the terror of its punishments."[21] Mobilizing the very fascination with suffering that distanced the display of degradation and opened the space for new styles of penal embodiment, Rush casts out the public punishment. But bodily sanction and the knowledge of that sanction remained. And both the casting out and the remains produced the satisfaction of enlightened distance.

This new penal distance presupposed the contradictory qualities of sympathy. As a central component of the emerging culture of sensibility, sympathy lay at the heart of the problematic nature of society itself. Most famously presented in Adam Smith's *The Theory of Moral Sentiments* but articulated widely on both sides of the Atlantic, sympathy connoted an intrinsic capacity to imagine the experience of others.[22] As such it made social intercourse viable. But this imaginary identification also marked the individual as always at risk. For it was possible for the self to become overwhelmed by sympathetic impressions, to lose itself—most often a development figured as female—or, and this is crucial in this context, to identify and sympathize with vicious or extreme experience. Sympathy,

20. Rush, "An Enquiry into the Effects of Public Punishments," p. 89.
21. Ibid., p. 88. This distanced aesthetic of punishment was also gaining support in late-eighteenth-century England, where it was rooted in part on theories of the terror produced through aesthetic mystery and the sublime. See John Bender, *Imagining the Penitentiary: Fiction and the Architecture of Mind in Eighteenth-Century England* (Chicago, 1987), pp. 231–52; Steven Wilf, "Imagining Justice: Aesthetics and Public Executions in Late-Eighteenth-Century England," *Yale Journal of Law and the Humanities* 5 (1993): 51–78; and V. A. C. Gatrell, *The Hanging Tree: Executions and the English People, 1770–1868* (New York, 1994), pp. 259–66.
22. Adam Smith, *The Theory of Moral Sentiments*, intro. E. G. West (1759; rpt., Indianapolis, 1969), pp. 1–6. For discussions of sympathy in Smith which link it to the contradictory and sometimes traumatic effects of theatricality, see Jean-Christophe Agnew, *Worlds Apart: The Market and the Theater in Anglo-American Thought, 1550–1750* (New York, 1986), pp. 177–88; Bender, *Imagining the Penitentiary*, pp. 218–28; and David Marshall, *The Figure of Theater: Shaftesbury, Defoe, Adam Smith, and George Eliot* (New York, 1986), pp. 167–92.

the root of the individual's capacity for friendly sociability, could also destroy the self.[23]

This two-edged quality of sympathy helped to justify the separation and confinement of criminals. The critique of the scaffold scene focused on false identification—with the criminal, with crime, or with violence. In a direct way, reformers expected the walls of the prison to break this process of identification. But Rush's fantasy of children eagerly listening to tales of the penal crypt indicates that neither sympathetic identification nor the pleasure that accompanied it were to be banished from the penal scene. As Smith suggested, sympathizing with the suffering Other produced its own fascination and pleasure. It was someone else's pain after all—sympathy was an imaginary identification, not a real substitution—and the fact that it was not you, that you were safely at a distance, meant that sympathy contained its own hedonistic rewards.[24] Eliminating the visibility of the public punishment protected against the overwhelming nature of observed sensations. But it also opened the possibility of other, more internalized enjoyment.

In this sense, the late-eighteenth-century doctrine of sympathy anticipated the Freudian dynamic of enjoyment and prohibition. Sympathy, after all, recognized both the identifications that demanded prohibition and the pleasures of prohibition itself. But the connections between psychoanalytic theory and penal history are even more intriguing. In the fantasy he titled " 'A Child Is Being Beaten'," Freud argued that some of his patients sought to escape the burdens of their own desires through a series of fantasmatic images. The first fantasy, in which the patient imagined watching a single child being beaten by her or his father, Freud interpreted as signifying a desire on the part of a child for its sibling to be beaten (thereby indicating that paternal love remained with the fantasizer). This first moment, however, produced unbearable guilt. The second phase, which Freud cautioned almost invariably remained unconscious prior to analytic treatment, was a fantasy of the child being beaten by her father (for Freud drew his cases from his female patients). Freud

23. For a powerful discussion of the contradictory effects of sympathy for psyche and society, see John Mullan, *Sentiment and Sociability: The Language of Feeling in the Eighteenth Century* (Oxford, 1988). On the gendered aspects of sympathy, see Michel Foucault, *Madness and Civilization: A History of Insanity in the Age of Reason*, trans. Richard Howard (New York, 1965), pp. 143–58, and Helen Deutsch, "Symptomatic Correspondences: The Case of the Author in Eighteenth-Century Britain," *Cultural Critique* 42 (Fall 1999), 40–103. On the figuration of loss in commerce as feminine, see Toby Ditz's essay in this volume.

24. Adam Smith, *Theory of Moral Sentiments*, discusses the dynamics of sympathetic identification throughout, but see in particular his discussion of "a malice in mankind" that takes pleasure in the small sufferings of others (p. 91), and the entire section that follows on the greater sensibility that accompanies sympathy with sorrow than with joy (pp. 93–108).

insisted that this stage had a double meaning, in which the patient simultaneously punished herself for her erotic desires for her father and achieved a regressive substitute for paternal love (the beating symbolizing an incestuous sexual relationship). This masochistic moment, in turn, produced even greater guilt and led finally to the third phase of the fantasy, where the child imagined an indefinite group of children (usually boys) being beaten by either an undetermined figure or an institutional authority (for example, a teacher). Just as important, whereas in the first two fantasies the fantasizer had been present within the scene, either as witness or victim, now she was absent. Here, Freud insists, the seeming depersonalization of the beating scene is itself another layer of fantasy, one that allows the patient to achieve erotic satisfaction without acknowledging that she is doing so.[25] The distancing of the scene allows identification to move from an "immediate" spectatorial connection to a more disembodied, imaginary one.[26]

Freud's patients therefore recapitulated in fantasy what late-eighteenth-century reform enacted in practice. The logic of eighteenth-century reform presupposed that public punishments failed because crowds either derived vicious pleasure from the pain imposed on criminals or inverted the ritual by identifying with those subject to punishment. In its stead Rush, and those allied with him, proposed not only ending the personalized nature of punishment but also institutionalizing a distanced relationship between the citizenry and the penal scene. And, as I have suggested above, a new sort of pleasure was produced in the fantasmatic reflection on that newly enclosed site of punishment.

Freud thereby met in his patients' psyches what had previously been enacted on the level of the law in the history of criminal punishment. In making this argument, I do not wish to suggest—perhaps in line with Freud's dictum that masochistic practices are "only a kind of make-

25. Sigmund Freud, " 'A Child Is Being Beaten': A Contribution to the Origin of Sexual Perversions," in Freud, *Collected Papers*, vol. 2, ed. Ernest Jones, trans. under the supervision of Joan Riviere (1924; rpt., London, 1948), pp. 172–201.

26. According to Freud, the male patients in whom he encountered a beating fantasy followed a very different and more truncated trajectory. Men, he reported, typically went through two phases, one in which they were being beaten by their fathers and a second in which they were being beaten by their mothers. Freud interprets this series as indicating a primary homosexual attachment to the father that is then inverted into a passive relationship with the mother. Thus to Freud, the meaning of the difference between male and female versions of the fantasy derives from the inversion and passivity that accompany the male attachment, a structure that he ties to the negative Oedipus complex. Ibid., pp. 194–96. But what is of equal interest here is that the boy in this case seems unable to achieve the abstraction or distancing that the girl does; he is not able to achieve the spectatorial distance that constitutes the superego, or the disciplinary state, for that matter. In some fundamental way, then, the construction of bourgeois femininity is foundational for the establishment of the forms of state authority that I discuss here.

believe performance of the [masochistic] fantasies"—that penal reform was a working out of tensions surrounding reformers' sadistic or masochistic fantasies.[27] Instead, I want to attend to the historical situation of the fantasies that psychoanalysis later encountered. The attempt by Freud's patients to overcome contradiction through distancing, depersonalization, and reversal reproduced within the psyche the efforts of late-eighteenth- and early-nineteenth-century reformers to spiritualize punishment. Freud pointed out that for his patients, seeing scenes of real flagellation or cruelty provided little pleasure, and he insisted that these patients "were very seldom beaten in their childhood, or were . . . not brought up by the help of the rod."[28] In these fantasies, "moreover, it was always a condition . . . that the punishment should do the children no serious injury."[29] Freud's bourgeois patients inhabited a space cleared of the physical display of legal punishment; the visible corporality of the eighteenth century returned in the shape of fantasy.[30]

In the very displacement from society to psyche, Freud's patients remind us of the importance not simply of visibility to punishment or even of the different structures of visibility in punishment but also of the investment in visibility itself. Each of the different moments in the beating fantasy evinced a desire to imagine the gaze, to use a fantasmatic observation of the body as a means to produce pleasure. "A Child Is Being Beaten" not only manifests the effects of the long-term transformation of displayed violence in bourgeois culture but also demands attention to the meanings of the processes through which we imagine ourselves watching that transformation itself. These fantasies point to the process begun by Enlightenment penal reformers who imagined a penal space shorn of overt violence to its charges. By the time that Freud wrote and his patients fantasized, the givenness of distanced punishment was deeply inscribed within liberal culture. But that distancing was accompanied by a continued desire to imagine the suffering body, indeed to imagine the imagining of the suffering body. The historical place of that desire needs to be attended to.[31]

27. Sigmund Freud, "The Economic Problem of Masochism," in *Collected Papers*, 2:258.

28. Freud, " 'A Child Is Being Beaten'," p. 174.

29. Ibid.

30. On the relationship between Anglo-American humanitarianism and the migration of violence from open display to privatized pleasures, see Karen Halttunen, "Humanitarianism and the Pornography of Pain in Anglo-American Culture," *American Historical Review* 100, no. 2 (1995): 303–34, esp. 330–34.

31. For suggestive discussions of the ways in which print mediated and transformed the desire to imagine suffering in the nineteenth century, see Daniel A. Cohen, *Pillars of Salt, Monuments of Grace: New England Crime Literature and the Origins of American Popular Culture, 1674–1860* (New York, 1993), pp. 167–246; Gatrell, *The Hanging Tree*, pp. 597–601; and Halttunen, "Humanitarianism and the Pornography of Pain," pp. 325–30.

Let me return, then, to Freud's text. Freud, as was his wont, insisted that the fantasy of "a child is being beaten" be traced back to early childhood. These fantasies, he argued, could lay dormant until the sight of a beating at school triggered them. But more interestingly, Freud reported that the fantasy could become dormant again, only to be reawakened with reading. "In my patient's *milieu*," Freud tells us, "it was almost always the same books whose contents gave a new stimulus to the beating-phantasies: those accessible to young people, such as the so-called *'Bibliotheque rose'*, *Uncle Tom's Cabin*, etc."[32] Somehow within the confines of bourgeois Vienna, the echoes of that most famous abolitionist assault on the lash could be heard. And with that reentry of history into Freud's narrative of psychodynamics, the problem of the whip in early-nineteenth-century America reappears.[33]

II.

Late-eighteenth-century reformers confidently condemned the use of the lash. And Pennsylvania's legislature outlawed the use of the whip not only as a public criminal sanction but also as a tool of discipline within Philadelphia's Walnut Street Jail. At the turn of the century, it appeared that whipping had been removed from Pennsylvania's penal apparatus definitively.[34]

Yet during the 1820s the lash reemerged as a flash point of penal discussion, only this time from within the evolution of penal form itself. By 1820, the failures of reformative incarceration had become evident. Prison officials and penal reformers pointed to high rates of recidivism, low labor productivity, prison violence, inmate resistance, and open rebellion, and they called for a new style of punishing. Initially, it appeared that an intensification of isolation in the form of separate confinement would emerge unchallenged in Pennsylvania's penal system. But New York had developed a modified form of imprisonment, one which combined congregate labor during the day with solitary quarters at night and which depended, at least in part, on the whip for maintaining penal discipline.

32. Freud, " 'A Child Is Being Beaten'," p. 173. Freud continues, "The child began to compete with these works of fiction by producing its own phantasies and by constructing a wealth of situations, and even whole institutions, in which children were beaten or were punished and disciplined in some other way because of their naughtiness and bad behaviour" (ibid.).

33. For another discussion, to which I am indebted, that both uses Freud's notions and distances itself from them historically in a treatment of the place of whipping in Melville's *White-Jacket* (1850), see Michael Paul Rogin, *Subversive Genealogy: The Politics and Art of Herman Melville* (New York, 1983), pp. 90–95.

34. New York also outlawed the whip as a tool of prison discipline. See Glenn, *Campaigns against Corporal Punishment*, p. 13.

Defenders of New York's Auburn system accused proponents of penitential discipline of misplaced and naïve sympathy with criminals. They
denied that whipping at Auburn was either excessive or cruel. Instead,
they asserted, it was carefully controlled and a necessary and acceptable
part of penal discipline.[35]

Although New York's defense of Auburn and especially its acceptance
of whipping obtained some allies in Pennsylvania, it ultimately received
little local support. Pennsylvanian Samuel Miller, for one, declared the
whip "the most impolitic and pernicious system ever resorted to for the
government and reformation of rational beings."[36] Charles Caldwell
argued that whipping instigated a dialectic of degradation. "If we are not
greatly mistaken," he affirmed, "it tends to the extinguishment of all high,
amiable and honourable feelings in the hirelings who pursue it, almost as
inevitably as in the convicts who are subjects to it. . . . Being exclusively
the offspring of animal propensity, its unavoidable effect is to brutalize
those who are daily concerned in it."[37] The lash, its critics charged, led not
to reform but to psychological and moral regression. Its practice, they
believed, threatened to reduce both Americans and the United States to
the level of "animal propensity."[38]

This horror of the whip, tied to a faith in the reformative powers of solitude, was deeply felt. Both the deep revulsion from the lash and the fascination with flagellation were linked to reformers' vision of the shape of
society. For the reemergence of whipping as an issue of penal policy coincided with the reemergence of slavery as an issue for bourgeois society.
The 1820s, of course, witnessed accelerated agitation over slavery. The
Missouri Compromise, attempts to extend slavery into Illinois, and calls
to strengthen the police power over fugitive slaves propelled the issue of
slavery back into the center of national political life. And many of those

---

35. Commissioners to Revise the Penal Code, *Report of the Commissioners on the Penal Code,
With the Accompanying Documents. Read in the Senate, January 4, 1828* (Harrisburg, 1828), pp.
62, 70–73.

36. Samuel Miller to Roberts Vaux, January 1, 1828, in *Hazard's Register* 1 (1828): 79.
Rumors that the commissioners were going to defend the Auburn system had been circulating among penitential advocates before issuance of the actual report; see Edward Livingston
to Roberts Vaux, December 15, 1826, Vaux Papers, Historical Society of Pennsylvania,
Philadelphia.

37. Charles Caldwell, *New Views on Penitentiary Discipline, And Moral Education, And Reform*
(Philadelphia, 1829), p. 4.

38. See also Roberts Vaux to Frederick Tuckett, January 21, 1834, Vaux Papers. Edward
Livingston, *On the Advantages of the Pennsylvania System of Prison Discipline* (Philadelphia,
1828). As Michael Rogin has argued, antiwhipping agitation also contained anxiety over an
erotic component in flagellation. Deploying the whip, reformers feared, produced a dangerous and destructive pleasure (Rogin, *Subversive Genealogy*, pp. 92–94).

actively pressing for penitential punishments were also involved in the struggles over slavery.[39]

The interconnectedness of slavery and punishment extended beyond mere contemporaneity or biographical fusion. Penitential reformers and antislavery writers imagined the meaning and effects of corporal punishments in ways that reinforced each other. Roberts Vaux, addressing the "impolicy of slavery," declared that "mankind have always been more forcibly operated upon by moral incentives, than by physical compulsion, and roused to greater exertions by the hope of a benefit, than by a fear of an evil. Among slaves," he maintained, "the inflictions of the lash supply the place of moral incentives, and the fear of punishment is substituted for the hope of reward."[40] Nor were masters unmarked. "In daily familiarity with cruel and degrading punishments," Vaux asked, "must not their feelings become callous and indifferent to human rights and sufferings? With evil examples constantly before them, with minds at leisure to multiply imaginary desires, with every facility to gratification and every temptation to crime, and unrestrained by discipline, necessity, or the moral feelings of the community, will they not become dissolute, licentious and criminal?"[41] Vaux's depiction of whipping under slavery doubled the assault on penal flagellation. In both cases, critics charged, the lash disinhibited its subject while debasing and demoralizing its object.

Yet if the dynamic of corporal punishment led to mutual degradation, the implications of the whip extended even further. Tellingly, in Vaux's mind, the evils of the slave system even prevailed on plantation mistresses who exercised the whip with undisguised pleasure. "Who will deny the tendency of slavery to corrupt the disposition and deprave the heart," he demanded, "when it is testified by credible witnesses . . . that 'respectable ladies' frequently order, and superintend, the infliction of cruel punishments on their naked slaves—nay, inflict them with their own hands! To be capable of such acts must they not have forfeited every claim to that humanity and delicacy of feeling which contribute so much to the interest and charm of the Sex!"[42] Acting through the body of the

---

39. Most notably involved in Pennsylvania were Roberts Vaux, John Sergeant, and Job Tyson. In fact, almost all the members of the Philadelphia Society for Alleviating the Miseries of Public Prisons (PSAMPP)—the organizational basis for the movement toward separate confinement—were also members of the Pennsylvania Abolition Society. Peter Jonitas and Elizabeth Jonitas, "Members of the Prison Society: Biographical Vignettes, 1776–1830, of the Philadelphia Society for Assisting Distressed Prisoners and the Members of the PSAMPP, 1787–1830," typescript, 2 vols. (1982), 2:337, Haverford College Library, Haverford, Pa.

40. Roberts Vaux, "An Address on the Impolicy of Slavery, delivered January 1, 1824 before an Association Formed for the Education of Men of Color," p. 2, American Philosophical Society, Philadelphia.

41. Ibid., p. 8.

42. Ibid., p. 9.

slave mistress and on the body of the slave, Vaux contended, slavery inverted human nature and social justice.

To Vaux's mind this female infliction of "cruel punishments on their naked slaves" clinched slavery's inhumanity. Vaux's outrage over southern women instigating whippings is not surprising. Plantation mistresses using the whip stood in direct contrast to that refined and delicate female sensibility that increasingly marked bourgeois self-understanding. The system of slavery, Vaux suggested, stripped plantation ladies of their very humanity and delicacy, producing a process of regression through which they took pleasure and satisfaction from the pain of others. Slavery's direct and violent seizure of the body symbolized its intrinsic inhumanity.[43]

Yet the stability of bourgeois identity was not maintained so easily. For when plantation mistresses used the whip, they also gave the lie to claims that the two sexes possessed irrevocable and uniquely different characteristics—characteristics, so the argument went, rooted in biology but manifested in female fragility, tact, and morality.[44] Women wielding the whip threatened to destabilize the gender distinctions that northern society was naturalizing—and that helped stabilize masculine identity and northern society in the process. At the same time as they provided Vaux with a powerful symbol of the distance between slavery and humanity, these women also threatened the very gendered ground on which he stood. Thus to the penitential imagination, whipping gave body to the injustice and inhumanity of slavery and tyranny. It was in "despotic governments," Job Tyson proclaimed, that "history informs us, excessive punishments almost always prevail."[45] And, of course, whipping flourished in the slave south. The presence or absence of whipping signified the distance traveled toward enlightened humanity. But that distance was anything but secure.

43. This linkage of eroticism with power under slavery was not limited to Vaux. It was a source of anxiety among a wide range of antislavery individuals. See Ronald Walters, *The Antislavery Appeal: American Abolitionism after 1830* (Baltimore, 1976), pp. 70–87.

44. On the spread of what he calls a "two-sex" model of biological incommensurability in the late eighteenth and early nineteenth centuries, see Thomas Lacqueur, *Making Sex: Body and Gender from the Greeks to Freud* (Cambridge, Mass., 1990), pp. 149–233. Lacqueur notes that the two-sex model never fully replaced the one-sex model. In making this argument, he focuses primarily on the discursive instability of the two models—on their tendencies to slide over into the other. But it is equally true that there were social reasons for this slippage, reasons that were rooted in distinctive gender structures in different social systems. The division between the bourgeois north and the slave south provides perhaps the most visible example of this social difference, but even within northern society, as Christine Stansell has shown, different classes had distinct gender systems. Consequently, the notion of womanhood presumed by Vaux and his allies was always a contested one. On this issue, see Stansell, *City of Women: Sex and Gender in New York, 1789–1860* (New York, 1986).

45. Job Tyson, *Essay on the Penal Law of Pennsylvania* (Philadelphia, 1827), p. 9.

III.

The paradoxes of the new penal philosophy emerge clearly in the case of Maccumsey's death.[46] Confronted with accusations of cruelty and abuse of power in the death of Maccumsey, the warden, the prison inspectors, and their allies responded in two complementary ways. First, they adduced evidence that the gag had been employed previously—and without fatality—within the penitentiary and other reformative institutions within the city.[47] And, second, they turned the responsibility for Maccumsey's death back on Maccumsey himself. George McClellan, a physician testifying on the likely effects of the gag, maintained that it would have been "impossible" for the gag itself to have caused his death: "If the man had remained cool, and patiently submitted to the punishment," McClellan concluded, "it could not have produced apoplexy."[48] Had Maccumsey patiently accepted his punishment, they implied, he would still have been alive. The fault lay not in the gag but in himself.

These arguments contained a certain penitential logic. Through the architectural mechanism of the separate cell (fig. 14.4), the penitentiary aimed to impose the space of reformation. Penitentiary discipline centered on silent submission, and the gag was designed to ensure that silence. Maccumsey had been caught trying to get "the men next him talking."[49] In so doing, he had challenged the fundamental design of the penitentiary. The gag was a more personalized version of the penitentiary. Like the walls of the cell it restrained the recalcitrant will of the inmate. And, its defenders believed, once in place, the gag, like the cell, eliminated the physical violence and struggle that marked the whipping scene.[50]

At the same time, none of the medical men or officials who testified about the gag denied that it imposed suffering. But this suffering was relative—and relatively necessary. William Gibson confidently asserted that if "drawn with moderate tightness," it would cause no "more effect than a common mouthing bit upon a horse."[51] In treating the gag as equivalent

46. Maccumsey's death, combined with charges of other irregularities at the penitentiary, provoked a legislative inquiry. For a fuller discussion of this investigation and its implications, see Meranze, *Laboratories of Virtue*, pp. 305–28.

47. *Report of the Joint Committee of the Legislature of Pennsylvania, relative to the Eastern State Penitentiary, at Philadelphia. By Mr. Anderson of Delaware, Read in the House of Representatives, March 26, 1835* (Harrisburg, 1835), p. 96.

48. McElwee, *Concise History of the Eastern State Penitentiary*, 2:37–38; for similar testimony limiting the dangerousness of the gag, see the testimony of William B. Gibson on p. 44.

49. "Warden's Daily Journal," June 27, 1833.

50. In reality, the actual placing of the gag could involve a good deal of physical struggle and force, as it did in the case of Maccumsey.

51. McElwee, *Concise History of the Eastern State Penitentiary*, 2:43. George McClellan concurred. Dismissing the notion that the gag could be truly dangerous, he suggested that it was "just like a machine for breaking young horses" (2:37).

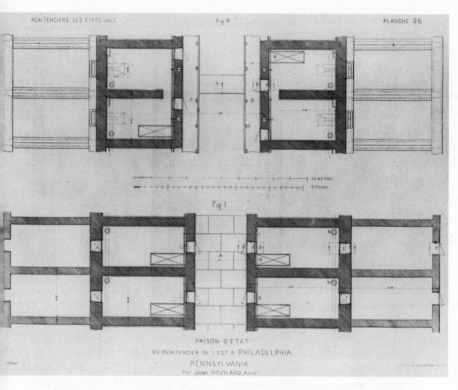

Fig. 14.4. Plans de détail de rez-de-chausée et du premier étage des cellules de l'aile S.O. From Frédéric-Auguste Demetz and Guillaume-Abel Blouet, *Rapports sur les pénitenciers des Etats-Unis* (Paris, 1837), plate 26; figure I shows a plan of the ground floor, and figure II shows that of the first floor. Key: A. corridors between cells on both levels; B. wooden door serving as passage in wall; B'. wooden door pierced with a small opening for the inspection of cell; C. iron grillwork with opening that serves as a small table for giving food to prisoners; D. embrasure in stone; F. wooden door to courtyard, visible to central pavilion; G. embrasure in wood; M. wooden bed against the wall; N. "seat of ease" or toilet that leads to a common drain serving all cells; S. ventilation chimneys for ground floor cells. (Photo: The Library Company of Philadelphia.)

to breaking a horse, the doctor implied that Maccumsey was somewhat less than fully human. A majority of the legislators investigating the Eastern State Penitentiary agreed. They reminded the public that although the penitentiary aimed for reformation, it acted on "men of idle habits, vicious propensities, and depraved passions." The first step in reformation, the legislators maintained, was securing "obedience." But "gentle means" were not always sufficient, and thus, they declared, "it becomes necessary to adopt some punishment beyond that which is inflicted under the sentence of the convict, and which is essential to secure his quiet subjection to that sentence."[52]

The penitentiary's defenders thus turned inmate recalcitrance into both object and cause of penitential discipline. Penal reformer and political theorist Francis Lieber made this point explicit. Declaring deprivation of food to be the ideal penalty to supplement solitude, Lieber explained that it "depends entirely upon the convict to remove it—and if he will abstain until he dies, I should say, let him die—as obedience is the first means of discipline."[53] From this perspective, punishments were the inmates' responsibility. Prisoners had only to accept the dictates of the sentence and thus free themselves from extra restraint.

Freedom through a willing acceptance of the law had deep roots within Christian tradition. And those roots were clearly manifest in what were, after all, punishments through penitence. But they also had striking parallels with liberal notions of the place of desire in a market society. Roberts Vaux, in his attack on slavery, insisted that to the slave, "whether the product of his labour is great or small, it is equally the same . . . he makes no acquisition, and sustains no loss, of property."[54] The freeman, on the other hand, operated under a different economy of desire, labor, and reward. "The freeman tastes the reward which," Vaux asserted, " 'sweetens labour.' "[55] Whereas the one system blocked the connection between desire and labor, the other reinforced it. The market was able to "sweeten" life and seize the "taste" of the laborer. And with this seizure of desire—as opposed to the seizure of the body under slavery—the incessant accumulation of improvement would begin.

As with the market, so with penitential punishments. Both penitential punishments and free labor ultimately aimed to create a productive and prudent workforce. They did so by denying that they acted on the body, insisting instead that they reformed and disciplined the will. The coercions of the market and the limits of penitential architecture would take the place of the lash. The theater of conscience and the incentive of property would replace the scaffold spectacle and the confrontation of master and slave. The denial of corporality would enable a new regime of submission.

Yet as the case of Maccumsey suggests, matters were a bit more complicated. For the turn to the reformation of character did not proceed smoothly. The emphasis on conscience opened up new realms of disobedience, struggles between inmates and authorities that, while seemingly trivial, signified incomplete reformation. The move beyond the body not

52. *Report of the Joint Committee*, p. 12.
53. Lieber quoted in McElwee, *Concise History of the Eastern State Penitentiary*, 2:56.
54. Vaux, "Address on the Impolicy of Slavery," p. 2.
55. Ibid.

only justified the penitential project but explained its failures as well. Inmate character became not only object and cause of the penal process but its limit as well. The "soul," in Foucault's sense, became fetishized, and the problems of the "soul" in turn helped ensure the fetishism of the prison.

Fetishism is an intersecting site of two of the most powerful modern discourses of the body: marxism and psychoanalysis. But they approach the problem of the fetish in distinctly different ways. In the famous section of *Capital* titled "The Fetishism of Commodities and the Secret Thereof," Marx argued that under capital, a critical reversal took place when commodities—the products of human labor—appeared to take on a life of their own and entered "into relation both with one another and the human race."[56] For Marx, fetishism marked the reversal of the animate with the inanimate, the created with the creative. This reversal is itself a sign of a greater repression—of the ultimately social character of production and the ways capital stamps value not only on commodities but also on labor itself. The animation of the commodity enables the concealment of the social network of the production of commodities. It is a part substituting for the whole.

If for Marx the fetishism of commodities helped to repress knowledge of the totality, for Freud fetishism worked to disavow knowledge of the impossibility of a totality. Freud saw fetishism as an attempt to disavow a lack or, more precisely, to deny the possibility of a potential lack.[57] For Freud, the male turns to the fetish for disavowal (unconsciously denying what he consciously knows). The fetishist disavows sexual difference and thereby the possibility of his own castration. The Freudian fetish is an object concealing the void at the heart of an identity.[58]

These two interpretations of fetishism, although contradictory in theory—one conceals the reality of a totality, the other the gap in that totality—highlight different elements of the structure of the penal soul. On the one hand, the penal soul, that imaginary doubling of the penal body, comes to seem a target apart—a target that demands the transformation of punishment itself. Like the marxist fetish, the soul appears to generate

56. Karl Marx, *Capital: A Critique of Political Economy*, vol. 1, *The Process of Capitalist Production*, ed. Frederick Engels, trans. Samuel Moore and Edward Aveling (New York, 1967), p. 72.

57. Freud, "Fetishism," in *Collected Papers*, vol. 5, ed. James Strachey (1924; London, 1950), pp. 198–204.

58. For a discussion of these differing perspectives on the fetish which draws out their wider implications for ideology critique, see Slavoj Žižek, *The Sublime Object of Ideology* (New York, 1989), pp. 49–53. Žižek here argues that the essential interpretative gesture of a marxist critique is to demonstrate a false universality, whereas the essential gesture of the Freudian critique is to demonstrate what he terms an *over-rapid historicization* (p. 50). Although I employ Freudian categories here, I emphasize the historical emergence of their conditions of possibility—a position that Žižek strenuously opposes.

out of itself the entire penitential network; the ways, as Foucault has shown, that the disciplinary network produced the penal soul are effaced. On the other hand, the character of the inmate marks the lack of the penitential process. Like the Freudian fetish, the inmate's soul offered a way to acknowledge the failing of the penitentiary yet deny that the penitentiary is responsible. For the incompleteness of penitential transformation was always—as it was with Maccumsey—the fault of the inmate.[59]

This structural doubling of fetishism paralleled a historical doubling. The emphasis on inmate conscience and the fascination with the whipped body were, if you will, soul mates. It was the entry of the soul into punishment that retroactively made the direct seizure of the body cruel. It was the entry of the soul that made the physical violences of the prison something more than mere sanguinary vengeance. And it was the entry of the soul that transformed punishment from a specific act of retribution into an ongoing process of reformation. But the entry of the soul took place against the scene of the body: not just any body but the body beneath the gallows or under the lash.

What is most striking here is the investment not in the whipped or hanged body so much as in the gaze on that body. In "Fetishism," Freud reported being initially puzzled by a young man "who had exalted a certain kind of 'shine on the nose' into a fetishistic condition." The solution to this puzzle, it turned out, came from the realm of language. For Freud had interpreted the patient's fetishism in German (where *glanz* would have indicated "shine"), but the fetishism took place in English—the fetish was a "*glance* at the nose."[60] Freud quickly assures us that the nose is the fetish. He thereby disavows that the full fetishistic obsession was with looking at the nose. It was the glance or the gaze that was fetishized.[61] Similarly, it was the gaze at the whipped body that sustained the investment in the soul. If the penal soul retroactively made corporal and capital punishments cruel, it is equally true that the power of that soul—its ability to hold together and conceal the contradictions of the entire penal network—drew its strength from the gaze upon the whipped body.[62]

59. This structure of blame does not always hold. It was also possible to blame the failures of the penitentiary on its own incomplete implementation. But I think that in this case the same logic holds.

60. Freud, "Fetishism," p. 198.

61. For the importance of this disavowal for Freud's larger disavowal of the social relations of the object, see Kaja Silverman, *The Acoustic Mirror: The Female Voice in Psychoanalysis and Cinema* (Bloomington, Ind., 1988), pp. 18–22.

62. Freud's disavowal is particularly striking because his patient was the "Wolf-Man." In a case structured by the traumatic effects of looking, Freud is unable to divert his own gaze from the transhistorical threat of castration. But perhaps his looking at the body to look away from the gaze is not entirely surprising, for it is in keeping with Freud's relentless emphasis on embodiment and away from the larger realm of social relations. Freud's tendency can be

The fascination with flagellation, then, had wide import. Inasmuch as they equated whipping with the tyrannies of aristocracy, monarchy, and slavery, penitential reformers defined the body—or at least its treatment—as a symptom of social organization. But this emphasis on whipping, with its seemingly frenzied degradation of the body, enabled reformers to refuse that symptomatic character to their own disciplinary apparatus. Instead, penitential reformers insisted, disciplinary sanctions were a sign of individual failing (the failings of individual prisoners, that is) and not indicative of structural inequity or organized cruelty. When, as with Maccumsey, the body emerged like the return of the repressed to demonstrate the excess of the penitentiary, prison officials and their defenders turned that excess back upon the prisoners themselves. It was impossible to escape bodily punishments, they admitted. But it was the spiritual character of inmates, not the nature of penitential punishments, which determined that impossibility. And what made that logic possible, what marked the violences of the soul's transformations as humane, was another scene, perhaps the primal scene of penal reform: a criminal is being beaten.

seen in the different ways in which he and Marx evoke the religious realm in their discussions of fetishism. For Marx, the gods themselves were fetishes: "In that world [the religious one] the productions of the human brain appear as independent beings endowed with life, and entering into relation both with one another and the human race." The fetish materializes social relations. But for Freud, modern fetishes "are with some justice likened to the fetishes in which savages believe that their gods are embodied." Once again, Freud insists that material embodiment, not social relations, is the essence of fetishism. Freud's concentration on embodiment has the paradoxical effect of removing the body from history and social relations. His disavowal of the possibility of the fetishized gaze mirrors his own interpretative technique vis-à-vis fetishism. Marx, *Capital*, 1:72; Sigmund Freud, *Three Essays on Sexuality*, intro. Steven Marcus, trans. and ed. James Strachey (New York, 1962), p. 19.

part four

Oral Performance, Personal Power

Massacred Language:
Courtroom Performance in
Eighteenth-Century Boston

ROBERT BLAIR ST. GEORGE

ON AUGUST 19, 1770, John Adams confided to his dairy that "Mr. Royal Tyler began to pick chat with me. Mr. Adams, have you ever read Dr. Souths sermon upon the Wisdom of this World?" Tyler's recommendation was timed to make Adams contemplate the wisdom of the difficult task he would begin later that fall, when he would be defending the soldiers accused of murdering five men during the confusion and violence of the "Bloody Massacre" in Boston's King Street marketplace earlier that year. South's sermons had first been preached at Westminster Abbey in 1676 on the text from 1 Corinthians 3:19, "For the wisdom of this World is Foolishness with God." When Adams consulted the sermon Tyler had recommended, he attended with special care to the first principle of worldly wisdom it set forth as conflicting with God's will: "A man must maintain a constant Course of Dissimulation, in the whole Tenor of his Behaviour." After considering that "constant Dissimulation, may be good or evil as it is interpreted," Adams revealed the lawyer's skill at drawing a rational argument in smooth language. "There are persons in my Heart I despize," he wrote, and "others I abhor. Yet I am not obliged to inform the one of my Contempt, nor the other of my Detestation. This Kind of Dissimulation, which is no more than Concealment, Secrecy, or Reserve, or in other Words, Prudence and Discretion, is a necessary

Versions of this paper were presented at the "Possible Pasts: Critical Encounters in Early America" conference at the University of Pennsylvania and the "Theorizing the Hybrid" conference held at the University of Texas at Austin. For constructive comments, I am indebted to Roger D. Abrahams, Richard Bauman, John Borneman, Peter Burke, Deborah A. Kapchan, and Natalie Z. Davis.

Branch of Wisdom, and so far from being immoral and unlawful, that [it] is a Duty and a Virtue."[1]

Adam's meditation on the ethics of dissimulation demonstrates how deeply colonial lawyers and their courtroom performances were indebted to a sense of critical disengagement and spectatorial distance that permeated public behavior in late-seventeenth- and eighteenth-century America. In his clever use of language to convert dissimulation from a transgressive practice to one of virtue, lawyer Adams revealed his skill at the trade in talk, or the symbolic economy of exchanging and mixing languages to fashion a respectable public self and pursue self-interest simultaneously. In this essay I explore the "many-languagedness" of legal discourse and the destabilizing impact it had on established standards for oral performance in colonial Anglo-American culture.

Over the past two decades, work at the intersection of folklore, the ethnography of communication, and cultural history has made apparent the internal logic of early modern speech communities. In Europe and its American colonies, from court circles to small villages, men and women used a variety of expressive strategies in their daily lives. More recently, historians have explored some of these in detail: the range and intensity of "heated speech" in early New England and the Chesapeake, and its role in constructing and regulating gender relations and family government; the functions of ritual insult in New France; the inversive nature of "antilanguages" in sixteenth-century England and Italy; and the functions of silence in such diverse settings as Catholic France and Quaker Philadelphia during the late sixteenth and seventeenth centuries.[2]

---

1. John Adams, *Diary and Autobiography of John Adams*, ed. L. H. Butterfield, 3 vols. (Cambridge, Mass., 1961), 1:362–63 (hereafter *DAJA*). The volume of sermons mentioned, Robert South, *Twelve Sermons Preached Upon Several Occasions*, 5th ed. (London, 1722), is in the collection of John Adams's books in the Boston Public Library; South drew his biblical citations from the King James Version. See also Francis Bacon, "On Simulation and Dissimulation," in *The Works of Francis Bacon*, ed. Basil Montagu, 3 vols. (Philadelphia, 1842), 1:14–15.

2. Robert Blair St. George, " 'Heated Speech' and Literacy in Seventeenth-Century New England," in *Seventeenth-Century New England*, ed. David D. Hall and David G. Allen (Boston, 1984), pp. 275–322; Mary Beth Norton, "Gender and Defamation in Seventeenth-Century Maryland," *William and Mary Quarterly*, 3d ser., 44, no. 1 (1987): 3–39; Peter Moogk, " 'Thieving Buggers' and 'Stupid Sluts': Insults and Popular Culture in New France," *William and Mary Quarterly*, 3d ser., 36, no. 4 (1976): 524–47; Jane Kamensky, *Governing the Tongue: The Politics of Speech in Early New England* (New York, 1997). See also M. A. K. Halliday, "Antilanguages," in his *Language as Social Semiotic: The Social Interpretation of Language and Meaning* (Baltimore, 1978), pp. 164–82; Peter Burke, "Language and Anti-Language in Early Modern Italy," *History Workshop* 11 (1981): 24–32; and Eric Partridge, "American Underworld and English Cant," in *American Tramp and Underworld Slang*, ed. Godfrey Irwin (New York, n.d.), pp. 255–64. On silence, see Richard Bauman, *Let Your Words Be Few: Symbolism of Speaking and Silence among Seventeenth-Century Quakers* (New York, 1983); Peter Burke, *The Art of Conversation* (Ithaca, 1993), pp. 123–41; and Susan Sontag, "The Aesthetics of Silence," in her *Styles of Radical Will* (New York, 1969), pp. 3–34.

What has emerged, with few exceptions, are two ways of speaking that are inversions of each other. Defenders of "Godly conversation" advocated the "language of Canaan," a speech genre modeled on the imagined unity of the perfect language of heavenly saints, a code that would restore the semiotic wreckage of Babel. Samuel Sewall delighted in believing that there "Shall be Language in Heaven," and remained confident that God's elect would have "no need to Learn Languages as now; which is a fruit of the Curse, since the Confusion." Illicit speech—including cursing, beggar's cant, insult, slander, defamation, and sedition—existed as the negative imprint of Canaan's transparent clarity. Predictably, court records map its railing (but riotous) contours. In December 1639, for example, John Woodcock was "warned to answer for his laughinge in Sermon tyme" in Springfield, Massachusetts. In 1677 Bridget Oliver stood with her husband "back to back, on a lecture day in the public market place" at Salem for having called him an "old rogue and old devil, on Lord's days." On the one hand, we feel what Cotton Mather termed the "honey-dripping," "heart-melting" words of meetinghouse and church. On the other, in the language of back alleys, rural paths, and public marketplaces, we hear curses, insults, sexual banter, scatological humor, the cony-catcher's cant, and sharp styles of verbal abuse: "railing," "affronting," "threatening," "swearing rashly."[3]

Not all speech in colonial Anglo-America, however, fell easily into these two discursive domains. The English metropolitan merchant, for instance, realized that altering one's speech style was useful, in the words of William Scott in *An Essay of Drapery* (1635), to convince "his Customer to the liking of his commodity." With the dissembling nature of commercial language in mind, Hobbes penned his critical definition of "person" as derived from the Latin *persona*, which "signifies the disguise, or outward appearance of a man, counterfeited upon the stage. . . . So that a *person*, is the same that an *actor* is, both on the stage and in polite conversation." Hobbes was likely drawing on George Pettie's 1581 translation of Stefano Guazzo's *La Civile Conversatione* (1574). Guazzo may have concurred with other courtesy-book writers in viewing polite conversation as the epitome of social relations, but he chose as the ideal locus for such talk neither church nor palace chamber but the marketplace. There he discov-

3. On ministers and "holy conversation," see Mason Lowance, *The Language of Canaan: Metaphor and Symbol in New England from the Puritans to the Transcendentalists* (Cambridge, Mass., 1980); Samuel Sewall, *Diary of Samuel Sewall, 1674–1729*, ed. M. Halsey Thomas, 2 vols. (New York, 1973), 1:564 (entry of March 31, 1707). See *The Pynchon Papers: Pynchon Court Record*, comp. Juliette Tomlinson, ed. Carl Bridenbaugh, Colonial Society of Massachusetts Publication 61 (Boston, 1982), p. 205, and *Records and Files of the Quarterly Courts of Essex County, Massachusetts*, ed. George Francis Dow, 9 vols. (Salem, Mass., 1911–78), 6:386. See also B. E., *A New Dictionary of the Terms Ancient and Modern of the Canting Crew* (London, n.d.).

ered "a numberlesse multitude walking upp and downe in every place, keeping a continuall mercate, where there is bargayning for all things." Dialogue at the center of commercial capitalism demanded that people "put of[f] as it were our own fashions and manners, and cloath our selves with the conditions of others, and imitate them so farre as reason will permit." To succeed at marketplace discourse, Guazzo argued, "We must alter our selves into an other."[4]

Hobbes's homology of "person" and "actor" thus described a commercial figure exchanging words in a milieu of displaced, exchanging selves. As language fed off the magic of merchant capitalists and theater's mimetic force, neo-Platonist critics—including the Puritan clergy—critiqued communication that threatened the sanctity of Canaan's code. But ministers too mixed languages even as they promised transparency. In Boston, for example, Cotton Mather grafted the "clipped talk" of local legends, remarkable providences, his own helpless stutter, and "plain style" exegesis into polished sermons. Similarly, Puritan missionaries knew the many points of slippage and negotiated meanings that fractured the predicted lines of translation at places where European and Native American cultures collided. And, in turn, the hybrid styles of ministers and missionaries circled back to influence nascent professional classes. New England merchants quickly co-opted the rhetorical flourishes they heard in sermons, and as Roy Porter has shown, English "quacks" drew on the puffery of the popular stage and "classical tongues to conjure up the mystique of venerable tradition."[5]

Linguistic exchange inevitably denies dualism. It demands and reproduces heterogeneity and multivocality, as recent ethnographic work on language and commerce demonstrates. Languages of the marketplace are a topic of ongoing interest and debate precisely because they highlight the creative and coercive force of creolization, hybridity, and dissimulation. This work extends and in many ways refines the high level of critical theory and situated fieldwork in the ethnography of speaking that has had a steady impact on historical research since the early 1970s.[6] More recent

4. William Scott, *An Essay of Drapery* (London, 1635), as quoted in Jean-Christophe Agnew, *Worlds Apart: The Market and the Theater in Anglo-American Thought, 1550–1750* (New York, 1986), p. 81; Thomas Hobbes, *Leviathan*, ed. Michael Oakeshot (Oxford, 1946), p. 105; Stefano Guazzo, *The Civil Conversation*, trans. George Pettie, 2 vols. (London, 1581), as quoted in Agnew, *Worlds Apart*, p. 77.

5. On Mather's debt to popular culture, see David D. Hall, *Worlds of Wonder, Days of Judgment: Popular Religious Belief in Early New England* (New York, 1989). On colonial contacts and linguistic colonialism, see Stephen Greenblatt, "Learning to Curse: Aspects of Linguistic Colonialism in the Sixteenth Century," in *First Images of America: The Impact of the New World on the Old*, ed. Fredi Chiappelli, 2 vols. (Berkeley, 1976), 2:562–64. Roy Porter, "The Language of Quackery," in *The Social History of Language*, ed. Peter Burke and Roy Porter (Cambridge, England, 1987), p. 90.

6. Mikhail Bakhtin, *Rabelais and His World*, trans. Hélène Iswolsky (Cambridge, Mass., 1968), pp. 145–95. On the ethnography of speaking, see Dell Hymes, *Foundations in Sociolin-*

work, however, emphasizes pragmatics of discourse in performance situations. Established concerns in the ethnography of communication—context, play, reflexivity, and the ways that performances call attention to, or highlight, aesthetic criteria for public consideration—have thus taken a turn toward the political, the historical, the ideological. Instead of viewing performance as a strictly aesthetic frame, work now centers on how, during performance, speakers lift a text out of discursive routine and mark it as decentered from the norms of daily conversation and open to appropriation.[7]

The ways that texts are marked or entextualized involves other aspects of spoken language, including such metalinguistic techniques as indexicality or deixis used for specifying spatial and temporal position, indirect and direct reported speech, and discourse that indexes or refers to other relevant genres and discourses. These features of language keep speech open-ended, admitting material phenomena outside the text to the ongoing negotiation of meaning within its formal or stylistic borders. Once certain utterances can be decentered as texts and marked for special consideration or appropriation by other performers or speech communities, performances become lenses for the critical observation of the relationship of speech and power. But as the sociologist Pierre Bourdieu has argued, linguistic pragmatics can remain vital to the ethnographer or the historian only if the social position of speakers and their particular and relative delegated powers in society are granted interpretive primacy:

> It is not enough to say, as people sometimes do, in order to avoid the difficulties inherent in a purely internalist approach to language, that the use made of language in a determinate situation by a determinate speaker, with his style, rhetoric and socially marked identity, provides words with "connotations" that are tied to a particular context, introducing into dis-

---

guistics: An Ethnographic Approach (Philadelphia, 1974), and Richard Bauman and Joel Sherzer, eds., Explorations in the Ethnography of Speaking (New York, 1974). On the importance of this work for social historians of language and ways of speaking, see the comments in Peter Burke, "Introduction," in The Social History of Language, ed. Burke and Porter, pp. 1–20, and its enlarged version in Burke, Art of Conversation, pp. 1–33.

7. On performance, see Hymes, "Breakthrough into Performance," in Folklore: Performance and Communication, ed. Dan Ben-Amos and Kenneth S. Goldstein (The Hague, 1975), pp. 1–74; Richard Bauman, Verbal Art as Performance (Rowley, Mass., 1977); and Richard Bauman, Judith T. Irvine, and Susan U. Philips, Performance, Speech Community, and Genre, Working Papers and Proceedings of the Center for Psychosocial Studies, no. 11 (Chicago, 1997): pp. 5–9. This discussion is also indebted to the following essays: Richard Bauman and Charles L. Briggs, "Poetics and Performance as Critical Perspectives on Language and Social Life," Annual Review of Anthropology 19 (1990): 59–88, esp. 66–78; William Hanks, "Text and Textuality," Annual Review of Anthropology 18 (1989): 95–127; Judith T. Irvine, "When Talk Isn't Cheap: Language and Political Economy," American Ethnologist 16, no. 2 (1989): 248–67; Irvine, "Status and Style in Language," Annual Review of Anthropology 15 (1985): 557–81; and Hanks, "Discourse Theory in a Theory of Practice," American Ethnologist 14, no. 4 (1988): 668–92.

course that surplus of meaning which gives it its "illocutionary force." In fact, the use of language, the manner as much as the substance of discourse, depends on the social position of the speaker, which governs the access he can have to the language of the institution, that is, to the official, orthodox and legitimate speech. It is therefore the participation in the authority of the institution which makes *all* the difference—irreducible to discourse as such—between the straightforward imposture of masqueraders, who disguise a performative utterance as a descriptive or constative statement, and the authorized imposture of those who do the same thing with the authorization and the authority of an institution.[8]

Although the position of the speaker has always been central to sociolinguistic interpretation, Bourdieu's admonitory statement warrants consideration. Because he makes the single issue of authority—its management, influence, and reproduction—central to his view of language as an extension of the market economy, his critique cautions against any metaphysics of "aesthetics" or "poetic language" existing outside the fields of power and interest. At the core of every utterance may lie difference, but at the heart of hybridity lurk strategies for the consolidation of influence.[9]

Public places of exchange are sympathetic environments for the hybridization and exchange of style and discursive power, as people come together in arenas where outsiders have always been present and where claims to authenticity as a local resident are often suspended. Marketplaces are open sites where orthodoxies and official languages may be subverted but where ambiguities over exchange, identities, and communication typically elude codification. In early-eighteenth-century England, for example, Jonathan Swift lashed out against the creeping changes he detected in the English language, mocking the fondness for adopting French terms "for a fashion" and lamenting "the affectation of some late Authors to introduce and multiply *Cant* words, which is the most ruinous corruption in any language." In short order John Oldmixon issued a retort, claiming Swift's letter was "meant to Bully us into his Methods for pinning down our Language, and making it as Criminal to

---

8. Pierre Bourdieu, "Authorized Language: The Social Conditions for the Effectiveness of Ritual Discourse," in his *Language and Symbolic Power*, ed. John B. Thompson (Cambridge, Mass., 1991), p. 109. See also Kurt Heinzelman, *The Economics of the Imagination* (Amherst, Mass., 1980), pp. 70–109.

9. Compare Bourdieu's comments, focused on issues of social agency and claims of authority in language, with the more general project signaled in Michel Foucault, "The Discourse on Language," in *The Archaeology of Knowledge and the Discourse on Language*, trans. A. M. Sheridan Smith (New York, 1972), p. 216: "I am supposing that in every society the production of discourse is at once controlled, selected, organised and redistributed according to a certain number of procedures, whose role it is to avert its powers and its dangers, to cope with chance events, to evade its ponderous, awesome materiality."

admit Foreign Words as Foreign Trades, tho' our Tongue may be enrich'd by the one, as much as our Traffick by the other."[10]

But if marketplaces are critical sites for subversion, two problems emerge in this interpretation that relate to the courtroom performances of lawyers in early America. The "open marketplace" so often imagined in ethnographic writing as a zone of inversive festivity was itself, in England and her North American colonies, an institution invented to guarantee the proper *surveillance* of exchanges. As a result, the hybridity of marketplace language in early Anglo-American culture may have enforced claims to legitimacy and protected power as often as it subverted or confounded them. In addition, to make such an argument requires one to avoid nostalgia for the "visibility" of the market as place; indeed, in the eighteenth century, language in the increasingly placeless market economy vied for attention with utterances in the urban square and merchant's walk.

Lawyers in colonial America used discursive hybridity as a strategy to protect their interests as a nascent professional group, the members of which, at least in Boston by the 1750s, were already consolidating their social ranks and political positions. In this case, mixed languages were used to assert an elite social identity, a plausible fiction of integrity, and not to subvert one. Part of the power of legal discourse lay in its ambiguous status as placed but somehow placeless, performed in the courthouse but also conditioned by legal texts that circulated standardized knowledge regardless of local context; in a Puritan colony both dependent on and long hostile to the social rise of lawyers, attorneys especially relied on hybrid speech, as it provided them a means of anchoring their trade in local "tradition"—of appearing part of a consensual, popular, and classless social formation—at the same moment as they pursued their own advancement.[11] Support for this argument requires complete documenta-

10. Jonathan Swift, *A Proposal for Correcting, Improving, and Ascertaining the English Tongue* (London, 1712; rpt., Menston, England, 1969), pp. 14–15; John Oldmixon, *Reflections on Dr. Swift's Letter . . . about the English Tongue* (London, 1712; rpt., Menston, England, 1970), p. 2. For an example of recent work on expressive strategies in the marketplace, see Deborah A. Kapchan, "Hybridization and the Marketplace: Emerging Paradigms in Folkloristics," *Western Folklore* 52, nos. 2–4 (1993): 307–8.

11. On the biases attending the rise of common lawyers, see Brian P. Levack, *The Civil Lawyers in England, 1603–1641* (Oxford, 1973), pp. 9–16, 34–43, 53–60; William J. Bouwsma, "Lawyers and Early Modern Culture," *American Historical Review* 78, no. 2 (1973): 303–27; C. W. Brooks, "The Common Lawyers in England, c. 1558–1642," and Stephen Botein, "The Legal Profession in Colonial North America," both in *Lawyers in Early Modern Europe and America*, ed. Wilfred Prest (New York, 1981), pp. 42–64, 129–46; John Dykstra Eusden, *Puritans, Lawyers, and Politics in Early Seventeenth-Century England* (New Haven, 1958), pp. 9–40, 55–63, 114–48; and Glenn W. Hatfield, "Quacks, Pettyfoggers, and Parsons: Fielding's Case against the Learned Professions," *Texas Studies in Literature and Language* 9, no. 1 (1967): 69–83. On plain speech, see Michael Clark, "The Word of God and the Language of Man: Puritan Semiotics and the Theological and Scientific 'Plain Styles' of the Seventeenth Cen-

tion of lawyers in action, and the record of the second Boston Massacre trial, held in Boston's Queen Street courthouse from November 27 to December 4, 1770, provides just such an opportunity.

I.

Thanks to Hiller B. Zobel's *The Boston Massacre* (1970), the details of the event are readily available. Briefly, soon after nine o'clock on the evening of March 5, 1770, the bells of Boston's meetinghouses began ringing. People quickly appeared in the King Street marketplace below the Town House (now the Old State House), thinking there was a fire. Rumors snaked through the crowd about some "boys" taunting a sentry at his post outside the customhouse. Rough play turned to outright violence. The sentry summoned support. A small detachment of between seven and twelve (here the narratives vary) British regulars arrived on the scene in about ten minutes. But by all accounts, citizens hurled verbal abuse as well as ice and snow at the troops. At some point muskets were leveled and fired, without orders. Three men instantly fell dead in the snow, a fourth perished shortly after the shooting, and a fifth lay mortally wounded and died several days later. From the patriot perspective, as shown in Henry Pelham's drawing of the incident (fig. 15.1), the British troops attacked an unarmed, innocent citizenry in a clear display of unwarranted martial force.

After numerous judicial delays and a vicious newspaper and pamphlet war, two legal cases—one for Captain Thomas Preston, followed by another for the eight British regulars under his command—came to trial in the fall of 1770. The Grand Jury of the Province of Massachusetts Bay had indicted each of these men with five separate counts of murder, accounting for the individuals who had died—Crispus Attucks, Patrick Carr, Samuel Maverick, James Caldwell, and Samuel Gray. With local sentiment moving strongly against the British troops, the decision on the part of attorney John Adams to serve in their defense was controversial. Indeed, the Boston Massacre trials remain famous in part because of his assertion that British law guaranteed every individual, regardless of assumed guilt or political party, adequate legal protection and a fair trial.

---

tury," *Semiotic Scene* 2, no. 2 (1978): 61–90, and Thomas Spratt's advocacy in his *History of the Royal Society* (1667) of a "close naked and natural way of speaking," as discussed in Nancy Armstrong and Leonard Tennenhouse, "Gender and the Work of Words," *Cultural Critique* 13 (Fall 1989): 258–61. On the grounding of "plain speech" in the "word and thing" debate generally, see Barbara J. Shapiro, *Probability and Certainty in Seventeenth-Century England* (Princeton, 1983), pp. 227–41, and Tony Davies, "The Burning Ark: Words and Things in the English Revolution," *LTP: Journal of Language Teaching Politics* 4 (1985): 63–84.

Fig. 15.1. Henry Pelham, *The Fruits of Arbitrary Power, or the Bloody Massacre, Perpetrated in King Street, Boston, on March 5th: 1770.* Engraving; H. 9 3/16" (23.3 cm), W. 8 3/4" (22.2 cm). (Photo: Courtesy of the American Antiquarian Society)

The law, Adams believed, was a bastion of equality because it insisted on rational argument and complete impartiality. As he prepared his defense notes for the Preston trial, which began on October 24, 1770, and went to the jury five days later, Adams drew on Algernon Sidney's *Discourses concerning Government* (1704). "Law," Adams maintained,

> no Passion can disturb. Tis void of Desire and Fear, Lust and Anger. Tis Mens Sine affectu, written Reason, retaining Some Measure of divine Perfection. It does not enjoin that which pleases a weak, frail Man, but without any Regard to Persons, commands that which is good, and punishes evil in all whether rich or poor, high or low. Tis deaf, inexorable, inflexible.[12]

When the Preston case returned from the jury on October 30, Adams's arguments and his examination of witnesses had prevailed. Preston was found not guilty on every count.

In this essay, however, I focus on the second trial, which began on November 27 and ended on December 4, 1770. Four lawyers worked this case: for the Crown's prosecution of the soldiers, Samuel Quincy and Robert Treat Paine; in their defense, John Adams and Josiah Quincy Jr. Samuel Quincy opened for the Crown, questioned the witnesses to establish evidence, and made the prosecution's main argument. Josiah Quincy Jr. opened for the defense, presented the evidence, and argued. Adams made the closing argument for the defense, followed by Paine for the Crown. Presiding over the proceedings in the Superior Court of Judicature of Suffolk County (Boston) were four magistrates: Benjamin Lynde, John Cushing, Peter Oliver, and Edmund Trowbridge. And a man named John Hodgson kept a shorthand transcript of the trial, which, along with related minute books, letters, and diaries, allows us to examine courtroom performance in detail.[13]

The first kind of speech the lawyers exploited was that of witnesses in the case, who narrated what they remembered having seen and heard that night. A total of eighty witnesses took the stand during the second trial: twenty-eight for the Crown, and fifty-two for the defense. We know the

12. Cited in "VII. Adams' Notes of Authorities for His Argument for the Defense," in "No. 63. Rex v. Preston," in *Legal Papers of John Adams* (hereafter *LPJA*), ed. L. Kinvin Wroth and Hiller B. Zobel, 3 vols. (Cambridge, Mass., 1965), 3:82.

13. On the transcript and other supporting documents and for critical remarks by John Adams and defense witness Richard Palmes on the biased inaccuracies in Hodgson's transcript, see the summaries in L. Kinvin Wroth and Hiller B. Zobel, "Editorial Note," in *LPJA*, 3:27–28; the Hodgson transcript of the second trial was published as *The Trial of William Wemms, James Hartegan, William McCauley, Hugh White, Matthew Killroy, William Warren, John Carrol, and Hugh Montgomery* (Boston, 1770). Although eight names are cited in this title, four others (a boatbuilder, two more soldiers, and a "gentleman") were initially indicted for having fired on the crowd from inside the customhouse, but charges on this latter group were dropped. A fifth attorney, Sampson Blowers, is listed as serving for the defense, but no evidence suggests he performed publicly in the trial; see *LPJA*, 3:101.

occupations of fifty-eight (72.5 percent) of the witnesses, and with some biases, they represent a full cross-section of the working population of Boston. Merchants and traders dominate the group (nineteen), with others drawn from the service trades (thirteen), shipbuilding and construction trades (nine), clothing trades (four), food and drink trades (two), unspecified apprentices (four), and soldiers and sailors (four). The group also included one free black, one slave, and one widow.[14]

In dialogue with the attorneys, most of the eighty witnesses employed such fundamental linguistic strategies as spatial and temporal indexicals (to contextualize their accounts by incorporating tight references to place and time); reported speech (to make other people's statements their own); and restatement (repetition as a means of stressing—indeed constructing—the "truth" of specific details). Because precise location during the events involved could be crucial to the power of one's testimony, many witnesses were careful to claim recall of their exact spatial position. A map of the King Street marketplace drawn shortly after the event by Paul Revere shows the key features involved: the town house (with market stalls below), the customhouse, the streets, shops, and location of firing soldiers and fallen citizens (fig. 15.2).

Witnesses packed their testimonies with locative references as part of the context of their narrative statements. Some of these are directive or relative and give their speech a sense of "having been there" which builds their claim to truth. As William Strong, clerk of the customhouse described, during the confusion on King Street, "I thought to go up to an acquaintance's house, and went in the *middle* of the street, and *coming opposite* to the soldiers, I saw two men lay, one on the *right* and one on the *left*, on their backs; I concluded they were dead."[15] Here, Strong combined the directives "middle," "right," and "left" with the relative "coming opposite." Archibald Bowman, an auctioneer, responded to a question from defense lawyer Josiah Quincy Jr. like this:

Q. Where did they stand?
A. They stood *opposite* Mr. *Lewis Deblois* shop.[16]

Such references to spatial location may have effectively tied legal claims to factual evidence. Yet the difficulty with either directive or relative spatial indexing is that such words as "to the right" or "opposite" fail to qualify how far to the right or exactly what something is oppo-

14. This breakdown of trades among witnesses is abstracted from testimony given in this case; see "No. 64. Rex v. Wemms," in *LPJA*, 3:101–222.

15. *LPJA*, 3:181 n; emphasis added. See also W. Lance Bennett, "Storytelling in Criminal Trials: A Model of Social Judgment," *Quarterly Journal of Speech* 64, no. 1 (1978): 1–22.

16. *LPJA*, 3:178 n; emphasis added.

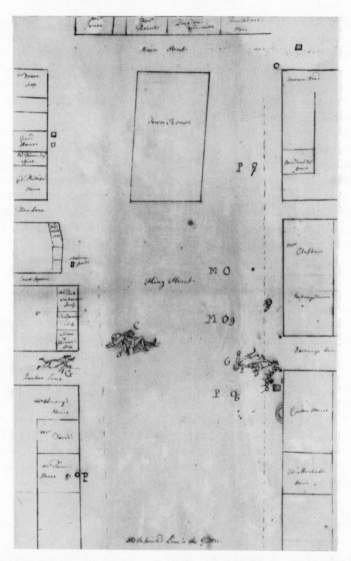

Fig. 15.2. Paul Revere, *Plan of the Scene of the Boston Massacre used at the Trial of Captain Preston*, Boston, 1770 [?]. Ink on paper. (Photo: Courtesy of the Trustees of the Boston Public Library.)

site, making legal argument based on them less than convincing. More satisfactory, perhaps, was the testimony of block-maker James Brewer, who, although he retained the directive "above" in his speech, referred to actual linear distance when questioned by prosecutor Samuel Quincy:

Q. How near were you to the soldiers when they fired?
A. I was about *ten or fifteen feet* from them. I stood in the street just *above* Royal-Exchange-lane, about *six or seven feet from the gutter*.
Q. Could you see the whole part?
A. Yes, they stood in a circle, or half moon.[17]

Still other witnesses compared distances in the marketplace with those in the courtroom's performance zone and in so doing anchored their speech in two places at once. The place of narration, or discursive domain of a given utterance, matters greatly to its indexical structure and also clarifies the interdependence of material setting and oral performance. When Samuel Quincy asked Joseph Croswell, tailor, "How near were you to the bayonet?" Croswell replied, as he looked toward Lynde, Cushing, Oliver, and Trowbridge on the high bench, "About the same distance I am from the judges, *viz.* six feet." When he asked James Carter, writing-school master, "How nigh were you to him?" the teacher responded, "As nigh as I am to you, Sir, *viz.* three feet off."[18]

Because narrative authority and claims to speaking the "real truth" are in part shaped by the spatial context of a performance—who is standing where and talking to whom, and how close or far apart they are while conversing—the interior arrangement of colonial courtrooms makes these witness statements more immediate. English prints commonly depicted the clutter of courtroom space, with sitting judges, the jury, a table for the clerk, lawyers, and the box for the witness all in close proximity (fig. 15.3). The trappings of Crown authority—red robes, wigs, royal coat of arms— were intimidating, especially in a colonial situation such as eighteenth-century Boston, a port that had seen its fair share of British imperial intervention in the forms of press gangs, currency loss, and taxation. Although no plan of Boston's 1769 Queen Street courtroom is extant (documents, however, reveal it was thirty-five feet wide), a "court chamber" in nearby Salem offers clues to its interior arrangement. In 1763, Salem refitted the courtroom in its old 1718 town house, and a measured plan was taken that shows the location of the judge's bench, the justices' benches, the jury seats, and in the middle of the room a large table for the work of the clerk. Before the table was the bar, with two witness boxes (one for the defense and one for prosecution?), and a seat for the lawyers (fig. 15.4).[19] The overall dimensions of the Salem courtroom were smaller than the Boston

17. Ibid., p. 113; emphasis added.
18. Ibid., p. 141 n.
19. Court of General Sessions of the Peace, Essex County, Massachusetts, Record Book, 6:2 (March 1764), Peabody-Essex Museum, Salem, Massachusetts. The plan is in "Essex County Courts," Mss. Collections, box 1, folder 1, Peabody-Essex Museum. I am indebted to Martha McNamara for bringing the plan to my attention.

Fig. 15.3. *Mr Alderman Wilkes in his Magisterial Character at the Sessions House in the Old Bailey.* Engraving, from the *Oxford Magazine* 4 (1770), opposite p. 221. (Photo: Bodleian Library, University of Oxford, Shelfmark: Hope Adds 284.)

space—it was only twenty feet wide—but the cramped placement of principal interior fittings resembled its English counterparts closely.

A variant plan survives in the courtroom in the Colony House in Newport, Rhode Island, designed in 1739 by architect Richard Mundy (fig. 15.5). In this case a similar configuration existed for the judge's high bench, side benches for justices or jury, and table below the judges for the clerk; location of bar, witness boxes, and lawyers' seats are unfortunately less clear. But while the seats for spectators are not indicated in the Salem plan, in Newport they were probably curved to afford spectators an ample view of the proceedings. In each case, these court chambers materialized relations of social hierarchy and deference.[20] Recall from the testimony of Croswell and Carter that witnesses sat about six feet from the judges and three feet from the lawyers. Operating in a constricted space

20. On the Newport courtroom, see Norman M. Isham, "The Colony House at Newport, Rhode Island," *Old-Time New England* 8, no. 2 (1917): 3–21. I am indebted to Carl Lounsbury for sharing his research on the Newport courtroom space with me; letter from Lounsbury to author, January 13, 1997.

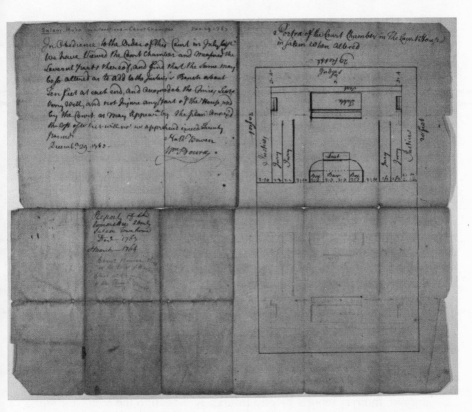

Fig. 15.4. Portra[it] of the Court Chamber in the Court House in Salem When Altered. December 29, 1763, ink on paper. (Photo: Courtesy, Peabody Essex Museum, Salem, Mass.)

between justices' bench and witness box, the lawyers thus held forth on a stage roughly four feet by nine feet. They felt the constant gaze of spectators, jury, and magistrates. As historians Greg Roeber and Rhys Isaac have argued for colonial Virginia, the courtroom was a theater where lawyers stood front and center as historical "actors," trading like merchants with other people's talk.[21]

As they told their stories of what had happened, witnesses also made common use of reported speech, a technique by which people create drama and lend truth to their statements by incorporating aspects of other people's utterances into their own. In legal discourse reported speech is

21. See A. G. Roeber, "Authority, Law, and Custom: The Rituals of Court Day in Tidewater, Virginia, 1720–1750," in *Material Life in America, 1600–1860*, ed. Robert Blair St. George (Boston, 1988), pp. 419–38, and Rhys Isaac, *The Transformation of Virginia, 1740–1790* (Chapel Hill, N.C., 1982), pp. 88–94.

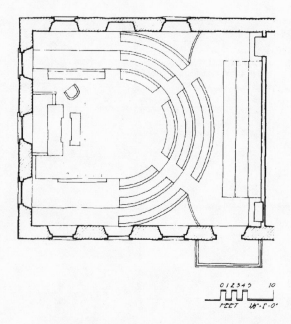

Fig. 15.5. Courtroom plan, Old Colony House, Newport, Rhode Island, with interior arrangement of ca. 1770–1840[?]. (Drawing: Douglas R. Taylor; courtesy of Carl Lounsbury.)

used frequently. As the linguistic anthropologist Susan U. Philips has argued, indirect reports help to insert a witness into the scene and build an evidentiary background for her or his claims. Indirect reports emerge constantly in the Massacre trial records, as individuals mustered force for their public narratives. Indirect reports often draw on other languages, such as slander, insults, and cursing. Richard Hirons, a physician, recalled action outside his house late on March 5: "The next thing I recollect in the affair was, a little boy came down the alley, clapping his hand to his head, and cried he was killed, he was killed; on which one of the officers took hold of him, and damned him for a little rascal, asking him what business he had out of doors; the boy seemed to be about seven or eight year old."[22] In this passage, Hirons described the small boy's gesture, as well as indirectly quoted the words the soldier said to the boy. He used indirect quotation as a means of interpreting what he heard to the speech situation of the courtroom; his statement evaluates the soldier's language based on what he thinks his listeners in court want to hear.

22. *LPJA,* 3:184. On the relative legal uses of direct and indirect quotation, see Susan U. Philips, "Reported Speech as Evidence in an American Trial," in *Languages and Linguistics: The Interdependence of Theory, Data, and Application,* ed. Deborah Tannen and James E. Alatis (Washington, D.C., 1986), pp. 154–55, 168–69.

This background documentation is very different from direct quotation, in which a speaker reframes the "actual words" of an individual to allow listeners to evaluate the words for themselves, to bring them into a dialogue from which they can take their own primary interpretations; Hirons stated the little boy "cried he was killed, he was killed." Merchant Richard Palmes described his interchange with Captain Preston before the firing began: "I went to Capt. *Preston*, and saw Mr. Theodore Bliss talking with him, who said to Capt. *Preston*,'Why do you not fire,''God damn you fire.' I slipt betwixt them and asked Capt. *Preston* if the soldiers were loaded he said yes, with powder and ball: I said I hope Sir you are not going to fire upon the inhabitants, he said by no means." Reported speech can also combine direct and indirect strategies, as in jeweler Alexander Cruckshank's account of hearing boys talking to the sentry: "Before the box stood about twelve or fourteen lads, I often saw the boys go towards them and back to the Sentinel with a fresh repetition of oaths, they said to him damn you, you son of a bitch, called him lobster and rascal, wished he was in hell's flames, often and often lowly rascal." Here, the "they said" cues a direct quotation ("damn you, you son of a bitch"), while the words "called him" and "wished he" signal a movement into indirection. Reported speech can be indirect, direct, or a combination of the two. This technique is common in narrative, a technique that good storytellers learn to manipulate. But in court, lawyers, jurors, and judges paid special attention to words set apart through the dramatic use of direct quotation, because these announce themselves as "true" and therefore more effective in legal argument. Direct quotation is a technique for deliberately foregrounding the criminal actions for which a person has been charged.[23] It is also a means, through heightened drama, of encouraging empathy for the defense argument as being imbued with direct human feeling.

II.

Witnesses claimed narrative legitimacy by contextually grounding their claims to truth through spatial deixis and reported speech. But the

23. Ibid., pp. 184 (Hirons), 118–19 (Palmes), 190 (Cruckshank). Philips,"Reported Speech as Evidence," is based on contemporary courtrooms and twentieth-century concepts of admissible evidence. While I agree that direct quotation certainly dramatizes the relevance of the testimony in some instances, there is simply too much of it going on in the Massacre trial records to support Philips's restrictive claim that "quoting is reserved for information being presented as evidence directly related to proof of the elements of a criminal charge" (p. 154). This may have been more the case, as we shall see, with the use of quoted materials by the lawyers; since the witnesses were not "coached" for dramatic statements, there is no way to insist that quotes were used in this manner during their narratives. For additional insight on oral strategies and the law, see Jane H. Hill and Judith T. Irvine, eds., *Responsibility and Evidence in Oral Discourse* (New York, 1993).

lawyers confronted the witnesses' rich use of these techniques by subtly transforming them into elements of their own arguments. They too drew heavily on reported speech to manipulate both directly and indirectly quoted materials to dramatic effect; indeed, the skill lawyers brought to English culture was an ability to manipulate dialogue as a means of constituting their own centralized authority. Their speech was infused with the aesthetics of mercantilism, a colonial cultural order based on media of symbolic exchange—money, labor, commodities, language—being channeled into concentrated zones of production and reproduction.[24]

Consider, for example, how the Massacre lawyers reported direct quotations. Crown prosecutor Samuel Quincy altered the literal sense of what one witness had earlier stated. Here, for example, is a portion of Edward G. Langford's dialogue with Quincy while on the stand. Langford begins by recalling his encounter with Samuel Gray, after which Quincy's questions turn to his exchange with Matthew Kilroy, one of the soldiers on trial:

A. . . . and *Samuel Gray* , who was shot that night, came and struck me on the shoulder, and said, *Langford*, what's here to pay.

Q. What said you to Gray then?

A. I said I did not know what was to pay, but I believed something would come of it by and bye. He made no reply. Immediately a gun went off. I was within reach of their guns and bayonets; one of them thrust at me with his bayonet, and run it through my jacket and great coat. . . .

Q. You spoke to him [Kilroy] you say before he fired, what did you say to him?

A. I said either damn you, or God damn you do not fire, and immediately he fired.

Q. What in particular made you say do not fire?

A. Hearing the other guns go off.

Q. How many guns went off before he fired?

A. Two: but I saw nobody fall. *Gray* fell close to me. I was standing leaning on my stick.

Quincy then summarized this exchange in his argument notes for his own purposes:

About this time *Gray*, one of the unhappy sufferers, came and clapped *Langford* on the shoulder, saying what's here to pay? *Langford* replies, I do not know, but something I believe will come of it by and by; . . . *Langford* spoke

24. See James H. Bunn, "The Aesthetics of British Mercantilism," *New Literary History* 11 (1980): 303–21.

to *Killroy*, and after two guns were discharged, seeing him present his piece, said to him, damn you are you going to fire? Presently upon this *Killroy* levelled his piece, and firing directly at *Gray*, killed him dead on the spot![25]

Along with embedding the witness's words in his own rhetorical flourish, Quincy also created direct quotations that were in variance with what, according to the transcript, Langford had actually said. The lawyer subtly changed certain words to boost their theatrical effect (from "struck" to "clapped"); altered the tense of some verbs from past to present to make actions represented in oral testimony more immediate (from "I said I did not know" to "I do not know"); and shifted the most crucial line from an indeterminate command to an interrogative (from "I said either damn you, or God damn you do not fire" to "*Langford* spoke to *Killroy*, and . . . said to him, damn you are you going to fire?"). Quincy thus modified Langford's testimony in preparing a public argument.

The trial transcript abounds with such instances, including ones in which indirect quotations by witnesses are transformed by the lawyers into direct quotations so as to heighten their dramatic value in court. Nathaniel Fosdick, a Boston hatter, narrated his encounter with a soldier's bayonet: "I asked one the reason of his pushing at me? he damn'd my blood, and bid me stand out of their way." In his argument, Samuel Quincy changed this statement to read, "Mr. *Fosdick*, deposes that upon his going down *King-street*, the first salutation he had, was the pressing of soldiers behind him with the points of their bayonets, crying out, damn your blood stand out of the way!"[26] Or consider the testimony of Nathaniel Thayer, describing the arrival of the soldiers: "There came seven soldiers from the *Main-Guard* without any coats on, driving along, swearing, cursing and damning like wild creatures, saying where are they? Cut them to pieces, slay them all." Samuel Quincy translated Thayer's words thus: "He saw seven soldiers in an undress coming down like wild creatures, with cutlasses in their hands, crying damn them, where are they?" Here Quincy dropped Thayer's description of the soldiers' speech style ("swearing, cursing and damning"), retained his "like wild creatures," added the flourished "cutlasses in their hands" from an altogether different witness's testimony, and dropped the directly quoted words "Cut them to pieces, slay them all" entirely from Thayer's statement.[27]

25. *LPJA*, 3:109–10, 146–47.

26. Ibid., pp. 129, 152. A similar instance of Samuel Quincy shifting a witness's indirect statement to a direct statement in argument appears with Samuel Hemmingway; see ibid., pp. 131, 152.

27. Ibid., pp. 138, 155.

Two additional examples will represent the many instances in which the lawyers subtly yet knowingly reformulated the reported speech of witnesses in order to strengthen the legal argument at hand. Closing for the defense, John Adams changed the verb tenses used by Crown witness Langford so as to heighten the dramatic impact of his testimony. Recall that Langford had described his encounter with Samuel Gray:

A. . . . and *Samuel Gray*, who was shot that night, came and struck me on the shoulder, and said, *Langford*, what's here to pay?
Q. What said you to Gray then?
A. I said I did not know what was to pay, but I believed something would come of it by and bye. He made no reply. Immediately a gun went off. I was within reach of their guns and bayonets; one of them thrust at me with his bayonet, and run it through my jacket and great coat.

In his jotted minutes of Crown testimony, defense attorney Adams transformed this passage of dialogue to read:

At the Party, S. Gray came to me, took me by the shoulder and said what is here to pay? I said I dont know but *I believe Something or other would come of it, by and by*. S. Gray was just by me, when the 1st Gun went off. I stood so near that they might have reached me, and they did. A Bayonet went thro my Cloaths.

Based on this transcribed note, Adams in his summary argument offered the following version of what Langford had "actually" said:

Langford goes on "*Gray* struck me on the shoulder and asked me what is to pay? I answered, I don't know but I believe something will come of it, by and bye."—Whence could this apprehension of mischief arise, if *Langford* did not think the assault, the squabble, the affray was such as would provoke the soldiers to fire?—"a bayonet went through my great coat and jacket," yet the soldier did not step out of his place.[28]

In his original testimony, Langford had used the past tense throughout: "I said I did not know," "I believed something would come of it." But when Adams jotted his minute, he changed both these to the present tense ("I don't know but I believe something will come of it"), a crucial temporal shift needed to bring the damaging implication of Gray's question more dramatically before the jury—namely, that an "apprehension of mischief" was already in the air. The present tense more effectively brought jury and court face-to-face, in temporal terms, with the incident at hand. In his

28. Ibid., pp. 109, 108, 267.

final argument Adams shifted Gray's key line from being quoted directly in Langford's own words ("*Gray* . . . came . . . and said, '*Langford*, what's here to pay?' ") to one embedded in another ("*Langford* goes on '*Gray* . . . asked me what is to pay?' "), therefore rendering it less compelling. With this single move, Adams reduced the impact of a Crown witness's words in a way that helped to support his own argument in the case—that the soldiers were hapless victims of the illegal "mobbishness" of a few alienated Irishmen, sailors, and one "Indian from Framingham" named Crispus Attucks.

In a final instance, Adams totally rearranged witness testimony to achieve a more compelling, compressed argument. When James Bailey was originally examined by Crown prosecutor Quincy, the sequence of his seeing Attucks, a Natick Indian but called a "molatto" throughout the trial, was key:

1 Q. Did you see a number of persons coming up *Royal-exchange-lane*, with sticks?
2 A. No, I saw a number going up *Cornhill*, and the Molatto fellow headed them.
3 Q. Was this before the guard came down or after?
4 A. It was before the guard came down.
5 Q. How many might there be of that party?
6 A. Betwixt twenty and thirty: they appeared to be sailors; some had sticks, some had none. The Molatto fellow, had a large cord-wood stick.
7 Q. Did they come down *King-street* afterwards?
8 A. I did not see them come down. I did not see the Molatto afterwards, till I saw him dead.
9 Q. Which way was the Molatto with his party going, when you saw them?
10 A. Right towards the Town-pump.
11 Q. Which way did you go into *King-street*?
12 A. I went up *Royal-exchange-lane*.
13 Q. How long before the firing, was it, you saw them in *Cornhill*?
14 A. Six, seven, or eight minutes, I believe.

From this dialogue Adams took his courtroom minute, which selected from Bailey's discourse only four lines and arranged them in the sequence lines 2, 6, 14, 13: "*Saw the Molatto at the Head of 25 or 30 sailors with Clubbs some of em. Molatto had a large Cord wood stick. It was 7 or 8 Minutes before the firing that I saw them in Cornhill.*" In his argument, however, Adams reordered these four pieces of Bailey's testimony—lines 2, 14, 13, 6—and presented them, despite his fabrication of Bailey's words, as a direct quote: "*Bailey* 'Saw the Molatto seven or eight minutes before the firing, at the head of twenty or thirty sailors in *Corn-hill*, and he had a large cord-wood stick.' "[29] Through a variety a linguistic means, including changing tenses, dropping phrases, shifting the relationship of indirect and direct reported speech, and selectively indexing known places and times, the Massacre lawyers reconstituted the words of witnesses to make their own words more persuasive.

Although lawyers had long depended on their skill in reformulating the testimony of others, it was precisely this skill that had brought accusations of falsehood and duplicity to their ranks. Antilawyer sentiment surfaced continually in colonial New England, despite the fact that many of its early political leaders and ministers had training in the common law. In 1690 Boston merchant John Saffin recorded a "Saying of Pius the 2d That those that went to law were the Birds, the Court the field, the Judge the Nett and the Lawyers the fowlers." A Massachusetts almanac of 1740 warned that "Politicians encrease daily. / While lawyers get, the People lose. / How raving Mad are Men big with Conceit." Nine years later another almanac rhymed an insult: "The Lawyer's Tongues they never freeze, / If warm'd with honest Client's fees." All this was before lawyers in Suffolk and Essex Counties decided to form associations to legitimize their professional standing.[30]

III.

People despised common lawyers because they made their living off the unfortunate affairs of fellow citizens and were generally people of middling birth using the law as an entree to higher levels of society and political power. One way lawyers sought to redress continual antilawyer sentiment was to trade on classical oratory and the language of civic virtue. As Stephen Botein has suggested, New England lawyers, as well as many ministers and educated merchants, were "infatuated" with Cicero, owing in part to the popularity of Thomas Gordon's 1744 edition of Cicero's orations against Catiline, a volume that quickly became required reading for the radical political community in both England and America. In Boston the "Sodalitas" for young lawyers formed by Jeremiah Gridley in the 1760s was, in member John Adams's words, "a private Association for the study of law and oratory," and regular reading in both Tullus and Cicero on "the Three sorts of orations, the Demonstrative,

29. Ibid., pp. 117–18, 115, 268.

30. See John Saffin, *John Saffin, His Book (1665–1708): A Collection of Various Matters of Divinity, Law, and State Affairs Epitomiz'd both in Verse and Prose* (New York, 1928), p. 46; *The Essays, Humor, and Poems of Nathaniel Ames, Father and Son, of Dedham, Massachusetts, from their Almanacs, 1726–1775,* ed. Samuel Briggs (Cleveland, 1891), pp. 138 (1740 almanac), 212 (1749 almanac).

Deliberative, and Judicial, and the several parts of an oration, the Exordium & c." suggests that learning to speak well in public may have been as important to professional success as arguing technicalities in feudal law. James Otis, Josiah Quincy Jr., and John Adams all recognized the force of classical oratory, which Adams termed "New England Ciceronian" speech. The popularity of classical style among these trained attorneys also suggests that the many Boston lawyers who became effective political leaders could do so, in part, because they had mastered the hybridized speech style necessary in local politics to cultivate the support and identification of diverse constituencies.[31]

Aware of lingering antilawyer bias that might lead some to see the law's "worldly wisdom" as a "foolishness" before God, lawyers also sought to anchor secular judgment in the sacred Word. Religious discourse appears throughout the Massacre trial proceedings. Perhaps this is to be expected, for as historian John M. Murrin has shown, most lawyers in early New England turned to the law only after first considering the ministry (as had John Adams) or actually having served in the pulpit.[32] Josiah Quincy's arguments for the defense are a case in point. Cautioning the jury not to capitulate to "eye for an eye" justice, he urged them not to be distracted by "any endeavour to mislead our judgment on this occasion; by drawing our attention to the precepts delivered in the days of *Moses*; and by disconnected passages of Scriptures, applied in a manner foreign to their original design or import." Having said that, Quincy himself went on to do a bit of "disconnected passage" selection, on the dangers that ensue from a return to a vengeful Mosaic law. He glossed Numbers 35:6–15 with the following statement: "For we find, the *Jews* had their six cities of refuge, to which the manslayer might flee, from the avenger of blood." And from Numbers 35:31, "You shall take no satisfaction for the life of a *murderer*, which is *guilty of death*." Quincy paused here to speculate that the phrase "guilty of death" was actually a mistaken translation of the original text, which he argued should instead read "faulty to die." He returned to this line in his concluding speech to the jury: "May the blessing of those, who were in jeopardy of life, come upon you—may the blessing of him who is *'not faulty to die'* [that is, Christ] discend and rest

31. *DAJA*, 1:251–55. See Stephen Botein, "Cicero as Role Model for Early American Lawyers: A Case Study in Classical 'Influence,' " *Classical Journal* 73, no. 4 (1978): 313–22, and Botein, afterword to *"Mr. Zenger's Malice and Falsehood": Six Issues of the "New-York Weekly Journal,"* 1733–34, ed. Botein (Worcester, Mass., 1985), p. 48. For another source of classical rhetorical style common in New England, see Thomas Gordon, *The Works of Sallus, Translated into English. With Political Discourses upon that Author* (London, 1744).

32. John M. Murrin, "The Legal Transformation: The Bench and Bar of Eighteenth-Century Massachusetts," in *Colonial America: Essays in Politics and Social Development*, ed. Stanley N. Katz (Boston, 1971), pp. 425–29.

upon you and your posterity."[33] John Adams had already likened law to religion when, in preparing his defense summation for the Preston case, he cited with approval Algernon Sidney's view that "Law no Passion can disturb," because it retains "Some Measure of divine perfection." Now he drew upon this same passage in summing up his defense for the accused soldiers. The law, like the Lord, "will preserve a steady, undeviating course" and "commands that which is good, and punishes that which is evil in all, whether rich, or poor, high or low,—'Tis deaf, inexorable, inflexible."[34]

With intertextuality thus at the center of their occupation's collective résumé, the Massacre lawyers, not surprisingly, drew at last on one another's speech throughout the proceedings. They referenced one another in their arguments, quoting (and often misquoting slightly) critical passages at the bar from the trial at hand and sometimes even from previous trials. Opening for the Crown, Samuel Quincy stated, "I remember at the last tryal [for Thomas Preston], my brother Adams made this observation, that 'Man is a social creature, that his feelings, his passions, his imaginations are contagious,' " a passage noted in Quincy's minutes simply as "Man is a Social Creature. His Passions and Ima[gi]nation Contagious." Not to be outdone, Josiah Quincy Jr. quoted the same statement during his argument for the defense: "For as was elegantly expressed, by a learned Gentleman at the late trial, 'The passions of man, nay his very imaginations are contagious.' " Such quotation usually functioned to undercut the opposition's argument, as when Samuel Quincy observed, "It has been represented 'that the life of a Soldier is thought to be less valuable among us than the life of a private Subject' than which nothing can be more ill founded."[35]

The Massacre lawyers also quoted published legal texts. Although we may be used to seeing lawyers in film and on television speaking extemporaneously, lawyers in the eighteenth century often read aloud from books in open court. Crown prosecutors Quincy and Paine limited their textual references to a total of six books. But defense lawyers Quincy and Adams cited a total of nineteen. These written (and printed) sources, ranging from such standards as Coke's *Institutes* and Blackstone's *Commentaries* to Dalton's *Country Justice* and Hawkins's *Pleas of the Crown*,

33. *LPJA*, 3:234–35, 241.

34. Ibid., p. 269, quoting Algernon Sidney, *Discourses concerning Government*, 2d ed. (London, 1704), p. 288.

35. *LPJA*, 3:155–56, 166, 271. Here the passage Samuel Quincy believed he actually was referencing from Josiah Quincy's opening defense argument agreed: "An opinion has been entertained by many among us, that the life of a soldier, was of little value: of much less value, than others of the community. The law Gentleman, knows no such distinction; the life of a soldier is viewed by the equal eye of the law, as estimable, as the life of any other citizen" (ibid., p. 160).

were thus drawn into the attorneys' oral performance. Samuel Quincy began his opening statement by clarifying "a distinction is made in the books betwixt malice and hatred, and a good distinction it is; I have it in my hand and will read it." Adams prefaced his argument for the defense by stating that "I will read the words of the law itself," continued with "I shall now, read to you a few authorities on this subject of self-defense," and concluded by reminding the court, "I have endeavoured to produce the best authorities, and to give you the rules of law in their words, for I desire not to advance any thing of my own."[36]

It is one thing to quote legal texts in extenso in open court, but quite another to alter them to fit the situation. Adams, for example, presented the court with a direct quotation on riots from Hawkins's *Pleas of the Crown*: "It is necessary to consider what is a riot. 1 Hawk. c. 65 2. I shall give you the definition of it, 'Wheresoever more than three persons use force or violence, for their accomplishment of any design whatsoever, all concerned are rioters.' " But the actual passage cited from Hawkins reads differently: "Where-ever more than three Persons use force and violence, in the Execution of any Design whatever wherein the law does not allow the Use of such Force, all who are concerned therein are Rioters."[37] Printed legal texts also allowed Adams to qualify his many quotations, some of which were themselves made up of quotes. In one instance he announced that Hale "quotes Crompton, 25. Dalton 93, p. 241," and in another, that Foster's *Crown Cases* referred to one case "mentioned by Hale" and another "cited by Hale."[38] By drawing into their oral performance reported writing, which typically employs a greater number of second- and third-person pronouns, simpler sentence structures, and standard-ized punctuation, the Massacre lawyers extended the range of styles they could deploy in argument and, in particular, the ways in which they could create and manipulate moral distance through language. The pub-lic reading from legal texts and such shorthand references as "Crompton, 25. Dalton 93, p. 241" also closely parallels the rehearsal of scriptural cita-tion at the center of Puritan liturgy and household devotional practice.[39]

As they sought to convert judges and jurors to the "truth" of their argu-

36. Ibid., pp. 147, 242, 245, 253.

37. Ibid., pp. 252, 253.

38. Ibid., p. 251.

39. See the critical overview in Wallace Chafe and Deborah Tannen, "The Relation between Written and Spoken Language," *Annual Review of Anthropology* 16 (1987): 383–407. Viewing the playful aspects of the relationship of oral and written language (rather than seeing them as part of a "crisis of representation") is especially useful in the early modern period, when both codes were still being standardized and when rules for writing and speaking were influencing one another; see Walter Ong, "Oral Residue in Tudor Prose Style," in his *Rhetoric, Romance, and Technology: Studies in the Interaction of Expression and Culture* (Ithaca, 1971), pp. 38–43, and Marshall McLuhan, "The Effect of the Printed Book on Language in the Sixteenth

ments, lawyers seem also to have drawn on the emotional preaching styles of New Light ministers, especially the kind of extemporaneous speaking known in the sermons of such celebrated itinerants as George Whitefield and James Davenport. The particular "searching" style of Gilbert Tennent's sermonizing was closely linked to the lawyer's need to "examine" and search out the truth in witnesses and to have witnesses "examine" their own hearts and consciences prior to the revelation of truth. But the intersections between the theatrics of preaching and court-room performance emerge most clearly in James Harris's *An Essay on the Action Proper for the Pulpit* (1753).[40]

Harris wrote to convince preachers that they could enhance their spiri-tual message by attending more carefully to style in speech and gesture. The problem, he observed, was that "we see not a few manly, spirited, and decent Speakers at the *Bar*, on the *Bench*, and in the *Parliament* . . . and several excellent and wonderful *Actors* on the Stage. What is the reason," he pondered, "that we see so few becoming, natural, pathetic *Preachers*?" Harris argued that ministers should follow the lead of lawyers, politi-cians, and actors; by transforming their speech and demeanor, these fig-ures had transformed themselves into other characters. Using the actor as his key example, Harris offered this summary as a model for the clergy (and an early concept of performance):

> What is still more surprising on the theatre is this; Even a Profligate Actor shall sometimes, by the Stretch of Genius merely, sustain with prodigious success the most worthy Character. Indeed it is evident in this case, that *such* an Actor must in a manner quit *himself* during his Performance, and, by a sort of temporary Transformation, *assume* that Worthy Character which he personates: But now a Virtuous Actor, supporting his Genius Equal, hath manifestly an unspeakable advantage here. He doth not need to step out of himself into an Opposite kind of Being: he is already in some measure what he *represents*: You see in this instance the *Man* rather than the *Actor*.[41]

In fact, lawyers exploited the theatrical play with voices and personae used by New Light preachers to shape linguistic hybridity in their own image.

If legal discourse gained legitimacy as it continually referenced other languages, so too did courtrooms strategically implicate other places in

Century," in *Explorations in Communication*, ed. Edmund Carpenter and Marshall McLuhan (Boston, 1960), pp. 125–35.

40. See Harry S. Stout, *The New England Soul: Preaching and Religious Culture in Colonial New England* (New York, 1986), pp. 192–94 ("The Orality of Whitefield's Message"), 198–99; James Harris, *An Essay on the Action Proper for the Pulpit* (London, 1753; rpt., New York, 1971).

41. Harris, *Essay on the Action Proper*, p. 21.

the minds of spectators. The placement of the judges' bench and clerk's table referenced the pulpit and deacon's table of the New England meetinghouse. The curved seats in the Newport courtroom indexed the plans of English theaters, including one Inigo Jones had designed early in the seventeenth century (fig. 15.6). Indeed, at times courtrooms and theaters *were* interchangeable seats of personation and judgment in British culture; in 1766 James Woodforde noted in his diary that "I went to a Play at the Court House." As theater, the Massacre trial depended on some of its participants—the prisoners, witnesses, and lawyers for the defense—to encourage empathy (in the manner of seventeenth-century masques) in the jury, judges, and spectators, while insisting those on the side of the Crown cultivate distance as a performative tactic.[42]

IV.

Colonial lawyers hybridized speech genres as a means of attaining professional authority. By borrowing the languages of classical Roman virtue and Holy Scripture in particular, lawyers tied their trade to ethical moorings. Viewed more critically, lawyers used these languages to counter the destabilizing effects of their own linguistic appropriations by indexing the steadied moral ground of republican history and God's Word. Through these borrowed languages, lawyers adopted (following Hobbes) the "disguise, or outward appearance of a man, counterfeited upon the stage," shifting at once from dialogic interlocutor with witnesses to legal scholar citing authoritative texts, to classical orator defending freedom, to New Light minister seeking to "convert" the jury to his truth.

The borrowing and combination of languages did not escape notice during the period. In December 1758, for example, a young John Adams heard a friend speak in "Language taken partly from Scripture and partly from the drunken Disputes of Tavern Philosophy." The mixed language of Massacre lawyers was locally placed in courthouse performances but at the same time tied to the legal authority recorded in books that moved throughout Britain's colonial possessions. Even the courtroom context could not secure the meaning of this new breed of hybridized speech, as architecture and furnishings referenced other places outside the sensory surrounds of the trial itself. Indeed, the novel coupling of placed language and placeless knowledge served to enhance the dramatic impact of legal performance. Consider, for example, two of Adams's most graceful

42. James Woodforde, *Diary of a Country Parson*, ed. John Beresford, 4 vols. (London, 1924–31), 1:37–38. See the excellent discussion in Gloria Flaherty, "Empathy and Distance: Romantic Theories of Acting Reconsidered," *Theatre Research International* 15, no. 2 (1990): 125–41.

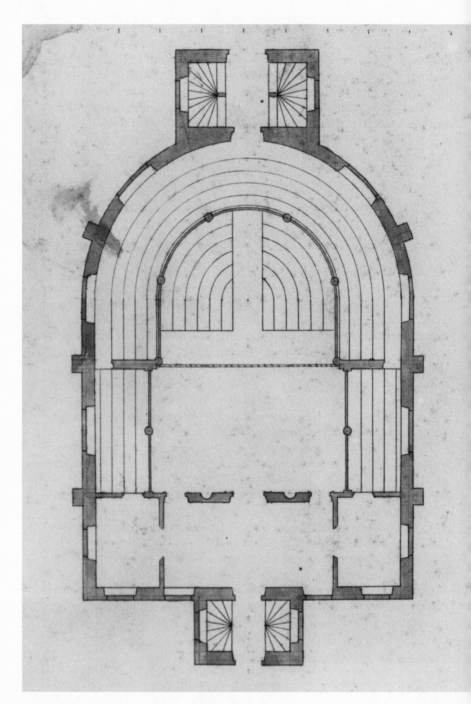

Fig. 15.6. Inigo Jones, design for theater, early seventeenth century. (Photo: The Provost and Fellows of Worcester College, University of Oxford.)

rhetorical flourishes during his lengthy defense summation. Knowing his colonial audience, Adams used language that, by tying ecclesiastical upheaval to the tradition of remarkable providences, would effectively resonate with the history of New England and gain local empathy:

> In the continual vicissitudes of human things amidst the shocks of fortune and the whirls of passion, that take place at certain critical seasons, even in the mildest government, the people are liable to run into riots and tumults. There are Church-quakes and state-quakes, in the moral and political world, as well as earth-quakes, storms, and tempests in the physical. This much however must be said in favour of the people and of human nature, that it is a general, if not universal truth, that the aptitude of the people to mutinies, seditions, tumults and insurrections, is in direct proportion to the despotism of the government.

Or take the powerful opening statement he fabricated by directly quoting the Marquis Bonesana Beccaria's *An Essay on Crimes and Punishments* (1767): "If I can but be the instrument of preserving one life, his blessing and tears of transport, shall be a sufficient consolation to me, for the contempt of all mankind."[43] With this single passage, Adams effectively fused his roles as religious orator (the lawyer as "instrument" for a higher good, as martyr gaining "consolation") and as liberal defender of English constitutional protection (despite universal "contempt").

Acutely aware of how language shaped understanding, Adams worked throughout the second Massacre trial to draw connections between law, religion, theater, the abstract world of legal texts, and the concrete world of the courtroom. The results, finally, were equally as concrete. On December 5, 1770, after just two and one-half hours of deliberation, the jury brought in its verdict: six of the eight soldiers were proclaimed not guilty, while two others, convicted of manslaughter, were punished solely by having their thumbs branded, and released. For Adams and Josiah Quincy Jr. the legal victory was rooted in careful research, philosophical commitment to the judicial process as a safeguard against tyranny, and a mastery of performative tactics in the crowded Boston courtroom. According to John Quincy Adams, he had "often heard, from individuals, who had been present among the crowd of spectators at the trial, the *elec-*

---

43. *DAJA*, 1:60; *LPJA*, 3:249–50, 242. See also John Locke, *An Essay concerning Human Understanding* (London, 1690), bk. 3, chap. 9 ("On the Imperfection of Words"), secs. 4–6. On the "implicative" or "reported" aspects of place, language, and event, see Robert Blair St. George, *Conversing by Signs: Poetics of Implication in Colonial New England Culture* (Chapel Hill, 1998), pp. 2–13. See also Terry Castle, "The Carnivalization of Eighteenth-Century Narrative," *Proceedings of the Modern Language Association* 99 (1984): 903–16.

trical effect produced upon the immense and excited auditory, by the first sentence with which he opened his defense."[44]

Legal discourse, like that of the eighteenth-century novel, cannibalized the speech genres and claims to authority of various social groups: local witnesses of different social ranks and occupations, philosophers, legal scholars, ancient orators, ministers, actors, and other lawyers. In so doing, these talkers charted new performative terrain that connected the ludic, dismantling tradition of the carnivalesque with an uncanny ability to anchor self-interest and political power in rhetorics of virtue and community morality, a terrain that would become more familiar as the Revolution approached. This new trade in talk destabilized both the sanctity of Canaan's code and its inversion in the dangerous words of insult, slander, and sedition. In colonial America, lawyers played the market economy of language to political advantage, using hybridity and dialogue not to subvert or massacre monologic authority but to claim it for themselves.

44. Quoted in *LPJA*, 3:28 (emphasis added).

"Neither male nor female": Jemima Wilkinson and the Politics of Gender in Post-Revolutionary America

SUSAN JUSTER

IN 1776, a memorable year in American history, a strange and (for some) truly wondrous occurrence took place in a small town in Rhode Island. A young woman named Jemima Wilkinson took to her bed with a lingering illness of vague origin, appearing several hours later with a miraculous tale of death and rebirth. She had, so she claimed, died and been reincarnated as the second coming of Christ, a transfiguration so complete that she refused from that point on to answer to the name "Jemima Wilkinson." In her new role as messiah and prophet, the "Publick Universal Friend"—as she now styled herself—took to the highways and byways of New England, preaching a message of apocalyptic destruction. The public fascination with this strange figure, who abandoned not only her given name but her identity as a woman as well, dressing in men's clothes and speaking in a "masculine, authoritative" voice, reached its peak just as the Revolutionary War was heating up. She aroused opposition wherever she preached; crowds jeered her in Rhode Island and mobbed the house where she was staying on a tour of Philadelphia, throwing "brick-bats" and other debris at her entourage. Her short but spectacular career as a religious visionary ended, as did so many others in the late eighteenth and early nineteenth centuries, in an obscure settlement in western New York she named "New Jerusalem," where she and a handful of devotees sought refuge after the debacle in Philadelphia.

Why was Jemima Wilkinson so fascinating to her fellow Americans in the 1770s and 1780s? And why should she, who made no lasting impression on American religious culture, interest us today? The answer, I think, lies not in her peculiar theology (which was a rather conventional brand of Old Testament millennialism) or even in her messianic ambitions but rather in the *figure* she presented to her audiences: the cross-dressed actress or impostor.[1] Everywhere she went she invited scorn and ridicule for her masculine dress and melodramatic retellings of the terrible script of revelation. As one observer recalled some years later, "What she said, or of the subject matter, nothing is remembered; but her person, dress and manner is as palpable . . . as though she thus looked and spake but yesterday."[2] Public hostility to her self-proclaimed status as the second Christ was surprisingly muted; audiences reacted more to her external appearance than her internal transformation. Jemima Wilkinson was an actress (and I mean this not as a judgment on her sincerity but as a statement about her public persona) on the stage of American religious theater in the 1780s, and her story is symptomatic of a larger conjunction of historical forces in the Revolutionary era that rendered the stage a fitting symbol of eighteenth-century culture.

The starting point for my discussion is the fascinating convergence now taking place between the language of feminist theory and the language of religious studies. At the same time that feminist theorists are coming to speak of gender as a "style" or an "act" that is in some sense external to identity, so too are historians of religion increasingly making use of theatrical or performative metaphors to convey the experiential and cultural dimensions of faith.[3] The "dramaturgical" approach used so effectively by Rhys Isaac to portray the evangelical challenge to gentry culture in Virginia has had a deep influence on the field of religious studies, from Harry Stout's fine biography of George Whitefield (the "Divine Dramatist") to Leigh Eric Schmidt's study of the rituals of communion and revival in Scotland and America. In these studies, the eighteenth century has emerged as the period in which the synthesis of stage and pulpit represented most unabashedly by Whitefield revitalized popular religious culture on both sides of the Atlantic. While Wilkinson's seventeenth-century Puritan forebears were notorious for their hostility to the theater, which seemed to them to mock the integrity of the human soul by celebrating the

1. Catherine A. Brekus explores Wilkinson's theology and her struggles as a female preacher in an era of unstable gender norms in *Strangers and Pilgrims: Female Preaching in America, 1740–1845* (Chapel Hill, NC, 1998), pp. 80–97.

2. Quoted in John F. Watson, *Annals of Philadelphia and Pennsylvania in the Olden Days* (Philadelphia, 1870), 1:554.

3. On gender as "styles of the flesh," see Judith Butler, *Gender Trouble: Feminism and the Subversion of Identity* (New York, 1990), and Nina Auerbach, *Private Theatricals: The Lives of the Victorians* (Cambridge, Mass., 1990). On "styles of manhood," see Clyde Griffen, "Reconstructing Masculinity from the Evangelical Revival to the Waning of Progressivism: A Speculative Synthesis," in *Meanings for Manhood: Constructions of Masculinity in Victorian America,* ed. Mark Carnes and Clyde Griffen (Chicago, 1990), p. 183.

artifice of the player, newer evangelical groups such as the Methodists succeeded in appropriating the conventions of the theater for their own purposes. Like those actors he so greatly admired, Whitefield was not afraid to assume female as well as male personas in his sermons, especially that of the laboring woman struggling to deliver the word of God. As a sarcastic observer wrote, "He talks of a Sensible New Birth—then belike he is in Labour, and the good Women around him are come to his assistance. He dilates himself, cries out [and] is at last delivered." Whitefield "played the woman" on numerous occasions to thousands of rapt listeners, eliciting "the woman" in his audience as well as they were reduced to tears and physical tremors by the sheer power of his words.[4]

The distance between Whitefield and his Puritan predecessors cannot be measured in time alone; there was a vast emotional and expressive gulf between the plain, asexual style of the Puritans and the flamboyant, highly sexualized style of eighteenth-century revivalists.[5] Whitefield represents a significant trend in the economy of religious expression from the seventeenth to the eighteenth centuries, as he strove to externalize—to make palpable—the passionate feelings that for Puritans were to remain subdued in the inner recesses of the heart. In embracing the theater, Whitefield also embraced a more overtly feminized form of religious expression, for the stage had always been indelibly associated with the dangers of feminization (the cross-dressed actor, the unleashing of passions) in early modern cultural commentary.

The rise and spread of itinerants throughout the American colonies in the years of the First Great Awakening heralded the arrival of a new market-based model of society, one that drew on theatrical metaphors to represent a spiritual community bound together more by language and the "performance" of piety than by locality or institutions. Itinerants like Whitefield and his American disciples, the Tennents, were "living metaphors for flux and disorder," in Timothy Hall's words, men who transgressed not only the spatial boundaries of church and town but also the cultural categories in which Americans were accustomed to think of themselves and their society. It was precisely this rupturing of the personal and collective categories of identity by market-based practices that, in Jean-Christophe Agnew's formulation, allowed the theater to become

4. Quoted in Harry Stout, *The Divine Dramatist: George Whitefield and the Rise of Modern Evangelicalism* (Grand Rapids, Mich., 1991), p. 40; see also Rhys Isaac, *The Transformation of Virginia, 1740–1790* (Chapel Hill, N.C., 1982), and Leigh Eric Schmidt, *Holy Fairs: Scottish Communions and American Revivals in the Early Modern Period* (Princeton, 1989).

5. On the sexualized nature of revivalist preaching, see George Rawlyk, *Ravished by the Spirit: Religious Revivals, Baptists, and Henry Alline* (Kingston, Canada, 1984), and Henry Abelove, *The Evangelist of Desire: John Wesley and the Methodists* (Stanford, 1990).

such a powerful tool of cultural representation in the early modern world, and we can see in itinerancy the seeds of a peculiarly American form of consumer culture.[6]

When Jemima Wilkinson first emerged on the public scene in Rhode Island in 1776, she thus appeared before audiences already well primed by two generations of traveling evangelists to expect a greater theatricality in public religious performances. Yet she never elicited the kind of popular response that her itinerant predecessors had enjoyed. Whitefield moved thousands to weep for their lost souls through the power of his oratory, but Wilkinson was more likely to draw jeers than tears. As a woman she perhaps did not have the same artistic license that male preachers had to experiment with different gender personas in their spiritual performances. Colonial audiences would accept a laboring Whitefield more readily than a woman who presumed to preach like a man; when Bathsheba Kingsley stole her husband's horse in 1741 to "wander about from house to house, and very frequently to other towns, under a notion of doing Christ's work and delivering his messages," she was ridiculed by the revivalist Jonathan Edwards as a "brawling woman." The disparity in the transgressive behaviors permitted men and women in the colonial period does not tell the whole story, however. For Jemima Wilkinson appeared at a particularly anxious moment in the history of American gender politics, a moment when, in the words of an anonymous contributor to the *Worcester Spy*, Americans had "broken the line that divided the sexes."[7] It is almost too neat a coincidence that the newspaper war occasioned by her disastrous tour of Philadelphia broke into print in 1787, the very year in which Americans were engaged in a bitter debate over the future of the fragile new republic.

Seventeen eighty-seven was also a watershed year in the history of American theater; Royall Tyler's *The Contrast*, the first drama written by an American playwright, premiered that spring in New York City. Appearing contemporaneously with the first professional theatrical troupes in the former colonies, Wilkinson seemed to many Americans to embody the best and the worst features of the stage. When her performances succeeded, she was hailed as a charismatic seer; when they failed, she was castigated as a designing impostor. Throughout the politically charged decades of the 1770s and, especially, the 1780s, she served as an unsettling metaphor for the future of the American republic itself. Would

6. Timothy D. Hall, *Contested Boundaries: Itinerancy and the Reshaping of the Colonial American Religious World* (Durham, N.C., 1994), p. 6; Jean-Christophe Agnew, *Worlds Apart: The Market and the Theater in Anglo-American Thought, 1550–1750* (New York, 1986). My admiration for and intellectual debt to Agnew's study will be readily apparent.

7. The case of Bathsheba Kingsley is discussed by Catherine Brekus in *Strangers and Pilgrims*, pp. 23–26 (quotations are on p. 24); *Worcester Spy*, April 24, 1788.

politics transcend the petty factionalism that threatened to turn government into a theater of empty gesture and meaningless rhetoric, or would civic virtue reassert itself as the "true" spirit of the revolution? Only by placing the commentary surrounding Wilkinson in the context of contemporary debates over the fragility of *all* social forms, from government to the human body, can we appreciate her significance as a cultural marker.

I.

Jemima Wilkinson's own account of her ministry begins with a story of transfiguration:

> The heavens were open'd and she saw [two] Archangels descending from the east . . . and the Angels said, the Spirit of Life from God had descended to earth, to warn a lost and guilty, perishing, dying World, to flee from the wrath which is to come. . . . And then taking her leave of the family between the hour of nine and ten in the morning, dropped the dying flesh & yielded up the Ghost. And according to the declaration of the Angels, the Spirit took full possession of the Body it now Animates.[8]

Once reborn as the spirit of Christ (and there is persistent and deliberate confusion throughout her writings about the extent to which her reincarnation was merely spiritual rather than corporeal), she cast off the external signs of her old identity and began a new life as a prophet and preacher. Draping herself in severe clerical garb (long black robes unadorned with any accessories save a plain black hat), refusing to answer to any name but the "Publick Universal Friend" (even forbidding her followers to address her in gendered pronouns), Wilkinson presented a tantalizing if ambiguously gendered persona. To most, she appeared "more like a man than a woman," and her only published work, an address entitled *Some Considerations by a Universal Friend of Mankind*, appeared anonymously under the signature "your friend and *brother* in the communion and fellowship of the gospel." Wilkinson's *sexual* identity was never really in doubt (at least among those who were unpersuaded by her claims to divine incarnation), but her *gender* identity floated somewhere in between two cultural types that would come to embody the moral ambiguities of post-Revolutionary America, the "confidence man" and the "painted woman." As a symbol of both imposture and seduction—vices that blended masculine power and feminine guile into a

---

8. "A Memorandum of the Introduction of the Fatal Fever," undated, Jemima Wilkinson Papers, 1771–1849, Department of Manuscripts and University Archives, Carl A. Kroch Library, Cornell University Library.

volatile mix—Jemima Wilkinson was a focal point for republican anxieties about the precarious nature of civic and familial bonds in a world of uncertain sexual boundaries.[9]

Wilkinson's supposed sexual transfiguration was the subject of a lively and occasionally heated exchange in contemporary newspapers and pamphlets from 1783 to 1787 in which her unusual physical appearance was subjected to intense scrutiny. From tip to toe, every aspect of her distinctive dress was noted, analyzed, ridiculed, and rebuked. Even the most sympathetic observers conceded that her dress was provocative, a loud "call or proclamation to the people at large to 'come, see, and hear.' " Abner Brownell, a disciple who later left the society and wrote a searing indictment of his former mentor, was startled by his first glimpse of the Friend. Her "outward Appearance seem'd to be something singular and extraordinary, appearing in a different Habit from what is common amongst Women, wearing her Hair curl'd in her Neck, without any other Covering on her Head, except it was when she travel'd out, she put on a Hat much like a Man's, only the Brim flap'd down."[10] Wilkinson made quite an impression on the young Brownell who immediately left his home and family and began to itinerate with the Friend.

Those who saw her could often not make up their minds whether she intended to appear as a man or a woman. One described her as "habited partially as a man." Another recalled that "she appeared beautifully erect, and tall for a woman, although at the same time the masculine appearance predominated; which, together with her strange habit, caused every eye to be riveted upon her." She spoke not with the genteel inflections of chaste womanhood but in a "Voice very grum and shrill for a Woman," a "feminine-masculine tone of voice" that was oddly compelling. Her closest female followers imitated her masculine dress and mannerisms. One, Sarah Richards, was described in 1787 as a woman who "would be a comely person were she to dress as becomes her sex. But, as she imitates

9. Abner Brownell claimed that some of Wilkinson's followers "call her *him*." See Brownell, *Enthusiastical Errors Transpired and Detected* (New London, 1783), p. 18; *Extracts from the Diary of Jacob Hiltzheimer of Philadelphia*, ed. Jacob Cox Parsons (Philadelphia, 1893), p. 85; [Jemima Wilkinson], *Some Considerations Propounded to the several Sorts and Sects of Professors of this Age . . . by a Universal Friend of Mankind* (Providence, 1779), p. 94 (emphasis added). See Karen Halttunen, *Confidence Men and Painted Women: A Study of Middle-Class Culture in America, 1830–1870* (New Haven, 1982); Liz Young first pointed out to me the parallels between Wilkinson's public persona and these two stock characters of Victorian popular culture in a session at the 1995 American Studies Association. See also Jan Lewis, "The Republican Wife: Virtue and Seduction in the Early Republic," *William and Mary Quarterly*, 3d ser., 44, no. 3 (1987): 689–721.

10. *American Museum* 1 (March 1787): 253–54. When confronted by a gentleman about her "improper" and "indecent" dress, the Friend retorted, "There is nothing indecent or improper in my dress or appearance; I am not accountable to mortals, *I am that I am*." *American Museum* 1 (April 1787): 335; Brownell, *Enthusiastical Errors*, pp. 4–5.

the person they call the friend in her external appearance and particularly in wearing her hair down like a man, she is by that means disfigured."[11] Whether "disfigured" or transfigured, Wilkinson and her followers presented unusual "figures" to be deciphered according to the stylistic and gendered conventions of the day. The choice of words here is important, for it suggests that the problem posed by the Friend was perceived as one of form rather than substance. There is remarkably little said (either positive or negative) about theology in these accounts; no one seemed bothered by the heretical notion that Wilkinson was the spirit of Christ incarnate. Rather, critics wrote to expose the "deformity" of Jemima Wilkinson's peculiar ministry, while supporters defended her cross-dressing on the grounds that her body was "animated" by the masculine spirit of Christ. Questions of form structured these debates over Wilkinson's authenticity as a prophet. Was the outer form consonant with the spirit that supposedly "animated" it? What was the relationship between body, soul, and costume in the figure of the Friend? Did her masculine dress reflect a masculine spirit (Christ) or a deformed sexuality?

Beneath the preoccupation with Wilkinson's external appearance was confusion about her true sexual identity. "As she is not supposed of either sex, so this neutrality is manifest in her external appearance," observed one viewer. Her long dark gown fascinated because of what it concealed rather than what it revealed. "It falls to the feet, without outlining her figure," one disappointed observer wrote, "and its sleeves reveal only the tips of her hands." Another wrote that her neck was "conformable to the line of beauty and proportion; that is, the proportion of it visible at the time, being partly hidden by her plain habit of coloured stuff, drawn closely round above the shoulders, by a drawing string knotted in front, without handkerchief or female ornament of any kind." Even her underclothes were cause for speculation: "Under [her robe], it is said, her apparel is very expensive; and the form of it conveys the same idea, as her external appearance, of being neither man nor woman."[12] The luxurious undergarments offered an eroticized glimpse of the sexuality hidden beneath the clerical robes of the Friend.[13]

An undercurrent of sexual scandal runs throughout the newspaper reports of Wilkinson's ill-fated tour of Philadelphia in the early 1780s, in

---

11. Quoted in Watson, *Annals of Philadelphia*, 1:553, 554; Brownell, *Enthusiastical Errors*, p. 5; *American Museum* 1 (February 1787): 153.

12. *American Museum* 1 (February 1787): 153; ibid.; *Our Revolutionary Forefathers: The Letters of François, Marquis de Barbe-Marbois*, trans. and ed. Eugene Parker Chase (New York, 1929), p. 164. Quoted in Watson, *Annals of Philadelphia*, 1:554.

13. Marjorie Garber, *Vested Interests: Cross-Dressing and Cultural Anxiety* (New York, 1992), p. 219, points out that in eighteenth-century masquerades, ecclesiastical dress (such as the clerical robe worn by Jemima) was "charged with erotic significance."

which she was accused of "having separated men from their wives, wives from their husbands, and made confusion wherever [she has] been." A satirical letter to the *Freeman's Journal* in 1787 ridiculed the supposed modesty of Wilkinson and her female disciples; like Jezebels, the female Friends "paint" their minds as well as their faces and "anoint" their bodies with "nasty stuff" which makes them "smell rather disagreeable." "You must know," scolded the writer, "this disgusts me a little as a lover of yours, and makes me imagine you are not quite so cleanly as I would wish you to be." The juxtaposition of descriptions of the plain outer attire of the Friend with hints of corrupt bodily functions underneath suggests just how unsettling was the sexual ambiguity of Wilkinson and her followers. The reluctance of one disciple, Abigail Daton, to spell out the word "bedpan" in a letter to the paper detailing her charitable activities on behalf of the Friend provoked ribald scorn: "You call it, I believe, the bed-p—. But what does p—stand for? I thought the Spirit which inspires you never spoke with *dashes*. If I am not mistaken, that *p* means something rather unbecoming the gravity of a prophetess, and you must have made a sweet figure in the act of performing that charitable office. I would give twenty pounds to have seen you at that precious moment, provided the spirit had not moved you to throw the contents of what you held in my face."[14]

If Wilkinson and her female disciples were ridiculed as sexually corrupt, her male followers were portrayed as desexualized and effeminate. One, James Parker, was characterized as "artful, conceited, and illiterate; and as the countenance of a man is sometimes a tell tale, so those who are skilled in physiognomy, may see in his face the cunning which lies hid in his heart, though varnished over with an apparent candour and freedom in conversation: and as he possesses none of the fire of a divine enthusiast, so neither does he possess that zeal which is necessary to complete the character of an imposter." Parker's vices are the archetypal female ones; he is artful, unlettered, deceitful, cunning, vain, and indolent, traits that are all readily apparent from the surface of his skin. Other male disciples had more alarming and visible marks of effeminacy than Parker's "cunning" physiognomy. The Marquis de Chastellux reported that in contrast to the severe and unadorned visage of the Universal Friend, the men in her entourage sported "large round flipped hats, and long flowing straight locks, with a sort of melancholy wildness in their countenances, and an effeminate dejected air." Where the masculine dress of Jemima was thought to hide a corrupt sexuality, the effeminate appearance of her male disciples signified the actual loss of sexuality; by "general assertion,"

14. *American Museum* 1 (May 1787): 392; "To the Most Holy Sybil, Abigail Daton, a Fool by birth and a Prophetess by Profession," *Freeman's Journal* 1 (August 1787).

they were believed to have "literally followed the precept of 'making eunuchs of themselves for Christ's sake.' "[15] Wilkinson's sexuality was obscured (and thereby deformed) by her ambiguous dress; that of her male followers was entirely effaced.

This debate over the sexual and gender identity of Wilkinson and her followers took place in the context of a sustained conversation among literate Americans about the nature of social and national identity after the Revolution. The new urban press, in which most contemporary observations of Wilkinson appeared, engaged its readers in serious and thoughtful inquiries into the latest scientific and philosophical traditions emanating from Europe. Lockean sensationalist psychology, modified by common sense thought, provided a new paradigm for understanding the role of environment in shaping the individual (and the national) character. A series of essays on "the causes of the variety of complexion and figure in the human species" surveyed the entire sweep of human history to conclude that "the features of the human countenance are modified, and its entire expression radically formed, by the state of society.... Every passion, and mode of thinking, has its peculiar countenance."[16] Social states were, so to speak, marked on the body in ways that both thrilled and discomfited post-Revolutionary Americans. The debilitating social effects of monarchy and aristocracy (effeminacy and enervation) could be erased by the institution of republican forms of government, but by the same token the republican polity was itself in danger of being deformed by the corrupting influence of "Others" (blacks, American Indians, women, the poor) in the population. The "poor labouring classes" could mark their social superiors with the same depravity that they exhibit in their "coarse ruddiness" if allowed to participate fully in political life, and more ominous, the white skin of southern planters was in danger of being permanently darkened by constant exposure to the vicious habits of their slaves. "A dark colour, once contracted," warned one writer, "will be

15. *Freeman's Journal* 1 (February 1787); Marquis de Chastellux, *Travels in North America in the Years 1780, 1781, and 1782*, trans. Howard C. Rice Jr., 2 vols. (Chapel Hill, N.C., 1963), 1:322.

16. *American Museum* 6 (September 1789): 186. For an overview of these new urban magazines, see Frank Luther Mott, *A History of American Magazines, 1741–1850* (Cambridge, Mass., 1930), and James Playsted Wood, *Magazines in the United States*, 3d ed. (New York, 1971). The Philadelphia magazine in which most of the articles about Jemima Wilkinson appeared, the *American Museum*, was the largest of these new urban periodicals, with a subscription list of about 1,250 (Mott, *History of American Magazines*, p. 101). See also David Paul Nord, "A Republican Literature: Magazine Reading and Readers in Late-Eighteenth-Century New York," in *Reading in America*, ed. Cathy N. Davidson (Baltimore, 1985), pp. 114–39, and Catherine Kaplan," 'We Have Joys ... They Do Not Know': Letters, Partisanship, and Sentiment in the New Nation, 1790–1812" (Ph.D. diss., University of Michigan, 1998). On the social diffusion of Lockean psychology, see Jay Fliegelman, *Prodigals and Pilgrims: The American Revolution against Patriarchal Authority, 1750–1800* (New York, 1982).

many ages before it can be entirely effaced. . . . The negro colour may, by the exposure of a poor and servile state, be rendered almost perpetual."[17]

The moral and physical boundaries of the self were thus conceived as permeable and malleable in the new scientific discourse of the late eighteenth century. The environment imprinted its features on the bodies and souls of its inhabitants through the benign influence of climate or the more invidious influence of social custom. The physical alteration observed in the pigmentation of white southerners was a consequence both of the tropical climate of the region and the moral erosion of civilized values by the proximity of brutish slaves. On occasion, this fantasy of altered bodies took on a macabre quality, as in Francis Hopkinson's grotesque account of the "Dialogues of the Dead" in an early issue of the *American Museum*. "Bodies have no palpable outlines," the Pennsylvania doctor insisted. "There is not to be found in all nature a truly solid body. [When] bodies lie so near each other, their atmospheres interfere, there must be actual intercourse of parts between them . . . and by a communication of parts, sentiments may be conveyed from one incarnate body to another." By this logic even the line separating death from life was breachable; in Hopkinson's nightmarish vision of post-Revolutionary society, dead bodies conversed with one another and with the living as their essences were dispersed into the "atmosphere."[18]

That such an insidious process of assimilation across boundaries of race, class, and gender was already in progress was all too evident to the editors and contributors of these (mostly conservative) periodicals. The urban press provided numerous examples of mutant bodies and sudden transfigurations, in response to an apparently insatiable appetite among post-Revolutionary Americans for stories about the bizarre and the inexplicable. "Motley coloured" or "pye Negroes," mermaids, and remarkable "alterations" of color in both Africans and Indians appear regularly in the pages of the *American Museum* and the *Columbian Magazine* in the 1780s and 1790s, juxtaposed to lengthy essays on the merits of the new federal constitution and the need to stamp out religious fanaticism. A graphic description of two mulatto children exhibited before the American Philosophical Society in 1784 was provided for the voyeuristic pleasure of the *American Museum*'s subscribers in 1788, followed several issues later by a detailed account of the physical deformities of the "free-martin" and other

17. *American Museum* 6 (August 1789): 125; 6 (October 1789): 276. Fliegelman notes the double-edged nature of Lockean sensationalist psychology, which provided a model for the molding of the human character by the environment (*Prodigals and Pilgrims*).

18. Francis Hopkinson, "Some Account of a New Work, Entitled 'Dialogues of the Dead,' " *American Museum* 1 (March 1787): 257–58.

"mutilated animals" whose genitals exhibit "an equal mixture of both sexes."[19]

Social hermaphroditism was also a recurring motif of essays on the pernicious habits of urban men and women in the new republic. The magazines chided men for assuming female manners, and women for acting like men. "Governing women" and "submitting husbands," both abominations of nature, had become all too common in domestic parlors, while a new category of "social being" made its appearance in the leisured spaces of the new city—the "*ambosexual* order of tatlers." Stock figures of transgressive behavior, like "Mrs. Jolly" the "manly" drunkard and "Renaldo" the effeminate tea drinker, acted out dramas of inversion that were meant to provoke both laughter and moral vigilance. Examples of the barbarous gender customs found abroad (especially in the "savage" continents of Africa and Asia) served to reinforce the moral lesson; in the archipelago island of Metelin, "manly ladies seem to have changed sexes with the men. The woman rides astride—the man sits sideways upon the horse."[20] In post-Revolutionary America, it was genteel men in particular ("ye macaronies of the age") who were in danger of losing their masculinity altogether in the presence of greedy women of leisure who consumed sex and foreign luxuries in equal measure. "The nearer a man assimilates himself to female manners, capacities, and softness, the more acceptable [to the fair sex]," complained one writer. "On no other principle can we account for the effeminacy, lepidity, and languid lassitude of our modern beaux."[21] The word "coxcomb" came to describe not a flirtatious woman, as prior usage would suggest, but increasingly a man who forfeited the rights of masculinity by "assimilating" to femininity.

Language itself was partially to blame for this profusion of heterodox forms; the "frothy" style of writing popularized by Dr. Samuel Johnson and his fellow rhetoricians broke apart the union of form and substance that was the hallmark of classical literature, substituting in its place a

19. See, for example, "Account of a remarkable alteration of colour in a negro woman" and "Remarkable change in the complexion of an Indian," *American Museum* 4 (December 1788): 501–2, 558; "Account of a white negro," *American Museum* 5 (March 1789): 234; "Account of an extraordinary lufus naturae," *American Museum* 6 (November 1789): 350; "Account of turtle with two heads," *American Museum* 8 (August 1790): 85; and "Account of mermaid," *American Museum* 8 (October 1790): 192. "Some account of a motley coloured, or pye negro girl, and mulatto boy," *American Museum* 3 (January 1788): 38, and "An Account of the Free-Martin, or Hermaphrodite Cow," *American Museum* 4 (December 1788): 521. See also "Account of the Free-Martin," *Columbian Magazine* 1 (September 1787): 651–52.

20. *Columbian Magazine* 2 (August 1788): 449; "Singular Customs at Metelin," *American Museum* 12 (October 1792): 230.

21. *American Museum* 10 (Appendix 1, 1791): 8; 3 (March 1788): 267; 3 (June 1788): 508; 6 (September 1789): 240.

"loose," "bombastic," and "heterogeneous" style. Jay Fliegelman's 1993 study of rhetoric draws attention to the "elocutionary revolution" of the eighteenth century in which the manner of speaking assumed greater importance than the meaning of the words spoken. The insistence of rhetoricians on the primacy of sound over sense in public performances of language (from political oratory to music to drama) focused attention on the physical body of the speaker (his facial expressions and gestures) rather than on the text itself. In the conservative press of the 1780s and 1790s, it was Johnson who personified this new, vulgar approach to language. "He frowns so *emphatically*," wrote a regular contributor to the *American Museum*, "that every muscle is a sentence. Talk of your lovers, & your languishers, and your fainters, and your expirer—'tis nothing, sir— 'tis all learned out of the looking-glass." The promiscuous mingling of sense and meaning found in such modern writing as Johnson's *Rambler* essays was really "no language at all. . . . The things he calls Ramblers are composed of Greek and Latin words, with English terminations."[22] To more conservative thinkers in the 1780s and 1790s, the mutant words coined by these frivolous writers were the linguistic representation of the hybrid social and natural forms spawned by the Revolutionary assault on conventional categories of social organization.[23]

One could be tempted to dismiss these accounts of bizarre deformities as evidence of the vulgar popularizing of literary tastes in the age of "democratic eloquence" were it not for the undercurrent of political anxiety that runs through the reports.[24] The Revolution, one writer lamented, had created social forms "which nature never intended to create," and the mutant offspring of the political experiment undertaken so rashly in 1776 included men who changed political positions as well as races or genders with bewildering ease. In an age of "changes and revolutions," man is the most "variable" being on earth. "He is a creature perpetually falling out with himself, and sustains two or three opposite characters every day he

22. *American Museum* 2 (November 1787): 498; 2 (August 1787): 197–98; Jay Fliegelman, *Declaring Independence: Jefferson, Natural Language, and the Culture of Performance* (Stanford, 1993).

23. One precedent for this disturbing trend toward linguistic polymorphism was the debased language of the American Indian; Euro-American linguists noted the absence of fixed grammatical structures and the "loose" meanings of words in savage tongues. Jonathan Edwards singled out the absence of gender specificity in the nouns and pronouns of the Muhhekanew Indians as a particular source of criticism—"the very same words express he and she, him and her," he noted. Edwards, "Observations on the language of the Muhhekanew Indians," *American Museum* 5 (January 1789): 25. It was, of course, the same disregard for gendered terminology that was one of the most striking features of Jemima Wilkinson's ministry, and it is not difficult to imagine that her linguistic practices would have fueled fears of cultural assimilation among learned observers of Native American customs.

24. Kenneth Cmiel, *Democratic Eloquence: The Fight over Popular Speech in Nineteenth-Century America* (New York, 1990).

lives."[25] In the sphere of urban sociability, hermaphrodite behavior was repulsive but relatively harmless; in the sphere of government, it could be lethal to the political health of the new nation. The fierce, overwrought debates over growing partisanship in the late 1780s and 1790s provided a troubling glimpse of the protean nature of political man in post-Revolutionary America. A man who was as variable in his political opinions as in his fashion habits, who changed his character to suit the prevailing political winds, was far more dangerous than the seducing coxcomb or effete aristocrat.

Yet it would be a mistake to make too great a distinction between the dangers of social and of political effeminacy, because they were so closely intertwined in public representations of the new American order. Urban periodicals not only juxtaposed essays on fashion with essays on government, warning of the need for constancy in both, but also often discussed political issues via the language of dress. "Peter Prejudice's Complaint," a sally on the licentiousness of those who preferred the old Articles of Confederation to the new Constitution, used the image of tattered old "breeches" to represent the conjoined dangers of sexual and political disorder that threatened in the 1780s. The roguish Peter rails against the "tailors" (constitutional convention) who "meditated the ruin of my old breeches, and conspired against the liberty of my thighs, knees, and loins, which they have insidiously attempted to confine and cramp by palming this 'gilded trap,' the new breeches, on me. . . . They have conspired to lay restraints upon my free-born members, which are utterly incompatible with our republican form of government!"[26] In this reading of the ratification debate, sexual and political license are restrained by the adoption of the new "breeches," a modest set of clothes more suited to an austere, manly republicanism. The counterpoint to this manly republicanism was the effete extravagance of European court life; "the etiquette of courts, like that of dress, is calculated to obscure the real character," argued one writer, who recommended abolishing aristocratic fashions along with titles of nobility. This general denunciation of the "deformities" of foreign dress and its antirepublican tendencies led several authors to argue for the creation of a "national dress" for all Americans. Since it is "the fair sex" who are "the arbiters of dress," one proposed calling "a convention of the ladies, for the express purpose of devising a mode of dress" suitable to American habits and tastes. In the same spirit an "Address to the Ladies of America" called for the invention of "a CONVENTION HAT, a FED-

25. *American Museum* 1 (January 1787): 54; 1 (June 1787): 559.
26. *American Museum* 3 (June 1788): 524–25. The licentious breeches of "Prejudice" are the counterpoint to Wilkinson's asexual black robe; the unrestrained sexuality of men and the inaccessible sexuality of women both violate the natural order of gender relations on which the new republic was founded.

ERAL BONNET, or a CONGRESS CAP" to signal America's cultural independence from Europe.[27]

Beginning with the nonconsumption and nonimportation movements
of the 1760s and 1770s and continuing through the debates over the ratification of the Constitution, clothes had carried a particularly charged
political meaning in public and private discourse. To wear "homespun"
was a badge of patriotic honor during the war years, and domestic textiles
continued to represent republican virtues long after the war had ended.
Enemies of the new nation, including both aristocrats and the "lower
orders," were portrayed in foppish apparel; discontented farmers who
formed the backbone of Shays's Rebellion, for instance, insolently sported
velvet and satin vests and breeches, ruffled Holland shirts, and fine
worsted stockings.[28] In part, the urban press was reacting against the vigorous resumption of foreign trade in the 1780s, as Americans rushed to
buy those goods that had been denied them for so long. The evils of foreign consumption (moral turpitude, cultural dependence, economic instability) were invoked everywhere as a convenient cultural shorthand for
political corruption.

This message was directed largely at women, as the prime consumers
of foreign fashions. The use of bustlers among American women, in slav-
ish imitation of foreign fashions, one writer sharply noted, was "injurious
to the constitution"—not only the physical constitution of the women
themselves but the federal constitution as well. "If this abominable practice should be continued, and become general throughout the state, I shall
despair of our ever having more than one representative in congress
under the proposed constitution." The dangers of the insatiable female
desire for luxury lay not only in the foreign origins of most fashions but
in the very nature of the fashions consumed, whose overriding object was
to conceal nature by art. "If there is one object in the world, more dis-
gusting than all the others," the contributors to these magazines declared,
"it is a girl whom nature formed to be innocent and artless, reducing
affectation and disguise to a system."[29] The natural beauties and virtues of
women were hidden or, worse, deformed, by the artificial means they
employed to enhance their figures—stays, bustlers, bishops, powders,

27. *American Museum* 5 (March 1789): 239–40; 2 (November 1787): 481."Address to the
Ladies of America" urged "the freeman inhabitants of the United States" to adopt a "national
dress from head to foot" that all prospective citizens would be required to display; see *American Museum* 2 (August 1787): 118–19.

28. *American Museum* 1 (June 1787): 537–38.

29. *American Museum* 2 (November 1787): 483; 11 (May 1792): 193. The image of the consuming woman was central to the construction of citizenship in the early republic, Carroll
Smith-Rosenberg has argued, as an antitype of civic virtue and political independence. See
her "Dis-Covering the Subject of the 'Great Constitutional Discussion,' 1786–1789," *Journal of
American History* 79, no. 4 (December 1992): 841–73.

perfumes, and artificial eyes, teeth, and hair, were all forms of deception. Face paint, in particular, was roundly condemned for its dissimulating effect. "The very act of painting the face, is equivalent to putting on a mask—it is calculated to deceive."[30] Some innovations in fashion practiced this deception so far as to turn women into men. "The new riding habits, particularly, that have been so fashionable, and even make their appearance in all public places, conceal everything that is attractive in a woman's person, her figure, her manner, and her graces. They wholly unsex her, and give her the unpleasing air of an Amazon or a virago." Under such "masculine apparel," the author sadly concluded, "we forget that you are a woman . . . and we forget to love."[31]

This preoccupation with clothes as a metaphor for political order (both the degraded, aristocratic variant and the undefiled, democratic one) makes the fascination with Jemima Wilkinson's peculiar dress all the more suggestive as a form of political commentary. We can reconstruct the cultural meaning of Wilkinson's appearance by reading contemporary descriptions of her person and ministry in situ, against the prevailing motifs and narrative strategies of the urban press. As a woman who wore "masculine apparel," whose "expensive" underclothes were sexually ambiguous, whose disciples "painted" their faces and perfumed their bodies, who used indeterminate language and ungendered grammar, and who violated most conventional categories of being (sacred and profane, body and soul, male and female, rich and poor, even life and death), she represented everything the new republic most detested and feared. She was, as a fable about political treason put it, a "mongrel form"—not male or female, sacred or profane, but permanently in between.[32] It was this ambiguity of sexual status more than her masculine appearance that most unsettled her audiences, and they responded by attempting to fix her identity via a searching examination of the external signs of dress, voice, gesture, and demeanor.

Above all, Jemima Wilkinson was, most emphatically, not a "natural" woman. The urban press devoted a great deal of energy to delineating the attributes and qualities of this sublime if elusive figure. One exemplar, the apocryphal "Louisa," "is (what nature intended her to be) wholly a woman. She has a quality, that is the direct opposite to manliness and vigour. Her voice is gentle; her pronunciation delicate; her passions are

30. *American Museum* 9 (May 1791): 246.
31. *American Museum* 11 (March 1792): 94.
32. "The Birds, the Beasts, and the Bat," *Columbian Magazine* 1 (March 1787): 346. In this fable, written during the Revolutionary War in 1778, the bat—"half-bird, half-beast"—cannot make up its mind which side of the battle between the birds and the beasts to support, presenting himself first in one form and then in another. In the end, his "mongrel form" leads to political exile, as he is not accepted by either camp.

never suffered to be boisterous; she never talks politics; she never foams with anger; she is seldom seem in any masculine amusements. . . . I will venture to prophecy, that she will never canvass for votes at an election. I never saw her in an unfeminine dress, or her features discomposed with play." On every score, Jemima Wilkinson was the perfect antithesis of "Louisa." And unnatural women—like the unnatural governments to which they were thought to give birth—were creatures marked for extinction in republican America.[33]

II.

How should we understand the peculiar gender "style" of Jemima Wilkinson? Did she wish to present herself as a man in order to escape association with the degraded qualities of women in the masculine culture of republican America, qualities that included a fatal susceptibility to fanaticism and superstition? I have argued elsewhere that Wilkinson's ministry represented a daring, if ultimately futile, attempt to reframe the democratic promises of the revolutionary movement in the language of patriarchal authority. In her apocalyptic sermons, the prevailing symbols of political tyranny (magistrates, the established clergy, monstrous women) are destroyed by a firestorm of populist anger, only to be replaced by an even more compelling male figure, that of the Old Testament Patriarch. The resurrection of masculine power in the form of a prophet would become the hallmark of antebellum religious culture, as Paul Johnson and Sean Wilentz's recent biography of Robert Mathews, the self-styled Prophet Matthias, illustrates. Matthias's potent blend of populism and patriarchy, in which he castigated women as "the capsheaf of the abomination of desolation—full of all deviltry," while denouncing the injustices of the new capitalist order, was no ideological aberration but a logical coda to the post-Revolutionary generation's struggle to justify the exclusion of women from the public sphere.[34] Like most Americans who had lived through the devastation of war and the chaos of the first decade of independence, Wilkinson knew that women were deemed unfit

33. *American Museum* 11 (May 1792): 195. As Carole Pateman and Joan Landes have argued, Lockean political theory was predicated on a reformulation of the categories of "nature" and "society." Characteristics (including gender) that had previously been part of the social order were reassigned to nature and thereby newly authenticated by Lockean liberalism; see Pateman, *The Sexual Contract* (Stanford, 1988), and Landes, *Women and the Public Sphere in the Age of the French Revolution* (Ithaca, 1988).

34. Susan Juster, "To Slay the Beast: Visionary Women in the Early Republic," in *A Mighty Baptism: Race, Gender, and the Creation of American Protestantism*, ed. Susan Juster and Lisa MacFarlane (Ithaca, 1996), pp. 19–37; Paul Johnson and Sean Wilentz, *The Kingdom of Matthias: A Story of Sex and Salvation in Nineteenth-Century America* (New York, 1994), p. 93.

to govern because of their uncontrollable passions and fickle loyalties; hence her sexual transfiguration into a stern and somber prophet of God.

Or, alternatively, did her ambiguous dress and demeanor signal an attempt to transcend gender categories altogether, to resurrect an earlier model of spiritual authority that Puritan and Quaker women had found so empowering? Androgyny was, after all, a powerful spiritual position in the religious culture of early America, one that evangelists as diverse as the flamboyant George Whitefield and the austere Jonathan Edwards both adopted at various points in their careers as revivalists. Embracing the biblical dictum that "in Christ there is neither male nor female," Anglo-American visionaries from the English Civil War prophets studied by Phyllis Mack to eighteenth-century revivalists had sought to liberate their spiritual voices from the constraints of gender, presenting themselves as empty vessels waiting to be filled with the spirit of Christ. Yet, unlike Wilkinson, few found it necessary to discard the external signs of their gender identity to fulfill their calling as divine mediums.[35] Early Puritan mystics such as Anne Hutchinson believed in an androgyny of the soul, not of the body.

Whatever her intentions (and we have no reason to suspect that Wilkinson was anything but sincere about her own transfiguration), it is clear that audiences placed her in a relatively new category: the spiritual transvestite. Transvestism was certainly not a new cultural practice in eighteenth-century British America. Indeed, Dianne Dugaw argues that the literary tradition of the female warrior reached its zenith in the late eighteenth century, and examples of women who disguised themselves as men to fight in the various imperial wars (including the American War of Independence) abound in the popular literature of the day. But these public displays of female transvestism were usually of short duration and for highly specific (and laudatory) purposes, such as the pursuit of patriotic acclaim, the heroic determination to escape parental tyranny, or the desire for love and adventure. Such women were more likely to be celebrated by their contemporaries for their courage than censored for their transgressive behavior; as the archconservative Edmund Burke remarked of the Chevalier d'Eon, the famous French diplomat who supposedly dressed

---

35. Stout, *Divine Dramatist;* Phyllis Mack, *Visionary Women: Ecstatic Prophecy in Seventeenth-Century England* (Berkeley, 1992); and Phyllis Mack, "Women as Prophets during the English Civil War," *Feminist Studies* 8 (Spring 1992): 19–45. On women visionaries as passive vessels of the Spirit, see Christine Krueger, *The Reader's Repentance: Women Preachers, Women Writers, and Nineteenth-Century Social Discourse* (Chicago, 1992). See also the biography of perhaps the most famous of the Civil War prophets, Dame Eleanor Davies, who refused to relinquish her identity or responsibility as a woman when acting the prophet: Esther Edwards Copes, *Handmaid of the Holy Spirit: Dame Eleanor Davies, Never Soe Mad a Ladie* (Ann Arbor, Mich., 1992).

like a woman to serve his king: "She is the most extraordinary person of the age. We have several times seen women metamorphosed into men, and doing their duty in the war; but we have seen no one who has united so many military, political, and literary talents."[36] Rarely was cross-dressing a lifelong habit, and rarely was it seen as symptomatic of much deeper confusions over one's real sexual identity. Women such as Deborah Sampson, the best-known female soldier of the American Revolution, dressed in men's clothes not because they believed themselves to be men but because male attire afforded them greater freedom and flexibility in pursuing their goals—goals that their contemporaries almost always accepted as consistent with proper gender norms. These conventional enactments of female transvestism, in other words, did not constitute a *category crisis*, as Marjorie Garber uses the term, but rather served to stabilize existing gender categories by allowing women a temporary space within which to experiment with masculine behaviors without forfeiting their essential femininity.[37]

Post-Revolutionary Americans would have had a difficult time comprehending the strange attire of the Universal Friend within the parameters of accepted female transvestism. The reasons for their confusion, I think, have as much to do with the changes taking place in the discourse of sex as with the simple but disturbing fact that Jemima Wilkinson not only dressed like a man but pretended to have been transformed into one. The distinction between androgyny (an interiorized state of sexual ambiguity) and transvestism (an external performance) threatened to collapse in public representations of the Friend at the same time that the two models of gender identity which these states inverted were themselves at an ideological crossroad. Reaching back into the literature on the history of sexuality, we can identify the late eighteenth century as a paradigmatic moment of transition in the Euro-American conceptualization of gender and sexual difference, the moment when an older notion of gender identity as flexible and contingent was being displaced by the modern notion of sexual identity as an immutable fact of nature. As Thomas Lacqueur describes it, the relationship of sex (biology) to gender (culture) was

---

36. Dianne Dugaw, *Warrior Women and Popular Balladry, 1650–1850* (New York, 1989); Burke quoted in Gary Kates, *Monsieur d'Eon Is a Woman: A Tale of Political Intrigue and Sexual Masquerade* (New York, 1995), p. 3. See also Julie Wheelwright, *Amazons and Military Maids: Women Who Dressed as Men in Pursuit of Life, Liberty, and Happiness* (London, 1989), and the discussion of d'Eon in Garber, *Vested Interests*, pp. 260–65. For examples of literary depictions of the female warrior in America after the Revolution and the War of 1812, see Daniel Cohen, " 'The Female Marine' in an Era of Good Feelings: Cross-Dressing and the 'Genius' of Nathaniel Coverly, Jr.," *Proceedings of the American Antiquarian Society* 103 (1994): 359–95.

37. Garber, *Vested Interests*.

inverted in the late eighteenth and early nineteenth centuries, as identity was increasingly seen to be rooted in biological sexual difference as opposed to cultural practice.[38]

Lacqueur's historical model of the changing relationship of sex to gender, or of substance to form, corresponds neatly to the distinction drawn by Foucault between the early modern and the modern discourse of sexuality. Put simply, Foucault argues that sex was transformed from an act to an identity sometime between the seventeenth and the nineteenth centuries. In his classic example, sodomy—a "category of forbidden acts"—became redefined in the nineteenth century as homosexuality, a "kind of interior androgyny, a hermaphroditism of the soul. The sodomite had been a temporary aberration; the homosexual was now a species."[39] For Foucault as for Lacqueur, the improvisational nature of sexual identity was a major casualty of the epistemological revolutions of the late eighteenth and early nineteenth centuries. Wilkinson can thus be seen as a kind of cultural "sodomite," a sexually indeterminate figure who represented an older (and disappearing) way of constructing gender. As contemporary gender theorists might put it, Wilkinson "performed" her ambiguous gender identity before an audience who wished desperately to believe that gender was part of the natural, not the constructed, world.

But if a culturally determined model of gender identity was on the way out in the waning decades of the eighteenth century under the relentless press of new forms of biological determinism, it had not disappeared entirely. The new epistemology of sexual difference whose victory Foucault and Lacqueur attribute to the political battles of the Age of Revolution had to contend with an equally powerful and tenacious mode of representing social behavior, one identified most fully with the ancien regimes of Europe and America: that of the *theatrum mundi*. Cultural historians have delighted in exposing the richly theatricalized nature of public life in the Anglo-American world in the eighteenth century. This was the Age of Public Man, in which a highly ritualized public life flourished and "manners"—the external signs of status and identity—were taken to be the measure of a man. Dress became extraordinarily stylized, how-to manuals for the aspiring gentleman proliferated, the "theater and countertheater" of repression and resistance that E. P. Thompson has described in popular life became ever more elaborate. What Agnew calls the "waning drama of paternalism and the waxing spectacle of the mar-

---

38. Thomas Lacqueur, *Making Sex: Body and Gender from the Greeks to Freud* (Cambridge, Mass., 1990).

39. Michel Foucault, *The History of Sexuality: An Introduction*, trans. Robert Hurley (New York, 1978), p. 43.

ket" were played out in street theater, the stock market, and the penny press.[40]

The theatricalized nature of eighteenth-century public life helped to promote an understanding of the self as, in Fliegelman's words, "an endless sequence of self-presentations structured for different audiences without an overarching and definable core self."[41] Until common sense philosophy arrived to save the day, the deconstructive dimension of the market revolution and its associated ideological allies (contractual political theory, Smithian liberalism, and Lockean psychology) had eroded popular confidence that one could accurately read the inner essence of a man from his position in a divinely ordered universe. If man was but an empty shell to be formed and reformed by the currents of social change, then he was an eternal cipher. In such a protean and contingent world, all individuals were actors—"liminal being[s] always on the verge of becoming something or someone else."[42] And in such a world, gender could hardly be inscribed on the body in a predetermined and determining manner or, for that matter, on the soul in a manner consistent with earlier notions of spiritual androgyny. Female visionaries such as Jemima Wilkinson thereby became reinterpreted as cross-dressing impostors.

In America, these protracted public discussions about the artifice of costume and custom, while never as elaborate as those taking place across the Atlantic, assumed a menacing shape as the Revolutionary crisis unfolded in the 1760s and 1770s. When the British spy Major André was found to have "changed his dress within our lines, and under a feigned name, and in a disguised habit," the artifice of costume became much more than an aesthetic problem. André's use of disguise was, literally, a question of life or death. The critical need to distinguish true patriots from disloyal traitors rendered modes of self-presentation a matter of politics rather than manners or even morals (recall the numerous literary representations of antirepublican dress in the urban press). Cross-dressers such as the Universal Friend were easy targets for those who saw the hand of treason in every fashion innovation, and indeed, Wilkinson was accused of harboring Tory sentiments throughout her public career. If the American Revolution constituted a new adventure in "self-fashioning"—or, perhaps more aptly, in self-making—for that generation of patriots exemplified by the picaresque hero of Benjamin Franklin's *Autobiography*, it was an experiment constantly in danger of being subverted by its own unstable premises. As Jeffrey Richards puts it, the theater of self-representation "[leaped] from metaphor to political act" in the wake of the Revolution. In

40. Agnew, *Worlds Apart*, p. 159; see Richard Sennett, *The Fall of Public Man* (New York, 1977), and E. P. Thompson, *Customs in Common* (New York, 1992).
41. Fliegelman, *Declaring Independence*, pp. 82–83.
42. Agnew, *Worlds Apart*, pp. 161, 95.

Britain, genteel self-fashioning may have been a rather complacent and politically neutral affair by the late eighteenth century, a matter more of satire than of real moral concern, but in post-Revolutionary America it was fraught with the same political urgency that had underwritten much of the frenzied self-fashioning of the Renaissance state.[43]

While the Revolutionary crisis accentuated the threat posed by transvestism by calling into question all identity, it created new forms of androgyny through its rhetorical innovations. In an intriguing analysis of the narrative of Hannah Snell, the "Female Soldier," Fliegelman argues that the language of revolution generated its own version of linguistic androgyny. The "androgynous characterization" of female heroines like Snell and the mythologized Molly Pitcher, he suggests, "replicates the rhetorical and oratorical ideals of the Revolution—a combination of compensating passive and aggressive postures." The rhetoric of revolution was itself cross-dressed by its synthesis of masculine and feminine modes of address.[44] Not until independence was fully secured could Revolutionary leaders abandon the morally suspect but emotionally invigorating position of scorned supplicants at the foot of a tyrannical master, a position indelibly associated with the vices and virtues of femininity.

With such confusions of identity and allegiance rampant in American cultural and political life, it is no wonder that the Revolutionary generation sustained a deeply ambivalent relationship to the theater, the ultimate symbol of artifice. Richards notes that the patriot assault during the Revolutionary War on the theater as a symbol of British corruption masks (or complements) the extent to which the patriots themselves conducted the war effort as a kind of political theater. We have recently come to appreciate just how theatrical the politics of revolution had become by the time the fighting was over—the toasts and processions; the rituals of humiliation and reconciliation; and the songs, masquerades, and gestures of defiance and solidarity, some distinctly plebian in origin, others partaking of a more generic nationalist sensibility.[45] What is less clear is

43. Jeffrey H. Richards, *Theater Enough: American Culture and the Metaphor of the World Stage, 1607–1789* (Durham, N.C., 1991), pp. 184, 261; Stephen Greenblatt, *Renaissance Self-Fashioning from More to Shakespeare* (Chicago, 1980).

44. Fliegelman, *Declaring Independence*, pp. 159–60. See also Sandra M. Gustafson's "Deborah Sampson Gannett Was a Woman Warrior . . . and So Was George Washington: The Framing of Gender Identity and Difference in Early Republican Politics," paper presented at the 1995 meeting of the American Studies Association, Pittsburgh, Pa., and her essay in this volume.

45. Ann Fairfax Withington, *Toward a More Perfect Union: Virtue and the Formation of American Republics* (New York, 1991); Alfred F. Young, "English Plebian Culture and Eighteenth-Century American Radicalism," in *The Origins of Anglo-American Radicalism*, ed. Margaret C. Jacob and James R. Jacob (Atlantic Highlands, N.J., 1984), pp. 185–213; David Waldstreicher, "Rites of Rebellion, Rites of Assent: Celebrations, Print Culture, and the Origins of American Nationalism," *Journal of American History* 82 (June 1995): 37–61.

whether this republican theater served to accentuate the confusions of identity and allegiance spawned by the revolutionary crisis or whether it helped to resolve them. The answer to this query will depend partly on how we choose to read the multiple texts of representation and misrepresentation that so captivated Americans in the anxious years after independence. Did the readers of the *American Museum* find the ambiguous dress and demeanor of the Universal Friend a threat to their own precarious sexual and political identities, or did they find it merely ridiculous? Did Wilkinson personify the constantly shifting world of republican politics, with its unstable gender conventions, or was she a figure of satirical humor? Did she disconcert or entertain? Those who wondered what exactly was under Jemima Wilkinson's long black robe were part of a larger chorus of seekers in post-Revolutionary America who felt simultaneously disoriented and liberated by the winds of epistemological change transforming their world; from our distant historical vantage point, it is probably impossible ever to recover the feelings and opinions of those eighteenth-century men and women who flocked to see the Friend perform. She remains, to us as to her audiences, an enigma.

As actress and prophet, Wilkinson invites an analysis that combines a theatrical perspective with an appreciation for the performative aspects of gender identity. She conveyed in her very person the powerful message that external appearance (including gender) was not the transparent reflection of an inner reality but a carefully constructed image. Such artifice could be deeply disturbing to a people recently emerged from the chaos of war and the disruptions of identity (national, social, even gendered) caused by the Revolution, and the physical violence that greeted the Friend on her prophetic travels reminds us that a thin line exists between scorn and fear. Later evangelicals would find more effective ways to manipulate the ambiguities and slippages of post-Revolutionary society than Wilkinson's awkward attempts at self-transformation. The most spectacularly successful preacher of the antebellum era was the Methodist circuit rider "Crazy" Lorenzo Dow; like Wilkinson, he cultivated a sexually ambiguous figure with his "bizarre appearance—long hair parted like a woman's, weather-beaten face, flashing eyes, crude gestures, and disheveled clothes."[46]

Dow was a charismatic performer, a storyteller, and an astute reader of Jacksonian sensibilities. Equal parts sacred clown and populist demagogue, he was able to voice the democratic aspirations of the early nineteenth century in a sexually transgressive manner, a feat Jemima Wilkinson could never pull off. But then, he was preaching in an age when the

---

46. See Nathan Hatch's wonderful description of Dow in *The Democratization of American Christianity* (New Haven, 1989), p. 37.

spectacle of democratic politics had become more important than the substance, an age in which those urban predators, the "confidence man" and
the "painted woman," had been reified as literary types and sacred theater had been institutionalized in the camp meeting and the revivalist's
"anxious bench." When Charles Grandison Finney purchased the Bowery
Street Theater in New York City and converted it into a tabernacle of God,
a new era in the history of American popular religion had begun.[47] By
then, Jemima Wilkinson was gone and the republican moment, a moment
of experimentation in the politics of gender, had passed as well.

47. Jeanne Halgren Kilde, "Worshipping in the Theater: Commercial Performance Space
and the Religious Audience," paper presented at the 1995 meeting of the American Studies
Association, Pittsburgh, Pa.

The Genders of Nationalism: Patriotic Violence, Patriotic Sentiment in the Performances of Deborah Sampson Gannett

SANDRA M. GUSTAFSON

ON THE evening of March 22, 1802, Deborah Sampson Gannett mounted the stage of Boston's Federal-Street Theatre and introduced herself to her audience with the following words:

> Not unlike the example of the patriot and philanthropist, though perhaps perfectly so in effect, do I awake from the tranquil slumbers of retirement, to active, public scenes of life, like those which now surround me. That genius which is the prompter of *curiosity*, and that spirit which is the support of *enterprize*, early drove, or, rather illured me, from the corner of humble obscurity—their cheering aspect has again prevented a torpid rest.[1]

The convoluted syntax and multiple, contradictory rhetorics represented in Gannett's opening words anticipated the complexities of the performance that followed. In her lengthy introduction, the American Revolution's most famous woman warrior justified transforming her *"tale of truth"* from "the soliloquy of a hermit" into a public lecture. She confessed that the deeds she was about to relate amounted to "a foible, an error and presumption," while insisting on "the *good intentions* of a *bad deed*" (pp.

I acknowledge the kind help of Al Young and Ellen Gustafson in the preparation of this essay.

1. Quotations from Gannett's address are from the reprinted version entitled "An Address on Life as a Female Revolutionary Soldier," in *Outspoken Women: Speeches by American Women Reformers*, ed. Judith Anderson (Dubuque, Iowa, 1984), pp. 135–41; the passage quoted here is from p. 135. Further references will be given parenthetically in the text. The address was originally published as *Addr[e]ss Delivered with Applause, At the Federal-Street Theatre, Boston . . . By Mrs. Deborah Gannet, The American Heroine* (Dedham, 1802).

135–36). The "review" that followed attributed her decision to disguise herself as a man and join the Continental army to a combination of inquisitiveness ("my juvenile mind early became inquisitive to understand . . . whether the principles, or rather the seeds of *war* are analogous to the genuine nature of *man*" [p. 136]), patriotism, and frustration with her helpless state as she observed the consequences of British brutality.

These explanations proved adequate only temporarily. After drawing on her audience's memory to fill in her "shade of a picture" (p. 139) of the battles of Charlestown, White Plains, Yorktown, and Schuyler's Canadian expedition, and after sketching the benefits of peace in an ode to liberty, Gannett returned to the central question of her address: What motivated her to disguise herself and fight? It was a question that Gannett insisted was ultimately unanswerable: "I would not purposely evade a pertinent answer; and yet I know not, at present, how to give a more particular one than has already been suggested" (p. 140). Rather than attempt to answer the question, Gannett concluded her address with an apology and an appeal to the women in the audience, who as wives and mothers occupied a rank "in the scale of beings . . . superior to that of man" (p. 141). Repeating the conventions of republican motherhood, Gannett insisted that such feminine superiority depended on women acquiescing in the belief that the "*field* and the *cabinet* are the proper spheres assigned to our MASTERS and our LORDS " while remaining content to govern in "our *kitchens* and in our *parlours*" and "rear an offspring in every respect worthy to fill the most illustrious stations of their predecessors" (p. 141). But Gannett quickly undermined her own delineation of separate spheres when, "equipt in complete uniform," she concluded her performance with a display of the manual exercise she learned as a soldier, a complex series of vigorous maneuvers with a large, heavy gun.[2] Throughout the address and the military drill, the pervasive texture of ambiguity characteristic of Gannett's opening words heightened attention to linguistic mediation and the theatrical dimension of everyday life, working to suspend the audience's understanding of conventional modes of experience, if only temporarily.

As an impoverished, female Revolutionary soldier claiming public

---

2. See the broadside reproduced in Elizabeth Evans, *Weathering the Storm: Women of the American Revolution* (New York, 1975), p. 319. For the drill, see Ernest W. Peterkin, *The Exercise of Arms in the Continental Army* (Alexander Bay, N.Y., 1989). Jane Elmes-Crahall, "Deborah Sampson Gannett," in *Women Public Speakers in the United States, 1800–1925: A Bio-Critical Sourcebook*, ed. Karlyn Kohrs Campbell (Westport, Conn., 1993), pp. 380–92, concludes that Gannett's "praise of Republican Motherhood" was "a heartfelt expression of her own beliefs, supported by concern for her children" (p. 389). While Gannett's diary does reveal her love of her children, this sentiment is not identical to republican motherhood, nor does Gannett's performance taken in its entirety suggest an unqualified embrace of that gender ideology.

stature, Gannett challenged the emergent post-Revolutionary ideology of gendered spheres that separated society into masculine public and feminine private domains (fig. 17.1). That ideology made universal claims but had limited explanatory power, particularly for women in the lower or working classes. Her rapid shifts between the rhetorics of domesticity and antidomesticity, of self-promotion and self-incrimination, reflected her multiple projects: the need to authenticate and justify her military experience at the same time as she attested to her feminine virtue. Gannett's performances oscillated between aggressive challenges to gender and class conventions and self-conscious submission to them. Staging violent disruptions of cultural categories, she then enacted her sentimental response to that violation. Through these acts of rhetorical and performative instability, Gannett presented her life story as the site of an ongoing battle over gender and class identities in the early republic.

The opening words of Gannett's oration repeated commonplaces of neoclassical rhetoric, specifically when she identified herself with the Cincinnatus-like hero who reluctantly leaves his rural retirement to serve his nation. George Washington self-consciously modeled his public persona on the farmer / patriot / warrior Cincinnatus, providing the most famous instance of this masculine rhetorical convention. Called to serve as the republic's first president, Washington claimed that it was his "sole desire to live and die, in peace and retirement on my own farm."[3] Gannett's wartime experience and subsequent life provided the basis for her claims to Cincinnatean rhetoric. In May 1782, she disguised herself as Robert Shurtliff and enlisted in the Continental army, where she served undetected for over a year until a doctor discovered her disguise while treating her for a fever. Discharged from the army in October 1783, she returned to the agricultural district outside Boston and later married Benjamin Gannett. The couple settled on a farm in Sharon, Massachusetts, where they struggled to make a living for themselves and their three children. Gannett had grown accustomed to heavy physical labor as a teenager bound out to a Middleborough family, and she was reported to don men's clothes (even her army uniform) while working in the fields beside her husband. But her war wounds took their toll on her strength, and despite her labor the family was poor. Paul Revere described her condition in an 1804 letter supporting her bid for a federal pension: "She is now much out of health; She has several children; her Husband is a good

3. Washington is quoted in Kenneth Silverman, *A Cultural History of the American Revolution* (New York, 1987), p. 603; on Washington's self-conscious adaptation of Whig literary ideals of the heroic leader, see pp. 430–31. For a thorough discussion of the iconography of Washington as Cincinnatus, see Garry Wills, *Cincinnatus: George Washington and the Enlightenment* (Garden City, N.Y., 1984).

Fig. 17.1. Joseph Stone, *Deborah Sampson: Drawn by Joseph Stone*, Framingham, [Massa-chusetts,] 1797. Oil on panel. (Photo: Courtesy of the Rhode Island Historical Society, RHi X3 2513.)

sort of a man, 'tho of small force in business; they have a few acres of poor land which they cultivate, but they are really poor."[4]

The tortured and self-qualifying syntax of the opening words of her address reflects the multiple ironies she involved herself in when she took the Cincinnatus role. Gannett's financial need disturbed her identification with the Cincinnatean gentleman farmer. While her military career allowed her to assert that she was "not unlike the example of the patriot and philanthropist" in returning to the public stage nearly twenty years after her discharge, the "retirement" from which she emerged was hardly one of "tranquil slumbers," nor was her rest "torpid." Her family's economic hardships lent urgency to her repeated attempts to receive the same compensation as male veterans, which included a successful petition for back pay approved in 1792 and an unsuccessful 1797 petition to win a military pension. Over the year following her appearance in Boston, Gannett performed her oration and display of arms before audiences in northeastern towns including Providence, Springfield, Northampton, and Albany.[5] Her lecture tour formed part of her renewed effort to win a pension by publicly establishing the legitimacy of her claim. While making her tour, she paid visits to her former commanding officers to renew their friendships and elicit their support. Gannett's diary of the tour reveals something of the "curiosity" that motivated her first to disguise herself as a man and enlist in the army, then to conduct her unprecedented lecture tour, but she records much more fully her suffering from ill health, anxiety about her children, and concern that her "enterprize" pay off. As her lecture tour indicates, Gannett had a strong sense of the need to make her case for a pension to the wider populace as well as to the Congress. She sought out men of letters who could publicize her adventures and make her a well-known figure. Both of Gannett's bids for a pension were conducted with the help of Herman Mann, a Dedham, Massachusetts, writer, editor, and printer who assisted her first effort by publishing her biography, *The Female Review* (1797). Mann later aided her in preparing her speech and arms drill.[6] About the time that *The Female Review* appeared,

---

4. Quoted in Vera O. Laska, *"Remember the Ladies": Outstanding Women of the American Revolution* (Boston, 1976), p. 84; Elizabeth D. Schafer, "Sampson, Deborah (1760–1827)," in *The American Revolution, 1775–1783: An Encyclopedia*, ed. Richard L. Blanco, 2 vols. (New York, 1993), 2:1473–75, reports that "after the Revolution, Deborah enjoyed wearing men's clothing and her uniform while performing physical labor on the farm" (p. 1475). While this account is not well substantiated, it is not unlikely that Gannett worked in the fields beside her husband, as she had when she was a bound servant.

5. She also performed in New York City; see George C. D. Odell, *Annals of the New York Stage*, 15 vols. (New York, 1927), 2:176. These performances do not appear in her diary.

6. Herman Mann, *The Female Review: Life of Deborah Sampson* (Dedham, Mass., 1797; rpt. New York, 1972). Further references will be given parenthetically in the text. For Mann's background, see Randall Craig, "Herman Mann (1771–1833)," in *American Writers before 1800:*

she visited Philip Freneau, convincing him of her authenticity and winning his support, which he offered in an ode calling on Congress to grant her a pension. Her attempt to win legitimacy in the eyes of the national government, and consequently a permanent income, concluded successfully in 1805 when she was awarded the pension. This outcome resulted from her public performances, the support of her commanding officers, and the efforts of Paul Revere and other prominent men.

If one central irony of Gannett's first words to her audience lay in the discrepancy between her neoclassical language of rural repose and her actual life as a poor farmer, the more obvious irony lay in her linguistic cross-dressing, the verbal counterpart to her Continental army uniform. Employing a vocabulary of masculine patriotism, she exposed the inadequacy of the distinct gendered languages of nationalism that emerged during the post-Revolutionary period, revealing their inability to account for her wartime experiences.[7] Gannett's performances revealed her to be a woman who eluded conventional categories by masquerading as a man on the battlefield and on the stage. She unfolded that revelation obliquely, tentatively, and self-contradictorily in the language of her speech.

Gannett's appearance heightened her audience's sense of incongruity. At five feet, seven inches in height, she made a convincing enough man in uniform that, as she noted with delight in her tour diary, one audience was "full of unblieff [sic]," claiming "that I was a lad of not more than Eighteen years of age." The success of her disguise pointed to the dependence of gender distinctions on cultural signs such as clothing. Distinct masculine and feminine modes of dress preoccupied early republican writers of diverse political commitments, suggesting widespread cultural anxieties about gender distinctions. In the same March 1792 issue of Matthew Carey's American Museum that carried a sympathetic account of Gannett's petition to the Massachusetts legislature, the British moralist John Bennett warned "a young lady" about the inappropriateness of mas-

---

A Biographical and Critical Dictionary, ed. James A. Levernier and Douglas R. Wilmes (Westport, Conn., 1983), pp. 939–40.

7. See Nancy F. Cott, The Bonds of Womanhood: "Woman's Sphere" in New England, 1780–1835 (New Haven, 1977); Mary Beth Norton, Liberty's Daughters: The Revolutionary Experience of American Women, 1750–1800 (Boston, 1980); and Linda Kerber, Women of the Republic: Intellect and Ideology in Revolutionary America (New York, 1986). These works provided the foundational description of post-Revolutionary gender ideologies, influentially characterizing separate spheres and republican motherhood as the predominant modes of constructing femininity in the new republic. Christine Stansell, City of Women: Sex and Class in New York, 1789–1860 (Urbana, 1987), stresses the inadequacy of republican motherhood and separate spheres as explanations of working-class women's experience, arguing that poor women had "only fragments of an ideological language with which to press their own claims" (p. 37). Women such as Gannett were deeply attentive to the problem of fitting diverse experiences into the straitjackets of accepted social roles, and thus they were themselves actively reflective about the processes of social construction that preoccupy modern scholars.

culine attire. Bennett singled out riding habits for criticism in terms that suggest he would not have approved of Gannett; riding habits on a woman "wholly unsex her, and give her the unpleasing air of an Amazon, or a virago," he wrote. Sometime radical republican and Wollstonecraft sympathizer Charles Brockden Brown echoed Bennett's sentiments when he painted the absence of gender-marked attire as the most troubling feature of Alcuin's imagined "paradise of women."[8] The transvestite woman proved so disquieting because she disrupted the binary gender system. She functioned as what the critic Marjorie Garber describes as the cultural "third term" that is *not a term* but rather "a space of possibility."[9] Throwing binary models of social identity into disequilibrium, she exposed uncharted social terrain.

It was the disequilibrium and instability of the transvestite that Gannett's address captured as she oscillated between the representation and the erasure of fixed gender distinctions. Her opening claim to be "not unlike" the male "patriot and philanthropist," which measured her distance from the male ideal, gave way to an asserted perfect identity "in effect." But her second sentence reasserts difference, disrupting her original effort to acknowledge and then erase gender categories. She first claimed that curiosity and enterprise "drove" her "from the corner of humble obscurity," an assertion resonant with the newly legitimated masculine ambitions of liberalism. But she immediately qualified the masculine language of drive with the feminine language of seduction, describing herself alternatively as "illured" into public activity. Unlike "drive," seduction implies uncontrolled, socially disruptive passions identified with its feminine objects.

The conflicts intrinsic to Gannett's role are nowhere more obvious than in her repeated insistence on the violence-laden potential of her speech. She explicitly linked her language to the socially disruptive nature of her experiences, claiming to present "a narration of facts in a mode as uncouth as they are unnatural" (p. 136). While she "bow[ed] submissive to an audience" p. (135), her submissiveness could not control the potentially destructive effects of her speech, which she claimed might be "wounding to the ear of more refined delicacy and taste" and "ring discord in the ear, and disgust to the bosom of sensibility and refinement"

8. "Diary of Deborah Sampson Gannett in 1802," p. 11, Sharon Historical Society, Sharon, Mass.; John Bennett, "Letters to a young lady. Letter X: On dress," *American Museum* 11 (March 1792): 94; Charles Brockden Brown, *Alcuin: A Dialogue* (Kent, Ohio, 1987), pp. 40–43. The American discussion of riding habits and other forms of "cross-dressing" echoed debates on the other side of the Atlantic. For the British context, see Linda Colley, *Britons: Forging the Nation, 1707–1837* (New Haven, 1992), chap. 6.

9. Marjorie Garber, *Vested Interests: Cross-Dressing and Cultural Anxiety* (New York, 1992), p. 11.

(p. 136). The power she attributed to her wounding words echoed her description of the effects of Revolutionary violence on Bostonians, whose "ears are yet wounded by the shrieks of [Charlestown's] mangled and her distressed" (p. 138). In a similar figural linking of her actions with Revolutionary upheaval, she compared the effects of the war to "the terrific glare of the comet . . . in its excentric orbit" (p. 138), a realm that she herself occupied as she traveled "like a bewildered star traversing out of its accustomed orbit" (p. 140) through the masculine domain of the battlefield.

Rhetorically joining her transvestite disguise with the violence and disruption of war itself, Gannett related her performance to the familiar popular culture icon of female disorderliness that the historian Natalie Zemon Davis has called the "woman-on-top." The cross-dressing woman of the early modern period provided a potent figure that could be used to restructure social relations. Her transgressive force was twofold: the unruly woman could operate, Davis writes, "first, to widen behavioral options for women within and even outside marriage, and, second, to sanction riot and political disobedience for both men and women in a society that allowed the lower orders few formal means of protest."[10]

While the woman-on-top provided Gannett with a broadly familiar figural means of linking her personal experiences to Revolutionary motifs of the world-turned-upside-down, the popular tradition of the woman warrior offered a set of narrative traditions that contributed to the shape of Gannett's oration. During the period of the woman warrior's widespread popularity from the early seventeenth through the mid–nineteenth century, she provided a general figure for transgression, violating class and genre boundaries as well as the boundaries of gender identity. Characterized by her physical and figural mobility, the woman warrior type existed in the life experiences of real women such as Hannah Snell, a British soldier at the battle of Pondicherry whose biography appeared in 1750 and was reprinted in *Thomas's New-England Almanack* in 1775; the improvisational performances of carnivals and masquerades; and the diverse scripted worlds of the broadside ballad, the novel, the political tract, and the stage.[11]

10. Natalie Zemon Davis, "Women on Top," in *Society and Culture in Early Modern France: Eight Essays* (Stanford, 1975), pp. 124–51; quotation on p. 131.

11. On passing women, see Rudolf M. Dekker and Lotte C. van de Pol, *The Tradition of Female Transvestism in Early Modern Europe* (New York, 1989), and Lynne Friedli, " 'Passing Women': A Study of Gender Boundaries in the Eighteenth Century," in *Sexual Underworlds of the Enlightenment*, ed. G. S. Rousseau and Roy Porter (Chapel Hill, N.C., 1988), pp. 234–60. Dianne Dugaw, *Warrior Women and Popular Balladry, 1650–1850* (Cambridge, England, 1989), traces the wide dissemination of the woman warrior ballad; many of those printed in England appeared in America. Jay Fliegelman, *Declaring Independence: Jefferson, Natural Language, and the Culture of Performance* (Stanford, 1993), pp. 155–60, discusses the version of the

In the transformative moment of the American Revolution, when patriots drew on popular ritual to reimagine political structure, the figure of the Amazonian woman suggested both a general rebelliousness against established authority and the overthrow of accepted gender roles. Philadelphia women defended their unaccustomed public efforts to collect funds for Washington's troops in a broadside of 1780 that offered historical women warriors as precedents for their actions. These included the biblical Deborah, the Israelite judge and military leader whose name Gannett bore, and Joan of Arc, "the Maid of Orleans who drove from the kingdom of France the ancestors of those same British, whose odious yoke we have just shaken off; and whom it is necessary that we drive from this Continent."[12] A few years earlier in the first American Crisis paper, Thomas Paine invoked the unifying power of Joan of Arc in a fight against British tyranny. Praying that "Heaven might inspire some Jersey maid to spirit up her countrymen, and save her fair fellow-sufferers from ravage and ravishment," Paine sought to mobilize women such as Gannett.[13]

Two decades later, Gannett's address made the Amazonian woman central to the Revolutionary mythos when she conflated her convention-breaking acts of personal heroism with nation formation. "I burst the tyrant bands, which *held my sex in awe*," she announced, identifying her personal liberation from gender constraints with the liberation of the American colonies from British rule. The myth-making imagination at work in her address accounts for her historically inaccurate assertion that she entered the army at a time of severe military crisis when the patriot cause was in danger of collapsing: "Whilst poverty, hunger, nakedness, cold and disease had dwindled the *American Armies* to a handful—whilst universal terror and dismay ran through our camps, ran through our country—while even WASHINGTON himself, at their head, though like a god, stood, as it were, on a pinacle tottering over the abyss of destruction," at that moment, she continued, "did I throw off the soft habiliments of *my sex*, and assume those of *the warrior*, already prepared for battle."[14] Her

Snell story printed in *Thomas's New-England Almanack*. For the original Snell narrative, see *The Female Soldier, or, The Surprising Life and Adventures of Hannah Snell* (Los Angeles, 1989).

12. See Esther DeBerdt Reed, "The Sentiments of an American Woman," in *American Women Writers to 1800*, ed. Sharon M. Harris (New York, 1996), pp. 255–59; the quotation is on p. 257. On elements of popular ritual and theater in Revolutionary politics, see Peter Shaw, *American Patriots and the Rituals of Revolution* (Cambridge, Mass., 1981); Silverman, *Cultural History of the American Revolution*; and Jeffrey H. Richards, *Theater Enough: American Culture and the Metaphor of the World Stage, 1607–1789* (Durham, N.C., 1991).

13. See Thomas Paine, "The American Crisis. Number 1. December 19, 1776," in *Collected Writings*, ed. Eric Foner (New York, 1995), pp. 91–99; the quotation is on p. 92.

14. Gannett, "An Address on Life," p. 137. One of the central controversies in the historical literature on Gannett concerns whether she joined the army in time to fight at Yorktown, as both her biography and her address claim. The most reliable documents suggest that she did not enlist until the spring of 1782, when the war was winding down.

language implied that by reversing conventional gender order she reversed American military fortunes.

As if this claim were not extraordinary enough, Gannett asserted that her actions staged yet another, related cultural reversal. Distinguishing herself from her "reputed Predecessor," Eve, Gannett suggested that her mythic revolution in gender superseded the biblical basis of gender differentiation. Identifying her own person and actions with the war for political independence, Gannett portrayed the Revolution as the source of a new social myth of female heroism that displaced the central biblical myth justifying female subordination.[15]

Gannett was not alone in her revisionary mythography. The woman warrior figure reached the zenith of her popularity in both England and America in the 1790s, when stage extravaganzas and ballads made her a pervasive feature of popular culture. During this decade, American writers evolved their own symbolic vesture for the cross-dressing female soldier, one woven of the disputed issues of political, economic, and gender identity. The exclusion of American women from the constitutionally established government converged with the French Revolution and the publication of Wollstonecraft's *Vindication of the Rights of Woman* (1792) to make the relationship between gender and citizenship in a republic a central cultural preoccupation in its own right, as well as a general figure for the problem of social order.[16] While the view from America was often deceptive and the response confused, the prominent role of French women in crowd actions and formal battles, intellectual debates, and revolutionary iconography made France seem a model of liberalized attitudes to those Americans who sought a broader public role for women.

In the decade before Gannett's lecture tour, as Americans defined the legacy of their own revolution in relation to the ongoing disruptions in France, a number of otherwise dissimilar American writers included a female warrior in works which differ in genre and sophistication but which, at some level, thematize the French connection. These works include the popular anonymous picaresque novel *The History of Constan-*

---

15. Jan Lewis, "The Republican Wife: Virtue and Seduction in the Early Republic," *William and Mary Quarterly*, 3d ser., 44, no. 3 (1987): 689–721, argues that the post-Revolutionary period saw the transformation of the family from patriarchal hierarchy into a model for republican political relations through the reimagining of Milton's Eve as an equal but deferential helpmate rather than a seductress. Gannett rejects Eve altogether, offering the woman warrior in her place.

16. Linda Kerber, "Separate Spheres, Female Worlds, Woman's Place: The Rhetoric of Women's History," *Journal of American History* 75, no. 1 (1988): 20, observes that in the late eighteenth century "issues of sexual asymmetry dominated political discourse to an unprecedented extent as people tried to define a place for women in postrevolutionary society. . . . [M]ajor changes in women's political life were associated with the radical stages of the French Revolution, and erasure of those changes was associated with the retreat from radicalism."

tius and Pulchera (1789–90); Herman Mann's seminovelized biography of Gannett, *The Female Review* (1797); Philip Freneau's ode of the same year celebrating Gannett's wartime heroism, "A Soldier Should Be Made of Sterner Stuff: On Deborah Gannett"; John Daly Burk's theatrical celebration of Joan of Arc, *Female Patriotism* (1798); and Charles Brockden Brown's *Ormond*, which appeared in 1799. Deborah Gannett both figured prominently in the symbolic debate and shaped her 1802 address in response to its changing dynamics. As American writers and audiences reflected on the competing definitions of their new nation, they framed their concerns about national identity in relation to a woman warrior in whom destabilized gender identity intersected with conflicting definitions of republicanism. These works reveal the range of significances attached to the warrior woman in the post-Revolutionary era, a cultural milieu that Gannett at first helped to create and then could not avoid engaging in her later efforts to define herself for the public during her lecture tour.

The anonymous *History of Constantius and Pulchera, or Constancy Rewarded*, patriotically subtitled *An American Novel*, first appeared in serial form between 1789 and 1790 and then in eight editions after 1794. This immensely popular novel translates the topoi of the woman warrior ballad into the picaresque tale.[17] Young Pulchera loves Constantius passionately, but her ambitious father forbids their union. The tyrannical patriarch forces her to depart for France, where she must marry the rich nobleman LeMonte. When pirates waylay her ship, Pulchera escapes her marital fate and embarks on a series of wild adventures, in the midst of which she dons a lieutenant's uniform and transforms herself into the delicate-looking but courageous soldier Valorus. She ends up in Paris several captivities and catastrophes later, still inexplicably clad in male attire. There she finds Constantius alive and preparing to marry the sister of the rehabilitated LeMonte. After assuring herself of his continuing love for her, Pulchera reveals her identity, and the happy couple returns to Pennsylvania for her father's blessing. The novel's thematic coherence, such as it is, centers on instability—cultural, economic, familial. Pulchera's wealthy farmer father rejects the suitable Constantius, son of a Philadelphia merchant, for the dazzling LeMonte. If the lure of French nobility initially disrupts an American domestic economy, LeMonte ultimately develops respect for the very contract to marry that he once sought to breach—perhaps reflecting the author's early, optimistic view

---

17. Cathy N. Davidson, *Revolution and the Word: The Rise of the Novel in America* (New York, 1986), p. 182. According to Dugaw, *Warrior Women*, pp. 92–93, the topoi shaping the basic plotline of woman warrior ballads include a disrupted courtship; a debate over the woman's decision to disguise herself; trials of the masquerading woman; tests of love imposed on the lover; and a happy resolution.

of the French Revolution's outcome. The cross-dressed warrior woman provides the figural center that redeems the French and restores a national community predicated on the union of agriculture and native merchandising.

Herman Mann began interviewing Deborah Sampson Gannett for her biography in 1795, the year after *Constantius and Pulchera* first appeared in book form from a Boston publisher. As a local publisher in the Massachusetts popular book trade, Mann may well have been familiar with the successful picaresque novel. He was almost certainly familiar with Hannah Snell's biography and shared its novelizing strategies as a way to appeal to a female readership.[18] Claiming that what the novelist "has painted in *embryo*, I have represented in *expansion*" (p. 42), Mann elaborated Gannett's life story to develop the woman warrior tale in radically new ways. The biography's interest resides in its movement away from the conventions of British woman warrior ballads and narratives through the incorporation of American Revolutionary ideology. While Deborah, like Pulchera, is a version of the pastoral heroine, she is the daughter not of a domineering, wealthy father but of a man disinherited, impoverished, and soon dead. In her orphaned condition she typifies Columbia, with whom Mann repeatedly identifies her before the Revolution. Bound out as a servant at the age of ten, she serves for eight years doing farm labor that gives her tall frame a muscular tone foreign to the delicate Pulchera. While she faces denial like a conventional romance heroine, it is denial of an uncommon sort. Not love but learning eludes her. Possessing "a fertile genius and an aspiring mind," Mann tells us, "she found less *opportunities*, than *inclinations*, for learning" (pp. 55–56). This longing for knowledge and travel provides the primary justification for Deborah's costumed departure for the war; her supposed desire to evade an unwelcome lover remains firmly secondary. Self-consciously transforming literary convention, Mann notes that Deborah was indeed "a *lover*" (p. 122), but a lover of her country. For Deborah, as for male patriots in the Whig commonplace, patriotism is a variant of conjugal love.[19] Displacing the

18. Their titles suggest that Snell's anonymously authored biography, *Female Soldier*, provided a model for Mann's *Female Review*. Both works insistently compare their heroines with the more conventionally feminine heroines of novels. Moreover, both Snell and Mann's Sampson suffer bullet wounds in their groin areas and are forced to extract the bullets themselves to avoid discovery. The location of the wounds suggests the desire to reinscribe the "wound" of female genitals on the transgressive female body. See Dianne Dugaw, introduction to *Female Soldier*, p. viii. Snell further anticipated Gannett in her performance of military exercises on the stage at Sadler's Wells in the 1750s. Judith Hiltner discusses the sources of Mann's biography, including the Snell narrative, in " ' She Bled in Secret': Deborah Sampson, Herman Mann, and the *Female Review*," *Early American Literature* 34, no. 2 (1999): 190–220, esp. 200–208.

19. Silverman, *Cultural History of the American Revolution*, p. 666.

object of love from an individual to a nation, Mann's Deborah combines the gendered virtues of patriotic violence and patriotic sentiment: "In cool blood, yet with firm attachment, we now see blended in her, the peerlessness of enterprise, the deportment, ardor and heroism of the veteran, with the milder graces, vigor and bloom of her secreted, softer sex" (p. 138).

In a move uncharacteristic of woman warrior literature, Mann makes no mention of historical or mythical precedents for Deborah's actions; he situates her in nature rather than in culture. The figure of Joan of Arc lies behind Mann's figure of Deborah, however, both in her French grandmother and in the features of the Joan myth that she embodies. Philip Freneau was the first writer explicitly to develop the analogy between Joan of Arc and Gannett. His poem supporting Gannett's petition for a federal pension appeared in his New York journal the *Time-Piece* after she came to his office soliciting his support in 1797, around the time that Mann's biography appeared. Freneau described Gannett as a "faithful amazon" who fought

> With the same vigorous soul inspired
> As Joan of Arc, of old,
> With zeal against the Briton fired,
> Her spirit warm and bold.

Celebrating Gannett's military prowess and her willingness to "scorn . . . a censuring age," he also condemned men "with contracted mind" who deny women military glory.[20]

Four months after Freneau published his ode painting Gannett as an American Joan of Arc, John Burk portrayed the French woman warrior on the New York stage in *Female Patriotism* (1798). Burk, who succeeded Freneau as editor of the *Time-Piece* in the same year that he wrote *Female Patriotism*, may have found inspiration for his play in Gannett's exploits. But his play had other precedents. Pantomime versions of the Joan of Arc story appeared on the bills of theaters in New York, Philadelphia, and Charleston between 1794 and 1796.[21] Burk drew on these precedents in the

---

20. Philip Freneau, "Ode XIII: A Soldier should be made of Sterner Stuff: On Deborah Gannet," in *The Poems of Philip Freneau*, ed. Fred Lewis Pattee, 3 vols. (Princeton, 1902–7), 3:182–84.

21. John Daly Burk, *Female Patriotism, or The Death of Joan D'Arc* (New York, 1798). Burk was an Irish radical who fled government persecution after his secret societies and liberationist military units were broken up in 1794. He entered New York disguised as a woman. See Ingvald Raknem, *Joan of Arc in History, Legend, and Literature* (Oslo, Norway, 1971), chap. 11. Odell, *Annals of the New York Stage*, 2:20–21, describes the production of Burk's *Female Patriotism*. The pantomime versions were "Female Heroism: The Siege of Orleans," Philadelphia, 1794; "Jeanne d'Arc: The Siege of Orleans," New York, 1795; and "Maid of Orleans: Joan of Arc," Charleston, 1796. See the listings in Susan L. Porter, *With an Air Debonair: Musical Theatre in America, 1785–1815* (Washington, D.C., 1991), pp. 449, 463, and 469 (appendix A). There were a number of other productions with martial women as lead characters,

elaborate staging of his play, which included a procession with Joan armed like Minerva leading the French army. The text of Burk's play bears much in common with Mann's *Female Review*, suggesting that they shared a narrative tradition. Together they reveal the cultural issues nego-tiated through the figure of the woman warrior in the 1790s. Like Pul-chera, both Joan and Deborah are country bred and celebrate rural life.[22] Both women seek knowledge beyond their sphere, Deborah through efforts at self-education, Joan with a learned kinsman who gives her clas-sical training. Each has a dream vision that inspires her patriotic actions, providing a sacred authority that transcends the conventions of formal religion, which the women disdain. They both give rousing speeches that demonstrate the power of female eloquence and inspire patriotism in their male comrades. While Joan finds love in the French camp, romance remains firmly secondary to her main mission of liberating France from British domination, and her compatriots celebrate her chastity. The emphasis on Joan's sexual virtue repeats a theme that dominates all con-temporary discussion of Gannett.[23] Finally and most important for my argument here, both women warriors cry on the battlefield, demonstrat-ing their susceptibility to wartime suffering that they themselves help to inflict. For Mann and Burk, the woman warrior as Revolutionary symbol blends redemptive feminine sentiment with the violence of war.

But while Burk celebrated his heroine as a figure prophesying the emer-gence of a radical republican movement, Mann's biography wandered into narrative ambivalence about the meaning of Deborah's experience. Charles Brockden Brown shared Mann's response to an age that he described as "particularly distinguished by female enterprize and hero-ism."[24] Through Martinette de Beauvais, the woman warrior of *Ormond*, Brown treats the French Revolution as a historical moment "which called forth talents and courage, without distinction of sex" (p. 205). Brown jux-taposes the radical republican Martinette with his American heroine, Constantia, to explore the female capacity for violence. The two women look alike and have similar educations; indeed, Constantia perceives "that all the differences between them, arose from diversities of situation" (p. 191). Brown writes that "Constantia's attention had been chiefly occupied

including the popular "Highland Reel: The Female Soldier" (first performed in 1793), and "The Shipwreck: The Female Sailor" (first performed in 1798); see Porter, *With an Air Debonair*, pp. 460, 487.

22. On pastoral myths in revolutionary ideology, see Lynn Hunt, *The Family Romance of the French Revolution* (Berkeley, 1992), pp. 85–86.

23. See, for example, the article entitled "Female Heroism" in *American Museum* 11 (March 1792), which states that she "did her duty without a stain on her virtue or honour" (p. 110). While presenting several titillating stories of Gannett's costumed flirtations with women, Mann similarly defends her chastity.

24. Charles Brockden Brown, *Ormond, or The Secret Witness* (Kent, Ohio, 1982), p. 205. Fur-ther references will be given parenthetically in the text.

by personal concerns" (p. 190), most notably caring for her blind and impecunious father in Philadelphia. Martinette, in contrast, has lived all over Europe and the Middle East and fought in two revolutions, the American and the French. Martinette's involvement in the American Revolution conforms to the pattern of the woman warrior ballads: attired in men's clothes, she follows her new husband onto the battlefield. There she participates in the fighting, but her main function is to rescue her husband and tend his wounds. After her husband's death in a British prison, she becomes a celebrity, "exhibited at operas and masquerades, made the theme of enquiry and encomium at every place of resort, and caressed by the most illustrious among the votaries of science, and the advocates of the American cause" (p. 203).

Such public celebration of her heroism cements Martinette's revolutionary sensibilities, and she eagerly joins the French Revolutionary forces on her own. Motivated, she claims, "by a generous devotion to liberty," she joins "whole regiments of women" (p. 207) on the battlefield. Constantia is shocked to learn that Martinette's "devotion to liberty" allows her to confront "so much bloodshed, and injustice" (p. 206), without a qualm. Indeed Martinette glories in her destructive power, celebrating the "fusil of two barrels" (p. 206) with which she killed thirteen officers, including two former friends who have joined the monarchists. Unlike Mann's Deborah Sampson and Burk's Joan of Arc, Martinette displays no ideal combination of feminine sentiment and masculine violence; rather, she reveals the female capacity for an impassive, even an enthusiastically murderous violence.

Despite her horror, Constantia soon performs an act as violent as Martinette's, exposing Brown's dark moral. At the end of the novel Constantia confronts her would-be rapist Ormond, who we later learn is Martinette's long-lost brother, and kills him with a penknife. At the moment of the fatal assault, Brown disrupts the narrative, shifting perspectives to omit a first-person account of the murder, which, the reader is led to assume, Constantia is incapable of providing. Like another Brown heroine Clara Wieland, who cannot forgive herself for killing her brother rather than committing suicide, Constantia's act of self-defense rather than self-sacrifice exposes the feminine capacity for violent aggression that Martinette openly celebrates. Neither Clara nor Constantia can reconcile herself to this potential for a violence that spins uncontrollably out of the orbit of feminine sentiment. That violence, in Brown's Hobbesian vision, proves the ultimate human reality that underlies distinctions of gender.[25]

25. Through Martinette and Constantia, Brown revises his position in *Alcuin*, where he celebrates women's domestic employments as protection from "profane violences" and "ghastly spectacles" (p. 20). Like Clara Wieland, Constantia finds violence at the heart of

Brown composed *Ormond* as American relations with France reached their nadir during the Adams presidency. His use of the French woman warrior as a figure for human savagery marks an important stage in his movement away from his youthful radicalism.[26] When Deborah Sampson Gannett made her lecture tour in 1802, the national political climate had shifted dramatically. She seized the moment following Jefferson's election to present her claim to a status equal to that of a male veteran, including a pension.

Gannett was already a figure in the cultural debates staged through the woman warrior thanks to Mann's biography and Freneau's ode. She sought the popular support she needed to win a pension through a lecture performance that blended elements of a theatrical presentation, a commemorative oration, and a spiritual narrative. In Boston she shared the bill with works celebrating disguise and patriotism, including Shakespeare's *Henry IV* (1598), Frederick Reynolds's *The Will* (1797), a farce called "The Soldier's Festival," a pageant titled "Columbus; or, America Discovered," and the pantomime piece "Harlequin's Frolic." The celebratory patriotism of these evenings can be inferred from the theater bill for March 24, which announced that the evening would conclude with Mrs. Gannett's performance of "the Manual Exercise" followed by "the Song and Chorus of 'God Save the Sixteen States.' "[27] Like the pageantry of Burk's *Female Patriotism*, Gannett's manual exercise provided a dramatic spectacle, while her lecture echoed themes from the plays. The main offerings on the bills, *Henry IV* and *The Will*, were dramas celebrating playful transformation followed by the restoration of cultural order. Prince Hal emerges from his tavern haunts to confess the error of his ways, defend his father's throne, and defeat the rebel Hotspur. Similarly, Albina, the heiress heroine of *The Will*, restores patriarchal order when she tears up her grandfather's unjust will disinheriting her father. Albina's act of filial dependence wins her the husband of her choice. Before conventional social order can be reestablished, however, Albina masquerades as a Navy lieutenant, testing the loyalty of her lover and her father. In *The Will*, as in *Constantius and Pulchera*, women disguise themselves in military uniforms to preserve existing society while ameliorating the injustices of patriarchal authority. Gannett's Boston performances, then, took place in a theatrical context that foregrounded masquerade elements of playful, temporary social transformation followed by the restoration of order. Outside the city she delivered her lecture in courthouses and masonic

---

domestic existence. In both instances, Brown links female violence to the violence of writing, through the choice of a penknife as weapon.

26. Steven Watts, *The Romance of Real Life: Charles Brockden Brown and the Origins of American Culture* (Baltimore, 1994), offers the most thorough and convincing discussion of Brown's political development.

27. See the broadside reprinted in Evans, *Weathering the Storm*, p. 319.

halls without the elaborate companion pieces of her Boston appearances. In these venues she had greater control over her performances.

The ideological elements that Gannett's performances shared with the woman warrior literature of the 1790s converged on the issues of violence and sentiment as they mutually constructed gender and national identities during the period. For Charles Brockden Brown, the woman warrior exposes human bloodthirstiness beneath the facades of culture, a fundamental nature that underlies and threatens to expose any pretensions to "higher" identity, whether of gender or of nation. For John Burk and Herman Mann, the woman warrior manifests the ideal tempering of violent action in a worthy cause with sympathy for the enemy's humanity. Her tears reflect both the suffering that redeems murderous violence and the patriotic transfer of affection from the individual to the nation. In Gannett's "Address on Life," the locus of emotion shifts from the scene of slaughter to the initial act of cross-dressing; not the response to physical violence but the response to violence against cultural categories preoccupies her. Focusing on "the tear of repentence . . . which many times involuntarily stole into my eye, and fell unheeded to the ground: And that too before I had reached the embattled field" (p. 137), she made little mention of her feelings while fighting. Gannett concentrated attention away from her personal battlefield experience and toward her own violation of gender roles. Earlier woman warrior narratives such as those of Christian Davies (1740) and Hannah Snell (1750) have little or nothing to say about the virago's psychological experience upon donning male garb.[28] In contrast, the act of cross-dressing preoccupied Gannett in her 1802 address.

What does this shift in attention from the woman warrior's actions to her psychological state reveal about her changing significance as American writers responded to events in France and at home? Gannett's oration was not unconcerned with the political questions of nationalism and republicanism that the earlier literature addresses. She celebrated national prospects in bland optimistic platitudes adapted from Fourth of July oratory, claiming the beneficent effects of "agriculture and commerce, industry and manufactures, arts and sciences, virtue and decorum, union and harmony" (p. 139). The ode to liberty echoed Burk's Joan of Arc in its cosmopolitan republicanism. It even discreetly conveyed abolitionist sentiments, urging liberty to extend its "beatific influence" over Africa as well as Europe (p. 139).

But the celebration of liberty's virtues and Columbia's economic future quickly gave way to the renewed query, included in the printed address as if spoken by the audience, *"What particular inducement could she have thus to elope from the soft sphere of her own sex?"* (p. 139). Gannett offered

---

28. See *The Life and Adventures of Mrs. Christian Davies* (London, 1740).

explanations that framed her experience in masculine terms which echo her introduction ("And dost thou ask what fairy hand inspired / A *Nymph* to be with martial glory fired? . . . Then ask—why *Cincinnatus* left his farm?" [p. 140]). Alternatively, she placed herself in the ballad tradition of the woman warrior who follows a man into battle, asking, "Was some hapless *lover* from her torn?" Finally, however, she could provide no paradigm adequate to explain her motivations, for she was fully identifiable with neither Cincinnatus nor the conventional woman warrior. If for Brown the lacuna opened up by the woman warrior is a gap in female consciousness that reveals the ungendered primacy of human aggression, for Gannett the lacuna opened around her motivation for taking on the woman warrior's role at all. The emergence of the inexplicable in this instance suggests that Gannett fell outside the available languages of female subjectivity, especially the increasingly hegemonic language of the novel.[29]

Rejecting the possibility of adequate explanation, she turned instead to a confession of "error and presumption" (p. 140). Her promise of *"repentance"* and "atonement to the SUPREME JUDGE of our offenses" (p. 140) echoed the conversion narrative, a form that may have been familiar to her from her brief experience as a Baptist convert before entering the army. Her rhetoric had another possible source in literature, for confession and reform are common to the reversals that structure literary forms. Both Hal in *Henry IV* and Albina in *The Will* confess their faults on the way to restored order. Like them, Gannett turned to conversion rhetoric when pleading for cultural acceptance. Employing the language of seduction, she acknowledged that she walked on the "precipice of feminine perdition" and "in the precipitancy of passion" prepared "a moment for repentance at leisure" (p. 140).

The concluding minutes of Gannett's lecture indicated a deep desire to elicit her audience's sympathy. She first titillated her auditors with a catalogue of dissipated characters familiar from sermons, including the prodigal, the libertine, the bacchanalian, the debauchee, and the *"baggage* in the streets" (p. 141), then testified that "I cannot, indeed bring the adventures, even of the worst part of my own life, as parallels with this black catalogue of crimes" (p. 141). Appealing to the women in the audience, she solicited their judgment in the language of conversion: "In what-

29. The question of motivation, which apparently preoccupied Gannett's audience, continues to puzzle scholars. Laska, *"Remember the Ladies,"* p. 64, offers as the final reward of scholarly efforts to decipher Gannett's life a "solution" to "the ultimate puzzle: what motivated her to become a soldier." Gannett's address suggests the impossibility of ever adequately answering this question because it presupposes a female subject modeled on the novel heroine; see Nancy Armstrong, *Desire and Domestic Fiction: A Political History of the Novel* (New York, 1987).

ever I may be thought to have been unnatural, unwise and indelicate, it is now my most fervent desire it may have a suitable impression on you— and on me, a penitent for every wrong thought and step" (p. 141). Here Gannett employed one of her characteristic rhetorical moves: she repeatedly voiced the worst thing that could be said of her, only to distance herself from that opinion while, nevertheless, submitting to those who held it. Her linguistic contortions revealed her subordinate position before her audience, particularly its female members. She was an object for their judgment, and she hoped to garner support through her humble appeal to the women in the audience, whose standards she had presumably violated.

Gannett's strategy reflected the class dynamics of her situation. The Boston advertisements highlight the "respectable" sponsors of her performance, and her diary exhibits her concern to have "respectable" people in the audience and to win the approval of "the Ladies."[30] Her conversion rhetoric staged her submission to an audience synecdochically representing the nation: if her auditors, particularly her female auditors, would accept her repentance, she could be sure to have won God's blessing and, presumably, the money that she needed to raise her family, perhaps even the pension that she sought. Despite her wandering from the path of convention, she stated, "I still hope for some claim on the indulgence and patronage of the public; as in such case I might be conscious of the approbation of my GOD" (p. 141). Conflating God and nation with "the public," Gannett submitted the disruptive energies of the woman warrior to the control of "this respectable circle" (p. 141).

The "ladies" to whom she addressed her remarks represented a model of femininity that was not fully available to Gannett and her class peers, but it was the approbation of these women that she sought to win through the language of patriotic motherhood and gendered domains. Yet her concluding celebration of republican womanhood and separate spheres undermined itself in its public articulation; her very act of giving such a performance stressed her distance from this mode of femininity, both because of the unconventional nature of her tour and because of its economic causes. Inhabiting and transforming the role of the woman warrior, Gannett made the icon speak in ways that subordinated her to the ideology of republican womanhood. Yet the performance dimension of her tour—the costume, the arms drill, Gannett's substantial physical presence—both aestheticized her own role and invited members of her audience to recognize the republican woman as a figure requiring a similar, if less dramatic, kind of role-playing.

Gannett's tears no longer validated patriotic violence as they did in the

30. See "Diary of Deborah Sampson Gannett," May 5, 1802.

male-authored woman warrior tales. They instead symbolized her confrontation with the inadequacy of the cultural roles that defined class and gender, not only the gendered roles of Cincinnatus and the republican woman that were the mainstays of post-Revolutionary ideology but also the conventional figure for category disruption, the woman warrior herself. By redirecting the rhetorics of violence and sentiment associated with the woman warrior's response to battle, training them instead on her own violent disruption of gender categories and her sentimental response to that violation, and then repeatedly staging both the violation and the emotion, Gannett presented her life story as the site of an ongoing battle over gender and class identities intimately tied to the life of the nation.

Gannett pointed to an occluded spot in the early republic's field of vision, the point where gender and class categories intersected and exposed the absence of a coherent ideology of ordinary women's experience. While making that spot visible, Gannett presented herself as an anomaly and a curiosity rather than a representative of a variety of female experience. Later women orators such as the Grimké sisters would shape a feminine political identity based on the moral superiority that middle-class domestic ideologues paradoxically attributed to all women while seeking to impose it on workingwomen through moral reform. Although Gannett's lecture tour did not directly provide women with an alternative rhetoric for entering public life, her continuing popularity as a figure and the ongoing debates about women in the military reveal the role that our most famous woman warrior continues to play in the nation's acts of cultural self-definition.[31]

31. For a discussion of some modern tributes to Gannett, including her selection as official Heroine of the Commonwealth in Massachusetts in 1983 and a movement for a commemorative stamp featuring her, supported by a 1988 resolution of the Massachusetts Senate, see Emil F. Guba, *Deborah Samson: Alias Robert Shurtliff, Revolutionary War Soldier* (Plymouth, Mass., 1994), chaps. 15 and 16.

Contributors

LOUISE M. BURKHART is Associate Professor of Anthropology and Latin American and Caribbean Studies at the University at Albany, State University of New York. A 1997 Guggenheim Fellow, she is the author of *The Slippery Earth: Nahua-Christian Dialogue in Sixteenth-Century Mexico* (1989), *Holy Wednesday: A Nahua Drama from Early Colonial Mexico* (1996), and the forthcoming *Before Guadalupe: The Virgin Mary in Early Colonial Nahuatl Literature*, as well as numerous articles on colonial Nahua religion.

TOBY L. DITZ is Professor of History at the Johns Hopkins University. She is the author of *Property and Kinship: Inheritance in Early Connecticut, 1750–1820* (1986) and is currently completing "Shipwrecked: Manly Identity and the Culture of Risk among Philadelphia Merchants," a cultural study of commerce and concepts of the gendered self among eighteenth-century elites.

SANDRA M. GUSTAFSON is Assistant Professor of English at the University of Notre Dame. She is completing *Eloquence is Power: Oratory and Performance in Early America*, which will be published by the Omohundro Institute of Early American History and Culture, where she held a postdoctoral fellowship. Her published works include essays on Sarah and Jonathan Edwards, Esther Edwards Burr, Margaret Fuller, and William Apess.

DAVID D. HALL teaches American history and religion at Harvard Divinity School. His many publications include *The Faithful Shepherd: A History of the New England Ministry in the Seventeenth Century* (1972), *The Antinomian Controversy, 1636–1638: A Documentary History* (1968, 1990), *Worlds of Wonder, Days of Judgment: Popular Religious Belief in Early New England* (1989), *Witch-Hunting in Seventeenth-Century New England: A Documentary History, 1638–1692* (1991), *Cultures of Print: Essays in the History of the Book* (1996), and, most recently, *Lived Religion in America: Toward a History of Practice* (1997).

PETER HULME is Professor of Literature at the University of Essex. He is the author of *Colonial Encounters: Europe and the Native Caribbean, 1492–1797* (1986) and *Remnants of Conquest: Visitors to the Caribs, 1877–1997* (2000), and coeditor of several books, most recently *Cannibalism and the Colonial World* (1999).

SUSAN JUSTER is Associate Professor of History at the University of Michigan. Her book *Disorderly Women: Sexual Politics and Evangelicalism in Revolutionary New England* (1994) won the 1995 Louis Gottschalk Prize for the best book in Eighteenth-Century Studies. She has also coedited (with Lisa MacFarlane) *A Mighty Baptism: Race, Gender, and the Creation of American Protestantism* (1996). She is currently working on a comparative study of radical prophecy in Britain, Canada, and the United States from 1780 to 1815.

MARGARETTA M. LOVELL is Associate Professor of History of Art and co-director of American Studies at the University of California, Berkeley. She has taught at Yale University, Harvard University, and the University of Michigan and has held the Dittman Chair in American Studies at the College of William and Mary, the Ednah Root Curatorial Chair for American Art at the Fine Arts Museum of San Francisco, and the R. Stanton Avery Visiting Chair at the Huntington Library. She is the author of *A Visitable Past: Views of Venice by American Artists, 1860–1915* (1989) and numerous essays on eighteenth- and nineteenth-century American art and material culture.

JOSÉ ANTONIO MAZZOTTI is Assistant Professor of Romance Languages and Literatures at Harvard University, where he specializes in Latin American literature. He has previously taught at Temple University. His books include *Coros mestizos del Inca Garcilaso* (1996) and, as coeditor, *Asedios a la heterogeneidad cultural* (1996). His research focuses now on epic poetry, formation of a creole identity, and popular culture in the Viceroyalty of Peru during the seventeenth and eighteenth centuries.

MICHAEL MERANZE is Associate Professor of History at the University of California, San Diego. He is the author of *Laboratories of Virtue: Punishment, Revolution, and Authority in Philadelphia, 1760–1835* (1996) and the editor of Benjamin Rush's *Essays—Literary, Moral, and Philosophical* (1988).

LAURA J. MURRAY is Associate Professor of English at Queen's University in Kingston, Ontario, where she teaches American and Native American literatures. The editor of *To Do Good to My Indian Brethren: The Writings of Joseph Johnson, 1751–1776* (1998), she is currently working on a literary and historical study of vocabularies and phrasebooks of American Indian languages from the eighteenth and nineteenth centuries.

ANNE G. MYLES is Assistant Professor of English at the University of Northern Iowa. She has essays published or forthcoming on Roger Williams and John Woolman and is at work on a manuscript tentatively entitled " 'Called Out': Languages of Dissent in Early America."

DANA D. NELSON is Professor of English and Social Theory at the University of Kentucky. She is the author of *The Word in Black and White: Reading "Race" in American Literature, 1638–1867* (1992) and *National Manhood: Capitalist Citizenship and the Imagined Fraternity of White Men* (1998), from which her essay in this volume is drawn. She is currently working on a study called "Representative/Democracy" and is coediting (with Russ Castronovo) a volume of essays titled *Materializing Democracy*.

ROBERT BLAIR ST. GEORGE is Associate Professor of History at the University of Pennsylvania. He has taught in the Winterthur Program in Early American Culture and at Boston University, and has held the Dittman Chair in American Studies at the College of William and Mary. His previous writings include *The Wrought Covenant: Source Materials for the Study of Craftsmen and Community in Southeastern New England, 1620–1700* (1979), *Material Life in America, 1600–1860* (1988), and *Conversing by Signs: Poetics of Implication in Colonial New England Culture* (1998).

IRENE SILVERBLATT is Associate Professor of Cultural Anthropology at Duke University. She is the author of *Moon, Sun, and Witches: Gender Ideologies and Class in Inca and Colonial Peru* (1987) and several articles on colonialism and gender in Peru, including "Becoming Indian in the Central Andes of Seventeenth-Century Peru" and "Andean Witches and Virgins: Seventeenth-Century Nativism and Subversive Gender Ideologies." She has previously received Guggenheim and Rockefeller Fellowships. Her current research is on the cultural dimensions of state-making and colonization in the Peruvian Andes.

CARROLL SMITH-ROSENBERG is Professor of History at the University of Michigan. She has previously taught at the University of Pennsylvania. Her many publications include *Religion and the Rise of the American City: the New York City Mission Movement, 1812–1870* (1971), *Disorderly Conduct: Visions of Gender in Victorian America* (1985), and numerous essays on gender, social reform, and women's history. Her current work explores the politics of representation in the early national period.

JOHN K. THORNTON teaches in the Department of History at Millersville University of Pennsylvania. His publications include *Africa and Africans in the Making of the Atlantic World, 1400–1680* (1992) and other essays on culture and politics in the African diaspora in the early modern period.

MICHAEL WARNER is Professor of English at Rutgers University. His most recent works include *The Trouble with Normal: Sex, Politics, and the Ethics of Queer Life* (1999) and *American Sermons: The Pilgrims to Martin Luther King* (1999). He is also the author of *The Letters of the Republic: Publication and the Public Sphere in Eighteenth-Century America* (1990); the editor of *Fear of a Queer*

Planet: Queer Politics and Social Theory (1993); the editor, with Myra Jehlen, of *The English Literatures of America, 1500–1800* (1997) and, with Gerald Graff, of *The Origins of Literary Studies in America: A Documentary Anthology* (1988). His essays and journalism have appeared in the *Village Voice, VLS, The Nation, The Advocate, POZ, In These Times,* and other magazines. He lives in Brooklyn.

Index